[redacted]

(W., G. & W.) Coll.Barg. 4th Ed. ACB—1

American Casebook Series
Hornbook Series and Basic Legal Texts
Black Letter Series and Nutshell Series

of

WEST PUBLISHING COMPANY
P.O. Box 64526
St. Paul, Minnesota 55164–0526

Accounting

FARIS' ACCOUNTING AND LAW IN A NUTSHELL, 377 pages, 1984. Softcover. (Text)

FIFLIS' ACCOUNTING ISSUES FOR LAWYERS, TEACHING MATERIALS, Fourth Edition, 706 pages, 1991. Teacher's Manual available. (Casebook)

SIEGEL AND SIEGEL'S ACCOUNTING AND FINANCIAL DISCLOSURE: A GUIDE TO BASIC CONCEPTS, 259 pages, 1983. Softcover. (Text)

Administrative Law

AMAN AND MAYTON'S HORNBOOK ON ADMINISTRATIVE LAW, Approximately 750 pages, 1993. (Text)

BONFIELD AND ASIMOW'S STATE AND FEDERAL ADMINISTRATIVE LAW, 826 pages, 1989. Teacher's Manual available. (Casebook)

GELLHORN AND LEVIN'S ADMINISTRATIVE LAW AND PROCESS IN A NUTSHELL, Third Edition, 479 pages, 1990. Softcover. (Text)

MASHAW, MERRILL, AND SHANE'S CASES AND MATERIALS ON ADMINISTRATIVE LAW—THE AMERICAN PUBLIC LAW SYSTEM, Third Edition, 1187 pages, 1992. (Casebook)

ROBINSON, GELLHORN AND BRUFF'S THE ADMINISTRATIVE PROCESS, Third Edition, 978 pages, 1986. (Casebook)

Admiralty

HEALY AND SHARPE'S CASES AND MATERIALS ON ADMIRALTY, Second Edition, 876 pages, 1986. (Casebook)

MARAIST'S ADMIRALTY IN A NUTSHELL, Second Edition, 379 pages, 1988. Softcover. (Text)

SCHOENBAUM'S HORNBOOK ON ADMIRALTY AND MARITIME LAW, Student Edition, 692 pages, 1987 with 1992 pocket part. (Text)

Agency—Partnership

DEMOTT'S FIDUCIARY OBLIGATION, AGENCY AND PARTNERSHIP: DUTIES IN ONGOING BUSINESS RELATIONSHIPS, 740 pages, 1991. Teacher's Manual available. (Casebook)

FESSLER'S ALTERNATIVES TO INCORPORATION FOR PERSONS IN QUEST OF PROFIT, Third Edition, 339 pages, 1991. Softcover. (Casebook)

HENN'S CASES AND MATERIALS ON AGENCY, PARTNERSHIP AND OTHER UNINCORPORATED BUSINESS ENTERPRISES, Second Edition, 733 pages, 1985. Teacher's Manual available. (Casebook)

REUSCHLEIN AND GREGORY'S HORNBOOK ON THE LAW OF AGENCY AND PARTNERSHIP, Second Edition, 683 pages, 1990. (Text)

SELECTED CORPORATION AND PARTNERSHIP STATUTES, RULES AND FORMS. Softcover. Revised 1991 Edition, 953 pages.

STEFFEN AND KERR'S CASES ON AGENCY-PARTNERSHIP, Fourth Edition, 859 pages, 1980. (Casebook)

STEFFEN'S AGENCY-PARTNERSHIP IN A NUTSHELL, 364 pages, 1977. Softcover. (Text)

Agricultural Law

MEYER, PEDERSEN, THORSON AND DAVIDSON'S AGRICULTURAL LAW: CASES AND MATERIALS, 931 pages, 1985. Teacher's Manual avail-

List current as of January, 1993

Agricultural Law—Cont'd

able. (Casebook)

Alternative Dispute Resolution

KANOWITZ' CASES AND MATERIALS ON ALTERNATIVE DISPUTE RESOLUTION, 1024 pages, 1986. Teacher's Manual available. (Casebook) 1990 Supplement.

NOLAN-HALEY'S ALTERNATIVE DISPUTE RESOLUTION IN A NUTSHELL, 298 pages, 1992. Softcover. (Text)

RISKIN AND WESTBROOK'S DISPUTE RESOLUTION AND LAWYERS, 468 pages, 1987. Teacher's Manual available. (Casebook)

RISKIN AND WESTBROOK'S DISPUTE RESOLUTION AND LAWYERS, Abridged Edition, 223 pages, 1987. Softcover. Teacher's Manual available. (Casebook)

RISKIN'S DISPUTE RESOLUTION FOR LAWYERS VIDEO TAPES, 1992. (Available for purchase by schools and libraries.)

American Indian Law

CANBY'S AMERICAN INDIAN LAW IN A NUTSHELL, Second Edition, 336 pages, 1988. Softcover. (Text)

GETCHES AND WILKINSON'S CASES AND MATERIALS ON FEDERAL INDIAN LAW, Second Edition, 880 pages, 1986. (Casebook)

Antitrust—see also Regulated Industries, Trade Regulation

BARNES AND STOUT'S ECONOMIC FOUNDATIONS OF REGULATION AND ANTITRUST LAW, 102 pages, 1992. Softcover. Teacher's Manual available. (Casebook)

FOX AND SULLIVAN'S CASES AND MATERIALS ON ANTITRUST, 935 pages, 1989. Teacher's Manual available. (Casebook) 1993 Supplement.

GELLHORN'S ANTITRUST LAW AND ECONOMICS IN A NUTSHELL, Third Edition, 472 pages, 1986. Softcover. (Text)

HOVENKAMP'S BLACK LETTER ON ANTITRUST, Second Edition approximately 325 pages, April 1993 Pub. Softcover. (Review)

HOVENKAMP'S HORNBOOK ON ECONOMICS AND FEDERAL ANTITRUST LAW, Student Edition, 414 pages, 1985. (Text)

POSNER AND EASTERBROOK'S CASES AND ECONOMIC NOTES ON ANTITRUST, Second Edition, 1077 pages, 1981. (Casebook) 1984–85 Supplement.

SULLIVAN'S HORNBOOK OF THE LAW OF ANTITRUST, 886 pages, 1977. (Text)

Appellate Advocacy—see Trial and Appellate Advocacy

Architecture and Engineering Law

SWEET'S LEGAL ASPECTS OF ARCHITECTURE, ENGINEERING AND THE CONSTRUCTION PROCESS, Fourth Edition, 889 pages, 1989. Teacher's Manual available. (Casebook)

Art Law

DUBOFF'S ART LAW IN A NUTSHELL, Second Edition, approximately 325 pages, 1993. Softcover. (Text)

Banking Law

BANKING LAW: SELECTED STATUTES AND REGULATIONS. Softcover. 263 pages, 1991.

LOVETT'S BANKING AND FINANCIAL INSTITUTIONS LAW IN A NUTSHELL, Third Edition, 470 pages, 1992. Softcover. (Text)

SYMONS AND WHITE'S BANKING LAW: TEACHING MATERIALS, Third Edition, 818 pages, 1991. Teacher's Manual available. (Casebook)

Statutory Supplement. *See Banking Law: Selected Statutes*

Bankruptcy—see Creditors' Rights

Business Planning—see also Corporate Finance

PAINTER'S PROBLEMS AND MATERIALS IN BUSINESS PLANNING, Second Edition, 1008 pages, 1984. (Casebook) 1990 Supplement.

Statutory Supplement. *See Selected Corporation and Partnership*

Civil Procedure—see also Federal Jurisdiction and Procedure

AMERICAN BAR ASSOCIATION SECTION OF LITIGATION—READINGS ON ADVERSARIAL JUSTICE: THE AMERICAN APPROACH TO ADJUDICATION, 217 pages, 1988. Softcover. (Coursebook)

CLERMONT'S BLACK LETTER ON CIVIL PROCEDURE, Third Edition, approximately 350 pages, May, 1993 Pub. Softcover. (Review)

COUND, FRIEDENTHAL, MILLER AND SEXTON'S

Civil Procedure—Cont'd

CASES AND MATERIALS ON CIVIL PROCEDURE, Fifth Edition, 1284 pages, 1989. Teacher's Manual available. (Casebook)

COUND, FRIEDENTHAL, MILLER AND SEXTON'S CIVIL PROCEDURE SUPPLEMENT. 476 pages, 1991. Softcover. (Casebook Supplement)

FEDERAL RULES OF CIVIL PROCEDURE—EDUCATIONAL EDITION. Softcover. 761 pages, 1992.

FRIEDENTHAL, KANE AND MILLER'S HORNBOOK ON CIVIL PROCEDURE, Second Edition, approximately 1000 pages, May 1993 Pub. (Text)

KANE AND LEVINE'S CIVIL PROCEDURE IN CALIFORNIA: STATE AND FEDERAL 1992 Edition, 551 pages. Softcover. (Casebook Supplement)

KANE'S CIVIL PROCEDURE IN A NUTSHELL, Third Edition, 303 pages, 1991. Softcover. (Text)

KOFFLER AND REPPY'S HORNBOOK ON COMMON LAW PLEADING, 663 pages, 1969. (Text)

LEVINE, SLOMANSON AND WINGATE'S CALIFORNIA CIVIL PROCEDURE, CASES AND MATERIALS, 546 pages, 1991. Teacher's Manual available. (Casebook)

MARCUS, REDISH AND SHERMAN'S CIVIL PROCEDURE: A MODERN APPROACH, 1027 pages, 1989. Teacher's Manual available. (Casebook) 1991 Supplement.

MARCUS AND SHERMAN'S COMPLEX LITIGATION–CASES AND MATERIALS ON ADVANCED CIVIL PROCEDURE, Second Edition, 1035 pages, 1992. Teacher's Manual available. (Casebook)

PARK AND MCFARLAND'S COMPUTER-AIDED EXERCISES ON CIVIL PROCEDURE, Third Edition, 210 pages, 1991. Softcover. (Coursebook)

SIEGEL'S HORNBOOK ON NEW YORK PRACTICE, Second Edition, Student Edition, 1068 pages, 1991. Softcover. (Text) 1992 Supplemental Pamphlet.

SLOMANSON AND WINGATE'S CALIFORNIA CIVIL PROCEDURE IN A NUTSHELL, 230 pages, 1992. Softcover. (Text)

Commercial Law

BAILEY AND HAGEDORN'S SECURED TRANSACTIONS IN A NUTSHELL, Third Edition, 390 pages, 1988. Softcover. (Text)

EPSTEIN, MARTIN, HENNING AND NICKLES' BASIC UNIFORM COMMERCIAL CODE TEACHING MATERIALS, Third Edition, 704 pages, 1988. Teacher's Manual available. (Casebook)

HENSON'S HORNBOOK ON SECURED TRANSACTIONS UNDER THE U.C.C., Second Edition, 504 pages, 1979, with 1979 pocket part. (Text)

MEYER AND SPEIDEL'S BLACK LETTER ON SALES AND LEASES OF GOODS, Approximately 300 pages, 1993. Softcover. (Review)

NICKLES' BLACK LETTER ON COMMERCIAL PAPER, 450 pages, 1988. Softcover. (Review)

NICKLES, MATHESON AND DOLAN'S MATERIALS FOR UNDERSTANDING CREDIT AND PAYMENT SYSTEMS, 923 pages, 1987. Teacher's Manual available. (Casebook)

NORDSTROM, MURRAY AND CLOVIS' PROBLEMS AND MATERIALS ON SALES, 515 pages, 1982. (Casebook)

NORDSTROM, MURRAY AND CLOVIS' PROBLEMS AND MATERIALS ON SECURED TRANSACTIONS, 594 pages, 1987. (Casebook)

RUBIN AND COOTER'S THE PAYMENT SYSTEM: CASES, MATERIALS AND ISSUES, 885 pages, 1989. Teacher's Manual Available. (Casebook)

SELECTED COMMERCIAL STATUTES. Softcover. 1897 pages, 1992.

SPEIDEL, SUMMERS AND WHITE'S COMMERCIAL LAW: TEACHING MATERIALS, Fourth Edition, 1448 pages, 1987. Teacher's Manual available. (Casebook)

SPEIDEL, SUMMERS AND WHITE'S COMMERCIAL PAPER: TEACHING MATERIALS, Fourth Edition, 578 pages, 1987. Reprint from Speidel et al., Commercial Law, Fourth Edition. Teacher's Manual available. (Casebook)

SPEIDEL, SUMMERS AND WHITE'S SALES: TEACHING MATERIALS, Fourth Edition, 804 pages, 1987. Reprint from Speidel et al., Commercial Law, Fourth Edition. Teacher's Manual available. (Casebook)

SPEIDEL, SUMMERS AND WHITE'S SECURED

Commercial Law—Cont'd

TRANSACTIONS: TEACHING MATERIALS, Fourth Edition, 485 pages, 1987. Reprint from Speidel et al., Commercial Law, Fourth Edition. Teacher's Manual available. (Casebook)

STOCKTON AND MILLER'S SALES AND LEASES OF GOODS IN A NUTSHELL, Third Edition, 441 pages, 1992. Softcover. (Text)

STONE'S UNIFORM COMMERCIAL CODE IN A NUTSHELL, Third Edition, 580 pages, 1989. Softcover. (Text)

WEBER AND SPEIDEL'S COMMERCIAL PAPER IN A NUTSHELL, Third Edition, 404 pages, 1982. Softcover. (Text)

WHITE AND SUMMERS' HORNBOOK ON THE UNIFORM COMMERCIAL CODE, Third Edition, Student Edition, 1386 pages, 1988. (Text)

Community Property

MENNELL AND BOYKOFF'S COMMUNITY PROPERTY IN A NUTSHELL, Second Edition, 432 pages, 1988. Softcover. (Text)

VERRALL AND BIRD'S CASES AND MATERIALS ON CALIFORNIA COMMUNITY PROPERTY, Fifth Edition, 604 pages, 1988. (Casebook)

Comparative Law

BARTON, GIBBS, LI AND MERRYMAN'S LAW IN RADICALLY DIFFERENT CULTURES, 960 pages, 1983. (Casebook)

FOLSOM, MINAN AND OTTO'S LAW AND POLITICS IN THE PEOPLE'S REPUBLIC OF CHINA IN A NUTSHELL, 451 pages, 1992. Softcover. (Text)

GLENDON, GORDON AND OSAKWE'S COMPARATIVE LEGAL TRADITIONS: TEXT, MATERIALS AND CASES ON THE CIVIL LAW, COMMON LAW AND SOCIALIST LAW TRADITIONS, 1091 pages, 1985. (Casebook)

GLENDON, GORDON AND OSAKWE'S COMPARATIVE LEGAL TRADITIONS IN A NUTSHELL. 402 pages, 1982. Softcover. (Text)

Computers and Law

MAGGS, SOMA AND SPROWL'S COMPUTER LAW—CASES, COMMENTS, AND QUESTIONS, 731 pages, 1992. Teacher's Manual available. (Casebook)

MAGGS AND SPROWL'S COMPUTER APPLICATIONS IN THE LAW, 316 pages, 1987. (Coursebook)

MASON'S USING COMPUTERS IN THE LAW: AN INTRODUCTION AND PRACTICAL GUIDE, Second Edition, 288 pages, 1988. Softcover. (Coursebook)

Conflict of Laws

CRAMTON, CURRIE AND KAY'S CASES–COMMENTS–QUESTIONS ON CONFLICT OF LAWS, Fourth Edition, 876 pages, 1987. (Casebook)

HAY'S BLACK LETTER ON CONFLICT OF LAWS, 330 pages, 1989. Softcover. (Review)

SCOLES AND HAY'S HORNBOOK ON CONFLICT OF LAWS, Student Edition, 1160 pages, 1992. (Text)

SIEGEL'S CONFLICTS IN A NUTSHELL, 470 pages, 1982. Softcover. (Text)

Constitutional Law—Civil Rights—see also First Amendment and Foreign Relations and National Security Law

ABERNATHY'S CIVIL RIGHTS AND CONSTITUTIONAL LITIGATION, CASES AND MATERIALS, Second Edition, 753 pages, 1992. (Casebook)

BARNES AND STOUT'S THE ECONOMICS OF CONSTITUTIONAL LAW AND PUBLIC CHOICE, 127 pages, 1992. Softcover. Teacher's Manual available. (Casebook)

BARRON AND DIENES' BLACK LETTER ON CONSTITUTIONAL LAW, Third Edition, 440 pages, 1991. Softcover. (Review)

BARRON AND DIENES' CONSTITUTIONAL LAW IN A NUTSHELL, Second Edition, 483 pages, 1991. Softcover. (Text)

ENGDAHL'S CONSTITUTIONAL FEDERALISM IN A NUTSHELL, Second Edition, 411 pages, 1987. Softcover. (Text)

FARBER AND SHERRY'S HISTORY OF THE AMERICAN CONSTITUTION, 458 pages, 1990. Softcover. Teacher's Manual available. (Text)

FISHER AND DEVINS' POLITICAL DYNAMICS OF CONSTITUTIONAL LAW, 333 pages, 1992. Softcover. (Casebook Supplement)

GARVEY AND ALEINIKOFF'S MODERN CONSTITUTIONAL THEORY: A READER, Second Edition, 559 pages, 1991. Softcover. (Reader)

LOCKHART, KAMISAR, CHOPER AND SHIFFRIN'S CONSTITUTIONAL LAW: CASES–COMMENTS–QUESTIONS, Seventh Edition, 1643 pages,

Constitutional Law—Civil Rights—Cont'd

1991. (Casebook) 1992 Supplement.

LOCKHART, KAMISAR, CHOPER AND SHIFFRIN'S THE AMERICAN CONSTITUTION: CASES AND MATERIALS, Seventh Edition, 1255 pages, 1991. Abridged version of Lockhart, et al., Constitutional Law: Cases–Comments–Questions, Seventh Edition. (Casebook) 1992 Supplement.

LOCKHART, KAMISAR, CHOPER AND SHIFFRIN'S CONSTITUTIONAL RIGHTS AND LIBERTIES: CASES AND MATERIALS, Seventh Edition, 1333 pages, 1991. Reprint from Lockhart, et al., Constitutional Law: Cases–Comments–Questions, Seventh Edition. (Casebook) 1992 Supplement.

MARKS AND COOPER'S STATE CONSTITUTIONAL LAW IN A NUTSHELL, 329 pages, 1988. Softcover. (Text)

NOWAK AND ROTUNDA'S HORNBOOK ON CONSTITUTIONAL LAW, Fourth Edition, 1357 pages, 1991. (Text)

ROTUNDA'S MODERN CONSTITUTIONAL LAW: CASES AND NOTES, Fourth Edition, approximately 1100 pages, April, 1993 Pub. (Casebook)

VIEIRA'S CONSTITUTIONAL CIVIL RIGHTS IN A NUTSHELL, Second Edition, 322 pages, 1990. Softcover. (Text)

WILLIAMS' CONSTITUTIONAL ANALYSIS IN A NUTSHELL, 388 pages, 1979. Softcover. (Text)

Consumer Law—see also Commercial Law

EPSTEIN AND NICKLES' CONSUMER LAW IN A NUTSHELL, Second Edition, 418 pages, 1981. Softcover. (Text)

SELECTED COMMERCIAL STATUTES. Softcover. 1897 pages, 1992.

SPANOGLE, ROHNER, PRIDGEN AND RASOR'S CASES AND MATERIALS ON CONSUMER LAW, Second Edition, 916 pages, 1991. Teacher's Manual available. (Casebook)

Contracts

BARNES AND STOUT'S THE ECONOMICS OF CONTRACT LAW, 127 pages, 1992. Softcover. Teacher's Manual available. (Casebook)

CALAMARI AND PERILLO'S BLACK LETTER ON CONTRACTS, Second Edition, 462 pages, 1990. Softcover. (Review)

CALAMARI AND PERILLO'S HORNBOOK ON CONTRACTS, Third Edition, 1049 pages, 1987. (Text)

CALAMARI, PERILLO AND BENDER'S CASES AND PROBLEMS ON CONTRACTS, Second Edition, 905 pages, 1989. Teacher's Manual Available. (Casebook)

CORBIN'S TEXT ON CONTRACTS, One Volume Student Edition, 1224 pages, 1952. (Text)

FESSLER AND LOISEAUX'S CASES AND MATERIALS ON CONTRACTS—MORALITY, ECONOMICS AND THE MARKET PLACE, 837 pages, 1982. Teacher's Manual available. (Casebook)

FRIEDMAN'S CONTRACT REMEDIES IN A NUTSHELL, 323 pages, 1981. Softcover. (Text)

FULLER AND EISENBERG'S CASES ON BASIC CONTRACT LAW, Fifth Edition, 1037 pages, 1990. (Casebook)

HAMILTON, RAU AND WEINTRAUB'S CASES AND MATERIALS ON CONTRACTS, Second Edition, 916 pages, 1992. Teacher's Manual available. (Casebook)

KEYES' GOVERNMENT CONTRACTS IN A NUTSHELL, Second Edition, 557 pages, 1990. Softcover. (Text)

SCHABER AND ROHWER'S CONTRACTS IN A NUTSHELL, Third Edition, 457 pages, 1990. Softcover. (Text)

SUMMERS AND HILLMAN'S CONTRACT AND RELATED OBLIGATION: THEORY, DOCTRINE AND PRACTICE, Second Edition, 1037 pages, 1992. Teacher's Manual available. (Casebook)

Copyright—see Patent and Copyright Law

Corporate Finance—see also Business Planning

HAMILTON'S CASES AND MATERIALS ON CORPORATION FINANCE, Second Edition, 1221 pages, 1989. (Casebook)

OESTERLE'S THE LAW OF MERGERS, ACQUISITIONS AND REORGANIZATIONS, 1096 pages, 1991. (Casebook) 1992 Supplement.

Corporations

HAMILTON'S BLACK LETTER ON CORPORATIONS, Third Edition, 732 pages, 1992. Softcover. (Review)

HAMILTON'S CASES AND MATERIALS ON CORPORATIONS—INCLUDING PARTNERSHIPS AND

Corporations—Cont'd

LIMITED PARTNERSHIPS, Fourth Edition, 1248 pages, 1990. Teacher's Manual available. (Casebook) 1990 Statutory Supplement.

HAMILTON'S THE LAW OF CORPORATIONS IN A NUTSHELL, Third Edition, 518 pages, 1991. Softcover. (Text)

HENN'S TEACHING MATERIALS ON THE LAW OF CORPORATIONS, Second Edition, 1204 pages, 1986. Teacher's Manual available. (Casebook)

Statutory Supplement. *See Selected Corporation and Partnership*

HENN AND ALEXANDER'S HORNBOOK ON LAWS OF CORPORATIONS, Third Edition, Student Edition, 1371 pages, 1983, with 1986 pocket part. (Text)

SELECTED CORPORATION AND PARTNERSHIP STATUTES, RULES AND FORMS. Revised 1991 Edition, 953 pages. Softcover.

SOLOMON, SCHWARTZ AND BAUMAN'S MATERIALS AND PROBLEMS ON CORPORATIONS: LAW AND POLICY, Second Edition, 1391 pages, 1988. Teacher's Manual available. (Casebook) 1992 Supplement.

Statutory Supplement. *See Selected Corporation and Partnership*

Corrections

KRANTZ' THE LAW OF CORRECTIONS AND PRISONERS' RIGHTS IN A NUTSHELL, Third Edition, 407 pages, 1988. Softcover. (Text)

KRANTZ AND BRANHAM'S CASES AND MATERIALS ON THE LAW OF SENTENCING, CORRECTIONS AND PRISONERS' RIGHTS, Fourth Edition, 619 pages, 1991. Teacher's Manual available. (Casebook)

Creditors' Rights

BANKRUPTCY CODE, RULES AND OFFICIAL FORMS, LAW SCHOOL EDITION. 910 pages, 1992. Softcover.

EPSTEIN'S DEBTOR-CREDITOR LAW IN A NUTSHELL, Fourth Edition, 401 pages, 1991. Softcover. (Text)

EPSTEIN, LANDERS AND NICKLES' CASES AND MATERIALS ON DEBTORS AND CREDITORS, Third Edition, 1059 pages, 1987. Teacher's Manual available. (Casebook)

EPSTEIN, NICKLES AND WHITE'S HORNBOOK ON BANKRUPTCY, Approximately 1000 pages, January, 1992 Pub. (Text)

LOPUCKI'S PLAYER'S MANUAL FOR THE DEBTOR-CREDITOR GAME, 123 pages, 1985. Softcover. (Coursebook)

NICKLES AND EPSTEIN'S BLACK LETTER ON CREDITORS' RIGHTS AND BANKRUPTCY, 576 pages, 1989. (Review)

RIESENFELD'S CASES AND MATERIALS ON CREDITORS' REMEDIES AND DEBTORS' PROTECTION, Fourth Edition, 914 pages, 1987. (Casebook) 1990 Supplement.

WHITE AND NIMMER'S CASES AND MATERIALS ON BANKRUPTCY, Second Edition, 764 pages, 1992. Teacher's Manual available. (Casebook)

Criminal Law and Criminal Procedure—see also Corrections, Juvenile Justice

ABRAMS' FEDERAL CRIMINAL LAW AND ITS ENFORCEMENT, 866 pages, 1986. (Casebook) 1988 Supplement.

BUCY'S WHITE COLLAR CRIME, CASES AND MATERIALS, 688 pages, 1992. Teacher's Manual available. (Casebook)

DIX AND SHARLOT'S CASES AND MATERIALS ON CRIMINAL LAW, Third Edition, 846 pages, 1987. (Casebook)

GRANO'S PROBLEMS IN CRIMINAL PROCEDURE, Second Edition, 176 pages, 1981. Teacher's Manual available. Softcover. (Coursebook)

HEYMANN AND KENETY'S THE MURDER TRIAL OF WILBUR JACKSON: A HOMICIDE IN THE FAMILY, Second Edition, 347 pages, 1985. (Coursebook)

ISRAEL, KAMISAR AND LAFAVE'S CRIMINAL PROCEDURE AND THE CONSTITUTION: LEADING SUPREME COURT CASES AND INTRODUCTORY TEXT. 802 pages, 1992 Edition. Softcover. (Casebook)

ISRAEL AND LAFAVE'S CRIMINAL PROCEDURE—CONSTITUTIONAL LIMITATIONS IN A NUTSHELL, Fourth Edition, 461 pages, 1988. Softcover. (Text)

JOHNSON'S CASES, MATERIALS AND TEXT ON CRIMINAL LAW, Fourth Edition, 759 pages, 1990. Teacher's Manual available. (Casebook)

JOHNSON'S CASES AND MATERIALS ON CRIMI-

Criminal Law and Criminal Procedure—Cont'd

NAL PROCEDURE, 859 pages, 1988. (Casebook) 1992 Supplement.

KAMISAR, LAFAVE AND ISRAEL'S MODERN CRIMINAL PROCEDURE: CASES, COMMENTS AND QUESTIONS, Seventh Edition, 1593 pages, 1990. (Casebook) 1992 Supplement.

KAMISAR, LAFAVE AND ISRAEL'S BASIC CRIMINAL PROCEDURE: CASES, COMMENTS AND QUESTIONS, Seventh Edition, 792 pages, 1990. Softcover reprint from Kamisar, et al., Modern Criminal Procedure: Cases, Comments and Questions, Seventh Edition. (Casebook) 1992 Supplement.

LAFAVE'S MODERN CRIMINAL LAW: CASES, COMMENTS AND QUESTIONS, Second Edition, 903 pages, 1988. (Casebook)

LAFAVE AND ISRAEL'S HORNBOOK ON CRIMINAL PROCEDURE, Second Edition, 1309 pages, 1992 with 1992 pocket part. (Text)

LAFAVE AND SCOTT'S HORNBOOK ON CRIMINAL LAW, Second Edition, 918 pages, 1986. (Text)

LOEWY'S CRIMINAL LAW IN A NUTSHELL, Second Edition, 321 pages, 1987. Softcover. (Text)

LOW'S BLACK LETTER ON CRIMINAL LAW, Revised First Edition, 443 pages, 1990. Softcover. (Review)

SALTZBURG AND CAPRA'S CASES AND COMMENTARY ON AMERICAN CRIMINAL PROCEDURE, Fourth Edition, 1341 pages, 1992. Teacher's Manual available. (Casebook) 1992 Supplement.

SUBIN, MIRSKY AND WEINSTEIN'S THE CRIMINAL PROCESS: PROSECUTION AND DEFENSE FUNCTIONS, Approximately 450 pages, February, 1993 Pub. Softcover. Teacher's Manual available. (Text)

VORENBERG'S CASES ON CRIMINAL LAW AND PROCEDURE, Second Edition, 1088 pages, 1981. Teacher's Manual available. (Casebook) 1990 Supplement.

Domestic Relations

CLARK'S HORNBOOK ON DOMESTIC RELATIONS, Second Edition, Student Edition, 1050 pages, 1988. (Text)

CLARK AND GLOWINSKY'S CASES AND PROBLEMS ON DOMESTIC RELATIONS, Fourth Edition. 1150 pages, 1990. Teacher's Manual available. (Casebook) 1992 Supplement.

KRAUSE'S BLACK LETTER ON FAMILY LAW, 314 pages, 1988. Softcover. (Review)

KRAUSE'S CASES, COMMENTS AND QUESTIONS ON FAMILY LAW, Third Edition, 1433 pages, 1990. (Casebook)

KRAUSE'S FAMILY LAW IN A NUTSHELL, Second Edition, 444 pages, 1986. Softcover. (Text)

KRAUSKOPF'S CASES ON PROPERTY DIVISION AT MARRIAGE DISSOLUTION, 250 pages, 1984. Softcover. (Casebook)

Economics, Law and—see also Antitrust, Regulated Industries

BARNES AND STOUT'S CASES AND MATERIALS ON LAW AND ECONOMICS, 538 pages, 1992. Teacher's Manual available. (Casebook)

GOETZ' CASES AND MATERIALS ON LAW AND ECONOMICS, 547 pages, 1984. (Casebook)

MALLOY'S LAW AND ECONOMICS: A COMPARATIVE APPROACH TO THEORY AND PRACTICE, 166 pages, 1990. Softcover. (Text)

Education Law

ALEXANDER AND ALEXANDER'S PUBLIC SCHOOL LAW, Third Edition, 880 pages, 1992. Teacher's Manual available. (Coursebook)

ALEXANDER AND ALEXANDER'S THE LAW OF SCHOOLS, STUDENTS AND TEACHERS IN A NUTSHELL, 409 pages, 1984. Softcover. (Text)

YUDOF, KIRP AND LEVIN'S EDUCATIONAL POLICY AND THE LAW, Third Edition, 860 pages, 1992. (Casebook)

Employment Discrimination—see also Gender Discrimination

ESTREICHER AND HARPER'S CASES AND MATERIALS ON THE LAW GOVERNING THE EMPLOYMENT RELATIONSHIP, Second Edition, 966 pages, 1992. (Casebook) Statutory Supplement.

JONES, MURPHY AND BELTON'S CASES AND MATERIALS ON DISCRIMINATION IN EMPLOYMENT, (The Labor Law Group). Fifth Edition, 1116 pages, 1987. (Casebook) 1990 Supplement.

PLAYER'S FEDERAL LAW OF EMPLOYMENT DIS-

Employment Discrimination—Cont'd

CRIMINATION IN A NUTSHELL, Third Edition, 338 pages, 1992. Softcover. (Text)

PLAYER'S HORNBOOK ON EMPLOYMENT DISCRIMINATION LAW, Student Edition, 708 pages, 1988. (Text)

PLAYER, SHOBEN AND LIEBERWITZ' CASES AND MATERIALS ON EMPLOYMENT DISCRIMINATION LAW, 827 pages, 1990. Teacher's Manual available. (Casebook) 1992 Supplement.

Energy and Natural Resources Law—see also Oil and Gas

LAITOS' CASES AND MATERIALS ON NATURAL RESOURCES LAW, 938 pages, 1985. Teacher's Manual available. (Casebook)

LAITOS AND TOMAIN'S ENERGY AND NATURAL RESOURCES LAW IN A NUTSHELL, 554 pages, 1992. Softcover. (Text)

SELECTED ENVIRONMENTAL LAW STATUTES—EDUCATIONAL EDITION. Softcover. 1296 pages, 1992.

Environmental Law—see also Energy and Natural Resources Law; Sea, Law of

BONINE AND MCGARITY'S THE LAW OF ENVIRONMENTAL PROTECTION: CASES—LEGISLATION—POLICIES, Second Edition, 1042 pages, 1992. (Casebook)

FINDLEY AND FARBER'S CASES AND MATERIALS ON ENVIRONMENTAL LAW, Third Edition, 763 pages, 1991. Teacher's Manual available. (Casebook)

FINDLEY AND FARBER'S ENVIRONMENTAL LAW IN A NUTSHELL, Third Edition, 355 pages, 1992. Softcover. (Text)

PLATER, ABRAMS AND GOLDFARB'S ENVIRONMENTAL LAW AND POLICY: NATURE, LAW AND SOCIETY, 1039 pages, 1992. Teacher's Manual available. (Casebook)

RODGERS' HORNBOOK ON ENVIRONMENTAL LAW, 956 pages, 1977, with 1984 pocket part. (Text)

SELECTED ENVIRONMENTAL LAW STATUTES—EDUCATIONAL EDITION. Softcover. 1296 pages, 1992.

Equity—see Remedies

Estate Planning—see also Trusts and Estates; Taxation—Estate and Gift

LYNN'S INTRODUCTION TO ESTATE PLANNING IN A NUTSHELL, Fourth Edition, 352 pages, 1992. Softcover. (Text)

Evidence

BERGMAN'S TRANSCRIPT EXERCISES FOR LEARNING EVIDENCE, 273 pages, 1992. Teacher's Manual available. (Coursebook)

BROUN AND BLAKEY'S BLACK LETTER ON EVIDENCE, 269 pages, 1984. Softcover. (Review)

BROUN, MEISENHOLDER, STRONG AND MOSTELLER'S PROBLEMS IN EVIDENCE, Third Edition, 238 pages, 1988. Teacher's Manual available. Softcover. (Coursebook)

CLEARY, STRONG, BROUN AND MOSTELLER'S CASES AND MATERIALS ON EVIDENCE, Fourth Edition, 1060 pages, 1988. (Casebook)

FEDERAL RULES OF EVIDENCE FOR UNITED STATES COURTS AND MAGISTRATES. Softcover. 549 pages, 1992.

FRIEDMAN'S THE ELEMENTS OF EVIDENCE, 315 pages, 1991. Teacher's Manual available. (Coursebook)

GRAHAM'S FEDERAL RULES OF EVIDENCE IN A NUTSHELL, Third Edition, 486 pages, 1992. Softcover. (Text)

LEMPERT AND SALTZBURG'S A MODERN APPROACH TO EVIDENCE: TEXT, PROBLEMS, TRANSCRIPTS AND CASES, Second Edition, 1232 pages, 1983. Teacher's Manual available. (Casebook)

LILLY'S AN INTRODUCTION TO THE LAW OF EVIDENCE, Second Edition, 585 pages, 1987. (Text)

MCCORMICK, SUTTON AND WELLBORN'S CASES AND MATERIALS ON EVIDENCE, Seventh Edition, 932 pages, 1992. Teacher's Manual available. (Casebook)

MCCORMICK'S HORNBOOK ON EVIDENCE, Fourth Edition, Student Edition, 672 pages, 1992. (Text)

ROTHSTEIN'S EVIDENCE IN A NUTSHELL: STATE AND FEDERAL RULES, Second Edition, 514 pages, 1981. Softcover. (Text)

Federal Jurisdiction and Procedure

CURRIE'S CASES AND MATERIALS ON FEDERAL COURTS, Fourth Edition, 783 pages, 1990. (Casebook)

CURRIE'S FEDERAL JURISDICTION IN A NUTSHELL, Third Edition, 242 pages, 1990.

Federal Jurisdiction and Procedure—Cont'd

Softcover. (Text)

FEDERAL RULES OF CIVIL PROCEDURE—EDUCATIONAL EDITION. Softcover. 761 pages, 1992.

REDISH'S BLACK LETTER ON FEDERAL JURISDICTION, Second Edition, 234 pages, 1991. Softcover. (Review)

REDISH'S CASES, COMMENTS AND QUESTIONS ON FEDERAL COURTS, Second Edition, 1122 pages, 1989. (Casebook) 1992 Supplement.

VETRI AND MERRILL'S FEDERAL COURTS PROBLEMS AND MATERIALS, Second Edition, 232 pages, 1984. Softcover. (Coursebook)

WRIGHT'S HORNBOOK ON FEDERAL COURTS, Fourth Edition, Student Edition, 870 pages, 1983. (Text)

First Amendment

GARVEY AND SCHAUER'S THE FIRST AMENDMENT: A READER, 527 pages, 1992. Softcover. (Reader)

SHIFFRIN AND CHOPER'S FIRST AMENDMENT, CASES—COMMENTS—QUESTIONS, 759 pages, 1991. Softcover. (Casebook) 1992 Supplement.

Foreign Relations and National Security Law

FRANCK AND GLENNON'S FOREIGN RELATIONS AND NATIONAL SECURITY LAW, 941 pages, 1987. (Casebook)

Future Interests—see Trusts and Estates

Gender Discrimination—see also Employment Discrimination

KAY'S TEXT, CASES AND MATERIALS ON SEX-BASED DISCRIMINATION, Third Edition, 1001 pages, 1988. (Casebook) 1992 Supplement.

THOMAS' SEX DISCRIMINATION IN A NUTSHELL, Second Edition, 395 pages, 1991. Softcover. (Text)

Health Law—see Medicine, Law and

Human Rights—see International Law

Immigration Law

ALEINIKOFF AND MARTIN'S IMMIGRATION: PROCESS AND POLICY, Second Edition, 1056 pages, 1991. (Casebook)

Statutory Supplement. *See Immigration and Nationality Laws*

IMMIGRATION AND NATIONALITY LAWS OF THE UNITED STATES: SELECTED STATUTES, REGULATIONS AND FORMS. Softcover. 519 pages, 1992.

WEISSBRODT'S IMMIGRATION LAW AND PROCEDURE IN A NUTSHELL, Third Edition, 497 pages, 1992. Softcover. (Text)

Indian Law—see American Indian Law

Insurance Law

DEVINE AND TERRY'S PROBLEMS IN INSURANCE LAW, 240 pages, 1989. Softcover. Teacher's Manual available. (Coursebook)

DOBBYN'S INSURANCE LAW IN A NUTSHELL, Second Edition, 316 pages, 1989. Softcover. (Text)

KEETON'S COMPUTER-AIDED AND WORKBOOK EXERCISES ON INSURANCE LAW, 255 pages, 1990. Softcover. (Coursebook)

KEETON AND WIDISS' INSURANCE LAW, Student Edition, 1359 pages, 1988. (Text)

WIDISS AND KEETON'S COURSE SUPPLEMENT TO KEETON AND WIDISS' INSURANCE LAW, 502 pages, 1988. Softcover. Teacher's Manual available. (Casebook)

WIDISS' INSURANCE: MATERIALS ON FUNDAMENTAL PRINCIPLES, LEGAL DOCTRINES AND REGULATORY ACTS, 1186 pages, 1989. Teacher's Manual available. (Casebook)

YORK AND WHELAN'S CASES, MATERIALS AND PROBLEMS ON GENERAL PRACTICE INSURANCE LAW, Second Edition, 787 pages, 1988. Teacher's Manual available. (Casebook)

International Law—see also Sea, Law of

BERMANN, DAVEY, FOX AND GOEBEL'S CASES AND MATERIALS ON EUROPEAN COMMUNITY LAW, Approximately 1200 pages, 1993. (Casebook) Statutory Supplement. *See European Economic Community: Selected Documents*

BUERGENTHAL'S INTERNATIONAL HUMAN RIGHTS IN A NUTSHELL, 283 pages, 1988. Softcover. (Text)

BUERGENTHAL AND MAIER'S PUBLIC INTERNATIONAL LAW IN A NUTSHELL, Second Edition, 275 pages, 1990. Softcover. (Text)

EUROPEAN ECONOMIC COMMUNITY: SELECTED DOCUMENTS. Approximately 550 pages,

International Law—Cont'd

1993. Softcover

FOLSOM'S EUROPEAN COMMUNITY LAW IN A NUTSHELL, 423 pages, 1992. Softcover. (Text)

FOLSOM, GORDON AND SPANOGLE'S INTERNATIONAL BUSINESS TRANSACTIONS—A PROBLEM-ORIENTED COURSEBOOK, Second Edition, 1237 pages, 1991. Teacher's Manual available. (Casebook) 1991 Documents Supplement.

FOLSOM, GORDON AND SPANOGLE'S INTERNATIONAL BUSINESS TRANSACTIONS IN A NUTSHELL, Fourth Edition, 548 pages, 1992. Softcover. (Text)

HENKIN, PUGH, SCHACHTER AND SMIT'S CASES AND MATERIALS ON INTERNATIONAL LAW, Second Edition, 1517 pages, 1987. (Casebook) Documents Supplement.

INTERNATIONAL LITIGATION AND ARBITRATION: SELECTED TREATIES, STATUTES AND RULES. Approximately 275 pages, 1993. Softcover

INTERNATIONAL ORGANIZATIONS IN THEIR LEGAL SETTING: SELECTED DOCUMENTS. Approximately 500 pages, March, 1993 Pub. Softcover

JACKSON AND DAVEY'S CASES, MATERIALS AND TEXT ON LEGAL PROBLEMS OF INTERNATIONAL ECONOMIC RELATIONS, Second Edition, 1269 pages, 1986. (Casebook) 1989 Documents Supplement.

KIRGIS' INTERNATIONAL ORGANIZATIONS IN THEIR LEGAL SETTING, Second Edition, approximately 1150 pages, March, 1993 Pub. Teacher's Manual available. (Casebook) Statutory Supplement.

LOWENFELD'S INTERNATIONAL LITIGATION AND ARBITRATION, Approximately 875 pages, 1993. (Casebook) Statutory Supplement. *See International Litigation: Selected Documents*

WESTON, FALK AND D'AMATO'S INTERNATIONAL LAW AND WORLD ORDER—A PROBLEM-ORIENTED COURSEBOOK, Second Edition, 1335 pages, 1990. Teacher's Manual available. (Casebook) Documents Supplement.

Interviewing and Counseling

BINDER AND PRICE'S LEGAL INTERVIEWING AND COUNSELING, 232 pages, 1977. Softcover. Teacher's Manual available. (Coursebook)

BINDER, BERGMAN AND PRICE'S LAWYERS AS COUNSELORS: A CLIENT-CENTERED APPROACH, 427 pages, 1991. Softcover. (Coursebook)

SHAFFER AND ELKINS' LEGAL INTERVIEWING AND COUNSELING IN A NUTSHELL, Second Edition, 487 pages, 1987. Softcover. (Text)

Introduction to Law—see Legal Method and Legal System

Introduction to Law Study

HEGLAND'S INTRODUCTION TO THE STUDY AND PRACTICE OF LAW IN A NUTSHELL, 418 pages, 1983. Softcover. (Text)

KINYON'S INTRODUCTION TO LAW STUDY AND LAW EXAMINATIONS IN A NUTSHELL, 389 pages, 1971. Softcover. (Text)

Judicial Process—see Legal Method and Legal System

Jurisprudence

CHRISTIE'S JURISPRUDENCE—TEXT AND READINGS ON THE PHILOSOPHY OF LAW, 1056 pages, 1973. (Casebook)

SINHA'S JURISPRUDENCE (LEGAL PHILOSOPHY) IN A NUTSHELL. Approximately 350 pages, 1993. Softcover. (Text)

Juvenile Justice

FOX'S JUVENILE COURTS IN A NUTSHELL, Third Edition, 291 pages, 1984. Softcover. (Text)

Labor and Employment Law—see also Employment Discrimination, Workers' Compensation

FINKIN, GOLDMAN AND SUMMERS' LEGAL PROTECTION OF INDIVIDUAL EMPLOYEES, (The Labor Law Group). 1164 pages, 1989. (Casebook)

GORMAN'S BASIC TEXT ON LABOR LAW—UNIONIZATION AND COLLECTIVE BARGAINING, 914 pages, 1976. (Text)

LESLIE'S LABOR LAW IN A NUTSHELL, Third Edition, 388 pages, 1992. Softcover. (Text)

NOLAN'S LABOR ARBITRATION LAW AND PRAC-

Labor and Employment Law—Cont'd

TICE IN A NUTSHELL, 358 pages, 1979. Softcover. (Text)

OBERER, HANSLOWE, ANDERSEN AND HEINSZ' CASES AND MATERIALS ON LABOR LAW—COLLECTIVE BARGAINING IN A FREE SOCIETY, Third Edition, 1163 pages, 1986. Teacher's Manual available. (Casebook) Statutory Supplement. 1991 Case Supplement.

RABIN, SILVERSTEIN AND SCHATZKI'S LABOR AND EMPLOYMENT LAW: PROBLEMS, CASES AND MATERIALS IN THE LAW OF WORK, (The Labor Law Group). 1014 pages, 1988. Teacher's Manual available. (Casebook) 1988 Statutory Supplement.

WOLLETT, GRODIN AND WEISBERGER'S COLLECTIVE BARGAINING IN PUBLIC EMPLOYMENT, (The Labor Law Group). Fourth Edition, approximately 600 pages, April, 1993 Pub. (Casebook)

Land Finance—Property Security—see Real Estate Transactions

Land Use

CALLIES AND FREILICH'S CASES AND MATERIALS ON LAND USE, 1233 pages, 1986. (Casebook) 1991 Supplement.

HAGMAN AND JUERGENSMEYER'S HORNBOOK ON URBAN PLANNING AND LAND DEVELOPMENT CONTROL LAW, Second Edition, Student Edition, 680 pages, 1986. (Text)

WRIGHT AND GITELMAN'S CASES AND MATERIALS ON LAND USE, Fourth Edition, 1255 pages, 1991. Teacher's Manual available. (Casebook)

WRIGHT AND WRIGHT'S LAND USE IN A NUTSHELL, Second Edition, 356 pages, 1985. Softcover. (Text)

Legal History—see also Legal Method and Legal System

PRESSER AND ZAINALDIN'S CASES AND MATERIALS ON LAW AND JURISPRUDENCE IN AMERICAN HISTORY, Second Edition, 1092 pages, 1989. Teacher's Manual available. (Casebook)

Legal Method and Legal System—see also Legal Research, Legal Writing

ALDISERT'S READINGS, MATERIALS AND CASES IN THE JUDICIAL PROCESS, 948 pages, 1976. (Casebook)

BERCH, BERCH AND SPRITZER'S INTRODUCTION TO LEGAL METHOD AND PROCESS, Second Edition, 585 pages, 1992. Teacher's Manual available. (Casebook)

BODENHEIMER, OAKLEY AND LOVE'S READINGS AND CASES ON AN INTRODUCTION TO THE ANGLO-AMERICAN LEGAL SYSTEM, Second Edition, 166 pages, 1988. Softcover. (Casebook)

DAVIES AND LAWRY'S INSTITUTIONS AND METHODS OF THE LAW—INTRODUCTORY TEACHING MATERIALS, 547 pages, 1982. Teacher's Manual available. (Casebook)

DVORKIN, HIMMELSTEIN AND LESNICK'S BECOMING A LAWYER: A HUMANISTIC PERSPECTIVE ON LEGAL EDUCATION AND PROFESSIONALISM, 211 pages, 1981. Softcover. (Text)

KEETON'S JUDGING, 842 pages, 1990. Softcover. (Coursebook)

KELSO AND KELSO'S STUDYING LAW: AN INTRODUCTION, 587 pages, 1984. (Coursebook)

KEMPIN'S HISTORICAL INTRODUCTION TO ANGLO-AMERICAN LAW IN A NUTSHELL, Third Edition, 323 pages, 1990. Softcover. (Text)

MEADOR'S AMERICAN COURTS, 113 pages, 1991. Softcover. (Text)

REYNOLDS' JUDICIAL PROCESS IN A NUTSHELL, Second Edition, 308 pages, 1991. Softcover. (Text)

Legal Research

COHEN AND OLSON'S LEGAL RESEARCH IN A NUTSHELL, Fifth Edition, 370 pages, 1992. Softcover. (Text)

COHEN, BERRING AND OLSON'S HOW TO FIND THE LAW, Ninth Edition, 716 pages, 1989. (Text)

COHEN, BERRING AND OLSON'S FINDING THE LAW, 570 pages, 1989. Softcover reprint from Cohen, Berring and Olson's How to Find the Law, Ninth Edition. (Coursebook)

Legal Research Exercises, 4th Ed., for use with Cohen, Berring and Olson, 253 pages, 1992. Teacher's Manual available.

ROMBAUER'S LEGAL PROBLEM SOLVING—ANALYSIS, RESEARCH AND WRITING, Fifth Edition, 524 pages, 1991. Softcover. Teacher's Manual with problems availa-

Legal Research—Cont'd

ble. (Coursebook)

STATSKY'S LEGAL RESEARCH AND WRITING: SOME STARTING POINTS, Fourth Edition, approximately 270 pages, 1993. Softcover. Teacher's Manual available. (Coursebook) Student Workbook.

TEPLY'S LEGAL RESEARCH AND CITATION, Fourth Edition, 436 pages, 1992. Softcover. (Coursebook)

Student Library Exercises, Fourth Edition, 276 pages, 1992. Answer Key available.

Legal Writing and Drafting

CHILD'S DRAFTING LEGAL DOCUMENTS: PRINCIPLES AND PRACTICES, Second Edition, 425 pages, 1992. Softcover. Teacher's Manual available. (Coursebook)

DICKERSON'S MATERIALS ON LEGAL DRAFTING, 425 pages, 1981. Teacher's Manual available. (Coursebook)

FELSENFELD AND SIEGEL'S WRITING CONTRACTS IN PLAIN ENGLISH, 290 pages, 1981. Softcover. (Text)

GOPEN'S WRITING FROM A LEGAL PERSPECTIVE, 225 pages, 1981. (Text)

MARTINEAU'S DRAFTING LEGISLATION AND RULES IN PLAIN ENGLISH, 155 pages, 1991. Softcover. Teacher's Manual available. (Text)

MELLINKOFF'S DICTIONARY OF AMERICAN LEGAL USAGE, 703 pages, 1992. Softcover. (Text)

MELLINKOFF'S LEGAL WRITING—SENSE AND NONSENSE, 242 pages, 1982. Softcover. Teacher's Manual available. (Text)

PRATT'S LEGAL WRITING: A SYSTEMATIC APPROACH, Second Edition, approximately 550 pages, April, 1993 Pub. Teacher's Manual available. (Coursebook)

RAY AND COX'S BEYOND THE BASICS: A TEXT FOR ADVANCED LEGAL WRITING, 427 pages, 1991. Softcover. Teacher's Manual available. (Text)

RAY AND RAMSFIELD'S LEGAL WRITING: GETTING IT RIGHT AND GETTING IT WRITTEN, 250 pages, 1987. Softcover. (Text)

SQUIRES AND ROMBAUER'S LEGAL WRITING IN A NUTSHELL, 294 pages, 1982. Softcover. (Text)

STATSKY AND WERNET'S CASE ANALYSIS AND FUNDAMENTALS OF LEGAL WRITING, Third Edition, 424 pages, 1989. Teacher's Manual available. (Text)

TEPLY'S LEGAL WRITING, ANALYSIS AND ORAL ARGUMENT, 576 pages, 1990. Softcover. Teacher's Manual available. (Coursebook)

WEIHOFEN'S LEGAL WRITING STYLE, Second Edition, 332 pages, 1980. (Text)

Legislation—see also Legal Writing and Drafting

DAVIES' LEGISLATIVE LAW AND PROCESS IN A NUTSHELL, Second Edition, 346 pages, 1986. Softcover. (Text)

ESKRIDGE AND FRICKEY'S CASES AND MATERIALS ON LEGISLATION: STATUTES AND THE CREATION OF PUBLIC POLICY, 937 pages, 1988. Teacher's Manual available. (Casebook) 1992 Supplement.

NUTTING AND DICKERSON'S CASES AND MATERIALS ON LEGISLATION, Fifth Edition, 744 pages, 1978. (Casebook)

STATSKY'S LEGISLATIVE ANALYSIS AND DRAFTING, Second Edition, 217 pages, 1984. Teacher's Manual available. (Text)

Local Government

FRUG'S CASES AND MATERIALS ON LOCAL GOVERNMENT LAW, 1005 pages, 1988. (Casebook) 1991 Supplement.

MCCARTHY'S LOCAL GOVERNMENT LAW IN A NUTSHELL, Third Edition, 435 pages, 1990. Softcover. (Text)

REYNOLDS' HORNBOOK ON LOCAL GOVERNMENT LAW, 860 pages, 1982 with 1990 pocket part. (Text)

VALENTE AND MCCARTHY'S CASES AND MATERIALS ON LOCAL GOVERNMENT LAW, Fourth Edition, 1158 pages, 1992. Teacher's Manual available. (Casebook)

Mass Communication Law

GILLMOR, BARRON, SIMON AND TERRY'S CASES AND COMMENT ON MASS COMMUNICATION LAW, Fifth Edition, 947 pages, 1990. (Casebook)

GINSBURG, BOTEIN AND DIRECTOR'S REGULATION OF THE ELECTRONIC MASS MEDIA: LAW

Mass Communication Law—Cont'd

AND POLICY FOR RADIO, TELEVISION, CABLE AND THE NEW VIDEO TECHNOLOGIES, Second Edition, 657 pages, 1991. (Casebook) Statutory Supplement.

ZUCKMAN, GAYNES, CARTER AND DEE'S MASS COMMUNICATIONS LAW IN A NUTSHELL, Third Edition, 538 pages, 1988. Softcover. (Text)

Medicine, Law and

FISCINA, BOUMIL, SHARPE AND HEAD'S MEDICAL LIABILITY, 487 pages, 1991. Teacher's Manual available. (Casebook)

FURROW, JOHNSON, JOST AND SCHWARTZ' HEALTH LAW: CASES, MATERIALS AND PROBLEMS, Second Edition, 1236 pages, 1991. Teacher's Manual available. (Casebook)

FURROW, JOHNSON, JOST AND SCHWARTZ' BIOETHICS: HEALTH CARE LAW AND ETHICS, Reprint from Furrow et al., Health Law, Second Edition. Softcover. Teacher's Manual available. (Casebook)

FURROW, JOHNSON, JOST AND SCHWARTZ' THE LAW OF HEALTH CARE ORGANIZATION AND FINANCE, Reprint from Furrow et al., Health Law, Second Edition. Softcover. Teacher's Manual available.

FURROW, JOHNSON, JOST AND SCHWARTZ' LIABILITY AND QUALITY ISSUES IN HEALTH CARE, Reprint from Furrow et al., Health Law, Second Edition. Softcover. Teacher's Manual available. (Casebook)

HALL AND ELLMAN'S HEALTH CARE LAW AND ETHICS IN A NUTSHELL, 401 pages, 1990. Softcover (Text)

JARVIS, CLOSEN, HERMANN AND LEONARD'S AIDS LAW IN A NUTSHELL, 349 pages, 1991. Softcover. (Text)

KING'S THE LAW OF MEDICAL MALPRACTICE IN A NUTSHELL, Second Edition, 342 pages, 1986. Softcover. (Text)

SHAPIRO AND SPECE'S CASES, MATERIALS AND PROBLEMS ON BIOETHICS AND LAW, 892 pages, 1981. (Casebook) 1991 Supplement.

Military Law

SHANOR AND TERRELL'S MILITARY LAW IN A NUTSHELL, 378 pages, 1980. Softcover. (Text)

Mining Law—see Energy and Natural Resources Law

Mortgages—see Real Estate Transactions

Natural Resources Law—see Energy and Natural Resources Law, Environmental Law

Negotiation

GIFFORD'S LEGAL NEGOTIATION: THEORY AND APPLICATIONS, 225 pages, 1989. Softcover. (Text)

TEPLY'S LEGAL NEGOTIATION IN A NUTSHELL, 282 pages, 1992. Softcover. (Text)

WILLIAMS' LEGAL NEGOTIATION AND SETTLEMENT, 207 pages, 1983. Softcover. Teacher's Manual available. (Coursebook)

Office Practice—see also Computers and Law, Interviewing and Counseling, Negotiation

HEGLAND'S TRIAL AND PRACTICE SKILLS IN A NUTSHELL, 346 pages, 1978. Softcover (Text)

MUNNEKE'S LAW PRACTICE MANAGEMENT: MATERIALS AND CASES, 634 pages, 1991. Teacher's Manual available. (Casebook)

Oil and Gas—see also Energy and Natural Resources Law

HEMINGWAY'S HORNBOOK ON THE LAW OF OIL AND GAS, Third Edition, Student Edition, 711 pages, 1992. (Text)

KUNTZ, LOWE, ANDERSON AND SMITH'S CASES AND MATERIALS ON OIL AND GAS LAW, Second Edition, approximately 1000 pages, 1993. Teacher's Manual available. (Casebook) Forms Manual. Revised.

LOWE'S OIL AND GAS LAW IN A NUTSHELL, Second Edition, 465 pages, 1988. Softcover. (Text)

Partnership—see Agency—Partnership

Patent and Copyright Law

CHOATE, FRANCIS AND COLLINS' CASES AND MATERIALS ON PATENT LAW, INCLUDING TRADE SECRETS, COPYRIGHTS, TRADEMARKS, Third Edition, 1009 pages, 1987. (Casebook)

HALPERN, SHIPLEY AND ABRAMS' CASES AND MATERIALS ON COPYRIGHT, 663 pages, 1992. (Casebook)

Patent and Copyright Law—Cont'd

MILLER AND DAVIS' INTELLECTUAL PROPERTY—PATENTS, TRADEMARKS AND COPYRIGHT IN A NUTSHELL, Second Edition, 437 pages, 1990. Softcover. (Text)

NIMMER, MARCUS, MYERS AND NIMMER'S CASES AND MATERIALS ON COPYRIGHT AND OTHER ASPECTS OF ENTERTAINMENT LITIGATION—INCLUDING UNFAIR COMPETITION, DEFAMATION, PRIVACY, ILLUSTRATED, Fourth Edition, 1177 pages, 1991. (Casebook) Statutory Supplement. See *Selected Intellectual Property Statutes*

SELECTED INTELLECTUAL PROPERTY AND UNFAIR COMPETITION STATUTES, REGULATIONS AND TREATIES. Softcover.

Products Liability

FISCHER AND POWERS' CASES AND MATERIALS ON PRODUCTS LIABILITY, 685 pages, 1988. Teacher's Manual available. (Casebook)

PHILLIPS' PRODUCTS LIABILITY IN A NUTSHELL, Third Edition, 307 pages, 1988. Softcover. (Text)

Professional Responsibility

ARONSON, DEVINE AND FISCH'S PROBLEMS, CASES AND MATERIALS IN PROFESSIONAL RESPONSIBILITY, 745 pages, 1985. Teacher's Manual available. (Casebook)

ARONSON AND WECKSTEIN'S PROFESSIONAL RESPONSIBILITY IN A NUTSHELL, Second Edition, 514 pages, 1991. Softcover. (Text)

LESNICK'S BEING A LAWYER: INDIVIDUAL CHOICE AND RESPONSIBILITY IN THE PRACTICE OF LAW, 422 pages, 1992. Softcover. Teacher's Manual available. (Coursebook)

MELLINKOFF'S THE CONSCIENCE OF A LAWYER, 304 pages, 1973. (Text)

PIRSIG AND KIRWIN'S CASES AND MATERIALS ON PROFESSIONAL RESPONSIBILITY, Fourth Edition, 603 pages, 1984. Teacher's Manual available. (Casebook)

ROTUNDA'S BLACK LETTER ON PROFESSIONAL RESPONSIBILITY, Third Edition, 492 pages, 1992. Softcover. (Review)

SCHWARTZ, WYDICK AND PERSCHBACHER'S PROBLEMS IN LEGAL ETHICS, Third Edition, approximately 400 pages, 1993. (Coursebook)

SELECTED STATUTES, RULES AND STANDARDS ON THE LEGAL PROFESSION. Softcover. 940 pages, 1992.

SMITH AND MALLEN'S PREVENTING LEGAL MALPRACTICE, 264 pages, 1989. Reprint from Mallen and Smith's Legal Malpractice, Third Edition. (Text)

SUTTON AND DZIENKOWSKI'S CASES AND MATERIALS ON PROFESSIONAL RESPONSIBILITY FOR LAWYERS, 839 pages, 1989. Teacher's Manual available. (Casebook)

WOLFRAM'S HORNBOOK ON MODERN LEGAL ETHICS, Student Edition, 1120 pages, 1986. (Text)

WYDICK AND PERSCHBACHER'S CALIFORNIA LEGAL ETHICS, 439 pages, 1992. Softcover. (Coursebook)

Property—see also Real Estate Transactions, Land Use, Trusts and Estates

BARNES AND STOUT'S THE ECONOMICS OF PROPERTY RIGHTS AND NUISANCE LAW, 87 pages, 1992. Softcover. Teacher's Manual available. (Casebook)

BERNHARDT'S BLACK LETTER ON PROPERTY, Second Edition, 388 pages, 1991. Softcover. (Review)

BERNHARDT'S REAL PROPERTY IN A NUTSHELL, Second Edition, 448 pages, 1981. Softcover. (Text)

BOYER, HOVENKAMP AND KURTZ' THE LAW OF PROPERTY, AN INTRODUCTORY SURVEY, Fourth Edition, 696 pages, 1991. (Text)

BROWDER, CUNNINGHAM, NELSON, STOEBUCK AND WHITMAN'S CASES ON BASIC PROPERTY LAW, Fifth Edition, 1386 pages, 1989. Teacher's Manual available. (Casebook)

BRUCE, ELY AND BOSTICK'S CASES AND MATERIALS ON MODERN PROPERTY LAW, Second Edition, 953 pages, 1989. Teacher's Manual available. (Casebook)

BURKE'S PERSONAL PROPERTY IN A NUTSHELL, Second Edition, approximately 400 pages, May, 1993 Pub. Softcover. (Text)

CUNNINGHAM, STOEBUCK AND WHITMAN'S HORNBOOK ON THE LAW OF PROPERTY, Second Edition, approximately 900 pages, May, 1993 Pub. (Text)

DONAHUE, KAUPER AND MARTIN'S CASES AND MATERIALS ON PROPERTY, AN INTRODUCTION TO THE CONCEPT AND THE INSTITUTION, Third

Property—Cont'd

Edition, approximately 1000 pages, 1993. Teacher's Manual available. (Casebook)

HILL'S LANDLORD AND TENANT LAW IN A NUTSHELL, Second Edition, 311 pages, 1986. Softcover. (Text)

JOHNSON, JOST, SALSICH AND SHAFFER'S PROPERTY LAW, CASES, MATERIALS AND PROBLEMS, 908 pages, 1992. Teacher's Manual available. (Casebook)

KURTZ AND HOVENKAMP'S CASES AND MATERIALS ON AMERICAN PROPERTY LAW, Second Edition, approximately 1350 pages, March, 1993 Pub. Teacher's Manual available. (Casebook)

MOYNIHAN'S INTRODUCTION TO REAL PROPERTY, Second Edition, 239 pages, 1988. (Text)

Psychiatry, Law and

REISNER AND SLOBOGIN'S LAW AND THE MENTAL HEALTH SYSTEM, CIVIL AND CRIMINAL ASPECTS, Second Edition, 1117 pages, 1990. Teacher's Manual available. (Casebook) 1992 Supplement.

Real Estate Transactions

BRUCE'S REAL ESTATE FINANCE IN A NUTSHELL, Third Edition, 287 pages, 1991. Softcover. (Text)

MAXWELL, RIESENFELD, HETLAND AND WARREN'S CASES ON CALIFORNIA SECURITY TRANSACTIONS IN LAND, Fourth Edition, 778 pages, 1992. Teacher's Manual available. (Casebook)

NELSON AND WHITMAN'S BLACK LETTER ON LAND TRANSACTIONS AND FINANCE, Second Edition, 466 pages, 1988. Softcover. (Review)

NELSON AND WHITMAN'S CASES AND MATERIALS ON REAL ESTATE TRANSFER, FINANCE AND DEVELOPMENT, Fourth Edition, 1346 pages, 1992. (Casebook)

NELSON AND WHITMAN'S HORNBOOK ON REAL ESTATE FINANCE LAW, Second Edition, 941 pages, 1985 with 1989 pocket part. (Text)

Regulated Industries—see also Mass Communication Law, Banking Law

GELLHORN AND PIERCE'S REGULATED INDUSTRIES IN A NUTSHELL, Second Edition, 389 pages, 1987. Softcover. (Text)

MORGAN, HARRISON AND VERKUIL'S CASES AND MATERIALS ON ECONOMIC REGULATION OF BUSINESS, Second Edition, 666 pages, 1985. (Casebook)

Remedies

DOBBS' HORNBOOK ON REMEDIES, Second Edition, approximately 1000 pages, April, 1993 Pub. (Text)

DOBBS' PROBLEMS IN REMEDIES. 137 pages, 1974. Teacher's Manual available. Softcover. (Coursebook)

DOBBYN'S INJUNCTIONS IN A NUTSHELL, 264 pages, 1974. Softcover. (Text)

FRIEDMAN'S CONTRACT REMEDIES IN A NUTSHELL, 323 pages, 1981. Softcover. (Text)

LEAVELL, LOVE AND NELSON'S CASES AND MATERIALS ON EQUITABLE REMEDIES, RESTITUTION AND DAMAGES, Fourth Edition, 1111 pages, 1986. Teacher's Manual available. (Casebook)

O'CONNELL'S REMEDIES IN A NUTSHELL, Second Edition, 320 pages, 1985. Softcover. (Text)

SCHOENBROD, MACBETH, LEVINE AND JUNG'S CASES AND MATERIALS ON REMEDIES: PUBLIC AND PRIVATE, 848 pages, 1990. Teacher's Manual available. (Casebook) 1992 Supplement.

YORK, BAUMAN AND RENDLEMAN'S CASES AND MATERIALS ON REMEDIES, Fifth Edition, 1270 pages, 1992. Teacher's Manual available. (Casebook)

Sea, Law of

SOHN AND GUSTAFSON'S THE LAW OF THE SEA IN A NUTSHELL, 264 pages, 1984. Softcover. (Text)

Securities Regulation

HAZEN'S HORNBOOK ON THE LAW OF SECURITIES REGULATION, Second Edition, Student Edition, 1082 pages, 1990. (Text)

RATNER'S SECURITIES REGULATION IN A NUTSHELL, Fourth Edition, 320 pages, 1992. Softcover. (Text)

RATNER AND HAZEN'S SECURITIES REGULATION: CASES AND MATERIALS, Fourth Edition, 1062 pages, 1991. Teacher's Manual available. (Casebook) Problems and Sample Documents Supplement.

Statutory Supplement. *See Securities*

Securities Regulation—Cont'd

Regulation, Selected Statutes

SECURITIES REGULATION, SELECTED STATUTES, RULES, AND FORMS. Softcover. Approximately 1375 pages, 1993.

Sports Law

CHAMPION'S SPORTS LAW IN A NUTSHELL,. Approximately 300 pages, January, 1993 Pub. Softcover. (Text)

SCHUBERT, SMITH AND TRENTADUE'S SPORTS LAW, 395 pages, 1986. (Text)

Tax Practice and Procedure

GARBIS, RUBIN AND MORGAN'S CASES AND MATERIALS ON TAX PROCEDURE AND TAX FRAUD, Third Edition, 921 pages, 1992. Teacher's Manual available. (Casebook)

MORGAN'S TAX PROCEDURE AND TAX FRAUD IN A NUTSHELL, 400 pages, 1990. Softcover. (Text)

Taxation—Corporate

KAHN AND GANN'S CORPORATE TAXATION, Third Edition, 980 pages, 1989. Teacher's Manual available. (Casebook) 1991 Supplement.

SCHWARZ AND LATHROPE'S BLACK LETTER ON CORPORATE AND PARTNERSHIP TAXATION, 537 pages, 1991. Softcover. (Review)

WEIDENBRUCH AND BURKE'S FEDERAL INCOME TAXATION OF CORPORATIONS AND STOCKHOLDERS IN A NUTSHELL, Third Edition, 309 pages, 1989. Softcover. (Text)

Taxation—Estate & Gift—see also Estate Planning, Trusts and Estates

MCNULTY'S FEDERAL ESTATE AND GIFT TAXATION IN A NUTSHELL, Fourth Edition, 496 pages, 1989. Softcover. (Text)

PEAT AND WILLBANKS' FEDERAL ESTATE AND GIFT TAXATION: AN ANALYSIS AND CRITIQUE, 265 pages, 1991. Softcover. (Text)

PENNELL'S CASES AND MATERIALS ON INCOME TAXATION OF TRUSTS, ESTATES, GRANTORS AND BENEFICIARIES, 460 pages, 1987. Teacher's Manual available. (Casebook)

Taxation—Individual

DODGE'S THE LOGIC OF TAX, 343 pages, 1989. Softcover. (Text)

GUNN AND WARD'S CASES, TEXT AND PROBLEMS ON FEDERAL INCOME TAXATION, Third Edition, 817 pages, 1992. Teacher's Manual available. (Casebook)

HUDSON AND LIND'S BLACK LETTER ON FEDERAL INCOME TAXATION, Fourth Edition, 410 pages, 1992. Softcover. (Review)

MCNULTY'S FEDERAL INCOME TAXATION OF INDIVIDUALS IN A NUTSHELL, Fourth Edition, 503 pages, 1988. Softcover. (Text)

POSIN'S FEDERAL INCOME TAXATION, Second Edition, approximately 650 pages, May, 1993 Pub. Softcover. (Text)

ROSE AND CHOMMIE'S HORNBOOK ON FEDERAL INCOME TAXATION, Third Edition, 923 pages, 1988, with 1991 pocket part. (Text)

SELECTED FEDERAL TAXATION STATUTES AND REGULATIONS. Softcover. 1686 pages, 1993.

Taxation—International

DOERNBERG'S INTERNATIONAL TAXATION IN A NUTSHELL, 325 pages, 1989. Softcover. (Text)

KAPLAN'S FEDERAL TAXATION OF INTERNATIONAL TRANSACTIONS: PRINCIPLES, PLANNING AND POLICY, 635 pages, 1988. (Casebook)

Taxation—Partnership

BERGER AND WIEDENBECK'S CASES AND MATERIALS ON PARTNERSHIP TAXATION, 788 pages, 1989. Teacher's Manual available. (Casebook) 1991 Supplement.

BISHOP AND BROOKS' FEDERAL PARTNERSHIP TAXATION: A GUIDE TO THE LEADING CASES, STATUTES, AND REGULATIONS, 545 pages, 1990. Softcover. (Text)

BURKE'S FEDERAL INCOME TAXATION OF PARTNERSHIPS IN A NUTSHELL, 356 pages, 1992. Softcover. (Text)

SCHWARZ AND LATHROPE'S BLACK LETTER ON CORPORATE AND PARTNERSHIP TAXATION, 537 pages, 1991. Softcover. (Review)

Taxation—State & Local

GELFAND AND SALSICH'S STATE AND LOCAL TAXATION AND FINANCE IN A NUTSHELL, 309 pages, 1986. Softcover. (Text)

HELLERSTEIN AND HELLERSTEIN'S CASES AND MATERIALS ON STATE AND LOCAL TAXATION, Fifth Edition, 1071 pages, 1988. (Case-

Taxation—State & Local—Cont'd

book)

Torts—see also Products Liability

BARNES AND STOUT'S THE ECONOMIC ANALYSIS OF TORT LAW, 161 pages, 1992. Softcover. Teacher's Manual available. (Casebook)

CHRISTIE AND MEEKS' CASES AND MATERIALS ON THE LAW OF TORTS, Second Edition, 1264 pages, 1990. (Casebook)

DOBBS' TORTS AND COMPENSATION—PERSONAL ACCOUNTABILITY AND SOCIAL RESPONSIBILITY FOR INJURY, 955 pages, 1985. Teacher's Manual available. (Casebook) 1990 Supplement.

KEETON, KEETON, SARGENTICH AND STEINER'S CASES AND MATERIALS ON TORT AND ACCIDENT LAW, Second Edition, 1318 pages, 1989. (Casebook)

KIONKA'S BLACK LETTER ON TORTS, 339 pages, 1988. Softcover. (Review)

KIONKA'S TORTS IN A NUTSHELL, Second Edition, 449 pages, 1992. Softcover. (Text)

PROSSER AND KEETON'S HORNBOOK ON TORTS, Fifth Edition, Student Edition, 1286 pages, 1984 with 1988 pocket part. (Text)

ROBERTSON, POWERS AND ANDERSON'S CASES AND MATERIALS ON TORTS, 932 pages, 1989. Teacher's Manual available. (Casebook)

Trade Regulation—see also Antitrust, Regulated Industries

MCMANIS' UNFAIR TRADE PRACTICES IN A NUTSHELL, Third Edition, approximately 450 pages, 1993. Softcover. (Text)

SCHECHTER'S BLACK LETTER ON UNFAIR TRADE PRACTICES, 272 pages, 1986. Softcover. (Review)

WESTON, MAGGS AND SCHECHTER'S UNFAIR TRADE PRACTICES AND CONSUMER PROTECTION, CASES AND COMMENTS, Fifth Edition, 957 pages, 1992. Teacher's Manual available. (Casebook)

Trial and Appellate Advocacy—see also Civil Procedure

APPELLATE ADVOCACY, HANDBOOK OF, Second Edition, 182 pages, 1986. Softcover. (Text)

BERGMAN'S TRIAL ADVOCACY IN A NUTSHELL, Second Edition, 354 pages, 1989. Softcover. (Text)

BINDER AND BERGMAN'S FACT INVESTIGATION: FROM HYPOTHESIS TO PROOF, 354 pages, 1984. Teacher's Manual available. (Coursebook)

CARLSON'S ADJUDICATION OF CRIMINAL JUSTICE: PROBLEMS AND REFERENCES, 130 pages, 1986. Softcover. (Casebook)

CARLSON AND IMWINKELRIED'S DYNAMICS OF TRIAL PRACTICE: PROBLEMS AND MATERIALS, 414 pages, 1989. Teacher's Manual available. (Coursebook) 1990 Supplement.

CLARY'S PRIMER ON THE ANALYSIS AND PRESENTATION OF LEGAL ARGUMENT, 106 pages, 1992. Softcover. (Text)

DESSEM'S PRETRIAL LITIGATION IN A NUTSHELL, 382 pages, 1992. Softcover. (Text)

DESSEM'S PRETRIAL LITIGATION: LAW, POLICY AND PRACTICE, 608 pages, 1991. Softcover. Teacher's Manual available. (Coursebook)

DEVINE'S NON-JURY CASE FILES FOR TRIAL ADVOCACY, 258 pages, 1991. (Coursebook)

GOLDBERG'S THE FIRST TRIAL (WHERE DO I SIT? WHAT DO I SAY?) IN A NUTSHELL, 396 pages, 1982. Softcover. (Text)

HAYDOCK, HERR, AND STEMPEL'S FUNDAMENTALS OF PRE-TRIAL LITIGATION, Second Edition, 786 pages, 1992. Softcover. Teacher's Manual available. (Coursebook)

HAYDOCK AND SONSTENG'S TRIAL: THEORIES, TACTICS, TECHNIQUES, 711 pages, 1991. Softcover. (Text)

HEGLAND'S TRIAL AND PRACTICE SKILLS IN A NUTSHELL, 346 pages, 1978. Softcover. (Text)

HORNSTEIN'S APPELLATE ADVOCACY IN A NUTSHELL, 325 pages, 1984. Softcover. (Text)

JEANS' HANDBOOK ON TRIAL ADVOCACY, Student Edition, 473 pages, 1975. Softcover. (Text)

LISNEK AND KAUFMAN'S DEPOSITIONS: PROCEDURE, STRATEGY AND TECHNIQUE, Law School and CLE Edition. 250 pages, 1990. Softcover. (Text)

MARTINEAU'S CASES AND MATERIALS ON APPELLATE PRACTICE AND PROCEDURE, 565 pages, 1987. (Casebook)

Trial and Appellate Advocacy—Cont'd

SONSTENG, HAYDOCK AND BOYD'S THE TRIALBOOK: A TOTAL SYSTEM FOR PREPARATION AND PRESENTATION OF A CASE, 404 pages, 1984. Softcover. (Coursebook)

WHARTON, HAYDOCK AND SONSTENG'S CALIFORNIA CIVIL TRIALBOOK, Law School and CLE Edition. 148 pages, 1990. Softcover. (Text)

Trusts and Estates

ATKINSON'S HORNBOOK ON WILLS, Second Edition, 975 pages, 1953. (Text)

AVERILL'S UNIFORM PROBATE CODE IN A NUTSHELL, Second Edition, 454 pages, 1987. Softcover. (Text)

BOGERT'S HORNBOOK ON TRUSTS, Sixth Edition, Student Edition, 794 pages, 1987. (Text)

CLARK, LUSKY AND MURPHY'S CASES AND MATERIALS ON GRATUITOUS TRANSFERS, Third Edition, 970 pages, 1985. (Casebook)

DODGE'S WILLS, TRUSTS AND ESTATE PLANNING–LAW AND TAXATION, CASES AND MATERIALS, 665 pages, 1988. (Casebook)

MCGOVERN, KURTZ AND REIN'S HORNBOOK ON WILLS, TRUSTS AND ESTATES–INCLUDING TAXATION AND FUTURE INTERESTS, 996 pages, 1988. (Text)

MENNELL'S WILLS AND TRUSTS IN A NUTSHELL, 392 pages, 1979. Softcover. (Text)

SIMES' HORNBOOK ON FUTURE INTERESTS, Second Edition, 355 pages, 1966. (Text)

TURANO AND RADIGAN'S HORNBOOK ON NEW YORK ESTATE ADMINISTRATION, 676 pages, 1986 with 1991 pocket part. (Text)

UNIFORM PROBATE CODE, OFFICIAL TEXT WITH COMMENTS. 863 pages, 1991. Softcover.

WAGGONER'S FUTURE INTERESTS IN A NUTSHELL, 361 pages, 1981. Softcover. (Text)

Water Law—see also Energy and Natural Resources Law, Environmental Law

GETCHES' WATER LAW IN A NUTSHELL, Second Edition, 459 pages, 1990. Softcover. (Text)

SAX, ABRAMS AND THOMPSON'S LEGAL CONTROL OF WATER RESOURCES: CASES AND MATERIALS, Second Edition, 987 pages, 1991. Teacher's Manual available. (Casebook)

TRELEASE AND GOULD'S CASES AND MATERIALS ON WATER LAW, Fourth Edition, 816 pages, 1986. (Casebook)

Wills—see Trusts and Estates

Workers' Compensation

HOOD, HARDY AND LEWIS' WORKERS' COMPENSATION AND EMPLOYEE PROTECTION LAWS IN A NUTSHELL, Second Edition, 361 pages, 1990. Softcover. (Text)

LITTLE, EATON AND SMITH'S CASES AND MATERIALS ON WORKERS' COMPENSATION, 537 pages, 1992. Teacher's Manual available. (Casebook)

WEST'S LAW SCHOOL ADVISORY BOARD

COLLECTIVE BARGAINING IN
PUBLIC EMPLOYMENT
Fourth Edition

By

Donald H. Wollett
Professor Emeritus, McGeorge School of Law,
University of Pacific
Former Director of Employee Relations,
New York State

Joseph R. Grodin
Professor of Law, University of California,
Hastings College of Law
Former Associate Justice of the California Supreme Court

June M. Weisberger
Kathleen M. and George Haight Professor,
University of Wisconsin Law School

for
The Labor Law Group

AMERICAN CASEBOOK SERIES®

WEST PUBLISHING CO.
ST. PAUL, MINN., 1993

610 Opperman Drive
P.O. Box 64526
St. Paul, MN 55164–0526
1–800–328–9352

Printed in the United States of America

Library of Congress Cataloging-in-Publication Data

Wollett, Donald H.
Collective bargaining in public employment. — 4th ed. / by Donald H. Wollett, Joseph R. Grodin and June M. Weisberger.
p. cm. — (American casebook series)
Includes index.
ISBN 0–314–01862–X
1. Collective labor agreements—Government employees—United States. I. Grodin, Joseph R. II. Weisberger, June. III. Title. IV. Series.
KF3409.P77W65 1993
344.73'0189041353—dc20
[347.304189041353]

93–14768
CIP

ISBN 0–314–01862–X

(W., G. & W.) Coll.Barg. 4th Ed. ACB

PRINTED ON 10% POST CONSUMER RECYCLED PAPER

TO
IDA KLAUS
who pointed the way.

*

Dedication

In 1977 Arnold Weber made a speech in Chicago to an institute on public sector labor relations sponsored by the American Bar Association Section on Labor Relations Law (now the Section of Labor and Employment Law). Weber started with the following remarks:

> Coming out on the plane [from Pittsburgh, Pennsylvania], I was reflecting how long public sector bargaining has been a phenomenon commanding the attention of academics, practitioners and the Bar Association, and probably it would date back to Executive Order 10988 in 1962 and beyond that to the Wisconsin and the New York [City] laws. . . . I remember that when I started teaching what we unfelicitously called labor relations at the University of Chicago, one rarely made reference to public sector unions at all. It was sort of an exercise in flashy pedantry to show that you knew that the letter carriers were unionized. . . . All of that has changed, and now the development of public sector unionism and collective bargaining in the public sector, at all levels, federal, state and local, is really hot property.

Remarkably, the singular moving person in all the developments which Weber identified as the wellsprings of public sector collective bargaining—the early attention of the Bar Association, the Federal Executive Order, and the New York City laws—was Ida Klaus.

It was Ida Klaus who wrote the nine monographs that formed the intellectual underpinnings of the Executive Order on the Conduct of Labor Relations between the City of New York and its employees, promulgated by Mayor Wagner in 1958. The Executive Order created for the first time for city employees a code of labor relations policies and procedures, and set up a definitive scheme for the administration and enforcement of those policies. The New York City program became a model for structural arrangements in the expanding field of labor relations in the public service.

It was Ida Klaus who persuaded the Council of the Labor Law Section of the American Bar Association to establish a committee on the law of government employee relations in the late 1950s, despite the fact that many members of the Section regarded as fanciful, the notion that collective bargaining had a proper place in the public sector. (Ida served as Chairperson of this committee from 1958 through 1964.)

It was Ida Klaus who was appointed as chief consultant to President Kennedy's task force on employee-management relations in the federal service, an assignment which culminated in the promulgation in January of 1962 of Executive Order No. 10988 on "Employee-Management Cooperation in the Federal Service."

It was Ida Klaus who was called in by the New York City Board of Education in 1962 to carry forward the Board's first efforts at collective bargaining for the system's teachers. (The educational system was exempt from the Mayor's 1958 Executive Order.) Ida functioned in that capacity, directing labor relations for more than 100,000 organized pedagogical and administrative school board employees, until 1975. Ida also served as one of the three members of the New York State Public Employment Relations Board from 1976 until 1984.

Ida Klaus' contribution to labor relations in the public sector, beginning in the middle 1950's and continuing for well over 30 years, compelled the authors to dedicate this course book to her. Ida Klaus was not only present at the creation; she was herself a creator.

Preface to Fourth Edition

When the first edition of this volume appeared in 1971, collective bargaining for public employees was still in its infancy. While a majority of states had by that time adopted statutes providing for some form of bargaining (or "meeting and conferring," to use the more typical public sector terminology) for some groups of employees, most of the statutes were only two or three years old, and experience under them was just developing. Federal employees had enjoyed a limited framework for bargaining since 1962, when President Kennedy promulgated Executive Order 10988, but it was only in 1970, with President Nixon's Executive Order 11491, that the framework began to approach the private sector model based on exclusive representation. Public employment was growing, money was available to fund increased wages and benefits, and the field was alive with excitement. The authors of that volume, Don Sears and Donald Wollett, summed the situation up in their preface when they observed: "To use the phrase which is current (if not choice), in labor relations the public sector is 'where the action is.' "

By the time of the second edition, in 1975, the field was continuing to grow and develop. Two more states had adopted legislation providing for some form of bargaining for public employees; the institution of bargaining had spread into new areas of public employment, particularly higher eduction; the membership of public employee organizations continued to increase; and significant judicial decisions interpreting and applying the statutes had begun to emerge. The authors of that volume, Donald Wollett and Joseph R. Grodin, stated in their preface that it had been necessary, as a result, to make substantial changes in the earlier edition.

Four years later, at the time of the third edition, public sector labor relations were going through a period of stormy adolescence. The basic right of public employees to bargain through representatives of their own choosing had been recognized at the federal level by statute, replacing the old Executive Order, and a number of states had amended their statutes in the direction of broader acceptance of the private sector model—speaking in terms of "collective bargaining" rather than "meeting and conferring," for example, and explicitly providing for exclusive recognition of bargaining units determined appropriate by a public agency. Public employee organizations had continued to grow in size, and public management had become more sophisticated in its approach to, and acceptance of, the institution of collective bargaining.

Fourteen years later, labor relations in the public sector has reached an era of maturity and stability. Beneath the surface, however, are old conflicts which have never been completely resolved, and these continue to pose problems.

At one level, these conflicts can be reduced to a single, overriding question: To what extent should labor relations principles and precedents developed for the private sector be applied to the public sector as well? That question has two branches. One turns upon evaluation of the private sector system apart from any differences which may exist between private and public employment. After all, the fact that the private sector system has been in operation for some time does not entitle it to automatic acceptance. The private sector system has come in for a good deal of criticism of late even within the private sector, and the relatively fluid state of public sector labor relations law provides an excellent opportunity for evaluation. A student of private sector labor will find in the public sector a kind of comparative jurisprudence which serves to keep the mind open to new alternatives.

The other branch of this basic question turns on whether there are differences in the public sector which require rejection or modification of private sector labor relations principles, even where those principles are considered to work well in the private sector. It is in this area that the most serious conflicts continue to exist. Are the criteria for unit determination in the private sector equally appropriate in the public, or are there characteristics of public sector bargaining which require different criteria? Can the private sector definition of the scope of bargaining serve to identify the area of negotiations in the public sector, or do considerations of public policy require a different, perhaps broader, definition of managerial prerogative? Is the system of grievance arbitration which has served so well in the private sector adaptable to the public sector without modification, or do considerations of public interest require different legal rules? Should public employees have the right to strike? Some of them, but not all? Under some circumstances, but not others? To the extent that public employees are denied the right to strike, what alternatives should be provided for the resolution of impasses in collective bargaining? Is arbitration of interests disputes an appropriate solution, or does that pose an even greater threat to the public interest than the strike itself?

The answers which have been given to these basic questions vary from jurisdiction to jurisdiction, and are nearly as numerous as the jurisdictions themselves. Some jurisdictions use private sector criteria for unit determinations; others emphasize different criteria. Some use the private sector definition of bargaining scope; others define scope in a narrower, or at least different, manner. Some accept the principles which have been developed in the private sector toward grievance arbitration, while others insist that different principles are required. Most states, and the Federal Government, continue to prohibit strikes by public employees, but a few recognize the right to strike on a limited basis, and there is considerable variation among states with respect to the means for implementing the strike prohibition. Many states are experimenting with interests arbitration for the resolution of public sector disputes.

Given this diverse state of affairs, a casebook cannot be expected to develop "the law" of public employee labor relations. What we attempt, rather, is to identify the policy issues implicit in any system of public sector labor relations law, and to present materials illustrative of the various arguments and solutions which have been brought to bear on these issues by legislatures, courts, and administrative agencies. Such an approach has obvious value for the lawyer in his or her role as policy formulator, but for the lawyer as advocate it has value as well.

We assume that the instructor who wishes to teach the law of a particular state will supplement this book with appropriate local material; but, in a field in which legal principles are in such a state of flux, to focus entirely upon the statutes, court decisions, and agency rulings in a particular jurisdiction at a particular time is extremely shortsighted. To the extent that there are similarities in many of the statutes, court or agency decisions interpreting them may prove persuasive elsewhere; but, more significantly, a student sensitive to the role of public policy in the development of legal principles will find the experience of other jurisdictions useful in obtaining perspective, and essential to the development of arguments and strategy. In a sense, this is a casebook in comparative law.

Although we have continued to focus on the question of the extent to which labor relations principles and precedents developed for the private sector shall be applied to the public sector, there are significant omissions. For example, there is little material dealing with unfair labor practices which interfere with the organizational rights of employees. While public employers may stoutly resist the enactment of legislation establishing collective bargaining, once it is established, they generally do not actively participate in election campaigns. Thus, there is nothing comparable in the public sector to the vast body of law which has developed under the National Labor Relations Act with respect to fair election campaigns.

The most significant omission from the materials is the statutory and decisional law that has developed in the federal sector. The authors' judgment was that the federal system is so different from the bargaining systems that have developed at the state and local level (primarily because of the narrow scope of bargaining which eliminates, among other things, money matters) that it cannot be treated properly unless it is developed as an entity. It did not seem feasible to give the federal sector material this much attention while at the same time dealing with developments at the state and local level in a reasonably comprehensive way. Something had to be eliminated. It was our judgment that the federal sector material should go rather than reducing the state and local government material because the former is an atypical form of collective bargaining.

There is a lot of new material in the Fourth Edition—new cases, new statutes and recent amendments to old statutes, and an increased number of descriptive and analytical notes and questions. We have expanded consideration of the problems, unique to the public sector, connected with identifying the accountable public employer. Strikes, the prohibition of which continues to raise many interesting issues, are treated more fully than in the Third Edition. This is also true of procedures and arrangements for facilitating the settlement of bargaining impasses over what the terms and conditions of the collective bargaining agreement should be.

The authors estimate that about twenty-five percent of the material in the Third Edition has been carried forward on the ground that it continues to have more teaching value than some of the later decisions and statutes. The Fourth Edition is larger than its predecessors, but it is still designed to fit about 30 class hours (plus local supplementary material).

There are a number of persons to whom we are indebted for assistance. Several of Mr. Wollett's former students made significant contributions: Richard Bromley, Barbara Christiansen, Martha Geiger, and Nalda Keller. We are also indebted to Joseph Bress, Director of the Governor's Office of Employee Relations in New York, for his thoughtful suggestions.

DONALD H. WOLLETT
Sacramento, California

JOSEPH R. GRODIN
San Francisco, California

JUNE M. WEISBERGER
Madison, Wisconsin

March, 1993

Foreword

The Labor Law Group is an association of law teachers, most of whom serve on faculties in the United States; others teach in Belgium, Canada, England and Israel.

At the December 1946 meeting of the Labor Law Roundtable of the Association of American Law Schools, Professor W. Willard Wirtz (who became Secretary of Labor in 1962) delivered a compelling paper criticizing the labor law coursebooks then available. His remarks so impressed those present that the Roundtable Council organized a general conference on the teaching of the subject. At the conference, held in Ann Arbor in 1947, some conferees agreed to exchange proposals for sections of a hoped-for new coursebook. The late Professor Robert E. Mathews served as coordinator. Beginning in 1948, a preliminary mimeographed version was used in 17 schools; each user supplied comments and suggestions for change. In 1953, a hard-cover version was published under the title *Labor Relations and the Law*. The thirty-one "cooperating editors" were so convinced of the value of multi-campus collaboration that they gave up any individual claims to royalties. Instead, those royalties were paid to a trust fund to be used to develop and "provide the best possible materials" for training students in labor law and labor relations. The Declaration of Trust memorializing this agreement was executed November 4, 1953, and remains the Group's charter.

Cooperative ventures among legal scholars are often centered around ideological orthodoxies or common experiences or identities. In contrast, the Labor Law Group has tried to expand the scope of perceptions and experiences represented within its membership. Consistent with this goal, it has attained significant diversification in the racial, sexual, national and ideological composition of its participants and, additionally, has drawn its membership and leadership from institutions that are varied in size, styles, status, and geography.

The founding committee's hope that the initial collaboration would bear fruit has been fulfilled. Under Professor Mathews' continuing chairmanship the Group's members produced *Readings on Labor Law* in 1955, and *The Employment Relation and the Law* in 1957 edited by Robert Mathews and Benjamin Aaron. A second edition of *Labor Relations and the Law* appeared in 1960, with Benjamin Aaron and Donald H. Wollett as co-chairmen, and a third edition was published in 1965, with Jerre Williams at the helm.

In June of 1969, the Group, now chaired by William P. Murphy, sponsored a conference to reexamine the labor law curriculum. The meeting, held at the University of Colorado, was attended by practitioners and by full-time teachers including nonmembers as well as members of the Group. The conference papers and discussion summaries were distributed to law school libraries and to participants. In meetings that followed the conference, the

Group decided to reshape its work substantially. It restructured itself into ten task forces, each assigned a unit of no more than 200 pages on a discrete topic, such as employment discrimination or union-member relations. An individual teacher could then choose two or three of these units as the material around which to build a particular course. This multi-unit approach dominated the Group's work throughout much of the 1970's under Professor Murphy and his successor as chairman, Herbert L. Sherman, Jr. As the decade progressed and teachers refined their views about what topics to include and how to address them, some units were dropped from the series while others increased in scope and length. Under Professor Sherman's chairmanship, the Group planned a new series of six enlarged books to cover the full range of topics taught by labor and employment law teachers.

Professor James E. Jones, Jr. was elected chairman in 1978 and shepherded to completion the promised set of six full size, independent casebooks. In addition, during this period supplements were published for some of the books. The Group continued to reevaluate its work and eventually decided that it was time to convene another conference of law teachers.

In 1984, the Group, now chaired by Robert Covington, sponsored another general conference to discuss developments in the substance and teaching of labor and employment law, this time at Park City, Utah. (The conference papers were distributed to law school libraries as well as participants.) Those discussions and a subsequent working session led to the conclusion that the Group should devote principal attention to three new conventional length coursebooks, one devoted to employment discrimination, one to union-management relations, and one to the individual employment relationship. In addition, work was planned on more abbreviated coursebooks to serve as successors to the Group's earlier works covering public employment bargaining and labor arbitration.

In 1989 the Group met in Breckenridge, Colorado, to assess its most recent efforts and develop plans for the future. In addition to outlining new coursebook projects, the Group discussed ways to assist teachers of labor and employment law in their efforts to expand conceptual horizons and perspectives. In pursuit of the latter goals it co-sponsored, in 1992, a conference held at the University of Toronto Faculty of Law at which legal and nonlegal specialists examined alternative models of corporate governance and their impact on workers.

At any one time, roughly twenty-five to thirty persons are actively engaged in the Group's work; this has proved a practical size, given problems of communication and logistics. Coordination and editorial review of the projects are the responsibility of the executive committee, whose members are the successor trustees of the Group. Governance is by consensus; votes are taken only to elect trustees and to determine whom to invite to join the Group. Since 1953, more than 70 persons have worked on Group projects; in keeping with the original agreement, none has ever received anything more than reimbursement of expenses.

The coursebook presented here is a successor to a series of Group sponsored books on public sector labor-management relations. The three preparers of this book are uniquely equipped for their task by experience as well as scholarship. Donald Wollett's long career in the labor relations field has combined extended periods of teaching (University of Washington, New York University, University of California-Davis, and McGeorge School of Law) with extended periods of law practice. The latter included service as Chief Negotiator and Director of Employee Relations for the State of New York during the 1970s. Joseph Grodin entered law teaching at Hastings Law School after a long period of labor law practice in San Francisco. His teaching career has been interrupted by service as one of the original members of the California Agricultural Labor Relations Board, service as an Associate Justice of the California Court of Appeal from 1979–82 and from 1982 to 1987 as an Associate Justice of the California Supreme Court. June Weisberger began her service in the public sector labor relations field in 1963 as a member of the Office of Corporation Counsel in Rochester, New York. From 1966 to 1972 she was legal counsel to the Rochester Board of Education. She began her law teaching career at Cornell's School of Industrial and Labor Relations and then joined the law faculty at the University of Wisconsin. Additionally, each of the coursebook preparers has made numerous contributions to the literature of the public sector labor law field.

THE EXECUTIVE COMMITTEE:

REGINALD ALLEYNE
ROBERT N. COVINGTON
JOSEPH GRODIN
ROBERT J. RABIN
EILEEN SILVERSTEIN
ALVIN L. GOLDMAN, *Chairman*

*

Summary of Contents

Table of Contents

Table of Cases

The principal cases are in bold type. Cases cited or discussed in the text are roman type. References are to pages. Cases cited in principal cases and within other quoted materials are not included.

COLLECTIVE BARGAINING IN
PUBLIC EMPLOYMENT

Fourth Edition

*

Chapter 1

INTRODUCTION

A. OVERVIEW AND ANALYSIS

Collective bargaining in the public sector has been a significant national phenomenon for less than thirty years. As late as 1966, in the entire State of New York, out of 8,600 governmental employing entities, the employees of which might have desired to exercise the right of association for the purpose of negotiating collectively the terms of their employment and the handling of their grievances, Governor Rockefeller's Committee on Public Employee Relations (the Taylor Committee) was able to find only eleven formal collective bargaining agreements.[1]

In the early 1960s, only about one million public employees belonged to unions. The largest employee group was in the postal service. There were state and local government unions such as the American Federation of Teachers and the American Federation of State, County and Municipal Employees, but they were not very important, either in membership or in influence. Indeed, except for some of the large cities such as Philadelphia and New York, there were few places where collective bargaining of the sort characteristic of the private sector even existed.

Why was there so little collective bargaining in the public sector as late as 1966?

1) First, and perhaps foremost, was the absence of an explicit legal framework.

In 1962, Wisconsin, which had the only state statute of significance covering public employees, improved its 1959 statute (which applied to local employees only) by authorizing an existing administrative agency (the Wisconsin Employment Relations Board) to enforce the public

1. 1966 report of the Taylor Committee at pp. 11, 55. The Taylor Committee was the architect of the omnibus public sector collective bargaining act enacted into law in New York State. The authors are indebted to this committee (George Taylor, Frederick Harbison, David Cole, John Dunlop and E. Wight Bakke) for many of the insights contained in this introductory note.

sector law.[2] In the same year, federal employees were given organizational impetus by the promulgation of Executive Order 10988 by President John F. Kennedy.[3] It called for a modified form of tiered collective bargaining, narrow in scope, but revolutionary for its time. The order called for arbitration of some kinds of disputes but, in deference to the concept of sovereignty, made the awards advisory only. There was nothing else of significance.

The National Labor Relations Act, as amended in 1947 and again in 1959, excluded from its coverage public employers and public employees.[4] This meant that public employees had no federal statutory guarantee of the right to form, join and assist labor organizations and no statutory basis protecting this right against invasion or abridgement by employers. It meant that there was no forum to which public employees might resort if they desired to organize in some formal way and achieve status for bargaining with their employer. And it meant that if public employees believed that they had grievances which required redress, they were limited to a civil service forum or a judicial forum where the process predictably would be lengthy and expensive. Finally, public employees were without any right, apart from political pressure, to force their employer to meet and treat with them if the employer was of a mind not to do so. And, there was no process which might produce some kind of agreement to which the employer could be held.

Second, the model of collective bargaining developed in the private sector did not fit very well within the structure and practice of fixing the terms and conditions of public employment.

In the first place, private sector unions were organized to bargain with management executives in order to reach a mutually acceptable agreement binding on both parties, both of whom had authority to reach a final agreement, and both of whom had economic power to veto terms with which they disagreed. But given the realities of the public sector, who was the employer with unitary authority to "make a deal?"

Herbert L. Haber, City Director of Labor Relations for New York in the middle 1960s, put the point as follows:

> The public employer is an artificial creature of the electorate established to minister to the needs and desires of that body and to provide the mechanical and administrative structure to carry out those functions. In this lie all the problems of sovereignty, which I am here using narrowly in the sense of control and determination of budget and tax rates and the setting of goals and priorities and policy. Here also lies the very essence of the question who, in fact, is the employer and who should have the ultimate responsibility for negotiating workable agreements.[5]

2. W.S.A. § 111.70.

3. E.O. 10988, 27 F.R. 551.

4. 29 U.S.C.A. § 152(2).

5. "The Relevance of Private Sector Experience to Public Sector Collective Bargaining", proceedings of a conference held

Fixing the terms and conditions governing public employment had historically been determined by statute or administrative regulation, with expenditures constrained by budget allocations, and tax decisions made by legislators responsive to the public. Decisions concerning public employment had to be related to the budget-making processes of the appropriate body—a legislature, a board of supervisors, a city council, or a fiscally-independent school board.

The total or partial separation of operational authority and funding authority made collective bargaining, private-sector style, very difficult. For example, two-thirds of the employees of the City of New York worked in agencies directly under the control and supervision of the Mayor and his administration. The other one-third were employed by the Board of Education, the Housing Administration, and the transit systems. These agencies were established directly by state legislation. However, they were supported by City funds. Thus, in 1968 the negotiations with both teachers and transit employees were conducted without a City presence at the bargaining table. The agencies did their own negotiating; the City's function was to pay the bill.[6]

The Taylor Committee expressed the problem somewhat differently.

> Let us take, for example, the case of an employee unit composed of the professional employees of the welfare agencies of a city. The corresponding employer unit with respect to determining and administering many of the terms of employment is the Welfare Department. The "employer" executives with whom negotiations are carried on are the Superintendents of the several Welfare services and ultimately the Commissioner of Welfare. It is within their authority to negotiate about the working rules, the provisions of facilities, services, equipment, and other aspects of the working environment not involving major expenditures with respect to such items. They are also likely to be the "employers" with respect to the administration and supervision of working routines and relationships, the handling of grievances, and the administration of discipline. But another stratum of employer, whose chief executive, the city manager or mayor, holds the administrative authority with respect to an over-all personnel policy for all employees of the city, with respect to the determination of costly city-wide benefits of various sorts, and wages, and concerning decisions as to the distribution of city funds among various uses (buildings, streets, sewers, new schools, payrolls for the several departments, etc.). But even that chief executive can only recommend such a distribution and the budget required to meet the expenditures involved. His budget proposals must be submitted to the next stratum of "employer," the legislative body which is responsible for approving

by the Institute of Management on Labor Relations, Rutgers University, May 23, 1968, at p. 8.

6. Haber at p. 10.

the overall budget and for levying the taxes with which to balance income with expenditures. If the negotiated items include any which have been mandated by state law or if they involve any modification of local or state civil service provisions, there is a further level of decision-makers who must approve the settlement.[7]

The kind of collective bargaining which is typical of the private sector could be approximated in negotiating with public authorities such as those that operate bridges, transit districts, and some school districts (those that are fiscally independent), whose governing boards are not only responsible for operating the services but have the authority to meet their needs by revenues from prices charged, from taxes, or from the sale of bonds. However, even in these cases, the revenues are usually supplemented by appropriations from the public treasury or are limited by public policy with respect to the level of prices or taxes which the legislature permits the governing body to impose.[8]

2) In the second place, public sector unions, to the extent that they existed, were usually geared to represent particular occupational groups such as transit employees, school teachers and sanitation workers. Advancement of the occupational interests of particular employees was fundamentally different from the civil service approach, characteristic of the public sector, under which basic working terms and conditions were specified by government-wide classifications of public employees of the State and of its political subdivisions. This "industry-wide" approach was the one historically followed by the civil service associations, the predominant form of employee organization in the public sector. They typically were organized for the purpose of promulgating civil service laws and other legislative enactments applied uniformly to classified public employees in diverse occupational groups performing varied functions.

The implications of "industry-wide" uniform treatment for all employees in the classified service versus "fragmentary" objectives for particular occupational or functional groups posed a difficult problem of accommodation.

Some terms of public employment were mandated by legislative enactment: hire and tenure procedures, trial periods, promotions, seniority and layoffs, discipline, general standards of compensation, minimum and maximum salaries and increment schedules, procedures for changes in individual salaries and wages, hours and overtime, and fringe benefits such as insurance, pensions, vacations, holidays, sick leaves, etc. To the extent that these terms were mandated for all state and many municipal employers by state and local civil service commissions, the opportunity for classified state employees and classified local government employees in particular occupational and functional groups to improve them was limited, if not for legal reasons, then for practical ones.

7. 1966 report of the Taylor Committee at p. 26.

8. 1966 report of the Taylor Committee at p. 60.

As Haber contended, such things as pensions, time and leave rules, holidays and vacations, should be uniformly applied across the board. He argued that where there was a single employer (like New York City), even though it did business with 90 different unions and 200 different bargaining units, employing from 2 persons up to 28,000 persons, one should not be required to provide different pensions, different vacations, different holidays, on a union-by-union negotiated basis. An employer should not have clerical workers belonging to one union having a different set of holidays or different vacation allotments from the same class of workers belonging to other unions.[9]

3) In the third place, the power of employee organizations to veto agreement terms with which they disagreed was different than it was in the private sector.

> Instead of the constraints of the market place on collective bargaining, including the right to strike, which are in the private sector, negotiations in the public sector are subject to the constraints imposed by democratic political processes. A work stoppage in the private sector involves costs primarily to the direct participants. They also undertake considerable risk in fixing the terms of settlement; the volume of sales and opportunities for employment are at stake. On the other hand, a strike of government employees (there can scarcely be a countervailing lockout) introduces an alien force in the legislative processes. With a few exceptions, there are no constraints of the market place. The constraints in the provision of free services by government are to be found in the budget allocation and tax decisions which are made by legislators responsive to the public will. * * * [T]he executive agencies are required to compensate their employees within the limits of the budgets for the State and for its political subdivisions. In New York, these budgets must balance, i.e., taxes must be levied to cover estimated expenditures. It is the budget, rather than the market place, which constrains collective negotiation in public employment.[10] XX

Thus, strikes, which gave unions in the private sector the economic power to veto proposals with which they disagreed, were often of doubtful effectiveness and legality in the public sector.

The traditional public sector associations, recognizing the pluralistic nature of the "employer," pursuing an "industry-wide" approach to collective action, and aware of the "bottom-line" political nature of the activity, had adapted their strategies and tactics to these realities. Their tactics involved discussion and consultation, followed ultimately by a unilateral decision by the executives or the legislative body of a governmental entity; joint studies of terms on the assumption that a joint commitment was desirable, but with the recognition that approval and appropriations to implement any agreement would have to follow

9. Haber at pp. 9–10.

10. 1966 report of the Taylor Committee at pp. 15–16.

from a legislative body; direct political action before a legislative body in order to acquire statutory confirmation of desired terms; and efforts to obtain a "prevailing rate" arrangement gearing wages and benefits to wages and benefits enjoyed by comparable groups in the private sector. They did not bargain collectively, private sector style, and most of them did not claim the right to strike.[11]

The "union" approach and the "association" approach did not turn out to be mutually exclusive. Again, the Taylor Committee made perceptive comments:

> Any organization representing public employees is "fully aware of the fact that there are normally strata of 'employers', including ultimately a legislature, to whom any agreements made with negotiating executives must be referred for approval and financial implementation. They are also aware that sometimes the most dependable process is to work directly for legislation favorable to their members, which legislation will be binding on the government agencies whose employees they represent. * * * [A]ny successful employee organization, whether of the Union or Association type, will understand and utilize the strategy and tactics associated with political activity as a major re-enforcement of, and, on occasion, as a substitute for, the strategy and tactics associated with skill in negotiating with government agency executives." [12]

This is why representatives of employers in the public sector often are faced with and complain about the problem of the "end run." Public employee unions and associations frequently lobby in an effort to gain from a legislative body those benefits which they failed to obtain or which they traded off at the negotiating table.

Why did the movement toward union-style collective bargaining acquire such impetus in the 1960's that by 1988 forty-three percent of government employees were covered by collective bargaining agreements and 35.8 percent of government employees belonged to bargaining organizations (as compared to 17.5 percent in the private sector)? [13]

There are many reasons, and there is no clear cause and effect.

One reason for the movement was the enactment of state statutes which brought public sector employees into the mainstream of American labor policy. These developments are discussed below.

A second reason was the fact that, as collective bargaining statutes were enacted, most public employee associations chose to take on the coloration of unions and to fight for formal status as exclusive bargaining representatives for discrete sets of employees in "bargaining units"

11. Many, perhaps most, of the civil service associations eschewed the right to strike. In the 1960's, the National Education Association regarded strikes as unprofessional and unethical activity.

See the 1966 report of the Taylor Committee at pp. 58–59.

12. 1966 report of Taylor Committee at p. 62.

13. Aaron, *The Future of Collective Bargaining,* Public Sector Bargaining, 2d Ed. (1988) p. 315.

vis-a-vis their "employers." Most of them, to use Arnold Weber's felicitous phrase, became "unionoids." Some became unions in a formal sense. Thus, New York's Civil Service Employees Association affiliated with the American Federation of State, County and Municipal Employees, AFL–CIO, and the California State Employees Association became part of the Service Employees International Union, AFL–CIO. Some of the private sector unions, anxious to expand their membership base, "got in on the action" with organizational campaigns, e.g., the International Brotherhood of Teamsters.[14]

Nowhere were these developments more pronounced than in the fight for representation rights in the public schools (grades Kindergarten through 12). The Industrial Union Department, AFL–CIO, and particularly the United Automobile Workers, decided in 1961 to target public schools as a lead-strategy in organizing white-collar professional employees. It lent support, financial and otherwise, to the organizational activities of its associate, the American Federation of Teachers.[15]

In December of 1961 the United Federation of Teachers, Local No. 2 of the AFT, won an election and achieved representative status for the certificated employees of the New York City School system. The National Education Association, heretofore a relatively benign confederation of powerful state associations,[16] chose as a matter of survival (as it saw it) to do battle with the AFT for bargaining agent status in every major urban area in the northeastern United States.

Most of the early collective bargaining elections in public school systems were extra-legal; that is, they were conducted pursuant to agreement of the parties rather than under statutes. Despite the fact that it had far fewer members than the NEA and its affiliates, the AFT did well north of the Ohio River and east of the Mississippi. In addition to New York City, it won elections handily in Chicago, Baltimore, the District of Columbia, Philadelphia, Boston, Hartford, and Detroit. The NEA affiliate won a victory in only one major city in this geographic area—Milwaukee, Wisconsin. However, the NEA did achieve success in some lesser but important cities such as Syracuse and Rochester, New York, and Newark, New Jersey (with challenged ballots after a 1373 to 1373 tie).

The battleground was not confined to claims over representational status in particular school districts. It reached into many state legislatures where the two organizations attempted (successfully) to gain enactment of favorable statutes. Connecticut, Massachusetts, New Jersey, Pennsylvania, Michigan, Rhode Island, and New York were the early battlegrounds. The NEA and its affiliates took positions which

14. See Weber, "Prospects for the Future," in *Labor Relations Law in the Public Sector,* (Andrea Knapp, Ed.1977).

15. See West, *The National Education Association: The Power Base for Education* (1980) pp. 53–55, 62–65, 75.

16. These were the days of little or no federal aid. The power of the educational establishment lay in the NEA's state affiliates.

moved them ever closer to "collective bargaining as practiced in the private sector." [17]

The vigor and intensity of the fight between the AFT and the NEA and its affiliates, coupled with significant public exposure, arguably gave a substantial boost to the push for collective bargaining among other public employees, as did the rapid enactment of statutes.[18]

> Some of the early laws limited the coverage to public school personnel. As experience was gained, however, the trend was toward state laws covering all public employees, including teachers. Two factors accounted for the trend. First, teachers' associations found they could secure fair treatment from the public administration agencies. Second, the added support of other public employees could be helpful in securing the approval of the governors and state legislatures to get the proposed law enacted.[19]

These were collective bargaining laws conforming generally (but not uniformly) to the model bill proposed in 1962 to the state education associations' officers by the NEA. Many of the state associations were not enthusiastic about the legislation, but they were moved by the fact, according to the NEA's Research Division, that teachers overwhelmingly supported it.

By 1980 thirty-one states, most of them with large industrial cities, had enacted public sector bargaining laws.[20]

B. LEGAL DEVELOPMENTS

The important public sector collective bargaining laws that developed, following Wisconsin, were state laws. The legal structure grew unevenly fragmented and diverse. The imperatives of national labor

17. West, at pp. 72–74.

18. Another problem for the growth of "collective bargaining as practiced in the private sector" was the fact that many of the public sector employee associations welcomed supervisors as members. Indeed, often their leadership consisted largely of supervisors or higher ranked management. This is, of course, contrary to the policies of the National Labor Relations Act which excludes supervisors and managers from coverage and frowns on their predominant influence in organizational affairs. NLRA: 29 U.S.C.A. § 152(3), (11); *NLRB v. Bell Aerospace Co., Div. of Textron, Inc.*, 416 U.S. 267, 94 S.Ct. 1757, 40 L.Ed.2d 134 (1974); Morris, The Developing Labor Law, 2d Ed., 1983, pp. 1491–92.

Nowhere was this more evident than in the ranks of the National Education Association and its state affiliates. The role of the superintendent, if collective bargaining was established in a school district, was particularly troublesome. Was he the chief executive officer and therefore a key member of the adversary? Or was he, as a member of the NEA and its state affiliate, the head of the profession and therefore on the same side as the teachers? The role of building principals and department chairmen was also a major source of controversy. Did they belong in the unit with teachers whom they supervised? Was the independence of an organization of certificated teachers compromised by the fact that supervisors were members and often officers?

The American Federation of Teachers, a prime proponent of the union model, suffered from no such ambivalence. Supervisors and management were excluded from membership, and the NEA and its affiliates were repeatedly attacked as company-dominated.

19. West, at p. 73.

20. Ibid.

and economic markets, which created a political impetus for uniform national labor policies in the private sector, were inoperative. The exemptions of state and local governments from the federal labor relations laws, particularly the National Labor Relations Act, remained intact.

The only federal models were Executive Order 19088, (promulgated on January 17, 1962) [21] and its successor, Executive Order 11491 (issued by President Nixon on October 29, 1969),[22] followed by Title VII of the Civil Service Reform Act in 1978 (enacted during the administration of President Jimmy Carter). They provided for an unusual form of collective bargaining in which economic issues are non-bargainable and many non-economic issues are wiped off the table by management rules, civil service regulations, and the provisions of the Federal Personnel Manual.

Today there are 36 states plus the District of Columbia with collective bargaining statutes of one sort or another. Some states—Ohio and Illinois—developed a substantial amount of public sector collective bargaining although they did not enact statutes until the 1980s. There were pockets, particularly in the sun belt (except for Florida), where not much happened.[23]

Some of the state laws are omnibus, that is, they cover all levels of government and virtually all occupational groups. Others are limited to particular types of governmental services, e.g., school districts. Still others are limited to specified occupational groups such as firefighters. The laws are diverse not only with respect to coverage, but also with respect to scope of bargaining, impasse procedures, strikes, and unfair labor practices. However, there are areas in which developments were sufficiently similar to justify the claim that they constituted a national norm.

(a) In the main, public employers (except for a few publicly-funded institutions of higher education), unlike their private sector counterparts, did not fight the organization of employees who wished to engage in collective bargaining after legislation was enacted.

(b) Most public employers, having lost the battle to prevent the enactment of collective bargaining legislation, attempted to protect their authority by restricting the scope of mandatory bargaining; early-

21. Executive Order 10988: promulgated January 17, 1962 E.O. 10988, 27 F.R. 551.

22. Executive Order 11491: promulgated October 29, 1969 E.O. 11491, 34 F.R. 17605.

23. The 36 states are: Alaska, California, Connecticut, Delaware, Florida, Hawaii, Idaho, Illinois, Indiana, Iowa, Kansas, Maine, Maryland, Massachusetts, Michigan, Minnesota, Missouri, Montana, Nebraska, Nevada, New Hampshire, New Jersey, New Mexico, New York, North Dakota, Ohio, Oklahoma, Oregon, Pennsylvania, Rhode Island, South Dakota, Tennessee, Vermont, Washington, Wisconsin and Wyoming. Five had authorized bargaining by statute for specified groups under restrictions (Alabama, Georgia, Kentucky, Louisiana and Texas). Nine had no statutes at all: Arizona, Arkansas, Colorado, Mississippi, North Carolina, South Carolina, Utah, Virginia and West Virginia. *Commerce Clearinghouse, Public Employee Bargaining Reporter,* Vol. I, pp. 905–1407 (1990).

on, questions of what is negotiable occupied the front line at the bargaining table and lay at the heart of a plethora of administrative and judicial decisions.

(c) Most of the statutes adopted the private sector principle of appropriate bargaining units and winner-take-all elections where one organization emerges as the exclusive representative. (Minnesota and California were the exceptions, but their experiments with proportional representation did not last long.) As a consequence, the organizations that survived (including the professional and civil service associations that Weber calls unionoids) acquired more members, more money, and more political influence than they had pre-collective bargaining.

(d) The unions paid a predictable price. They were saddled with the duty of fair representation. These developments are also discussed below at Chapter 9.

(e) Despite predictions that they would atrophy and blow away after collective bargaining came into being, civil service systems survived. Indeed, they appear today to be healthy, if not prosperous. This seems to be the function of a process of accommodating public sector collective bargaining to pre-existing institutions and procedures for dealing with employer-employee relations. This is roughly the reverse of what happened in the private sector where personnel systems were a response to collective bargaining rather than its predecessor. This is also true of self-governance systems (e.g., faculty senates) in publicly-funded institutions of higher education. They have proved to be very durable. See Chapter 5.

(f) Binding grievance arbitration, despite some early judicial foot-dragging, grew almost as rapidly as it did in the private sector and is now the preferred method for dealing with questions of contract interpretation. When confronted with the enforceability of an executory promise to arbitrate or the confirmance of an arbitral award, most courts have tried to follow the principles enunciated in the *Trilogy* (*United Steelworkers of America v. American Mfg. Co.,* 363 U.S. 564, 80 S.Ct. 1343, 4 L.Ed.2d 1403 (1960); *United Steelworkers of America v. Enterprise Wheel & Car Corp.,* 363 U.S. 593, 80 S.Ct. 1358, 4 L.Ed.2d 1424 (1960); *United Steelworkers of America v. Warrior & Gulf Navigation Co.,* 363 U.S. 574, 80 S.Ct. 1347, 4 L.Ed.2d 1409 (1960).) These developments are discussed at Chapter 6.

(g) With the exception of 13 states (Alaska, California, Hawaii, Idaho, Illinois, Louisiana, Minnesota, Montana, Ohio, Oregon, Pennsylvania, Vermont, and Wisconsin) that gave a limited and conditional right to strike, strikes were outlawed or severely constrained by statutory or decisional law. Of course, they occurred anyhow. The fact of illegality increased the cost to employees. This fact, coupled with the reality that many public employee strikes were ineffective or counterproductive and made settlement of the disputes more difficult, caused some unions to push for strike substitutes.[24] The major issues are discussed below at Chapter 7.

(h) The search for strike substitutes led to extensive experimentation with fact-finding with recommendations and/or compulsory binding interest arbitration, both conventional and last-best offer, particularly for firefighters and police officers. Little of this experimentation involved state employees. Most of it occurred in local government. See Chapter 8.

(i) Agency shop arrangements, some imposed by statute and some reached by agreement, became common and withstood constitutional challenge although the use of fees-payer contributions was severely regulated by courts and administrative agencies. These developments are discussed below at Chapter 9.

C. THE POLITICAL NATURE OF DECISION-MAKING

ABOOD v. DETROIT BOARD OF EDUCATION

Supreme Court of the United States, 1977.
431 U.S. 209, 97 S.Ct. 1782, 52 L.Ed.2d 261.

MR. JUSTICE STEWART delivered the opinion of the Court:

The State of Michigan * * * enacted legislation authorizing a system for union representation of local government employees. A union and a local government employer are specifically permitted to agree to an "agency shop" arrangement, whereby every employee represented by a union—even though not a union member—must pay to the union, as a condition of employment, a service fee equal in amount to union dues. The issue before us is whether this arrangement violates the constitutional rights of government employees who object to public sector unions as such or to various union activities financed by the compulsory service fees. [The Court held that it was unconstitutional for the union to use the service fees for political and ideological purposes unrelated to collective bargaining. See Chapter 9.]

* * *

[D]ecisionmaking by a public employer is above all a political process. The officials who represent the public employer are ultimately responsible to the electorate, which for this purpose can be viewed as comprising three overlapping classes of voters—taxpayers, users of particular government services, and government employees. Through exercise of their political influence as part of the electorate, the

24. At the 1976 meeting of the National Academy of Arbitrators, Abe Zwerdling, counsel to the American Federation of State, County, and Municipal Workers, stated during a panel discussion his preference for arbitration in lieu of strikes. The consensus of the 1976 Spring meeting of the National Association of Teacher Attorneys, a nation-wide group of lawyers representing affiliates of the National Education Association, was the same.

employees have the opportunity to affect the decisions of government representatives who sit on the other side of the bargaining table. Whether these representatives accede to a union's demands will depend upon a blend of political ingredients, including community sentiment about unionism generally and the involved union in particular, the degree of taxpayer resistance, and the views of voters as to the importance of the service involved and the relation between the demands and the quality of service. It is surely arguable, however, that permitting public employees to unionize and a union to bargain as their exclusive representative gives the employees more influence in the decisionmaking process than is possessed by employees similarly organized in the private sector.

The distinctive nature of public-sector bargaining has led to widespread discussions about the extent to which the law governing labor relations in the private sector provides an appropriate model. To take but one example, there has been considerable debate about the desirability of prohibiting public employee unions from striking, a step that the State of Michigan itself has taken, Mich.Comp.Laws § 423.202. But although Michigan has not adopted the federal model of labor relations in every respect, it has determined that labor stability will be served by a system of exclusive representation and the permissive use of an agency shop in public employment. * * *

BARGAINING IN THE GOVERNMENT'S BUSINESS: PRINCIPLES AND POLITICS *

Clyde Summers

18 Univ. of Toledo L.Rev. 265–268 (1987).

I. Introduction

Public employee bargaining chronically suffers from cognitive dissonance. There is repeated acknowledgment that collective bargaining in the public sector is different from collective bargaining in the private sector. At the same time, the statutes enacted for public sector bargaining, and the administrative rules and decisions announced under those statutes are modeled on the statutory rules and decisions of the private sector. Often the same paragraph or even the same sentence affirms both of these perspectives with equal confidence and no overt recognition of the dissonance. This dissonance confuses our discussion and obscures our understanding of many of the problems in public employee bargaining.

II. The Political Character of Public Bargaining

From the union perspective, the public and private sectors have much in common. Both sectors involve the same kind of work; jobs in the public sector are matched by jobs in the private sector—truck drivers, building maintenance, typists, record keepers, teachers, guards,

* Reprinted by permission of the University of Toledo Law Review and the author.

safety personnel, and firefighters. The employees' goals are the same—wages, medical insurance, pensions, holidays, working conditions, job security, and protection against arbitrary supervision. Workers in both sectors seek to protect these interests by the same means—collective representation and collective agreements which secure those rights and make them enforceable through a reasonably prompt and reliable procedure.

From the public employer's side, the perspective is quite different because bargaining is framed by legal and political considerations. Pension benefits may be statutorily defined, public services may be legally required, and personnel matters may be governed by civil service rules. More importantly, employer representatives at the bargaining table have limited authority to make binding agreements because wage increases or benefits are dependent on the budget, which is dependent on taxes, and these are matters for the legislative body, not the negotiators.

The crucial difference is that in the public sector the collective agreement is not a private decision, but a governmental decision; it is not so much a contract as a legislative act. Labor costs may be seventy percent of a city's budget. Bargaining on wages and other economic items, therefore, inevitably involves the level of taxes and the level of services. An agreement to increase wages requires either an increase in taxes or a decrease in services. Negotiated holidays close city services for the day. Other contractual provisions may affect the kind or quality of public services provided.

In the public sector the ultimate employer is not the mayor or the council but the voters. They are the ones who pay the taxes and receive the services. They are the ones to whom those who make the collective agreement are answerable. From the employer's side, the collective agreement is not an economic decision but a political decision; it shapes policy choices which rightfully belong to the voters to be made through the political processes. Collective bargaining in the public sector is properly and inevitably political; to try to make it otherwise denies democratic principles.

I would suggest that the main source of cognitive dissonance in public sector bargaining is that the participants on both sides are reluctant to confront the implications which follow from recognizing the inherently political character of the process. They feel much more comfortable following the familiar market model of the private sector, giving little more than lip service to the existence of a difference. But, there is a suppressed or subconscious awareness that the difference is fundamental and has implications which require examination.

A. Bargaining and the Political Process

It may be helpful to compare how certain decisions are made with and without collective bargaining. Consider, for example, the question of whether the salaries of teachers should be raised. In the absence of bargaining, individual teachers or teacher organizations will try to persuade the superintendent by petition, discussion or otherwise to provide for an increase in the next school budget. When the budget comes before a public hearing, the teachers, perhaps reinforced by parents or the PTA, will argue for the fairness and need for an increase. Taxpayers, individualized and organized, will argue against the increases and protest the level of taxes the budget will require. The school board or finance committee will retire to executive session and reach a decision. Consider a second question of class size. The process will be much the same, with perhaps more vigorous advocacy by the PTA, but less vigorous advocacy by the taxpayers who may not recognize the relation to taxes. Consider third the question of the teacher's authority to discipline students. Here the teachers will not speak with one voice; some will ask for authority to paddle, and some will ask that paddling be prohibited. The parents will also be divided, and the PTA's may be paralyzed. In both cases, the school board will listen, go into executive session and decide.

Collective bargaining significantly changes the political process. The union, as an exclusive bargaining representative, formulates its demands, and on each of these issues, proceeds to negotiate with the school board's representative behind closed doors. The board is required to respond by giving reasons for its positions, meeting arguments with arguments, and having those arguments examined. Parent organizations and taxpayer organizations are not present. Individual teachers with different views are not present. When an agreement is reached, it is then presented as part of a package decision including many other issues. The taxpayer, the parents and the dissenting teachers do not know the background information, the competing considerations, or the compromises which led to the decision. They have no active voice until the next election when they may by vote change the composition of the school board.

It becomes immediately evident that collective bargaining gives the teachers' collective representative a much more effective voice in the decision-making. The union has more direct access in the decision-making than the taxpayers, the parents or any other voters, and they purport to represent the viewpoint of all teachers although many may disagree. The union is able to deal with public decision-makers behind closed doors without other interests being heard, and to arrive at agreements which are politically difficult, if not legally impossible to change.

Giving employees and their collective representatives this special role in government decision-making is a significant departure from our traditional political processes. This is the discomfort of our cognitive dissonance; how do we reconcile this process with our democratic principles? I do not raise this question to argue against public employee bargaining. On the contrary, my purpose is to try to understand more exactly why we have public employee bargaining. With that understanding we may better shape the structure and scope of the system.

B. The Need for Bargaining on Public Decisions

The first, and for me, compelling reason for public employee bargaining is that our political system has a built-in bias which requires it. The ultimate public employer is the electorate, the taxpayer and the users of public service. Much like other employers they want from their employees high production and low labor costs. In political terms, they want more public service with lower taxes. With labor costs making up seventy percent or more of the public employer's budget, the political pressure of the whole electorate—taxpayers and service users—is to hold down wages and other economic benefits. No matter how well organized public employees are and what strategic positions they occupy, they are massively outnumbered in votes. The voter is not as compelled by self-interest as a private employer confronting non-union competition, but may be more resistant to wage demands than an employer whose competitors are also unionized and subject to standardized wage terms. Public employees are always at risk that the political demands for low taxes and more service will be placated at their expense.

The collective bargaining process which gives public employees more direct access and ability to persuade the political decision-makers helps offset this built-in political disadvantage.

Notes and Questions

Is Professor Summers right in his assertion that the compelling reason for public employee bargaining is that our political system has a built-in bias against public employee demands that could increase taxes?

Is it true that bargaining units (voting precincts) defined by employee community of interest, winner-take-all elections, majoritarianism and the principle of exclusivity, formal negotiations monitored by a public agency, and enforceable labor agreements of fixed duration are the best way to protect the standard of living of public employees? Prior to the middle '60s there was a long history of protecting the interests of public employees in other ways.

What happens if the scope of bargaining is severely limited? What happens if the strike—the motivational force at the bargaining table in the private sector—is either unavailable or ineffective? What happens if the employer asserts its power to reject consistently the recommendations of fact-finders or to frustrate the creation of a binding interest arbitration system as an alternative to strike action?

Abood asserted that he should not have to help finance an organization that does not represent his point of view regarding either his interests as an employee or the proper resolution of public employment issues. Does the Court satisfactorily respond to his constitutional challenge? Can such bargaining representation be separated from political decision-making? If Professor Summers' thesis regarding a bias against fair treatment of public employees is correct, why would such an employee reject Union representation?

D. EXAMPLES OF PRIVATE SECTOR DOGMA IN CONFLICT WITH PUBLIC SECTOR REALITIES

1. WHO ARE THE ADVERSARIES: EMPLOYER VS. EMPLOYEE OR EMPLOYEE VS. EMPLOYEE?

EXCERPT FROM NEW YORK TIMES [25]

July 15, 1978.

More than 19,000 municipal employees went on strike here today, crippling most governmental services other than firefighting and law enforcement.

The strike began at 12:01 a.m., just an hour after city representatives had offered wage increases of 7 percent this year and 5 percent next year to the two bargaining units involved, District Councils 33 and 47 of the American Federation of State, County and Municipal Employees.

The union took the proposal under consideration, but proceeded with the strike. The strike stopped garbage and trash collections; severely limited services at 10 city health centers; closed 48 libraries and the Philadelphia Museum of Art; left playgrounds, pools and recreation centers without staffs, and removed clerical and custodial help at city facilities.

In addition, three prisons were left without guards and two nursing homes were making do with volunteer aid.

District Council 33 is a union of blue-collar workers with average annual earnings of $11,267. District Council 47 is negotiating for white-collar workers with an average yearly income of $17,436.

BOTH WANT ONE-YEAR CONTRACT

Both councils want a one-year contract commensurate with one given to city policemen in arbitration several weeks ago. In that settlement, law enforcement officers won a one-year contract that called for 9 percent salary raises at a cost of $19.2 million to the city.

To pay for the police settlement, Mayor Frank L. Rizzo said, more than 3,000 nonuniformed city employees would have to be furloughed. This announcement formed the kernel of the dispute that resulted in the current strike.

"Nine percent!" and "No layoffs!" pickets screamed outside city buildings today. * * * A spokesman for the municipal employees' union said this afternoon: "It's not right and it's not fair that our

25. *Philadelphia is crippled by a strike of more than 19,000 employees,* by Gregory Jaynes. Copyright 1978 by the New York Times Company. Reprinted by permission.

members face layoffs to pay the package for police officers. What our members are looking for is a fair and equitable distribution of taxpayers' money for all city employees."

2. THE FORUM OF FINALITY: POWER OR JUSTICE?

One of the alternatives to strike action and one which is employed in New York State for state employees is the device of the legislative hearing. If mediation and fact-finding fail, the dispute goes to a joint legislative committee for hearing and decision. The appeal of this mechanism is that it recognizes that the bottom line in public sector collective bargaining is political.

Dispute settlement under this procedure has little to do with justice, equity, or fairness. It is driven primarily by considerations of votes, elections, and re-elections.

In 1976, the State of New York and the Civil Service Employees Association were at impasse. They went to fact-finding. The fact-finders recommended a six percent across the board salary increase. The State (per the Governor) rejected this recommendation and offered nothing; the Union accepted the fact-finders' recommendation.

The dispute went to a hearing before a joint committee of the State Assembly and the State Senate. The committee adopted the State's position.

> A spokesperson for the Governor's office made the following statement some years later: "We were not worried about the outcome. The democratically controlled Assembly was not about to overrule the second Democratic governor that the state had had in thirty years; and the Republican controlled Senate was not likely to try to 'outliberal' a Democratic governor, in a context of genuine fiscal crisis bordering on bankruptcy created by the problems of New York City, by requiring him to spend $74 million more for state employee salaries." [26]

3. END RUNS: HEREIN OF SUPPLEMENTAL POLITICAL SETTLEMENTS OF PUBLIC SECTOR LABOR DISPUTES

The political nature of public sector collective bargaining is exemplified by some illustrations drawn from New York State.

In 1977 there were 39 bills sponsored by public sector unions, all of them bearing more than an incidental relationship to the terms and conditions of employment, which passed both houses of the legislature and wound up on the governor's desk. Thirteen of these bills were "end runs" where the unions manipulated through the legislature proposals which they had either traded off or otherwise lost at the

26. The vote was 10 to 2. The majority consisted of 6 Democrats and 4 Republicans. The dissenters were Republicans. Authors' files.

bargaining table. These included such matters as disability benefits, time off with pay whenever work is unavailable because of snow conditions, arbitration of dismissal cases involving tenured teachers, compensatory time off, seniority, leave benefits, and extension of preferred lists for recall. Nineteen of the bills involved subjects excluded from the bargaining table by statutory or decisional law, including certain retirement proposals, work standards, and insurance for upper echelon supervisory personnel.

Nine of the bills, five of them dealing with retirement, were mandates by the state to local governments to increase expenditures to improve the terms and conditions of their employees, particularly police and firefighters.

The Advisory Commission on Intergovernmental Relations has noted: "Local authorities are especially bitter over the 'end-run play' by which local employee representatives (especially police and firemen) successfully obtain from the state legislature more generous personnel benefits on a mandated basis than they could through negotiation with locally elected officials." [27]

In 1978 approximately 40 bills manifesting more than an incidental relationship to the terms and conditions of employment went to the governor for approval or veto. Ten of these were again "end runs." These included such matters as time off with pay (without charge to leave credits) for absence due to severe weather conditions or power failures and employee participation on certain boards or panels, as well as greater benefits than had been negotiated in such areas as tenure or retention of employment, retiree dental insurance participation, and continuity of employment. In addition, there were approximately 30 bills which went to the governor which involved subjects either excluded from the collective bargaining process by statutory or decisional law, or rendered inappropriate for disposition at the bargaining table because of the multiplicity of parties in interest or the functional structuring of government. Included among these were various retirement proposals, employment status changes, and other civil service law amendments. Furthermore, as had been the case in 1977, a significant number of the bills were mandates or authorization by the state to local governments to increase expenditures to improve benefits (principally retirement) for or on behalf of local employees, particularly police and firefighters.

New York's Civil Service Employees Association lost an arbitration decision which held that the leave provisions of the labor agreement did not entitle the state employees whom they represented time off with pay when work was unavailable because of snow conditions. Thereafter, CSEA put enough pressure on the governor, who was tooling up for his re-election campaign, to get him to direct the Civil Service Commis-

27. Advisory Comm'n on Intergovernmental Relations, Intergovernmental Perspective, Vol. 3, No. 3 (Summer 1977), p. 9.

sion to award paid leaves for such days, in effect thereby gaining a retroactive amendment to the collective bargaining agreement.

Notes and Questions

1. Does the foregoing material support Professor Summers' assertion that our political system has a built-in bias against the public employee?

2. Can our political institutions ever be insulated from such end-runs by public employee labor organizations?

3. Does the end-run technique support the Supreme Court's thesis in *Abood*?

4. Suppose a public employer, after bargaining to impasse with a union representing its employees, unilaterally puts into effect its last, best offer on (a) wages and (b) health care premium contributions. Specifically, the employer reduces salaries by five percent as proposed in its last, best offer, and increases the costs to employees of contributions to the health benefits program.

Suppose further that the union brings an action in the appropriate court requiring the public employer to desist and refrain from reducing wages, a result grounded on a specific section of a state statute which prohibits employee establishment of salaries in a bargaining unit where a union has been chosen to represent its members.

Should the court defer action on the ground that the Public Employee Relations Board has exclusive primary jurisdiction over the cause?

A California appellate court gave a negative answer to this question in part because the Public Employee Relations Board disavowed jurisdiction over the dispute. *Department of Personnel Administration v. Superior Court,* 5 Cal.App. 4th 155, 6 Cal.Rptr.2d 714 (1992).

The court went on to hold that where a collective bargaining agreement has expired by its terms and the parties have bargained to an impasse, the employer cannot unilaterally adjust wages.

Under this holding what is the forum for resolving a wage dispute? The court addressed this question as follows:

> "Considering * * * the highly political nature of this dispute, it makes * * * sense that it will be ultimately resolved in the political branch." (at p. 729)

[The court reached a different result on the merits of the unilateral adjustment in health benefit contributions.]

Chapter 2

ORGANIZING ACTIVITIES AND BARGAINING UNIT ISSUES

A. ORGANIZING ACTIVITIES

1. CONSTITUTIONAL RIGHTS

In *Keyishian v. Board of Regents,*[1] the Supreme Court repudiated the distinction in constitutional status between public and private employees whereby "public employment, including academic employment, may be conditioned upon the surrender of constitutional rights which could not be abridged by direct government action."[2] Adopting the language of the court below, the Court stated: "[T]he theory that public employment which may be denied altogether may be subjected to any conditions, regardless of how unreasonable, has been uniformly rejected."[3] Public employees cannot be "relegated to a watered-down version of constitutional rights" solely because they are public employees.[4] Since private employees have a constitutional right to organize into associations for the purpose of self-help[5] and public employees cannot be relegated to "watered-down" constitutional rights, it follows that the latter have the right to belong to employee organizations, to engage in organizational activities, and through such organizations, to importune their employers for improvements in the terms and conditions of employment.

1. 385 U.S. 589, 87 S.Ct. 675, 17 L.Ed.2d 629 (1967).

2. Id. at 605, 87 S.Ct. at 684.

3. Id. at 605–606, 87 S.Ct. at 684–685, quoting from 345 F.2d 236, 239 (2d Cir. 1965).

4. *Garrity v. New Jersey,* 385 U.S. 493, 500, 87 S.Ct. 616, 620, 17 L.Ed.2d 562 (1967).

5. See *NAACP v. Button,* 371 U.S. 415, 83 S.Ct. 328, 9 L.Ed.2d 405 (1963); *NAACP v. Alabama ex rel. Patterson,* 357 U.S. 449, 78 S.Ct. 1163, 2 L.Ed.2d 1488 (1958); *Brotherhood of Railroad Trainmen v. Virginia ex rel. Virginia State Bar,* 377 U.S. 1, 84 S.Ct. 1113, 12 L.Ed.2d 89 (1964); *Shelton v. Tucker,* 364 U.S. 479, 81 S.Ct. 247, 5 L.Ed.2d 231 (1960).

AMERICAN FEDERATION OF STATE, COUNTY & MUNICIPAL EMPLOYEES A.F.L.–C.I.O. v. WOODWARD

United States Court of Appeals, Eighth Circuit, 1969.
406 F.2d 137.

HEANEY, CIRCUIT JUDGE: The principal question raised on this appeal is whether public employees, discharged because they joined a labor union, have a right of action for damages and injunctive relief under Section 1 of the Civil Rights Act of 1871, 42 U.S.C. § 1983,[1] against the public official who discharged them. The answer to this question turns on whether public employees have a constitutionally protected right to belong to a labor union.[3]

The District Court dismissed the plaintiffs' complaint on the grounds that it failed to allege facts constituting a claim under 42 U.S.C. § 1983. We reverse.

The complaint alleged: that LeRoy Gage and John Engleman had been employed by the Street Department of the City of North Platte, Nebraska; that in May 1967, the Union began an organizational campaign among the employees of the Street Department; that a number of employees, including Gage and Engleman, became members of the Union; that Defendant Woodward, the City Commissioner in charge of the Street Department, learned of the Union activities and of the fact that Gage and Engleman had become members of the Union; that Woodward "purposely and maliciously and solely for the purpose of discriminating against such employees of the Street Department * * * as joined or wanted to join a Union, threatened said employees with possible discharge; * * * [and] did in fact discharge * * * Gage and Engleman" solely because they joined the Union; and that Woodward reduced the salaries of other employees for the same reason.

Engleman and Gage claimed damages in the sum of $5,000 and, along with the plaintiff Union, sought an injunction prohibiting the defendant from discriminating against any employee of the Street Department because of membership or nonmembership in a union and interfering with the organization of the employees of the department.

To invoke the remedies provided by the Civil Rights Act of 1871, the plaintiffs must show that the Commissioner deprived them of rights, privileges or immunities secured by the United States Constitu-

1. [Footnotes numbered as in original.—Ed.] Section 1, Civil Rights Act of 1871, 42 U.S.C. § 1983, provides:

"Every person who under color of any statute, ordinance, regulation, custom, or usage, of any State or Territory, subjects, or causes to be subjected, any citizen of the United States or other person within the jurisdiction thereof to the deprivation of any rights, privileges, or immunities secured by the Constitution and laws, shall be liable to the party injured in an action at law, suit in equity, or other proper proceeding for redress."

3. Nebraska law prohibits strikes by public employees, Reissue Revised Statutes of 1943, § 48–821, and provides that no governmental subdivision can be compelled to enter into a collective bargaining agreement with a labor organization. Reissue Revised Statutes of 1943, § 48–810.01. The Union does not contend on this appeal and we express no opinion as to whether a union has a federally protected right to engage in either activity.

tion or by the laws of the United States, and that the Commissioner acted under color of law. The plaintiffs argue that this was done here as the commissioner deprived them of the right to freedom of association under the First Amendment made applicable to the states by the Fourteenth Amendment.

The First Amendment protects the right of one citizen to associate with other citizens for any lawful purpose free from government interference. The guarantee of the "right of assembly" protects more than "the right to attend a meeting; it includes the right to express one's attitudes or philosophies by membership in a group or by affiliation with it or by other lawful means. * * * " *Griswold v. Connecticut,* 381 U.S. 479, 483 (1965); *NAACP v. Alabama, ex rel. Patterson,* 357 U.S. 449, 460–61 (1958).

Union membership is protected by the right of association under the First and Fourteenth Amendments. *Thomas v. Collins,* 323 U.S. 516 (1945); *McLaughlin v. Tilendis,* 398 F.2d 287 (7th Cir.1968). The Court commented in *Thomas:*

> "* * * Great secular causes, with small ones, are guarded. The grievances for redress of which the right of petition was insured, and with it the right of assembly, are not solely religious or political ones. And the rights of free speech and a free press are not confined to any field of human interest.
>
> "The idea is not sound therefore that the First Amendment's safeguards are wholly inapplicable to business or economic activity. * * * " *Id.* 323 U.S. at 531.
>
> "* * * This Court has recognized that in the circumstances of our times the dissemination of information concerning the facts of a labor dispute must be regarded as within that area of free discussion that is guaranteed by the Constitution. * * * Free discussion concerning the conditions in industry and the causes of labor disputes appears to us indispensable to the effective and intelligent use of the processes of popular government to shape the destiny of modern industrial society'. *Thornhill v. Alabama,* 310 U.S. 88, 102, 103. * * * The right * * * to discuss, and inform people concerning, the advantages and disadvantages of unions and joining them is protected not only as part of free speech, but as part of free assembly. * * * "

Id. at 532.

In *Tilendis,* the Court held that a complaint alleging that a nontenure teacher was dismissed because of his membership in a union stated a claim upon which relief could be granted under the Civil Rights Act of 1871. The Court stated:

> "It is settled that teachers have the right of free association, and unjustified interference with teachers' associational freedom violates the Due Process clause of the Fourteenth Amendment.... Public employment may not be subjected to unreasonable condi-

tions, and the assertion of First Amendment rights by teachers will usually not warrant their dismissal.... Unless there is some illegal intent, an individual's right to form and join a union is protected by the First Amendment...."

McLaughlin v. Tilendis, supra 398 F.2d at 288–89 (citations omitted).

The defendant argues that the plaintiffs have no federally protected right to be continued in public employment. The Supreme Court disposed of his argument in *Wieman v. Updegraff,* 344 U.S. 183, 191–92 (1952):

"* * * [T]he facile generalization that there is no constitutionally protected right to public employment is to obscure the issue. For, in United Public Workers, though we held that the Federal Government through the Hatch Act [18 U.S.C.A. §§ 118j, 118*l*] could properly bar its employees from certain political activity thought inimical to the interests of the Civil Service, we cast this holding into perspective by emphasizing that Congress could not 'enact a regulation providing that no Republican, Jew or Negro shall be appointed to federal office, or that no federal employee shall attend Mass or take any active part in missionary work,' 330 U.S. at [page] 100. See also *In re Summers,* 1945, 325 U.S. 561, 571. We need not pause to consider whether an abstract right to public employment exists. It is sufficient to say that constitutional protection does extend to the public servant whose exclusion * * * is patently arbitrary or discriminatory."

This same theme has been repeated by the Supreme Court on a number of occasions. In *Beilan v. Board of Public Ed. of Phila.,* 357 U.S. 399, 405 (1958), the Court stated that, "By engaging in teaching in the public schools, petitioner did not give up his right to freedom of belief, speech or association. * * * " Again, in *Keyishian v. Board of Regents of University of State of New York,* 385 U.S. 589, 605 (1967), the Court specifically rejected the theory that public employment "may be conditioned upon surrender of constitutional rights which could not be abridged by direct government action." See, *Pickering v. Board of Education,* 391 U.S. 563 (1968).

Notes and Questions

1. A number of federal cases have relied on the First Amendment to protect the right of public employees to form or join a labor organization, association, or union. For example, in *United Federation of Postal Clerks v. Blount,* 325 F.Supp. 879, 883 (D.D.C.1971), *affirmed mem.* 404 U.S. 802, 92 S.Ct. 80, 30 L.Ed.2d 38 (1971), in the course of holding that federal employees do not have a constitutional right to strike, a three-judge court in the District of Columbia stated that the right to form a labor organization and to select an organizational representative for the purpose of collective negotiations is a *fundamental* constitutionally protected right.

It does not follow, however, that there is a duty requiring a public employer to bargain collectively with representatives of groups of its employees, unless such a duty is imposed by an executive order or statute. In addition, bargaining rights established by executive order or statute may limit some rights to organize. For example, some states limit organizational rights of law enforcement officers by allowing such employees to form or join their own organization but prohibit such employees from joining organizations which bargain collectively for other employees of the public employer. Similarly, in jurisdictions which provide for bargaining rights for public employee supervisors, there may be restrictions preventing a bargaining unit of supervisors from being represented by the same labor organization that represents nonsupervisory employees of the public employer. Where these limitations have been challenged, they have typically been upheld.

What policy considerations support such limitations on a public employee's right of association?

2. In the private sector, under the NLRA, many critical issues have arisen concerning the right of a private sector employer to oppose a pro-union vote during a union organizing campaign. With rare exception, public employers do not take a public position about the pros or cons of union representation and the merits of collective bargaining during a union organizing campaign.

Why would, or should, a public employer (in contrast to a private sector employer) choose to remain silent during a union organizing campaign?

3. In *Aurora Educ. Ass'n v. Board of Educ.*, 490 F.2d 431, 434 (7th Cir.1973), the court held invalid, as violative of First Amendment rights, a school board policy excluding from bargaining rights any organization "which asserts the right to strike against any * * * agency of the government, or to assist or to participate in any such strike, or which imposes a duty or obligation to conduct, assist or participate in any such strike. * * *" The opinion of Judge Wyzanski declared: "We need no recital of literary authorities from John Milton to Harold J. Laski or of judicial luminaries from Justices Holmes, Brandeis, and Cardozo to Black, Frankfurter, and Harlan (to mention only the dead) to buttress the principle that the teacher, like any other citizen, is free to think as he likes, and to express those views academically provided action is not advocated but merely adumbrated."

4. The New York State Taylor Law provides:

> **Sec. 207. Determination of Representation Status.**—For purposes of resolving disputes concerning representation status, pursuant to section two hundred five or two hundred six of this article, the board or government, as the case may be, shall
>
> * * *
>
> certify or recognize an employee organization upon (a) the determination that such organization represents that group of public employees it claims to represent, and (b) the affirmation by such organization that it does not assert the right to strike against any government, to assist or participate in any such strike, or to impose an obligation to conduct, assist or participate in such a strike.

This section was declared constitutional in *Rogoff v. Anderson*, 34 A.D.2d 154, 310 N.Y.S.2d 174 (1970), *affirmed* 28 N.Y.2d 880, 322 N.Y.S.2d 718, 271 N.E.2d 553 (1971), *appeal dismissed for want of a substantial federal question* 404 U.S. 805, 92 S.Ct. 108, 30 L.Ed.2d 37 (1971). If a union advocated repeal of subsection (b) of Section 207 of the New York law, would it be disqualified from serving as a bargaining representative?

2. STATUTORY RIGHTS

Nearly all state public employee labor relations statutes contain declarations of organizational rights, and prohibitions against interference and discrimination, though there is some variation in language. The similarity in language between these public sector statutory provisions and Sections 7, 8(a)(1), (2), and (3) of the National Labor Relations Act has led to extensive reliance upon federal precedents. The pertinent provisions from two statutes, the California State Employer–Employee Relations Act and New York's Taylor Law (applicable to all public employees) follow:

CALIFORNIA

"Sec. 3515. Except as otherwise provided by the Legislature, state employees shall have the right to form, join, and participate in the activities of employee organizations of their own choosing for the purpose of representation on all matters of employer-employee relations. State employees also shall have the right to refuse to join or participate in the activities of employee organizations, except that nothing shall preclude the parties from agreeing to a maintenance of membership provision, as defined in subdivision (h) of Section 3513, pursuant to a memorandum of understanding. In any event, state employees shall have the right to represent themselves individually in their employment relations with the public agency.

"Sec. 3510. It shall be unlawful for the state to:

"(a) Impose or threaten to impose reprisals on employees, to discriminate or threaten to discriminate against employees or otherwise to interfere with, restrain, or coerce employees because of their exercise of rights guaranteed by this chapter.

"(b) Deny to employee organizations rights guaranteed to them by this chapter.

"(d) Dominate or interfere with the formation or administration of any employee organization, or contribute financial or other support to it, or in any way encourage employees to join any organization in preference to another."

NEW YORK

"Sec. 202. Public employees shall have the right to form, join and participate in, or to refrain from forming, joining, or participating in, any employee organization of their own choosing.

"Sec. 209–a. *Improper employer practices.* It shall be an improper practice for a public employer or its agents deliberately (a) to interfere with, restrain or coerce public employees in the exercise of their rights guaranteed in section two hundred two for the purpose of depriving them of such rights; (b) to dominate or interfere with the formation or administration of any employee organization for the purpose of depriving them of such rights; (c) to discriminate against any employee for the purpose of encouraging or discouraging membership in, or participation in the activities of, any employee organization. . . ."

Question

Under Section 208(2) of New York's "Taylor Law" a union organization which enjoys a negotiated agreement with a public employer has the right to exclusive and unchallenged representation until seven months before the end of the public employer's fiscal year in which the employment agreement terminates. (The seven-month challenge period for incumbent unions having a contract with the State of New York, accordingly, begins August 1 of the year before the termination of such contract.) Concerned that the state's operations might be unreasonably interrupted, the Governor's Office of Employee Relations promulgated guidelines permitting access to state facilities by professional union organizers for campaigning purposes only for a period of 90 days prior to the beginning of the challenge period (May 1).

Do restrictions on access to public facilities during a union organizing campaign by a public employer raise special issues which are not involved when a private sector employer imposes similar limitations?

B. ESTABLISHMENT OF REPRESENTATION STATUS

1. TYPES OF REPRESENTATION

The system of exclusive representation which prevails in the private sector (one union representing all the employees in a bargaining unit on an exclusive basis) was not uniformly accepted in the early days of public sector bargaining. California's first comprehensive public sector statute, for example, adopted in 1961, provided that the public employer was to meet and confer with representatives of an employee organization "on behalf of its members." Thus, two or more employee organizations could be recognized simultaneously, each on behalf of its members only, within the same grouping of employees.

Minnesota and California experimented with a second system of recognition based on proportional representation. Organizations representing teachers were allowed representation on a negotiating council in proportion to their membership within the bargaining unit. Both states have since abandoned that system in favor of exclusive representation. Consider the following observation:

> "* * * There are inherent difficulties with this system which make it much more unstable than a system of exclusive recognition

> * * * Each of the organizations on the council is caught in a competitive milieu where it must continuously strive to outdo the other organizations in order to hold present members and gain new ones. The minority organization has nothing to lose and everything to gain by taking militant and even irresponsible positions * * *
>
> "Moreover, to the extent that negotiations are productive, there is likely to be maneuvering by each organization in an effort to claim credit * * *
>
> "School boards may be tempted to exploit the competitive tensions * * * Ultimately, however, the hostilities and anxieties created among teachers by the failure of the system to produce dividends and the intensity of organizational competition may produce a strident and extremist majority organization with demagogic leadership." *

Remnants of nonexclusive representation systems remain—in California, for example, where the statute pertaining to local government employees appears to permit a "members only" arrangement. See Grodin, *Public Employee Bargaining in California: The Meyers–Milias–Brown Act in the Courts,* 23 Hast.L.J. 719 (1972). The federal statutes and nearly all state statutes, however, have adopted the private sector model of exclusive recognition within bargaining units.

SUMMERS, BARGAINING IN THE GOVERNMENT'S BUSINESS: PRINCIPLES AND POLITICS **

18 U.Tol.L.Rev. 265, 269, 270 (1987).

* * *

The principle of exclusive representation is considered fundamental in our labor law. It approaches being the First Commandment with the deification of the majority union. "I am the Lord thy God, Thou shalt have no other gods before me." But it is not written on stone from Sinai; it has more practical origins. The historical purpose of exclusive representation was to prevent an employer from playing one union against another to divide and conquer, and its practical purpose was to establish a single contract with standardized terms.

The principle has been carried over from the private sector to the public sector with little recognition that in the public sector it is at most only half viable. The need for standardized terms is even greater in the public than the private sector, for traditions of classified service and insistence on equal treatment generates nearly irresistible demands of equal pay for equal work, and an increase for one group must be matched by equal increases for other groups. But exclusive repre-

* Wollett & Chanin, The Law and Practice of Teacher Negotiations. (Washington, D.C.:BNA Books, 1974), pp. 2:22–23.

** Reprinted by permission of the University of Toledo Law Review and the author.

sentation in bargaining units carved out according to the private sector pattern denies the political reality.

If city officials negotiate first with the union representing employees in the public works department, that agreement will provide the benchmark for other bargaining units represented by other unions, from the parks department to the city clerk's office. The contract made with the police will be the blueprint for the contract with the firefighters. The increases won by the teachers union will determine the increases for the administrators. The public works union, the police union and the teachers union become, for purposes of negotiating wages and other economic benefits, the effective representatives of employees who have selected different exclusive representatives.

City officials, in negotiating economic terms of one contract, must calculate its impact on other employees, for all of the money comes out of the same budget and is reflected in a single tax millage. In this respect, exclusive representation is a misleading myth. It is not the instrument for standardizing terms—that is done by the employer, and it does not produce unity on the employee side, but insures fragmentation and provides opportunity for manipulation by the public employer.

Multiple bargaining units do, of course, serve the purpose of enabling special groups to deal with special problems, to make variations to fit particular preferences, and at times to make adjustments in the general wage structure. Perhaps most important, multiple units give employees greater control over selection of those who represent them daily in handling their grievances. What is plainly needed in the public sector is some form of two-level bargaining [one level in issues which are special to each bargaining unit and a second level where standardized terms for all units are needed.] But the idolizing of principles from the private sector has obstructed serious consideration of such needed solutions.

Exclusive representation is only half, or less than half, viable in the public sector in another respect. One accepted corollary of exclusive representation in the private sector is that the employer cannot consult or discuss terms and conditions of employment with an individual employee or any other employee representative. In the public sector such a rule curbing open communication has serious implications for the political process.

* * *

Notes and Questions

Do you agree or disagree with Professor Summers' unconventional viewpoint on the appropriateness of exclusivity in the public sector? Why has exclusive union representation become the dominant United States public sector labor law pattern with so little debate, particularly when no other country except Canada has adopted it?

The exclusive bargaining representative has a duty of fair representation to each member of the bargaining unit. This duty is further explored in Chapter 9. If a public employee who is a member of a bargaining unit has exercised a statutory right not to join the union which has exclusive bargaining rights, may the union refuse to represent that bargaining unit member in a grievance arbitration case unless that member pays a share of arbitration costs or is this an unfair labor practice? This issue is also explored in Chapter 9.

2. METHODS OF OBTAINING RECOGNITION

1. In most states a union may obtain recognition either on the basis of a secret ballot election to determine majority status or on the basis of voluntary recognition by the employer. There is some variation among the statutes with respect to the type of evidence upon which an employer may rely, short of an election, in determining that a union in fact represents a majority of employees in the bargaining unit. The Civil Service Reform Act (§ 7111) and a few states (e.g., Alaska Stats. § 23.40.100) make an election the only route to recognition. What arguments support or reject such a policy?

2. Where recognition is based upon an election, the procedure is typically quite similar to that under the National Labor Relations Act: The election is conducted by an independent agency; in the absence of a consent agreement a preelection hearing is conducted to determine unit questions and other disputed issues; employees vote by secret ballot; the ballot permits a choice among one or more unions and "no union"; and if no alternative receives a majority vote, there is a runoff. There is some variation, however. The California statute pertaining to local government employees, for example (West's Ann.Cal.Gov't.Code § 3500), is not administered by any agency, and rules regarding elections are left up to the governmental employers themselves. Vermont appears to require that a union receive a majority of votes within the bargaining unit, rather than a majority of votes cast. (Vt.Stats.Ann. § 1583.) And in Oregon, college and university professors vote separately (a) for or against representation, and (b) for the particular labor organization, if any, they wish to have represent them. If a majority votes against representation, the ballots for particular organizations are not counted. What are the practical differences between such a system and the typical model in which "no union" is simply a choice on the ballot?

3. In *Decatur Federation of Teachers, AFL–CIO v. ELRB,* 199 Ill.App.3d 190, 145 Ill.Dec. 162, 556 N.E.2d 780 (4th Dist.1990) the court affirmed an order of the Board adopting in full a hearing officer's recommendation and order which set aside a representation election and ordered a new election. The case illustrates that state public employment relations boards (PERBs) supervise elections in the same manner as does the NLRB, although the standards of review may be somewhat different. The court required a finding in the *Decatur* case that the misconduct which was the basis for the challenge to the election's validity in fact affected the election results.

4. The possibility of a union obtaining recognition on the basis of a bargaining order to remedy employer unfair labor practices appears not to have arisen in the public sector. Can you think of why that might be so?

C. BARGAINING UNIT ISSUES

1. WHAT IS AT STAKE IN REPRESENTATION DECISIONS—OR, WHY DO THE PARTIES CARE ABOUT THE COMPOSITION OF BARGAINING UNITS?

Unit determinations serve a dual function in both the public and private sectors. They determine the constituency for purposes of selecting the majority representative, and they mold the structure of collective bargaining which takes place after a representative, if any, is selected. Unions, particularly where two or more unions are competing for representation of overlapping groups, are likely to be more interested in the first function. For example, if Union A traditionally represents counselors and psychologists employed by school districts, Union A's survival may be at stake in a unit contest where Union B seeks a unit consisting of counselors, psychologists, and classroom teachers. It may be that Union A could not win an election in the larger unit. This aspect of unit determination is present in both private and public sectors, but it tends to be intensified in the public sector where one of the competing organizations is an association which preexisted collective bargaining, and which represented employees (e.g., all civil service employees) on a basis which had nothing to do with a collective bargaining relationship. A statewide civil service association, for example, is likely to have a vital stake in seeing that bargaining units are broadly drawn; indeed, the best of all possible worlds for such an association is likely to be one in which only a single statewide civil service unit is permitted. In sum, unit determination contests with more than one union party tend to be manifestations of interunion as well as union-employer conflict. Interunion tensions in the public sector are highlighted by the competition for representation that is sometimes provided by an employee association which existed long before collective bargaining became authorized and necessarily operated in a manner entirely out of character with the conventional relationship between an employer and a union.

The following excerpt from a 1969 article remains a classic description of unit determination issues posed in the public sector. The author was the labor relations advisor to the City of Philadelphia between 1952 and 1962 where, as he notes, there is a single bargaining unit for municipal employees (excluding police and firefighters). The author refers to the unit determination provisions of New York State's Taylor Law which are set forth in their entirety in the next subsection.

ROCK, THE APPROPRIATE UNIT QUESTION IN THE PUBLIC SERVICE: THE PROBLEM OF PROLIFERATION

67 Mich.L.Rev. 1001 (1969).

I. Introduction

It is becoming increasingly clear that of the numerous problems which complicate the practice of collective bargaining in the public sector, none is more important than the appropriate unit question. In the public sector as well as in private industry, determination of the size and composition of the bargaining unit at the initial stages of organization and recognition can be decisive of the question of which employee organization will achieve majority recognition, or whether any organization will win recognition. Save for the employee organization which limits its jurisdiction along narrow lines such as the craft practiced by its members, the normal tendency may be to request initially a unit whose boundaries coincide with the spread of the organization's membership or estimated strength. The public employer, on the other hand, may seek to recognize a unit in which the no-union votes will be in the majority, or a favored employee organization will have predominant strength; or the employer may simply seek to avoid undue proliferation of bargaining units.

The problem in the public sector, however, is of far greater depth than the initial victory-or-defeat aspect of recognition. In the private sector, it is clear that the scope and nature of the unit found to be appropriate for bargaining has acted as an important determinant of the union's basic economic strength—that is, its bargaining over bread-and-butter economic issues. In the public sector, it seems clear that the scope and nature of the unit found to be appropriate will also affect the range of subjects which can be negotiated meaningfully, the role played in the process by the separate branches of government, the likelihood of peaceful resolution of disputes, order versus chaos in bargaining, and ultimately, perhaps, the success of the whole idea of collective bargaining for public employees.

Although the appropriate unit question has received much attention in the private sector during the past thirty years, it has not received the same attention for public sector employees until recently.

* * *

Traditionally, the public employer and union have given little thought to the appropriateness of a unit that requested recognition. More often than not, in the years prior to the enactment of definitive rules for recognition of public employees, a union requesting and receiving some form of recognition was considered the spokesman for its members—in whatever job classifications, functional departments, or physical locations they happened to be. This lenient approach was facilitated by (and perhaps had its start in) the fact that "recognition" frequently carried no legal consequences beyond the ability to appear before legislative or executive bodies hearing budgetary requests or the power to lobby with key political figures. Even when recognition was followed by a procedure similar to bargaining—including in some instances an embodiment of the bargain in a written agreement or memorandum—little if any consideration was given to the appropriateness of the unit being dealt with. Apart from the obvious problems stemming from the failure to grant "exclusive bargaining rights" to these early public employee units and from the inattention to the matter of excluding supervisors from the units representing those whom they supervise, a groundwork was laid for the creation of illogical unit lines. All too frequently the result was a proliferation of bargaining units.

* * *

At the state and local levels, virtually all of the significant legislation passed since 1960 has spelled out standards of some type of unit determination. In many instances these state enactments made possible further proliferation by adding to the existing illogical patterns of recognition new units made possible through espousal of the federal "community of interest" standard and its converse, separate units for groups having "conflicting interests"; * * * [and in some states] by permitting the government agency to rely on the extent of employee organization. Notwithstanding the fact that some of the state laws embody specific standards used by the National Labor Relations Board for the private sector, observers familiar with bargaining conditions in both sectors have contended that the degree of fragmentation in some of the states exceeds that of the private sector.

Clearly, at both state and federal levels the standards place a high premium on the subjective judgment of the decision-making body or individual, and results are also shaped to a high degree by the happenstance of the petitioning organization's requested unit at the time of the petition. Particularly when there is no rival organizational claim for a larger unit—which is often the case—the over-all effect has been to encourage recognition of the smaller unit. Even if a union succeeds in winning recognition in a large unit, employees in that unit are generally not required to become members of the union. The relative lack of union security clauses in the collective bargaining agreements of the public service assures that, to a degree unparalleled in the private sector, dissident small-unit groups are able to maintain their separate identities and to prolong the battle for break-off from the larger group's exclusive bargaining agent.

The Case for and Against the Small Unit

It cannot be assumed automatically that the pattern of many small units is wrong. A single craft, classification, department, or installation which would otherwise constitute a small minority if included in a larger unit can argue with some justification that its specialized interests and needs may be subordinated to the wishes of the larger unit's majority. Moreover, the smaller unit which performs a particularly essential function may also be capable of striking a better bargain for itself when left to do its own negotiating.

"Community of interest" is more than a catch phrase. It not only points up that like-situated employees will better understand their own problems and press their unique needs, but it also recognizes the instinct of exclusiveness which causes employees to *want* to form their own organization rather than become part of a larger organization in which they may feel themselves strangers. The desire to possess such "freedom of choice" or "self-determination" should, it can be argued, receive greater weight for public employees, because they are "public," than for those in the private sector.

There is nothing inherently wrong in permitting an employee organization to gain a foothold in a smaller unit, if the employees in that unit select it; and, if the union is effective in the small unit, it may grow and achieve recognition in other separate units or in a single large unit. This consideration may be particularly significant in the early period after the promulgation of legislation or executive orders encompassing a vast group of employees whose right to representation had not previously been formally legitimized. It is frequently easier for unions to secure employees' allegiance in smaller, distinctive groups than in larger, heterogeneous ones.

At the same time, there are important considerations which, it seems, point toward a unique, long-range need for larger units in the public sector. The special problems of unit determination in the public sector were most clearly recognized legislatively in 1967 in New York's Taylor Law, which included, in addition to the common standards of community of interest and necessity to promote the public welfare, the further requirement that in defining an appropriate unit the following standard should be taken into consideration: "the officials of government at the level of the unit shall have the power to agree, or to make effective recommendations to other administrative authority or the legislative body with respect to, the terms and conditions of employment upon which the employees desire to negotiate. * * *" [§ 207(1)(b)]. The latter clause clearly reflects awareness of the fact that the employer-negotiator in the public service frequently has only limited authority, and that this condition will affect the scope of bargaining. As pointed out by the New York Governor's Committee on Public Employee Relations, the picture in the public sector is fundamentally different from that in the private sector. In private business, the authority to bargain on all of the normally bargainable matters is present or can be delegated, no matter what the size or make-up of the bargaining unit. By contrast, in the public service the necessary authority may not be delegable to lower-level functional units; legal requirements and tradition often call for uniformity of certain working conditions for like categories of employees throughout the governmental entity, regardless of bargaining unit categorization; and, even at the top of the particular level of government involved, authority is normally divided at least three ways—among the executive branch, the legislative branch, and a civil service commission.

Inherent in the previously quoted section of the Taylor Law, therefore, is the necessity that some consideration be given to the nature of the subject matter sought to be bargained upon in seeking to arrive at the appropriateness of a unit. This provision of the Taylor Law also recognizes that the subject matter of bargaining must normally be limited by the scope of the "employer's" authority to make agreements or effective recommendations, and a likely consequence is that the smaller the unit decided upon, the more restricted the scope of the bargaining by that unit will be.

Apart from this inhibiting effect on the bargaining experience, an approach which permits or favors small units makes it very difficult to resolve other institutional complications which arise in bargaining in the public service. The New York Governor's Committee, in both its 1966 Report and its 1968 Report, pointed out the unique importance of completing a negotiation with public employees in time to incorporate the agreement's financial essence in the budget of the governmental unit—which, by law, generally must be submitted to the legislature by a specified date. However, many of the annual bargaining sessions in the public sector today are extraordinarily prolonged, starting with direct negotiation, followed by resort to mediation and the frequently used machinery of fact-finding or impasse panels. After all of this there may be further extensive dealings with upper-echelon individuals or groups in the executive and legislative branches. Thus, the sheer weight of the process may lead to its breakdown if the trend toward proliferation of bargaining units in numerous jurisdictions continues unabated. It is noteworthy that in the City of Philadelphia—which is frequently cited as an example of well-established, peaceful, and effective bargaining at the municipal level—all employees except policemen and firemen have been represented by a single unit for most of the last two decades. Even with only a single unit and without use of impasse resolution machinery, however, the experience in Philadelphia has been marked by many instances of abnormally prolonged annual negotiations. The Philadelphia experience also demonstrates the need to establish detailed liaison between the executive branch, the legislative branch, and the civil service commission during the course of an annual bargaining program in order to minimize the chaotic effects of overlapping authority on the government side.

While it is possible that a city the size of Philadelphia might also have had a history of successful labor relations in the public sector under a pattern which broke down the public employee bargaining group into a small number of separate units, there is little question that the success could not have been achieved under the patterns of excessive fragmentation found elsewhere. In any event, the existence of the single large unit clearly contributed significantly to that city's ability to surmount effectively the institutional obstacles complicating public sector bargaining. Moreover, proliferation can and does breed excessive competition among rival organizations. One consequence of this may be a high incidence of breakdowns in peaceful bargaining. To be sure, competition in bargaining is to some extent unavoidable; this condition is not necessarily undesirable socially, and will continue to characterize the experience in private and public sector alike, regardless of the size of units involved. Nevertheless, there is hardly a permanent justification for permitting what appears to be a greater proliferation of bargaining units in the public sector than that now prevailing in the private sector. The institutional factors discussed above add a unique dimension to the task of achieving peaceful and successful bargaining in the public sector. Because of this, and because of the likelihood that proliferation will result in an increased number of breakdowns in the bargaining process, larger units must become the accepted norm in the public sector.

* * *

Another interesting development [took] place in New York City. With the creation of the Office of Collective Bargaining, New York City began to consolidate its bargaining units through techniques such as recognition by citywide job classifications. This transition was followed, in the spring of 1968, by the truly basic step of recognizing one exclusive bargaining agent for *all* the employees of the mayoral agencies for purposes of those citywide working conditions which are required to be uniform for such employees. Separate representation in smaller units continues for purposes of other issues, and this condition is no doubt prolonging the same problems that are found elsewhere; but the basic trend appears to be a salutary one.

A third experience of interest involve[d] the employees of the State of New York. Prior to the enactment of the Taylor Law, which defined the first set of rules for bargaining by both state and local government personnel, the majority of the state's 124,000 employees had belonged to the statewide Civil Service Employees Association (CSEA)—an organization which, at least in its earlier years, had shunned the concept of formalized collective bargaining. Following enactment of the Taylor Law, the state, as employer, recognized the CSEA as the bargaining agent for a "general unit" of all the employees. After nearly a year of bargaining by this unit, the Public Employment Relations Board (PERB), the state agency charged with administering the Taylor Law, received petitions challenging the appropriateness of the general unit. In opposition to the CSEA, twelve separate employee organizations requested recognition in twenty-five different bargaining units. The proposed units were drawn along highly diverse occupational, departmental, or installation lines.

Shunning the extremes of either one general unit or twenty-five separate units, the PERB ruled in favor of five separate statewide negotiating units and directed elections to determine the majority agent in each of those units. The units were constituted along lines cutting across departments; instead, the employees were grouped into families of occupations primarily on the basis of function and training. In denying the requested continuance of the general unit, the PERB adopted an earlier finding of its Director of Representation regarding the unit's inconsistency with the "community of interest" standard of the law and, noting that the employees were divided among ninety occupational groupings, encompassing more than 3,700 separate job classifications, held: "The enormity of this diversity of occupations and the great range in the qualifications requisite for employment in these occupations would preclude effective and meaningful representation in collective negotiations if all such employees were included in a single unit." On the other hand, the PERB concluded that accepting the opposite extreme of twenty-five separate units would foster a proliferation of small groups and would cause "unwarranted and unnecessary administrative difficulties" which "might well lead to the disintegration of the State's current labor relations structure." In addition to these policy considerations, the PERB relied upon the provision of the Taylor Law requiring that the bargaining unit be "compatible with the joint responsibilities of the public employer and public employees to serve the public." This standard, the PERB determined, "requires the designation of as small a number of units as possible consistent with the overriding requirement that the employees be permitted to form organizations of their own choosing" in order to achieve meaningful representation.

The PERB did not make specific reference to the statutory standard requiring consideration of a requested unit in terms of the employer-agency's existing authority to deal effectively with possible bargaining subject matter within such a unit. There seems to be little question, however, that the size and nature of the five designated statewide units insure adequate authority, on the side of the state's negotiating representatives, to make meaningful agreements or recommendations with respect to a large portion of the substantial issues normally deserving of consideration in an effective collective bargaining relationship. Moreover, since the employees were geographically dispersed and because the general unit presented serious problems of providing direct representation, the PERB's breakdown of the employees into five large families of jobs probably maximizes the possibilities for self-determination and adequate union responsiveness in representing the various segments within each family.

The New York experience is also noteworthy because the direct confrontation between the two opposite extremes presented by the requested patterns at the inception of newly formalized public sector collective bargaining afforded an opportunity to weigh the basic implications of excessive fragmentation. In contrast to policy makers in cities like New York and Detroit * * *, the New York State PERB was able to adopt a coherent policy at a time when the damage had not yet been done. At the same time, the Board's decision rejected a monolithic bargaining unit which would have been neither proper nor realistic for public employees at this stage of history.

* * *

Note

D. BOK AND J. DUNLOP, LABOR AND THE AMERICAN COMMUNITY.[5]

"The breadth of election districts in the public sector should also be influenced by the wage-determining principles that are likely to be applied in the negotiation to follow. If the government and its employees are genuinely committed to the principle of prevailing wages by occupation, then very narrow units, such as craft occupations, may be entirely appropriate, and few administrative problems can be expected within the groups accepting this wage criterion. The T.V.A. is an example. But if this principle is not fully understood and accepted within a group, or if it does not apply to all employees in the particular government, there are prospects of serious conflict and escalation. One unit of employees will emphasize their wage comparisons with outside industry, while other units may stress the internal wage relationships and the principle of equality of treatment among all government employees performing similar tasks. A wage increase to a small unit of government employees, such as those in a craft or specialized occupation, under the prevailing wage standard is likely to be followed by a wage increase to other units which prefer the principle of equality of compensation within public employment. The result is likely to involve serious and continuing conflict and wage escalation.

* * *

"The dangers just described would be greatly reduced in a large unit represented by a single union. In federal white-collar employment, for example, Congress adopted both the principle of comparability with private enterprise and that of equal pay for substantially equal work. But the unit is so wide—effectively, the whole white-collar civil service—that tactical escalation among units is precluded.

* * *

"(2) It is often presumed that all terms and conditions of employment should be negotiated in the same election district. But this is not true of the private sector, and the design of bargaining relations in public employment would do well to vary negotiators with the nature of the issue, particularly where many units have been established. Thus, where pensions are involved, a strong case can be made to require that the issue be negotiated by representatives of all employee organizations

5. Pp. 325–26 from *Labor and the American Community* by Derek C. Bok and John T. Dunlop. Reprinted by permission.

as a group.* The single negotiating group may permit lower administrative costs. It is essential, also, to secure uniform pension benefits or to secure general acceptance from all employees for any differential pension benefits to apply to specialized classes of employees. The competitive escalation of pension benefits is extremely expensive, as New York City is discovering in negotiations involving firemen, police, and transit and sanitation workers. For similar reasons, there are other conditions of employment, such as sick leave and health benefits, which may also be appropriately handled by a group representative of all employees.

"At the other extreme, it is appropriate that many grievances and disputes over specialized working conditions be negotiated in relatively small units, provided that reasonable care is given to the wider implications of any agreement. While there are, no doubt, dangers of fostering union rivalry, it is even possible to find instances in which one union should negotiate wages and other broad issues for a large group of employees, while a different union, chosen by a subgroup, should handle the subgroup's working-conditions problems within the framework agreed upon in the larger unit.

"(3) The range of subjects negotiated between employee organizations and public managers varies a great deal among governments. A threefold division is to be made between topics determined by legislative bodies, those left exclusively to civil-service regulations and public managers, and those within the scope of negotiation and agreement. In federal employment, negotiation is narrowly limited to certain matters of personnel policy, practices, and working conditions; wages, benefits, and many major conditions of employment are fixed by Congressional legislation or by civil-service regulations. In local governments, the range of subjects for bargaining is typically much broader, although the precise limits are not drawn at the same place in all relations."

2. A STATUTORY SAMPLING

The following reflects the diversity in statutory provisions relating to unit determinations:

HAWAII

§ 89–6

"Appropriate bargaining units. (a) All employees throughout the State within any of the following categories shall constitute an appropriate bargaining unit:

"(1) Nonsupervisory employees in blue collar positions;

* [Footnote as in original.—Ed.] This will remain true even though different retirement ages and benefits may be established for those in uniformed services (police and fire departments) in some cities under the influence of a military type of retirement policy.

"(2) Supervisory employees in blue collar positions;

"(3) Nonsupervisory employees in white collar positions;

"(4) Supervisory employees in white collar positions;

"(5) Teachers and other personnel of the department of education under the same salary schedule;

"(6) Educational officers and other personnel of the department of education under the same salary schedule;

"(7) Faculty of the University of Hawaii and the community college system;

"(8) Personnel of the University of Hawaii and the community college system, other than faculty;

"(9) Registered professional nurses;

"(10) Nonprofessional hospital and institutional workers;

"(11) Fireman;

"(12) Policeman; and

"(13) Professional and scientific employees, other than registered professional nurses.

"Because of the nature of work involved and the essentiality of certain occupations which require specialized training, units (9) through (13) are designated as optional appropriate bargaining units. Employees in any of these optional units may either vote for separate units or for inclusion in their respective units (1) through (4). If a majority of the employees in any optional unit desire to constitute a separate appropriate bargaining unit, supervisory employees may be included in the unit by mutual agreement among supervisory and nonsupervisory employees within the unit; if supervisory employees are excluded the appropriate bargaining unit for such supervisory employees shall be (2) or (4), as the case may be."

NEW YORK

§ 207. **Determination of Representation Status.**—For purposes of resolving disputes concerning representation status, pursuant to section two hundred five or two hundred six of this article, the board or government, as the case may be, shall

1. define the appropriate employer-employee negotiating unit, taking into account the following standards:

(a) the definition of the unit shall correspond to a community of interest among the employees to be included in the unit;

(b) the officials of government at the level of the unit shall have the power to agree, or to make effective recommendations to other administrative authority or the legislative body with respect to, the terms and conditions of employment upon which the employees desire to negotiate; and

(c) the unit shall be compatible with the joint responsibilities of the public employer and public employees to serve the public.

WISCONSIN

§ 111.70(d) Municipal Employment Relations Act

2. a. The commission shall determine the appropriate bargaining unit for the purpose of collective bargaining and shall whenever possible avoid fragmentation by maintaining as few units as practicable in keeping with the size of the total municipal work force. In making such a determination, the commission may decide whether, in a particular case, the employes in the same or several departments, divisions, institutions, crafts, professions or other occupational groupings constitute a unit.

* * *

ILLINOIS

§ 9(b)

(b) The Board shall decide in each case, in order to assure public employees the fullest freedom in exercising the rights guaranteed by this Act, a unit appropriate for the purpose of collective bargaining, based upon but not limited to such factors as: historical pattern of recognition: community of interest including employee skills and functions; degree of functional integration; interchangeability and contact among employees; fragmentation of employee groups; common supervision, wages, hours and other working conditions of the employees involved; and the desires of the employees. For purposes of this subsection, fragmentation shall not be the sole or predominant factor used by the Board in determining an appropriate bargaining unit.

MICHIGAN

§ 423.213 Appropriate collective bargaining unit, firefighting personnel

Sec. 13. The commission shall decide in each case, to insure public employees the full benefit of their right to self-organization, to collective bargaining and otherwise to effectuate the policies of this act, the unit appropriate for the purposes of collective bargaining * * * Provided, That in any fire department, or any department in whole or part engaged in, or having the responsibility of, fire fighting, no person subordinate to a fire commission, fire commissioner, safety director, or other similar administrative agency or administrator, shall be deemed to be a supervisor.

KANSAS

§ 75–4327

(e) Any group of public employees considering the formation of an employee organization for formal recognition, any public employer considering the recognition of an employee organization on its own volition and the board, in investigating questions at the request of the parties as specified in this section, shall take into consideration, along with other relevant factors: (1) The principle of efficient administration of government; (2) the existence of a community of interest among employees; (3) the history and extent of employee organization; (4) geographical location; (5) the effects of overfragmentation and the splintering of a work organization; (6) the provisions of K.S.A. 75–4325 and amendments thereto; and (7) the recommendations of the parties involved.

OHIO

§ 4117.06 Appropriate bargaining unit

(A) The state employment relations board shall decide in each case the unit appropriate for the purposes of collective bargaining. The determination is final and conclusive and not appealable to the court.

(B) The board shall determine the appropriateness of each bargaining unit and shall consider among other relevant factors: the desires of the employees; the community of interest; wages, hours, and other working conditions of the public employees; the effect of over-fragmentation; the efficiency of operations of the public employer; the administrative structure of the public employer; and the history of collective bargaining.

(C) The board may determine a unit to be the appropriate unit in a particular case, even though some other unit might also be appropriate.

(D) In addition, in determining the appropriate unit, the board shall not:

(1) Decide that any unit is appropriate if the unit includes both professional and nonprofessional employees, unless a majority of the professional employees and a majority of the nonprofessional employees first vote for inclusion in the unit;

(2) Include guards or correction officers at penal or mental institutions, special policemen or policewomen appointed in accordance with sections 5119.14 and 5123.13 of the Revised Code, psychiatric attendants employed at mental health forensic facilities, youth leaders employed at juvenile correction facilities, or any public employee employed as a guard to enforce against other employees rules to protect property of the employer or to protect the safety of persons on the employer's premises in a unit with other employees;

(3) Include members of a police or fire department or members of the state highway patrol in a unit with other classifications of public employees of the department;

(4) Designate as appropriate a bargaining unit that contains more than one institution of higher education; nor shall it within any such institution of higher education designate as appropriate a unit where such designation would be inconsistent with the accreditation standards or interpretations of such standards, governing such institution of higher education or any department, school, or college thereof. For the purposes of this division, any branch or regional campus of a public institution of higher education is part of that institution of higher education.

(5) Designate as appropriate a bargaining unit that contains employees within the jurisdiction of more than one elected county office holder, unless the county-elected office holder and the board of county commissioners agree to such other designation;

(6) With respect to members of a police department, designate as appropriate a unit that includes rank and file members of the department with members who are of the rank of sergeant or above.

This section shall not be deemed to prohibit multiunit bargaining.

IOWA

§ 20.4. Exclusions

The following public employees shall be excluded from the provisions of this chapter:

1. Elected officials and persons appointed to fill vacancies in elective offices, and members of any board or commission.

2. Representatives of a public employer, including the administrative officer, director or chief executive officer of a public employer or major division thereof as well as the officer's or director's deputy, first assistant, and any supervisory employees.

Supervisory employee means any individual having authority in the interest of the public employer to hire, transfer, suspend, layoff, recall, promote, discharge, assign, reward or discipline other public employees, or the responsibility to direct them, or to adjust their grievances, or effectively to recommend such action, if, in connection with the foregoing, exercise of such authority is not of a merely routine or clerical nature, but requires the use of independent judgment. All school superintendents, assistant superintendents, principals and assistant principals shall be deemed to be supervisory employees.

3. Confidential employees.

4. Students working as part-time public employees twenty hours per week or less, except graduate or other postgraduate students in

preparation for a profession who are engaged in academically related employment as a teaching, research, or service assistant.

5. Temporary public employees employed for a period of four months or less.

6. Commissioned and enlisted personnel of the Iowa national guard.

7. Judicial officers, and confidential, professional, or supervisory employees of the judicial department.

8. Patients and inmates employed, sentenced or committed to any state or local institution.

9. Persons employed by the state department of justice, except nonsupervisory employees of the consumer advocate division who are employed primarily for the purpose of performing technical analysis of nonlegal issues.

10. Persons employed by the credit union division of the department of commerce.

11. Persons employed by the banking division of the department of commerce.

12. Persons employed by the savings and loan division of the department of commerce.

Notes and Questions

1. Why would a state legislature (such as Hawaii) mandate statutory bargaining units while other state legislatures follow the private sector and delegate the responsibility for unit determinations to an administrative agency with few specific guidelines?

Why is there special concern about proliferation of bargaining units in the public sector (in contrast to the private sector)?

2. With few exceptions, the NLRB has broad leeway to determine what constitutes "an" appropriate bargaining unit.

Ohio § 4117.06(C) states: "The board may determine a unit to be the appropriate unit in a particular case, even though some other unit might also be appropriate." What policies support this legislative choice? What policies support a requirement in the public sector that a unit be the "most appropriate unit"? On the general subject of "an" versus "most" appropriate unit, see Crowley, *The Resolution of Representation Status Disputes Under the Taylor Law,* 37 Fordham L.Rev. 517, 518–20 (1969); and Rhemus, *The Role of The Neutral in Public Employment Disputes,* in The Arbitrator, The NLRB and the Courts (1967), p. 253.

3. Although the NLRB and most state labor relations agencies with public sector jurisdiction have rule making powers, there have been few instances of substantive rules relating to bargaining units. The Supreme Court affirmed the NLRB's rare foray into rule-making relating to general rules defining bargaining units in acute care hospitals in *American Hosp. Ass'n v. NLRB,* ___ U.S. ___, 111 S.Ct. 1539, 113 L.Ed.2d 675 (1991). Why

have there been so few examples of substantive administrative rules relating to bargaining units in both the private and public sectors?

3. DEFINING THE PUBLIC EMPLOYER

One of the thorniest decisions which must be made in jurisdictions where collective bargaining in the public sector is authorized concerns identifying the public employer. While the issue may be initially debated in the legislature in connection with the passage of collective bargaining legislation, the issue is often raised after a union has been recognized or certified as the representative of employees in an appropriate unit and a duty to bargain arises.

The main discussion of issues relating to defining who is the public employer for purposes of collective bargaining is contained in the next chapter on the duty to bargain—Chapter 3.

4. SPECIAL REPRESENTATION ISSUES

a. Supervisors

One of the noteworthy distinctions between public and private sector collective bargaining is the manner in which supervisors are treated for unit purposes. Since 1947, private sector supervisors have been expressly excluded from National Labor Relations Act coverage; they are not eligible for inclusion in bargaining units of employees that an employer is obligated to recognize. In the public sector, larger numbers of supervisory levels and the long-term association of supervisors with pre-collective bargaining employee associations have made pressures to include supervisors in the collective bargaining process difficult to resist. To counter the problem of conflict-of-interest which would exist with the inclusion of supervisors and nonsupervisors in the same bargaining unit, most statutes provide that public sector supervisors and nonsupervisors may not be included in the same bargaining unit. Other statutes, such as California's Educational Employment Relations Act [West's Ann.Cal.Gov't Code § 3545(b)(2)], go further and provide, in addition, that a "negotiating unit of supervisory employees * * * shall not be represented by the same employee organization as employees whom the supervisory employees supervise."

A notable exception to modified coverage of supervisors in public sector collective bargaining statutes is the Civil Service Reform Act covering federal employees. Like the NLRA, it expressly excludes supervisors from the Act's definition of employee.

BOARD OF EDUCATION OF WEST ORANGE v. WILTON

Supreme Court of New Jersey, 1971.
57 N.J. 404, 273 A.2d 44.

The opinion of the Court was delivered by FRANCIS, J.

After the Legislature adopted the New Jersey Employer–Employee Relations Act, L.1968, C. 303, N.J.S.A. 34:13A–1 *et seq.*, certain administrative employees of the West Orange Board of Education organized the Administrators Association of the West Orange Public Schools and requested the Board to recognize it as the collective negotiating unit for all supervisory personnel, except the Superintendent of Schools. * * * On February 10, 1969, the Board recognized the Association as negotiating representative for principals, assistant principals, subject matter directors, and administrative assistants but excluded from the unit "Directors who act in supervisory capacity" over such personnel. Pursuant to this resolution, the Board refused to accept the Association as the appropriate negotiating unit for Elizabeth Wilton who holds the supervisory position of Director of Elementary Education.

* * *

After reviewing the testimony and noting the fact that her salary for the year 1969–1970 was computed on a basis different from that of the teachers and principals, the Hearing Officer found that Miss Wilton was a "top level managerial employee rather than a rank and file supervisory employee," and that of the "top echelon managerial group" she was the only member of the Association. He agreed that the evidence weighed heavily in favor of the Board's view that to have Miss Wilton "in the same negotiating unit as the people she supervises constitutes a conflict of interest that could seriously reduce her effectiveness as an administrator." He concluded and so reported to the Commission, that it would be "inappropriate for her to be included in the same negotiating unit as administrators whom she supervises."

* * *

On July 2, 1969 PERC reversed the holding of the Hearing Officer and ruled as a matter of law that Miss Wilton had such a "community of interest" with the other members of the Association as warrants her inclusion in the collective negotiating unit. In doing so, it said:

"The Act provides that supervisors may not be represented by an organization that admits non-supervisory personnel and that supervisory personnel and non-supervisory employees may not be combined in the same unit in the absence of established practice, prior agreement or unusual circumstances. The Act is clear and unambiguous in not prescribing the right of various ranks of supervisors to be combined in the same unit or belong to the same organization."

Therefore, PERC declared that the Director of Elementary Education may be included in the specific "unit of supervisors and administrators and may be represented by the Association." Thereafter, the Board of Education sought a review in the Appellate Division which affirmed in an unreported *per curiam* opinion and we granted certification. * * *

In reaching its decision, PERC construed Sections 13A–3(d) and 13A–6(d) to mean that in school districts only the superintendent of schools is excluded from an employees' unit and that all persons who qualify as supervisors may properly be assigned to an organization of supervisors, irrespective of their relation to each other, the nature of the authority of one or more over the others, or whether the public employer has placed one employee on a higher plane of authority in the organizational structure of the school system than other supervisors. We cannot agree with such a broad interpretation. If followed unqualifiedly in all situations, it might seriously weaken the effectiveness of the statute as an instrument of meaningful public employer-employee relations. In some situations, obviously it might put the *employer,* in the form of a high echelon supervisor, on both sides of the negotiating table to the detriment of the *employees* in the unit; in other situations it might put an employee on both sides of that table and deprive the employer of the loyalty he has the right to expect from an employee entrusted with administration of management supervisory policy.

In seeking out the proper solution for the present case, two factors, apparently considered to have been significant by PERC, should be evaluated. First, it pointed out that despite a degree of supervision by principals over assistant principals both classes are included in the Association negotiating unit. That fact has no particular bearing here because, as noted above, both grades of supervisors are members of the Association and the Board of Education has raised no issue with respect to their membership. Secondly, PERC referred to Miss Wilton's desire and consent to be a part of the unit. Her consent is an element which may be considered but, as in the private employment sector, it should not be deemed controlling. See *NLRB v. Delaware–New Jersey Ferry Co.,* 128 F.2d 130, 137 (3 Cir.1941). The determinative factor, so far as Miss Wilton is concerned, in ascertaining the appropriateness of a unit is neither what she wants nor what the public employer wants, but rather whether her inclusion in the unit will serve and not subvert the purpose of the Act, i.e., establishment and promotion of fair and harmonious employer-employee relations in the public service.

There is no doubt that the Legislature intended to authorize appropriate independent negotiating units for supervisory employees (except the superintendent of schools or his counterpart) of the Board of Education. But there is no clear and unqualified direction in Section 13A–5.3 and 13A–6(d) to permit all such supervisory employees to join a single negotiating representative, regardless of gradations of duties of particular supervisors.

Ordinary considerations of employer-employee relations make it sensible to say that if performance of assigned duties by a particular supervisor bespeaks such an intimate relationship with the management and policy-making function as to indicate actual or potential substantial conflict of interest between him and other supervisory personnel in a different or lower echelon of authority, such supervisor should not be admitted to the same negotiating unit. Admission would not be fair either to the other supervisory employees or to the employer. Obviously no man can serve two masters.

* * *

Whether the matter under discussion is concerned with the propriety of supervisors joining the same organization as ordinary employees, or the propriety of supervisors in various degrees of managerial proximity in relation to the employer and each other belonging to the same organization, the issue would seem to be substantially the same. Are the duties, authority and actions of the employee in question, vis-a-vis the other employees in the Association, primarily related to the management function? To what extent does the reasonable and good faith performance of the obligations a supervisor owes to his employer have capacity, actual or potential, to create a conflict of interest with other supervisors whose work he is obliged to oversee and evaluate for his employer?

Unfortunately it cannot be said that the language used in Sections 13A–5.3 and 13A–6(d) regarding the appropriate negotiating unit for supervisors in a school system clearly expresses the solution intended by the Legislature. The superintendent of schools or his equivalent is excluded beyond question. Further, except where "established practice, prior agreement or special circumstances, dictate the contrary" no "supervisor having the power to hire, discharge, discipline, or to effectively recommend the same" shall "have the right to be represented in collective negotiations by an employee organization that admits nonsupervisory personnel to membership. * * *"

* * *

"Supervisory employee" means "any individual having authority, in the interest of the employer, (i) to hire, transfer, suspend, lay off, recall, promote, discharge, assign, reward, or discipline other employees, or (ii) responsibility to direct them, or (iii) to adjust their grievances, or (iv) effectively to recommend such action, if in connection with the foregoing the exercise of such authority is not of a merely routine or clerical nature, but requires the use of independent judgment." Section 2(2).

* * *

The fact that potential conflict of interest in a given case may bar supervisors from representation by an organization of nonsupervisory employees does not mean that the former have no organizational rights. Under our statute supervisors are employees and ordinarily have the right to join and be represented by an organization of their own, i.e., an organization of supervisory personnel. But here again, if there are grades or echelons of supervisors having differing relations to each other because of the quantum of managerial or supervisory authority or duty delegated by the employer, the general exclusory language of N.J.S.A. 34:13A–5.3, quoted above, would seem to throw some light on the legislative intention with respect to the organizational rights of such supervisors. Should not the language of that section by reasonable implication be deemed to bar a supervisor from the same unit as other supervisors if he has such a degree of supervision over others as to reveal a potential, substantial conflict of interest between them? In addition to exclusory language, Section 13A–5.3 contains a further qualification for unit membership. It prescribes that "[t]he negotiating unit shall be defined with due regard for the community of interest among the employees concerned. * * *" No express definition of the phrase "community of interest" is contained anywhere in the statute. Nor was it defined in the Final Report of the Public and School Employees' Grievance Procedure Study Commission on which L.1968, c. 303 (N.J.S.A. 34:13A–1 *et seq.*) was based. That Report limited itself to the single statement that in determining the appropriate unit "community of interest" among the employees and the structure of the appointing authority should be considered. Report at 23.

The 1969 Report of the Advisory Commission on Intergovernmental Relations, *supra,* mentions "community of interest" as a major criterion used in determining the appropriate unit for purposes of collective negotiation. But it refers to the test as a "somewhat elusive concept." ACIR Report, *supra,* at p. 74. It says also that since supervisors by definition include those having authority to effectively recommend hiring, transfer, suspension, promotion, discharge or discipline and to assign and direct work as well as to adjust grievances, their inclusion in a unit with nonsupervisory personnel has been opposed on grounds that it makes for conflict rather than community of interest. *Id.*

We have found no court decision in the public employment relations field which undertook to set out an explicit or mathematically precise definition of community of interest. We recognize that traditional connotations of "management" and "employee" in private sector labor relations may not be identical in the public arena because of the more complex personnel systems and wage and promotion controls of state and local governments. Nevertheless, decisions in the private sector, which speak in terms of the nature of the interests involved with regard to the issue of inclusion of supervisory and nonsupervisory employees in the same bargaining unit, throw light on the present problem.

* * *

In the Matter of New York State Division of State Police et al., Case No. 0062, C–0130, C–0133, N.Y.PERB Decisions § 1–399.92 (July 1, 1968), [the New York Board] * * * [i]n deciding whether certain of the employees who wish to join a unit of other employees over the objection of the public employer should be permitted to do so * * * looks for conflict of interest between the groups with respect to the obligations they owe to the employer and to each other. Obviously it considers substantial potentiality for conflict of interest as incompatible with the community of interest required for single unit membership. Significant indications of such conflict are existence of a duty in some of the group to evaluate the performance of others in the unit in the interest of the employer, and exercise by some of an influential part in matters of discipline or grievance procedures with respect to the others.

If sufficient conflict of interest appears, the fact that all of the employees desire to be included in the same negotiating unit is not deemed controlling or determinative. See *In the Matter of Johnson City Central School District Board of Education et al,* Case No. C 0135, N.Y.PERB decisions, § 1–399.55 (Sept. 17, 1968); Opinions of Counsel to N.Y. PERB, § 1–551 (June 28, 1968); and *cf. In the Matter of George McNamee et al.,* Case No. R–042, N.Y.PERB Misc. Opinions, § 3–8006 (Feb. 25, 1970).

* * * Except where established practice, prior agreement or special circumstances dictate the contrary, inclusion of nonsupervisory personnel in the same unit as supervisors who have "the power to hire, discharge discipline, or to effectively recommend the same" is prohibited. Aside from these specifications, the nature of the negotiating unit is to be determined generally "with due regard for the community of interest among the employees concerned. * * * "

* * *

In dealing with Miss Wilton specifically, PERC considered her simply as another supervisor and, as such, entitled by unquestionable statutory prescription to a determination that the Association is an appropriate unit for her. The nature of her authority over the other supervisors or of her obligations to the employer vis-a vis the others in the unit, or the fact that her compensation was fixed on a basis different from the others was not felt to be significant. We cannot agree.

One underlying concept which emerges from a study of statutes, texts and judicial decisions in employer-employee relations, whether in the public or private employment sector, is that representatives of the employer and the employees cannot sit on both sides of the negotiating table. Good faith negotiating requires that there be two parties confronting each other on opposite sides of the table. Obviously both employer and employee organizations need the undivided loyalty of their representatives and their members, if fair and equitable settlement of problems is to be accomplished. Unless the participation is of that calibre, the effectiveness of both protagonists at the discussion table would be sharply limited. * * *

In the present case, PERC made no evaluation, in terms of conflict of interest, of the facts relating to Miss Wilton's position as Director of Elementary Education and the nature of the supervision she was obliged to exercise over other supervisors, such as elementary school principals in the lower echelon of authority. There is no doubt that it was her duty, among other things, to supervise the work of the principals of the nine elementary schools and to evaluate their performance for the purpose of reporting and making recommendations to the Superintendent of Schools with respect to salary increases and tenure for them. In the performance of such tasks she owed undivided loyalty to the Board of Education. If she were joined in an employees unit which included the principals whose work she was duty bound to appraise in the Boards interest, would she be under pressure, real or psychological, to be less faithful to the Board and more responsive to the wishes of her associates in the negotiating unit? She is obliged, of course, to be fair and nondiscriminatory in evaluating the principals, and if the Association felt that she was consciously or unconsciously in error in doing so, presentation of a grievance would undoubtedly result. In that event she would have to defend against a complaint made by an organization of which she was a member.

In this connection it must be noted that the by-laws of the Association provide for a grievance committee. Section 2 thereof says that the committee shall be a representative body "to include but not be limited to: 1 Director; 1 Secondary Principal; 1 Junior High; 2 Elementary; 1 Assistant Principal." Thus, while the record is silent on the point, it appears that Miss Wilton may well be a member of the committee designed to process grievances against her own actions.

* * *

* * * PERC did not perform its fact-finding function. It assumed existence of the necessary community of interest between Miss Wilton and the other supervisors in the unit simply because she was classified as a supervisor. * * * PERC must decide whether, on a fair appraisal, her role puts her on the management side of the negotiating table. If so, a temporary or short term advantage to the Association that might come from allowing her to be in the supervisors' unit would be more than outweighed by the long term disadvantage to effective and healthy labor relations.

Under the circumstances the determination of PERC and the affirmance thereof by the Appellate Division are reversed. * * *

* * *

APPENDIX

Public employer-employee relations statutes often have detailed definitions of supervisory employees. Some of them may be noted:

The Connecticut Act says:

"The board shall have the power to determine whether a supervisory or other position is covered by * * * [this act] in the event of a dispute between the municipal employer and an employee organization. In determining whether a supervisory position should be excluded from coverage under * * * [this act] the board shall consider, among other criteria, whether the principal functions of the position are characterized by not fewer than two of the following:

"(A) Performing such management control duties as scheduling, assigning, overseeing and reviewing the work of subordinate employees:

"(B) performing such duties as are distinct and dissimilar from those performed by the employees supervised;

"(C) exercising judgment in adjusting grievances, applying other established personnel policies and procedures and in enforcing the provisions of a collective bargaining agreement; and

"(D) establishing or participating in the establishment of performance standards for subordinate employees and taking corrective measures to implement those standards. * * *" Conn.Gen. Stat.Ann. § 7–471(2)

The Hawaii Act provides:

" 'Supervisory employee' means any individual having authority in the interest of the employer, to hire, transfer, suspend, layoff, recall, promote, discharge, assign, reward, or discipline other employees, or the responsibility to assign work to and direct them, or to adjust their grievances, or effectively to recommend such action, if, in connection with the foregoing, the exercise of such authority is not of a merely routine or clerical nature, but requires the use of independent judgment."

* * *

Rhode Island has a special statute applying only to teachers. However, superintendents of schools, assistant superintendents, principals and assistant principals are excluded from representation by an association or labor organization. R.I.Gen.Laws § 28–9.3–2 (P.L.1966, c. 146, § 1).

In Vermont the State Employees Labor Relations Act, provides that in determining the appropriate collective bargaining unit the state employee labor relations board shall consider certain factors.

Among them are the "authority of governmental officials at the unit level to take positive action on matters subject to negotiation," and the "appropriateness of the proposed unit to represent all employees within the unit having regard for the similarity or divergence of their interests, needs, and general conditions of employment. * * *" 3 Vt.Stat.Ann. § 941(f)(1), (2).

The Wisconsin State Employment Labor Relations Act excludes from an employee organization employees "who are performing in a supervisory capacity, and individuals having privy to confidential matters affecting employer-employee relationship. * * *" L.1966, c. 612, § 111.81(12). * * *

* * *

Note

Since the New Jersey court compiled the above Appendix, several states listed have made statutory changes. The two most significant are Connecticut and Wisconsin. Connecticut now permits separate units of supervisors except that mixed single units of supervisory and nonsupervisory fire and police department employees are specifically provided for. Wisconsin has added the following to its State Employment Labor Relations Act (§ 111.825(5)):

> Although supervisors are not considered employes for purposes of this subchapter, the commission may consider a petition for a statewide collective bargaining unit of professional supervisors or a statewide unit of nonprofessional supervisors in the classified service, but the representative of supervisors may not be affiliated with any labor organization representing employees. For purposes of this subsection, affiliation does not include membership in a national, state, county or municipal federation of national or international labor organizations. The certified representative of supervisors may not bargain collectively with respect to any matter other than wages and fringe benefits.
> * * *

MILTON DERBER, MANAGEMENT ORGANIZATION FOR COLLECTIVE BARGAINING IN THE PUBLIC SECTOR *

Public–Sector Bargaining 90, 96–99 (2d ed. 1988).

* * *

Supervisors as Part of Management

The problem of defining management for purposes of collective bargaining has one other aspect that merits note. This pertains to the drawing of management boundaries, i.e., which supervisory or managerial staff members are to be treated as "management" and therefore to be excluded from appropriate bargaining units or to be confined to special units separate from the employees they supervise. For the private sector, the federal Labor Management Relations Act defines management boundaries broadly, encompassing first-line supervisors who are excluded from the protective definition of "employee" under the act. In the public sector, however, employee organizations *historically* counted even middle and upper supervisory and managerial officials not only as members but often as leaders. This was particularly true in the specialized services of education, health care, firefighting, and police protection, but it also applied to the general civil service. As a result there was strenuous resistance among some employee organizations, as well as some managers, against proposals to adopt private-sector policies on management boundaries.

One of the strongest attacks on the effort to maintain a distinction between the public and the private sector in this (and other) respects was made by former NLRB chairman, Edward B. Miller. In a speech to the National Public Employer Labor Relations Association, he assailed those public employers who seemed bent on proving they were different. Some public employers, for example, insisted on ignoring all the experience about bargaining units which had been developed in the private sector under the National Labor Relations Act. * * *

> We also saw units which included supervisors and managers. You probably read some of the same scholarly articles that I did wherein lines were "blurred" in the public sector. We were told that in schools and in police departments and in fire departments, existing associations of employees ignored these kinds of lines, and thus we would have to accept that when bargaining took place in this public institutional framework we would have to have units quite different from those in the private sector.[14]

Tim L. Bornstein of the University of Massachusetts similarly concluded, in discussing the fire department problem, that

> in the long run, it is all but inevitable that your deputies and your captains, and perhaps even your lieutenants, will systematically be excluded from collective bargaining. The reason is that collective bargaining, which can be a very helpful, useful, constructive institution in the conduct of public affairs, has to operate according to rules which assure that both sides have a reasonable measure of leverage. And if, in a community, only the fire chief or one or two deputies are excluded from the bargaining unit, then who is left to assure that policy is carried out faithfully and effectively?[15]

Most states with public-employee relations legislation have, indeed, incorporated a Taft–Hartley-type definition of supervisor as part of management into their laws, as has the federal government in its executive orders. In some branches of government, most notably education, top and middle managers, like superintendents and principals, have been obliged to abandon their dual role of management and employee.

Nonetheless, as Stephen Hayford and Anthony Sinicropi have concluded, after a comprehensive national survey, "The bargaining rights status of public sector supervisors is far from being settled. While it is clear that * * * federal employment experience has paralleled that of the private sector, several state legislatures and/or administrative agencies have chosen a more expansive approach. * * *"[16] This approach has taken two principal forms: (1) many individuals with supervisory titles are not held to be supervisors for statutory purposes because they "are not really managers"; (2) "bona fide supervisors" are granted bargaining rights but are usually placed in bargaining units separate from the employees whom they supervise.

14. 702 GERR 39–40 (April 4, 1977).

15. 718 GERR 12 (July 25, 1977).

16. Stephen L. Hayford and Anthony V. Sinicropi, *Bargaining Rights Status of Public Sector Supervisors,* 15 Indus.Rel. 44, 59 (February, 1976).

* * *

A few cases may be illustrative. The Minnesota law provides that supervisory and confidential employees, principals, and assistant principals may form their own organizations and the latter may receive exclusive representation rights for the purpose of negotiating terms and conditions of employment as though they were essential employees, i.e., with the right to invoke binding arbitration (Sec. 179.65(6)). Wisconsin's *municipal* employment relations act generally does not consider a supervisor to be a covered employee, but it distinguishes firefighters from other municipal employees and explicitly defines supervisors as the chief and the officer directly below him in single-station communities and all offices above the rank of the highest ranking officer at each single station in municipalities with more than one station. Firefighting and law-enforcement supervisors may organize separate units for the purpose of negotiating with their municipal employers, although the statute's other provisions do not apply to them. Moreover, the Wisconsin Employment Relations Commission (WERC) may require a supervisory unit of firefighters or police to be organized separately from the local employee unit, but it may not prevent affiliation by a supervisory representative with the same parent state or national organization as the employee representative (Secs. 111.70(1)(b), (1)(*o*)(2), and (3)(d)).

Wisconsin's *state* employment relations act authorizes the WERC to establish two statewide units of professional and nonprofessional supervisory employees, but the certified representatives may not be affiliated with labor organizations representing other categories of nonsupervisory employees. Moreover, the supervisory representatives may not bargain on any matter other than wages and specified fringe benefits (Sec. 111.81(3)(d)). Hawaii's public-employee bargaining law, like Wisconsin's, specifies appropriate bargaining units, but it distinguishes between supervisory employees in blue-collar positions and those in white-collar positions. In New Jersey, the schools receive a bit of special attention in this area with the provision that the term "managerial executive" shall mean the superintendent of schools or his equivalent, and the law further provides that no supervisor shall have the right to be represented in collective negotiations by an employee organization that admits nonsupervisory personnel to membership "except where established practice, prior agreement or special circumstances, dictate the contrary" (Sec. 34:13A–5.3).

Practice often indicates even wider divergence. A 1977 survey in New York City noted that, among others, deputy chiefs in the fire and police departments, supervisors below the level of borough superintendents in the sanitation department, and housing-project managers in the housing authority belong to a union. The conclusion reached was that "many managers identify not with the City but with the union they belong to." [17] In Boston in 1986 some 410 middle-level managers

17. *Reporter at Large,* The New Yorker (August 1, 1977), 38.

were reportedly affiliated with a salaried employees' division of the United Steelworkers of America.[18]

The foregoing provisions and practices, and others like them, reflect the tensions and the ambiguities of public-sector management. On the one hand, many top executives (particularly those in elective positions) have failed to appreciate the importance of adequately motivating, training, and rewarding middle and lower managerial and supervisory personnel so as to bind them to the management side. On the other hand, many supervisory personnel have been impressed by the organizational achievements of the people whom they supervise and are determined to keep pace.

Most of the foregoing discussion on the definition of management is based on experience in the period before 1980. In the ensuing decade the central tendency appears to have been a further sharpening and broadening of boundary lines between management and other employees. Although considerable diversity among states and localities continued, this tendency was promoted by the Reagan administration and reinforced by the courts. The tough managerial stand of the federal government in the Air Traffic Controllers strike (1981), the U.S. Supreme Court's decision in the private-sector *Yeshiva University*[19] case, the defensive posture of public- as well as private-sector unions during the deep recession of the early eighties, the growing concerns over public-sector budgets and expenditures, and the increased knowledge and sophistication in managerial circles—all contributed to the trend.

Note

In Douglas, *"Collective Bargaining and Public Sector Supervisors: A Trend Toward Exclusion?"*, 47 Public Administrative Review 485 (1987), it is reported that in a study of the rights of public sector supervisors (PSS), "four models emerged concerning the statutory treatment and framework for PSS bargaining. PSS were either: (1) excluded from coverage without any reference to particular job title, (2) excluded form coverage based on job title, (3) placed in autonomous supervisory units or, (4) allowed to bargain with rank-and-file employees in mixed units. Of the 88 statutes identified for analysis, 27% provide for PSS exclusion, 30% require separate supervisory unions, and 43% permit inclusion in mixed units. When measured from a longitudinal viewpoint a modest trend toward the exclusion of PSS from the right to bargain collectively is noted."

APPEAL OF MANCHESTER BOARD OF SCHOOL COMMITTEE

Supreme Court of New Hampshire, 1987.
129 N.H. 151, 523 A.2d 114.

BROCK, CHIEF JUSTICE.

The underlying issue in this case is whether a group of school principals, certified as a bargaining unit under RSA 273–A:8, II by the

18. 24 GERR 627–628 (May 5, 1986).

19. 444 U.S. 672, 103 LRRM 2526 (1980).

New Hampshire Public Employee Labor Relations Board (the PELRB), may be represented by the same union representative as the teachers whom they supervise. The PELRB ruled that they could, and after a representative election held on September 26, 1985, the PELRB formally certified the Manchester Education Association (the Association), also the teachers' representative, as the representative of the school principals.

The Manchester Board of School Committee (the School Committee) appeals from the PELRB's certification decision, claiming *inter alia* that it is erroneous as a matter of law because of the inherent conflicts of interest that exist in such an arrangement. Specifically, the School Committee argues that the Association's status as exclusive representative for both supervisory and non-supervisory personnel is contrary to RSA 273–A:8, II and would lead to actual and potential conflicts of interest and/or a division of loyalties between the Association and the principals and teachers.

We have stated on numerous occasions that the PELRB is vested with the authority to initially define and interpret the terms of RSA chapter 273–A. *Appeal of Town of Pelham,* 124 N.H. 131, 134, 469 A.2d 1295, 1297 (1983); *Appeal of City of Concord,* 123 N.H. 256, 257, 459 A.2d 285, 286 (1983). However, it is well-established that "this court is the final arbiter of the intent of the legislature as expressed in the words of a statute considered as a whole." *City of Concord v. PELRB,* 119 N.H. 725, 727, 407 A.2d 363, 364 (1979). A ruling made by the PELRB will not be disturbed unless the appealing party meets its burden of showing that the PELRB's determination was erroneous as a matter of law, or that it was unjust or unreasonable. *Appeal of Internat'l Assoc. of Firefighters,* 123 N.H. 404, 408, 462 A.2d 98, 101 (1983).

RSA 273–A:8, II explicitly prohibits "[p]ersons exercising supervisory authority involving the significant exercise of discretion [from belonging] to the *same bargaining unit* as the employees they supervise." (Emphasis added.) In *City of Concord v. PELRB, supra,* 119 N.H. at 727, 407 A.2d at 364, we further interpreted RSA chapter 273–A as a whole, and § 8, II in particular, as requiring that supervisory personnel be kept separate from the employees they supervise, not only by maintaining separate bargaining units, but also by refraining from commingling in the *same negotiating teams.* In the present appeal, the School Committee urges us to further interpret RSA 273–A:8 as prohibiting supervisors from being represented by the same union that is already representing the rank-and-file employees whom they supervise.

In adopting RSA chapter 273–A, the legislature declared that "it is the policy of the state to foster harmonious and cooperative relations between public employers and their employees and to protect the public by encouraging the orderly and uninterrupted operation of government." Laws 1975, 490:1 (statement of policy). With this purpose in mind and because we agree with the statement of the Nebraska

Supreme Court that "[t]o permit supervisory personnel to retain the same bargaining agent as the employees union would be tantamount to permitting them to enter the same bargaining unit," *Nebraska Ass'n of Pub. Emp. v. Nebraska Game & Parks Commission,* 197 Neb. 178, 180, 247 N.W.2d 449, 450 (1976), we hold that supervisory personnel may not retain the same exclusive representative as the rank-and-file employees they supervise.

In *City of Concord v. PELRB,* 119 N.H. at 726, 407 A.2d at 364, we recognized that the basis of the requirement of RSA 273–A:8, II, that supervisory personnel not be in the same unit with the rank-and-file, was "to avoid conflicts between the two groups because of the differing duties and relationships which characterize each group." Giving logical effect to the "inten[t] to keep supervisory personnel separate from the rank and file," *Id.* at 727, 407 A.2d at 364, we held that supervisory and non-supervisory personnel should "not be allowed to commingle on each other's negotiating teams." *Id.* In the present case, we see the same potential for conflicts of interest arising due to the differing duties and relationships of the groups.

At oral argument, counsel for the Association conceded that there was the theoretical potential for conflicts of interest under such an arrangement, but argued that the absence of conflicts of interest in actual practice should be controlling. We reject this argument. Even if it is true that the Manchester school system has generally functioned well and has experienced good relations between its principals and teachers, it is not necessary for us to sit by and "allow events to unfold to the extent that the disruption of the [school] and the destruction of working relationships is manifest before taking action." *Vicksburg Firef. Etc. v. City of Vicksburg, Miss.,* 761 F.2d 1036, 1040 (5th Cir.1985) (citing *Connick v. Myers,* 461 U.S. 138, 152 (1983)). To the contrary, "[a]n identity of interests on the part of supervisors with the rank and file poses a significant threat that the loyalties of the supervisors will be divided and that consequently the discipline and effectiveness of [the school system] will be impaired." *Vicksburg supra,* thus warranting preventive action. *See Germann v. City of Kansas City,* 577 S.W.2d 54, 56 (Mo.Ct.App.1978).

One such example of an inherent conflict of interest was recognized in *Elk Grove Firefighters Local No. 2340 v. Willis,* 400 F.Supp. 1097 (N.D.Ill.1975), *aff'd unpublished order,* 539 F.2d 714 (7th Cir.1976). In *Elk Grove,* the court noted that an inherent conflict of interest exists where a union takes a position against involuntary overtime and a supervisory official decides that such overtime is necessary for efficient operation of the department. *Elk Grove, supra* at 1102. *Germann, supra* at 56. A conflict of this kind is not out of the realm of possibility in the Manchester school system.

The Association further alleges that if joint representation is prohibited in this case, we will be impinging upon the right of the principals to join the labor union of their choice. In effect, however, our decision precludes principals from choosing a particular representative, the one already chosen by the teachers. The principals are free to choose any other bargaining representative. We conclude that this limitation on their ability to choose a representative is reasonable in view of the purpose and mandates of RSA chapter 273–A.

The PELRB's certification order is vacated and the case remanded for further proceedings consistent with this opinion.

Reversed and remanded.

BATCHELDER, J., concurred specially; the others concurred.

Questions

1. Why have there been difficulties in coming to a consensus about public sector supervisors' statutory bargaining rights?

2. Why do some statutes which generally prohibit the placement of supervisors in the same bargaining unit as nonsupervisory employees nevertheless authorize placement of protective services (police and firefighters) supervisors such as sergeants, lieutenants, and captains in the same bargaining unit as rank-and-file employees?

b. Managerial and Confidential Employees

Unlike supervisors, with their qualified right to participate in the collective bargaining process, as provided in most public sector statutes, managers are excluded from the definition of employee in virtually all public sector enactments. The definition of management employee most commonly found in public sector legislation is derived from decisions interpreting the National Labor Relations Act, which does not contain a definition of management employee nor a statutory exclusion for such employee. See *NLRB v. Bell Aerospace Co.,* 416 U.S. 267, 94 S.Ct. 1757, 40 L.Ed.2d 134 (1974), which approves the definition of management employee fashioned by the National Labor Relations Board: "[persons] who are in a position to formulate, determine, and effectuate management policies."

In the bargaining unit context, confidential employees are only those who are involved in the employer's labor-management relations activities and thus have access to confidential information about the employer's labor relations as part of the employee's regular job duties. They are excluded from the definition of employee by decisional law in the private sector and often by express statutory terms in the public sector.

NEW YORK PUBLIC EMPLOYEES' FAIR EMPLOYMENT ACT § 201(7)

(a) The term "public employee' means any person holding a position by appointment or employment in the service of a public employer, except that such term shall not include for the purposes of any provision of this article other than sections two hundred ten and two hundred eleven of this article, judges and justices of the unified court system, persons holding positions by appointment or employment in the organized militia of the state and persons who may reasonably be designated from time to time as managerial or confidential upon application of the public employer to the appropriate board in accordance with procedures established pursuant to section two hundred five or two hundred twelve of this article, which procedures shall provide that any such designations made during a period of unchallenged representation pursuant to subdivision two of section two hundred eight of this chapter shall only become effective upon the termination of such period of unchallenged representation. Employees may be designated as managerial only if they are persons (i) who formulate policy or (ii) who may reasonably be required on behalf of the public employer to assist directly in the preparation for and conduct of collective negotiations or to have a major role in the administration of agreements or in personnel administration provided that such role is not of a routine or clerical nature and requires the exercise of independent judgment. Employees may be designated as confidential only if they are persons who assist and act in a confidential capacity to managerial employees described in clause (ii).

(b) For the purpose of this article, assistant attorneys general, assistant district attorneys, and law school graduates employed in titles which promote to assistant district attorney upon admission to the bar of the state of New York shall be designated managerial employees, and confidential investigators employed in the department of law shall be designated confidential employees.

* * *

Questions

1. Why would a public manager want to be part of a bargaining unit?

2. Since a confidential employee may be a loyal union member, how effective is the confidential employee exclusion?

c. Mixed Professional and Nonprofessional Employee Bargaining Units

In the private sector, professional employees (defined by 2(12) NLRA) may not be placed in the same bargaining unit with employees who are not professional employees unless a majority of the professional employees vote for such a mixed unit. Some public sector collective bargaining statutes include a similar rule while others require a vote for the mixed unit by both the professional employees and the nonprofessional employees.

What arguments support the private sector rule? Are there any special features of the public sector which support a rule requiring a majority of *each* group to vote affirmatively for inclusion in a mixed unit? Would this rule be equally sound for the private sector?

d. *Special Higher Education Issues*

Many institutions of higher education are public. When the jurisdiction in which they are located has enacted collective bargaining legislation which covers such institutions in whole or in part, special representation issues may arise.

REGENTS OF THE UNIVERSITY OF CALIFORNIA v. PUBLIC EMPLOYMENT RELATIONS BOARD

Supreme Court of California, 1986.
41 Cal.3d 601, 224 Cal.Rptr. 631, 715 P.2d 590.

BIRD, C.J.—The Regents of the University of California (University) petitions for review of a decision by the Public Employment Relations Board (PERB or the Board). The Board found that housestaff [interns, residents, and clinical fellows] who are paid by the University while participating in residency programs at clinics, institutes or hospitals owned or operated by the University, are "employees" within the meaning of Government Code section 3562, subdivision (f) of the Higher Education Employer–Employee Relations Act (HEERA or the Act) (§ 3560 et seq.). Therefore, they are entitled to collective bargaining rights. This court must review the propriety of that ruling.

I.

Prior to July 1, 1979, Physicians National Housestaff Association (PNHA) chapters representing housestaff at the Irvine, San Francisco and Davis campuses participated in meet-and-confer sessions with representatives of different hospital administrations. During this period, PNHA also received payroll dues deductions from its members' paychecks.

In 1978, the California Legislature enacted HEERA, which extended collective bargaining rights to employees of the University of California. Hastings College of the Law and the California State University (§ 3560, subd. (b).) Shortly after HEERA became effective (July 1, 1979), the University notified PNHA that it did not consider housestaff to be "employees" within the meaning of the Act. It then ceased making payroll deductions from housestaff salaries to pay PNHA dues. On July 20, 1979, PNHA responded by filing an unfair labor practice charge against the University, alleging that the University had violated section 3571, subdivisions (a) and (b) and section 3585, by refusing to make such deductions.

A hearing before a PERB hearing officer ensued. The evidence consisted of the following:

The University operates medical schools at five of its campuses: Los Angeles (UCLA), San Diego (UCSD), San Francisco (UCSF), Irvine (UCI) and Davis (UCD). Through its medical schools, the University provides residency training programs in most medical specialty and subspecialty areas and operates hospitals at which housestaff gain clinical experience. Other hospitals, both public and private, are also affiliated with these medical schools. Many housestaff rotate through these hospitals during the course of their training.

In the spring of 1979, approximately 4,500 housestaff were participating in University residency programs. Approximately 2,000 of them were on the University payroll. The others were paid by the affiliated institutions at which they served.

In order to participate in a University residency program, an individual must have graduated from medical school with a doctor of medicine (M.D.) degree. To qualify to practice medicine in California and in most other states, such an individual must complete at least one year in an approved residency program. In California, he or she must also obtain a "physician's and surgeon's certificate" from the Board of Medical Quality Assurance. Until receipt of such a certificate, housestaff may practice medicine only under an approved residency program. (Bus. & Prof.Code, § 2065.)

Most residency programs take between two and six years to complete, depending upon the specialty. The programs are structured so that housestaff rotate through different hospital services relevant to their specialty. Upon successful completion of a residency, an individual receives a certificate entitling him or her to take a specialty board examination leading to board certification in a particular specialty. Board certification is not a requirement for specialty practice, but attests to the physician's competence in that field.

Board certification requires participation in a training program approved by the Liaison Committee on Graduate Medical Education (LCGME). LCGME sets standards for residency programs, reviews programs for compliance and grants accreditation to programs which meet those standards. In order for University residency programs to acquire LCGME approval, they must comply with the general requirements contained in an LCGME document entitled "Essentials of Accredited Residencies."

On April 9, 1980, the PERB hearing officer concluded that housestaff are not employees under HEERA and recommended that PNHA's unfair labor practice charge be dismissed.

PNHA filed exceptions to the proposed decision. On February 14, 1983, PERB rendered a written decision adopting the hearing officer's findings of facts and making additional factual findings. The Board found that the educational objectives were subordinate to the services housestaff perform and coverage of housestaff under HEERA would further the purposes of the Act. Based on these findings, the Board concluded that housestaff are "employees." It further held that the University had violated HEERA by refusing to make payroll deductions. The Board issued a cease and desist order and directed the

University to reimburse PNHA for the dues lost during the period for which the University made no payroll deductions.

This matter is before the court on the University's petition for a writ of review.

II.

The first question to be resolved is whether HEERA precludes housestaff from being considered employees under the Act.

* * *

The statute provides in relevant part that "[t]he board may find student employees whose employment is contingent on their status as students are employees only if the services they provide are unrelated to their educational objectives, or, that those educational objectives are subordinate to the services they perform and that coverage under this chapter would further the purposes of this chapter." (§ 3562, subd. (f).)

Although the statute is silent on the subject of housestaff, it clearly leaves open the possibility that such persons may come within it. As the words of the statute make clear, the Legislature intended that PERB determine whether a particular student qualifies as an employee under the Act.

The legislative history which accompanied the passage of HEERA supports this conclusion. HEERA was enacted by Assembly Bill No. 1091 during the 1977–1978 session. When that bill was first introduced, subdivision (f) contained no reference to students. That provision simply defined "employees" as "any employee" except managerial and confidential employees. (Assem.Bill No. 1091 (1977–1978 Reg.Sess.) Mar. 24, 1977.) This section was subsequently amended to exclude "managerial, and confidential employees, and employees who are students on the same campus where they are employed and who work less than 10 hours per week." (Assem.Amend. to Assem.Bill No. 1091 (1977–1978 Reg.Sess.) May 23, 1977.)

However, the bill was not passed in this form. On the Senate side, an amendment was passed which eliminated the distinction between student employees based on the number of hours worked. That amendment, which was enacted into law, prescribed a case-by-case assessment of the degree to which a student's employment is related to his or her educational objectives. The determination of student employee status was expressly left to PERB. (Sen.Amend. to Assem.Bill No. 1091 (1977–1978 Reg.Sess.) Aug. 7, 1978.) Although this amendment arguably made the status of housestaff more uncertain, it is clear that they were not eliminated from coverage under the Act.

When this statutory history is considered in conjunction with a Legislative Counsel's opinion prepared while the bill was pending, the conclusion is inescapable that the Legislature did not intend to exclude housestaff from coverage under the Act.

The Legislature responded to this opinion by amending subdivision (f) to *include* a "more definitive statement" as to the status of student employees. That action strongly suggests that the Legislature intended to promulgate a new standard for determining this issue rather than to follow NLRB precedent and deny housestaff employee status.[7] That action also indicates that the Legislature did not intend to foreclose the issue of housestaff organizational rights. Instead, its creation of a statutory standard distinct from NLRB precedent was intended to permit PERB to make an independent determination of the status of housestaff.

* * *

Under HEERA, the Board may find students who are employed in a capacity *unrelated* to their course of study to be "employees" within the meaning of the Act and therefore entitled to collective bargaining rights. Further, PERB may find students who are employed in a capacity *related* to their educational program entitled to such rights depending on a case-by-case evaluation of (1) whether their educational objectives are subordinate to the services they perform, and (2) whether coverage under HEERA would further the purposes of the Act.

Thus, in defining "employees" under HEERA, the Legislature specifically rejected the NLRB rulings. Under the NLRB precedent, the relevant inquiry is whether the student's objectives are primarily academic. Under HEERA, even if PERB finds that housestaff are motivated by "educational objectives," it may nevertheless classify them as "employees" if their objectives are "subordinate to the services they perform" and if granting collective bargaining rights would further the purpose of the Act. It is, therefore, clear that instead of denying collective bargaining rights to student employees of public educational institutions, the Legislature intended to permit PERB to grant such rights in situations not permitted under NLRB precedent. If, as the dissent suggests, the Legislature had intended to retain NLRB precedent, it could have easily done so by adopting the language of the NLRA verbatim.

* * *

This interpretation, moreover, is not what the Legislature intended. Subdivision (f) makes clear that PERB should determine in each case whether "[the student's] educational objectives are subordinate to the services they perform."

The dissent argues that this language cannot be applied as written because it would require PERB to " 'balance' apples and oranges." (Dis.opn., *post,* at p. 639.) That is to say, a student's "subjective"

7. Amicus AFL–CIO also argue that certain letters written by and to Assemblyman Berman, the sponsor of Assembly Bill No. 1091, support this conclusion. This court may not consider those letters in determining legislative intent, as they simply reflect the motives and understandings of individual legislators. (See *San Mateo City School Dist. v. Public Employment Relations Bd.* (1983) 33 Cal.3d 850, 863 [191 Cal.Rptr. 800, 663 P.2d 523].)

educational objectives cannot be "balanced" against the "objective" "services they perform." From this premise, the dissent takes a gargantuan leap and concludes that PERB may look only to the students' subjective balancing as to which aspect of the students' job *they* believe is more important. (Dis.opn., *post,* at p. 640.) The dissent then takes another leap and states that the *University's* subjective balancing of these factors is also a determinative factor. (*Ibid.*) The dissent cites absolutely no authority for this latter proposition.

While applying the Legislature's command may be difficult, that is no excuse for disregarding it altogether. The Legislature has clearly *not* instructed PERB to confine its inquiry to the students' state of mind. Moreover, nothing in the language of subdivision (f) even *hints* that the *University's* subjective perceptions of the functions of housestaff duties should be taken into consideration.

The Legislature has instructed PERB to look not only at the students' goals, but also at the services they actually perform, to see if the students' educational objectives, however personally important, are nonetheless subordinate to the services they are required to perform. Thus, even if PERB finds that the students' motivation for accepting employment was primarily educational, the inquiry does not end here. PERB must look further—to the services actually performed—to determine whether the students' educational objectives take a back seat to their service obligations.

This interpretation is the only one which remains true to the statutory language. Moreover, it makes sense in light of the events surrounding the passage of HEERA. As noted above, the housestaff issue was clearly on the mind of the Legislature when it enacted this provision. The NLRB had just rendered two controversial decisions on the issue. In those decisions a majority of the Board concentrated primarily on the students' motivation for entering into housestaff programs. The NLRB dissenter thought the focus should be confined to the services they actually perform, disregarding as irrelevant their motive for taking such jobs. (See *ante,* at pp. 609–611.)

Subdivision (f), as enacted, represents a compromise between the majority and dissenting opinions expressed in the NLRB decisions. HEERA took a middle road, requiring both factors to be considered. It is not the prerogative of this court to act as a super-legislature and alter that legislative choice merely because it may be unwise. (*People v. Dillon* (1983) 34 Cal.3d 441, 463 [194 Cal.Rptr. 390, 668 P.2d 697].)

Another provision of HEERA corroborates the conclusion that housestaff were not excluded, per se, from the benefits of collective bargaining. Section 3562, subdivision (*o*)(1) defines a "professional employee" as a person engaged in work (i) predominantly intellectual and varied in character, (ii) involving the consistent exercise of discretion, (iii) impossible to standardize with respect to output, and (iv) requiring knowledge of an advanced type acquired through a course of specialized intellectual instruction and study in an institution of higher learning or a hospital. A professional employee is also defined as an individual who has completed the courses of specialized intellectual instruction and study described in clause (iv) above and is performing related work under the supervision of a professional person to qualify to become a professional employee. (§ 3562, subd. (*o*)(2).) Housestaff fit precisely within this definition. The fact that housestaff so clearly fall within the definition of professional employee reinforces the view that the Legislature did not intend housestaff to be excluded under the Act.

It is noteworthy that at the time HEERA was enacted the vast majority of decisions from other jurisdictions had concluded that housestaff are employees within the meaning of their respective collective bargaining statutes. * * * Although these collective bargaining statutes did not contain a provision like subdivision (f), many of the factors which led to the conclusion that housestaff are employees are similar to those which are appropriately considered under a subdivision (f) analysis.

In view of the foregoing, it is clear that the Legislature did not intend to preclude housestaff from coverage under the Act. Rather, it left that determination to PERB. Under subdivision (f), the Board determines whether students are employees under the Act by assessing whether the educational objectives are subordinate to the services students perform and whether according them collective bargaining rights would further the purposes of the Act. Since PERB made such a finding here, the only remaining issue is whether there is substantial evidence to support it.

III.

[This section reviews whether the PERB decision was supported by substantial evidence.]

* * *

PERB's review of the evidence revealed that the patient care services performed by housestaff were an important part of the hospital's overall service delivery. The Board also found that although housestaff did receive educational benefits in the course of their programs, this aspect was subordinate to the services they performed. The Board made this determination based on (1) the substantial quantity of time housestaff spend on clinical activities and direct patient care, (2) the nature of the procedures housestaff perform with little or no supervision, (3) the professional guidance they provide for interns, medical students and other hospital employees such as nurses and technicians, (4) the extensive indicia of employment that characterize housestaff as employees rather than students, and (5) the extent of the educational benefit and training received by housestaff. A review of the record demonstrates that the Board's finding was supported by substantial evidence.

* * *

Since there is substantial evidence to support the Board's finding that educational objectives are subordinate to the services performed by housestaff and granting collective bargaining rights to them will further the purposes of the Act, the Board's conclusion that housestaff are employees must be affirmed.

IV.

The HEERA does not preclude housestaff from being considered employees. The Legislature specifically intended that PERB determine whether students are employees under the Act by assessing whether the educational objectives are subordinate to the services students perform and whether according them collective bargaining rights would further the purposes of the Act. Here, the Board's determination to that effect is supported by substantial evidence. Therefore, the Board properly concluded that housestaff are employees under HEERA.

The Board's decision is affirmed. The matter is remanded to the Board for reconsideration of its remedy in light of the defunct status of PNHA.

MOSK, J., BROUSSARD, J., and REYNOSO, J., concurred. [Dissent omitted.]

Notes and Questions

1. Why did the parties take such pains to develop a full factual record in this case?

2. What implications does this decision have for the growing number of public institutions where graduate student teaching assistants have been organizing?

In *Association of Graduate Student Employees v. Regents of the University of California,* 13 PERC 20087 (1989), PERB held that neither graduate student instructors nor graduate student researchers were employees for purposes of coverage under HEERA because the students educational objectives outweighed services actually performed for the university. PERB also concluded that the purposes of HEERA would not be advanced by collective bargaining between the university and its graduate student instructors and researchers.

The PERB decision noted that the factual backdrop of *The Regents of the University of California v. Public Employment Relations Board,* 41 Cal.3d 601, 224 Cal.Rptr. 631, 715 P.2d 590 (1986), was so unique that it severely limited *Regents'* application to the case at hand. In *Regents,* the housestaff were no longer students but were graduate M.D.s who received no grades, took no examinations, and did not obtain a degree at the end of the residency. By way of contrast, graduate student employees must be registered students, are limited to a maximum of half-time employment, pay the required tuition and student fees, receive credit for their teaching and research positions, and receive a graduate degree upon completion of their research dissertation. Finally, the appointment and reappointment to a particular graduate student instructor or researcher position is based upon several factors, including whether the graduate student is making appropriate progress towards a graduate degree and is in good academic standing.

In applying the first prong of West's Ann.Cal.Gov't.Code Section 3562, subd. (f), providing that student employees may not be considered university employees unless their educational objectives are subordinate to the services they perform, PERB "recalibrated" the test by examining how the two interests (academic and employment) interrelate and determining which side ultimately prevails when the two interests conflict. In applying this newly calibrated scale, PERB concluded that the students' educational objectives were not subordinate to the services they performed as graduate student instructors and researchers.

PERB went on to examine whether finding graduate student instructors and researchers employees under HEERA would further the purposes of the Act. PERB concluded that HEERA's policy of encouraging the pursuit of excellence in teaching, research and learning would not be furthered by covering the graduate students.

The Association of Graduate Student Employees appealed the PERB decision and in *Association of Graduate Student Employees v. Public Employment Relations Board,* 6 Cal.App. 4th 1133, 8 Cal.Rptr.2d 275 (1992), the First District Court of Appeal affirmed. The court initially held that PERB had misapplied the first prong of West's Ann.Cal.Gov't.Code Section 3562, subd. (f). The court held that this Section required PERB to examine not only the students' subjective educational goals, but also to look at the actual services performed, in order to determine whether their educational objectives were subordinate to their employment obligations. The court went on to hold, however, that PERB properly concluded that granting collective bargaining rights to graduate student instructors and researchers would not further the purposes of HEERA. The record showed that collective bargaining would interfere with the mentor-student relationship, damaging the stature of the university and its ability to attract the best students and faculty.

3. In the private sector, the United States Supreme Court reviewed an NLRB determination that a university committed an unfair labor practice by refusing to bargain with a unit of full-time faculty. It determined that faculty members at Yeshiva University who participated in a governance system were part of management and thus not entitled to bargaining rights. *NLRB v. Yeshiva University,* 444 U.S. 672, 100 S.Ct. 856, 63 L.Ed.2d 115 (1980). "It is clear that Yeshiva and like universities must rely on their faculties to participate in the making and implementation of their policies. The large measure of independence enjoyed by faculty members can only increase the danger that divided loyalty will lead to those harms that the Board traditionally has sought to prevent." At 689–90.

The Court's decision has been criticized. For example, Getman and Pogrebin argue that *Yeshiva* provides a "tempting technique for those employers who seek to avoid unionization in enterprises that differ significantly from the traditional manufacturing and retailing enterprises in which the Act has been applied." *Labor Relations, The Basic Processes, Law and Practice,* The Foundation Press (1988) at p. 21. They point to *FHP, Inc. and Union of American Physicians,* 274 N.L.R.B. 168 (1985), where the NLRB found a group of physicians to be managers because the governance system of the hospital in which they worked included committees of physicians that played a role in determining some aspects of health care policy.

The logic of *Yeshiva* also suggests that the management of publicly-funded colleges and universities may prevent the establishment of a collective bargaining system by establishing or emphasizing a procedure pursuant to which management receives, weighs, and takes into account faculty opinions with respect to academic status and standards. If management follows faculty advice with respect to enough issues with sufficient frequency, the principle of the *Yeshiva* decision may come into play.

In some jurisdictions, faculty at public institutions of higher education are entitled to bargaining rights (e.g., New York and California), while in other jurisdictions (e.g., Wisconsin), faculty and academic staff of the university are not. Do you have an explanation for such diversity?

4. Where employees of public institutions of higher education are covered by collective bargaining statutes, a number of uniting questions arise. Where there are multiple campuses, should employees at a single campus constitute an appropriate bargaining unit or should the unit include all campuses?

Section 207 of the Taylor Act (Civil Service Law § 200 et seq.) prescribes two criteria for unit determination in addition to "community of interest": "the officials of government at the level of the unit shall have the power to agree, or to make effective recommendations to other administrative authority or the legislative body with respect to, the terms and conditions of employment upon which the employees desire to negotiate"; and the unit "shall be compatible with the joint responsibilities of the public employer and public employees to serve the public." The significance of the latter two criteria is illustrated in *State University of New York,* 2 PERB § 2–4010 (1969). The campuses involved in that case were four university centers, two medical centers, twelve colleges of arts and science, seven specialized contract colleges, six two-year agricultural and technical colleges, and thirty-one locally sponsored two-year community colleges. The community colleges were excluded from consideration by stipulation, as were four of the contract colleges. The Public Employment Relations Board also excluded the College of Ceramics at Alfred University, leaving a group of 26 campuses.

The basic issue for the PERB was whether the boundaries of the unit should be campuswide or inclusive of all 26 campuses. First, with respect to the locus of managerial decisionmaking authority over the subject matter of bargaining, the evidence showed that the power to set general personnel and education policies, fringe benefits, salary scales, and to determine other economic and noneconomic terms and conditions of employment resides in the Chancellor or the Board of Trustees subject to legislative approval where necessary.

"Any power the campus presidents have is effectively circumscribed by the existence of the master plan and the comprehensive budget for the entire university, both of which are under the control and implementation of the Board of Trustees. Centralized control of the planning and budget processes also means that almost all allegedly 'local' issues will have serious state-wide ramifications, either of an economic or policy nature. For these reasons, it is only during the course of state-wide negotiations with the Board of Trustees, if at all, the 'local' issues could be properly defined and the scope of authority of campus presidents to negotiate on them could be insured. Any attempt to frame local issues independently would be putting the cart before the horse. Until such state-wide negotiations are conducted with a certified employee organization, it is clearly impossible for any sort of meaningful negotiations to take place at the campus level. Thus, the conclusion is inescapable that the establishment of negotiating units on a campus level would run counter to the statutory requirement that a negotiating unit be established at a level where officials of the employer have the power to make determinations or effective recommendations concerning terms and conditions of employment."

Second, the New York statute commands a unit determination which is compatible with the responsibilities of the particular public enterprise to the community which it serves. On this point the record established that SUNY is operated pursuant to a "Master Plan" which constitutes the blueprint for every significant University development or program and from which emanates all current and long-range programs affecting every aspect of the University's mission, including its educational structure, personnel policies, enrollment capacities and capital development. Each campus is deliberately designed to perform one or more of the various educational missions committed to the University. "[I]t would be sheer chaos if we were to have a system whereby each campus set up its own personnel policies with all of its conditions of employment set up according to the views of that particular campus.... [I]t would drain away this effort we have made toward unifying the University * * * it would create an unhealthy kind of competition among the campuses. * * * " Testimony of Chancellor Samuel Gould, Record of the Proceedings, pp. 3588–89 and 3591.

The centralized locus of decision-making authority and the responsibility of SUNY to plan and execute a state-wide strategy for the delivery of higher education services dependent upon such factors as the number of high school graduates aspiring to go to college, the projected interests of the students, the skill needs of the state, budgetary needs and abilities, and the number, location and mission of private institutions, impelled the determination that a multi-campus unit was appropriate.

5. In a multi-campus state university, is the employer the chief executive official of a campus, the head of the state wide system, the board of regents or board of higher education, the governor, the state legislature, or the state administrative agency designated to represent the public employer in state employee bargaining?

6. What arguments support the recognition of a separate medical school (or law school) bargaining unit at a large state university campus? What arguments oppose such recognition?

7. May a faculty senate be an "employee organization" (union) for purposes of representing the faculty in collective bargaining?

5. WHAT IS THE "PUBLIC SECTOR" ANYWAY?

The National Labor Relations Act excludes from the definition of "employer" the "United States or any wholly owned Government corporation * * * or any State or political subdivision thereof." § 2(2), 29 U.S.C.A. § 152(2). Questions have arisen concerning such entities as a local utility district organized pursuant to state statute.

Even though an entity does *not* meet the NLRA test for exemption under Section 2(2), the NLRB has in the past declined to assert jurisdiction if the public employer has retained sufficient control over the entity's labor relations to preclude meaningful collective bargaining.

The fact that the NLRB declines to assert jurisdiction over an entity because of its governmental aspects or functions does not, of course, mean that the entity qualifies as a "public employer" under a state statute. In *Nassau Library System,* 196 N.L.R.B. 864 (1972), the NLRB decided it would not "effectuate the purposes" of the NLRA to assert jurisdiction over a library system which was chartered pursuant to state law, received state and county financial assistance, and performed a public service in close coordination with governmental functions. New York's PERB ruled, however, that the library system was not an "instrumentality or unit of government" for purposes of the state's Taylor Law, 1 PERB Par. 399.47 (1968). The New York Court of Appeals affirmed PERB's position in *Matter of New York Public Library v. New York State Public Employment Relations Bd.,* 45 A.D.2d 271, 357 N.Y.S.2d 522 (1974), holding that the Taylor Law applies "only to employment which is unequivocally or substantially public." Judge Fuchsberg, in a dissenting opinion, argued that the real question was whether the state's PERB or its State Labor Relations Board (having jurisdiction over nongovernmental employers excluded from coverage under the NLRA) should have jurisdiction. Considering the close relationship between the Public Library and the City of New York, he would have held them to be joint employers, subject to Taylor Law application.

6. JUDICIAL REVIEW

In the private sector, there are very few circumstances which permit direct judicial review of a unit determination once the NLRB has made a decision or has certified a union which has won an election. Why have many public sector jurisdictions permitted direct judicial review of a state agency's unit determination decision involving public employees? If direct judicial review is permitted, what should be the standard of judicial review for the administrative agency's decisions—rational basis, *de novo,* or some "middle" standard? Why would the Ohio legislature enact the following?

§ 4117.06 Appropriate bargaining unit

(A) The state employment relations board shall decide in each case the unit appropriate for the purposes of collective bargaining.

The determination is final and conclusive and not appealable to the court.

In *South Community v. State Employment Relations Board,* 38 Ohio St.3d 224, 527 N.E.2d 864 (1988), the Ohio Supreme Court held that this section was not applicable to the initial issue of whether certain employees were public employees covered by the Act and, therefore, eligible to vote in a representation election. The court found that the general appeal section applied. Does this judicial result surprise you?

Chapter 3

DUTY TO BARGAIN IN GOOD FAITH *

A. GOOD FAITH BARGAINING

The National Labor Relations Act (NLRA) imposes upon the parties the obligation to bargain collectively which, since 1947, has been defined as "the performance of the mutual obligation of the employer and the representative of the employees to meet at reasonable times and confer in good faith * * * and the execution of a written contract incorporating any agreement reached if requested by either party, but such obligation does not compel either party to agree to a proposal or require the making of a concession." [§ 8(d).] A key issue raised by this language is what constitutes "good faith" bargaining. In the public sector, similar issues have been raised about the bargaining process.

One early issue in the public sector (which has still not been put to rest in all jurisdictions) is whether a requirement to "meet and confer" should be interpreted literally so that the public employer retains the right to make unilateral decisions after mandated "discussions." This "pure" form of "meet and confer" has been rare, however, and the obligation imposed by statute now is commonly understood to be a bilateral process by parties who approach one another at the bargaining table with the intent to reach an agreement and with a free exchange of relevant information, opinions, and proposals.

NATIONAL EDUCATION ASSOCIATION OF SHAWNEE MISSION v. BOARD OF EDUCATION

Supreme Court of Kansas, 1973.
212 Kan. 741, 512 P.2d 426.

FOTH, COMMISSIONER: In this case we are called upon for the first

* The two chapters following this one deal with the *subjects* of bargaining; This chapter focuses on the bargaining process.

time to examine the substantive provisions of the Kansas professional negotiations act ("the act"), which expressly recognizes the right of professional employees of school boards to negotiate collectively with respect to terms and conditions of professional service. Our only previous encounter with the act was limited to its recognition-nonrecognition procedures, in *Liberal NEA v. Board of Education,* 211 Kan. 219, 505 P.2d 651, 82 LRRM 2815.

The plaintiff, National Education Association of Shawnee Mission, Inc. ("NEA"), is a voluntary association of certificated teachers employed by the defendant Board of Education of Shawnee Mission Unified School District No. 512, Johnson County, Kansas ("the Board"). At the time of trial NEA had a membership of about 1500, out of approximately 2250 teachers employed by the Board.

The controversy before us is an immediate aftermath of the 1970 legislative enactment of the act. * * * It became effective July 1, 1970, and within two weeks NEA applied for recognition as the exclusive representative of all professional employees of the district (except administrative employees) for the purpose of professional negotiations. Such recognition was duly granted on August 10, 1970.

There followed the first tentative groping for position: In September NEA requested negotiation of the 1970–71 school calendar; the Board noted some urgency in settling the matter, but solicited suggestions. In November negotiating teams from each side held three meetings, reached a consensus, and submitted the agreed calendar to their respective principals for ratification. Both agreed, and the first negotiating effort under the new act was successfully concluded.

This, however, was but a preliminary skirmish: the main battle was yet to come. On December 1, the last date for doing so * * * the parties exchanged notices of the items about which they desired to negotiate for the following school year. The Board's notice contained two items: an acknowledgment that management rights were vested in the Board, and a no-strike no-lockout agreement. NEA's notice contained a proposed master contract of 123 pages, containing 22 sections and 122 subsections covering everything from sick leave to curriculum.

It seems fair to say that these two proposals epitomized the parties' positions throughout the ensuing proceedings; the Board took the position that virtually nothing was negotiable, while NEA claimed that everything was.

With the lines thus drawn the parties proceeded the next day to the first order of business, which was drawing up ground rules for their future meetings. This proved to be the first insurmountable hurdle; they were unable to agree on ground rules at meetings held on December 2, 10 and 18, 1970, and on January 5, 14, 21 and 26, 1971. It is apparent that this was the first test of strength. After seven meetings over two months the antagonists were still unable to agree on how many meetings there would be, how long they would negotiate, or a procedure for resolving impasses. At this point the negotiators decided by mutual consent to go on to consider substantive proposals, without ground rules.

On February 2, 1971, substantive negotiations began. At this meeting the Board's basic position was solidified: all matters, whether "negotiable" under the act or not, which represented Board "policies" must always remain subject to unilateral change by the Board. Hence the Board would not consider entering into a master contract concerning terms and conditions of professional service, nor would any of its policies with respect thereto be incorporated by reference in an individual teacher's contract. The Board would lend a respectful ear to the teachers' suggestions as to what its policies should be, but it reserved not only the final say on adopting policy but also on changing it at will.

NEA, on the other hand, retreated from its demand for a comprehensive master contract, but insisted that agreed upon policies affecting terms and conditions of professional service be at least incorporated in individual contracts so as to bind the Board during the contractual period. This fundamental difference continued throughout all subsequent negotiations and throughout this litigation.

On February 9 the teams met again, and at this meeting the Board announced its intention to cease negotiations on March 8, 1971. This, it was claimed, was necessary in order to submit contracts to teachers on or before March 15, the last date to terminate a teacher's employment under the continuing contract law. * * * To support its position the Board had an opinion of counsel to that effect.

The next meeting was a week later, on February 16; thereafter the pace picked up somewhat. Meetings were held on February 18, 23 and 25. At the last mentioned meeting the Board's team enumerated an extensive list of items of the NEA proposal which the Board considered "non-negotiable," most because they were regarded as "prerogatives of management," or because they were existing policy, or both. The Board reaffirmed its determination to break off negotiations on March 8, adopt a salary schedule on March 9, and issue teacher contracts before March 15.

On March 1, 1971, this mandamus action was filed by NEA, asking that the Board be compelled to continue negotiations and for a temporary restraining order and a temporary injunction against the impending termination of negotiations. The temporary restraining order was granted *ex parte,* and the trial court held a hearing on March 8 on the temporary injunction. On March 11 the court entered findings of fact and conclusions of law resulting in a temporary order in mandamus requiring the Board to continue negotiations and restraining it from issuing teacher contracts before April 15.

Two meetings were held in early March, before the March 8th hearing, and as a result of the court's order some fourteen more were held between March 11 and April 15. On the latter date the last meeting of the year was held. Although some NEA suggestions were unilaterally adopted as Board policies, no binding agreement was ever reached on anything, and in particular no salary schedule was agreed upon. On April 22, the Board adopted the salary schedule it had last proposed, and it issued teachers' contracts around May 6.

Beginning June 25, 1971, this case was tried to the court. On December 10, 1971, it filed extensive and detailed findings of fact and conclusions of law resulting in (1) a permanent order of mandamus compelling the Board to negotiate with NEA, but only in the rather limited manner which the court found was all the law required, and which will be discussed later, and (2) denying attorney fees to the plaintiff NEA. The court specifically found that both parties had negotiated in a good faith effort to comply with the law as they understood it.

NEA has appealed from that part of the judgment which limited the Board's duty to negotiate and which denied attorney fees: the Board cross-appealed from the part of the judgment which compelled negotiations after March 15. Initially the Board also challenged the constitutionality of the act, but that point has now been abandoned. Both parties seek guidance as to their rights and duties under the act.

1. The Duty to Negotiate

The first and most fundamental issue separating the parties is their different view of the underlying objective of negotiations. Each approaches the problem by seeking to pin a label on the act: NEA would have it be a "collective bargaining" act, under which the parties are required to reach a binding agreement; while the Board says it is but a "meet and confer" act, under which its duty is merely to listen to the teachers and then make up its own mind.

The terms are defined in the Report on Labor–Management Policies for State and Local Government by the Advisory Commission on Intergovernmental Relations, 1969. (Superintendent of Documents, U.S. Government Printing Office, Washington, D.C. 20402. Hereinafter cited as "the Commission Report."):

"*Collective Bargaining or Negotiations.* A method of determining conditions of employment through bilateral negotiations between representatives of the employer and employee organizations. These parties are required by law to reach a settlement which is set forth in writing and which is mutually binding. The National Labor Relations Act defines the process as 'the performance of the mutual obligation of the employer and the representative of the employees to meet at reasonable times and confer in good faith with respect to wages, hours, and other terms and considerations of employment, or the negotiation of an agreement, or any question arising thereunder, and the execution of a written contract incorporating any agreement reached if requested by either party, but such obligation does not compel either party to agree to a proposal or require the making of a concession. * * *'

"*Meet and Confer.* A method of determining conditions of public employment through discussions between representatives of the employer and employee organizations. These parties are required by law to endeavor to reach an agreement on matters within the scope of representation. If agreement is reached, it is reduced to a memorandum of understanding and presented to a jurisdiction's governing body or its statutory representative for final determination.

"*Memorandum of Understanding, Meet and Confer.* A written, nonbinding record of recommendations mutually agreed upon by an employer and employee organization concerning the conditions of employment (wages, hours vacations, holidays, overtime, etc.), and the procedures to be followed in settling disputes or handling issues that arise during the terms of the memorandum. Such memoranda are prepared for submission to the executive or legislative body and shall become effective when such executive or legislature takes the necessary implementary action."

The court below apparently agreed generally with the Board, for it concluded: "The collective negotiation statutes, in essence, require mandatory meet and confer negotiations between teacher representatives and the school board in anticipation that such negotiations will provide agreement. They do not require and make mandatory collective bargaining that is customary in collective bargaining as is found with labor unions and industry."

We would caution that we are not concerned at this point with what are proper *subjects* for negotiation under the act—that issue will be treated later. What we are talking about now is the *objective* of negotiations, on matters which are undeniably "negotiable."

At the outset a broad outline of the entire act may be helpful. We quote where exact language is important to the present case, and emphasize that which seems controlling:

Section 72–5413: Definitions: The key definition in this case is (g):

" 'Professional negotiation' means meeting, conferring, consulting and discussing *in a good faith effort by both parties to reach agreement* with respect to the terms and conditions of professional service."

Section 72–5414: Authorizes employees to form and join organizations and "to participate in professional negotiation with boards of education through representatives of their own choosing for the purpose of establishing, maintaining, protecting or improving terms and conditions of professional service."

Section 72–5415: Authorizes recognition of exclusive representatives.

* * *

Section 72–5421: "A board of education and a representative selected or designated pursuant to the provisions of sections 3 (72–5414) to 8 (72–5420) of this act may enter into an agreement covering terms and conditions of professional service. *Such agreements become binding when ratified* by a majority of the members of the board of education and a majority of the members of the applicable negotiating unit ..."

* * *

Section 72–5423: "(a) Nothing in sections 1 (72–5413) to 12 (72–5421), inclusive, of this act shall be construed to change or affect any right or duty conferred or imposed by law upon any board of education, *except that boards of education are required to comply with this act in recognizing professional employees' organizations,* and when such an organization is recognized, the board of education and the professional employees' organization *shall enter into professional negotiations* prior to issuance of the annual teachers' contracts or renewal of the same on request of either party. * * *

* * *

"(c) Any agreement lawfully made under the provisions of this act may be adopted by reference and made a part of the employment contract between any professional employee of the applicable negotiating unit and a board of education for a period of not to exceed two years."

Section 72–5424: Authorizes agreements to contain enforceable binding arbitration clauses.

* * *

In support of its position the Board points to the absence from the act of any procedure for resolving impasses, and to the use of the permissive "may" in 72–5421, providing that the parties "may" enter into an agreement covering terms and conditions of professional service. It notes also [2] constitutional provision * * * and statutes * * * which in general terms vest the management and control of the affairs of a school district in its board of education. All such power, says the Board, is reserved to it by the express terms of 72–5423(a) quoted above.

We think the Board's analysis glosses over some important terms. The reservation-of-powers in 72–5423(a) is subject to the important exception that the Board is "*required* to comply with this act in recognizing professional employees' organizations" as exclusive representatives for professional negotiations. Further, when such an organization is recognized, the Board "*shall* enter into professional negotiations." This is a limitation on the Board's autonomy of no small dimensions, particularly when one re-examines the definition of "professional negotiations."

That term, under 72–5413(g), means not only meeting and conferring but doing so in "in a good faith effort by both parties *to reach agreement.*" We think this is where the Board's determination not to be bound runs afoul of the act. If a board were merely required to "meet and confer" there would be no need for the legislative mandates of good faith and a mutual effort to reach agreement. "Agreement," in particular, is hardly necessary if the Board is to be free to ignore what is agreed upon.

By the same token, the act's elaborate procedures dealing with recognition * * * would seem an exercise in futility if the duly selected and exclusive negotiating agent could do no more than make suggestions, which the Board is then free to ignore. Although many unadulterated "meet and confer" acts do contain such provisions, we can only say that such acts are, for that reason, subject to the same observation. They offer more to the eye than to the touch.

The feature of the act which we think militates most strongly against the rigidity of the Board's position is the statutory provision that agreements when ratified by *both parties* are "binding." This is in contrast to the unilateral "implementary action" to make a "memorandum of agreement" effective, as contemplated by the "meet and confer" definitions of the Commission Report, *supra.* * * * In addition, the act states that such agreements may provide for binding arbitration of disputes. That any such agreement is in severe derogation of the traditional powers of a board of education is obvious, yet the legislature saw fit to authorize them.

If we understand the Board correctly it concedes its duty to meet and confer, and the requirement of a good faith effort to reach agreement. We think the act, read as a whole, requires it to go one step farther: if it does reach agreement we think the Board is required to reduce the agreement to writing and be bound by it. This may be done either by a master contract with the professional employees organization (72–5421) or by agreed policies incorporated by reference in the individual teachers' contracts (72–5423[c]).

Of course, and we emphasize this, agreement by the negotiating teams is not enough. Board ratification is required on the one hand, which presumably will be recommended in good faith by the Board's team and considered in good faith by the Board. On the other, ratification is required by a majority of the entire negotiating unit, not just of the negotiating organization. Again, a good faith recommendation of ratification by the organization's negotiating team is to be expected. Only when so ratified does an agreement become binding.

In reaching this conclusion we recognize the differences, noted by the court below, between collective negotiations by public employees and "collective bargaining" as it is established in the private sector, in particular by the National Labor Relations Act. Because of such differences federal decisions cannot be regarded as controlling precedent, although some may have value in areas where the language and philosophy of the acts are analogous. * * * We do not, however, believe those differences prevent our reaching the conclusion that a public employer may negotiate and be bound by its agreements relating to terms and conditions of employment.

The prime subject of most negotiating encounters will suffice to illustrate the point. While public employers have limited resources with which to pay wages and salaries demanded across the bargaining table, they do have some flexibility in ordering priorities in their budget. A school board can, for example, pay larger salaries at the expense of supplies or library books. Thus proposals and counter-proposals for a salary schedule played a prominent role in the "negotiations" in this case. No agreement was reached, but in due course contracts calling for fixed salaries were offered to the district's teachers.

We note at this point that if the Board's argument were pushed to its limits, it would necessarily follow that such contracts are not binding upon it—they do, after all, purport to limit the Board's prerogative to change its mind on the most vital and fundamental matter entrusted to its custody and control, i.e., the expenditure of the taxpayer's money. The Board, of course, does not so contend and at least to that extent concedes that it *can* make agreements on terms and conditions of professional service which will be binding upon it.

[The remainder of the opinion dealing with subjects and timing of negotiations and the effect of unilateral acts, is omitted.]

Questions

1. During negotiations for a collective bargaining agreement covering classified employees of a school district, the union submitted a proposal which would have required that the school district give 90 days' notice to all classified employees who were to be laid off at the end of the school year. The proposed language specified that layoffs could occur only at the end of a school year; and, if the employees were not given 90 days' notice, they would be considered rehired for the following school year. The school district's negotiators rejected the proposal and asserted that they would make no counter proposal. Furthermore, the district's negotiators did not make the reason for the rejection of the union's proposal clear, although they did make a tangential reference to the fact that the Education Code required only 30 days' notice of layoff for permanent, classified employees instead of 90 days. At no time did the district contend that the union's proposal was beyond the scope of mandatory bargaining.

Did the school district, by refusing to offer any counter proposal to the union's layoff proposal and failing to clarify its reasoning, fail to negotiate in good faith? See *Oakland School Employees Assn. v. Oakland Unified School District,* 5 PERC 12149 (1981).

2. Some statutes governing public sector collective bargaining use the term "negotiations." Is there any substantive difference between "negotiations" and "bargaining?" Why would a legislature impose a duty to negotiate while hesitating to impose a duty to bargain?

3. The union representing State Troopers agreed to a settlement with the State, the employing entity. The agreement, which was subject to ratification by the union membership, contained a provision which guaranteed that if any other union of state employees received a superior agreement, the State Troopers would receive the same treatment. The tentative agreement was submitted to the membership in a mail vote. The ballots that were received by the mail deadline were still unopened when the state reached an agreement with another union. The Executive Board of the

State Troopers Union took the position that this agreement was superior to its agreement, destroyed the ballots before opening them, and advised the state negotiators formally that their agreement had been vitiated and was open for renegotiations. Has the union representing the State Troopers failed to bargain in good faith? If so, what is the remedy?

4. Is it a breach of the duty to bargain in good faith for a school district to publish in the local newspaper a listing of all bargaining unit teachers, their current salaries, and their salaries based upon the union's bargaining proposal? What purpose does the school district have in publishing such information?

B. SPECIAL PUBLIC EMPLOYER ISSUES CONCERNING BARGAINING OBLIGATIONS

The general and difficult issue of identifying who is the public employer for purposes of labor negotiations was briefly noted in the prior chapter (see page 44). Some bargaining outcomes require implementation by legislative bodies; other bargaining outcomes may be implemented by public executives without legislative action. There are numerous constraints on public management decision making, constitutional, statutory, and political, which have no private sector counterparts. The issue of identifying who is the public "employer" arises both for negotiating collective bargaining agreements and for their subsequent administration.

ASSOCIATION OF NEW JERSEY STATE COLLEGE FACULTIES v. BOARD OF HIGHER EDUCATION

Superior Court of New Jersey, Law Division, 1970.
112 N.J.Super. 237, 270 A.2d 744.

FELLER, J.S.C.: This is an action in lieu of prerogative writs. Plaintiff requests summary judgment commanding defendant Board of Higher Education to meet at reasonable times and negotiate in good faith with plaintiff Association (hereinafter referred to as plaintiff), and to enjoin the Deputy Director of the Office of Employee Relations from interfering with the negotiations between plaintiff and defendant Board of Higher Education.

Defendants have made a cross motion for summary judgment. They contend that the Governor and his duly constituted representatives may exercise authority over the conduct of collective negotiations in the State government.

The New Jersey Employer–Employee Relations Act, N.J.S.A. 34:13A–1 *et seq.,* L.1968, c. 303 was adopted in 1968 as an amendment and supplement to the New Jersey Mediation Act. This statute created the Public Employment Relations Commission consisting of seven members to be appointed by the Governor by and with the consent of the

Senate. Of such members two shall be representatives of public employers, two shall be representatives of public employee organizations and three shall be representatives of the public, including the appointee who is designated as chairman. It followed a long study by a legislative commission of the need for establishing a procedure for considering the grievances of public employees. L.1966, c. 70. The commission recommended "legislation setting forth a procedure that is fully compatible with and complementary to existing Civil Service systems and present laws and regulations governing personnel matters in public employment at all government levels in New Jersey." In particular, it said that such legislation, among other things, "should establish the obligation of public employers * * * to meet with employees through representatives of their own choosing for the mutual resolution within the law of grievances and proposals."

* * *

On July 15, 1969, the Public Employment Relations Commission created by L.1968, c. 303, *supra,* issued a certification of Public Employee Representative to the effect that plaintiff is the duly certified collective negotiations representative of the faculties of the six State colleges. Plaintiff and defendant Board of Higher Education commenced collective negotiations on July 19, 1969, and met periodically until February 18, 1970, when an impasse in negotiations was declared by plaintiff and a mediator was appointed by the Public Employment Relations Commission according to the provisions of N.J.S.A. 34:13A–6(b); L.1968, c. 303 *supra.* Mediation sessions were held between February 20, 1970 and May 6, 1970 whereupon the mediator was unable to resolve the impasse in collective negotiations, thereby resulting in the appointment of a fact-finder by the Commission on May 15, 1970, also according to the terms of N.J.S.A. 34:13A–6(b), *supra.* Fact-finding hearings were held on May 26 and 27, at which hearings defendant Frank Mason, the Deputy Director of the Office of Employee Relations, presented the position of the State and participated in the negotiations.

On April 2, 1970, Governor Cahill issued Executive Orders Nos. 3 and 4 creating the Governor's Employee Relations Policy Council and the Office of Employee Relations. The purpose of the Council as set forth in the Executive Order was to make recommendations to the Governor concerning employee relations and relative matters involving State employees. The purpose of the Office of Employee Relations as set forth in Executive Order No. 4 was to assist the Council and to act as the Governor's agent in collective negotiations. The Director of Employee Relations was also empowered to make recommendations and reports to the Council on State employee relations.

1. [The argument presented by plaintiff is that the Board of Higher Education is the "public employer" as provided in N.J.S.A. 34:13A–3(c). The pertinent part of this statute provides as follows]:

> * * * This term shall include 'public employers,' and shall mean the State of New Jersey, or the several counties and municipalities thereof or any other political subdivision of the State or a school district, or any special district or any authority, commission or board, or any branch or agency of the public service."

Plaintiff contends that defendant Board of Higher Education or its representatives is the "public employer" in these negotiations and that the Governor, through his representative, the Deputy Director of the Office of Employee Relations, Frank Mason, has interfered and continues to interfere in the conduct of negotiations and in the means for the resolution of the impasse.

In support of its argument plaintiff cites Art. V. sec. VI, par. 1 of the 1947 Constitution of New Jersey, which provides *inter alia* as follows:

> "all Executive and Administrative Offices, Departments, and Instrumentalities of the State Government, * * * shall be allocated by law among and within not more than twenty principal departments, in such manner as to group the same according to major purpose so far as practicable. * * * "

Pursuant thereto the Legislature enacted L.1966, c. 302 (18.A:3–1 *et seq.*) which provides:

> "An Act concerning higher education, establishing a Department of Higher Education as a principal department in the Executive Branch of State Government and providing an appropriation therefor."

By virtue of said N.J.S.A. 18A:3–1, the Department of Higher Education consists of a Board of Higher Education, a Chancellor, and such divisions, bureaus, branches, committees, officers and employees as are specifically referred to in the Higher Education Act.

General supervision of higher education in the State is reposed in the Board of Higher Education by N.J.S.A. 18A:3–13 wherein it provides:

> "It shall be the duty of the Board of Higher Education to advance long range planning for the system of higher education as a whole in the State; establish general policy for the governance of the separate institutions; coordinate the activities of the individual institutions which, taken together, make up the system of higher education in New Jersey; and maintain general financial oversight of the State system of higher education. The Board shall not administer the individual institutions of higher education, its own administration being specifically reserved unto each of such institutions.
>
> Within the limitations imposed by general legislation applicable to all agencies of the State and the provisions of this chapter, the Board is hereby granted exclusive jurisdiction over higher education in this State and its constituent parts and the requisite

> power to do all things necessary and proper to accomplish the aims and carry out the duties provided by law."

Additional powers and duties are granted to the Board of Higher Education in N.J.S.A. 18A:3–14(h) which commands the Board to:

> "Set policy on salary and fringe benefits, and establish personnel policies for the public institutions of higher education; . . ."

In N.J.S.A. 18:3–16, the Board of Higher Education is granted all powers in addition to those specifically provided by law, requisite to the performance of its duties.

As stated, defendants contend that the Board of Higher Education is not a public employer within the meaning of the 1947 *Constitution* and the New Jersey Employer–Employee Relations Act (N.J.S.A. 34:13A–3(c)), but that the Governor of the State is the public employer.

The Legislature in L.1968, c. 303 did not define the "representative of the public employer" in the State government obligated to negotiate the terms and conditions of employment. N.J.S.A. 34:13A–3(c), N.J.S.A. 34:13A–5.3. In the absence of any express or clearly implied legislative authorization to the Board of Higher Education in this respect, resort must be had to applicable principles of constitutional law with due deference to the power of the Governor to superintend the internal administration of the Executive Branch of the State government. Art. V, sec. 1, par. 1 of the 1947 *Constitution* provides in pertinent part:

> "The executive power shall be vested in a Governor."

Art. V, sec. VI, par. 2 provides in pertinent part:

> "Each principal department shall be under the supervision of the Governor."

The question is: Who is the employer in relation to plaintiff? Is it the Board of Higher Education within the meaning of the act, or is the Governor of the State of New Jersey as the Chief Executive of the State, the employer within the meaning of the act? In reading the definition of "employer" as set forth in N.J.S.A. 34:13A–3, *supra,* it is clear that the term shall include "public employer" and shall mean the State of New Jersey.

The Board of Higher Education is a principal department within the Executive Branch of the government. This court takes judicial notice that the custom and practice in industry and other business organizations is that a department, or department head within an organization, is not an employer. The organization itself is the employer. It is true that under the provisions of N.J.S.A. 34:13A–3(c) a school district is designated as a public employer. It is also true that under this statute the Board of Higher Education is *not* designated as a public employer. * * *

* * *

The initial policy determination to restrict the scope of authority of the various executive departments and to centralize administration and control in the office of the Governor for purposes of collective negotiations among State employees is supported by the reason and spirit of L.1968, c. 303. A written collective negotiations agreement is a commitment on the part of a public employer to implement and effectuate the terms and conditions of employment in conformity with its terms. N.J.S.A. 34:13A:5.3. The "public employer" is charged with the responsibility of effectively negotiating a meaningful agreement. In this regard, the ultimate responsibility is imposed on the Governor for the executive administration of the State government.

N.J.S.A. 18A:64–6(g) provides in pertinent part: that the Board of Trustees of a State college may:

> "* * * appoint a Treasurer and such deans and other professional members of the academic, administrative and teaching stalls as shall be required and fix their compensation and terms of employment in accordance with salary ranges and policies adopted by the Board of Higher Education and *concurred in by the Governor* which salary policies shall prescribe qualifications for the various classifications * * *". (Emphasis added).

N.J.S.A. 52:27B–14 provides:

> "On or before October first in each year each department of the State Government, board, commission, officer or other State agency, hereinafter in this article called 'spending agency,' shall file with the commissioner a request for appropriation or permission to spend, as the case may be, which shall specify all expenditures proposed to be made by such spending agency during the next ensuing fiscal year." L.1944, c. 112, art. 3, p. 290, sec. 5.

N.J.S.A. 52:27B–19 provides:

> "On or before December thirty-first of each year, or at such other time or times as the Governor may request, the commissioner shall certify and transmit to the Governor and Governor-elect the requests of the spending agencies, together with his findings, comments and recommendations thereon."

N.J.S.A. 52:27B–20 provides in pertinent part:

> "The Governor shall examine and consider *all requests for appropriations,* together with the findings and recommendations of the commissioner and shall formulate his budget recommendations which shall be transmitted to the Legislature as a budget message on or before the third Tuesday following the first meeting of the Legislature in each year, except a year in which a Governor shall be inaugurated, when he shall do so on or before February fifteenth following the commencement of his term." (Emphasis added.)

L.1970 c. 96 provides in part that no salary range or rate of pay shall be increased or salary adjustment paid in any higher education institution without *the prior approval* of the President of the Civil Service Commission, the State Treasurer, the Director of the Division of Budget and Accounting and the Legislative Budget and Finance Director.

Therefore it is consistent with the statutory procedure set out above and with constitutional responsibility for a balanced budget that the Governor and his representatives shall formulate the complete economic program for the State government, including the Board of Higher Education. The Office of the Governor is, therefore, the appropriate agency of the State to supervise the conduct of negotiations with units of State employees and to intercede and supersede the departments in collective negotiations on the substantial terms and conditions of employment. * * *

* * *

It is therefore the opinion of this court that the motion for summary judgment commanding defendant Board of Higher Education to negotiate with plaintiff should be denied. It is also the opinion of this court that summary judgment should be entered in favor of defendants. * * *

Notes

1. In some bargaining systems the "employer" is the executive branch of government. Thus, for example, the employer in New York State negotiations is the governor. The parties to negotiations are the governor or his designee and the union representing the employees in the bargaining unit. The legislature is not involved in the process, nor are the operational heads of state agencies and departments, except in an advisory sense. For instance, the union representing the professional staff of the State University of New York negotiates with the Governor's Office of Employer Relations. The collective agreement which evolves runs between the governor and the union: the principal signatories are the president of the union and the director of the Governor's Office of Employer Relations. The legislature gets involved, but only after the fact. Provisions of collective agreements that require legislative action in order to permit their implementation (e.g., appropriation of funds) do not become effective until the legislature has taken action. See § 204–a.

Other statutes, such as California's section 3560, which applies to employees of publicly funded higher education, specify that the "employer" is the governing board of each institution. These boards, together with the unions representing each bargaining unit, constitute the parties to the process. They, and only they, have the duty to bargain in good faith; the agreement which comes out of the process is between them. However, in recognition of gubernatorial and legislative interests in bargaining outcomes, Section 3572 provides for three political intervenors in negotiations involving employees of the California State University and Colleges system (but not the University of California) where the matters under consideration would require an appropriation or other legislative action. The governor, the speaker of the assembly, and the senate rules committee are each entitled to have a representative present. Moreover, all higher education negotiators (CSUC and UC alike) are directed to maintain a close liaison with the department of finance and the legislature over money matters. Sections 3572 and 3572.3 also provide that terms in an agreement requiring budgetary or curative action by the legislature or other funding agency shall not be effective until such action has been taken. If the legislature or the governor fail to fully fund the provisions, the entire package goes back to the parties for further negotiations. However, they may agree that provisions that do not require funding shall take effect independently.

In *AFSCME v. IELRB,* 197 Ill.App.3d 521, 143 Ill.Dec. 541, 554 N.E.2d 476 (1990), the court held that the State University's Civil Service Board was not a joint employer with the constituent universities themselves. The Merit Board did not meet the definition of an education employer under Section 2 of the Illinois Educational Labor Relations Act. The Merit Board has some influence on the terms of employment, but in the main it is limited to the approval of terms negotiated by the universities and the recruiting of employees in accordance with statutory criteria and prescribed rules.

2. A 1977 study by the Labor–Management Services Administration of the U.S. Department of Labor (*Public Management's Internal Organizational Response to the Demands of Collective Bargaining in the Twelve Midwestern States,* pp. 71–73) reached the following conclusions, among others:

(1) Conflict with respect to the distribution of authority and responsibility on the management side frequently arises between central administration and departmental or agency heads. This arises when the latter resist the efforts of the chief executive, as collective bargaining expands, to shift responsibility and authority into the hands of a specialized bargaining component of his staff, with the ultimate decision resting with him. Chief executive officers favor centralized responsibility and control because they facilitate the administrative process, enable their officers to control budgeting, and reduce the likelihood of successful whipsawing tactics by the unions.

(2) Management's organizational response to bargaining may influence the structure of the bargaining units; in turn, that response is influenced by unit configurations. Thus, if bargaining units are based on occupations that cut across departmental or agency lines, management is compelled to centralize responsibility either for direct bargaining or for the coordination of bargaining. On the other hand, if units are based on departmental or agency dimensions, operational administrators may successfully claim bargaining responsibility and authority, with the central labor relations office playing the role of reviewer to prevent whipsawing and to maintain uniformity.

(3) The wider the bargaining unit, the greater the need for centralization. Multiple tier bargaining where the law mandates coalition bargaining on pay and fringe benefits but allows agency or departmental bargaining on other issues creates a mixed bag of centralization and decentralization.

(4) Where bargaining encompasses general money items, centralized management responsibility is virtually a necessity. On the other

hand, where bargaining is limited to work rules and conditions, management may decentralize responsibility. However, the concept of rule uniformity is so deeply imbedded in civil service systems that it sometimes carries over into a collective bargaining system and results in centralized negotiations with respect to those matters.

(5) Where bargaining is extensive and involves pay and fringe benefits, the chief executive officer maintains a tight rein over bargaining, including the setting of negotiating limits. The chief executive officer of government is uninvolved only where collective bargaining is limited and monetary issues are excluded.

(6) Where agreements do not involve pay or fringe benefits, legislative approval is normally not necessary. However, where they do involve money matters, they are treated through the regular appropriation process. The Wisconsin procedure which provides for consultations between the state labor negotiator and a joint legislative committee prior to both the negotiations and approval or rejection of negotiated agreements, has won strong support in Wisconsin and merits careful consideration in other states.

(7) Governments with decentralized bargaining and limited bargaining scope rarely involve their budget agencies in the bargaining process. However, where collective bargaining includes pay and fringe benefits, budget makers are usually involved in three aspects of the process: (a) the establishment of expenditure limits; (b) the timing of bargaining in relation to the budget-making process; and (c) evaluation of the potential impact of collective bargaining on the performance of state services.

3. In New York State, all public sector agreements must contain the following language: "It is agreed * * * that any provision of this agreement requiring legislative action to permit its implementation by amendment of law or by providing the additional funds therefor, shall not become effective until the appropriate legislative body has given approval." Why?

4. FLA. 447.309 provides:

(1) In conducting negotiations with the bargaining agent, the chief executive officer or his representative shall consult with, and attempt to represent the views of, the legislative body of the public employer. Any collective bargaining agreement reached by the negotiators shall be reduced to writing, and such agreement shall be signed by the chief executive officer and the bargaining agent. Any agreement signed by the chief executive officer and the bargaining agent shall not be binding on the public employer until such agreement has been ratified by the public employer and by public employees who are members of the bargaining unit, subject to the provisions of subsections (2) and (3). However, with respect to statewide bargaining units, any agreement signed by the Governor and the bargaining agent for such a unit shall not be binding until approved by the public employees who are members of the bargaining unit, subject to the provisions of subsections (2) and (3).

(2) Upon execution of the collective bargaining agreement, the chief executive shall, in his annual budget request or by other appropriate means, request the legislative body to appropriate such amounts as shall be sufficient to fund the provisions of the collective bargaining agreement. If less than the requested amount is appropriated, the collective bargaining agreement shall be administered by the chief executive officer on the basis of the amounts appropriated by the legislative body. The failure of the legislative body to appropriate funds sufficient to fund the collective bargaining agreement shall not constitute, or be evidence of, any unfair labor practice.

(3) If any provision of a collective bargaining agreement is in conflict with any law, ordinance, rule, or regulation over which the chief executive officer has no amendatory power, the chief executive officer shall submit to the appropriate governmental body having amendatory power a proposed amendment to such law, ordinance, rule, or regulation. Unless and until such amendment is enacted or adopted and becomes effective, the conflicting provision of the collective bargaining agreement shall not become effective.

(4) If the agreement is not ratified by the public employer or is not approved by a majority vote of employees voting in the unit, in accordance with procedures adopted by the commission, the agreement shall be returned to the chief executive officer and the employee organization for further negotiations.

Is the Florida legislation a reasonable procedure to address the complexities of public employer ratification?

5. Are there practical, functional differences between the governments of a state, a city and a school district that affect the identity of the "employer"?

LOS ANGELES BUILDING & CONSTRUCTION TRADES COUNCIL v. COUNTY OF LOS ANGELES

Los Angeles County Employee Relations Commission, 1971.
No. UFC 2.1.

Before LENNARD, Chairman; NATHANSON and ALLEYNE, Members:

BACKGROUND

The question for decision in this case whether the County of Los Angeles has violated Section 12(a)(3) of the Los Angeles County Employee Relations Ordinance. That section provides that it shall be an unfair employee relations practice for the County of Los Angeles to "refuse to negotiate with representatives of certified employee organizations on negotiable matters." The certified employee organization in this case, the Los Angeles Building and Construction Trades Council, filed an unfair employee relations charge with this Commission on January 22, 1971, alleging a violation of Section 12(a)(3) of the Ordinance. Following investigation of the charge by the Commission's

Executive Secretary, the Commission, on February 10, 1971, issued a Charge and Notice of Hearing alleging that the County of Los Angeles violated Section 12(a)(3) of the Ordinance in that County management reneged on an agreement to recommend that the County Board of Supervisors implement a signed Memorandum of Understanding which County management and Local 45 of the International Brotherhood of Electrical Workers had negotiated. The County Board of Supervisors was not named in the Charge.

On due notice to all of the parties, the Commission on February 19 and 26, 1971, held a hearing on the allegation set out in the Charge. Both Local 45 and the County were represented by counsel at the hearing. On the basis of the evidence presented at the hearing, we issued a brief written Order on March 26, 1971, deciding this case in favor of the charging party. This decision and opinion supplements the findings in our Order dated March 26, 1971, that the management of Los Angeles County has committed an unfair employee relations practice.

Facts and Decision

I

The material facts in this case are essentially undisputed. Acting pursuant to the County Employee Relations Ordinance (herein referred to as Ordinance) this Commission held hearings in April and May 1969 to determine the appropriate employee representation unit for a class of communications employees involved in the present dispute. Following those hearings and an election supervised by this Commission, Los Angeles Building and Construction Trades Council (BCTC) was certified as the majority representative for the employees involved in this dispute as well as other employees. Thereafter, International Brotherhood of Electrical Workers Local Union 45 (herein referred to as Local 45) was duly designated by BCTC to negotiate with the County on behalf of the communications classes.

Negotiations between Local 45 and County management commenced. They were unsuccessful. This Commission appointed a mediator; and his efforts were unsuccessful. Then, at the joint request of the parties, this Commission appointed a fact-finder mutually selected by the negotiating parties. The fact-finder conducted a hearing during which he heard and considered evidence and argument from both sides. On December 8, 1970 the fact-finder filed Findings of Fact and Recommendations which favored granting substantial benefits to the employees. These recommendations were not accepted by County management. It requested Local 45 to negotiate a settlement in substitution for the provisions recommended by the fact-finder. The union reluctantly accepted the County's request to negotiate a substitute settlement, and further negotiations resulted in an agreement dated December 30, 1970.

Local 45's leadership then recommended to the employees involved that they accept the compromise settlement. This recommendation was based in part upon the County Personnel Department's written promise of December 30, 1970 that it would "move swiftly to present a joint recommendation to the Board of Supervisors for effectivity [sic] the legally required thirty (30) days following Board approval." Affected employees accepted their union leader's recommendations and voted to ratify the agreement. The Director of Personnel, Mr. Gordon T. Nesvig, then recommended to the Board of Supervisors that the agreement be approved and implemented and that agreed salary increases be enacted. His letter to the Board was dated January 6, 1971. The Director of Personnel's letter noted that this agreement was not a midyear increase. He described it as "the terminal point of a negotiating process that started prior to July 1, 1970." He noted further in his letter of January 6, 1971 that money to fund these increases was included in the 1970–71 budget and that the total cost of the increases amounted to $30,249.

On January 21, 1971 the recently appointed Chief Administrative Officer, Mr Arthur G. Will, recommended to the Board that Mr. Nesvig's letter of January 6, 1971 be tabled. The Director of Personnel, Mr. Nesvig, concurred in that recommendation and the Board accepted the joint recommendation to table the letter and the negotiated agreement.

The object of the tabling motion, as described at the hearing by the County Administrative Officer, was to delay indefinitely the implementation of the agreement by the Board of Supervisors. It was the County Administrative Officer's intention to recommend implementation of the agreement at an indefinite time in the future when the County's financial condition improved. When asked at the hearing whether the tabling action meant that the implementation of the agreement would be given retroactive effect when implemented in the future, the County Administrative Officer replied that he could not answer that question. On the same subject, the County Director of Personnel was emphatic. He said that the agreement, if and when implemented, would not be given retroactive effect. It was this joint recommendation to table, offered by the County Administrative Officer and the County Director of Personnel, which led to the unfair employee relations charge in this case.

II

It is the County's position that the existence of a $59 million County deficit, the exact nature and size of which was not discovered until shortly before the Memorandum of Understanding was signed, made it incumbent upon County management to recommend to the Board of Supervisors that implementation of the agreement be tabled indefinitely. The County Administrative Officer testified that shortly after taking office on December 12, 1970 he received instructions from the Board of Supervisors to ascertain the County's financial condition.

The County Administrative Officer immediately undertook this task and by Christmas weekend, 1970, he had projected a County deficit of between $8 and $30 million. By the following weekend he had projected a County deficit of $50 million. The following Monday, January 3, 1971, a study of other projected budget items added $9 million to the deficit.

While Mr. Will was determining the size of the County's deficit, the County's Personnel Director worked closely with him and was party to all information concerning the size and scope of the deficit. Thus, when the Memorandum of Understanding was signed by County management on December 30, 1970 both the County Administrative Officer and the County Director of Personnel knew that the County had a sizeable deficit. When the Director of Personnel wrote the Board of Supervisors on January 6, 1971, recommending that the Board of Supervisors put the Memorandum of Understanding into effect, the nature of the deficit and its full implications were known to him and to the County Administrative Officer. At no time on or prior to January 6, 1971 was it made known to Local 45 that County management would not take steps to recommend approval of the agreement. Failure to so recommend, it has been charged, was a breach of that obligation. We agree.

We infer from the County Administrative Officer's testimony that he believed that he was not bound by the commitment of the Director of Personnel to seek the Board's approval of the settlement. He had the right and the obligation, as he saw it, to use his own judgment whether or not to support the commitment of Mr. Nesvig. That view is not our view. We think that the Director of Personnel did purport to bind, and did indeed bind, all of County management, including the Chief Administrative Officer, when he executed the Memorandum of Understanding. It is clear then that County management was committed to seek the Board's approval of the agreement. County Counsel concedes that there was at least an implied obligation to take certain action to implement the Memorandum of Understanding. We believe that on the basis of the facts presented to us there was both an implied obligation and an express obligation on management's part to seek the Board's approval. All of County management, including Mr. Will, was bound by that obligation.

In the context of this case, we think tabling and rejection of the negotiated agreement are almost synonymous. Tabling is not as final as rejection but it is almost as final. Tabling has had the effect of denying approval of this agreement and of denying the benefits provided for; that is the equivalent up to this point of rejection. Outright disapproval by the Board may seem to be, without actually being, more nearly final. The Director of Personnel's testimony that there will be no retroactivity if and when this agreement is ever approved means that there has been a permanent rejection of at least part of the negotiated benefits.

III

The Los Angeles County Employee Relations Ordinance was enacted by the Board of Supervisors on September 3, 1968, following receipt of a report by a distinguished panel of consultants who drafted the Ordinance and recommended its adoption by the Board of Supervisors. Section 12(a)(3) of the Ordinance provides that it shall be an unfair employee relations practice for the County "to refuse to negotiate with representatives of certified employee organizations on negotiable matters." A similar duty is imposed upon employee organizations by Section 12(b)(2) of the Ordinance, which makes it an unfair employee relations practice for a certified employee organization or their representatives or members to "refuse to negotiate with County officials on negotiable matters." Section 3(*o*) of the Ordinance defined negotiation as follows:

> " 'Negotiation' means performance by duly authorized management representatives and duly authorized representatives of a certified employee organization of their mutual obligations to meet at reasonable times and to confer in good faith with respect to wages, hours, and other terms and conditions of employment, *and includes the mutual obligation to execute a written document incorporating any agreement reached.*" (Emphasis added.)

The Ordinance is careful to protect both bargaining parties from any duty to make a concession to the other party. If the parties in good faith are unable to resolve their differences after a good faith attempt to do so, no negotiated agreement comes into existence and the Ordinance, under those circumstances, does not compel them to reach an agreement.

The obvious purpose of these provisions is to assure that County management and the employee organizations authorized to represent County employees make a good faith effort to reach a negotiated agreement which is to their mutual satisfaction. Needless to say, the obligation of negotiating parties to make a good faith effort to iron out their differences and to reach accommodation, if possible, is the very heart and essence of the collective negotiations process.

In this case, Section 12(a)(3) of the Ordinance required that the agreement reached by County management and Local 45 be reduced to writing and signed by the parties. By signing the agreement, County management necessarily became obligated to make every effort to seek implementation of the agreement by recommending to the Board of Supervisors that it be implemented. If signing a negotiated agreement does not so obligate County management, then signing a negotiated agreement is a meaningless act on the part of County management.

If signing a negotiated agreement is a meaningless act, then that portion of the Ordinance requiring that negotiated agreements be reduced to writing and signed is a meaningless provision, of no use to employee organizations or the County of Los Angeles. If negotiated agreements need not be reduced to writing and signed, it follows that no attempts need be made by County management or a certified employee organization to negotiate an agreement. In that event, the entire Ordinance would consist of a mere collection of words on paper, without meaning and without purpose.

We assume, as we must, that the Los Angeles County Employee Relations Ordinance was not enacted with the understanding that it would have no meaning. It follows that an interpretation of the Ordinance which would effectively render it meaningless must be rejected. We accordingly find that County management is in violation of Section 12(a)(3) of the Ordinance by virtue of its failure to recommend approval of the Memorandum of Understanding which it reached with Local 45. We reject County management's defense that a fiscal crisis precluded it from recommending that the Memorandum of Understanding be approved. The County's financial condition was known when the Memorandum of Understanding was signed; the County's financial condition was known when the County's Director of Personnel recommended that the Board of Supervisors implement the Memorandum of Understanding. Plainly, this defense is without merit.

We do not suggest that there was malice or evil intent on the part of County management. On the contrary, it is argued that Mr. Will felt bound by a more pressing obligation—as the Board's chief staff adviser—to recommend tabling of their settlement (and freezing of other County obligations and capital expenditures unless they were "already legally committed") because of the County's large fiscal deficit. Certainly Mr. Nesvig was not motivated by any malice or intention to do an injustice. But, good intentions, such as those described to us, have limited weight in the Commission's determination whether the Ordinance has been violated. We have found that County management, not including the Board, did violate the Ordinance, as charged.

Having found that County management violated the Ordinance in this case, the Ordinance requires that we fashion a remedy for the charging party. In this case, we withhold fashioning a remedy at this time, as the principal parties to this dispute, having been made aware of our decision by means of our written order of March 26, 1971, have agreed to attempt to fashion a remedy consistent with our decision in this case. If the parties are unable to agree upon an acceptable remedy this Commission will fashion a remedy in accordance with its obligations as set out in Section 12(e) of the Ordinance. At our meeting scheduled for April 16, 1971 we will consider what progress the parties have made to this end.

* * *

Questions

1. A school board by resolution hires a lawyer who is authorized, together with the superintendent, to negotiate with the teachers' union. The board's resolution says nothing concerning the authority of the superintendent to negotiate at times when the lawyer is not present. During

negotiations in June, when the lawyer was absent, the superintendent submitted written counterproposals to the union. Each was thoroughly discussed and evaluated, and modifications were made before the superintendent submitted the next counterproposal. At the conclusion of these month-long negotiations, the superintendent stated to the union that all changes and modifications of the board's counterproposals to which he had agreed were subject to the approval of the lawyer not only as to language but also as to substance. Is this bad faith bargaining?

2. The mayor of a city, having received notice of tentative agreements reached between his negotiators and the negotiators for a welfare workers' union, waited a month (after notification) and then repudiated some of those agreements. Is this bad faith bargaining?

3. A thruway authority and the union representing its toll takers and clerical employees negotiated for five months. Finally, they reached tentative agreement on a package settlement. The thruway's chief negotiator recommended to the governing board that it adopt the package settlement. The executive director of the authority opposed the recommendation and urged the board to repudiate several of the agreements in the package and insist upon renegotiations. The board went along with the executive director. Is this a failure to bargain in good faith? If yes, what conduct constitutes the improper practice—the board's refusal to follow the negotiator's recommendation? Or the intrusion by the executive director into negotiations after five months of letting them take their course?

4. Sometimes a party engages in "end run" bargaining and attempts to use whatever political or institutional advantage it may have to secure an agreement which it might not have been able to do at the bargaining table. Should there be any restrictions on a public employer's "end run" bargaining which appeals directly to employees or the public about the status of labor negotiations? Should there be any restrictions on a public employee who is dissatisfied with the results at the bargaining table and contacts a "higher up" public official to press bargaining demands?

EDWARDS, THE EMERGING DUTY TO BARGAIN IN THE PUBLIC SECTOR *

71 Mich.L.Rev. 885, 903–907 (1973).

* * *

[Other structural questions] pale by comparison to the problem of attempting to identify the real public "employer" in any given public sector negotiations. Should the executive branch, which has over-all responsibility for the bureaucracy, be designated as the employer? Or does that title belong to the legislature, which appropriates the money and approves the financial terms of contracts? What role should the personnel division of a civil service system play?

These questions take on great practical importance when the state statute provides sanctions for a refusal to bargain in good faith. One

* Reprinted by permission.

element of good faith bargaining is the presence of bargaining representatives on both sides of the negotiating table who have the authority to make genuine proposals. Of course, final authority need not be possessed by negotiators for either side; for example, it is an accepted practice in the private sector for union representatives to submit a contract for final ratification by the membership before execution. A different situation, however, is faced by public employees when the representative of the public employer lacks even the authority to arrive at a *conditional* agreement. Absent a statute clearly identifying the participants on the public employer's side of the bargaining table the question must be resolved on a case-by-case basis. A public employee relations board could serve a vital function in this area, by shaping the collective bargaining process through unfair labor practice proceedings.

A good example of the usefulness of the case-by-case method of establishing the identity of the employer is seen in *Typographical Union* v. *Personnel Division,*[93] decided by the Oregon Public Employee Relations Board (PERB). When the state personnel division refused to recommend approval of the wage adjustments called for in a joint agreement between state printing trade employees and the state printer, an unfair labor practice charge was filed. Even though a contract approved by the personnel division would still be subject to final approval by the governor and the making of the necessary appropriations by the legislature, the Oregon PERB held that the personnel division should have participated in the bargaining process rather than waiting to reject the completed agreement, because the state, as well as the state agencies, is a "public employer" by definition under the Oregon statute.[94]

The Oregon Board quite properly took a functional approach in defining the relation between the employees and the component parts of the employer's authority structure. The Board stressed that "individuals engaged in the actual bargaining process must be persons empowered to present the facts * * * in support of their own position and to weigh and evaluate the arguments * * * presented by their colleagues across the table." [95] The fact that the Oregon statute contemplates only a conditional agreement did not, in the Board's view, eliminate the employer's obligation to develop a bargaining approach common to all elements of the bureaucracy having an input into the process. The Board noted specifically that "[t]here is nothing to prevent the parties from negotiating to a point at which the governor has either accepted or not accepted a proffered agreement." [96]

Only recently has a state legislature addressed itself to the problem of identifying the employer of state employees. The revised Wisconsin statute provides that "the state shall be considered as a single employer * * * [and that] [i]t is the responsibility of the executive branch to

93. [Footnotes numbered as in original.–Ed.] GERR No. 400, at B–6 (Case No. C–39, March 31, 1971).

94. Ore.Rev.Stat. § 213.711(5) (1971).

95. GERR No. 400, at B–7.

96. GERR No. 400, at B–7.

negotiate collective bargaining agreements, and to administer such agreements. * * * "[97] The statute also spells out the responsibility for the handling of employer functions within the executive branch and for the coordination of collective bargaining activities.[98] Finally, the Wisconsin law makes it clear that the legislature must take specific steps to approve or disapprove those portions of agreements which require legislative action.[99] Statutes of this type should help to eliminate the frustration and waste of time and money which occur in those all-too-frequent instances where a union concludes an agreement only to find that it has been dealing with an agency with insufficient authority to negotiate effectively.

While the Wisconsin statute states in detail the tasks that the Wisconsin legislature must perform in public sector bargaining, it also brings out the fact that the role of the legislature in the bargaining process is conceptually ambiguous, absent a statute. On the one hand, the state legislature or its equivalent in a political subdivision, although it is the final legitimating authority, at least for fiscal matters, is wholly outside the negotiating process, which is completed before the legislature is called upon to act. On the other hand, the need for legislative approval necessarily affects the bargaining process. For example, the bargaining position of the employer is likely to be strengthened if the parties believe that the legislature will not approve settlements beyond a certain percentage or dollar increase over present benefits.

The Wisconsin statute provides an example of how the legislature may not only legitimate public sector contracts, but also participate more directly in the bargaining process. It requires that agreements, once approved by the unions involved, be approved by a joint legislative committee. The committee then introduces bills in both houses to implement those portions of the agreement, such as wage adjustments and fringe benefits, which require legislative approval. If the committee rejects the agreement or the legislature rejects the resultant bills, the agreement is sent back to the parties for renegotiation.[100] Thus, the parties must remain aware of the attitudes of both the legislative committee and the legislature itself.[101]

Participation by the legislature in the bargaining process raises the question whether a legislative body can be regarded as the "employer." The legislature, as approving authority, is a part of the same government as the executive branch, which acts as the negotiating authority. May the executive be regarded as the "agent" of the legislature, in the

97. Wis.Stat.Ann. § 111.81(16) (Supp. 1973).

98. Wis.Stat.Ann. §§ 111.80(4), 111.-81(16) (Supp.1973).

99. Wis.Stat.Ann. § 111.92 (Supp.1973).

100. Wis.Stat.Ann. § 111.92(1) (Supp. 1973).

101. In this respect, the role of the Wisconsin legislature is to be contrasted with that of its New York counterpart. The provision of the Taylor Law requiring legislative approval of the negotiated contract, N.Y.Civ.Serv.Law § 204–a(1) (McKinney 1973), involves a significantly lower level of legislative participation in the process than the Wisconsin statute provides.

sense that it has actual authority to negotiate only those contracts which the legislature will approve? Should the executive be charged with actual or constructive knowledge of legislative tolerance limits, and should both the executive and the legislature be subject to unfair labor practice charges if the executive negotiates a contract knowing the legislature will disapprove it? These interesting questions were raised with respect to a *local* legislative body in a recent decision by the New York Public Employment Relations Board. In *Board of Trustees of the Ulster County Community College,*[102] the college board of trustees agreed to a wage hike in excess of the maximum raise authorized by the county legislature. The legislature then repudiated the authority of the trustees and sought to renegotiate the contract. The hearing officer found that the trustees had in fact exceeded their authority; however, he found that the legislature had committed an improper practice in renouncing the authority of the board and rejecting the contract. By reference to agency principles, the hearing officer determined that the act of the agent (the trustees) should be attributed to the principal (the legislature) where the agent is clothed with apparent authority to negotiate an agreement. This finding of an improper practice was rejected by the New York PERB, on the ground that an agent should be free to agree to a proposal in excess of his authority if he has the good faith belief that his principal may be persuaded to agree also. The decision by the Board did not reject the agency concept, however, and left open the possibility that the Board may return in later cases to the view expressed by the hearing officer that where a legislative body directly involves itself in the negotiating process, such action is reviewable by the Board and may be the subject of an improper practice proceeding. In an earlier New York decision, in which the legislative body did involve itself in the negotiating process, a hearing officer ruled that only the executive branch could be charged with an improper practice since only that branch, and not the corresponding legislature, actually "negotiates." [103]

The *Ulster County Community College* case dealt with the role of a *local* legislative body in the bargaining process. Different questions are raised when dealing with state legislatures. County and municipal governments, even where "home rule" statutes grant considerable freedom of action to localities, are agencies of the state, subject to the superior authority of the state government.[104] State courts, therefore, have more freedom to evaluate the behavior of local legislative bodies according to the dictates of state law than they have to challenge the state legislature on its own ground. Attribution of "employer" status to the state legislature for the purpose of enforcing its own laws against itself is unlikely. But the fact that the legislature may not be a

102. 4 New York Public Employment Relations Board [hereinafter N.Y. PERB] 4639.971) (hearing officer's decision): 4 N.Y.PERB 3749 (1971) (board decision).

103. Town of Huntington, 3 N.Y. PERB 4501 (1970).

104. E. Stason & P. Kauper, Cases and Materials on the Law of Municipal Corporations 2 (3d ed. 1959).

designated participant in the bargaining process does not alter the reality of its influence on that process.

* * *

MILTON DERBER, MANAGEMENT ORGANIZATION FOR COLLECTIVE BARGAINING IN THE PUBLIC SECTOR *

Public Sector Bargaining, 90–123 (2d ed. 1988).

* * *

I start with an analysis of what may seem a peculiar question: Who is public management? I hope to demonstrate that this is indeed a question of considerable practical as well as theoretical importance.

* * *

WHO IS PUBLIC MANAGEMENT?

From a collective bargaining perspective, the concept of public management poses problems not normally found in the private sector. The private employer is readily identified as an entity, and the line of management responsibility for bargaining is usually clear and direct. But in the public sector the formal responsibility often differs from the actual.

Constitutional, Political, and Bureaucratic Considerations

The reasons for such confusion and ambiguity are many.[1] One major factor is the constitutional system of checks and balances that distributes authority for policy making and implementation among the legislative, executive, and judicial branches. Even the executive or legislative responsibilities may be legally shared among separately elected executive officers (e.g., the governor and the secretary of state) or among legislative bodies (e.g., the state legislature and home-rule municipal councils). Legislative bodies in turn often delegate rule-making authority to other agencies, such as a civil service commission, a school board, or a municipality. Arvid Anderson has pointed out that

> the education law, civil service law, welfare laws, statutes affecting police and fire [sic], prevailing wage statutes, pension statutes, statutes affecting the fiscal authority of the municipal employer and the timetable for budgetmaking, all affect and may operate as constraints on the authority of the public employer.[2]

Another significant factor is that apart from the federal Congress and the state legislatures, few public agencies have either the authority

* Reprinted by permission of The Bureau of National Affairs, Inc. and the author.

1. See, for example, my article, *Who Negotiates for the Public Employer,* in Perspective in Public Employee Negotiation, ed. Keith Ocheltree (Chicago: Public Personnel Association, 1969), 52–53.

2. *The Structure of Public Sector Bargaining,* in Public Workers and Public Unions, ed. Sam Zagoria (Englewood Cliffs, N.J.. Prentice–Hall, 1972), 43.

or the means to raise all or most of the money they need to perform their functions. Furthermore, to an increasing extent, public bodies obtain their funds from a multiplicity of sources rather than a single source. When a lower level of government receives grants from a higher level, the transfer is often accompanied by constraints on the use of the funds or conditions are specified about the qualifications or methods of the personnel involved.[3]

Finally, but not least in importance, political forces may shape the allocation of responsibility for collective bargaining. A strong mayor or governor typically prefers a centralized bargaining system under his direct control: a weak chief executive may be obliged to share responsibilities with other elected officials in executive or legislative or even administrative positions, resulting in a highly fragmented management approach. In some cases (e.g., where a union is linked to a party machine), the ultimate authority for bargaining may lie with a political leader or group that holds no formal governmental position but operates behind the scene.

The appointed bureaucracy or professional staff may also exercise widely varying degrees of responsibility in collective bargaining in relation to the elected officials who are formally their superiors. A city manager, a school superintendent, or the head of a municipal or state department, possessing a strong personality as well as labor relations expertise and long experience, may assume a dominant role in collective bargaining, whereas less well-endowed counterparts may have little or no role.

* * *

Citizen Interest Groups

Public management's bargaining structure may also be strongly influenced by the activities of interest groups that believe they (as members of the sovereign public) are entitled to a voice in the collective bargaining process. In some instances the group may desire representation on management's bargaining team, in others the right to attend the bargaining sessions, in still others the opportunity to present their views to the bargaining team or to the legislative body prior to the approval of a collective agreement. Illustrations of such interest-group desires are found in laws in Montana, Oregon, and Florida requiring student representation in university negotiations and in the court petition of a Parents' Union to obtain the right to participate in negotiations during the 1972–1973 Philadelphia teachers' strike.[5]

3. An example is the Urban Mass Transportation Act which specifies that before any federal funds are provided to a state or local government for the operation of a transit system, the U.S. Secretary of Labor must certify that arrangements have been made to protect the interests of affected employees, including the continuation of collective bargaining rights.

5. Richard P. Schick and Jean J. Couturier, The Public Interest in Government Labor Relations (Cambridge, Mass.: Ballinger Publishing Co., 1977), 43–67.

Because general government services must be paid for by the public through the tax system, public management has a relationship to its public that is very different from that of private management to its firm's customers. In the latter case, typically, a concerned customer can exercise the choice of buying or not buying, but lacks the power to influence the private management's collective bargaining policies or procedures. In the former case, a concerned public may seek to replace the responsible managers or force a change in bargaining policies.

Thought about the public's role in negotiations led Sam Zagoria, then director of the Labor–Management Relations Service, a public-employer organization, to advocate

> giving either party by law the right to take [a] contested issue to public referendum, hitching the factfinders' recommendation on the next regular or special election ballot. In effect, the issue would be taken to the citizens of the community, the ultimate public employer, for them to decide whether they want to supersede the instructions implicit in their earlier election of municipal officials by giving them newer directives based on the issue before them.[6]

Although the idea has not won wide support, at least three cities in Colorado adopted the use of the public referendum as the terminal point for an impasse procedure. The public referendum mechanism was also used in San Francisco in November 1975 when Proposition B was passed by a two-to-one margin abolishing a formula that tied pay for city craft workers to the prevailing wage rate for similar occupations in private industry.[7]

Frank P. Zeidler, former mayor of Milwaukee and a specialist in public-sector labor relations, has noted that taxpayers often believe that they are not represented at the bargaining table because they are not sure that the public-employer representatives represent them. "The taxpayer recognizes that the negotiator or negotiators for his side have several pressures at work on them other than taxpayer interests."[8]

A Theory of Diffused Management Responsibility

The diffused character of public management has been stressed by a number of students. Thomas Kochan, for example, in a study of fire-service bargaining in 228 cities, observed that "a number of semi-autonomous management officials (both administrative and elected) often share decision-making power over issues traditionally raised by unions in collective bargaining."[9] Community interest groups were

6. *Resolving Impasses by Public Referendum,* 96 Monthly Lab.Rev. 37–38 (May 1973).

7. 651 GERR B22 (April 5, 1976).

8. *The Public Interest in Collective Bargaining,* in Perspective in Public Employee Negotiation, *supra* note 1, at 9.

9. *A Theory of Multilateral Bargaining in City Governments,* 27 Indus. & Lab.Rel. Rev. 525, 526 (July 1974). *See also* Thomas A. Kochan, George P. Huber, and L.L. Cummings, *Determinants of Intraorganizational Conflict in Collective Bargaining in*

also found by Kochan (and others) [10] to become involved in the bargaining process. Kochan concluded that multilateral bargaining was a function of several variables, most notably the extent of internal conflict among management officials and the degree to which employee organizations use political pressure tactics. In short, the political context of municipal collective bargaining may lead to a fragmented management authority structure in contrast to the more unified management approach in private-sector bargaining.

One possible consequence of such fragmentation in management bargaining responsibility is the use by unions of the "end run." It is a rare public-employee organization that does not have friends and supporters among elected public officials. At every level of government the unions and associations devote often considerable resources (personnel, communication channels, financial contributions) in support of the election of particular candidates as well as in general lobbying. Sometimes these officials may "leak" information to employee representatives during or prior to bargaining. In other cases, if the employees cannot achieve their demands from the management negotiators, they may appeal informally to their elected friends to try to influence management positions or to secure more favorable consideration at a higher decision-making level. Numerous examples come to mind: the schoolboard member who urges the finance committee to approve the police association's wage demands, the party professional who advises a county board to make bargaining concessions as a trade-off for union support in a forthcoming election.[11]

Need for Legal Specification of Management Responsibility

Because of these potentially negative results of fragmentation, there seems to be widespread agreement among practitioners and students that management responsibility for collective bargaining should be clearly specified in law or administrative guidelines, although no specific uniform rule may be feasible. Where the constitutional structure requires a sharing of responsibility, agreements entered into in one forum should be clearly contingent on action in another, with an obligation on the part of both sides to the initial agreement to support it fully and wholeheartedly in its progress through any other requisite decision-making forum.

* * *

the Public Sector, 20 Ad.Sci.Q. 10–23 (March 1975).

10. Kenneth McLennan and Michael H. Moskow, *Multilateral Bargaining in the Public Sector,* in Proceedings of the 21st Annual Meeting, Industrial Relations Research Association (Madison, Wis.: IRRA. 1968), 34–41; Hervey A. Juris and Peter Feuille, Police Unionism: Power and Impact in Public Sector Bargaining (Lexington, Mass.; D.C. Heath & Co., 1973), 45–52.

11. For the observations of one experienced management negotiator, *see* R. Theodore Clark, Jr., *Politics and Public Employee Unionism: Some Recommendations for an Emerging Problem,* 44 U.Cin.L.Rev. 680–689 (1975).

Centralization of Management Authority for Bargaining

The distribution of management responsibility for bargaining appears to be at least partly related to the structure of the bargaining unit. The wider and more comprehensive the bargaining unit, the greater the likelihood that management responsibility for bargaining will be centralized. When bargaining units are smaller, narrower, and more numerous, centralized authority is more difficult to maintain, and there is a tendency for responsibility to be dispersed (formally or informally) among a variety of agencies, departments, and institutions. Several empirical surveys support this thesis.

After an extensive study in 1968–1969 of local government in some 40 cities and towns (part of The Brookings Institution's Studies of Unionism in Government), John Burton concluded that "bargaining forces a centralization of authority within management which overcomes the fragmentation of control over various [personnel] issues typical in a nonunionized unit of local government." [20] As bargaining develops, "[c]ollective bargaining will shift authority for personnel issues to the executive branch at the expense of the legislative branch and the civil service system," and within the executive branch, "[a]uthority for bargaining will be centralized and primary responsibility assigned to an individual or officer directly responsible to the chief executive." [21]

The relationship between management authority and bargaining structure suggested by the foregoing is by no means an iron law. In the cases of New York State and New York City, we find centralized managerial responsibility for bargaining with widely divergent bargaining-unit systems. The state has five broad horizontal units and three vertical units covering about 180,000 employees; the city has about 100 units (reduced from 400) covering some 250,000 employees. Bargaining for the state is conducted by the governor's Office of Employee Relations; bargaining for the city is the responsibility of the mayor's Office of Labor Relations. The history of management labor relations policy in both state and city is one of increasing centralization under the chief executive.[22] In the city, this centralization has occurred not only within the executive branch, but also as between the executive and legislative branches. In the state, the legislature has retained its

20. John F. Burton, Jr., *Local Government Bargaining and Management Structure,* 11 Indus.Rel. 123, 124 (May 1972).

21. *Id.* at 138.

22. For a history of the city's labor relations, see Raymond D. Horton, Municipal Labor Relations in New York City (New York: Praeger Publishers, 1972); Horton, *Report to State Charter Revision Commission on Reforming New York City's Labor Relations Process,* 594 GERR EI–ES (February 24, 1975); and Jack Bigel, *Municipal Finance and Its Implications for Negotiations, A Case History,* in The Evolving Process—Collective Negotiations in Public Employment, Association of Labor Relations Agencies publication (Fort Washington, Pa., Labor Relations Press, 1985), 530–546. The state's structure is described in Donald H. Wollett, *State Government: Strategies for Negotiations in an Austere Environment—A Management Perspective,* in Proceedings of the 1976 Annual Spring Meeting, Industrial Relations Research Association (Madison, Wis.: IRRA.1976), 504–511.

traditional power over appropriations, but has invariably assented to the collective-bargaining agreements.

Raymond Horton, David Lewin, and James Kuhn, however, have cautioned against overgeneralizing the centralization thesis. They offer three reasons for a "diversity" hypothesis:

> First, the formal dispersion of political power, particularly at the local government level in American cities, is so well-advanced that political "end-runs" around newly designated labor relations agencies and actors remain possible. Second, and closely related to the above point, one must distinguish between formal and informal power structures. The mere act of creating new labor relations institutions and delegating to them responsibilities to make decisions previously reached elsewhere in government does not mean, in fact, that the focus of control over decision-making also changes. Third, in certain cities where public employees are well-organized and politically strong, formal bargaining programs may result in a redistribution of power from public officials to municipal unions. This may represent a form of centralization, but not of the kind customarily anticipated by academics or public officials.[23]

A Lewin study of the evolution of management structure in the City and County of Los Angeles lends some support to the diversity thesis.[24] Despite an apparent formal centralization of public-management authority in these two major governmental units, multiple sources of authority remain. In the city, the Personnel Department, departmental commissioners, the city council, and the council's personnel committee, as well as the city administrative officer (the chief negotiator) and the mayor have all been participants to one degree or another in municipal labor relations. In the county, where decision making is more highly centralized than in the city, a five-member board of supervisors controls virtually all of the departments. Nevertheless, the county administrative officer (the chief negotiator), the personnel department, and the board of supervisors share negotiating responsibility.

Bargaining by state employees reflects the same tendency to centralize, as two separate 1974–1975 surveys of state government collective bargaining, by Ralph T. Jones and this author indicate. Jones (after a study of eight widely spread states) perceived the appearance of a "life cycle" pattern wherein "management structure evolves into and through distinctive growth and maturity patterns characterized by an almost instinctive thrust toward increasing centralization."[25] His

23. Raymond D. Horton, David Lewin, and James W. Kuhn, *Some Impacts of Collective Bargaining on Local Government,* 7 Ad. & Soc'y 509 (February 1976).

24. David Lewin, *Local Government Labor Relations in Transition: The Case of Los Angeles,* 17 Lab.Hist. 191 (Spring 1976).

25. Ralph T. Jones, *Public Management's Internal Organizational Response to the Demands of Collective Bargaining,* draft final report prepared by Contract Research Corp., Belmont, Mass., for Labor–Management Services Administration, U.S. Department of Labor, Contract No. L–74–207, undated, mimeo, 27.

study found that state bargaining was initiated under a variety of environmental circumstances which greatly affected the first management structures. Vertical units involving department-level contracts resulted in decentralized administration within state management. Horizontal units resulted in centralized administration. "Whatever the initial structure, however, subsequent events lead to further centralization. Decentralized administration becomes inappropriate as statewide units are established. These in turn begin to fade as pressures for coalition bargaining surface." [26]

My own research in the 12 midwestern states discovered three main bargaining patterns in which the allocation of management bargaining authority, the nature of the bargaining unit, and the scope of bargaining issues were interrelated.[27] Where bargaining coverage was widespread and the scope of bargaining was comprehensive (including pay, hours, and fringe benefits), government responsibility for bargaining tended to be centralized at the level of the governor or a civil service commission. Wisconsin, one of the pioneers in state government bargaining, illustrated the evolutionary process from widely dispersed, limited-scope management bargaining to a highly centralized system including the formal intermeshing of the executive and legislative roles. Iowa, influenced by its neighbor's experience, adopted a centralized bargaining system controlled by the governor's office from the outset. Other states with limited bargaining coverage and, typically, limited scope of issues reflected two different patterns. In some of these states (e.g., Missouri and North Dakota), responsibility was left to the heads of the agencies involved, and the chief executive followed a hands-off policy. In others of this group (e.g., Ohio, Nebraska), there was a centralized unit acting on behalf of the governor to maintain a measure of statewide uniformity. However, in such states, a tradition of departmental autonomy often resisted the centralization effort. As bargaining units evolved to a statewide scale, the centralization process tended to be strengthened.

MANAGEMENT'S INTERNAL ORGANIZATION FOR BARGAINING

Centralization of management responsibility in collective bargaining was fostered by a mounting recognition that the bargaining process demands professional skills, specialized knowledge, quick access to relevant data, and quantities of time and energy. After a few exposures to the process, many executives and legislators were happy to relinquish the function to others on their staff. Most recruited bar-

26. *Id.* at 32. This trend toward centralized state government bargaining must be distinguished from multiemployer local government bargaining as discussed earlier.

27. Milton Derber, Charles Maxey, and Kurt Wetzel, Public Management's Internal Organizational Response to the Demand of Collective Bargaining in the Twelve Midwestern States (Washington: U.S. Department of Labor, Labor–Management Services Administration, 1977). *See also* Milton Derber, Peter Pashler, and Mary Beth Ryan, Collective Bargaining by State Governments in Twelve Midwestern States (Champaign: Institute of Labor and Industrial Relations, University of Illinois, 1974).

gaining specialists, on a part-time or full-time basis, to represent them in bargaining and to advise them on policy.

In his 1969 Brookings survey of municipal and county management, David Stanley found that the

> largest group of cities and counties [in a sample of 15] are relying on their personnel or civil service staffs to assume labor relations responsibilities. Only large cities with a multiplicity of bargaining units have set up full-time labor specialists or units. More cities can be expected to follow their lead. * * * The larger more thoroughly unionized governments can be expected to move toward the industrial pattern—a department of labor relations headed by a vice mayor or an assistant manager for labor relations, who will supervise not only bargaining and employee relations but also selection and training activities.[28]

An Iowa study of the city manager's role in collective bargaining in 1975, shortly after the state enacted a comprehensive public-employee bargaining law, revealed a similar tendency.[29] Nine of sixteen managers had initially assumed the role of chief negotiator, either because they had been explicitly hired with the function in mind (two cases) or were required to assume the responsibility by city charter or by an ordinance adopted by the city council. However, most of the group indicated that the excessive time demanded by negotiations and the difficulty of maintaining consistency across multiple bargaining units had led them to consider seriously the appointment of a full-time labor relations specialist. The other seven managers had decided, for lack of experience in bargaining, to delegate the function to a committee (typically the city's chief finance officer, a personnel officer, and several department heads) or had hired an outside consultant, usually a lawyer with labor relations expertise. A 1986 report by the International City Managers Association revealed that 91 percent of the cities surveyed give responsibility for collective bargaining to the personnel department.[30]

Functional specialization in bargaining has raised a number of interesting questions and problems for management generally. Where in the management structure should the bargaining specialists be located? What role should department administrators play in the bargaining process, and how should their department interests be protected? How should communication lines be maintained with legislators who must approve any agreed items or vote appropriations to finance the agreements? Once negotiations have been completed, who

28. David T. Stanley, Managing Local Government Under Union Pressure (Washington, The Brookings Institution, 1972), 27–28.

29. Peter A. Veglahn and Stephen T. Hayford, *An Investigation into the City Manager's Role in the Collective Bargaining Process,* 5 J.Coll Neg.Pub. Sector 289 (1976).

30. 18 Labor–Management Relations Service Newsletter No. 1 and 3, 7 (April/May 1986).

should be responsible for contract administration and the settlement of grievances?

The answers to these and related questions have varied widely, not only at different levels of government but also within the same level. Contributory factors are numerous—the size and complexity of the bargaining unit, the legal framework, the distribution of political power, and the attitudes of management leaders, among others.

The Location of the Bargaining Specialist

Small governmental units (municipality, school board, or state institution) often hire a lawyer or industrial relations specialist on an ad hoc basis to represent management at the bargaining table. The consultant confers mainly with the chief executive (city manager or mayor) or a governing board, performs his function of negotiating an agreement with the union, and then withdraws from the scene. No systematic information is available on the characteristics or the role of these part-time representatives. General observation indicates that they are numerous, that they satisfy an essential need, and that a corps of such specialists have acquired multiple clients in various regions of the country.

Larger government units often appoint a full-time specialist as employee-relations director in the manner of a private corporation. Sometimes the labor-relations director handles all personnel matters; sometimes personnel and labor relations are treated as separate functions. As a staff specialist, the labor-relations director is usually responsible to a top administrative officer—the mayor or city manager, the civil service head, the superintendent of schools, the administrator of a hospital, the state director of administration or director of personnel, or the governor, as the case may be. Numerous variations may be cited.

In a national study of police unionism, Hervey A. Juris and Peter Feuille found that bargaining responsibility rested with the executive branch (mayor or city manager) or the city council. In "strong mayor" cities (Buffalo, Boston, New York, New Haven, Seattle), the executive branch prepared the budget, the city negotiators received instructions from the mayor, and at critical times the latter would enter the negotiations himself. In "weak mayor" cities (Milwaukee, Omaha, Los Angeles), the council was the dominant management factor. In council-manager cities, although the labor-relations specialists were attached to the city manager's office, the council typically provided negotiating directions or guidelines to them either directly (Oakland, Rochester, Vallejo) or through the manager (Cincinnati, Hartford, Dayton). In one instance, however, Juris/Feuille reported that the manager was able to persuade the council that "it was less costly politically to let him handle labor relations than to become involved themselves." [31]

31. Juris and Feuille, *supra* note 10, esp. 62–63.

In state government, as collective bargaining expanded, professional negotiators were employed increasingly to represent management at the bargaining table. In New York,[32] for example, Governor Rockefeller initiated the bargaining process shortly after the passage of the Taylor Law in 1967 by appointing a management negotiating team composed of his secretary, the president of the Civil Service Commission, and the director of the budget. It became clear in the following two years that these three top officials were far too involved in other functions to carry the collective bargaining responsibility. As a consequence, the governor requested the legislature to establish by law an Office of Employee Relations (OER) to bargain and administer contracts for the state. The director of the OER reported directly to the governor and became part of the governor's informal cabinet. The director's subordinates included a deputy director, who also served as director of the division of contract negotiation and administration, a research director who also served as director of the grievance division, and a legal counsel who served as the director of the legal division. Five assistant directors were responsible for preparing for negotiations and contract administration.

In Wisconsin, as in New York, comprehensive centralized bargaining followed the passage of a new bargaining law in 1971.[33] Bargaining responsibility for the state was conferred upon an Employment Relations Section established within the Department of Administration (DOA), with easy access through the DOA secretary, a cabinet member, to the governor. The Director of Employment Relations was designated the chief state negotiator. Together with a staff of five professionals, he developed management positions prior to bargaining, conducted bargaining, monitored all third-step (department) grievances, and represented management in all grievance cases submitted to arbitration. Whereas under an earlier law the Bureau of Personnel (which administered the merit system) acted as adviser to department negotiators, the post–1971 system separated responsibility for the labor relations function from that of the personnel function. In late 1977, following a comprehensive review of the state's personnel system, a bill was enacted that removed personnel functions from the Department of Administration and created a new Department of Employment Relations (headed by a secretary) with responsibility for the administration of the state civil service system, the affirmative action program, and collective bargaining.

Minnesota provides an example of a shift in labor relations responsibility from an independent Civil Service Board to the governor, with a team of top management officials as the governor's surrogates.[34] Under an initial "meet and confer" law (1965), state employee relations were controlled by the Civil Service Department, whose head was appointed

32. Derived mainly from Jones, *supra* note 25, at App. A, State Report.

33. Derber, Maxey, and Wetzel, *supra* note 27, at 6–7.

34. *Id.* at 10–12.

by a part-time Civil Service Board. When a bargaining law was enacted in 1971, negotiating responsibility was given jointly to the Director of Civil Service and the Commissioner of Administration, a key member of the governor's cabinet. In 1972 two state negotiators were hired within the Civil Service Department. The following year (1973) statutory revisions changed the title of Director of Civil Service to Commissioner of Personnel, made him a gubernatorial appointee instead of an appointee of the Civil Service Board, and limited the power of the board mainly to merit-employment procedures and merit appeals.

In Oregon [35] more than a decade of experimentation and change produced a comparatively weak central Employee–Relations Section (ERS) located in the Executive Department, but not strongly supported by the governor or the legislature. The supervisor of the Employee–Relations Section reports to the director of the Personnel Division who in turn reports to the director of the Executive Department. The ERS negotiators obtain their guidelines from the director of the Executive Department who consults with the governor. On occasion unions have made "end runs" to the governor to obtain concessions that the state negotiator has rejected. Agreements reached at the bargaining table may be altered at different levels—by either the Personnel Division (after a public hearing) or the Public Employment Relations Board if a merit-system rule is involved, by the governor, or (as has frequently happened) by the legislature. In addition, some 45 agencies or departments have the power to bargain on local issues such as work schedules, travel pay, supervisory appraisals, and maternity leave. All agency appointments must be reviewed and approved by the Personnel Division and the Executive Department director.

While the more highly developed collective-bargaining systems have led to the employment of centrally located professional negotiators, as illustrated above, numerous municipal, county, and state agencies continue to rely on line or staff officers with little or no expertise or experience.

Relations With Line Officials

When responsibility for negotiations is assigned to a central labor relations office, or is retained by the chief executive, a major problem arises as to the involvement of the heads of the operating departments and agencies. At least two reasons support some degree of such involvement. One is the specialized knowledge possessed by the administrator. The other is the concern of the administrator with the impact of the labor agreement on the functioning of his agency. If an agreement is to be meaningfully applied, it must be understood and, for best results, accepted by the people who must live with its provisions. Not the least of the negotiator's problems in some jurisdictions is the

35. Jones, *supra* note 25, at App. A. State Report.

hostility of managers at various levels to the idea of collective bargaining and their reluctance to help make it work. In some cases elaborate steps may be taken to frustrate bargaining.

The chief executive (mayor, city manager, school superintendent) who handles negotiations directly usually communicates informally with his main subordinates, asking for information or ideas as needed. Sometimes one or more line administrators may sit in on the negotiations. On the other hand, it is not uncommon for such officials to remain wholly in the dark about the negotiations and even to learn about them later than some of their unionized employees. The negative consequences for administrative morale and efficiency are obvious.

* * *

It seems clear that for management to neglect the interrelationships between bargaining and budget making is to incur serious risks respecting the effectiveness of collective bargaining and the fiscal stability of government. Structure must be adapted to function. The negotiators and the budget makers can contribute to each other's area of responsibility. Whether this communication is done formally or informally matters less than that it be recognized by public management as a necessary activity for both.

Relations With the Legislative Body

One of the distinctive features of public collective bargaining is that agreements about money (pay, fringe benefits) usually require legislative approval, and those concerning certain nonfinancial matters (civil service rules and regulations) often do. As noted earlier, some legislative bodies have, for this reason, retained responsibility for collective bargaining rather than leaving it to top-management officers. Most legislative bodies, however, have found the technical intricacies and time requirements of collective bargaining too demanding and have adopted a more limited role. Questions about the legislative role include a number of different aspects: whether the legislature should be involved in the preparation of the bargaining guidelines, whether it should be represented at the bargaining table, whether legislative leaders should approve the agreement before it is formally signed, whether the legislature should have the authority to revise the terms of an agreement or merely approve or disapprove, and whether it should remain wholly aloof from the collective-bargaining process and simply act on relevant appropriations and legal rules.

In most school districts and many municipalities, the legislative body (school board or city council) is totally involved from preparation for bargaining to approval of the agreement and voting of necessary funds. Members of the legislative body may even participate in the bargaining team, although as the specialized character of collective bargaining becomes increasingly appreciated, the legislators tend to withdraw to the background except in crises. At the other extreme are the cases in which the legislature (typically state legislatures and large city councils) try to disassociate themselves from the bargaining process and act on appropriations and other bills as in the days before bargaining. In between are the legislative bodies that accept a limited responsibility for collective bargaining by requiring the submission to them of negotiated agreements for approval or disapproval.

The argument for a shared responsibility for the legislative body and the executive branch is that both represent the community or public interest and therefore should coordinate their actions in relation to the employee organizations. A division between the two branches of government, it is found, will encourage "end runs" and undermine the effectiveness of the negotiators. An opposing view is that public managers (including the chief executive) have a different role in government than legislators and that the latter must take into account the interests of both management and nonmanagement employees as well as the interests of other public groups that are not ordinarily represented at the bargaining table.

Such philosophic differences are usually overridden by pragmatic political considerations and the distribution of power. In New York City the virtual exclusion of the city council and the Board of Estimate from collective bargaining and the supremacy of the mayor have been attributed to the former's inability to develop strong public or official confidence. In Chicago, the mayor's dominant role (until the Democratic Party split in the 1980s) can be explained by his party's monopoly of power and the integration of most of the unions into the party machinery. At the state level, however, in both New York and Illinois, a vigorous two-party system has given the governor responsibility for bargaining, while the legislature retains the final voice on appropriations.

One of the most ingenious and atypical systems of linking the state negotiators from the executive branch with a closely divided two-party legislature is found in Wisconsin. There the collective bargaining law provides for the establishment of a Joint Legislative Committee on Employment Relations (JOCER) on which the leaders of both parties in both houses are represented. The state negotiator must consult prior to bargaining with this committee in order to secure tacit approval of his bargaining position. After negotiations with the union, he must return to the committee for its approval or disapproval of the tentative bargaining agreement. If the agreement is disapproved, he must return for further negotiations. The agreement finally approved can then expect quick appropriations support in the legislature without the likelihood of an "end run" by either party from the bargaining table. The JOCER system worked well until 1977 when a strike of state employees occurred and communications between the negotiators and the legislators broke down. A settlement was rejected by JOCER, and it became necessary for the bargainers and the union to renegotiate the agreement. To avoid a recurrence, the legislature subsequently tightened up the consultation procedure between the state negotiators and JOCER in the 1977 statute.

Michigan, in contrast, has virtually insulated state employee relations from legislative impact by virtue of a constitutional provision that grants the state Civil Service Commission plenary power over all conditions of employment and authority to set wage rates and fringe benefits subject only to a veto of two-thirds vote in both houses of the legislature. There has not been such a veto since the rule was adopted in the mid-1930s.

* * *

CONCLUSION

As the preceding discussion indicates, public management has been confronted with a variety of structural and procedural problems emanating from the rapid growth of public unionism and collective bargaining since the middle 1960s. Experimentation, consciously contrived or unplanned, has been rife throughout the country and at all levels of government. A large number of outside labor relations specialists have been attracted by the challenges and rewards. Both personnel staff and line administrators from within have sought to develop new, needed skills by formal training and trial-and-error experience. Old management structures and practices have been discarded or revised; new ones have been introduced. But the time period has been short (few systems go back more than a decade or two), and the problems are complex. Hence, most of the basic issues remain at least partially unresolved despite a noticeable advance in knowledge and understanding and a substantial development in bargaining expertise.

Questions

1. In certain private sector industries, voluntary multi-employer bargaining units have been formed and recognized. Although cities and states have sought to avoid fragmentation of bargaining units by consolidating occupations, departments, and agencies under a single bargaining authority, there has been surprisingly little interest among local management groups in establishing public multi-employer arrangements. Why?

2. In the private sector, there have been instances when one bargaining unit's union has attempted "coordinated" bargaining by inviting representatives of the employer's other bargaining units to join the union's bargaining team as nonvoting members. In a leading case, *General Electric Co. v. NLRB,* 412 F.2d 512 (2d Cir.1969), the court upheld the NLRB's determination that the employer's refusal to bargain with such a bargaining team was an unfair labor practice. Should a public employer be required to bargain at the same time with several bargaining units representing its employees? (Why would several separate bargaining units wish to bargain in this manner?)

3. Although issues relating to the identification of the public employer for collective bargaining purposes have been discussed in the literature (such as Professor Derber's publication), why do these issues persist—even

in jurisdictions where public sector bargaining was authorized several decades ago?

C. A ROLE FOR THE PUBLIC?

Concerns have been expressed by some commentators, courts, and policy makers that democratic process values are endangered when "the public" is excluded from bilateral bargaining sessions between a public employer and the exclusive representative of public employees, particularly when the bargaining covers topics which have broad policy ramifications. A few states have responded to these concerns by requiring all or some negotiations sessions to be conducted in the "sunshine," like meetings of public bodies. This is in contrast to the conventional (and majority) position that, in order to be productive, bargaining sessions should not be public, unless both parties agree to public meetings.

BETHLEHEM AREA SCHOOL DISTRICT

Pennsylvania Labor Relations Board, 1973.
3 Pa.Pub.Employee Rptr. 102.

A charge of unfair practices was filed with the Pennsylvania Labor Relations Board * * * by the Bethlehem Education Association, hereinafter called the "Complainant," alleging that the Board of School Directors of the Bethlehem Area School District * * * engaged in unfair practices contrary to the provisions of the Public Employe Relations Act * * * Section 1201, subsection (a), clauses (1), (5) and (9) of Article XII.

In its charge of unfair practices, the Complainant alleged that the Respondent has refused and continues to refuse to negotiate with the Complainant unless the representatives of the press are permitted to attend the negotiation meetings.

FINDINGS OF FACT

* * *

4. That the Complainant and the Respondent entered into a collective bargaining agreement, which by its terms began on September 1, 1971, and was to continue in full force and effect until August 31, 1974. However, under the terms of the collective bargaining agreement salaries would be open to renegotiation for the period September 1, 1973, to August 31, 1974.

5. That on or about December 10, 1972, Joseph Kimock, President of Complainant, contacted representatives of the Respondent for the purposes of beginning negotiations pursuant to the collective bargaining agreement.

6. That the parties scheduled their first meeting for January 10, 1973.

7. That at the January 10, 1973, meeting the Complainant and the Respondent were present, and in addition to the parties, a representative of the press, namely, Mr. Clapp of the Bethlehem Globe Times was also in attendance at the invitation of the Respondent.

8. That at the January 10, 1973, meeting Joseph Kimock advised the Respondent that the presence of a reporter was not agreed to by the parties, and that he would not negotiate with the Respondent if Respondent insisted on having a reporter present at the negotiating session. The Respondent's representative, Mr. Guidon, a School Board member and Chief of the Negotiations Committee, advised Mr. Kimock that the reporter would be present because the Respondent's Board had voted for an open meeting which meant that the press would be present at the negotiating session.

9. That subsequent to January 10, 1973, meetings were held between the parties on January 17, 1973 and January 24, 1973, and at each of the two subsequent meetings the press was invited by the Respondent; and Complainant reiterated its position that it would not negotiate in the presence of a third party, and that the conduct of the Respondent amounted to a refusal to bargain.

10. That Respondent's President, Dr. Gary Pochlein, testified that all the Respondent's meetings are open to the press and public and all subjects are discussed in front of the press and public with the exception of items dealing with the buying or selling of real estate and items dealing with personalities.

11. That the collective bargaining agreement executed between the parties and effective at all times relevant hereto is silent on the subject of the press or other third parties attending negotiating sessions involving the Complainant and the Respondent.

Discussion

Article VII. Section 701 of the Act reads as follows:

> "Collective bargaining is the performance of the mutual obligation of the public employer and the representative of the public employes to meet at reasonable times and confer in good faith with respect to wages, hours and other terms and conditions of employment, or the negotiation of an agreement or any question arising thereunder and the execution of a written contract incorporating any agreement reached but such obligation does not compel either party to agree to a proposal or require the making of a concession."

The Act mandates collective bargaining between the public employer and the representative of the public employes. The Act does not, by its terms, provide for general supervision of the parties involved in negotiations by a "public representative," ombudsman, or representative of the press.

This matter is a case of first impression for the Board in that no decisions of the Board or the courts of this Commonwealth touch this issue. However, several of our sister states have dealt with the issues presented herein. [The Board's discussion of *Bassett v. Braddock,* on the Florida Sunshine Law, is omitted.]

In the matter of *Mayor Samuel E. Zoll and City of Salem and IAFF Local 1780,* decided December 14, 1972 by the Massachusetts Labor Relations Board, a decision similar to that of the Florida Supreme Court was reached on the issue of the presence of third parties at the collective bargaining table. In that case, the City of Salem insisted upon the presence of the public at bargaining sessions as a precondition to any agreement with the union. The union objected to the City unilaterally imposing such a condition and in upholding the union's position, the Massachusetts Labor Relations Board turned to similar duty-to-bargain language of the NLRA inasmuch as the Massachusetts statute was patterned after the NLRA. The Board pointed out that under the NLRA, parties must bargain on wages, hours and other terms and conditions of employment and are free to bargain or not on other subjects. The Board stated that an employer or a union may insist on mandatory bargaining subjects as a precondition to any agreement but it is unlawful to insist on non-mandatory bargaining subjects. The Board reasoned that since public bargaining clearly does not fall within "wages, hours and other conditions of employment" the insistence upon public view bargaining was illegal and constituted a lack of good faith by the City. The Board pointed out that the National Labor Relations Board (NLRB) has held that the insistence by an employer upon the presence of rank-and-file members of the union is contrary to uniform bargaining practice, not conducive to the orderly, informal and frank discussion of the issues confronting the negotiators necessary to reach a contract and violates the duty to bargain in good faith. (See *L.G. Everist, Inc.* (1953), 103 NLRB 308). In addition, the Board stated that it constitutes interference with the employes' right to bargain through representatives of their own choosing.

There are provisions in the Pennsylvania Public Employes Relations Act for public disclosure at a time when the legislature thought that public disclosure would have a beneficial effect in the public interest. Article VIII, Section 802 of the Act dealing with fact finding provides for public disclosure of the fact finder's report under certain circumstances. The purpose of such public disclosure is obvious.

Historically, collective bargaining has always been done "in camera" between the parties. The positions taken at the beginning of bargaining, if done in front of the public monitor, such as the press, would scarcely favor the elected official or the union official who through the course of negotiations modifies, weakens or compromises his position. Yet, such compromise is often the very art involved in the collective bargaining process.

Neither the Act nor the Rules and Regulations of the Board prevent either or both parties from giving media representatives an account of the bargaining sessions. The parties can give information they desire to the media before or after the bargaining sessions. Perhaps, wisdom would dictate that the parties take counsel with themselves during the course of bargaining, but the option to air views through the press is open to either or both parties.

There is nothing in the existing agreement between the parties requiring public monitoring of bargaining over future wages. The agreement is silent on the issue. * * *

The real issue involved in this matter is whether or not one of the parties involved in collective bargaining can compel the other party to bargain in front of a public monitor. By imposing the presence of a third party on the Complainant, the Respondent has refused to bargain with the Complainant. Bargaining is the mutual obligation of the parties. The parties can only impose their presence upon each other. Bringing in non-mutually-agreed-upon third parties is a violation of the obligation of the party who brought the third party into the negotiations.

* * *

The Respondent by its insistence of press coverage of the bargaining sessions has violated Section 1201(a)(1) of the Act in that it has interfered with employes' rights set forth in Article IV of the Act which grants them the right to bargain collectively with the Employer. When an Employer refuses to so bargain he denies his employes this right. Respondent also violated Section 1201(a)(5) of the Act by refusing to bargain with the duly certified representative of its employes.

Question

Under what circumstances might a public employer and union voluntarily agree to bargain in the "sunshine"?

As the following case indicates, Florida is one state which has experimented statutorily in this area of the law.

CITY OF FORT MYERS v. NEWS–PRESS PUBLISHING CO.

District Court of Appeals of Florida, Second District, 1987.
514 So.2d 408.

DANAHY, CHIEF JUDGE.

In this appeal the City of Fort Myers, the appellant, contends that once an impasse in collective bargaining is declared pursuant to the Public Employee Relations Act (PERA),[1] Florida's "Sunshine Law" [2] no longer applies to the ongoing bargaining process between the City's bargaining representative and the bargaining representative for the

1. § 447.403, Fla.Stat. (1985).

2. § 286.011, Fla.Stat. (1985).

employees' unions. The trial judge disagreed with that contention and held that section 447.605(2), Florida Statutes (1985), required that the continuing meetings held after impasse to resolve the disputed issues be held in the "sunshine." We agree with the trial judge and affirm his order which granted injunctive relief to the appellee, News–Press Publishing Company, Inc.

* * *

The City and the police union were unable to agree on a wage level as well as a few other minor economic matters for the new contract. The City and the police union declared that negotiations were at an impasse and, pursuant to procedures of chapter 447, Florida Statutes (1985), a special master was appointed to hear the dispute.[3] The special master scheduled the hearings to be held on December 10 and 11, 1985.

On December 9, the eve of the special master hearing for the police union, the attorney who was the representative leading the City's bargaining team contacted his counterpart, also an attorney, on the police union's team and arranged a meeting between the representatives for both sides to be held at 7:00 p.m. in a conference room at City Hall. No notice was posted, the appellee was not notified, and no media representatives were noticed or attended. The stated purpose of the meeting was an attempt to settle the terms and conditions of the employer-employee relationship which had caused the impasse.

The meeting was futile. The City presented a take-it-or-leave-it proposal with the condition that if this proposal were rejected, no mention of it was to be made at the next day's special master hearing. The police union rejected the settlement offer, and the parties anticipated the next day's hearing based on the City's last negotiation proposal, not the final offer of December 9.

The City had posted public notice of the special master hearing which was convened on the morning of December 10. The appellee's reporter and other media representatives were present.

Shortly after the special master convened the hearing, the police union's representative requested a recess so that the City's representative could step out into the hall to speak with him. The appellee's reporter, covering his first special master hearing, did not follow the attorneys as they left the conference room. Out in the hall, the union's representative offered another settlement proposal which the City's representative accepted. The two representatives agreed not to reveal the terms of the settlement offer until the following day. The purpose of this agreement was to avoid prejudice to the City by the special master knowing the terms of the agreed contract since that same

3. The negotiations between the City and the general employees' union also came to an impasse. The same procedures for public notice and participation of the appellee had been followed. The same special master was selected to hear both disputes on consecutive days. The dispute between the City and the police union was scheduled for the first day; the general employees' union had the special master for the second day.

master was to hear the general employees' dispute the next day. The police union also wanted the opportunity to present the settlement to its membership for ratification.

The two bargaining representatives reentered the conference room and announced to the special master that a settlement had been reached. The special master adjourned the proceedings but retained jurisdiction in the event of a later disruption regarding the settlement. The appellee's reporter next asked the two representatives to tell him the terms of the settlement. Both declined, citing the need for confidentiality.

The next day the special master proceedings began with the general employees' dispute with the same special master presiding. Once again, the representatives for the City and for the union met outside the hearing room in the hall for a private meeting. The same reporter followed the parties out of the hearing room and the two representatives made no effort to exclude him from this "off-the-record" encounter. After the second day's special master hearing was terminated, the appellee was informed of the settlement terms between the City and the police union. The membership of the police union ratified the settlement. The City Council, at a public meeting with notice, subsequently approved the contract, including the terms of the settlement agreed to during the private meeting on December 10.

We focus our attention, as did the trial judge, on the following pertinent part of PERA, section 447.605:

> (1) All discussions between the chief executive officer of the public employer, or his representative, and the legislative body or the public employer relative to collective bargaining shall be exempt from s. 286.011 [the Government in the Sunshine Law].
>
> (2) The collective bargaining negotiations between a chief executive officer, or his representative, and a bargaining agent shall be in compliance with s. 286.011.
>
> (3) All work products developed by the public employer in preparation for negotiations, and during negotiations, shall be exempt from chapter 119.

The City would have us note the use of different terms relating to the collective bargaining process in subsection (1)—"collective bargaining"—and subsection (2)—"collective bargaining negotiations." The City argues that there are four distinct phases of the collective bargaining process: (1) Recognition of the bargaining agent, (2) negotiations, (3) impasse resolution, and (4) contract administration. The City contends that because the legislature only submitted "negotiations" to the dictates of the Sunshine Law, the remaining phases of "collective bargaining" remain out of the sunshine. The trial judge was not persuaded by this view, nor are we.

Impasse only means a deadlock during negotiations where the parties refuse to compromise further to reach an agreement. Impasse is a feature of negotiations and is cured by further negotiation. The duty to negotiate is not extinguished by a declaration of impasse. *See* Vause, *Impasse Resolution in the Public Sector—Observations on the First Decade of Law and Practice Under the Florida PERA,* 37 U.Fla. L.Rev. 105 (1985). The City's attempts to characterize the collective bargaining process into categories which serve no meaningful distinction only avoid the obligation to carry out negotiations in the sunshine. The clear policy the legislature has established for Florida is simple to understand: To have the public's business carried out in public. As has been aptly stated by our supreme court:

> Various boards and agencies have obviously attempted to read exceptions into the Government in the Sunshine Law which do not exist. Even though their intentions may be sincere, such boards and agencies should not be allowed to circumvent the plain provisions of the statute. The benefit to the public far outweighs the inconvenience of the board or agency. If the board or agency feels aggrieved, then the remedy lies in the halls of the Legislature and not in efforts to circumvent the plain provisions of the statute by devious ways in the hope that the judiciary will read some exception into the law.

Canney v. Board of Public Instruction, 278 So.2d 260, 264 (Fla.1973) (construing section 268.011 in situation where board working in quasi-judicial capacity). Furthermore, it seems to us that the whole intent of the legislature—that public employee collective bargaining be conducted in the sunshine—could be thwarted by a declaration of impasse at a very early stage in the negotiations. In this way, the public could easily be shut out of a majority of the negotiating sessions which could be held in secret. The City's position would inevitably lead to this result, a result which would prevent public scrutiny and undermine public understanding of and confidence in the bargaining process. Such a result would hardly promote "harmonious and cooperative relationships between government and its employees." § 447.201, Fla. Stat. (1985).

As an alternative argument, the City cites *Bassett v. Braddock,* 262 So.2d 425 (Fla.1972), the only Florida Supreme Court case directly dealing with the question whether public employee collective bargaining must be held in the sunshine. In that case, decided before enactment of the collective bargaining statute, our supreme court said such bargaining need not be held in the sunshine. The court emphasized that, even though three legislative sessions had passed since the present constitutional provision guaranteeing collective bargaining for employees was adopted, the legislature had not yet passed the implementing statute necessary to give it meaning. *Id.* at 426. The court, therefore, merely affirmed the trial court order which refused to enjoin the holding of public employee contract negotiations out of the sunshine. The court, in dicta, speculated that negotiations in the sunshine "quite possibly would conflict with the protective umbrella of the constitutional guarantee of [article I] § 6." *Id.* Spurred by the urging of the supreme court in *Bassett* and the report of the court-appointed Supreme Court Public Employees Rights Commission, the legislature responded by implementing the constitutional provision when it enacted the Public Employee Relations Act in chapter 74–100, Laws of Florida. That act, which became chapter 447, provided that public employee collective bargaining negotiations between the contending parties be held in the sunshine. § 447.605(2), Fla.Stat. (1985). The following portion of the trial judge's final order succinctly clarifies the issue and points to our disposition:

> [I]t appears that the legislature has divided the total policy question into two catagories [sic]. One in which the public employer is meeting with its own side and one in which the public employer is meeting with the other side. The first it has exempted from the Sunshine Law F.S. 447.605(1). The second it has specifically required be under the Sunshine Law F.S. 447.605(2). Therefore once the collective bargaining process provided for under Chapter 447 of the Florida Statutes begins whenever one side or *any* of its representatives meet with the other side or *any* of its representatives at *any* time, irrespective of whether it is before or after the declaration of an impasse, to discuss *any* thing relevant to the terms and conditions of their employer-employee relationship, such meeting is subject to the Sunshine Law F.S. 286.011 and such meetings must be arranged or held so the Sunshine Law may be given effect and the Sunshine Law must be complied with. In the absence of this, such discussions may not be had irrespective of any agreement between the parties and no matter how beneficial it may be to the public interest.

The Florida Supreme Court has recently clarified the broad language of *Bassett* in *Neu v. Miami Herald Publishing Co.,* 462 So.2d 821, 824 (Fla.1985), wherein it held that meetings between a city attorney and a city council for the purpose of discussing settlement of pending litigation to which the city was a party had to be held in the sunshine. Specifically, the court stated that:

> [O]ur decision [in *Bassett*] was restricted to and rested on what we saw to be a *constitutional exception* to the Sunshine Law, to wit: the article I, section 6 right of public employees to bargain collectively.

Neu, 462 So.2d at 824 (emphasis added). At the time the court decided *Bassett,* it did not have the benefit of the legislature's pronouncements on the constitutional right of public employees to bargain collectively. The court was forced to analogize to private employees who can negotiate out of the sunshine in furtherance of their same right to collectively bargain. The court's discussion of a constitutional exception to the Sunshine Law in *Bassett* does not determine the issue before us which is based on construction of the post-*Bassett* statutory enactment implementing the constitutional provision.

The City lastly suggests to us that we reverse so that we may avoid a confrontation between public employees' constitutional right to bargain collectively and the Sunshine Law. We see no such confrontation. Florida public employees have the constitutional right to bargain collectively subject to the reasonable conditions of PERA, including application of the Sunshine Law. § 447.605(2), Fla.Stat. (1985). The burden of negotiating in the sunshine is hardly more onerous than being constitutionally deprived of the right to strike in article I, section 6. The right to strike is the mightiest weapon available to private employees in the collective bargaining process. Our holding that all phases of the public employee collective bargaining process between the contending parties must be held in the sunshine merely reiterates the strong public policy in Florida in place since the enactment of our Sunshine Law in 1967. *See, e.g., Board of Public Instruction v. Doran,* 224 So.2d 693 (Fla.1969); *Canney.* Further, the coverage of sunshine in Florida is general, whereas exemptions must be specific. *Wood v. Marston,* 442 So.2d 934 (Fla.1983). When it enacted PERA, the legislature did not exempt post-impasse negotiations between the contending parties from compliance with the Sunshine Law; on the contrary, it specifically included them. Because that is so, we find that the trial court correctly interpreted the statute. Accordingly, we affirm the order before us.

SCHOONOVER and HALL, JJ., concur.

Questions

1. If the "sunshine" principle is a good one, how far should it extend? To individual caucus sessions of management and labor? To the memoranda kept by the mediator?

2. California statutes applicable to public school, state employees, and higher education employees (West's Ann.Cal.Gov't Code §§ 3547, 3523, 3595) provide that all initial bargaining proposals and counterproposals are to be presented at a public meeting of the employer, to become a public record. In addition, proposals on new subjects are to be made public within 24 hours. Given that most collective bargaining agreements reached after serious negotiations differ materially from the initial proposals of both parties, how illuminating is this "sunshine" likely to be?

3. Another alternative was adopted by the Rochester, New York school district where a parent serves as a full-fledged member of the management bargaining team. How do you evaluate this unusual practice?

4. Yet another alternative responding to the issue of public access to the collective bargaining process in the public sector is a public referendum to ratify the tentative agreement. What are the pros and cons of this procedure?

5. Do all these "innovations" in collective bargaining reflect a concern that public management cannot or will not represent the public's interests in the bargaining process—or that the election process is an insufficient vehicle for the public to indicate its concerns?

D. CONSTITUTIONAL DIMENSIONS OF EXCLUSIVITY

In addition to "sunshine" issues, the process of public sector collective bargaining has raised constitutional questions—particularly involving first amendment rights of bargaining unit members as citizens or members of "the public."

CITY OF MADISON, JOINT SCHOOL DISTRICT NO. 8 v. WISCONSIN EMPLOYMENT RELATIONS COMMISSION

Supreme Court of the United States, 1976.
429 U.S. 167, 97 S.Ct. 421, 50 L.Ed.2d 376.

MR. CHIEF JUSTICE BURGER delivered the opinion of the Court.

The question presented on this appeal from the Supreme Court of Wisconsin is whether a State may constitutionally require that an elected Board of Education prohibit teachers, other than union representatives, to speak at open meetings, at which public participation is permitted, if such speech is addressed to the subject of pending collective-bargaining negotiations.

The Madison Board of Education and Madison Teachers Inc. (MTI), a labor union, were parties to a collective-bargaining agreement during the calendar year of 1971. In January 1971 negotiations commenced for renewal of the agreement and MTI submitted a number of proposals. One among them called for the inclusion of a so-called "fair-share" clause, which would require all teachers, whether members of MTI or not, to pay union dues to defray the costs of collective bargaining. Wisconsin law expressly permits inclusion of "fair share" provisions in municipal employee collective-bargaining agreements. Wis.Stat. § 111.70(2) (1973). Another proposal presented by the union was a provision for binding arbitration of teacher dismissals. Both of these provisions were resisted by the school board. The negotiations deadlocked in November 1971 with a number of issues still unresolved, among them "fair share" and arbitration.

During the same month, two teachers, Holmquist and Reed, who were members of the bargaining unit, but not members of the union, mailed a letter to all teachers in the district expressing opposition to the "fair share" proposal. Two hundred teachers replied, most commenting favorably on Holmquist and Reed's position. Thereupon a petition was drafted calling for a one year delay in the implementation of "fair share" while the proposal was more closely analyzed by an impartial committee. The petition was circulated to all teachers in the district on December 6, 1971. Holmquist and Reed intended to present the results of their petition effort to the school board and to MTI at the school board's public meeting that same evening.

Because of the stalemate in the negotiations, MTI arranged to have pickets present at the school board meeting. In addition, 300 to 400 teachers attended in support of the union's position. During a portion of the meeting devoted to expression of opinion by the public, the president of MTI took the floor and spoke on the subject of the ongoing negotiations. He concluded his remarks by presenting to the board a petition signed by 1,300–1,400 teachers calling for the expeditious resolution of the negotiations. Holmquist was next given the floor, after John Matthews, the business representative of MTI, unsuccessfully attempted to dissuade him from speaking. Matthews had also spoken to a member of the school board before the meeting and requested that the board refuse to permit Holmquist to speak. Holmquist stated that he represented "an informal committee of 72 teachers in 49 schools" and that he desired to inform the Board of Education, as he had already informed the union, of the results of an informal survey concerning the "fair share" clause. He then read the petition which had been circulated to the teachers in the district that morning and stated that in the 31 schools from which reports had been received 53 percent of the teachers had already signed the petition.

Holmquist stated that neither side had adequately addressed the issue of "fair share" and that teachers were confused about the meaning of the proposal. He concluded by saying: "Due to this confusion, we wish to take no stand on the proposal itself, but ask only that all alternatives be presented clearly to all teachers and more importantly to the general public to whom we are all responsible. We ask simply for communication, not confrontation." The sole response from the school board was a question by the president inquiring whether Holmquist intended to present the board with the petition. Holmquist answered that he would. Holmquist's presentation had lasted approximately two and one-half minutes.

Later that evening, the board met in executive session and voted a proposal acceding to all of the union's demands with the exception of "fair share." During a negotiating session the following morning, MTI accepted the proposal and a contract was signed on December 14, 1976.

(1)

In January 1972 MTI filed a complaint with the Wisconsin Employment Relations Commission (WERC) claiming that the Board had committed a prohibited labor practice by permitting Holmquist to speak at the December 6 meeting. MTI claimed that in so doing the board had engaged in negotiations with a member of the bargaining unit other than the exclusive collective-bargaining representative, in violation of Wis.Stat. § 111.70(3)(a)1, 4.[4] Following a hearing the

4. [Footnotes numbered as in original.—Ed.] The statute provides in relevant part:

"(3) PROHIBITED PRACTICES AND THEIR PREVENTION.

"(a) It is a prohibited practice for a municipal employer individually or in concert with others:

Commission concluded that the board was guilty of the prohibited labor practice and ordered that it "immediately cease and desist from permitting employees other than representatives of Madison Teachers, Inc., to appear and speak at meetings of the Board of Education, on matters subject to collective bargaining between it and Madison Teachers, Inc." The Commission's action was affirmed by the Circuit Court of Dane County.

The Supreme Court of Wisconsin affirmed. The court recognized that both the Federal and State Constitutions protect freedom of speech and the right to petition the government, but noted that these rights may be abridged in the face of "a clear and present danger that (the speech) will bring about the substantive evils that [the legislature] has a right to prevent." 69 Wis.2d at 211, citing *Schenk v. United States,* 249 U.S. 47 (1919). The court held that abridgment of the speech in this case was justified in order "to avoid the dangers attendant upon relative chaos in labor-management relations." 69 Wis.2d at 212.

(2)

The Wisconsin court perceived "clear and present danger" based upon its conclusion that Holmquist's speech before the schoolboard constituted "negotiation" with the board. Permitting such "negotiation," the court reasoned, would undermine the bargaining exclusivity guaranteed the majority union under Wis.Stat. § 111.70(3)(a)4. From that premise it concluded that teachers' First Amendment rights could be limited. Assuming, *arguendo,* that such a "danger" might in some circumstances justify some limitation of First Amendment rights, we are unable to read this record as presenting such danger as would justify curtailing speech.

The Wisconsin Supreme Court's conclusion that Holmquist's terse statement during the public meeting constituted negotiations with the board was based upon its adoption of the lower court's determination that, "[e]ven though Holmquist's statement superficially appears to be merely a 'position statement,' the court deems from the total circumstances that it constituted 'negotiation.' " This cryptic conclusion seems to ignore the ancient wisdom that calling a thing by a name does not make it so.[5] Holmquist did not seek to bargain or offer to enter into any bargain with the board, nor does it appear that he was

"1. To interfere with, restrain or coerce municipal employers in the exercise of their rights guaranteed in sub. (2).

* * *

"4. To refuse to bargain collectively with a representative of a majority of its employes in an appropriate collective bargaining unit. Such refusal shall include action by the employer to issue or seek to obtain contracts, including those provided for by statute, with individuals in the collective bargaining unit while collective bargaining, mediation or fact-finding concerning the terms and conditions of new collective bargaining agreement is in progress, unless such individual contracts contain express language providing that the contract is subject to amendment by a subsequent collective bargaining agreement."

5. The determination of the state courts that certain conduct constituted "negotiation" under state law, standing alone, would not ordinarily be open to our review; only its use as a predicate for restraining speech opens it to review here.

authorized by any other teachers to enter into any agreement on their behalf. Although his views were not consistent with those of MTI, communicating such views to the employer could not change the fact that MTI alone was authorized to negotiate and to enter into a contract with the board.

Moreover the school board meeting at which Holmquist was permitted to speak was open to the public.[6] He addressed the school board not merely as one of its employees but also as a concerned citizen, seeking to express his views on an important decision of his government. We have held that teachers may not be "compelled to relinquish the First Amendment rights they would otherwise enjoy as citizens to comment on matters of public interest in connection with the operation of the public school in which they work." *Pickering v. Board of Education,* 391 U.S. 563, 568 (1968). See also *Keyishian v. Board of Regents,* 385 U.S. 589 (1967); *Shelton v. Tucker,* 364 U.S. 479 (1960); *Wieman v. Updegraff,* 344 U.S. 183 (1952). Where the State has opened a forum for direct citizen involvement, it is difficult to find justification for excluding teachers who make up the overwhelming proportion of school employees and are most vitally concerned with the proceedings.[7] It is conceded that any citizen could have presented precisely the same points and provided the board with the same information as did Holmquist.

Regardless of the extent to which true contract negotiations between a public body and its employees may be regulated—an issue we need not consider at this time—the participation in public discussion of public business cannot be confined to one category of interested individuals.[8] To permit one side of a debatable public question to have a monopoly in expressing its views to the government is the antithesis of constitutional guarantees.[9] Whatever its duties as an employer, when the board sits in public meetings to conduct public business and hear

6. This meeting was open to the public pursuant to a Wisconsin statute which requires certain governmental decisionmaking bodies to hold open meetings. Wis. Stat. § 66.77(1) (1973). There are exceptions to the statute, and one of these has been interpreted to cover labor negotiations between a municipality and a labor organization. 54 Op.Atty.Gen. of Wis. vi (1965), cited with approval, *Board of School Directors v. Wisconsin Employment Relations Comm'n* 42 Wis.2d 637, 653 (1969). Thus, in contrast to the open session where the public was invited, the true bargaining sessions between the union and the board were conducted in private.

7. We need not decide whether a municipal corporation as an employer has First Amendment rights to hear the views of its citizens and employees. It is enough that Holmquist and other teachers and citizens have a protected right to communicate with the board. Since the board's ability to hear them is "inextricably meshed" with the teachers' right to speak, the board may assert those rights on behalf of Holmquist. *Procunier v. Martinez,* 416 U.S. 396, 409 (1974).

8. Plainly, public bodies may confine its meetings to specified subject matter and may hold nonpublic sessions to transact business. See n. 6, *supra.*

9. The WERC order does not prohibit all speech to the board on the subject of collective bargaining. Union representatives would continue to be entitled to come before the board at its public meetings and make their views known. The impact of such a rule is underscored by the fact that the union need not rely upon public meetings to make its position known to the school board; it can also do so at closed negotiating sessions. See n. 6, *supra.*

the views of citizens, it may not be required to discriminate between speakers on the basis of their employment, or the content of their speech. See *Police Department v. Mosley,* 408 U.S. 92, 96 (1972).[10]

(3)

The Employment Relations Commission's order was not limited to a determination that a prohibited labor practice had taken place in the past; it also restrains future conduct. By prohibiting the school board from "permitting employees * * * to appear and speak at meetings of the Board of Education" the order constitutes an indirect, but effective, prohibition on persons such as Holmquist from communicating with their government. The order would have a substantial impact upon virtually all communication between teachers and the school board. The order prohibits speech by teachers "on matters subject to collective bargaining." [11] As the dissenting opinion below noted, however, there is virtually no subject concerning the operation of the school system that could not also be characterized as a potential subject of collective bargaining. Teachers not only constitute the overwhelming bulk of employees of the school system, but they are the very core of that system; restraining teachers' expressions to the board on matters involving the operation of the schools would seriously impair the board's ability to govern the district. The Wisconsin court's reliance on *Broadrick v. Oklahoma,* 413 U.S. 601 (1973), for the proposition that one whose conduct falls squarely within an otherwise valid proscription may not challenge that proscription on grounds of vagueness, is inapposite. The challenged portion of the order is designed to govern speech and conduct in the future, not to punish past conduct, and as such it is the essence of prior restraint.

The judgment of the Wisconsin Supreme Court is reversed and the case is remanded to that court for further proceedings not inconsistent with this opinion.

Reversed and remanded.

MR. JUSTICE BRENNAN, with whom MR. JUSTICE MARSHALL joins, concurring in the judgment: By stating that "the extent to which the true contract negotiations may be regulated [is] an issue we need not

10. Surely no one would question the absolute right of the nonunion teachers to consult among themselves, hold meetings, reduce their views to writing, and communicate those views to the public generally in pamphlets, letters or expressions carried by the news media. It would strain First Amendment concepts extraordinarily to hold that dissident teachers could not communicate those views directly to the very decisionmaking body charged by law with making the choices raised by the contract renewal demands.

11. Counsel for the union conceded at oral argument that the WERC order was constitutionally overbroad, but asked the Court to narrow it simply to prohibit the board to negotiate with employees in the bargaining unit. It is not the function of this Court to undertake that task.

On the other hand, it is not the case that Holmquist was speaking "simply as a member of the community." On the contrary, as noted, p. 4, *supra,* Holmquist opened his remarks to the Board by stating that he represented "an informal committee of 72 teachers in 19 schools." Thus, he appeared and spoke both as an employee and a citizen exercising First Amendment rights.

consider at this time," *ante*, at 175, the Court's opinion treats as open a question the answer to which I think is abundantly clear. Wisconsin has adopted, as unquestionably the State constitutionally may adopt, a statutory policy that authorizes public bodies to accord exclusive recognition to representatives for collective bargaining chosen by the majority of an appropriate unit of employees. In that circumstance the First Amendment plainly does not forbid Wisconsin from limiting attendance at a collective-bargaining session to school board and union bargaining representatives and denying Holmquist the right to attend and speak at the session. * * *

[Concurring opinions of JUSTICES BRENNAN and STEWART are omitted.]

MINNESOTA STATE BOARD FOR COMMUNITY COLLEGES v. KNIGHT

Supreme Court of the United States, 1984.
465 U.S. 271, 104 S.Ct. 1058, 79 L.Ed.2d 299.

JUSTICE O'CONNOR delivered the opinion of the Court.

The State of Minnesota authorizes its public employees to bargain collectively over terms and conditions of employment. It also requires public employers to engage in official exchanges of views with their professional employees on policy questions relating to employment but outside the scope of mandatory bargaining. If professional employees forming an appropriate bargaining unit have selected an exclusive representative for mandatory bargaining, their employer may exchange views on nonmandatory subjects only with the exclusive representative. The question presented in these cases is whether this restriction on participation in the nonmandatory-subject exchange process violates the constitutional rights of professional employees within the bargaining unit who are not members of the exclusive representative and who may disagree with its views. We hold that it does not.

* * *

Appellees do not and could not claim that they have been unconstitutionally denied access to a public forum. A "meet and confer" session is obviously not a public forum. It is a fundamental principle of First Amendment doctrine, articulated most recently in *Perry Education Assn. v. Perry Local Educators' Assn.*, 460 U.S. 37, 45–46 (1983), that for government property to be a public forum, it must by long tradition or by government designation be open to the public at large for assembly and speech. Minnesota college administration meetings convened to obtain faculty advice on policy questions have neither by long tradition nor by government designation been open for general public participation. The District Court did not so find, 571 F.Supp., at 9, and appellees do not contend otherwise.

* * *

The Constitution does not grant to members of the public generally a right to be heard by public bodies making decisions of policy. In *Bi–*

Metallic Investment Co. v. State Board of Equalization, 239 U.S. 441 (1915), this Court rejected a claim to such a right founded on the Due Process Clause of the Fourteenth Amendment. Speaking for the Court, Justice Holmes explained:

> "Where a rule of conduct applies to more than a few people it is impracticable that every one should have a direct voice in its adoption. The Constitution does not require all public acts to be done in town meeting or an assembly of the whole. General statutes within the state power are passed that affect the person or property of individuals, sometimes to the point of ruin, without giving them a chance to be heard. Their rights are protected in the only way that they can be in a complex society, by their power, immediate or remote, over those who make the rule." *Id.,* at 445.

In *Madison Joint School District No. 8 v. Wisconsin Employment Relations Comm'n,* which sustained a First Amendment challenge to a restriction on access to a public forum, the Court recognized the soundness of Justice Holmes' reasoning outside the due process context. The Court stated: "Plainly, public bodies may confine their meetings to specified subject matter and may hold nonpublic sessions to transact business." 429 U.S., at 175, n. 8.

Policymaking organs in our system of government have never operated under a constitutional constraint requiring them to afford every interested member of the public an opportunity to present testimony before any policy is adopted. Legislatures throughout the Nation, including Congress, frequently enact bills on which no hearings have been held or on which testimony has been received from only a select group. Executive agencies likewise make policy decisions of widespread application without permitting unrestricted public testimony. Public officials at all levels of government daily make policy decisions based only on the advice they decide they need and choose to hear. To recognize a constitutional right to participate directly in government policymaking would work a revolution in existing government practices.

* * *

The academic setting of the policymaking at issue in these cases does not alter this conclusion. To be sure, there is a strong, if not universal or uniform, tradition of faculty participation in school governance, and there are numerous policy arguments to support such participation. See American Association for Higher Education—National Education Association, Faculty Participation in Academic Governance (1967); Brief for American Association of University Professors as *Amicus Curiae* 3–10. But this Court has never recognized a constitutional right of faculty to participate in policymaking in academic institutions.

* * *

Although there is no constitutional right to participate in academic governance, the First Amendment guarantees the right both to speak and to associate. Appellees' speech and associational rights, however, have not been infringed by Minnesota's restriction of participation in "meet and confer" sessions to the faculty's exclusive representative. The State has in no way restrained appellees' freedom to speak on any education-related issue or their freedom to associate or not to associate with whom they please, including the exclusive representative. Nor has the State attempted to suppress any ideas.

It is doubtless true that the unique status of the exclusive representative in the "meet and confer" process amplifies its voice in the policymaking process. But that amplification no more impairs individual instructors' constitutional freedom to speak than the amplification of individual voices impaired the union's freedom to speak in *Smith v. Arkansas State Highway Employees, supra.* Moreover, the exclusive representative's unique role in "meet and negotiate" sessions amplifies its voice as much as its unique role in "meet and confer" sessions, yet the Court summarily affirmed the District Court's approval of that role in these cases. Amplification of the sort claimed is inherent in government's freedom to choose its advisers. A person's right to speak is not infringed when government simply ignores that person while listening to others.

* * *

The District Court erred in holding that appellees had been unconstitutionally denied an opportunity to participate in their public employer's making of policy. Whatever the wisdom of Minnesota's statutory scheme for professional employee consultation on employment-related policy, in academic or other settings, the scheme violates no provision of the Constitution. The judgment of the District Court is therefore reversed.

[Justice Marshall's concurring opinion, Justice Brennan's dissenting opinion, and Justice Stevens' opinion (in which Justice Powell joined in part) are omitted.]

Question

The legislation challenged in *Knight* states the following:

Minnesota Public Employees Labor Relations Act

179A.03. Definitions

Subdivision 10. Meet and confer. "Meet and confer" means the exchange of views and concerns between the employer and their employees.

179A.08. Policy consultants

Subdivision 1. Professional employees. The legislature recognizes that professional employees possess knowledge, expertise, and dedication which is helpful and necessary to the operation and quality of public services and which may assist public employers in developing their policies. It is, therefore, the policy of this state to encourage close cooperation between public employers and professional employees by providing for discussions and the mutual exchange of ideas regarding all matters that are not terms and conditions of employment.

Subd. 2. Meet and confer. The professional employees shall select a representative to meet and confer with a representative or committee of the public employer on matters not specified under section 179A.03, subdivision 19, relating to the services being provided to the public. The public employer shall provide the facilities and set the time for these conferences to take place. The parties shall meet at least once every four months.

Do these statutory "meet and confer" provisions give new life and content to the earlier "pure" form of meet and confer legislation which was viewed as an alternative to "full" collective bargaining rights in the public sector? (For discussion of earlier meet and confer legislation, review Professor (now Judge) Harry Edwards' 1973 article earlier in this Chapter.)

E. MAINTAINING THE "STATUS QUO" DURING BARGAINING

A special issue arises in both the private and public sectors when the parties' collective bargaining agreement expires and the parties have not yet reached agreement on a successor contract. In the private sector, an employer may not unilaterally change any mandatory subject of bargaining (the scope of mandatory bargaining is covered in Chapters 4 and 5) without first negotiating these changes with the union. However, neither party may change the status quo until an impasse in bargaining is reached. These rules have generally been followed in the public sector although there have been disputes about what constitutes the "status quo," particularly when the expired contract contained features such as longevity increments (annual salary increases based upon years of service).

VIENNA SCHOOL DISTRICT NO. 55 v. ILLINOIS EDUCATIONAL LABOR RELATIONS BOARD.

Appellate Court of Illinois, Fourth District, 1987.
162 Ill.App.3d 503, 515 N.E.2d 476.

JUSTICE MCCULLOUGH delivered the opinion of the court:

The Vienna Elementary Education Association, IEA/NEA (Association), exclusive bargaining agent for Vienna teachers in Vienna School District No. 55 (District), filed charges with the Illinois Educational Labor Relations Board (Board) alleging the District's failure to provide annual incremental salary increases constituted a violation of the Illinois Educational Labor Relations Act (Act). The Board found the

District in violation of the Act for unfair labor practices. (Ill.Rev.Stat. 1985, ch. 48, pars. 1714(a)(1), (a)(5).) On appeal, the District maintains that it was not required to implement salary increments pursuant to an expired contract during collective bargaining. We disagree and affirm the Board's order.

The facts involved were not in dispute. The only issue pending was an interpretation of the "status quo" with respect to salary subsequent to expiration of the Association's employment contract. The District argues the status quo is the actual dollar amount paid under the terms of the existing contract while the Association maintains it is the salary structure.

In September of 1984, the District and Association entered into their first collective-bargaining agreement under the Act. This agreement was effective September 10, 1984, through one day prior to the beginning of the 1985–86 school term. The agreement incorporated a salary schedule which provided for incremental increases in salary. At the beginning of the new school year, teachers moved vertically along the salary schedule to reflect an additional year of experience and horizontally if they had acquired any additional education. This particular method of annual salary increments had been utilized by the District for the past 10 years and was automatically implemented prior to the opening of the new school term.

Prior to the expiration of the 1984–85 agreement, the District and Association negotiated a new contract. Negotiations for the 1985–86 contract, however, were still in progress at the beginning of the new school term. On August 15, 1985, eight days before school began, the teachers made their first salary demand. The District, however, refused to implement the annual step increments and compensated the teachers at the previous year's salary. The District continued to compensate the teachers at the 1984–85 rates until January of 1986 when negotiations for the 1985–86 collective-bargaining agreement were finally concluded. The agreement provided for step increments to be paid retroactive to the beginning of the school year.

In its order, the Board stated there was a duty to maintain the status quo during contract negotiations. Status quo, in this particular context, is a subjective determination requiring a consideration of the particular facts of the case involved. Status quo has been defined as a teacher's reasonable expectations deemed from the express provisions of the expired agreement and any relevant bargaining history and past practice. In light of the salary schedule contained in the 1984–85 agreement, and the past practice of automatically implementing annual step increments for additional education and experience, the Board found the Vienna teachers had a reasonable expectation of receiving the increase at the beginning of the 1985–86 school term. The Board further noted that withholding the expected advancements after the teachers opted to engage in collective bargaining might foster the impression of employer retaliation to collective bargaining. Thus, the

Board concluded that the District had violated the Act by unilaterally altering the status quo during contract negotiations.

* * *

The question presented here is one of first impression in Illinois. Consequently, we turn to the precedent of other jurisdictions to guide our interpretation of the State Act.

The Illinois Educational Labor Relations Act was adopted to "promote orderly and constructive relations between all educational employees and their employers" and to alleviate situations injurious to the public which are caused by educational employee-employer disputes. (Ill.Rev.Stat.1985, ch. 48, par. 1701.) An educational employer commits an unfair labor practice in violation of the Act where he interferes, restrains, or coerces employees in the exercise of rights guaranteed under the Act (Ill.Rev.Stat.1985, ch. 48, par. 1714(a)(1)), or where it refuses to bargain collectively in good faith. Ill.Rev.Stat.1985, ch. 48, par. 1714(a)(5).

In *NLRB v. Katz* (1962), 369 U.S. 736, 82 S.Ct. 1107, 8 L.Ed.2d 230, the United States Supreme Court established that an employer's unilateral alteration of prevailing terms and conditions of employment under negotiation during the course of bargaining constitutes an unlawful refusal to bargain. (*NLRB v. Katz* (1962), 369 U.S. 736, 743–47, 82 S.Ct. 1107, 1111–13, 8 L.Ed.2d 230, 236–38.) "Unilateral" changes are those alterations implemented without prior negotiation to impasse. (*NLRB v. Katz* (1962), 369 U.S. 736, 82 S.Ct. 1107, 8 L.Ed.2d 230.) Such changes are prohibited so the status quo might be maintained until new terms and conditions of employment are arrived at through bilateral negotiation and by mutual agreement. (*NLRB v. Katz* (1962), 369 U.S. 736, 82 S.Ct. 1107, 8 L.Ed.2d 230; see also *Galloway Township Board of Education v. Galloway Township Education Association* (1978), 78 N.J. 25, 393 A.2d 218.) Unilateral changes are unlawful because they frustrate the "statutory objective of establishing working conditions through bargaining." *NLRB v. Katz* (1962), 369 U.S. 736, 744, 82 S.Ct. 1107, 1112, 8 L.Ed.2d 230, 236.

A term or condition of employment is something provided by an employer which intimately and directly affects the work and welfare of the employees and which has become a mandatory subject of bargaining. (See *Board of Education of the Township of Bernards v. Bernards Township Education Association* (1979), 79 N.J. 311, 399 A.2d 620.) Typical terms and conditions include: wages (*General Motors Acceptance Corp. v. NLRB* (1st Cir.1973), 476 F.2d 850), health insurance, pension contributions (*Stone Boat Yard v. NLRB* (1983), 715 F.2d 441, *cert. denied* (1984), 466 U.S. 937, 104 S.Ct. 1910, 80 L.Ed.2d 459), life insurance, medical insurance (*In re Appeal of Cumberland Valley School District,* (1978), 483 Pa. 134, 394 A.2d 946), and hours (*School Board of Orange County v. Palowitch* (Fla.Dist.Ct.App.1979), 367 So.2d 730). During collective bargaining, an employer may not take unilateral action on these subjects absent an impasse in negotiations.

A term or condition of employment must be an established practice to constitute the status quo. The test for determining whether a specific practice is sufficiently established is objective. (See *Plasticrafts, Inc. v. NLRB* (10th Cir.1978), 586 F.2d 185.) With respect to wage increases, the focus is whether the status quo would have been clearly apparent to an objectively reasonable employer at the time in question. *Plasticrafts, Inc. v. NLRB* (10th Cir.1978), 586 F.2d 185.

Status quo requires the further consideration of the amount of discretion vested in an employer with respect to an established practice. (See *Gossen Co. v. NLRB* (7th Cir.1983), 719 F.2d 1354.) Where an employer engages in merit reviews at regular intervals with a view to granting preestablished salary increases, this is sufficient to constitute a status quo. When, however, the timing of reviews and amounts of increase is within the sole discretion of the employer with no established practice, such evaluations could not constitute a status quo. *Gossen Co. v. NLRB* (7th Cir.1983), 719 F.2d 1354.

Finally, in determining the status quo, it is necessary to consider the reasonable expectations of the employees in the continuance of existing terms and conditions of employment. (*Indiana Education Employment Relations Board v. Mill Creek Classroom Teachers Association* (Ind.1983), 456 N.E.2d 709.) Where employees receive regular salary increases based upon years of service or additional education, it is reasonable for employees to expect these increments even though negotiations for a new contract are still pending. *Indiana Education Employment Relations Board v. Mill Creek Classroom Teachers Association* (Ind.1983), 456 N.E.2d 709.

In a situation factually analogous to this case, the Indiana Supreme Court found that failure to grant teachers annual salary increments pending negotiations constituted an unfair labor practice. The court specifically noted:

> "Other jurisdictions have found that school corporations are legally required to pay wage increments which are part of an existing contract in order to maintain the status quo pending negotiation of a new contract. *Nassau Teachers Association v. School Board of Nassau County,* 8 FPER ¶ 13206 (Fla.1982); *In the Matter of Communications Workers of America & State of New Jersey,* 7 NJPER ¶ 12235 (N.J.1981); *California School Employees Association v. Davis Unified School District,* 4 PERC ¶ 11031 (Cal. 1980); *Springfield Board of Education v. Springfield Educational Association,* 47 Ill.App.3d 193, 5 Ill.Dec. 374, 361 N.E.2d 697, 95 LRRM 3000 (4th DCA 1977); *NLRB v. Allied Products Corp.,* 548 F.2d 644, 94 LRRM 2433 (6th Cir.1977)." (*Indiana Education Employment Relations Board v. Mill Creek Classroom Teachers Association* (Ind.1983), 456 N.E.2d 709, 712.)

See also *Galloway Township Board of Education v. Galloway Township Educational Association* (1978), 78 N.J. 25, 393 A.2d 218 (failure to pay annual step increments during collective bargaining constitutes refusal to bargain).

The salary increments herein were clearly a term and condition of employment which were unilaterally altered during contract negotiations. All parties agreed that the alteration occurred without prior negotiation to impasse. The step salary increments had been utilized by the District for some 10 years. It was an established practice. The evaluations were completely objective based upon years of experience and education attained. The evaluations were conducted annually prior to the beginning of each school term. There was little discretion afforded the District. Consequently, it was reasonable for the Vienna teachers to expect salary increases prior to the beginning of the 1985–86 school year based upon education and experience. The status quo required such yearly evaluations. By withholding the salary increments, the District unilaterally altered the status quo. The precedent from other jurisdictions is in accord.

* * *

The policy underlying the Act, as well as the weight of authority from other jurisdictions, supports the concept of status quo which includes an evaluation of past history, past bargaining practice, existing contract terms and the reasonable expectations of the employees. This concept prevents unfair bargaining tactics on behalf of the employer and promotes effective negotiations. We note, however, that this concept of status quo involves a subjective determination and, as such, must be made on a case-by-case basis.

Affirmed.

SPITZ, P.J., and GREEN, J., concur.

Questions

1. The result reached in this case has been referred to as the "dynamic status quo." The holding has also been called the *Triborough* doctrine after a 1977 New York State Public Employment Relations Board case involving the Triborough Bridge and Tunnel Authority, 5 P.E.R.B. ¶ 4505, *affirmed* 5 P.E.R.B. 3037 (1972). The New York State Legislature later codified the Board's decision into law. New York Civil Service Law § 209–a.1(e). Does the doctrine alter the dynamics of bargaining in favor of public employees? Does the opposite rule (referred to as the "static status quo") adopted by some jurisdictions tip the balance in favor of public employers?

2. In Illinois and other jurisdictions which reach similar results, may the parties negotiate an agreement which expressly limits the negotiated salary schedule to the stated term of the agreement and thus place themselves outside of the reach of the doctrine? In New York State, the Board has answered yes. See *Suffolk County and Faculty Association of Suffolk County Community College,* 18 P.E.R.B. ¶ 3030 (1985).

3. The *Triborough* doctrine is limited to the mandatory subjects of bargaining. However, its codification by the legislature was not. The

statute specified that it is an improper practice to fail to continue *all* the terms of an expired agreement until a new agreement is reached. This applies to permissive as well as mandatory subjects; the employer is thus required to continue all of the agreement's provisions, even those which cover nonmandatory topics.

The failure of the codification of *Triborough* to distinguish between permissive and mandatory subjects creates difficult problems in states like New York which mandate procedures for the resolution of impasses over interest disputes. These issues are discussed in Chapter 8.

F. BARGAINING STRATEGY

Are efforts to resolve disputes by negotiations significantly facilitated by rules and regulations? Roger Fisher and William Ury make the case for what they call "principled negotiation." They define that term as the process of deciding uses by examining the parties' needs rather than through a haggling process focused on what each side says it will and will not do. Principled negotiation suggests that you look for mutual gains whenever possible, and that where your interests conflict, you should insist that the result be based on some fair standards independent of the will of either side. Fisher and Ury, "Getting to Yes," Penguin Books, 1983.

Do decisions as to whether the parties are negotiating in good faith and if not, how they should behave, have anything to do with the question of whether negotiations produce settlements?

In the following example, the Chief Negotiator for the State of New York worked from erroneous assumptions about the law governing good faith negotiations. (He asserted that the State might terminate payment of health care premiums when the current agreement expired unless a successor contract had been reached. Later decisions established that this was probably an unfair labor practice under the *Triborough* doctrine.) Yet the State negotiator reached an agreement with the unions without great difficulty and with little travail.

Is this an example of what Fisher is talking about or was the state's negotiator just lucky?

WOLLETT, STRATEGIES FOR NEGOTIATIONS IN AN AUSTERE ENVIRONMENT: A MANAGEMENT PERSPECTIVE *

27 Lab L.J. 504 (1976).

* * *

Assume the following facts: Inflation has sent the costs of government up; recession has impaired the growth of revenues; the tax base

* Reproduced from the August, 1976, issue of the Labor Law Journal published and copyrighted 1976 by Commerce Clearing House, Inc., 4025 W. Peterson Ave., Chicago, Ill. 60646

has shrunk; hidden legacies of past mismanagement have been uncovered. In fiscal 1975–76 there was a serious budgetary gap between income and expenditures. The projected budget for 1976–77 is balanced, but precariously. Salary and fringe-benefit demands cannot be met without drastically curtailing services to the public or seeking major increases in a severely burdensome tax structure. Given these fiscal realities, state management's objective at the bargaining table is to yield nothing or next to nothing without provoking job action.

This has been the setting for negotiation in New York State. In the hope that our experiences may have general and instructive value, I propose to tell you how we operated.

Our strategies were predicated upon two articles of faith. First, collective bargaining is a flexible instrumentality that can be made to work in an austere environment. Second, trade unions and the employees whom they present will take "no" for an answer provided they are persuaded that (a) the economic crisis is "real," (b) they have a stake in the solution of the economic problems of the governmental enterprise, and (c) they are not being singled out, not being discriminated against—that sacrifice is being shared by all, not fastened upon a few.

* * *

Management Self-Discipline

The operational and structural arrangements should be similar to those that obtain in the private sector. The dimensions of the chief negotiator's authority should be derived directly from the governor. The sole responsibility to deal with the unions and the authority within those dimensions to make agreements should be fixed in the negotiator. End runs should be prohibited. The governor must set the tone. His door should be shut to the unions; only the chief negotiator's door should be open. This rule should apply to all top gubernatorial aides and agency heads.

Management must also maintain internal discipline. Let me give a personal example. On February 2, 1976, Albany was hit by a blizzard. Many employees were unable to get to work. The Director of State Operations decided that state offices in the Albany area should be shut down. The question then arose as to whether or not the day of absence should be counted against employee leave accruals, specifically five-day personal leave. Historically, so-called snow days have been counted, time off has been recorded as personal-leave time, and employees who manage to get to work are not entitled to compensatory time off. This time one of the governor's key advisers, in the belief that reversal of past practice would redound to the governor's political advantage, persuaded him to take that position.

Since we had a proposal on the bargaining table to reduce the five days' personal leave time to three days, and since the effect of the governor's decision was to add a day, our position at the bargaining table on this matter was fatally undermined. * * *

A TOTAL STRATEGY

Management must keep in mind at all times the impact of agreements with one union on the political imperatives of other unions. The twin phenomena of "me-too-ism" and "one-ups-manship" belong in the forefront of the bargaining strategy. State police troopers will not accept less money than prison guards; prison guards will want some advantage over maintenance workers; registered nurses will want more than licensed vocational nurses; * * *.

In New York State we * * * have five broad horizontal units that cut across agency and departmental lines:

Administrative Services Unit, 40,000 employees; represented by the Civil Service Employees Association (CSEA); communication equipment operators, examiners, office support staff, such as secretarial and clerical personnel.

Institutional Services Unit 47,000 employees; represented by CSEA; employees providing therapeutic and custodial care to persons in state institutions, *e.g.,* therapy aides.

Operational Services Unit, 25,000 employees; represented by CSEA; craft workers, maintenance and repair personnel and machine operators.

Professional, Scientific, and Technical Services Unit, 39,000 employees; represented by CSEA; employees who are primarily licensed professionals, *e.g.,* engineers, cartographers, kosher-food inspectors, bursars, psychiatrists.

Security Services Unit, 9,000 employees; represented by Council 82, American Federation of State, County and Municipal Employees; prison guards and security personnel other than state troopers, such as narcotic correction officers, lifeguards, and park and parkway patrolmen.

We have three vertical units:

*State University Professional Services * * * Unit,* 18,000 employees; represented by the United University Professions, Inc., affiliated with the American Federation of Teachers, AFL–CIO; all faculty and nonteaching professional staff of the State University system, including faculty, librarians, bursars, guidance counselors, environmental health and safety officers, museum curators, and pharmacists.

State Police Troopers, 3,300 employees; represented by the State Police Benevolent Association, all noncommissioned officers, investigators, and troopers of the Division of State Police.

State Police Officers, 100 employees; represented by CSEA; all captains, lieutenants, and majors in the Division of State Police

* * *

Management must reduce employee expectations to realistic levels, thus making it possible for union representatives to take acceptable positions and survive politically. This is a subliminal strategy that requires a public relations campaign designed to implant in the public subconscious the fiscal setting of the negotiations. * * *

Our theme was austerity—belt-tightening and survival. We were benefited by the continuous financial crisis in New York City with its fall-out impact on the state's fiscal situation, as well as such threatening events as a 3 percent reduction in force at the start of the fourth quarter of the fiscal year. Obviously, these events were not a part of any plan, but were fortuitous circumstances that worked to create a climate hospitable to low-cost settlement. However, we arranged for frequent repetition of the theme by as many sources as we could reach. * * *

We did two other things: First, we developed a set of affirmative management demands, utilizing the labor-relations directors of state agencies to set forth the felt needs of their operational people. We carefully sifted these, resolved inconsistencies, removed ambiguities, and excised all demands except those which could be justified by compelling operational problems or by a desire to return specified state benefits to comparable levels in the private sector. We initiated negotiations instead of waiting for the unions to come to us, and we publicized them in the media at the outset, making such statements as:

"The State has presented a set of proposals to eliminate employee benefits which exceed those found in the private sector. A report from the Division of the Budget demonstrates that some employee benefits are excessive. For instance, in the first year of State service a new employee is entitled to 42 days of leave with pay, including five days of personal leave. In 1974–75 paid leave, not including time off for union business, cost the State $384 million. There can be some dollar savings in this area and some increases in productivity by recapturing 14 million man-hours of work without increasing the number of State employees who presently work 37 hours a week to 40 hours a week. Our proposals will save the State $28½ million in out-of-pocket costs."

Finally, we gave public exposure to unrealistic positions taken by the unions where we felt that it was warranted. Thus, when the Civil Service Employees Association proposed salary increases ranging from 25 to 36 percent at an aggregate cost to the state of $460 million per annum, we did not hesitate to issue a critical press release, pointing out that these demands could not be met without raising taxes by that amount or laying off over 40,000 employees (or some combination of the two). Without exception, mass media editorial comment urged CSEA to abandon these unrealistic positions and adjust to the realities of the bargaining environment.

Risks

Management must be prepared to take risks. First, there is the risk of unpopularity.

* * *

A second risk is legal. The execution of strategies which are conceived to be sound from a labor relations point of view should not be inhibited by legal doctrines of doubtful validity, e.g., *Triborough.*

* * *

Finally, if public management is to pursue aggressive strategies, it must take a hard look at the possibility of strike action and be prepared to take a strike if bargaining objectives cannot otherwise be attained.

* * *

Realistic Expectations

Management must prepare to meet employee expectations that are realistic. Management should identify those areas of significant employee concern about which something can be done, thus creating feasible trade-offs without violating fiscal constraints or crippling operations. Three illustrations drawn from our recent New York experience make the point.

(1) A long-standing grievance of the members of the Operational Services Unit stems from the practice of discriminating against labor-class employees who are laid off. Employees in other classes have the right, after one year of credited service, to be laid off pursuant to seniority rules and to be placed on a preferred rehiring list. Labor-class employees do not acquire these rights until they have five years of credited service. The reason for the discrimination is political—a management desire to be free to lay off and rehire on the basis of patronage considerations.

(2) Some members of the Administrative Services Unit felt sorely abused when the New York State Lottery was abruptly closed last December because of defects in the conception and management of the "game plan," and all the employees were laid off with three weeks' notice.

(3) The correctional officers in the Security Services Unit have jammed our grievance docket with cases claiming that work directly affecting the health, safety, or security of inmates has improperly been assigned from time to time to civilian personnel, thus depriving prison guards of overtime opportunities and, according to their allegations, creating hazardous conditions.

A management that is pushing for a no-cost settlement must be prepared to make concessions with respect to matters of this sort.

Timetables

Where multiple sets of negotiations are in progress, management must work to a timetable. What should be the order of settlement?

In orthodox whipsaw strategy, you would go after the weakest adversary first. But this will not work here because patterns established with weak unions are not likely to have any impact on strong unions. What is needed is agreement with a union that has clout.

In our case we turned to the PBA, representing the State Police troopers. There were four reasons for this. First, PBA had just stood off an election challenge to its status as the bargaining representative by a three-to-one margin. As a consequence, it was secure. Second, PBA has strong, effective, and realistic leadership. Third, the State Police have a proud history of rising to emergencies. Fourth, they have a strong professional (no-strike) tradition and are held together by the amalgam of a nomadic and hazardous job.

The choice proved to be a wise one. The agreement with PBA established a pattern of extending the operative provisions of the present agreement, with no increase in the salary schedule or in fringe benefits. The only economic benefit was to service the present salary schedule by paying increments to eligible employees (which amounts to an increase in the aggregate payroll of about 1.25 percent).

The Memorandum of Agreement with PBA was signed February 9, 1976. The pattern was extended to the four units of 147,000 employees represented by the Civil Service Employees Association on March 12, and was accepted by Council 82 of AFSCME, representing the 9,000 members of the Security Service Unit, on April 29. Thus, the pattern is now established in six of the eight units (160,000 employees) with whom we have collective bargaining relationships.

The price for these settlements was to meet some of the employee concerns which neither pierced our fiscal ceiling nor crippled operations. Thus, we agreed to nondiscriminatory treatment of labor-class employees; to give notice of closedowns of agencies, facilities, and major departments; to create a committee to deal with labor-displacement problems patterned after the Armour Automation Committee established in the meat packing industry in 1959; to give permanent employees preference over provisional and temporary employees in layoff situations; and, except in emergencies, to assign correctional officers' work in the prison system to members of the Security Services Unit.

And, of course, we traded away most of our affirmative management demands.

Do These Strategies Work?

This question cannot be answered categorically.

It is clear, as far as our experience in New York State is concerned, that we complied with our marching orders and achieved our objectives: no increases in salary schedules or fringe benefits; some concessions in areas of special concern to employees, concerns which could be met with little or no cost; no job actions, with our collective bargaining systems alive and well.

It is not clear that these strategies were a *sine qua non* of ending up on target. * * * Nor can one accurately assess the long range consequences of pursuing these strategies. In this business there is always next year, and the question remains: "Did we pay too high a price in terms of employee morale and attitudes?" It is axiomatic that sometimes a deal is too tight and results in consequences that cost more than the agreement is worth. My judgment is that the price was about right. My evidence is the ratification-vote results, which were as follows:

Sixty-three percent of the State Police troopers approved the agreement.

In the four basic CSEA units, one agreement was ratified three-to-one, another two-to-one, a third five-to-two, and the final one seven-to-five.

The Security Services Unit agreement has not yet been ratified, but the 24 members of the negotiating committee approved it unanimously, suggesting that it has broad-based political support.

These data are by no means conclusive, but I find them reassuring, as I do the fact that our relationships with the union leaders seem to me to have been improved by our experiences in the crucible of hard bargaining.

There is also the question of the political cost to the first Democratic administration in New York State in 16 years. I do not feel competent to answer this question, although it does seem clear to me that our negotiations next year must turn to more constructive and dynamic directions than we have managed in the past two years of fiscal crisis.

Notes and Questions

1. Under different economic circumstances, would you recommend a different management strategy?

2. What are effective union strategies to deal with this type of management strategy?

3. Another approach to analyzing strategic choices in bargaining starts with the proposition that each side's bargaining strength is based on the other side's perceptions respecting the elements of bargaining power. Thus, Side A's bargaining strength is increased if Side B perceives that A is offering to meet more of B's needs. (In such a situation B has an increased motivation to accept A's offer.) This element, A's offer to meet B's needs, is modified by the extent to which Side B perceives that A has a high or low probability of performing on its promises. Bargaining strength is diminished, on the other hand, to the extent that the other side perceives that it has attractive alternatives to the proposed agreement and to the extent that it perceives that it faces high costs of continued negotiating before agreement will be reached. It is also diminished if the other side has a high level of confidence in its ability to assess the value of its alternatives and costs of impending negotiations. Hence, a goal of effective bargaining tactics is to

alter the other side's perceptions regarding one or more of these elements of bargaining power so as to swing the balance further in the direction of one's own interests. See A. Goldman, *Settling for More: Mastering Negotiating Strategies and Techniques* (BNA Books 1991).

To what extent, if any, does the above model for analyzing bargaining dynamics help explain the preceding New York bargaining experience?

Chapter 4

SCOPE OF BARGAINING

A. HISTORY AND TERMINOLOGY

WEISBERGER, THE APPROPRIATE SCOPE OF BARGAINING IN THE PUBLIC SECTOR: THE CONTINUING CONTROVERSY AND THE WISCONSIN EXPERIENCE

1977 WIS.L.REV. 685.

Deciding what issues should be resolved by labor-management negotiations has been controversial from the time collective bargaining was first proposed for public employees. Much of the heated debate which has surrounded the beginnings of public sector bargaining during the past decade has centered upon this problem of public policy.[2] Not only has this key aspect of the collective bargaining process evoked intense interest in state legislatures whenever public sector collective bargaining legislation is first introduced, but the controversy will continue unabated before administrative agencies and state courts in an increasing number of jurisdictions when parties litigating cases raise conflicting policy arguments in their efforts to secure favorable administrative or judicial rulings on the appropriate scope of bargaining in a wide variety of situations facing public employees and employers. No consensus is yet evident. * * *

* * *

Basically, the issue of the scope of bargaining deals with conditions of employment which may (or may not) be appropriately resolved by

2. *See* P. Prasow, Scope of Bargaining in the Public Sector—Concepts and Problems (U.S. Dep't of Labor 1972) [hereinafter cited as Prasow]; H. Wellington & R. Winter, Jr., The Unions and The Cities (1971); Blair, *State Legislative Control Over the Conditions of Public Employment: Defining the Scope of Collective Bargaining for State and Municipal Employees,* 26 Vand.L.Rev. 1 (1973) [hereinafter cited as Blair]; Edwards, *The Emerging Duty to Bargain in the Public Sector,* 71 Mich. L.Rev. 885 (1973); Wollett, *The Bargaining Process in the Public Sector: What is Bargainable?,* 51 Ore.L.Rev. 177 (1971).

Public sector employees, from the very beginning of public sector bargaining, have pushed hard to obtain a wide scope of bargaining, unlike their private sector counterparts.

labor and management utilizing the negotiations process. In the private sector, the National Labor Relations Act established a duty to bargain for covered employers, but did not enumerate the specific subjects over which bargaining must take place. Despite congressional attempts to legislate an explicit list of bargainable subjects,[5] the role of defining the required subjects has been assumed by the National Labor Relations Board, the agency established in 1935 to administer federal labor policies for the private sector. From its early years on, the Board issued a number of decisions, in the context of adjudicatory administrative proceedings, interpreting what elements of the employment relationship were covered by the requirement in the National Labor Relations Act that there be bargaining over "wages, hours, or other working conditions."

In *NLRB v. Wooster Division of the Borg–Warner Corp.*,[8] the United States Supreme Court affirmed and adopted the approach of the Board and the circuit courts of appeals in classifying subjects of bargaining as mandatory (the subjects over which labor and management *must* bargain), permissive (the subjects over which labor and management *may* bargain), and illegal or prohibited (the subjects over which labor and management *cannot* bargain). The analysis of scope in terms of mandatory, permissive, and prohibited subjects of bargaining has been criticized but it continues to be applied by the Board and the courts. Decisions subsequent to *Borg–Warner* have attempted to clarify and apply the very general guidelines adopted by the majority in *Borg–Warner.* Litigation before the Board and the courts continues to raise novel scope issues which test the meaning of *Borg–Warner.* Recent split decisions among decisionmakers in both administrative and judicial forums indicate a lack of consensus in this area of private sector labor law although the *Borg–Warner* terminology clearly controls both the majorities and the dissenters.

Meanwhile, in the public sector, there is a recurring question as to whether it is appropriate to utilize the *Borg–Warner* analysis, particularly in the permissive category for bargainable subjects. The main public sector justification for excluding a legal topic from the mandated bargaining process is that the demand involves a significant public policy question which should not be determined in the isolation of the bargaining process in which other vital public interests are not directly represented. If a topic is "too significant" to be classified as a mandato-

5. In 1947, a majority of the House Committee on Labor and Education and of the full House supported a bill listing definitively the subjects of bargaining. *See* Feinsinger, *The National Labor Relations Act and Collective Bargaining,* 57 Mich. L.Rev. 807 (1959) for a history of § 8(d).

8. 356 U.S. 342 (1958). The employer had insisted that the collective bargaining agreement include (1) a recognition clause solely with the local union as bargaining representative and not with the parent international although only the latter had received Board certification, and (2) a ballot clause which required a secret ballot vote of all members of the bargaining unit on the employer's last offer. If rejected, the employer would have 72 hours to modify its position followed by a repetition of the voting process. Only after these procedures were exhausted would the union be free to strike.

ry subject of bargaining, does it make any sense to say it may be bargained about if labor and management agree? * * * [T]his argument has exerted some influence on legislation and decisional law covering public employees although few legislatures, administrative agencies, or courts have chosen to eliminate the permissive category from public sector bargaining and adopt instead a system of classifying bargaining demands as mandatory or illegal only.

When a bargaining demand is labelled mandatory, permissive, or prohibited, certain well-established legal consequences result under interpretations of the National Labor Relations Act. First, during negotiations for a labor agreement, one party has a legal right to refuse to bargain over the opposing party's demand if that demand is permissive. No party may refuse to bargain over a mandatory demand. Second, if a party insists upon a permissive demand to the point of impasse or utilizes a primary economic strike or lock-out to support a permissive bargaining demand in the face of the opposing party's lack of consent to negotiate, the Board will find a violation of the statutory duty to bargain. A mandatory demand, however, may be pushed to impasse and may be supported by a primary economic strike or lock-out. Third, either party at any time may implement unilaterally any matter which is labelled permissive, in the absence of a contract provision restricting that right. A mandatory matter may not be implemented unilaterally unless a contract provision explicitly gives a party the right to take unilateral action or the opposing party has by some other act waived his right to insist upon bargaining over the mandatory matter. In the public sector where public employees are prohibited from striking and the negotiation processes are subjected to mandated impasse procedures when there is a breakdown in negotiations, must not the legal consequences flowing from the labelling of bargaining demands be modified?

In addition to devising guidelines for labelling bargaining demands and attaching consequences to the classification, other legal doctrines have been developed under the National Labor Relations Act to delineate the scope of the bargaining duty. For example, managerial decisions to subcontract, to automate, to relocate, or to close down a business operation in whole or in part have been subjected to special scrutiny by the Board and the courts to determine whether or not such decisions should be subjected to a bargaining requirement. In *Fibreboard Paper Products Corp. v. NLRB,*[14] a majority of the United States Supreme Court pragmatically stressed the suitability of the negotiations process to resolve one employer's economic problems if the employer wished to substitute a subcontractor's employees for the regular maintenance workers. Particularly since there was extensive industrial experience negotiating subcontracting clauses with unions and a likelihood that bargaining discussions on the problem could be fruitful, the majority did not hesitate to impose a bargaining duty. The concur-

14. 379 U.S. 203 (1964).

ring opinion emphasized that the majority's holding was limited to situations where "larger entrepreneurial questions" were not involved. There has been much post-*Fibreboard* litigation testing its meaning and application to a wide range of managerial decisions. In general, the approach of the concurring opinion has been adopted by the circuit courts of appeals and, more recently, by the Board. * * *

* * *

Although, under *Fibreboard* and subsequent cases, a "basic" managerial decision will not be held to be a mandatory subject of bargaining if it is made for an economic reason, in all instances the effects or impact of a "basic" managerial decision upon the affected employees' terms and conditions of employment will be subjected to a bargaining requirement. Effects bargaining, bargaining over the rights of employees whose employment status will be altered by the managerial decision, may include such questions as severance pay, order of layoffs, recall or preferential employment rights, and layoff or termination notification procedures. If work is to be shifted to other workers, mandated effects bargaining will also include the impact of these changes upon the retained employees' terms and conditions of employment. * * *

* * *

Some prominent practitioners and researchers have suggested that the legal doctrines relating to scope of bargaining described briefly above have been unduly emphasized. They point to many instances where the legal doctrine rarely determined what was actually bargained. For these pragmatists, there is little practical difference between a mandatory and a permissive demand because bargaining outcomes depend upon bargaining power and pressures and not upon technical legal distinctions. Thus, if a public employee union is strong enough to exert effective pressure, often political, then it will be successful in securing desired concessions regardless of the labels attached to bargaining demands. Similarly, weak unions will be unable to secure agreement at the bargaining table upon admittedly mandatory demands despite the presence of a duty to bargain. Indeed, even prohibited demands may be secured by effective union bargaining since legislation may be enacted to modify existing statutory constraints.

Any person knowledgeable about the dynamics of collective bargaining must acknowledge that there is much truth in the above-stated position that, in many instances, bargaining results are not primarily determined by the legal rules related to the scope of bargaining. This does not mean, however, that the law which defines scope is irrelevant to the bargaining process. At the very least, legal scope doctrines may be used tactically by one or both parties during the bargaining process to manipulate timing and secure delays. The large volume of public sector scope litigation is one clear-cut indication that legal scope determinations must indeed play some role in the bargaining process. At times, legal doctrines relating to scope may be used as a sword by a weak union or weak management to provide additional bargaining leverage or as a shield to provide some protection against granting undesired bargaining concessions. Moreover, in the "real" bargaining world, parties usually seek to arrange workable tradeoffs. These may be easier to arrange when there is a broad scope of bargaining which gives the parties greater flexibility. For a variety of reasons, therefore, it appears reasonable to assume that the "legalities" do play some role in most bargaining relationships although it is not clear what specific effects the legal rules on scope may have on the actual bargaining process.

* * *

When collective bargaining was first contemplated and introduced into the public sector, the differences between the private and public sectors tended to be emphasized. Special features of the public sector were often stressed and policy arguments relating to its uniqueness were particularly popular in debates over the appropriate scope of bargaining.

* * *

During the initial phase of considering public sector collective bargaining legislation, policy arguments concerning uniqueness produced an array of legislative solutions which usually rejected the National Labor Relations Act formulation in favor of some experiments with substantive scope restrictions. Statutory formulations of management rights became an integral part of some enabling legislation to protect public officials from being required to bargain on specified subjects or to prohibit officials from bargaining on these enumerated subjects. In other instances, the public sector collective bargaining statutes were drafted to include different explicit restrictions on scope or they set forth an exclusive list of items subject to the bargaining requirement. Several statutes were drawn to include explicit guarantees that if a conflict arose between the collective bargaining obligation and other legislated obligations, the latter would prevail. Private sector terminology was usually rejected or combined with new language to form hybrid variations.

* * *

During the period following legislative enactment, significant scope litigation has been initiated in virtually every jurisdiction. In contrast, in the private sector, scope litigation was rarely engaged in either during the period immediately following enactment of the National Labor Relations Act or during the initial stage of a bargaining relationship. During the second phase of defining the scope of public sector bargaining, administrative agency or court rulings have been sought to clarify the limitations of the statutory language adopted. This is true regardless of whether scope has been described using National Labor Relations Act terminology, statutory management rights provisions, listings of specified mandatory subjects of bargaining and exclusions from bargaining, or hybrid provisions which have been fashioned which combine features of each.

Notes and Questions

1. In *First National Maintenance Corp. v. NLRB,* 452 U.S. 666, 101 S.Ct. 2573, 69 L.Ed.2d 318 (1981), the Court held that an employer could terminate a contract with a customer without first bargaining with the union representing the discharged employees about this decision. The Court's majority expressed its concern for the employer's need for speed, flexibility, and secrecy which, in its view, outweighed the possible advantage to be gained from the bargaining process. The Court articulated a balancing test to determine the appropriate scope of mandatory bargaining required by the NLRA: the benefits for labor-management relations by requiring bargaining must be greater than the burden placed upon an employer being subjected to the bargaining requirement. In the required balancing, special weight was given to the employer interests to be free from bargaining constraints "for the running of a profitable business" but, in order for an employee interest to be considered in the balancing, it must be found to "vitally affect wages, hours, and other terms and conditions of employment."

The NLRB and reviewing courts have applied *First National Maintenance* in some cases to conclude that management decisions such as plant relocations, sales, and partial plant closing are not subject to mandatory bargaining (even though their effects or impact remain mandatory subjects of bargaining to the extent that they affect "wages, hours, and other terms and conditions of employment"). Recently, the NLRB formulated new and more expansive standards to determine when an employer must bargain about a decision to relocate. It noted, however, that unusual circumstances might require an expedited employer decision and, in such situations, an employer might not be required to bargain over a relocation decision or the bargaining may be foreshortened. *Dubuque Packing Co.,* (Dubuque II) 303 N.L.R.B. No. 66 (1991).

Based upon shifting private sector decisions, this area of labor law remains unstable. Predictability of outcomes in court review of NLRB scope determinations is even more difficult because some reviewing court decisions give great, express deference to the NLRB's expertise while others follow a more activist path giving little, if any, deference to the administrative agency's decisions.

In the public sector, the judicial response to scope litigation is also difficult to predict. Diverse statutory language covering scope of bargaining in the public sector accounts for some of the significant differences in results. However, even after public sector bargaining has been in place for several decades, there are few discernible stable trends in legislation or judicial interpretation. Some legislatures and courts continue to use and apply private sector terminology and concepts (such as mandatory, permissive, and prohibited subjects) while others have fashioned unique doctrines for the public sector. (For an example of the latter, see infra page 159 for New Jersey's judicial approach to scope of bargaining in the public sector.)

2. What are the reasons which support a scope of bargaining for public employees which is broader than the scope of bargaining for private sector employees? What reasons support a scope of bargaining for public employees which is narrower than the scope of bargaining for private sector employees?

3. Can parties realistically separate a requirement that they must only bargain over the effects of a management decision from a requirement that they bargain about the decision itself?

B. STATUTORY DIVERSITY

WISCONSIN STATE EMPLOYMENT RELATIONS ACT

111.90 Management rights. Nothing in this subchapter shall interfere with the right of the employer, in accordance with this subchapter to:

(1) Carry out the statutory mandate and goals assigned to the agency utilizing personnel, methods and means in the most appropriate and efficient manner possible.

(2) Manage the employes of the agency; hire, promote, transfer, assign or retain employes in positions within the agency; and in that regard establish reasonable work rules.

(3) Suspend, demote, discharge or take other appropriate disciplinary action against the employe for just cause; or to lay off employes in the event of lack of work or funds or under conditions where continuation of such work would be inefficient and nonproductive.

History: 1971 c. 270.

111.91 Subjects of bargaining. (1)(a) Except as provided in pars. (b) to (e), matters subject to collective bargaining to the point of impasse are wage rates, consistent with sub. (2), the assignment and reassignment of classifications to pay ranges, determination of an incumbent's pay status resulting from position reallocation or reclassification, and pay adjustments upon temporary assignment of classified employes to duties of a higher classification or downward reallocations of a classified employe's position; fringe benefits consistent with sub. (2); hours and conditions of employment.

(b) The employer shall not be required to bargain on management rights under § 111.90, except that procedures for the adjustment or settlement of grievances or disputes arising out of any type of disciplinary action referred to in § 111.90(3) shall be a subject of bargaining.

(c) The employer is prohibited from bargaining on matters contained in sub. (2).

(cm) Except as provided in sub. (2)(g) and (h) and §§ 40.02(22)(e) and 40.23(1)(f)4, all laws governing the Wisconsin retirement system under ch. 40 and all actions of the employer that are authorized under any such law which apply to nonrepresented individuals employed by the state shall apply to similarly situated employes, unless otherwise specifically provided in a collective bargaining agreement that applies to those employes.

(d) Demands relating to retirement and group insurance shall be submitted to the employer at least one year prior to commencement of negotiations.

(e) The employer shall not be required to bargain on matters related to employe occupancy of houses or other lodging provided by the state.

(2) The employer is prohibited from bargaining on:

(a) The mission and goals of state agencies as set forth in the statutes.

(b) Policies, practices and procedures of the civil service merit system relating to:

1. Original appointments and promotions specifically including recruitment, examinations, certification, policies with respect to probationary periods and appointments, but not including transfers between positions allocated to classifications that are assigned to the same pay range or an identical pay range in a different pay schedule, within the same collective bargaining unit or another collective bargaining unit represented by the same labor organization.

2. The job evaluation system specifically including position classification and reclassification, position qualification standards, establishment and abolition of classifications, and allocation and reallocation of positions to classifications; and the determination of an incumbent's status, other than pay status, resulting from position reallocations.

(c) Disciplinary actions and position abandonments governed by § 230.34(1)(a), (am) and (ar), except as provided in those paragraphs.

(d) Amendments to this subchapter.

(e) Matters related to grants made by the department of transportation under § 85.107(3)(b).

(f) Family leave and medical leave rights below the minimum afforded under § 103.10. Nothing in this paragraph prohibits the employer from bargaining on rights to family leave or medical leave which are more generous to the employe than the rights provided under § 103.10.

(g) An increase in benefit adjustment contribution rates under § 40.05(2n)(a)3.

(h) The rights of employes to have retirement benefits computed under § 40.30.

WISCONSIN MUNICIPAL EMPLOYMENT RELATIONS ACT

111.70 Municipal employment. (1) Definitions. As used in this subchapter:

(a) "Collective bargaining" means the performance of the mutual obligation of a municipal employer, through its officers and agents, and the representatives of its employes, to meet and confer at reasonable times, in good faith, with the intention of reaching an agreement, or to resolve questions arising under such an agreement, with respect to wages, hours and conditions of employment, and with respect to a requirement of the municipal employer for a municipal employe to perform law enforcement and fire fighting services under § 61.66, except as provided in § 40.81(3) and except that a municipal employer shall not meet and confer with respect to any proposal to diminish or abridge the rights guaranteed to municipal employes under ch. 164. The duty to bargain, however, does not compel either party to agree to a proposal or require the making of a concession. Collective bargaining includes the reduction of any agreement reached to a written and signed document. The employer shall not be required to bargain on subjects reserved to management and direction of the governmental unit except insofar as the manner of exercise of such functions affects the wages, hours and conditions of employment of the employes. In creating this subchapter the legislature recognizes that the public employer must exercise its powers and responsibilities to act for the government and good order of the municipality, its commercial benefit and the health, safety and welfare of the public to assure orderly operations and functions within its jurisdiction, subject to those rights secured to public employes by the constitutions of this state and of the United States and by this subchapter.

NEW YORK CIVIL SERVICE LAW

§ 201

4. The term "terms and conditions of employment" means salaries, wages, hours, agency shop fee deduction and other terms and conditions of employment provided, however, that such term shall not include agency shop fee deduction for negotiating units comprised of employees of the state or any benefits provided by or to be provided by a public retirement system, or payments to a fund or insurer to provide an income for retirees, or payment to retirees or their beneficiaries. No such retirement benefits shall be negotiated pursuant to this article, and any benefits so negotiated shall be void.

ILLINOIS PUBLIC LABOR RELATIONS ACT

Section 4. Management rights.—Employers shall not be required to bargain over matters of inherent managerial policy, which shall include such areas of discretion or policy as the functions of the employer, standards of services, its overall budget, the organizational structure and selection of new employees, examination techniques and direction of employees. Employers, however, shall be required to bargain collectively with regard to policy matters directly affecting wages, hours and terms and conditions of employment as well as the impact thereon upon request by employee representatives.

* * *

Section 7. Duty to bargain.—A public employer and the exclusive representative have the authority and the duty to bargain collectively set forth in this Section.

For the purposes of this Act, "to bargain collectively" means the performance of the mutual obligation of the public employer or his designated representative and the representative of the public employees to meet at reasonable times, including meetings in advance of the budget-making process, and to negotiate in good faith with respect to wages, hours, and other conditions of employment, not excluded by Section 4 of this Act, or the negotiation of an agreement, or any question arising thereunder and the execution of a written contract incorporating any agreement reached if requested by either party, but such obligation does not compel either party to agree to a proposal or require the making of a concession.

* * *

MICHIGAN PUBLIC EMPLOYMENT RELATIONS ACT

§ 423.215

A public employer shall bargain collectively with the representatives of its employees * * * and is authorized to make and enter into collective bargaining agreements with such representatives. For the purposes of this section, to bargain collectively is the performance of the mutual obligation of the employer and the representative of the employees to meet at reasonable times and confer in good faith with respect to wages, hours, and other terms and conditions of employment * * *.

IOWA PUBLIC EMPLOYMENT RELATIONS ACT

§ 20.9 Scope of negotiations.

The public employer and the employee organization shall meet at reasonable times, including meetings reasonably in advance of the public employer's budget-making process, to negotiate in good faith with respect to wages, hours, vacations, insurance, holidays, leaves of absence, shift differentials, overtime compensation, supplemental pay, seniority, transfer procedures, job classifications, health and safety matters, evaluation procedures, procedures for staff reduction, in-service training and other matters mutually agreed upon. * * * Such obligation to negotiate in good faith does not compel either party to agree to a proposal or make a concession.

Nothing in this section shall diminish the authority and power of the merit employment department, board of regents' merit system, educational radio and television facility board's merit system, or any civil service commission established by constitutional provision, statute, charter or special act to recruit employees, prepare, conduct, and grade examinations, rate candidates in order of their relative scores for certification for appointment or promotion or for other matters of classification, reclassification or appeal rights in the classified service of the public employer served.

The public employee retirement systems * * * shall be excluded from the scope of negotiations.

PENNSYLVANIA PUBLIC EMPLOYEE RELATIONS ACT

Sec. 701. Scope of Bargaining.—Collective bargaining is the performance of the mutual obligation of the public employer and the representative of the public employes to meet at reasonable times and confer in good faith with respect to wages, hours and other terms and conditions of employment, or the negotiation of an agreement or any question arising thereunder and the execution of a written contract incorporating any agreement reached but such obligation does not compel either party to agree to a proposal or require the making of a concession.

Sec. 702. Managerial Policy.—Public employers shall not be required to bargain over matters of inherent managerial policy, which shall include but shall not be limited to such areas of discretion or policy as the functions and programs of the public employer, standards of services, its overall budget, utilization of technology, the organizational structure and selection and direction of personnel. Public employers, however, shall be required to meet and discuss on policy matters affecting wages, hours and terms and conditions of employment as well as the impact thereon upon request by public employe representatives.

Questions

1. Generally, what are the advantages and disadvantages of each of the following:

(a) a "laundry list" approach (statute contains listing of subjects of bargaining);

(b) a "pure" NLRA approach (statute requires bargaining on "wages, hours, and terms and conditions of employment" and gives an administrative agency the duty to interpret the general statutory language);

(c) a "modified" NLRB approach (statute contains general NLRA language and some express prohibited subjects of bargaining or some specific examples of required subjects of bargaining)?

2. Why would the Wisconsin legislature choose a "laundry list" approach for the appropriate scope of state employee collective bargaining while it requires a broader scope of bargaining for municipal employers such as cities and school districts?

3. Some statutory provisions relating to management rights in the public sector make these prohibited subjects of bargaining while other statutes make management rights a permissive subject of bargaining. What arguments support (or oppose) each approach?

C. DIVERSE JUDICIAL RESPONSES

(1) CLASS SIZE

TUALATIN VALLEY BARGAINING COUNCIL v. TIGARD SCHOOL DISTRICT 23J

Court of Appeals of Oregon, 1991.
106 Or.App. 381, 808 P.2d 101.

Before BUTTLER, P.J., and ROSSMAN and EDMONDS, JJ.

BUTTLER, PRESIDING JUDGE.

Tigard Education Association (Union)[1] is the exclusive bargaining representative under the Public Employee Collective Bargaining Act (PECBA), ORS 243.650 *et seq.* for teachers employed by Tigard School District 23J (District). During negotiations for a new collective bargaining agreement, among Union's proposals was one entitled "Workload," which specified grade-by-grade class size limits.[2] District refused

1. When the original agreement was signed, Union was named Tualatin Valley Bargaining Council.

2.

"ARTICLE 14
"WORKING CONDITIONS

"A. Work Load

"The District agrees to strive to make every reasonable effort to limit the number of students per classroom as dictated by the financial condition of the District, the building facilities available and special program needs as recommended by the District's administrative staff.

"*1. Individual employee workloads shall not exceed the following standards:*

a. Kindergarten—20 students per class.

b. Grades 1, 2, 3 and 3–4 splits—24 students per class.

c. Grades 4, 5 and 6—26 students per class.

d. Grades 7, 8, and 9—28 students per class.

e. Grades 10, 11 and 12—28 students per class.

f. Special Education:

(1). Learning Disabled—30 student caseload.

(2). Seriously Emotionally Disabled—10 student caseload.

(3). Educable Mentally Retarded—10 student caseload.

"*2. Each Talented and Gifted, mainstreamed learning disabled and/or handicapped student and each English as a Second Language student shall be counted as two (2) students for the purpose of workload computation.*

"*3. Workloads for each elementary specialist shall not exceed four hundred (400) students.*

"B. Working Conditions

to bargain, contending that class size is not a mandatory subject of bargaining. Union filed a charge with the Employment Relations Board (ERB), alleging that District's refusal to bargain over the proposal was an unfair labor practice under ORS 243.672(1)(e). ERB held, contrary to one of its earlier decisions, that the proposal to limit the number of students assigned to each teacher addresses a matter that relates to and significantly affects a teacher's workload and, therefore, is a mandatory subject of bargaining on which District must bargain in good faith. District appeals, and we affirm.

Both a union and an employer must, at the other's request, bargain collectively "with respect to employment relations." ORS 243.650(4); ORS 243.672(1); ORS 243.672(2)(b). The question is what subjects are matters concerning "employment relations" as defined in ORS 243.-650(7):

> "'Employment relations' includes, but is not limited to, *matters concerning* direct or indirect monetary benefits, hours, vacations, sick leave, grievance procedures and *other conditions of employment.*" (Emphasis supplied.)

Because neither the subject of workload nor a proposal for class size is specifically identified in the statute, the question becomes whether either is an "other condition of employment."

In *Springfield Education Assn. v. School Dist.*, 290 Or. 217, 233, 621 P.2d 547 (1980), the court said:

> "The wording of [ORS 243.650(7)] indicates that the legislature chose to define 'employment relations' by example[.] * * * The reference to 'other' such subjects was not a delegation to ERB to make different choices; rather, it is, in effect, a direction to ERB to replicate the same choice by regarding as 'employment relations' only those subjects which embody the same characteristics as 'monetary benefits, hours, vacations, sick leave, grievance procedures,' and no others."

The question of whether any subject is like or unlike the listed matters is "one of interpretation, not of discretion." 290 Or. at 233.

District contends that ERB erroneously interpreted ORS 243.650(7), requiring reversal. ORS 183.482(8)(a). Whether it erred depends on the meaning of *Springfield* and *Portland Fire Fighters Assoc. v. City of Portland,* 305 Or. 275, 751 P.2d 770 (1988). In attempting to carry out *Springfield's* mandate that "other conditions of employment" must embody the "same characteristics" as "monetary benefits, hours, vacations, sick leave [and] grievance procedures," ERB considered each of those subjects to determine what characteristics they had in common

"The District and the Association agree to work together to promote safe working conditions. The number of students enrolled in classes in which hazardous materials or equipment is used: e.g. science, industrial arts, etc., shall not exceed the number of student stations in the classroom as prescribed by safety precautions that are jointly determined by the teacher and the building administrator." (Emphasis in original.)

and concluded that each was a generic term that was generally applicable to all public employees. That is consistent with *Springfield's* mandate that other subjects be of like kind.

That interpretation is also consistent with the court's analysis in *Portland Fire Fighters,* where the city had refused to bargain over the union's proposal responding to the city's announcement that it would limit the number of fire fighters who were permitted to be on vacation at any given time. ERB had applied a "balancing test," resulting in its concluding that the terms of the *proposal* would have less effect on conditions of employment than they would have on management rights; therefore, it did not concern a condition of employment and was not a mandatory subject of collective bargaining. We affirmed. *Portland Firefighters Assoc. v. City of Portland,* 86 Or.App. 662, 740 P.2d 228 (1987). In reversing, the Supreme Court pointed out that the *subject* of the proposal related to vacations, which is specifically identified in the statute as a matter concerning "employment relations" and was, therefore, a subject for mandatory bargaining, unless the union's proposal was a sham. Because ERB had not found it to be a sham, the city was required to bargain on the proposal. There was no occasion for ERB to apply a "balancing test."

The balancing test that ERB has used to determine what subjects with the same characteristics as those identified in the statute are "other conditions of employment" is set out in *IAFF Local 314 v. City of Salem,* Case No. C–61–83, 7 PECBR 5819, 5825 (1983):

> "Where a *subject generally* has a greater effect on working conditions than on management's rights, that subject is a condition of employment and is mandatory. Where a *subject generally* has a greater effect on management's rights than on working conditions, that subject is not a condition of employment and is permissive." (Emphasis in original.)

That application of the balancing test was approved generally in *Springfield Education Assn. v. School Dist., supra.*[4] ERB, however, has incorrectly applied that balancing test to determine whether *proposals* are mandatory or permissive. In *Portland Fire Fighters Assoc.,* the court pointed out that balancing was appropriate only in determining whether a *subject* was an "other condition of employment." 305 Or. at 282, 751 P.2d 770.

Once ERB has concluded, after applying the balancing test, that an unenumerated subject is an "other condition of employment" within the meaning of ORS 243.650(7), no further balancing is appropriate, because that subject must be treated the same as an enumerated

4. We note that, in *Portland Fire Fighters Assoc. v. City of Portland, supra,* 305 Or. at 283, 751 P.2d 770, the court said: "ORS 243.650(7) is worded very broadly, including not only 'matters concerning * * * other conditions of employment,' but also a caution that the definition of 'employment relations' is not limited to conditions of employment."

subject and is, therefore, one for mandatory bargaining.[5] Workload has been determined by ERB, by use of the balancing test, to be an "other condition of employment" and, thus, a subject for mandatory bargaining. *OPEU v. State of Oregon,* Case No. UP–64–87, 10 PECBR 51, 79 (1987).

Because the subject of Union's proposal here purports to be workload, the question is whether characterizing the proposal that way is a sham. Merely characterizing a proposal as workload does not make workload the subject of the proposal. *See Portland Fire Fighters Assoc. v. City of Portland, supra,* 305 Or. at 284, 751 P.2d 770. ERB found that the terms of the proposal, in fact, relate to workload. ERB put the question this way:

> "The appropriate inquiry is whether the proposal addresses a matter concerning a condition of employment; i.e., does the number of students assigned to a teacher significantly affect that teacher's workload?"

As we understand *Portland Fire Fighters,* the question is whether a proposal *relates* to a subject requiring bargaining, not whether it "significantly affects" that subject, which ERB posed as the question. Substantial evidence supports ERB's finding that the proposal significantly affects workload: *a fortiori,* it relates to workload. Before negotiations, Union had conducted a survey of District's teachers that showed that class size was the single most critical factor in determining workload. It determines the number of parent-teacher conferences, the number of papers to be graded and the hours spent on assistance to individual students, all of which relate to workload. There was also testimony to support the survey's findings.

District also contends that ERB failed to give an adequate explanation for rejecting its earlier holding that class size was not a mandatory subject of bargaining. *Springfield Educ. Assn. v. Springfield School Dist.,* Case No. C–278, 1 PECBR 347, 358 (1975). ERB has held that it "will not re-apply the balancing test to previously-adjudicated bargaining subjects unless [it is] presented with a compelling reason to do so." *OPEU v. State of Oregon,* 10 PECBR at 69. That is merely an application of ORS 183.482(8)(a)(B).

Actually, ERB did not re-apply the balancing test in this case to conclude, contrary to its precedent, that class size relates to a mandatory subject of bargaining. It concluded, rather, that its earlier decision was incorrect, given its understanding of the Supreme Court's decisions in *Springfield* and *Portland Fire Fighters,* requiring a different interpretation of the statute: Only subjects of general applicability to public employees may fall within the statutory phrase "other conditions of

5. ERB has held that "[a]ll [mandatory] subjects—whether expressed in the statute or found through case law to be conditions of employment—are equally mandatory for bargaining, for the legislative policy inherent in ORS 243. 650(7) * * * is to require good faith bargaining over all 'employment relations[.]' " *IAFF v. City of Salem,* Case No. C–61–83, 7 PECBR 5819, 5825 (1983).

employment." The balancing test is only appropriate to determine whether a subject should be considered an "other condition of employment." ERB pointed out that class size, as such, is not of general applicability to public employees; therefore, it could not be a *subject* requiring bargaining. ERB concluded that its earlier analysis was wrong, because it had failed to determine whether the class size proposal *related to a subject* that is an "other condition of employment." Its use of the balancing test was therefore skewed. ERB's explanation of its refusal to follow its decision in *Springfield Educ. Assn. v. Springfield School Dist., supra,* is sufficient. It explained, we believe correctly, why it changed its previous analysis.

Additionally, District contends that ERB's interpretation of ORS 243.650(7) is inconsistent with legislative policy. In *Portland Fire Fighters,* the court stated the legislative policy underlying ORS 243.-650(7):

> "If negotiation and mediation are to be effective means of resolving labor disputes, the scope of the definition of those matters subject to mandatory negotiation and mediation must be broad enough to encompass all matters over which labor disputes are likely to arise." 305 Or. at 283, 751 P.2d 770.

Not only is ERB's interpretation consistent with the policy of channelling potential disputes into the bargaining process, it is also consistent with the analysis of the statute employed by the Supreme Court in *Portland Fire Fighters* and *Springfield.*

Finally, District argues that ERB erred in stating that *Portland Fire Fighters* compels the result that it reached. As indicated, we believe that that decision, combined with *Springfield Education Assn. v. School Dist., supra,* requires the interpretation of ORS 243.650(7) that ERB followed.

Affirmed.

Notes and Questions

1. The above is a minority approach. The majority approach is reflected in *West Irondequoit Teachers Association v. Helsby,* 35 N.Y.2d 46, 358 N.Y.S.2d 720, 315 N.E.2d 775 (1974) where the court stated:

> The issue here presented is whether, as argued by appellant teachers association, class size in a public school is a term or condition of employment so as to be a mandatory topic of bargaining under the Taylor Law (Civil Service Law, art. 14, Consol.Laws, c. 7); or whether, as held by a majority of the Public Employment Relations Board (PERB) and a unanimous Appellate Division, the question of class size is one of educational policy and as such susceptible of independent action by respondent employer, the board of education.
>
> The facts are stipulated. In May, 1970 at the beginning of negotiations between the board and teachers association for the 1970–1971 contract, the association submitted a proposal which would, *inter alia,*

have set class sizes in kindergarten and the first grade at 20 pupils as the number "for whom a teacher is responsible during a single period in a single day" and for grades two through six at 25 pupils. It was further proposed that any increase beyond those minimums would have to be agreed upon by the teacher and building principal, and any disagreement would be subject to grievance procedures elsewhere set forth. The board did not agree to this, but in turn proposed in writing that the relationship between effective learning and class size and teacher load should be subject to continued examination by the parties, and that it was desirable to maintain administrative flexibility in arranging class sizes and teacher loads in order to allow for program diversity and innovation, and to allow for equitable arrangements among teachers. In this connection the board agreed to consider New York State Teachers Association guidelines in planning for the 1971–1972 school year. In this proposal the board recognized that "Excessive class size or teacher load may affect the emotional or mental well-being of the teacher."

The association commenced this improper practice proceeding alleging that the board failed to negotiate in good faith and had therefore violated subdivision 1 of section 209–a of the Civil Service Law. The board's answer rested mainly on the contention that negotiations are mandatory only with respect to terms and conditions of employment (§ 204, subd. 2), and that class size was not such a term or condition. There was thus presented a problem of legal dimensions. The hearing examiner ruled for the association on the ground that class size had nothing to do with the formulation of primary educational policy; that, rather, it had significant impact on teachers' working conditions.

The PERB majority recognized, as the board of education conceded, that class size bore on teacher load and that as a consequence of class size this impact on the teachers would be subject to mandatory negotiation; but it was held that the fixing of class size initially was purely the subject of educational policy made in light of the employers' resources and the needs of its constituency. The dissenting member could not make the division between the original designation of class size and the resulting impact on working conditions and stated that the causal chain was so direct as not to admit of the distinction imposed by the majority.

The Appellate Division unanimously upheld the PERB majority stating that the distinction was well taken and provided a reasonable basis for the majority's decision. We agree.

* * *

As a reviewing court in an article 78 proceeding where the question is whether the administrative agency made a correct legal interpretation, our task is merely to see whether the determination "was affected by an error of law or was arbitrary and capricious or an abuse of discretion" (CPLR 7803, subd. 3). So long as PERB's interpretation is legally permissible and so long as there is no breach of constitutional rights and protections, the courts have no power to substitute another interpretation on the strength of what the NLRB or the Federal courts might do in the same or a similar situation. The Legislature, in article 14 of the Civil Service Law, has provided that terms and conditions of employment are subject to mandatory negotiation (§ 204, subd. 2; *Board of Educ. v. Associated Teachers of Huntington,* 30 N.Y.2d 122, 127, 331 N.Y.S.2d 17, 282 N.E.2d 109), defined "terms and conditions of employment" [to mean] salaries, wages, hours and "other terms and conditions of employment" (§ 201, subd. 4), created PERB (§ 205), and lodged with PERB the power to resolve disputes arising out of negotiations (§ 209). Inherent in this delegation is the power to interpret and construe the statutory scheme. Such construction given by the agency charged with administering the statute is to be accepted if not unreasonable.

* * *

It is to be noted that PERB has held only that determination of class size is not negotiable. It has not been held that the impact of class size on the teachers is not negotiable. As stated in PERB's majority opinion: "Nevertheless, impact is a matter for negotiations. Thus, it is not the thrust of this decision that an employer is not required to negotiate on subjects which affect the allocation of resources because salaries clearly have such an effect; rather, the thrust of this decision * * * is that basic policy decisions as to the implementation of a mission of an agency of government are not mandatory subjects of negotiations." PERB's rationale could, we believe, be crystallized with this example: The decision whether, say, sections of the fourth grade should contain 25, 28 or 32 pupils is a policy decision and not negotiable; whereas whether the teachers responsible for the sections are to receive varying consideration and benefits depending on the ultimate size of each section as so determined is mandatorily negotiable as a condition of the employment.

2. What accounts for the different results in the *Tualatin* case and the *West Irondequoit* case?

3. Courts often talk about deferring to an administrative agency's "expertise" in cases such as these but what type of expertise does the agency have?

(2) CONTRACTING AND SUBCONTRACTING

LOCAL 195, IFPTE v. STATE OF NEW JERSEY

Supreme Court of New Jersey, 1981.
88 N.J. 393, 443 A.2d 187.

The opinion of the Court was delivered by PASHMAN, J.

The New Jersey Employer–Employee Relations Act, *N.J.S.A.* 34:13A–1 to –21, provides for collective bargaining between the State of New Jersey and public employee unions. During contract negotiations between the State and Local 195 of the International Federation of Professional and Technical Engineers, AFL–CIO (Local 195)[1] and be-

1. Local 195 is the majority representative of the Inspection and Security Unit, the Operations, Maintenance and Services Unit, and the Crafts Unit of the State of New Jersey.

tween the State and State Supervisory Employees Association (Association),[2] disputes arose over the negotiability of several provisions. Once again we must determine the scope of collective bargaining for public employees.

I

Facts and Procedural History

A. *In the Matter of Local 195*

From late 1978 to early 1979, the State and Local 195 were engaged in collective negotiations on a contract to run from July 1979 to June 1981. During the course of the negotiations, the negotiability of several contractual provisions came into question. The disputed clauses concerned (1) limitations on contracting and subcontracting, (2) the establishment of a workweek, and (3) transfer and reassignment determinations. Unable to reach agreement, the parties filed a joint petition for a scope of negotiations determination with the Public Employment Relations Commission (PERC) on May 31, 1979.[3] *N.J.S.A.* 34:13A–5.4(d).

On January 4, 1980, PERC held that the disputed contracting/subcontracting and workweek provisions, and portions of the transfer and reassignment provisions, were mandatorily negotiable. *In re Local 195, IFPTE, AFL–CIO,* PERC No. 80–85, 6 *NJPER* 32 (1980). In deciding that subcontracting was a negotiable issue, PERC relied on its earlier cases, arguing that subcontracting must be mandatorily subject to negotiation since

> a decision to subcontract would effectively terminate the employment relationship vis-a-vis the employees in a negotiations unit and would have a "cataclysmic effect on wages, hours, and working conditions. * * *" [Slip op. at 6]

On October 6, 1980, the Appellate Division substantially affirmed PERC's determinations regarding the workweek and the transfer and reassignment provisions. 176 *N.J.Super.* 85, 422 *A.*2d 424 (1980). The court divided on the negotiability of subcontracting. The majority reversed PERC and held that the determination to subcontract work is an inherent managerial prerogative. Judge Morgan dissented, arguing that the majority had failed to consider the interests of public employees in reaching its decision. Applying a balancing test, Judge Morgan would have found subcontracting to be a mandatorily negotiable issue.

2. The Association represents the Administrative and Clerical Services Unit, the Professional Unit, and the Primary Level Supervisory Unit.

3. No specific dispute has arisen about the application of any of the provisions. Rather, the State sought to remove the disputed clauses from the agreements under negotiation. Thus, there is no present factual context against which to measure the effect of the clauses.

Because of the dissent below, this case comes before the Court on appeal as of right. *R.* 2:2–1(a)(2).

B. In the Matter of State Supervisory Employees Association

The State of New Jersey and the New Jersey State Supervisory Employees Association, New Jersey Civil Service Association and the New Jersey State Employees Association began negotiations in late 1978 for a contract to run from July 1979 to June 1981. During the negotiations, dispute arose over the negotiability of the same three topics at issue in *Local 195.*

The State filed three petitions for scope of negotiations determinations with PERC on May 25, 1979. On August 28, 1979, PERC held that the subcontracting and workweek provisions were mandatorily negotiable. It further held some of the reassignment provisions negotiable because they reflected procedural concerns of the employees rather than substantive policy determinations by the employer. *In the Matter of State and State Supervisory Employees Association.* PERC No. 80–19, 5 *NJPER* 381 (1979). Those provisions that were substantive in nature were held to be non-negotiable.

Relying on the majority opinion in *Local 195, supra,* the Appellate Division again held subcontracting to be a non-negotiable subject. As in *Local 195,* Judge Morgan dissented on the issue of subcontracting. The Appellate Division also substantially affirmed PERC's determinations regarding the workweek and reassignment provisions. Unlike PERC, however, the Appellate Division held that provisions regarding (1) the applicability of seniority in transfer determinations, and (2) the transfer of Association officers and stewards, were non-negotiable subjects.

An appeal as of right was taken by the Association on the subcontracting provision, under *R* 2:2–1(a)(2). In addition, the Supreme Court granted certification on the transfer and reassignment provisions, upon petition by the Association, and on the workweek provision, upon petition by the State.

II

Scope of Negotiability

Public employees in New Jersey have a constitutional right to organize and present "grievances and proposals" to public employers through representatives of their own choosing. *N.J.Const.* (1947), Art. I. par. 19. The parameters of collective negotiations about such proposals were established in 1968 by the New Jersey Employer–Employee Relations Act, *N.J.S.A.* 34:13A–1 to –21, and later by judicial decisions.

The central issue in a scope of negotiations determination is whether or not a particular subject matter is negotiable. This depends on careful consideration of the legitimate interests of the public employer and the public employees. The process of balancing those competing interests is constrained by the policy goals underlying relevant statutes and by the Constitution.

The Legislature has recognized that, like private employees, public employees have a legitimate interest in engaging in collective negotiations about issues that affect "terms and conditions of employment." *N.J.S.A.* 34:13A–5.3. However, the scope of negotiations in the public sector is more limited than in the private sector.[7] This is so because the employer in the public sector is government, which has special responsibilities to the public not shared by private employers.[8] What distinguishes the State from private employers is the unique responsibility to make and implement public policy.

Matters of public policy are properly decided, not by negotiation and arbitration, but by the political process. This involves the panoply of democratic institutions and practices, including public debate, lobbying, voting, legislation and administration. We have stated that

> the very foundation of representative democracy would be endangered if decisions on significant matters of governmental policy were left to the process of collective negotiations * * * Our democratic system demands that governmental bodies retain their accountability to the citizenry. [*Ridgefield Park Ed. Ass'n v. Ridgefield Park Bd. of Ed.*, 78 *N.J.* 144, 163, 393 *A.*2d 278 (1978)]

We have therefore divided subjects of public employment negotiation into two categories: "mandatorily negotiable terms and conditions of employment and non-negotiable matters of governmental policy." *Id.* at 162, 393 A.2d 278.

The role of the courts in a scope of negotiations case is to determine, in light of the competing interests of the State and its employees, whether an issue is appropriately decided by the political process or by collective negotiations. In making this sensitive determination, the mere invocation of abstract categories like "terms and conditions of employment" and "managerial prerogatives" is not helpful. To determine whether a subject is negotiable, the Court must balance the competing interests by considering the extent to which collective negotiations will impair the determination of governmental policy.

Our opinions on public employment have established a three-part test for scope of negotiations determinations. First, a subject is nego-

7. For example, there are generally no permissive subjects of negotiation in New Jersey public employment. *Board of Education of Woodstown–Pilesgrove Regional School District v. Woodstown–Pilesgrove Regional Education Association,* 81 *N.J.* 582, 588 n. 1, 410 *A.*2d 1131 (1980); *Ridgefield Park Education Association v. Ridgefield Park Board of Education,* 78 *N.J.* 144, 162, 393 *A.*2d 278 (1978).

8. Thus, we have consistently held that federal precedents concerning the scope of collective bargaining in the private sector are of little value in determining the permissible scope of negotiability in the public sphere. *In the Matter of Paterson Police PBA Local No. 1 v. Paterson,* 87 *N.J.* 78, 90, 432 *A.*2d 847 (1981); *Ridgefield Park,* 78 *N.J.* at 159, 393 A.2d 278. For this reason, the United States Supreme Court decision holding subcontracting to be a negotiable subject in the context of a private employer is not persuasive authority in this case. *See Fibreboard Paper Products Corp. v. NLRB,* 379 U.S. 203, 85 S.Ct. 398, 13 L.Ed.2d 233 (1964).

tiable only if it "intimately and directly affect[s] the work and welfare of public employees * * *." The prime examples of subjects that fall within this category are rates of pay and working hours. Any subject which does not satisfy this part of the test is not negotiable.

Second, an item is not negotiable if it has been preempted by statute or regulation. If the Legislature establishes a specific term or condition of employment that leaves no room for discretionary action, then negotiation on that term is fully preempted. If the statute sets a minimum or maximum term or condition, then negotiation may be confined within the parameters established by these limits. However, the mere existence of a statute or regulation relating to a given term or condition of employment does not automatically preclude negotiations. Negotiation is preempted only if the "statutory or regulatory provisions * * * speak in the imperative and leave nothing to the discretion of the public employer."

Third, a topic that affects the work and welfare of public employees is negotiable only if it is a matter "on which negotiated agreement would not *significantly* interfere with the exercise of inherent management prerogatives pertaining to the determination of governmental policy." This principle rests on the assumption that most decisions of the public employer affect the work and welfare of public employees to some extent and that negotiation will always impinge to some extent on the determination of governmental policy. The requirement that the interference be "significant" is designed to effect a balance between the interests of public employees and the requirements of democratic decision making. As Justice Schreiber wrote in *Woodstown–Pilesgrove,*

> The nature of the terms and conditions of employment must be considered in relation to the extent of their interference with managerial prerogatives. A weighing or balancing must be made. When the dominant issue is [a governmental] goal, there is no obligation to negotiate and subject the matter, including its impact, to binding arbitration. Thus these matters may not be included in the negotiations and in the binding arbitration process even though they may affect or impact upon the employees' terms and conditions of employment. [81 *N.J.* at 591, 410 *A.*2d at 1135]

Thus negotiation will be allowed on a subject that intimately and directly affects the work and welfare of public employees unless such negotiated agreement would significantly interfere with the determination of governmental policy.

To summarize, a subject is negotiable between public employers and employees when (1) the item intimately and directly affects the work and welfare of public employees; (2) the subject has not been fully or partially preempted by statute or regulation; and (3) a negotiated agreement would not significantly interfere with the determination of governmental policy. To decide whether a negotiated agreement would significantly interfere with the determination of governmental policy, it is necessary to balance the interests of the public employees and the public employer. When the dominant concern is the government's managerial prerogative to determine policy, a subject may not be included in collective negotiations even though it may intimately affect employees' working conditions.

III

CONTRACTING AND SUBCONTRACTING

The proposed contract provision at issue in *State Supervisory Employees Ass'n* states:

> The State shall meet with the Association to *negotiate* all incidents of contracting or subcontracting whenever it becomes apparent that a layoff or job displacement might result. [Article XXXII (emphasis added)]

The contract provision in *Local 195* states:

> The State agrees to meet with the Union to *discuss* all incidences of contracting or subcontracting whenever it becomes apparent that a layoff or job displacement will result. [Article XXXIV (emphasis added)]

These provisions would require negotiation or discussion only if subcontracting might result in layoffs or displacement. "Nothing more directly and intimately affects a worker than the fact of whether or not he [or she] has a job." *State v. State Supervisory Employees Ass'n,* 78 *N.J.* at 84, 393 A.2d 233. The clause clearly meets the requirements of the first part of the test for negotiability.

We next decide whether negotiation about subcontracting has been preempted by statute. * * * [and hold that] the regulation does not preempt subcontracting as a negotiable subject.

Finally, we consider whether negotiation on the substantive decision to contract or subcontract would significantly interfere with the determination of governmental policy. The issue of subcontracting does not merely concern the proper technical means for implementing social and political goals. The choice of how policies are implemented, and by whom, can be as important a feature of governmental choice as the selection of ultimate goals. It is a matter of general public concern whether governmental services are provided by government employees or by contractual arrangements with private organizations. This type of policy determination does not necessarily concern solely fiscal considerations. It requires basic judgments about how the work or services should be provided to best satisfy the concerns and responsibilities of government. Deciding whether or not to contract out a given government service may implicate important tradeoffs.

Allowing such decisions to be subject to mandatory negotiation would significantly impair the ability of public employers to resort to subcontracting. We have previously held that decisions to reduce the work force for economy or efficiency are non-negotiable subjects. The decision to contract out work or to subcontract is similarly an area where managerial interests are dominant. This is highlighted by the fact that allowing subcontracting to be negotiable may open the road to grievance arbitration. Imposing a legal duty on the state to negotiate all proposed instances of subcontracting would transfer the focus of the decision from the political process to the negotiating table, to arbitrators, and ultimately to the courts. The result of such a course would significantly interfere with the determination of governmental policy and would be inimical to the democratic process.

We therefore hold that to the extent the contractual provision at issue in *State Supervisory Employees' Ass'n* includes negotiation on the ultimate substantive decision to subcontract, it is a non-negotiable matter of managerial prerogative. We recognize that our ruling on subcontracting is at odds with decisions in other jurisdictions. *Unified School Dist. No. 1 of Racine County v. Wisconsin,* 81 *Wis.*2d 89, 259 *N.W.*2d 724 (1977); *In re Saratoga Springs City School Dist. v. New York State Public Employment Relations Bd.* 68 *A.D.*2d 202, 416 *N.Y.S.*2d 415 (App.Div.1979); *Van Buren Public School Dist. v. Wayne Cty. Circuit Judge,* 61 *Mich.App.* 6, 232 *N.W.*2d 278 (Ct.App.1975). These decisions rest on the assumption that subcontracting "does not represent a choice among alternative social or political goals or values." As we have stated, we do not agree that the decision to contract out work necessarily concerns merely the technical means of implementing policy. The decision can be an important policy choice in its own right.

These out-of-state decisions also emphasize the wisdom of pursuing discussion between public employers and employees. We fully agree that such discussions are valuable and should be fostered. They would undoubtedly promote labor peace and harmony, a major goal of the New Jersey Employer–Employee Relations Act. *N.J.S.A.* 34:13A–2. Moreover, they may even result in greater efficiency or economy. If a public employer is considering subcontracting as a means to achieve these goals, employees may be motivated to suggest changes in working conditions that could accomplish the same or better results.

For these reasons, we fully expect that discussion between public employers and employees will be undertaken by the State. It is clearly in the interest of the State to do so. At oral argument, the representatives of the State voiced a commitment to pursue discussion with public employees before resorting to subcontracting. This is altogether appropriate. We do not mean to stifle discussion. We encourage it. State officials would be derelict in their public responsibilities if they did not pursue such discussions.

To this end, we hold that a public employment contract may include a provision reciting an agreement by the State to *discuss* decisions to contract or subcontract whenever it becomes apparent that a layoff or job displacement will result, if the proposed subcontracting is based on solely fiscal considerations. In such situations, the public would clearly benefit from suggestions by public employees directed toward improving economy or efficiency. While the public employees have no right to negotiate on the ultimate decision to subcontract, they may have a procedural right to present their position on the economic issue. Thus, for example, they could seek to show the employer that the employees are willing to perform the same job at a price competitive with the private replacements.

Discussion of subcontracting which is contemplated for purely fiscal reasons does not implicate governmental policy to the extent that it would if the decision were based on non-fiscal reasons. Replacing public employees with private employees solely to save money does entail a choice about the level of government spending, a matter of great public concern. However, discussion about such a replacement would not significantly interfere with the determination of public goals. In fact, as we have explained, such discussions would be in the public interest, since employees could demonstrate that they would do the same work more efficiently than a private contractor.

In *Local 195,* the contract provision would be acceptable if it limited discussion to occasions of subcontracting or contracting likely to result in job layoffs only when the subcontracting is done solely for fiscal or economic reasons. However, as written, the provision is overly broad. Placing a legal duty on the State to discuss subcontracting when proposed for broader policy purposes would place too great a burden on the determination of governmental policy. Only when the contracting out is proposed for purely economic reasons does the employee interest in discussion of alternative solutions become dominant.

Both contract provisions appear to allow negotiation or discussion not only on the ultimate issue of subcontracting but on the effects of subcontracting on public employees. To the extent the provisions impose a duty on the State to negotiate procedural aspects of the subcontracting decision as they affect employees, the clauses are negotiable. For example, negotiation could occur on the issue of adequate notice to employees that they are going to be laid off. We have held that, although substantive policy decisions may be non-negotiable matters, procedural aspects of the decision are negotiable. Negotiation about the procedures for laying off employees will not significantly interfere with the underlying policy determination. They are therefore negotiable terms and conditions of employment.

We emphasize that our holding today does not grant the public employer limitless freedom to subcontract for any reason. The State could not subcontract in bad faith for the sole purpose of laying off public employees or substituting private workers for public workers. State action must be rationally related to a legitimate governmental purpose. Our decision today does not leave public employees vulnerable to arbitrary or capricious substitutions of private workers for public employees.

We conclude that, as written, both proposed contractual provisions relating to contracting and subcontracting are non-negotiable matters of managerial prerogative.

IV

WORKWEEK PROVISIONS

The workweek provision in dispute in *State Supervisory Employees Association* states: [13]

> Where practicable: the normal workweek shall consist of five (5) consecutive workdays. [Article VIII, A.3.]

We find that this provision intimately and directly affects the work and welfare of public employees.

We further find that the clause is not preempted by statute. The disputed provision does not constrain the right of the State to determine the number or classification of employees on duty at any time. It merely governs negotiations concerning which employees within a given classification will work at any particular time. No statutes set the workweek for individual employees. *N.J.S.A.* 52:14–17.13 and –17.14 merely provide that the basic workweek shall be 40 hours, where practicable, and that any employee working longer than this shall receive overtime. Like *N.J.A.C.* 4:1–18.1 and –18.2, these provisions leave considerable discretion to the public employer in deciding who shall work when. Likewise, *N.J.S.A.* 11:14–1 empowers certain administrative officials of the Civil Service to prepare regulations concerning work hours, holidays, attendance and leaves of absence. This statute again leaves considerable discretion to public authorities.

We have previously held that, while the establishment of a school calendar, *In re Burlington Cty. College Faculty Ass'n v. Bd. of Trustees,* 64 *N.J.* 10, 311 *A.*2d 733 (1973), or the hours of instruction in a school day, *Woodstown–Pilesgrove, supra,* are non-negotiable subjects, the days and hours worked by individual employees are negotiable. The contract provision in this case concerns the negotiable subject of individual work schedules rather than the formation of an overall calendar. The provision does not interfere with the State's power to determine the number of classification of employees working at any given time. Nor does it interfere with the determination of the hours or days during which a service will be operated. The Association wishes only to negotiate the hours of employment of individual employees within the system established by the State. Negotiation on this issue will not significantly interfere with the determination of governmental policy, particularly since the term applies only "[w]here practicable." It is true that negotiation on the issue of practicability would impinge on the State's power to deviate from the provision. Nonetheless, the interests of the employees predominate and negotiation on the subject

13. PERC held this provision negotiable.

would not significantly interfere with determination of governmental policy.[14]

We therefore conclude that the workweek provision in dispute is a negotiable term and condition of employment.

[The portion of the decision covering the disputed transfer and reassignment provisions is omitted.]

CONCLUSION

We hold that in public employment law, the substantive decision to subcontract or to contract out work is a non-negotiable subject of managerial prerogative. However, a public employment contract could contain a provision requiring the State to discuss the economic aspects of subcontracting contemplated for purely fiscal reasons when a job layoff may result. Moreover, negotiation may take place on the procedural aspects of subcontracting as they affect public employees. The provision relating to the workweek is negotiable. As elaborated in this opinion, transfer and reassignment provisions relating to procedure are negotiable while those relating to the substantive criteria for transfer or reassignment are not. The provisions relating to the transfer or reassignment of Association officers and stewards are mandatorily negotiable, as written.

Affirmed in part and reversed in part.

Justices Handler and O'Hern concurred in part and dissented in part.

Questions

1. What are the advantages and disadvantages of the New Jersey Supreme Court's determination that all nonmandatory subjects of bargaining are prohibited subjects of bargaining?

2. In applying a balancing test, what factors are being balanced by the court and what weight does the court give to the various factors?

(3) LAY OFFS

CITY OF BROOKFIELD v. WISCONSIN EMPLOYMENT RELATIONS COMMISSION

Supreme Court of Wisconsin, 1978.
87 Wis.2d 819, 275 N.W.2d 723.

COFFEY, JUSTICE.

This is an appeal of a July 16, 1976 judgment that reversed an April 16, 1975 order of the Wisconsin Employment Relations Commis-

14. We do not hold that the decision as to which employees are working at a given time would never significantly interfere with the determination of governmental policy. In certain instances, such a decision may impinge on the ability of the governmental entity to determine policy.

sion (hereinafter WERC). The appellant, WERC, ordered the respondent, City of Brookfield (hereinafter Brookfield) to reinstate and reimburse five city firefighters laid off due to a decrease in the funds allocated to the fire department by the city budget. The ordered remedy was based upon the WERC's finding that Brookfield in the 1973 bargaining agreement had violated its duty to collectively bargain when it refused to negotiate the decision to lay off the five firefighters or the effects of the lay off decision, contrary to sec. 111.70(1)(d), Stats. The circuit court reversed the WERC order and found that Brookfield was not required to negotiate the lay off decision; the WERC conclusion in regard to the duty to bargain the effects of the lay off decision was affirmed and is not at issue in this appeal.

The parties do not dispute the facts of this case. Prior to and including the calendar year 1972 Brookfield and Firefighters Local 2051, International Association of Firefighters, AFL–CIO (hereinafter Local 2051) were parties to collective bargaining agreements. The 1972 agreement did not contain a minimum daily manpower clause as proposed by Local 2051, nor a specific waiver of bargaining clause, a management's rights clause or a lay off of unit employees clause.

Mike Sueflohn, a department fireman and member of Local 2051's bargaining team, testified before the WERC hearing examiner that as early as October 2, 1972 the possibility of personnel reductions, numbering 5 firefighters, was discussed. According to Sueflohn, the Brookfield bargaining representative described the city's financial condition as "very tight."

During the negotiations for the 1973 collective bargaining agreement, Local 2051 again requested a minimum manpower clause. Brookfield representatives told the union that the subject was not negotiable. At the November 13, 1972 bargaining session, Local 2051 demanded the discussion of bargaining proposals concerning the possibility of lay offs in the department. Brookfield's bargaining agent rejected the proposal, countering with the argument that any decision regarding lay off was an inherent right reserved to management.

On November 14, 1972 the Brookfield City Council reduced the fire department's 1973 budget allocation by $80,000. The budgets of other city departments were also reduced. The city council requested department heads to submit proposals on how these budget reductions could be met. The fire chief suggested personnel lay offs and also expressed concern over the reduction in the quality of services provided. Members of Local 2051 were aware of the anticipated lay offs resulting from the $80,000 budget cut and, in the words of Mike Sueflohn, "tried very hard through the news media and other avenues (distribution of fliers and newsletters) open to us to educate citizens of the city what was going to happen to their fire service." The fliers that were distributed were designed to encourage Brookfield residents to attend and voice at opinion at a city council meeting on November 28, 1972 at which time the $80,000 budget cut would be discussed and implemented by lay offs or other appropriate action. The fliers read in part:

> BROOKFIELD LIVES AND PROPERTY IN JEOPARDY * * * UNLESS YOU SAY NO!
>
> "The proposal to cut firefighters from the department means placing your family life in danger, higher homeowners and business insurance rates.
>
> "Learn the facts about what this proposal really means by attending a public meeting.
>
> "PLEASE ATTEND * * * for your FAMILY'S SAKE.
>
> "Citizens Committee to Protect Brookfield. Dr. R.A. Toepfer, Mr. & Mrs. David Ninstil and Brookfield Fire Fighters Association."

Local 2051 efforts to prevent the lay off of firemen were unsuccessful, despite the appearance at the November 28th city council meeting of 17 people who spoke on behalf of Local 2051. Speaking against the cut in manpower was John Pavlik, a former fire chief.

The city council's action on November 28th was described in a Local 2051 newsletter in the following language:

> "CITY OF BROOKFIELD VOTES TO LAY OFF FIRE FIGHTERS: Despite strong efforts of Local 2051, with the help of the IAFF and their neighboring locals, the Aldermen voted 8 to 5 to cut 6 men from the Fire Department. This means the 6 men hired just 2½ years ago to man a new Aerial will be put out of a job as will the Aerial as a first line rig.
>
> "All department heads have been told to cut their budgets, but only the Fire Chief submitted a proposal on how it could be done. He later pointed out that this was not good for the fire protection, but the Finance Committee had by then taken a public stand and we all know how politicians hate to admit they may have been wrong."

At the contract bargaining session on December 5th Local 2051 asked for the discussion of severance pay for the five firefighters who were about to be laid off. The Brookfield representative stated that the matter would have to be considered by the city finance committee. A committee member had previously stated during the negotiation sessions that because of the city's financial crunch, he was going to propose a return to an all volunteer fire department. On December 8, 1972 Brookfield notified the five firefighters of lowest seniority that they would be laid off effective December 31, 1972. At the December 13, 1972 bargaining conference, a city representative stated that no unemployment benefits would be accorded and that the matter was not negotiable as it was a management prerogative. The five firefighters were laid off on December 31, 1972 without any collective bargaining discussion as to the decision or the implementation of the lay offs. On that date, the number of employees on a twenty-four hour shift was reduced from 15 employees to 13.

Local 2051 filed separate unfair labor practice complaints with the WERC and a hearing examiner was subsequently appointed. This complaint alleged that Brookfield refused to negotiate the lay off decision and, secondly, they refused to bargain the impact of the decision in violation of sec. 111.70(1)(d), Stats., of the Municipal Employment Relations Act (hereinafter M.E.R.A.). * * *

* * *

The *Racine County* decision emphasized that:

> "[I]n the public sector, the principal limit on the scope of collective bargaining is concern for the integrity of political processes." *Unified School Dist. No. 1 of Racine County v. WERC, supra* at 96, 259 N.W.2d at 730.

We hold that economically motivated lay offs of public employees resulting from budgetary restraints is a matter primarily related to the exercise of municipal powers and responsibilities and the integrity of the political processes of municipal government. The citizens of a community have a vital interest in the continued fiscally responsible operation of its municipal services. Thus, it is imperative that we strike a balance between public employees' bargaining rights and protecting the public health and safety of our citizens within the framework of the political and legislative process.

* * *

[The decision again cited *Racine County:*

"In municipal employment relations the bargaining table is not the appropriate forum for the formulation or management of public policy. Where a decision is essentially concerned with public policy choices, no group should act as an exclusive representative; discussions should be open; and public policy should be shaped through the regular political process. Essential control over the management of the school district's affairs must be left with the school board, the body elected to be responsible for those affairs under state law."]

The court recognizes that unions, such as Local 2051, are not powerless in their ability to formulate and influence the direction of public policy decisions. As demonstrated in this case, unions can and do attend public budget meetings and can and do lobby with legislative bodies and organize and motivate the general public regarding the union's position. The distribution of informational fliers, newsletters and media releases as well as the solicitation of prominent and influential speakers are but a few of the ways in which unions can and do have a significant impact on the political processes. Local 2051 exerted acceptable political pressures upon the Brookfield City Council to halt the lay offs resulting from the budget cut. To decide the issue to be a mandatory subject of bargaining would destroy the equal balance of power that insures the collective bargaining rights of the union and protects the rights of the general public to determine the quality and level of municipal services they consider vital. The legislature has made it clear that a budgetary lay off decision is not a subject of mandatory bargaining. If it were, the right of the public to voice its opinion would be restricted as to matters fundamentally relating to the community's safety, general welfare and budgetary management.

* * *

Question

If courts are so concerned about the integrity of the political process and the continued fiscal responsible operation of municipal services, why are wages and economic benefits such as health insurance generally regarded as mandatory subjects of bargaining?

(4) WORK RULES

DEPARTMENT OF TRANSPORTATION v. PENNSYLVANIA LABOR RELATIONS BOARD

Commonwealth Court of Pennsylvania, 1988.
117 Pa.Commw. 427, 543 A.2d 1255.

Before DOYLE, BARRY and MCGINLEY, JJ.

OPINION

BARRY, JUDGE.

The Commonwealth of Pennsylvania, Department of Transportation (DOT) appeals from an order of the Pennsylvania Labor Relations Board (the Board) which, in short, ordered DOT to cease and desist from refusing to collectively bargain with its employee representative and rescind its revised work rules issued on March 1, 1984. For the reasons set forth below we vacate and remand.

On June 19, 1984, the American Federation of State, County and Municipal Employees, Council 13 (the Union) filed a charge of unfair labor practices against DOT with the Board. The charge alleged that DOT violated Sections 1201(a)(5) and (9) of the Public Employe Relations Act. The facts giving rise to the charge are not complicated. Since 1978 DOT has established work rules for its employees. In 1980 DOT revised its work rules and in March of 1984 it revised its rules again. The Union first became aware of the 1984 revisions following their publication and submission to the employees by DOT's Director of Personnel.

The Union contacted DOT and requested a meeting to discuss the rule changes. The requested meeting never took place due to a disagreement as to the number of Union employees who would be allowed to attend the meeting. The Union then filed its charge with the Board.

Following a hearing before a Board Hearing Examiner, a proposed decision and order was issued which concluded that DOT had violated

Sections 1201(a)(5) and (9) of the Act by failing to collectively bargain in good faith over the issue of changes to the work rules. The Hearing Examiner reached this conclusion by finding that the implementation of the revised work rules was a subject of mandatory collective bargaining under Section 701 of the Act rather than one of "inherent managerial policy" within the meaning of Section 702 of the Act.

DOT filed exceptions to the Hearing Examiner's proposed decision and order with the Board. The Board, without oral argument, dismissed DOT's exceptions and affirmed the Hearing Examiner. DOT then appealed to this Court.

Our scope of review is limited to determining whether there has been a constitutional violation or an error of law, and whether the findings of fact are supported by substantial evidence.

DOT's principal argument to this Court is that the Board applied the balancing test as set forth by our Supreme Court in *Pennsylvania Labor Relations Board v. State College Area School District,* 461 Pa. 494, 337 A.2d 262 (1975) in an improper manner. In *State College* the Court addressed one of the aspects of the relationship between Sections 701 and 702 of the Act. In determining that a balance must be struck between the mandatory subjects of bargaining of Section 701 and those managerial prerogatives of Section 702 the Court stated, "In striking this balance the paramount concern must be the public interest in providing for the effective and efficient performance of the public service in question." *Id.* at 506, 337 A.2d at 268. It went on to explain that:

> [w]here an item of dispute is a matter of fundamental concern to employees' interest in wages, hours and other items and conditions of employment, it is not removed as a matter subject to good faith bargaining under section 701 simply because it may touch upon basic policy. It is the duty of the Board in the first instance and the courts thereafter to determine whether the impact of the issue on the interest of the employe in wages, hours and terms and conditions of employment outweighs its probable effect on the basic policy of the system as a whole. If it is determined that the matter is one of inherent managerial policy but does affect wages, hours and terms and conditions of employment, the public employer shall be required to meet and discuss such subjects upon request by the public employe's representative pursuant to section 702.

Id. at 507, 337 A.2d at 268.

In *Chambersburg Area School District v. Pennsylvania Labor Relations Board,* 60 Pa.Commonwealth Ct. 29, 430 A.2d 740 (1981) this Court determined that the balancing approach of *State College* must be applied on a case-by-case basis. The proper application of the *Chambersburg* direction necessarily leads us to the conclusion that *State College* must be applied not only on a case-by-case basis but on an issue-by-issue basis as well.

This approach was specifically adopted by the United States Court of Appeals for the District of Columbia in *Newspaper Guild of Greater Philadelphia, Local 10 v. National Labor Relations Board,* 636 F.2d 550 (D.C.Cir.1980). As Chairman Scalera of the Pennsylvania Labor Relations Board noted in his dissent in the case before us the Court in *Newspaper Guild* determined that *each* substantive work rule implemented by the employer in that case should have been evaluated individually by the National Labor Relations Board to determine whether there was a duty to bargain over that provision. That Court stated:

> In regard to substantive rules, the [National Labor Relations] Board made no attempt to distinguish between those provisions of the Code [of Ethics] which, while central to the [employer's] interest in the preservation of its legitimate managerial prerogatives, affect the employees only minimally, and those which, although not essential to the [employer's] freedom to conduct its business, do have a significant impact on the employees. Yet such a distinction must be made. * * *

Id. at 561.

The factual situation in the case before us illustrates the wisdom of the adoption of the approach taken by the court in *Newspaper Guild.* Here, DOT implemented at least ten different changes to its work rules. It is possible that some of the changes would fall within the scope of Section 701 and must be collectively bargained while others would fall within the scope of Section 702 requiring only that the parties meet and discuss those changes, while still others may fall within that portion of Section 702 which does not require the parties to meet and discuss.

This Court lacks the expertise necessary to engage in a *State College* analysis of each work rule implemented by DOT. Accordingly, having found that the Board improperly examined DOT's changes to its work rules by analyzing the changes as a whole we vacate its order and remand the case for a rule-by-rule analysis not inconsistent with this opinion.

* * *

Questions

1. In reaching its conclusion, how important to the court was the management rights clause in the Pennsylvania Public Employment Relations Act (see Statutory Section in this Chapter)?

2. When refusing to bargain about some union demands, public officials commonly rely upon management rights set forth in collective bargaining statutes or concepts of implied management prerogatives borrowed from the private sector. Do these management rights theories hide the issue of whether certain public decisions should be made by means of the collective bargaining process where the public's participation is typically restricted?

(5) POLICE USE OF WEAPONS

SAN JOSE PEACE OFFICERS v. CITY OF SAN JOSE

California Courts of Appeal, First Appellate Division, 1978.
78 Cal.App.3d 935, 144 Cal.Rptr. 638.

BROWN, JUDGE: Defendants City of San Jose, a chartered city, its city manager and its chief of police (hereinafter appellants) appeal from a judgment declaring that they must meet and confer with the San Jose Police Officer's Association (hereinafter respondent) before changing the portion of their use of force policy governing when a peace officer may discharge his firearm. Respondent has cross-appealed from the portion of the judgment refusing to award it attorney's fees. For the reasons hereinafter stated, we reverse the judgment of the trial court, except for the portion refusing to award respondent attorney's fees, as to which we affirm.

Respondent is a recognized employee organization within the meaning of the Meyers–Milias–Brown Act (hereinafter the MMBA). Government Code sections 3500–3510, representing peace officers of the San Jose Police Department below the level of assistant chief.

Prior to the incidents involved herein, San Jose's police department adopted a regulation effective May 1, 1972, governing the circumstances under which a policeman would be permitted to discharge a firearm. As conceded by counsel for respondent during argument, this regulation was adopted unilaterally by the police department, and no request was made that the police department meet and confer with respondent with respect to its adoption. Said regulation provided as follows:

PART XI—USE OF FIREARMS

"311.1. *Firearm Regulations.*

"a. *When Firearms May be Discharged.* Firearms may be discharged in the performance of a police duty only under the circumstances listed below.

"If, in the opinion of the officer involved, he can safely accomplish the ends described in (3), (4) and (5) by firing a warning shot or shots, he may do so.

"(1) At an approved range.

"(2) When killing seriously wounded or dangerous animals when other disposition is impractical.

"(3) When necessary in the defense of his own life when all other reasonable means have failed.

"(4) When necessary in the defense of another person's life when all other reasonable means have failed.

"(5) When necessary to effect the capture of, or prevent the escape or rescue of a person whom the member has reasonable cause to believe has committed a felony involving the use or a threat to use deadly force, when all other reasonable means have failed.

"b. *When Firearms Will Not be Discharged.* Firearms will not be discharged under the following circumstances:

"(1) At misdemeanants.

"(2) To effect the capture or prevent the escape or rescue of a person whom the member has reasonable cause to believe has committed a felony which did not involve the use or a threat to use deadly force.

"(3) At moving or fleeing vehicles involved in violations of the Vehicle Code (including felony violations such as 20001, 10851, 23105) unless necessary to defend the life of the officer or another person."

Representatives of San Jose and respondent entered into a memorandum of understanding pursuant to the MMBA, covering the period July 1, 1972 through June 30, 1975. This memorandum of understanding was later adopted by San Jose's city council. On January 23, 1975, the chief of police issued a new policy governing the use of firearms. Appellants did not meet and confer with respondent before doing so. The policy of January 23, 1975 provided in part as follows:

"BACKGROUND AND PURPOSE.

* * *

"* * * Thus, it is seen that our new policy is not a radical departure from the evolving standards, but rather it reflects some generally accepted values of our modern society and the criminal justice system; to wit, the use of deadly force is justifiable only as a means of preserving life. The discharge of firearms is never justifiable solely for the purpose of apprehension. It should be emphasized that there is nothing in this policy that prohibits police officers from protecting themselves or another person from a danger of death or of great bodily injury."

"3111.1. *Definition of Deadly Force.*

* * *

"e. *An honest and reasonable belief* is a judgment based on a set of circumstances that would cause a person of ordinary caution and prudence to reasonably entertain (have in mind) a strong suspicion amounting to a belief that a certain condition exists that requires the use of deadly force. In determining reasonableness, the officer should honestly believe (in fact entertain) certain conditions exist that require the use of deadly force. The judgment is not reasonable if the officer is negligent in surveying the facts or is negligent in acquiring any knowledge needed to understand the set of circumstances, the applicable laws, or the policies of his Department.

" 'The San Jose Police Department qualifies its members by periodic training as stated elsewhere in this policy and each officer must demonstrate the ability to understand laws and policies, analyze combat situations, and defend himself and others.'

"P. *Force necessary to protect* is that force required to protect against a manifest peril to life or great bodily injury. Manifest peril occurs when there is a combination of time, space and reason to believe a perilous action will occur. There are three general situations of manifest peril involving these combinations which justify the use of deadly force:

"(1) Instant Peril—At this moment and this place the officer has reason to believe that this person has the ability to kill or do great bodily injury and will do so.

"(2) Near Peril—At the next moment and in this place, the officer has reason to believe that this person will have the ability to kill or do great bodily injury and will do so.

"This place, as used in (1) and (2), is defined as that area in proximity to the officer in which he can, at this time, personally observe the activity of the person.

"(3) Foreboding Peril—At another time and in an unknown place, the officer has reason to believe that this person will have the capacity to kill or do great bodily harm and will do so because he has demonstrated a wanton disregard for human life."

"3111.2. *When deadly force may be used.* A police officer may use deadly force when all other reasonable means have failed and the officer honestly and reasonably believes that such force is necessary to protect himself or another person from death or great bodily injury."

"3111.3. *When firearms may be discharged.* A police officer may discharge a firearm:

"a. As provided in Section 3111.2.

"b. At a firing range pursuant to all safety rules and instructions.

"c. To kill seriously injured or dangerous animals when no other disposition is practical and the public safety is not jeopardized by the discharge."

On February 25, 1975, respondent's counsel sent a letter to the city manager alleging that respondent had not received a copy of the new policy until February 10, 1975, and requesting that San Jose meet and confer concerning the policy. On February 26, 1975, counsel wrote another letter stating that, having read the memorandum of understanding between San Jose and respondent, he was of the opinion that

San Jose could only change the use of force policy if respondent was willing to meet and confer on the issue.

Thereafter respondent filed an action in superior court seeking a temporary restraining order and a preliminary and permanent injunction restraining appellants from giving effect to the new use of force policy until they met and conferred with respondent. Respondent also sought a judgment declaring that the use of force policy was a "meet and confer" item under the MMBA and the memorandum of understanding and that San Jose's unilateral action violated both the MMBA and the memorandum of understanding.

On March 7, 1975, the trial court issued a temporary restraining order granting the injunctive relief prayed for. On April 2, 1975 appellants answered the complaint and the chief of police withdrew the new use of force policy and reinstated the former policy. Following a trial to the court, the trial court rendered judgment for respondent and issued a permanent injunction which enjoined appellant from altering the 1972 use of force policy without meeting and conferring with respondent and from changing the 1972 use of force policy prior to June 30, 1975, without permission from respondent. The trial court further declared that the use of force policy regarding firearms was a mandatory subject of the meet and confer process under the MMBA. Finally the trial court denied respondent attorney's fees.

The principal issue presented by this appeal is whether appellants were required, under the MMBA, to notify respondent of the proposed change in the use of force policy and to meet and confer with respondent before changing that policy. Counsel have cited no controlling authority, and our own research has disclosed none. The issue appears to be one of first impression.

The MMBA applies to all local government employees in California. It provides for negotiation ("meet and confer") and mediation but not for fact finding or arbitration. (Sections 3505 and 3505.2.) "Meet and confer in good faith" is defined in section 3505 as exchanging information, opinions and proposals, and endeavoring "to reach an agreement on matters within the scope of representation. * * *" (Emphasis supplied.) Section 3504 defines the scope of representation as follows:

> "The scope of representation shall include all matters relating to employment conditions and employer-employee relations, including, but not limited to, wages, hours, and other terms and conditions of employment, except, however, that the scope of representation shall not include consideration of the merits, necessity or organization of any service or activity provided by law or executive order."

Respondent argues that the use of force policy relates to "terms and conditions of employment" and thus is within "the scope of representation." Appellants argue that the use of force policy relates to the "merits, necessity or organization of any service or activity provided by law or executive order" and thus is without "the scope of representation."

The issue thus presented is a most delicate one requiring the resolution of significant competing considerations. Respondent argues that the 1975 use of force policy issued by appellants curtailed the situations under which an officer may pull his firearm and fire. Respondent further argues that the 1975 use of force policy subjected peace officers, and the citizenry in general, to greater danger because it limits the situations in which a firearm may be discharged to the firing range, to the killing of a seriously injured or dangerous animal, and to situations where deadly force is involved. The trial court so found in its findings of fact. Appellants argue that it is contrary to the MMBA and to public policy for the conditions under which a police officer may kill a person to be placed on the bargaining table, to be traded off against increases or decreases in wages, hours, and fringe benefits. Appellants further argue that the conditions under which a police officer may kill are a fundamental governmental prerogative, a management decision, the formulation of which should be left to the appropriate elected representatives of the people whose lives and safety are directly affected by such decisions.

In *Fire Fighters Union v. City of Vallejo* (1974) 12 Cal.3d 608, the leading case on the meaning and interpretation of the MMBA, the court examined the problem of "reconciling the two vague, seemingly overlapping phrases of the statute: 'wages, hours and working conditions,' which, broadly read could encompass practically any conceivable bargaining proposal; and 'merits, necessity or organization of any service' which, expansively interpreted, could swallow the whole provision for collective negotiation and relegate determination of all labor issues to the city's discretion." (*Id.* at p. 615.)

The court pointed out that because of the similarities in language between the MMBA and the National Labor Relations Act (hereinafter the NLRA) (29 USC § 158(d)) federal precedents provide useful analogies in determining the parameters of the phrase "wages, hours and other terms and conditions of employment." However, the court also explained:

> "The origin and meaning of the second phrase—excepting 'merits, necessity or organization' from the scope of bargaining—cannot claim so rich a background. Apparently the Legislature included the limiting language not to restrict bargaining on matters directly affecting employees' legitimate interests in wages, hours and working conditions but rather to forestall any expansion of the language of 'wages, hours and working conditions' to include more general managerial policy decisions." (p. 616.)

The court further concluded, however, that

> "Although the NLRA does not contain specific wording comparable to the 'merits, necessity or organization' terminology in the city charter and the state act, the underlying fear that generated this

language—that is, that wages, hours and working conditions would be expanded beyond reasonable boundaries to deprive an employer of his legitimate management prerogatives—lies imbedded in the federal precedents under the NLRA. As a review of federal case law in this field demonstrates, the trepidation that the union would extend its province into matters that should properly remain in the hands of employers has been incorporated into the interpretation of the scope of 'wages, hours and terms and conditions of employment.' Thus, because the federal decisions effectively reflect the same interests as those that prompted the inclusion of the 'merits, necessity or organization' bargaining limitation in the charter provision and state act, the federal precedents provide reliable if analogous authority on the issue." (pp. 616–617.)

One of the most often cited analyses of the federal standard is the concurring opinion of MR. JUSTICE STEWART in *Fibreboard Corp. v. NLRB* (1964) 379 U.S. 203, 217, 57 LRRM 2609, which contains a careful and detailed discussion of the history of the NLRA and the limitations and exceptions in the term "working conditions" as that term applies in the private sector to employment security vis-a-vis entrepreneurial decisions. MR. JUSTICE STEWART said:

"While employment security has thus properly been recognized in various circumstances as a condition of employment, it surely does not follow that every decision which may affect job security is a subject of compulsory collective bargaining. Many decisions made by management affect the job security of employees. Decisions concerning the volume and kind of advertising expenditures, product design, the manner of financing and sales, all may bear upon the security of the worker's jobs. Yet it is hardly conceivable that such decisions so involve 'conditions of employment' that they must be negotiated with the employees' bargaining representative.

"In many of these areas the impact of a particular management decision upon job security may be extremely indirect and uncertain, and this alone may be sufficient reason to conclude that such decisions are not 'with respect to * * * conditions of employment.' Yet there are other areas where decisions by management may quite clearly imperil job security or indeed terminate employment entirely. An enterprise may decide to invest in labor-saving machinery. Another may resolve to liquidate its assets and go out of business. Nothing the Court holds today should be understood as imposing a duty to bargain collectively regarding such managerial decisions, which lie at the core of the entrepreneurial control. Decisions concerning the commitment of investment capital and the basic scope of the enterprise are not in themselves primarily about conditions of employment, though the effect of the decision may be necessarily to terminate employment. If, as I think clear, the purpose of § 8(d) is to describe a limited area subject to the duty of collective bargaining, those management decisions which are fundamental to the basic direction of a corporate enterprise or which impinge only indirectly upon employment security should be excluded from that area."

In *Fire Fighters,* in its discussion of the union's proposal that more fire fighters be added, our Supreme Court shed some light on the considerations which govern the resolution of the issue in this case. The City of Vallejo argued that the level of manpower in the fire department was inevitably a matter of fire prevention policy, and thus not within the scope of representation under the MMBA. The court commented that if the union's manpower proposal was aimed at maintaining a particular level of fire protection in the community the city's argument would be well taken. The union argued, however, that the more firemen the city employed, the less the workload of each would be and that because of the hazardous nature of the job, the number of men available to fight a fire directly affected the safety of the firemen. The court pointed out that under federal decisions, questions of employee workload and safety are recognized as mandatory subjects of bargaining (*Fire Fighters, supra,* at pp. 619–20). The court disposed of the issue by sending the case to an arbitrator, pursuant to provision of the City of Vallejo Charter similar to the MMBA, to decide in the first instance whether the manpower question "*primarily* involves the workload and safety of the men ('wages, hours and working conditions') or the policy of fire prevention of the City ('merits, necessity or organization of any governmental service')." [Emphasis supplied.] (*Fire Fighters, supra,* at pp. 620–21.)

A similar test has been applied to cases arising under the NLRA by the Court of Appeals for the Ninth Circuit. * * *

* * *

It is undoubtedly true, as the trial court found, that a change in the use of force policy, particularly when such a change inhibits the ability of a police officer to fire at a suspected criminal, has some effect on the safety of the police officer—clearly a term or condition of employment. It is equally true, however, that the use of force policy is as closely akin to a managerial decision as any decision can be in running a police department, surpassed only by the decision as to whether force will be used at all. While private managerial concepts do not translate easily to the public sector, we can imagine few decisions more "managerial" in nature than the one which involves the conditions under which an entity of the state will permit a human life to be taken. In a different context, involving issues of due process and equal protection rather than the MMBA, the Court of Appeal for the second district in *Long Beach Police Officers Assn. v. City of Long Beach* (1976) 61 Cal.App.3d 364, 371, stated the following with respect to the adoption of a use of force policy:

"The formulation of a policy governing use of deadly force by police officers is a heavy responsibility involving the delicate balancing of different interests: the protection of society from criminals, the protection of police officers' safety, and the preservation of all human life if possible. This delicate judgment is best exercised by the appropriate legislative and executive officers. The effort of the appropriate officials of the City of Long Beach to make that determination in the interests of its citizens and its police officers should be upheld if it is consistent with state law and constitutional standards."

It is, unfortunately, true that the job of a police officer is a dangerous one. The danger, however, is inherent in the calling: a police officer's situation is unique, and in today's world, oftentimes unenviable. Unlike the normal job in the private sector, or indeed, the job of a fire fighter, police work presents danger from third parties, rather than from dangerous working conditions. Thus the employer cannot eliminate safety problems merely by purchasing better equipment or by increasing the work force, as in *Fire Fighters.* The danger posed to a police officer by a suspected criminal must be balanced against difficult considerations of when an escaping criminal should pay the price of death for ignoring a peace officer's command to stop. Viewed in this context, the safety of the policeman, as important as it is, is so inextricably interwoven with important policy considerations relating to basic concepts of the entire system of criminal justice that we cannot say that the use of force policy concerns "primarily" a matter of wages, hours or working conditions.

It is important to note that San Jose's 1975 use of force policy does not restrict a police officer's right to defend himself from the threat of great bodily harm. The danger presented is an indirect one, in that a suspect who is able to escape because the police officer is not permitted to discharge his firearm in capturing the suspect, may later harm the police officer. While expressing no opinion as to the wisdom of such a decision by appellants, we observe that any such danger obviously extends equally as much to the public at large as it does to the individual police officer. Such an effect on public safety lends further support to our conclusion that the use of force policy is primarily a matter of public safety and therefore not a subject of meeting and conferring under the MMBA. While the policy may impinge on a condition of employment, it impinges only indirectly.

The power of a city to enact and enforce regulations relating to the use of firearms by police officers is in the exercise of the police power granted by Article XI, section 7 of the California Constitution (*Long Beach Police Officers Assn. v. City of Long Beach, supra,* at p. 372). A governmental agency may not suspend, bargain or contract away its police power. * * *

Respondent argues correctly that appellants are not required to come to an agreement with respondent on the use of force policy, but only to negotiate the policy. (Gov.Code, § 3505; *Los Angeles County Employees Association, Local 660 v. County of Los Angeles* (1973) 33

Cal.App.3d 1.) However, the MMBA does require the parties to meet and confer in good faith and "endeavor to reach an agreement" (Section 3505) on matters which are within the scope of representation. * * *

* * *

The real vice in respondent's position is demonstrated by its argument in its post trial brief to the trial court. There, in arguing that the trial court should grant declaratory relief as a guide for the parties' future conduct, respondent said: "Here both parties should know while they're carrying on meet and confer sessions whether or not they are bound to negotiate the gun policy if same is brought up, *whether or not they should bring it up as a possible exchange for favor or concession by the other side,* and the like. That is, the parties will more effectively be able to carry on negotiations if they have a judicial determination of the negotiability of a gun policy; *they should not, at least in part, have to base negotiating strategies and postures on the possible outcome of a suit* to be brought when and if the City refuses to negotiate on a gun policy and/or attempts unilaterally to change the policy again." [Emphasis supplied.] The forum of the bargaining table with its postures, strategies, trade-offs, modifications and compromises (*Glendale City Employees Association v. City of Glendale* (1975) 15 Cal.3d 328, 340, *cert. den.,* 424 U.S. 943) is no place for the "delicate balancing of different interests; the protection of society from criminals, the protection of police officers' safety, and the preservation of all human life, if possible." (*Long Beach Police Officers Assn. v. City of Long Beach, supra,* at p. 371.)

We conclude that San Jose's use of force policy falls within the exception delineated in section 3504. Respondent in fact challenged the merits or necessity of a "service or activity provided by law or executive order" (Section 3504), i.e., the policy of when and under what circumstances San Jose will permit a human life to be taken. This policy clearly constitutes a managerial decision which is not properly within the scope of union representation and collective bargaining. As our Supreme Court has pointed out, the analogous federal precedents have established substantive limitations upon the extent to which "working conditions" may be defined under the NLRA, so that decisions which are plainly within the realm of managerial discretion are excluded from the meet and confer requirements of the MMBA (see *Fire Fighters Union v. City of Vallejo, supra,* at pp. 616–17). As stated in *NLRB v. Transmarine Navig. Corp.* (9th Cir.1967) 380 F.2d 933, 939: "A decision of such fundamental importance as to the basic direction of the corporate enterprise is not included within the area of mandatory collective bargaining." This is consistent with the language in *Long Beach Police Officers Assn. v. City of Long Beach, supra,* at p. 371, that the heavy responsibility and delicate balancing of the different interests referred to above, involved in a use of force policy, are best exercised by the appropriate legislative and executive officers, who are then directly responsible to the people for such decisions.

* * *

The judgment of the trial court is reversed. * * *

Questions

1. Many of the scope of bargaining cases in the public sector have been initiated by police unions—and teachers' unions. What explains this phenomenon?

2. Are the different outcomes in the above cases solely or primarily explainable in terms of different statutory language covering scope of bargaining?

3. On the one hand, it has been argued that restricting the scope of bargaining for public employees will prevent responsiveness to changing conditions and new problems, make collective bargaining a frustrating and dysfunctional experience, and encourage lobbying by unions for legislated public employee benefits when they are outside the restricted scope of bargaining. On the other hand, it has been argued that the price paid by public employees for lesser bargaining rights than their private sector counterparts have is more than compensated for by the many advantages of public employment such as statutory benefits and the right to participate as citizens in employment-related decision making. Which side of this debate has the stronger arguments?

4. In discussing whether a particular subject should be labeled mandatory, some jurisdictions require that the subject must be "primarily" or "materially" or "significantly" or "fundamentally" related to or "vitally" or "directly" affect "wages, hours, and other terms and conditions of employment." In predicting the outcome of scope litigation, are any of these phrases helpful? Also, when a balancing test is applied, what factors should be considered and how much weight should be assigned to each factor?

5. It has already been noted that there are no general trends regarding scope of bargaining. What accounts for this notable lack of rethinking or developing a consensus on scope of bargaining in the public sector? What aren't jurisdictions "learning" and "borrowing" from each other in the area of legal scope of bargaining?

6. Should the following be subject to mandatory bargaining with a union representing classroom teachers: a school board's decision to "mainstream" students with disabilities into "regular" classrooms?

Should the following be subject to mandatory bargaining with a union representing county nursing home employees: a county's decision to sell its nursing home facility and go out of the business of providing public nursing home services because the cost of operating the facility is a "drain" on a "tight" county budget?

Should a city which wishes to improve its community relations by requiring all police officers to reside within the city be legally bound to bargain on this decision with the police officers' union?

Should a school district which wishes to discourage student smoking by establishing a strict no-smoking policy for employees be required to bargain about its no-smoking policy with the unions representing its employees? (In answering this question, should the outcome differ depending upon whether the employees represented are teachers or white collar or blue collar workers?)

7. Should a statutory right to strike or mandatory impasse arbitration procedures (explored further in Chapters 7 and 8) affect legislative or judicial decisions governing what subjects are within the appropriate scope of mandatory bargaining in that jurisdiction?

D. NOTE ON THE SIGNIFICANCE OF SCOPE OF BARGAINING DETERMINATIONS*

When management takes a unilateral action which will have a perceptible impact on the terms and conditions of employment, there are significant risks involved. If the matter is within the scope of mandatory bargaining, the action is an unfair labor practice unless management has given the union notice and negotiated to an impasse. If on the other hand, the matter is outside the mandatory scope of negotiations, it may be taken without giving collective bargaining a chance to work.

The risk to management of improper classification is obvious.

If management is correct that the judgment is outside the scope of the bargaining, it has nothing to worry about. But if management is wrong about this, the action exposes it to significant liability. Thus, for example, if a school board decides to contract out busing services, it may be required to rescind the contract, bargain with the union and offer to rehire its former bus driver employees and give them back pay.

Where the scope question arises in the context of a claim of bad faith bargaining, i.e., management refuses to discuss the matter on the ground that it is outside the scope of mandatory bargaining, the risks are minimal. This is so because if management is wrong, the worst that can happen to it is an order requiring it to bargain. Such a remedy has little or no practical significance. Management may, accordingly, be tempted to refuse to negotiate over matters which it regards as falling within its bundle of prerogatives. If management wants the bargaining process to work and to facilitate peaceable settlement, such a strategy is counter-productive.

Suppose, hypothetically, that a teacher organization lays on the bargaining table a package of proposals which includes the following subjects: a school calendar of specified holidays, vacations, and recesses; a guarantee of academic freedom; an increase in annual sick leave allowances; reimbursement of teachers for tuition for courses taken beyond the bachelors degree; prohibition of transfer from one building to another without the affected teacher's consent; teacher participation in decision-making with respect to appointments and tenure; teacher

* Unpublished lecture by one of the authors.

participation in decision-making with respect to curriculum, special programs, teaching methods, selection of textbooks, grading standards, and testing procedures; and a guarantee of staffing levels.

Some practitioners hold the view that the first thing for a school board to do when presented with this kind of list is to categorize which of these are negotiable, which are consultative, and which are non-negotiable, and, failing union agreement on the proposed classifications, to initiate or precipitate litigation.

A different view, and one which arguably is more consistent with the obligation to bargain in good faith, is to find out early-on which of these proposals is seriously made. If a union is functioning properly, its package of demands will be a political document, containing items of concern to every identifiable voting group in the constituency. Some of these proposals will doubtless be made for the record; others will be for real. One way to find out which is which is to take those proposals which management feels belongs in the category of non-negotiability and put them to one side, usually by the simple expedient of not responding to them. If they are on the table for political reasons, they will wash out as the negotiations move along.

What about the items which management regards as putatively non-negotiable but which stay alive because the union continues to push for them? Should they be the subject of litigation—precipitated by the board's refusal to consider them?

If management desires to move the bargaining process along without prejudice to its rights, a wiser course of action is to try to find out what these proposals mean, how they would work, and why the union has made them. At least three salutary things can come from this process.

First, the union may be persuaded to drop the proposal when its implications are understood.

Does the union want responsibility for deciding tenure questions? Is it willing to say "No" to a popular teacher of marginal competence and face the internal political consequences? Does the union have members who are willing to spend 10–15 hours of their own time per week on curricular and programmatic planning, special education, and pedagogic techniques?

Second, management may learn about a problem which, while it may not be appropriate for resolution at the bargaining table, needs to be dealt with. Why would the union propose that no teacher be involuntarily transferred from one building to another without his consent—a demand which is unreasonable on its face? Is there some underlying concern which demands school board attention and correction? For example, perhaps the personnel people in central administration have been transferring teachers for disciplinary reasons. This is hardly a sound basis for deploying teachers. Good school management should be as interested as the union is in stopping this practice.

Third, the union may reformulate its proposal, thereby removing management's objection to its negotiability. For instance, a school board decision to retrench operations is probably not negotiable, but the impact of the decision probably is. This means that a union proposal requiring a board to maintain present staffing patterns and levels may not be within the scope of negotiations but that a proposal dealing with the effects of a decision to layoff teachers, e.g., the impact on workload of the survivors—is. It is probably only the latter that the union was seriously interested in in the first place. What is to be gained from litigation when the scope issue can be resolved by agreement?

At least one unfortunate consequence is avoided by dealing this way with putatively non-negotiable proposals. The first teachers strike under the New York Taylor law was probably made inevitable by the school board's initial bargaining stance that academic freedom, special education, the school calendar, class size, textbook selection, and appointments and tenure were non-negotiable, i.e., none of the teacher's business. This position, formally and nakedly expressed, converted a teachers' organization with only benign interest in the negotiations into a militant, foot-stomping group.

Are there any risks that are run by taking this approach? Some have argued that a school board or other public employer that talks with the union about a subject may thereby waive its right to claim that the matter is non-negotiable. Perhaps, but surely the school board would not be found to have waived the right that really counts—the right to say "No" and to stand on the well settled proposition that good faith bargaining does not require the reaching of an agreement or the making of a concession.[1]

Comment

The point of view set forth above has been criticized as superficial and simplistic. It ignores the frustrations of interest groups other than public employee unions that are frozen out by collective bargaining from participating in decision-making. It also ignores the fact that public employee unions are usually very active politically and that their impact has been increased greatly with the spread of public employee unionism. This means, among other things, that public employees have influence on the

1. These views do not apply where the question is legality, not permissibility. Does the employer have the power to make a bilateral arrangement concerning the matter at issue? If it does not, any agreement may be vulnerable to being set aside. Moreover, if the school board performs the promise, it may be exposed to liability. But these questions need not foreclose a negotiated settlement. A severability clause will probably protect the rest of the agreement against an adverse decision on the questionable provisions. And a "hold harmless" promise from the union will protect the board against liability losses. Or the parties might agree that performance of the questionable commitment is contingent upon the determination that it is valid, with the understanding that if such determination is adverse, the provisions of the agreement affected will be renegotiated.

The right to take a subject out of bargaining on the ground that it is not negotiable may be important where the governing statute forces unsettled disputes into binding arbitration. See Chapter 8.

selection of who represents management. There is nothing in private sector bargaining even remotely comparable to the potential power of public employees to participate in the selection of public management. Management's ability and willingness to say "no" is thus undermined. Who is to stand guard against the efforts of public employee unionism to reach into areas that have only tangential relevance, if that, to the terms and conditions of employment and which may adversely affect the quality and level of services?

Evaluate the above arguments.

Chapter 5

COMPETING SYSTEMS OF WORKPLACE GOVERNANCE

A. INTRODUCTION

One of the striking developments in the private sector over the last several decades has been the growth in legal regulation of the workplace through statutes, common law rules, and even the application of state constitutions. Prior to that development, legal regulation was sparse—consisting mainly of wage and hour laws and workers compensation statutes—and workplace governance, in the absence of collective bargaining, was primarily a matter of individual employer decision-making.

The history of the public sector has been quite different. Long before the advent of collective bargaining, and long before the growth of regulation in the private sector, the public sector workplace was governed to a considerable extent by the provisions of constitutions, charters, or statutes. In some instances the law provided a specific workplace rule—decreeing, for example, that workers would have certain designated holidays, or vacation leave, or that teachers would be paid in accordance with a statutory salary schedule, or that police officers had to reside within city limits. In other instances, the law provided a general standard, for example that salaries were to be set on the basis of wages prevailing in other private or public employment for comparable work. And, in still others, the law allocated decision-making authority over certain employment conditions to a particular individual or body, such as a police chief or a school board, sometimes in connection with a generalized system of regulation, as in the case of civil service and tenure systems.

When collective bargaining was introduced, therefore, questions arose as to the relationship between that process and these pre-existing forms of workplace governance. Except for constitutional provisions, such questions were subject to being answered by the state legislatures; and some legislatures accepted that responsibility. Their answers varied substantially, however; indeed, in some cases the answers varied from one collective bargaining statute to another within the same state.

In Illinois, for example, the statute applicable to state and local government employees provides that any collective bargaining agreement negotiated pursuant to the statute supersedes conflicting laws (Ill.—S.H.A. ch. 48, para. 1607), while the statute applicable to educational employees provides that the parties shall not effect or implement contract provisions in violation of or inconsistent with other statutes. (Ill.—S.H.A. ch. 48, para. 1717(b) (1986)).

California's statute pertaining to state employees adopts a middle course: it lists the statutory provisions which may be preempted by a collective agreement, and those that may not be preempted absent approval by the legislature, and those that may be preempted unless the State Personnel Board finds the collective agreement to be inconsistent with the merit principle. (West's Ann.Cal.Gov't Code § 3527.6 (1980 & Supp.1990)).

A Florida statute provides that if a collective agreement conflicts with a law, ordinance, rule, or regulation which the negotiating employer has no power to amend, the negotiating employer is under an obligation to propose an amendment to the appropriate body; meanwhile, the conflicting provision is inoperative. (West's Fla.Stat.Ann. § 447.309(3) (1981)).

Notes and Questions

(1) What considerations would you expect (a) a public employer and/or (b) a union to take into account in deciding what position to take with respect to the relationship between collective bargaining and various external regulations and systems?

(2) If you were advising a legislative body with respect to an appropriate public policy concerning such relationships, what would you recommend?

Often the collective bargaining statute either fails to address the question of the relationship to pre-existing systems or rules of workplace governance, or fails to provide a clear answer in a particular case. When that is true, or when the pre-existing system or rule is provided for in a constitution beyond the reach of the collective bargaining statute, the question is likely to reach the courts.

Such questions may arise in a variety of procedural contexts: a generalized attack on the collective bargaining statute, a dispute over the scope of bargaining, a dispute over the arbitrability of a particular issue, or a dispute over the enforceability of an arbitrator's award. For that reason, it is difficult to isolate such questions in a single chapter without disturbing the organization of other chapters. To minimize that disturbance, we have confined the case examples in this chapter to the two most pervasive systems of workplace governance that preceded collective bargaining: civil service and teacher tenure.

B. CIVIL SERVICE SYSTEMS AND COLLECTIVE BARGAINING

PACIFIC LEGAL FOUNDATION v. BROWN

Supreme Court of California, 1981.
29 Cal.3d 168, 172 Cal.Rptr. 487, 624 P.2d 1215.

TOBRINER, J.—Over the past 20 years, the California Legislature has enacted a series of legislative measures granting public employees, at both the state and local level, a variety of organizational and negotiating rights somewhat analogous to the rights long afforded most employees in the private sector by the federal labor relation laws of the 1930's. In the instant mandate proceeding, petitioners have mounted a sweeping constitutional challenge to one of the most recent of these public labor relations measures, the State Employer–Employee Relations Act (SEERA), enacted in 1977 to regulate the state's labor relations with state employees. (Stats.1977, ch. 1159, § 4, p. 3751, codified in Gov. Code, § 3512 et seq.)[1] Petitioners principally contend that SEERA is unconstitutional on its face because it allegedly conflicts with the "merit system" of employment embodied in the civil service provisions of article VII of the California Constitution, and, in particular, with the powers that article VII assertedly assigns exclusively to the jurisdiction of the State Personnel Board. On the basis of these constitutional contentions, petitioners seek a writ of mandate striking down the 1977 statute and compelling the various respondent public officers and agencies to conduct their operations without regard to the provisions of SEERA.

* * *

1. BACKGROUND AND DESCRIPTION OF THE PROVISIONS OF SEERA.

Prior to 1961, public employees in California enjoyed no formal rights to participate in the decision-making processes which determined the terms and conditions of their employment. In 1961, the evolution of public employee rights in this state began with the enactment of the George Brown Act (Stats.1961, ch. 1964, § 1, pp. 4141–4142, now codified in §§ 3525–3536). As originally enacted, the act applied to employees of the state, cities, counties, school districts and institutions of higher education, granting such employees the right to join employee organizations of their choosing, and requiring public employers to "meet and confer" with employee organizations prior to undertaking

1. Unless otherwise indicated, all statutory references are to the Government Code.

action on "all matters relating to employment conditions and employer-employee relations."

Although it represented a significant first step, the George Brown Act omitted a number of key elements that have proven to be important factors in formulating peaceful labor relations in the private sector. Thus the act did not provide any mechanism for recognizing an employee organization as the exclusive representative of a group of employees, and placed no obligation on either the employer or employees to attempt to reach an agreement on terms and conditions of employment, i.e., to negotiate in good faith. Moreover, the act afforded the parties no explicit authority to reach binding agreements and did not establish an expert labor relations agency with authority to oversee the process and devise appropriate remedies for improper conduct by employees or employers.

Subsequent legislative and gubernatorial actions over the past decade and a half have been aimed, in large part, in overcoming these deficiencies and in tailoring the labor relations process to the special conditions of different segments of the public labor force. In 1965, the Winton Act (Stats.1965, ch. 2041, § 1, p. 4660) expanded the "meet and confer" rights of public school employees, and in 1968, the Legislature enacted the Meyers–Milias–Brown Act (MMBA) (Stats.1968, ch. 1390, § 1, p. 2725, codified at § 3500 et seq.) to provide a more structured collective bargaining process for most local government employees. (See *Glendale City Employees' Association, Inc. v. City of Glendale* (1975) 15 Cal.3d 328, 334–338 [124 Cal.Rptr. 513, 540 P.2d 609].)

The early 1970's brought an increasing demand among state employees for a formal system of collective bargaining that would provide them with a more meaningful role in establishing the terms and conditions of their employment. (See King, Deliver Us From Evil: A Public History of California's Civil Service System (1979) p. 51.) In response, Governor Reagan in March 1971 issued an executive order centralizing the "meet and confer" process by designating one state official, chosen by the Governor, to be responsible for meeting and conferring with employee organizations for the purpose of reaching an agreement on salary and employee benefits (Exec.Order No. R–25–71.) [2]

In 1972, following the first major state employee strike, the Legislature created the Assembly Advisory Council on Public Employee Relations, chaired by UCLA Professor Benjamin Aaron, to formulate recommendations "for establishing an appropriate framework within which disputes can be settled between public jurisdictions and their employees." (Assem.Res. No. 51 (1972 Reg.Sess.).) In its 1973 report the Advisory Council recommended the enactment of a comprehensive state law, modeled on the National Labor Relations Act, which would afford formal collective bargaining rights to all public employees.

2. In 1975, Governor Brown transferred these duties to a newly created Office of Employee Relations. (Exec.Order No. B–7–75.)

The Legislature, however, was unable to agree on a comprehensive bill covering all public employees and decided instead to draft separate collective bargaining statutes directed to the specific needs and problems of different categories of public entities. In line with this approach, the Legislature in 1975 first enacted the Educational Employment Relations Act (EERA) (Stats.1975, ch. 961, § 2, p. 2247, codified in § 3540 et seq.); EERA repealed the Winton Act, established formal negotiating rights for public school employees, and created the Educational Employment Relations Board, an expert, quasi-judicial administrative agency modeled after the National Labor Relations Board, to enforce the act. In 1977, the Legislature adopted SEERA, the legislation challenged in the instant proceeding, to provide formal collective bargaining rights to state employees. Finally, the legislative sequence was completed in 1978 with the adoption of the Higher Education Employer–Employee Relations Act (HEERA) (Stats.1978, ch. 744, § 3, p. 2312, codified in § 3560 et seq.), granting similar rights to employees in the state university and University of California systems. As this brief historical overview demonstrates, SEERA constitutes one significant component in a network of recent statutes affording collective bargaining rights to California public employees.

Although a detailed discussion of all of SEERA's provisions is not necessary for the purposes of this decision, it may be helpful to highlight the major features of the statute. To begin with, the act modifies the George Brown Act in a number of respects in order to strengthen the role of employees and to increase the efficiency of the employer-employee negotiation process. First, the act establishes the principle of exclusive representation on matters of employment relations by employee organizations chosen by a majority of employees in administratively designated bargaining units. (§§ 3520.5, 3521.) Second, the act requires the Governor and the exclusive employee representatives to meet and confer in good faith for the purpose of reaching agreement on wages, hours and other terms and conditions of state employment. (§ 3517.) Finally, the act specifically directs that any such agreement that the parties do reach be set forth in a written memorandum of understanding. (§ 3517.5.)

Although the act thus affords state employees significant new rights, the Legislature at the same time placed definite limits on the scope of representation and retained substantial control over state employee compensation and many other terms and conditions of state employment. SEERA specifically precludes bargaining over "the merits, necessity, or organization of any service or activity provided by law or executive order." (§ 3516.) The act also provides that as to matters within the scope of representation, a memorandum of understanding requiring the expenditure of funds does not become effective unless it is approved by the Legislature in the annual Budget Act (§ 3517.6); under this provision, virtually all salary agreements are subject to prior legislative approval.

The act further provides that, except with respect to a number of specific statutes which the Legislature has expressly determined may be superseded by a memorandum of understanding, any provision of a memorandum of understanding in conflict with a statutory mandate shall not be effective unless approved by the Legislature. (*Ibid.*) In addition, the act provides that any terms of a memorandum of understanding in conflict with specified statutes relating to layoffs or demotions shall not be controlling if the State Personnel Board finds those terms to be inconsistent with the merit employment principles of article VII of the California Constitution. (*Ibid.*)

Finally, to protect the rights and enforce the obligations of employees, employee organizations and the state, SEERA expanded the jurisdiction and changed the name of the Educational Employment Relations Board to the Public Employment Relations Board (PERB). Under SEERA, PERB's principal responsibilities and duties include: (1) determining appropriate units of employees, (2) determining whether a particular item is within the scope of representation, (3) arranging for and supervising representation elections and resolving disputes relating to certification or decertification, (4) establishing a list of available mediators, arbitrators and factfinders, and (5) investigating unfair practice charges relating to alleged violations of SEERA, and taking such actions with respect to such charges as are necessary to effectuate the purposes of the act. (§§ 3513, subd. (g), 3541.3, 3514.5.)

* * *

3. (4) SEERA does not conflict with the general "merit principle" of civil service employment embodied in article VII of the California Constitution.

In challenging the constitutionality of SEERA, petitioners rely primarily on the asserted conflict between the act and several sections of article VII of the California Constitution, the article pertaining to the state civil service.[5] Although, as we discuss below, the principal thrust of petitioners' challenge relates to the legislation's alleged conflict with the duties and powers afforded the State Personnel Board by

5. Article VII, sections 1, 2 and 3, the constitutional sections most relevant to the present case, provide in pertinent part:

"Section 1. (a) The civil service includes every officer and employee of the state except as otherwise provided in this Constitution.

"(b) In the civil service permanent appointment and promotion shall be made under a general system based on merit ascertained by competitive examination.

"Section 2. (a) There is a Personnel Board of 5 members appointed by the Governor and approved by the Senate, a majority of the membership concurring, for 10–year terms and until their successors are appointed and qualified. * * *

"(b) * * *

"(c) The Board shall appoint and prescribe compensation for an executive officer who shall be a member of the civil service but not a member of the board.

"Section 3. (a) The board shall enforce the civil service statutes and, by majority vote of all its members, shall prescribe probationary periods and classifications, adopt other rules authorized by statute, and review disciplinary actions.

"(b) The executive officer shall administer the civil service statutes under rules of the board."

article VII, section 3, subdivision (a), petitioners apparently also assert more broadly that the entire collective bargaining process adopted by SEERA conflicts with the "general system" of merit appointment and promotion mandated by article VII, section 1, subdivision (b). Because a review of the origins of the constitutional civil service provisions sheds considerable light on all of petitioners' contentions with respect to article VII, we turn directly to the history of the constitutional provision.

In 1913, the California Legislature enacted a statute creating California's first civil service system in an attempt to combat the "spoils system" of political patronage in state employment. (Stats. 1913, ch. 590, p. 1035.) By the early 1930's, however, the existing statutory civil service system was obviously failing in its primary task. The deficiencies in the system stemmed from several principal sources. First, acceding to political pressure, both the Legislature and the statutory civil service commission itself had over the years exempted numerous departments and positions from the civil service restrictions: indeed, by 1932 the exemptions had become so widespread that "[o]f the 23,222 full-time state employees, only 11,917 held permanent civil service positions." (King, Deliver Us from Evil: A Public History of California's Civil Service System (1979) p. 26.) Thus, fully one-half of the permanent state employees were exempt from the civil service law.

"A second abuse of the Civil Service Act was the gross misuse of authorizations for temporary employment [which was not subject to the civil service act]. * * * Officially, temporary appointments followed the three month rule, but this had never been followed. By August 1931, temporary employees constituted more than a third of the entire state service." (*Id.*)

Finally, in the early 1930's considerable public attention was focused on the problem by widespread newspaper accounts of the allegedly numerous politically motivated appointments made by the incumbent Governor. (*Id.* at pp. 26–29.)

It was in this milieu and in response to the specific problems of the times that in 1934 the people adopted article XXIV of the state Constitution. The ballot argument accompanying the 1934 initiative measure sets forth in clear terms both the objectives and the limits of the proposed constitutional provision.

The ballot argument stated: "The purpose of this constitutional amendment is to promote efficiency and economy in State government. *The sole aim of the act is to prohibit appointments and promotion in State service except on the basis of merit, efficiency and fitness ascertained by competitive examination.* Appointments of inefficient employees for political reasons are thereby prohibited, thus eliminating the 'spoils system' from State employment. [¶] * * * [T]his constitutional amendment provides: (1) Employment in the classified service based solely on merit and efficiency; (2) a nonpartisan Personnel Board; (3) prohibition against exemptions from the merit system of employment; (4) correction of the temporary political appointment evil. [¶] *Having by constitutional mandate prohibited employment on any basis except merit and efficiency, thereby eliminating as far as possible the 'spoils system' of employment, the Legislature is given a free hand in setting up laws relating to personnel administration for the best interests of the State,* including the setting up of causes for dismissal such as inefficiency, misconduct or lack of funds." (Italics added.) (Ballot Pamp., Proposed Amends. to Cal. Const. with arguments to voters, Gen. Elec. (Nov. 6, 1934), argument in favor of Prop. 7, p. 12.)

As this ballot argument demonstrates, the "sole aim" of the amendment was to establish, as a constitutional mandate, the principle that appointments and promotions in state service be made solely on the basis of merit. Having established this "merit principle" as a matter of constitutional law, and having established a nonpartisan Personnel Board to administer this merit principle, the constitutional provision left the Legislature with a "free hand" to fashion "laws relating to personnel administration for the best interests of the State."

From this description, we conclude that the collective bargaining process established by SEERA does not on its face conflict with the basic constitutional principles of article VII, section 1, subdivision (b). As we have seen, nothing in the history of the amendment suggests that the establishment of a general system of appointment and promotion based on merit proposed to prohibit the Legislature from adopting a labor relations policy affording employees a meaningful voice in determining the terms and conditions of their employment; instead, the amendment simply sought to eliminate the "spoils system" of public employment.

We recognize, of course, that theoretically the *product* of the collective bargaining process may possibly in specific instances conflict with the merit principle of employment embodied in article VII. Such a conflict would be most evident, for example, if the Governor and an exclusive bargaining representative agreed to a memorandum of understanding purporting to authorize hiring or promotion on a politically partisan basis. The provisions of SEERA, however, neither explicitly nor implicitly authorize any such encroachment on the merit principle of article VII through the collective bargaining process. On the contrary, in drafting SEERA the Legislature explicitly reaffirmed the primacy of the merit principle of employment and crafted the statute carefully so as to minimize any potential conflict with such principle.

* * *

Moreover, in designating the statutes that may be superseded by a memorandum of understanding without legislative approval, the Legislature excluded those statutes relating to classification, examination, appointment, or promotion, areas in which a potential conflict with the merit principle of employment would be most likely to occur. Finally, the Legislature's sensitivity to the preservation of the merit principle is additionally evident in the numerous legislative modifications contained in the 1978 "clean-up" legislation to SEERA, changes which were made largely upon the recommendation of the State Personnel Board to avoid any potential clash with the merit principle.[9]

These numerous provisions demonstrate beyond question that the Legislature drafted SEERA with the merit principle of article VII firmly in mind, fashioning the statute specifically to avoid any conflict with that constitutional mandate. As noted earlier, under familiar principles the legislative judgment in this regard is entitled to great weight, and in light of our own review of the history of article VII, we find no conflict between the general collective bargaining process authorized by SEERA and the merit principle of civil service employment guaranteed by the California Constitution. (Cf. *Los Angeles County Civil Service Com. v. Superior Court* (1978) 23 Cal.3d 55, 62–66 [151 Cal.Rptr. 547, 588 P.2d 249] (local civil service charter provision does not conflict with county's statutory "meet and confer" obligation).)

4. (5) SEERA does not contravene article VII in authorizing the ultimate setting of civil service salaries by the Governor and the Legislature rather than by the State Personnel Board.

Petitioners additionally claim that even if the collective bargaining process established by SEERA does not conflict with the merit principle of civil service employment, SEERA nonetheless is unconstitutional because it assigns the task of setting the salaries of civil service employees to the Governor and the Legislature rather than to the State Personnel Board. In this regard, petitioners rely on section 3, subdivision (a) of article VII, the constitutional provision describing the powers and duties of the State Personnel Board, which provides: "The [State Personnel Board] shall enforce the civil service statutes and, by majority vote of all of its members, shall prescribe probationary periods and classifications, adopt other rules authorized by statute, and review disciplinary actions." Although neither section 3, subdivision (a), nor its constitutional antecedent, explicitly endows the State Personnel Board with the authority to set salaries, petitioners argue nonetheless that the State Personnel Board's constitutional salary setting authority flows both from the Board's authority to "prescribe * * * classifications" and from its duty to "enforce the civil service statutes." We address each of these contentions in turn.

9. In the 1978 amendments to SEERA, the Legislature (1) deleted several statutes from the list of statutes subject to supersession which the State Personnel Board indicated might pose a conflict with the merit principle, (2) provided that nine additional statutes, relating to layoffs and demotions, which had been originally subject to supersession, would not be superseded by a memorandum of understanding if the State Personnel Board finds the terms of the memorandum to be inconsistent "with merit employment principles as provided for by article VII of the California Constitution" and (3) modified two additional statutes which had originally been subject to supersession, transferring the potentially merit-related portions of the statutes into different statutes not subject to supersession, and leaving the nonmerit related subjects in the statutes that remained subject to supersession. (Stats. 1978, ch. 776, §§ 5, 80, 81, 82, 83, pp. 2413–2414, 2452–2453.)

(a) The State Personnel Board's constitutional authority to prescribe classifications does not encompass the power to set the particular salary for such classifications.

On its face, SEERA clearly does not conflict with the State Personnel Board's constitutional authority to prescribe classifications for the state civil service. No provision of the act purports to authorize any other agency to classify positions in the civil service, and the act excludes the numerous statutory provisions relating to the State Personnel Board's classification power (§§ 18800–18806, 18523) from the list of statutes that may be superseded by the terms of a memorandum of understanding. (§ 3517.6.) Furthermore, the act provides that the State Personnel Board's existing classification structure is one of the specific criteria PERB must consider in determining the appropriate units for the selection of an exclusive representative. (§ 3521, subd. (b)(2).) [10]

Petitioners argue, however, that an integral part of the State Personnel Board's authority to prescribe classifications is the power to establish salaries for the classifications so set. An almost identical contention came before the Colorado Supreme Court in *Vivian v. Bloom* (1947) 115 Colo. 579 [177 P.2d 541]. * * *

In *Vivian,* the Colorado Supreme Court rejected the plaintiffs' contention, stating: "It is insistently urged that the power to classify carries with it by necessary implication the power to fix compensation. In this contention we cannot concur. Elsewhere, systems are set up with like divisions of authority. * * * [¶] We are constrained to conclude that the power to fix compensation within the classified service still abides in the [Legislature]. The [Legislature] has the burden of determining and providing for the amount of revenue to be made available for payment of salaries and is immediately responsible to the people's will therein, so it seems not improper that it should retain ultimate control of its ancient prerogative." (177 P.2d at p. 544.)

As the *Vivian* decision suggests, although the power to classify positions has frequently been lodged in civil service commissions or personnel boards, the actual authority to set salaries has traditionally been viewed as a legislative function, with ultimate authority residing in the legislative body. A host of California decisions demonstrate that this fundamental principle has long been followed in this state in jurisdictions operating under civil service provisions. [citing cases]

Petitioners assert, however, that the classification authority granted the State Personnel Board by article VII, section 3, subdivision (a) should be interpreted to include the power to set salaries because under the civil service statutory schemes in force in California since 1913, the State Personnel Board or its predecessor, the Civil Service Commission,

10. During the course of these proceedings, PERB determined the appropriate units for state employees; in its unit determination, PERB did not split any individual classifications established by the State Personnel Board. (See *Unit Determination for the State of California* (Nov. 7, 1979) PERB Dec. No. 110–S; (Jan. 11, 1980) PERB Dec. No. 110b–S.)

has continually been accorded the task of both classifying positions and also establishing salary ranges for the classifications it establishes. (See Stats.1913, ch. 590, § 5, p. 1036; Stats.1927, ch. 719, § 1, p. 1314; Stats.1937, ch. 753, § 70, p. 2094; § 18850.) Petitioners insist that this long-standing practice demonstrates that the power to set salaries is part of the State Personnel Board's constitutional power under article VII.

With the exception of one decision discussed below, however, judicial authorities have uniformly indicated that the State Personnel Board's authority to establish salary ranges rests simply on a delegation of legislative authority under the relevant statutes, and does not reside in the board by virtue of any constitutional mandate. * * *

This view of both the source and the extent of the salary setting power exercised by the State Personnel Board in the past is directly confirmed by an examination of the actual legislative practice that has been followed in this state since the inception of the civil service system. * * *

* * *

Petitioners argue, however, that while these actions by the Legislature and Governor may demonstrate that the State Personnel Board does not have unlimited power to set salaries in excess of authorized appropriations, such actions do not conflict with a recognition of the board's constitutional authority over the setting of salaries and distribution of funds within appropriated limits. Although the actions noted above may not be inconsistent with such a view, a host of other legislative actions over the years clearly conflicts with even this more limited version of the State Personnel Board's constitutional authority.

* * *

These numerous legislative actions, reaching back more than 40 years, demonstrate an unvarying legislative view that the salary setting authority for civil service employees has not been ceded to the State Personnel Board by article VII or its constitutional predecessors, but rather has been left with the Legislature. This consistent legislative interpretation is, of course, entitled to great weight, particularly since the constitutional civil service provision was revised and updated in 1970 without any indication that the drafters intended to alter this established interpretation. (See, e.g., *In re Governorship* (1979) 26 Cal.3d 110, 117–120 [160 Cal.Rptr. 760, 603 P.2d 1357].)

Moreover, the State Personnel Board itself has consistently concurred in the view that its constitutional authority to prescribe classifications does not encompass the ultimate authority to set civil service salaries.

* * *

Although we have determined that SEERA's salary setting provisions are not inconsistent with the State Personnel Board's authority to prescribe classifications, we do not intend to suggest that the board's classification decisions will have no effect whatsoever on the salary measures to which the parties may properly agree under SEERA. (Cf. *Vivian v. Bloom, supra,* 177 P.2d at p. 545.) Because we face no specific salary measures which assertedly conflict with the personnel board's classification scheme, we do not believe that we should at this stage attempt to determine precisely what constraints the board's classification decisions will place on permissible salary agreements.[16] As with other aspects of the "merit principle" of civil service employment, however, the parties are not free to adopt salary measures that interfere with any fundamental "merit principle" element that the classification system serves. This caveat, of course, in no sense renders SEERA unconstitutional on its face; if any improper salary measure should be agreed to by the Governor and approved by the Legislature in the future, petitioners or other interested parties will be free to challenge such measures at that time.[17]

(b)(6) SEERA does not conflict with the State Personnel Board's authority to "enforce the civil service statutes."

As noted above, in addition to contending that the salary setting provisions of SEERA conflict with the State Personnel Board's authority to "prescribe classifications," petitioners claim that the act's delegation to the Governor of the power to negotiate and agree to salaries conflicts with the portion of article VII, section 3, subdivision (a) which provides that "[t]he [State Personnel Board] shall enforce the civil service statutes." Recognizing that the language of the present constitutional provision affords little support to their argument, since SEERA would not normally be thought of as a "civil service statute," petitioners rely instead on the language of former article XXIV, section 3, subdivision (a), the provision from which the current section 3, subdivision (a) derives. (See fn. 8, *ante.*) As we shall explain, however, the provision's history and its consistent interpretation belie petitioners' suggested interpretation. * * * [That portion of the opinion which examines history and interpretation is omitted.]

16. For similar reasons, we have no occasion in this case to determine whether the "like-pay-for-like-work" concept is a constitutionally based doctrine embedded in either the merit principle of article VII, section 1, subdivision (b) or the State Personnel Board's classification power under section 3, subdivision (a), or alternatively is solely of statutory origin. (See, e.g., §§ 18500, subd. (c)(1); 18850.)

17. In its brief, the State Personnel Board indicates that it intends to promulgate "guidelines" identifying those areas of salary setting that may potentially conflict with the board's classification authority and with the merit principle. The board requests that this court "make clear that the Governor must observe the limits established" by such guidelines.

In our view, any ruling on such guidelines is premature. As of this time, the board has not even formally promulgated the guidelines and there is no indication that the Governor will not voluntarily agree to be guided by the board's advice. Until a concrete controversy arises, it would not be appropriate to express an opinion either upon the authority of the board to promulgate such guidelines or on the substantive validity of any particular guideline.

4. (7) PERB's jurisdiction to investigate and devise remedies for unfair practices is not unconstitutional on its face.

Petitioners contend that the provisions of SEERA granting PERB jurisdiction to investigate and devise remedies for unfair practices are irreconcilably in conflict with the State Personnel Board's jurisdiction to "review disciplinary actions" under article VII, section 3, subdivision (a).[18] Although petitioners do not complain of any specific issue that has arisen to date, they urge our court to invalidate PERB's authority to act in this area because of an alleged inevitable conflict with the State Personnel Board's powers. We conclude that petitioners' challenge to the facial validity of PERB's jurisdiction fails on several grounds.

First, as the State Personnel Board itself recognizes, many areas of PERB's unfair practice jurisdiction do not overlap with the State Personnel Board's "disciplinary action" jurisdiction at all. In these areas, obviously, no constitutional problems arise. Thus, for example, if the state denies rights which SEERA grants to employee organizations, or the state fails to meet and confer in good faith, PERB could clearly adjudicate unfair practice charges against the state without any danger of conflict with the personnel board's disciplinary action jurisdiction. Moreover, even in the case of employer reprisals against an employee for protected activity, PERB's unfair practice jurisdiction would clearly pose no conflict with the State Personnel Board's jurisdiction if the reprisal took a form that did not constitute a "disciplinary action" reviewable by the board. Because there is thus a substantial area in which PERB's unfair practice jurisdiction can unquestionably operate without damage to the State Personnel Board's jurisdiction, the provisions in question are not unconstitutional on their face.

Second, even in those areas in which the jurisdiction of the State Personnel Board and PERB do overlap, familiar rules of construction counsel our court to attempt to harmonize the disparate procedures, rather than simply to invalidate one or the other on broad constitutional grounds.[19] As a New Jersey court recently observed in reviewing a

18. The State Personnel Board, asserting that its jurisdiction in the areas of examination, selection, probation, promotion and discipline is "exclusive," joins with petitioners in arguing that PERB's unfair practice jurisdiction is unconstitutional insofar as it authorizes PERB to act with reference to discriminatory or retaliatory actions in any of these areas.

In taking this position in the instant case, the State Personnel Board has modified the views it expressed in its 1974 position paper on collective bargaining. In that document, the State Personnel Board expressly advocated the creation of a Public Employment Relations Commission which would, inter alia, "hear unfair practice complaints." (A Perspective on Collective Bargaining in the State Civil Service, *supra,* p. 9.) The document also stated that the State Personnel Board had considered whether it would be advisable for it to assume the duties of such a commission but had ultimately decided against the board's assumption of such a role because "we believe that the administering agency would be more acceptable to both management and employees if it were an entity with no other involvement in the personnel management process." (*Id.*)

19. The parties have advanced differing views as to whether, under article XIV, section 1 of the California Constitution, PERB's adjudicatory jurisdiction, like that of the State Personnel Board, flows from the Constitution itself. Although it may

conflict between quasi-judicial rulings of a civil service commission and the Public Employee Relations Board in that state: "The inquiry is properly not so much which statutory scheme prevails [over the other], but rather how each can be harmonized to give them reasonable and full effect. [Citations.] Each agency operates under different statutory schemes, but not to defeat each other's authority." (*City of Hackensack v. Winner* (1978) 162 N.J.Super. 1 [392 A.2d 187, 198], affd. (1980) 82 N.J. 1 [410 A.2d 1146].)

As the *Hackensack* decision suggests, PERB and the State Personnel Board are not in competition with each other; rather, each agency was established to serve a different, but not inconsistent, public purpose. The State Personnel Board was granted jurisdiction to review disciplinary actions of civil service employees in order to protect civil service employees from politically partisan mistreatment or other arbitrary action inconsistent with the merit principle embodied in article VII. As we noted in *Skelly v. State Personnel Bd.* (1975) 15 Cal.3d 194, 202 [124 Cal.Rptr. 14, 539 P.2d 774]: "To help insure that the goals of civil service are not thwarted by those in power, the statutory provisions implementing the constitutional mandate of article XXIV [now article VII] * * * invest employees with substantive and procedural protections against punitive actions by their superiors." (Fn. omitted.)

PERB, on the other hand, has been given a somewhat more specialized and more focused task: to protect both employees and the state employer from violations of the organizational and collective bargaining rights guaranteed by SEERA. Although disciplinary actions taken in violation of SEERA would transgress the merit principle as well, the Legislature evidently thought it important to assign the task of investigating potential violations of SEERA to an agency which possesses and can further develop specialized expertise in the labor relations field. Thus, insofar as possible, we should construe the relevant provisions to permit an accommodation of the respective tasks of both the State Personnel Board and PERB.

* * *

Because no actual jurisdictional conflict between PERB and the State Personnel Board confronts us in this proceeding, we have no occasion to speculate on how some hypothetical dispute that might be presented for decision in the future should properly be resolved. As numerous authorities in other jurisdictions make clear, however, any conflicts which may arise in this area can be resolved either by administrative accommodation between the two agencies themselves [21] or, failing that, by sensitive application of evolving judicial principles.

well be that PERB should be considered a constitutional agency by virtue of article XIV, section 1 (cf. *Perry Farms Inc. v. Agricultural Labor Relations Bd.* (1978) 86 Cal. App.3d 448, 460–462 [150 Cal.Rptr. 495]), we need not definitively decide that issue in this case because even if PERB's authority derives only from statute the accommodation of the two agencies' respective jurisdictions would still be appropriate.

21. In Los Angeles County, a jurisdictional conflict between a charter-established civil service commission and a local

Accordingly, we conclude that the fact that PERB's jurisdiction over unfair practices may in some cases overlap with the State Personnel Board's jurisdiction to review disciplinary actions provides no basis for finding the applicable provisions of SEERA unconstitutional on their face.

5. SEERA is not an unlawful delegation of legislative authority nor does it infringe on the gubernatorial veto power.

Finally, petitioners contend that even if SEERA does not fatally conflict with any of the provisions of article VII of the California Constitution, our court should strike down the collective bargaining statute on its face as either an unlawful delegation of legislative authority or as an unconstitutional infringement on the gubernatorial veto power. Both of these contentions are plainly without merit.

[The balance of the court's opinion, and the dissent by Richardson, J., are omitted.]

Notes

Disciplinary grievances. Civil service systems typically provide for a right of appeal by disciplined employees to an "independent" public agency called a civil service board, or personnel board. Public sector unions are often distrustful of such procedures, over which they have no control, and seek to negotiate independent review of discipline or other employment decisions through bilateral grievance and arbitration procedures. Thus, questions arise as to the relationship between these two regimes: Are civil service procedures exclusive, so that the parties are not free to negotiate a bilateral alternative? Or, if civil service and bilateral procedures may coexist, what is their relationship to one another? May an employee pursue either (or both) at his option? If so, what is the effect of a determination under one or the other?

In some states, statutes address such questions specifically, though their answers vary. The Wisconsin statute pertaining to state employees requires that agreements contain procedures for grievance and arbitration, and stipulates that such procedures displace civil service. (Wis.Stat.Ann. § 230.34(1)). In New Jersey, on the other hand, the parties are precluded from negotiating over any proposal relating to discipline that is covered by the Civil Service Act or regulations of the Civil Service Commission. (N.J.S.A. § 34:13A–5.3 (1988)). In some states statutes are silent on the subject, and the questions are open for litigation. *E.g. Pontiac Police Officers Association v. City of Pontiac,* 397 Mich. 674, 246 N.W.2d 831 (1976) (Collective bargaining law, as a later enactment, takes priority over civil

employment relations commission created by a county ordinance was ultimately resolved by an agreement of each agency to adopt corresponding regulations "which in effect, establish a policy of not hearing any part of a complaint that is within the jurisdiction of, and has been heard by, either an arbitrator or the other commission." (See Assem. Advisory Council on Public Employee Relations, Final Rep., *supra,* pp. 156–158; see also 29 C.F.R. § 1977.18 (OSHA regulation directed to the problem of overlapping jurisdiction when an employee's complaint as to discrimination is also subject to arbitration or some other agency's resolution).)

service law for local government employees, so that an agreement providing for binding arbitration of suspension and discharge of police officer is enforceable); *cf. AFSCME v. County of Lancaster,* 200 Neb. 301, 263 N.W.2d 471 (1978) (Civil service statute, enacted subsequent to collective bargaining law, controls).

Consider the following analysis: "States can resolve the perceived conflict between civil service law and bargaining over employee discipline without interfering with the goals of either statute. Although statutory provisions may appear to conflict, permitting negotiation over disciplinary procedures and standards does not hinder and may, in fact, promote merit employment. Accordingly, states should allow unions and employers to negotiate over these issues and to determine the appropriate disciplinary procedures and standards for the relevant employment setting." Hodges, *The Interplay of Civil Service Law and Collective Bargaining in Public Sector Employee Discipline Cases,* 32 Boston College L.Rev. 1 (1990).

C. TEACHER TENURE AND COLLECTIVE BARGAINING

ASSOCIATION OF NEW JERSEY STATE COLLEGE FACULTIES, INC. v. DUNGAN

Supreme Court of New Jersey, 1974.
64 N.J. 338, 316 A.2d 425, 85 LRRM 2625.

[On September 15, 1972, the defendant Board of Higher Education adopted a resolution which set forth general guidelines for the granting of tenure to faculty members in the State Colleges and for the periodic evaluation of tenured faculty members. The resolution followed recommendations made by the Office of the Chancellor, Department of Higher Education. On October 20, 1972, the Board adopted a similar resolution with respect to County Colleges. The State College resolution embodied the following principles]:

> "1) Each college Board of Trustees shall prepare a ten-year plan for its institution indicating the steps it plans to take to achieve a future balance of faculty in which no more than a reasonable proportion are ultimately tenured. The purpose of limiting the proportion of tenured faculty on each campus is to retain flexibility to enable the institution to respond to changing educational needs in the future. The plan established by each board shall include the proportion of tenured faculty projected each year during the ten-year period. The college trustees shall report their plan to the Board of Higher Education and shall inform the Board each year of the progress being made in achieving their goals.
>
> "2) Each State College Board of Trustees shall establish internal policies which indicate either that it will impose specific restrictions or more intensive and rigorous review procedures for any reappointment conferring tenure which brings the proportion of

individuals in a department (or other major academic sub-unit) or in the college as a whole above its present level. Reappointments conferring tenure which raise the tenure rate above that level shall be made only as an unusual action when judged by the college Board of Trustees as being in the best interests of the college.

"3) A reappointment conferring tenure may be offered only to faculty members who possess an appropriate terminal degree or its equivalent, except under unusual circumstances when the granting of tenure to an individual not having these qualifications is judged by a college Board of Trustees as being in the best interests of the institution.

"4) Tenure should be awarded only to individuals whose performance during their probationary period gives clear evidence of the ability and willingness to make a significant and continuing contribution to the growth and development of the institution.

"5) Tenure should be awarded after presentation of positive evidence of excellence in teaching, scholarly achievement, contribution to college and community, and fulfillment of professional responsibilities, and not solely because negative evidence to the contrary is not presented.

"6) Each college Board of Trustees should establish a procedure which the college will employ to regularly evaluate the performance of tenured faculty members. Such evaluations should occur not less frequently than every five years. These evaluations, which should include student input, should comprehend such factors as continued teaching competence, professional preparation and attainments which are directly related to teaching or administrative assignments, contributions to campus life beyond formal, assigned instructional activity and significant research, scholarly or community activity."

[Plaintiff association attacked the resolutions on the ground, among others, that they were adopted without benefit of bargaining.]

In their third and final point the plaintiffs contend that "the unilateral adoption of the Tenure Rules violated the New Jersey Employer–Employee Relations Act." That Act provides in section 7 (N.J.S.A. 34:13A–5.3) that a majority representative of public employees in an appropriate unit may act for all employees in the unit and that the majority representative and designated representatives of the public employer shall meet at reasonable times and "negotiate in good faith" with respect to grievances and "terms and conditions of employment." It also provides that proposed new rules or modifications of existing rules governing "working conditions" shall be negotiated with the majority representative before they are established. The Act is unclear in failing to define "working conditions" or "terms and conditions of employment" as used in section 7 and in failing to specify what subjects are mandatorily negotiable and what subjects are exclusively within management's prerogatives. But it makes clear that its statutory terms may not be viewed so expansively as to negate the Board of Higher Education's overall supervisory responsibilities as set forth in New Jersey's Education Law (Title 18A). See e.g., section 10 (N.J.S.A. 34:13A–8 1) which explicitly provides that no provision in the Act shall "annul or modify any statute or statutes of this State."

In *Dunellen Board of Education v. Dunellen Education Association,* 64 N.J. 17, 85 LRRM 2131 (1973), we were recently called upon to decide whether the local board of education's determination to consolidate the chairmanships of the Social Studies Department and the English Department was a proper subject of mandatory negotiation or arbitration under the Employer–Employee Relations Act. We held that it was not, pointing out that the determination to consolidate was predominantly a matter of educational policy within the exclusive management prerogatives of the local board. Similarly in *Burlington County College Faculty Association v. Board of Trustees, Burlington County College,* 64 N.J. 10, 84 LRRM 2857 (1973), we held that the fixing of the college calendar involved a major educational determination within the exclusive responsibility of those entrusted with administering the college.

In the aforecited cases we noted that it was "our clear judicial responsibility to give continuing effect to the provisions in our Education Law (Title 18A) without, however, frustrating the goals or terms of the Employer–Employee Relations Act (N.J.S.A. 34:13A–1 et seq.)." *Dunellen, supra,* 64 N.J. at 24–25, 85 LRRM at 2134. As pointed out earlier in this opinion, the tenure resolutions of the Board of Higher Education were adopted well within the statutory powers and duties set forth in N.J.S.A. 18A:3–13; N.J.S.A. 18A:3–14(h); N.J.S.A. 18A:3–15; N.J.S.A. 18A:3–16; N.J.S.A. 18A:64–6(g)(h)(i). They represent major educational policy pronouncements entrusted by the Legislature to the Board's educational expertise and objective judgment. While the guidelines towards institutional excellence and greater administrative care in the granting of tenure undoubtedly entail individual consequences, they embody only matters not mandatorily negotiable under the principles expressed in *Dunellen, supra,* 64 N.J. 17, 85 LRRM 2131, *Burlington, supra,* 64 N.J. 10, 84 LRRM 2857, and *Englewood, supra,* 64 N.J. 1, 85 LRRM 2137. Cf. Faculty Tenure report (Jossey–Bass Series) *supra* at 90: "The commission recommends that collective bargaining in colleges and universities not extend to academic freedom and tenure and related faculty personnel matters and that grievances involving issues of freedom and tenure be referred to academic procedures outside the collective bargaining process."

The legislature has not indicated any disagreement with the *Dunellen* principles (64 N.J. 17, 85 LRRM 2131) or their application to date. Nor has it expressed itself on tenure in relation to negotiation except in section 4 of Chapter 163 of the Laws of 1973. That section provides in effect that, notwithstanding the prescribed five-year probationary period, the board of trustees of the college may "as an exceptional action," and by a two-thirds majority of all of its members, grant tenure to "an individual faculty member" after employment for two consecutive academic years. Section 4 then concludes with the following: "The provisions of this section shall not be negotiable as a term and condition of employment under the 'New Jersey Employer–Employee Relations Act'." It is noteworthy that in this single statutory mention of tenure in relation to negotiation, mandatory negotiation is specifically excluded. It appears evident to us, particularly in the light of the continuing effect of section 10 of the Employer–Employee Relations Act (N.J.S.A. 34:13A–8.1), that the legislative silence elsewhere may not fairly or sensibly be construed as impairing the Board of Higher Education's exclusive statutory power under the Education Law to promulgate tenure guidelines which are reasonable in nature and which are not in conflict with any specific statutory provision dealing with tenure.

Although our present decision supports the Board of Higher Education's position that its tenure guidelines were not mandatorily negotiable, it is not to be taken as support for any notion that such guidelines or alterations therein should be promulgated without full and timely prior consultation with accredited faculty representatives and others interested. On the contrary, we take this occasion to reiterate the views expressed in the following concluding paragraph in Dunellen which may be taken to have general application:

"The holding that the consolidation was predominantly a matter of educational policy not mandatorily negotiable does not indicate that the Board would not have been well advised to have voluntarily discussed it in timely fashion with the representatives of the teachers. Peaceful relations between the school administration and its teachers is an ever present goal and though the teachers may not be permitted to take over the educational policies entrusted by the statutes to the Board they, as trained professionals, may have much to contribute towards the Board's adoption of sound and suitable educational policies. Before the passage of New Jersey's Employer–Employee Relations Act (N.J.S.A. 34:13A–1 *et seq.*) it was recognized that public employees had the right to be heard through their representatives on their proposals and grievances. The Act significantly broadened that right and, with the goal of peaceful labor relations in mind, created fields of mandatory negotiation. It would seem evident that, when dealing in fields with which the teachers are significantly concerned though outside the fields of mandatory negotiation, the end of peaceful labor relations will generally be furthered by some measure of timely voluntary discussion between the school administration and the representatives of its teachers even though the ultimate decisions are to be made by the Board in the exercise of its exclusive education prerogatives." 64 N.J. at 31–32, 85 LRRM 2137.

Affirmed.

Notes and Questions

1. What assumptions underlie the New Jersey court's conclusions in *Dungan?* Are they different from the assumptions underlying the Califor-

nia court's conclusion in the preceding case? Are there differences between a civil service system and a tenure system which are relevant to the scope of bargaining?

2. In addition to questions relating to the bargainability of tenure rules, considered in *Dungan,* are questions relating to the arbitrability of tenure decisions. Such questions are considered in Chapter 6.

3. A further example of the impact of external law upon public employer-union relationship is New York's statute (Education Laws 1950(4)(bb)) permitting a Board of Cooperative Educational Services (BOCES) to offer academic summer programs, providing a procedure for two or more local school districts to request the services of BOCES, and providing that when BOCES takes over a program formerly operated by a school district, teachers whose positions are abolished as a result have certain rights to employment with BOCES. When a union attempted to bargain over a school district's decision to subcontract summer teaching to BOCES, the New York Court of Appeal held that these provisions evidence the legislature's intent that such a decision not be subject to bargaining. (*Webster Central School District v. PERB,* 75 N.Y.2d 619, 555 N.Y.S.2d 245, 554 N.E.2d 886 (1990)).

4. In HEERA, the act covering higher education employees, the California legislature attempted to guarantee that academic or faculty senates would survive the advent of collective bargaining and have an independent sphere of operation by (1) declaring its desire to preserve and encourage the tradition of joint decision-making between administration and faculty or academic employees through shared governance mechanisms or practices, including the academic senates of the University of California and the California State University and Colleges and other faculty councils (§ 3561[b]) (2) specifying that senates are not labor organizations (§ 3562[g]), (3) permitting academic management to consult with senates apparently on any and all matters (§ 3571[f]), and (4) excluding from the scope of representation many of the subjects typically dealt with by governance systems: the merits, necessity, or organization of any service, activity or program; student fees; admission requirements; standards for awarding degrees; content and conduct of courses, curricula, and research programs; and (for CSUC) "criteria and standards" used for appointment, promotion, evaluation and tenure of academic employees (§ 3562[r][4]) or (for U.C.) "procedures and policies" used for appointment, promotion, and tenure as well as procedures used for evaluation and the processing of grievances (§ 3562[q][4]).

These sections of the statute accomplish two significant things. First, they legitimize governance and senate structures. Second, they keep the subjects of governance off the bargaining table unless the regents or the trustees withdraw a matter covered by 3562(q)(4) or (r)(4), respectively, from the senates in U.C. or CSUC, in which case it becomes bargainable or (in U.C. only) the academic senate (without relinquishing any of its own jurisdiction) decides that one or all of the subjects is bargainable. The power of a U.C. academic senate to do this is constrained by § 3579(e) which limits the scope of bargaining by a union representing a single campus unit to "matters which have customarily been determined on a division [campus] basis."

Chapter 6

ADMINISTRATION OF THE AGREEMENT

A. INTRODUCTION

Once the parties enter into a collective bargaining agreement, there must be some mechanism for resolving disputes ("grievances") which arise out of its interpretation or application. There are several possibilities:

(1) Either party could be permitted to engage in self-help—for example through strike or lockout—in an effort to "persuade" the other party. This used to be common practice in the private sector, until arbitration became common during World War II.

(2) By law or agreement. One party or the other could be given unilateral authority to decide the dispute. There might be grievance procedures, which allowed the employee (or her union) to pursue a dispute to higher levels of authority. Or, provision might be made for the employee to appeal to "advisory arbitration" by an outside arbitrator. In either event, however, the public authority had the last word. Such arrangements were formerly common in the public sector, and still exist in some jurisdictions.

(3) The parties could seek judicial enforcement, as with other contracts. In the absence of some other procedure established by agreement or by law, that option presumably exists. (See *Glendale City Employees' Association v. City of Glendale,* 15 Cal.3d 328, 124 Cal.Rptr. 513, 540 P.2d 609 (1975) ("Successful bargaining rests upon the sanctity and legal viability of the given word")).

(4) Violation of the agreement could be made an unfair labor practice, subject to the jurisdiction of a labor relations board, as in Wisconsin.

(5) The grievance could be submitted to binding arbitration by a third party. This procedure, almost universal under private sector agreements, has gained widespread acceptance in the public sector as

well. Indeed, statutes in a few states mandate inclusion of a provision for arbitration in every agreement.

Such arbitration is called "grievance arbitration", to distinguish it from arbitration over the terms of a new agreement. Typically, the agreement provides for a bilateral "grievance procedure" preliminary to arbitration, in which the dispute may be jointly considered by one or more levels of management and union representatives.

Question: Which of these approaches would you favor for the public sector if you were (a) a member of the governing body of the public entity? (b) manager of the public entity? (c) a union representative? (d) a public employee? (e) a taxpayer?

B. VALIDITY AND ENFORCEABILITY OF THE AGREEMENT TO ARBITRATE

GRODIN AND NAJITA, JUDICIAL RESPONSE TO PUBLIC–SECTOR ARBITRATION *

While it is sometimes said that courts at common law disapproved the arbitration of public-sector labor grievances as an unlawful delegation of governmental power, close examination of the cases cited in support of that proposition reveal either that the court was not talking about arbitration at all, or that it confused grievance arbitration with interest arbitration, or that its objection to arbitration stemmed from the court's view that the underlying collective bargaining agreement was itself beyond the authority of the public entity. In any event, once legislatures in many states came to give their blessing to collective bargaining in the public sector, courts began to accept grievance arbitration as an appropriate means of giving effect to an otherwise valid contract even in the absence of express statutory authority.

In the leading *City of Rhinelander* case, for example, [*AFSCME Local 1226 v. City of Rhinelander,* 35 Wis.2d 209, 151 N.W.2d 30, 65 LRRM 2793 (1967)], the Wisconsin Supreme Court held that a statute which authorized binding agreements by implication permitted binding agreements to arbitrate grievances, and it brushed aside the city's arguments based on sovereignty and home rule with the observation that the arguments failed to distinguish between grievance and interest arbitration.

Similarly, in *Associated Teachers of Huntington* [*Board of Education v. Associated Teachers of Huntington, Inc.,* 30 N.Y.2d 122, 331 N.Y.S.2d 17, 282 N.E.2d 109, 79 LRRM 2881 (1972)], the New York Court of Appeals found that legislative authorization for unions to represent employees "in the administration of grievances" necessarily implies the legitimacy of arbitration, since (quoting from one of the

* Reprinted by permission from Aaron, Najita and Stern (eds.) Public–Sector Bargaining, Research Volume of the Industrial Relations Research Association Series (Washington D.C.: BNA Books, 2d Ed., 1988), Ch. 7, pp. 229, 232–34.

Trilogy cases) "arbitration is, of course, part and parcel of the administration of grievances." And like its sister tribunal in Wisconsin, the New York court dealt summarily with the school board contention that its province was being invaded:

"Nor can we agree that a board of education is better qualified than an arbitrator to decide whether a teacher in its employ should be dismissed for incompetency or misconduct. It may not be gainsaid that arbitrators, selected because of their impartiality and their intimate knowledge of school board matters, are fully qualified to decide issues such as those under consideration."

Many of the modern statutes explicitly authorize, and in at least two cases actually mandate, provisions for binding grievance arbitration. Thus, except in Delaware where the statute forbids third-party decisions in the case of school districts, or in states where collective bargaining agreements are not yet permitted, there appears to be no question as to the general validity of agreements to arbitrate public-sector labor grievances.

There [were], however, a number of cases, particularly [early] ones, in which courts have refused to enforce arbitration agreements, or have set aside arbitration awards, on the stated ground that some law or public policy external to the agreement precludes the public agency from "bargaining away" or "delegating" its authority or discretion with respect to the particular issue in dispute. * * *

SCHOOL COMMITTEE OF DANVERS v. TYMAN

Supreme Judicial Court of Massachusetts, 1977.
372 Mass. 106, 360 N.E.2d 877.

WILKINS, JUSTICE: The defendants appeal from an order, under G.L. c. 150C, § 2(b), granting a stay of arbitration concerning certain grievances asserted on behalf of the defendant Tyman, a nontenured teacher in the Danvers school system. * * * We conclude that arbitration should not have been stayed and that an order should be entered under G.L. c. 150C, § 2(b), directing the parties to proceed to arbitration.

The basic circumstances are not in dispute. The Danvers Teachers' Association (association) and the Danvers school committee (school committee) entered into a collective bargaining agreement for the period from September 1, 1973, to June 30, 1975. The agreement provided that a grievance, as defined therein,[2] could be processed through four levels, the last of which called for final and binding arbitration. The agreement also set forth certain procedures to be followed in the evaluation of the work performance of a teacher. Those

2. [Footnotes numbered as in original.—Ed.] Article III A of the agreement defined a "grievance" as follows: "A 'grievance' is a claim based upon an event or condition which affects the wages, hours, or conditions of employment of a teacher or group of teachers and/or the interpretation, meaning, or application of any of the provisions of this Agreement or any subsequent agreement entered into pursuant to this Agreement."

procedures included notice to a teacher of any material placed in his or her file which was derogatory to the teacher's conduct, service, character or personality; an opportunity to review that material; and a right to reply in writing. Each teacher was entitled to be advised promptly in detail of any complaints about him or her made to the school administration or to the school committee. The agreement contained a provision that "[t]he Committee retains its statutory right to rehire or not to rehire non-tenure teachers. * * *"

The defendant Tyman was hired as a teacher of English for the school year commencing September, 1971. In the early part of April, 1974, during the third year of her employment and, hence, during the last possible year of nontenured status (G.L. c. 71, § 41), the school committee voted not to rehire Tyman and on April 12, 1974, notified her in writing of its decision. A grievance was filed in May which alleged a failure to follow appropriate evaluation procedures, inadequate classroom observations and evaluations, and discrimination. The defendants did not seek explicitly to arbitrate the school committee's decision not to reappoint Tyman to a fourth year as a teacher in the school system. Arbitration was requested by the association in July, and, after a continuance a hearing was scheduled for September 10, 1974.

On September 9, 1974, the school committee filed a complaint in the Superior Court seeking, in effect, an order granting a stay of the arbitration proceeding. It is clear from the complaint that the school committee's argument was that arbitration of the grievance was barred because, under G.L. c. 71, § 41, the school committee had an absolute power to pass on the question whether a non-tenured teacher's contract should be renewed. On that same day, the matter was argued by counsel and, on the basis of the complaint and the arguments of counsel, the judge entered an order granting a stay of arbitration because "the claim sought to be arbitrated does not state a controversy covered by the provision for arbitration." The defendants have appealed. On our own motion, we transferred the case here for decision.[3]

3. The school committee objects to the inclusion in the record of an answer which the judge permitted to be filed over a year after the order staying arbitration was entered. That answer expanded on the grounds of the grievance asserted on behalf of Tyman. Because the judge allowed the late filing of the answer, we assume that the grounds asserted were matters which were before him when he ordered the stay of arbitration or, at least, be regarded the matters raised in the answer to be of no consequence to his original order. Our decision does not depend, however, on the answer being a part of the record on appeal because the nature of the grievance is sufficiently clear from the complaint itself. General Laws c. 150C, § 2(b), inserted by St.1959, c. 546, § 1, states that an application for a stay "shall be forthwith and summarily determined. * * *" The judge and the parties should exercise care, however, to assure that an adequate record is made of the material which was before the judge in order that any appeal from an order granting a stay may be heard properly. See Mass.R.A.P. 8(c), 365 Mass. 849 (1974), for one method of establishing a proper record in such a situation. We view the judge's action in allowing the defendants' motion to file an answer as a means of developing an adequate appellate record in this case.

The fundamental issue in this case arises from the tension between (1) the terms of the lawfully authorized collective bargaining agreement between the association and the school committee providing for final and binding arbitration (see G.L. c. 150E, § 8), and (2) the traditional authority of school committees in the matter of contract renewal resulting in tenure for teachers. The Legislature could have, but has not, resolved this dispute by stating explicitly, as it has in other instances (see G.L. c. 150E, § 7), whether and how far the agreement may override existing law. Our function in this case is to assess the Legislature's over-all intention in light of (1) its apparent grant of full authority to school committees to agree to arbitration of "any dispute concerning the interpretation or application of * * * [a collective bargaining] agreement" (G.L. c. 150E, § 8, inserted by St.1973, c. 1078, § 2), and (2) the continuing, apparently unfettered, statutory authority of a school committee to determine that a non-tenured teacher "is not to be employed for the following school year." G.L. c. 71, § 41, as amended through St.1973, c. 847, § 6.

Views of various State courts have not been consistent concerning the extent to which, if at all, a school committee may assert an absolute authority to grant or deny tenure to probationary teachers in opposition to a claim of arbitrability of questions relating to nonrenewal of the teacher's contract. See Note, *Public Sector Grievance Procedures, Due Process, and the Duty of Fair Representation,* 89 Harv.L.Rev. 752, 757 n. 28 (1976). Because traditions and statutory provisions vary among States, the divergence of opinion is understandable.

In some States, the courts have held that a probationary employee may be discharged as a matter of discretion and that resort to contractual grievance procedures is impermissible. See, e.g., *Van Gorder v. Matanuska–Susitna Borough School Dist.,* 513 P.2d 1094, 1096, 84 LRRM 2683 (Alas.1973). In Illinois, a school board's duties in appointing teachers have been held to be nondelegable, and the failure to follow contractual evaluation procedures does not restrict a school board's statutory rights and powers to decide in its discretion not to renew a probationary teacher's contract. *Illinois Educ. Ass'n Local Community High School Dist. 218 v. Board of Educ. of School Dist. 218, Cook County,* 62 Ill.2d 127, 130–131, 90 LRRM 3207 (1975). *Wesclin Educ. Ass'n v. Board of Educ. of Wesclin Community Unit School Dist.,* 30 Ill.App.3d 67, 77, 90 LRRM 2342 (1975). Thus, in Illinois an arbitrator may not award an employment contract as a remedy for the violation of evaluation procedures contained in a collective bargaining agreement. *Trustees of Junior College Dist. No. 508, County of Cook v. Cook County College Teachers Union, Local 1600,* 62 Ill.2d 470, 476, 93 LRRM 2804 (1976).

In Michigan, on the other hand, the question whether a school board agreed to arbitrate the nonrenewal of a probationary teacher's contract has been left to determination by an arbitrator. *Kaleva–Norman–Dickson School Dist. No. 6 v. Kaleva–Norman–Dickson School Teachers' Ass'n.,* 393 Mich. 583, 595, 89 LRRM 2078 (1975). In that opinion, no particular consideration was given to any argument that the school board had no authority to delegate to an arbitrator the question of the propriety of its failure to renew a nontenured teacher's contract.

In New York, where the tenure statute is somewhat similar to ours, the Court of Appeals recently has taken an intermediate view of the status of the terms of a collective bargaining agreement in relation to the powers of a school board to determine whether a non-tenured teacher's contract will be renewed. In *Board of Educ., Bellmore–Merrick Cent. High School Dist., Nassau County v. Bellmore–Merrick United Secondary Teachers, Inc.,* 39 N.Y.2d 167, 92 LRRM 2509 (1976), the court had to decide whether an arbitrator properly could order the temporary reinstatement of a probationary teacher as a remedy for breach of certain procedural guaranties contained in a collective bargaining agreement. The teacher sought arbitration of a grievance because, contrary to the terms of the collective bargaining agreement, she was not apprised of certain parental complaints and was not afforded the opportunity to refute them. The school board there, as in this case, responded in effect that it had the absolute power to terminate the services of the teacher. The arbitrator concluded that the agreement had been violated and ruled that an appropriate remedy was reinstatement, without tenure, for a reasonable period sufficient to enable the school board to reevaluate the teacher in accordance with the prescribed procedures. The Court of Appeals upheld the arbitrator's award. That court recognized that the arbitrator could not grant tenure to the teacher because that was a power under the sole control of the board.[4] However, it viewed evaluation procedures guaranteed in a collective bargaining agreement as independent of the school board's ultimate authority to pass on nonrenewal. Those procedures could be followed without infringing on the school board's prerogative. See *Cohoes City School Dist. v. Cohoes Teachers Ass'n.,* 40 N.Y.2d 774, 778, 94 LRRM 2192 (1976); *Legislative Conference of the City Univ. of N.Y. v. Board of Higher Educ. of the City of N.Y.,* 31 N.Y.2d 926, 928, 82 LRRM 2848, *aff'g* 38 App.Div.2d 478, 482, 80 LRRM 2340 (1972).

Arbitration should not have been stayed in this case. Judicial intervention is not warranted where no conflict has arisen between the consequences of the arbitration proceedings called for in the collective bargaining agreement and any nondelegable authority of the school committee.

We accept the school committee's argument that, against its will, it may not delegate to an arbitrator its authority to make decisions concerning tenure. The nondelegable authority of an incumbent school committee in the appointment and reappointment of academic personnel has a long tradition * * * Although the Legislature has granted

4. See that court's even more recent opinion in *Cohoes City School Dist. v. Cohoes Teachers Ass'n,* 40 N.Y.2d 774, 94 LRRM 2192 (1976) (five to two decision), affirming that conclusion.

procedural safeguards to nontenured teachers who have been teaching for more than ninety days, where they are threatened with dismissal during a school year (G.L. c. 71, § 42), no such protection has been granted to such teachers when the subject of renewal or nonrenewal of their contracts is involved. Indeed, the Legislature has expressly indicated that the procedural safeguards applicable to dismissal of nontenured teachers do not apply to the renewal of their contracts. St.1970, c. 388, § 2. It is true that the tenure statute (G.L. c. 71, § 41) has the effect of reducing the traditional, wide discretion of school committees by granting protection to teachers who have acquired tenure. It is also true that by failure to send a timely notice a teacher may acquire tenure without a conscious, affirmative act by a school committee. [citation omitted] But the fact remains that a school committee's authority to determine questions of contract renewal and tenure during the first three years of a teacher's term of employment has been left unchanged by legislation. We do not find in legislative authorization for schoolteachers to bargain collectively concerning "wages, hours, and other terms and conditions of employment" (G.L. c. 150E, § 2, inserted by St.1973, c. 1078, § 2), and to arbitrate grievances (G.L. c. 150E, § 8), an intent to permit a school committee to bargain away its traditional authority to make tenure decisions if it so wishes.[5] Whenever the Legislature has limited the powers of school committees, it has done so in express terms, and it is expected that a radical departure from prior policy would be clearly indicated, and not left to doubtful implication. [citations omitted] For much the same reason that we have expressed, the Court of Appeals of New York has declined recently to enforce that portion of a collective bargaining agreement which arguably called for arbitration of a tenure decision. *Cohoes City School Dist. v. Cohoes Teachers Ass'n, supra* at 777–78.

Although a school committee may not surrender its authority to make tenure decisions, there is no reason why a school committee may not bind itself to follow certain procedures precedent to the making of any such decision. In this case, the school committee agreed to submit to arbitration on a wide range of subjects. Unless there is positive assurance that an arbitration clause is not susceptible to an interpretation that covers the asserted dispute, or unless no lawful relief conceivably can be awarded by the arbitrator, an order to arbitrate should not be denied. See *United Steelworkers of America v. Warrior & Gulf Navigation Co.,* 363 U.S. 574, 582–83 (1960); G.L. c. 150C, § 2(b). In this case, no occasion for a stay of the arbitration arises merely from

5. We recognize that, if, as a matter of educational policy, a school committee wishes to submit a particular tenure question to arbitration and to accept the result of the arbitration, it may do so as part of its prerogative. Such an arbitration proceeding and award would not be inconsistent with the school committee's educational policy and, indeed, might be consistent with it. *Teachers Local 66 v. School Comm. of Boston,* ___ Mass. ___, ___–___, 93 LRRM 2205 (1976) (Mass.Adv.Sh. [1976], 1515, 1527–1528). In this case, however, the incumbent school committee has indicated an unwillingness to accept any decision of the arbitrator granting tenure.

the possibility of an arbitrator's award which might purport to intrude into the school committee's inviolate authority.

Any threat to the school committee's authority has not matured yet because it is far from clear that the arbitrator's award will encroach on the school committee's exclusive domain. The agreement to follow certain procedures preliminary to exercising its right to decide a tenure question, and to permit arbitration of a claim that it has failed to follow those procedures, does not impinge on a school committee's right to make the ultimate tenure decision. If a violation is found by the arbitrator, he may not grant tenure to the teacher, but he may fashion a remedy which falls short of intruding into the school committee's exclusive domain. Some violations of evaluation procedures may be trivial and not justify any relief. Not all violations of a teacher's rights, even constitutional rights, will justify reinstatement. *Mt. Healthy City School Dist. Bd. of Educ. v. Doyle,* 429 U.S. 274 (1977). The arbitrator might direct merely that the omitted procedures be followed and the teacher's record corrected as appears appropriate. However, in other cases, the failure to follow evaluation procedures may be shown to have so prejudiced a teacher's position that more substantial relief may be in order. It would be premature in this case to announce any limits on the scope of an arbitrator's award in such a case, provided it does not award tenure to the teacher. See *School Comm. of West Bridgewater v. West Bridgewater Teachers' Ass'n,* ___, ___–___, 360 N.E.2d 886 (Mass.Sup.Jud.Ct.1987) for a discussion of the validity of an arbitrator's award which ordered reinstatement of a teacher. We leave open the question of the validity of an award which imposes sanctions because of the failure of a school committee to follow evaluation procedures although no teacher was harmed by the omission.

If a school committee wishes to deny the application of evaluation procedures to nontenured teachers or to deny such a teacher the right to arbitrate any failure to follow such agreed procedures, the school committee can say so explicitly in the collective bargaining agreement. Once a school committee agrees to follow certain procedures and to permit binding arbitration concerning its alleged failure to adhere to those practices, we see no public policy considerations which prevent full implementation of the terms of the agreement subject, however, to the retention in favor of the school committee of its nondelegable rights. Indeed, adherence to the evaluation procedures may be expected to provide information to the school committee which will permit it to make a fairer and more informed judgment concerning a teacher. The fact that ultimately the school committee may make the tenure decision without regard to information produced pursuant to evaluation procedures in no way justifies a school committee's failure to follow the terms of its agreement both to make such evaluations and to permit arbitration of its alleged failure to do so.

The collective bargaining agreement provides that the meaning of the agreement is a "grievance" which can be submitted to arbitration.

See n. 2 *supra.* The meaning of the agreement is for the arbitrator and not for the courts. The school committee may argue to the arbitrator that the grievances asserted here are not ones which may be the subject of arbitration because of the reservation by the committee of its statutory right "not to rehire non-tenure teachers." The decision of the arbitrator on such a question of interpretation will be final and not subject to review.

The order granting a stay of arbitration is vacated, and an order shall be entered pursuant to G.L. c. 150C, § 2(b), directing the parties to proceed to arbitration.

So ordered.

Notes

1. The court says a school committee "against its will * * * may not delegate to an arbitrator its authority to make decisions concerning tenure." What does the court mean by "against its will"? And what does it mean by the word "delegate"? If the school committee agreed that it would not deny tenure arbitrarily or unreasonably, and that its agreement on that score could be enforced in court, rather than through arbitration, would that constitute a "delegation" to the court?

2. Compare with the principal case, *Bradley v. School Comm. of Boston,* 373 Mass. 53, 364 N.E.2d 1229 (1977), holding that a dispute over whether a school committee properly denied applications of school principals for transfers from one school to another could be arbitrated without offending the committee's statutory authority. The test, said the court, is "whether the issues of educational policy which are implicated in [the committee's decision] so outweigh the similarly implicated issues of employment conditions that the [school] committee cannot make even voluntary agreements on this subject". Is this a workable test? See Comment, *Developments in the Law of Public Employment,* 97 Harv.L.Rev. 1161 (1984).

3. The Michigan Supreme Court has been supportive of arbitration, approving its use in disputes involving nonrenewal of a probationary teacher's contract and the discharge of a police officer, but there are limits. When it came to a dispute over the dismissal of probation officers serving under the supervision of judges, the court in a 4–3 decision held that arbitration was inappropriate. Stressing the "sensitive" nature of the probation officer's function, the majority reasoned that arbitration "could result in reinstatement of a probation officer in which the court could no longer place trust or confidence". Are the functions of a probation officer more "sensitive" in that respect than the functions of a teacher or police officer? *AFSCME v. Recorder's Court Judges,* 399 Mich. 1, 248 N.W.2d 220 (1976).

4. In *Board of Education, Yonkers City School District v. Cassidy,* 59 A.D.2d 180, 399 N.Y.S.2d 20 (1977), the parties entered into a contract under which all persons in the bargaining unit were to receive a 5% salary increase. The Board of Education failed to pay the increase because of the adoption by the New York State Legislature in 1975 of the Financial

Emergency Act (FEA) for the City of Yonkers. Section 10 of the Act suspended all increases in salary or wages of covered organizations including the Yonkers City School District Unit of the Civil Service Employees Association, Inc. (CSEA). The union sought to enforce the arbitration provisions of the contract and the Board of Education sought a stay of the arbitration. The court held that Section 10 of the FEA was not an unconstitutional impairment of a contractual obligation because it was an extension of state power to protect public welfare. The motion to compel arbitration was granted with the caveat that if the arbitrator should grant a remedy in conflict with Section 10, the award would be illegal and unenforceable.

Compare this decision on the point of constitutional law with *Association of Surrogates and Supreme Court Reporters Within the City of New York v. State of New York,* 940 F.2d 766 (2d Cir.1991).

The New York State Legislature, in 1990, enacted a "lag payroll" system for certain state employees. The legislation provided that the salary or wages of the affected employees should be payable by the state two weeks after they became due, effective March 31, 1991. 1990 N.Y.Law Ch. 190, § 375(b).

Under this provision the State Controller decided that in order to "phase in" the two week lag, employees would be paid 9–days salary for each 10–day salary period, for ten such periods. In other words, the employees would be paid for 50 weeks rather than 52 weeks of employment in that fiscal year. The union argued (a) that the lag payroll violated the collective bargaining agreements covering these employees because those agreements specified payment every second Wednesday for the two-week period which ended on the date of payment and (b) that it violated the contract clause of the United States Constitution which prohibits states from passing laws impairing the obligation of contracts. The union prevailed on both points.

5. Assuming the collective agreement so provides, should a court order arbitration of a grievance claiming that a public school board engaged in reverse racial bias when it failed to appoint a white teacher as assistant basketball coach? See *Teaneck Bd. of Education v. Teaneck Teachers Association,* 94 N.J. 9, 462 A.2d 137 (1983).

6. In the famous "Steelworkers Trilogy" cases of 1960, the U.S. Supreme Court set forth certain guidelines to govern lower courts in deciding questions of arbitrability in the private sector. Courts are not to pass upon the merits of the underlying dispute, but only to determine whether the party seeking arbitration is making a claim which "on its face is governed by the contract." *United Steelworkers of America v. American Mfg. Co.,* 363 U.S. 564, 80 S.Ct. 1343, 4 L.Ed.2d 1403 (1960). And courts are not to deny arbitration "unless it may be said with positive assurance that the arbitration clause is not susceptible to an interpretation that covers the asserted dispute." *United Steelworkers of America v. Warrior & Gulf Navigation Co.,* 363 U.S. 574, 80 S.Ct. 1347, 4 L.Ed.2d 1409 (1960). The court distinguished the commercial arena, where arbitration is the substitute for litigation, from the labor arena, where it is the "substitute for industrial strife." (*Ibid.*) And it spoke of the collective bargaining agree-

ment as "more than an ordinary contract," as an "effort to erect a system of self-government" in which grievance and arbitration machinery serve as a "means of solving the unforeseeable by molding a system of private law for all the problems which may arise." (*Ibid.*) It characterized the labor arbitrator as a person "usually chosen because of the parties' confidence in his knowledge of the common law of the shop and their trust in his personal judgment." (*Ibid.*) Are these same policy considerations applicable to the public sector? If not, are there other policy considerations which support similar rules of judicial abstinence?

ACTING SUPERINTENDENT v. UNITED LIVERPOOL FACULTY ASS'N

New York Court of Appeals, 1977.
42 N.Y.2d 509, 399 N.Y.S.2d 189, 369 N.E.2d 746.

JONES, JUDGE: We hold that in arbitrations which proceed under the authority of the Taylor Law, the scope of the particular arbitration clause, and thus whether the question sought to be submitted to arbitration is within or without the ambit of that clause, is to be determined by the courts. In making such determinations the courts are to be guided by the principle that the agreement to arbitrate must be express, direct and unequivocal as to the issues or disputes to be submitted to arbitration; anything less will lead to a denial of arbitration.

In this case Liverpool Central School District and the United Liverpool Faculty Association entered into a collective bargaining agreement which provided a grievance procedure, the fourth and final step of which called for submission of an unresolved grievance to arbitration. Tracking the provisions of section 682(4) of the General Municipal Law, the School District and the faculty association defined a grievance as follows:

"*Grievance* shall mean any claimed violation, misinterpretation, or inequitable application of the existing laws, rules, procedures, regulations, administrative orders or work rules of the District, which relates to or involves Teachers' health or safety, physical facilities, materials or equipment furnished to teachers or supervision of Teachers; provided, however, that such term shall not include any matter involving a Teacher's rate of compensation, retirement benefits, disciplinary proceeding or any matter which is otherwise reviewable pursuant to law or any rule or regulation having the force and effect of law."

In November, 1974, Mrs. Lorraine Gargiul, an elementary school teacher, was obliged to take sick leave due to illness. In February, 1975 she notified the School District that she would be able to return to her teaching duties the following month. On February 26th she was advised that pursuant to the provisions of § 913 of the Education Law she would be required to submit to a complete medical examination by the School District physician, Dr. Paul Day, before being permitted to return to the classroom. The teacher took the position that she would participate only in an examination by a female physician. Following further correspondence of similar tenor, on March 17, 1975, the Board of Education passed a resolution directing her to be examined by Dr. Day before returning to her teaching responsibilities, if, after reviewing her health history, he determined that such examination was necessary. On the same day, based on the teacher's refusal to be examined by Dr. Day, she was placed on leave of absence without pay until the matter was resolved.

On April 10, 1975, the faculty association instituted grievance procedures on behalf of Mrs. Gargiul. When the issue was not resolved, the faculty association demanded arbitration in accordance with the provisions of the collective bargaining agreement. The School District promptly applied for a stay of arbitration which was granted at Special Term. The Appellate Division reversed. We now reverse the determination of that court and reinstate the disposition of Special Term.

It will be useful to place this case, and indeed all arbitration under the Taylor Law, in a broader context. Generally speaking, as the law of arbitration between private parties has developed and progressed, a difference in perspective and approach has evolved between arbitration in commercial matters and arbitration in labor relations. In the former it is the rule that the parties will not be held to have chosen arbitration as the forum for the resolution of their disputes in the absence of an express, unequivocal agreement to that effect; absent such an explicit commitment neither party may be compelled to arbitrate (*Gangel v. DeGroot,* 41 N.Y.2d 840, 841; *Matter of Riverdale Fabrics Corp.* [*Tillinghast–Stiles Co.*], 306 N.Y. 288, 289, 292). In the field of labor relations, by contrast, the general rule is the converse. Because of the recognition that arbitration has been demonstrated to be a salutary method of resolving labor disputes, because of the public policy (principally expressed in the Federal cases) which favors arbitration as a means of resolving such disputes, and because of the associated available inference that the parties to a collective bargaining agreement probably intended to resolve their differences by arbitration, the courts have held that controversies arising between the parties to such an agreement fall within the scope of the arbitration clause unless the parties have employed language which clearly manifests an intent to exclude a particular subject matter (*Matter of Howard & Co. v. Daley,* 27 N.Y.2d 285, 289–90; *Matter of Long Is. Lbr. Co.* [*Martin*], 15 N.Y.2d 380, 385.)[1]

Arbitration agreements that derive their vitality from the Taylor Law (Civil Service Law, Art. XIV) are sufficiently different that they cannot properly be categorized under either of these headings. Initially

1. [Footnotes numbered as in original—Ed.] In our view the not infrequent reference to a "presumption of arbitrability," while understandable, does not advance analysis and indeed in some instances serves rather to obfuscate. In the field of labor relations, however, experience has demonstrated that an inference may usually be drawn that the signatories to a collective bargaining agreement between private parties intended to submit their differences to arbitration.

we observe that our Court has never held that boards of education, unless authorized by specific legislation, are free to delegate to arbitrators the resolution of issues for which the boards have official responsibility. The enactment of the Taylor Law, establishing authority for the use of voluntary arbitration, confirmed rather than vitiated the principle of the nondelegable responsibility of elected representatives in the public sector. Hence, we approach consideration of the scope of arbitration clauses in public employment from this perspective.

When challenge is raised to the submission to arbitration of a dispute between employer and employee in the public sector the threshold consideration by the courts as to whether there is a valid agreement to arbitrate (CPLR 7503[a]) must proceed in sequence on two levels. Initially it must be determined whether arbitration claims with respect to the particular subject matter are authorized by the terms of the Taylor Law. The permissible scope of arbitration under that law is variously limited. * * * If, of course, the subject matter of the dispute between the parties falls outside the permissible scope of the Taylor Law, there is no occasion further to consider the language or the reach of the particular arbitration clause (Matter of Candor Cent. School Dist. [*Candor Teachers Assn.*], 42 N.Y.2d 266; *Matter of Cohoes City School Dist. v. Cohoes Teachers Assn.*, 40 N.Y.2d 774).

If it is concluded, however, that reference to arbitration is authorized under the Taylor Law, inquiry then turns at a second level to a determination of whether such authority was in fact exercised and whether the parties did agree by the terms of their particular arbitration clause to refer their differences in this specific area to arbitration. In the field of public employment, as distinguished from labor relations in the private sector, the public policy favoring arbitration—of recent origin—does not yet carry the same historical or general acceptance, nor, as evidenced in part by some of the litigation in our Court, has there so far been a similar demonstration of the efficacy of arbitration as a means for resolving controversies in governmental employment. Accordingly, it cannot be inferred as a practical matter that the parties to collective bargaining agreements in the public sector always intend to adopt the broadest permissible arbitration clauses. Indeed, inasmuch as the responsibilities of the elected representatives of the taxpaying public are overarching and fundamentally nondelegable it must be taken, in the absence of clear, unequivocal agreement to the contrary, that the board of education did *not* intend to refer differences which might arise to the arbitration forum. Such reference is not to be based on implication.

We turn then to the appeal now before us to make the necessary judicial determinations both with respect to Taylor Law authorization and as to the scope of this arbitration clause, i.e., whether Mrs. Gargiul's present complaint falls within the contract definition of grievance. We have no difficulty at the first level in concluding that there is nothing in statute, decisional law or public policy which would preclude the Board of Education, acting in behalf of the District, and the Association, should they agree to do so, from referring disputes of the present nature to arbitration.

At the second level, we address the particular language employed by the parties for the articulation of their agreement to arbitrate. Surely their definition of grievances does not approach the breadth of provisions which in other contexts are referred to as "broad arbitration clauses." This clause is explicitly a limited one. Indeed in form it expresses two separate agreements. First, the parties agree that certain disputes ("claimed violation, misinterpretation or inequitable application of existing laws, rules, procedure, regulations, administrative orders or work rules of the District which relate to or involve Teachers' health or safety, physical facilities, materials or equipment furnished to teachers or supervision of Teachers") shall be submitted to arbitration. In the same paragraph they then agree that other disputes shall not be referred to arbitration ("any matter involving a Teacher's rate of compensation, retirement benefits, disciplinary proceeding").[2] Thus, the question is not to determine the outer boundaries of a single definition; the problem is rather to determine into which of two different classifications the present dispute falls, or more precisely in this instance, how it shall be treated when it may reasonably be included within both groups.

As is evident from the arguments pressed by the parties, as well as from the decisions in the courts below, the present controversy could be classified both in surface description and substantive context in either category. On the one hand, although contending principally that the issue of arbitrability is for the arbitrator and not for the courts, the Faculty Association has labeled the board's action a claimed violation or inequitable application of existing laws and rules relating to the teacher's health, thus in the included category. On the other hand, the School District classifies the dispute as a matter involving disciplinary proceedings, in the excluded category. The labels attached by the parties, each evidently for its own advantage, can never be determinative. A very reasonable assertion can be made that this particular controversy falls within both the included and the excluded categories.

In this circumstance, we cannot conclude that the present dispute falls clearly and unequivocally within the class of claims agreed to be referred to arbitration. Accordingly the application of the School District for a stay of arbitration was properly granted.

For the reasons stated, the order of the Appellate Division should be reversed, without costs, and the order of Supreme Court, Onondaga County, reinstated.

Notes and Questions

1. What is the relevance, in the context of this case, that there are some issues which school boards may not legally agree to arbitrate? Wasn't this dispute legally subject to arbitration?

2. No claim is made that the present dispute falls within the very broad category of "any matter which is otherwise reviewable pursuant to law."

2. What does the court mean when it says that arbitration in the public sector does not yet carry with it the "same historical or general acceptance" as in the private sector? This same court, in *Board of Education v. Associated Teachers of Huntington,* 30 N.Y.2d 122, 331 N.Y.S.2d 17, 282 N.E.2d 109 (1972), accepted the private sector teaching that arbitration is "part and parcel of the administration of grievances." Has something happened to change the court's mind? And what does the court have reference to when it says that there had not yet been a "demonstration of the efficacy of arbitration as a means of resolving controversies in governmental employment"? Is the court trying to protect public agencies against their own ineptitude in agreeing to broad arbitration clauses?

3. Judge Gabrielli, in a concurring opinion, argued it was unnecessary to reach the arbitrability issue in the case because the teacher, by appealing to the Commissioner of Education from the Board's action, had waived her right to arbitrate. That raises an issue to be considered later, but might it have played an unarticulated role in the majority's view?

4. *Liverpool* is an aberration. Even in New York, subsequent decisions pay it only lip service (e.g. *South Colonie Central School District v. Longo,* 43 N.Y.2d 136, 400 N.Y.S.2d 798, 371 N.E.2d 516 (1977)). Most state courts have accepted Trilogy principles as governing questions of arbitrability in the public sector. See, e.g., *Kaleva–Norman–Dickson School District v. Kaleva–Norman–Dickson School Teachers Association,* 393 Mich. 583, 227 N.W.2d 500, 89 LRRM 2078 (1975). A careful practitioner, however, will want to look behind the language which courts use in the results in particular cases. In some cases, for example, courts while espousing Trilogy principles have intruded rather deeply into the merits. The Connecticut Supreme Court, for example, has held that although an agreement made reference to existing retirement plans, a dispute concerning those plans was not arbitrable under the agreement because the court considered it "impossible to say that the substantive provisions of the pension plan were made part of the agreement." *Policemen's & Firemen's Retirement Board v. Sullivan,* 173 Conn. 1, 376 A.2d 399 (1977). In Oregon an appellate court held that a teacher organization was not entitled to arbitrate over a claimed violation of a state administrative rule specifying class size, though the applicable contract defined a grievance to include claimed violation of "administrative rules and regulations." The Court concluded that "the only rational interpretation" of this provision was that the school district agreed to arbitrate over its *own* rules and regulations and not those of the state agency. *Portland Association of Teachers v. School District No. 1,* 27 Or.App. 247, 555 P.2d 943 (1976).

C. JUDICIAL REVIEW OF THE ARBITRATION AWARD

In the private sector, under Steelworkers Trilogy principles, courts are not to review the merits of an arbitration award "so long as it draws its essence from the collective bargaining agreement". *United Steelworkers of America v. Enterprise Wheel & Car Corp.,* 363 U.S. 593,

80 S.Ct. 1358, 4 L.Ed.2d 1424 (1960). Most courts have come to accept that standard in the public sector as well. See, generally, Craver, *The Judicial Enforcement of Public Sector Grievance Arbitration,* 58 Tex. L.Rev. 329, 1980, 341 et seq. The congruence is not perfect, however. There are some situations in which courts appear to be more intrusive in reviewing a public sector arbitrator's award on the merits. And, while an award may be set aside even in the private sector on grounds of illegality or public policy, the chances of that occurring in the public sector are, for a number of reasons, significantly greater. The following materials illustrate this greater vulnerability of public sector arbitral awards.

COUNTY OF ALLEGHENY v. ALLEGHENY COUNTY PRISON EMPLOYEES

Supreme Court of Pennsylvania, 1977.
476 Pa. 27, 381 A.2d 849, 96 LRRM 3396.

[A union representing guards at the Allegheny County jail in Pennsylvania filed grievances claiming (1) that the officers' lounge where the guards took their meals should be supervised at mealtime by a guard, and (2) that the guards should be able to select for their meals any food available from the jail kitchen rather than being limited to the menus offered to the prisoners. In support of the grievance, the union relied upon practices which existed prior to the collective agreement. The agreement itself made no mention of those practices, nor did it mention past practices in general. It contained an "integration clause", stating the agreement to represent "the full and complete agreement and commitment between the parties thereto". The arbitrator ruled in favor of both grievances on the basis of past practices, but the Commonwealth Court of Pennsylvania set the award aside, and the Supreme Court of that state affirmed.] [8]

POMEROY, JUSTICE: * * *

II.

Turning to the substantive question of whether the arbitrator's award had a rational basis in the collective bargaining agreement, we

8. [Footnotes numbered as in original—Ed.] The pertinent clauses are as follows:

"Article III—Grievance Procedure

"1. Grievance Procedure Definitions:

"A. Grievance—An alleged breach or violation of this Agreement or a dispute arising out of the interpretation or application of the provisions of this Agreement. * * *

"2. Scope of Grievance Procedure:

"A. Any matter not specifically defined as a grievance in Section 1 above, as well as any matter reserved to the discretion of the County by the statutes, legal precedents and regulations of the Commonwealth of Pennsylvania, and/or by the terms of this Agreement is not a grievance and will not be construed as a grievance. * * *

* * *

"Article XII—Management Rights

"The County retains and reserves unto itself all powers, rights, authority, duties and responsibilities including but not limited to the security of the prison conferred upon and vested in it by the Commonwealth of Pennsylvania and all matters not covered by this Agreement. * * *"

must conclude that it did not. The agreement contains no provision whatever which deals either with the question of security arrangements for the employees' mealtimes or with what food should be available to the employees from the prison kitchen.[9]

The arbitrator's decision that the union members were entitled to choose for their luncheons any food available in the prison kitchen and were not limited to the items available on the daily prison menu was based on what he found to have been the past practice of the parties over a period of time, a practice which, so the arbitrator held, had been implicitly incorporated in the collective bargaining agreement which became effective in 1972.[10]

A recognized commentator [11] in the field of labor law identifies four situations in which evidence of past practice [12] is used in arbitrations:

9. The only clause of the agreement which refers to meals is found in Article VII, Section 4:

> "A lunch period of 30 minutes shall be made available to all employees before their sixth hour of work. * * * "

The Union argued to the arbitrator that implicit in this clause are both a choice of foods to be served to the guards and a requirement that security be provided during mealtimes. The arbitrator did not address himself to this contention in his opinion and award, nor did he in his award purport to interpret either the 30 minute lunch clause or the integration clause (Article XXIV, Sec. 1), discussed *infra.* The dissenting opinion of Mr. Justice Roberts, post, has ascribed to the arbitrator interpretations that simply are not to be found in his decision.

10. The facts shown by the record are as follows:

Before 1967, prison guards at the Allegheny County jail ate their meals in the prison kitchen, either bringing their lunches from outside or choosing from any of the food available within the prison. In May of 1967, the warden directed employees to cease bringing their own lunches. The Union protested this directive and submitted a grievance to a three member panel authorized by the predecessor statute to PERA, the Act of June 30, 1947, P.L. 1183, § 1 *et seq.,* 43 P.S. § 215.1 *et seq. as amended* (1964). This panel recommended that the prohibition against lunches brought from outside be continued but that the guards be given a choice of any food available in the prison kitchen. For some time this recommendation, although not legally binding, was followed. When later an officers' lounge was established the guards were permitted to take their luncheons from the kitchen to the lounge to be eaten. In December, 1970, the warden issued an order, which although objected to was apparently complied with, restricting the prison guard personnel to a choice of food from the daily prison menu. After the collective bargaining agreement became effective in May of 1972, the Union filed the present grievance challenging the 1970 directive of management. When, apparently in response to the filing of this grievance, the prison authorities issued further orders restricting the guards' privileges, the Union filed an unfair labor practice charge with the Pennsylvania Labor Relations Board. This charge was settled by the County's agreement to rescind the later restrictions, with the understanding that the processing of the grievance would continue. After this settlement, the old practice of allowing each employee to select any food available was, according to the arbitrator, gradually reinstated.

11. R. Mittenthal, *Past Practice and the Administration of Collective Bargaining Agreements,* Proceedings of the 14th Annual Meeting of the National Academy of Arbitrators 30 (1961).

12. In a frequently cited passage in an arbitration award, the meaning of "past practice" has been stated as follows:

> "A custom or practice is not something which arises simply because a given course of conduct has been pursued by Management or the employees on one or more occasions. A custom or a practice is a usage evolved by men as a normal reaction to a recurring type situation. It must be shown to be the *accepted* course of conduct characteristically repeated in response to the given set of underlying circumstances. This is not to say that the course of conduct must be *accepted* in the sense of both parties having agreed

(1) to clarify ambiguous language; (2) to implement contract language which sets forth only a general rule; (3) to modify or amend apparently unambiguous language which has arguably been waived by the parties; and (4) to create or prove a separate, enforceable condition of employment which cannot be derived from the express language of the agreement. In the case at bar, the arbitrator concluded that the implementation by the County of the advisory recommendation of a panel of arbitrators in 1967 [13] created a binding past practice, a clear example of the fourth use of past practices in the above formulation. With this implementation, the arbitrator held,

> "* * * the Guards acquired a working condition which constituted a recognizable benefit. Its constant, continual use caused the benefit to ripen into a binding practice. * * * The privilege given to each Guard to choose his meal from the available kitchen foods became one of the many day-to-day facets of the working relationship between the Prison administration and its Guards. * * *" Record at 13a.[14]

to it, but rather that it must be *accepted* in the sense of being regarded by the men involved as the *normal* and *proper* response to the underlying circumstances presented." Sylvester Garrett, Chairman, Board of Arbitration, U.S. Steel–Steelworkers, Grievance No. NL–453, Docket No. N.–146, January 31, 1953. Reported at 2 *Steelworkers Arbitration Bulletin* 1187. (Emphasis in original).

13. See n. 10, *supra.*

14. The arbitrator gave the following rationale in support of his conclusion that the past practice was implicitly included in the bargaining agreement:

> "The Warden was, or should have been, aware that a contractual grievance procedure provided the only practicable way by which the Union could attack his December 1970 edict [restricting the employees to food on the daily menu]. . . . During the negotiations leading up to the 1972 collective bargaining agreement, which first provided that type of grievance procedure, this awareness must be imputed to the County. It would obviously be impossible, in such an agreement, to incorporate all of the work practices and customs previously accepted by the mutual consent of the parties. If the County wished to bar this particular matter from the grievance procedure, the County had the duty to seek specific contract language on the subject. In this particular instance, the absence of a past practice clause does not eliminate the eating customs in effect as of December 1970 nor prevent the Union from setting aside the Warden's directive by filing a grievance. It is fair to conclude that the working condition at issue was one of the many implicitly incorporated into the corrective bargaining agreement." Record at 13–14a.

In contrast, the Commonwealth Court, in an alternative ground for its decision concluded as follows from its review of the record:

> "If there did, in fact, exist a past policy regarding luncheon procedure, it was a policy of constant change. Being aware of the ever-varying nature of appellant's practice towards guards' luncheons, to escape the application of * * * [those provisions of the agreement dealing with management's discretion over all matters not covered by the agreement], it was incumbent upon * * * [the Union] to have negotiated and explicitly reached an agreement upon this particular condition of employment." 20 Pa.Cmwlth. at 178, 341 A.2d at 580.

In light of our disposition of this case there is no need for us to resolve the question of which, if either, party had the responsibility to take the initiative in making past practices a subject of negotiation. Similarly, we are not called upon to decide whether a practice which was legally but unilaterally terminated by employer direction a year and a half before the collective bargaining agreement was entered into, but which termination has been a subject of continuing controversy between the parties, is properly to be considered a "past practice" as a matter of law. See

As for the Union demand for protection of its members by a guard posted in the officers' lounge at mealtimes, the arbitrator concluded that a "slightly different" problem was involved but that the contractual reservation to the County in Article XII of all responsibility relating to security, see n. 8, *supra,* "must be interpreted in a reasonable fashion. The Union is not seeking to interfere with the security of the Prison. On the contrary, it is trying to insure the physical safety of its member Guards. * * * The Prison was sufficiently concerned about the problem to provide a Guard over the residents when employees ate in the Prison kitchen. There is no reason why the same protection ought not to be afforded to employees while they are eating in the Officers' Lounge." Record at 15a.

The question for decision is whether the arbitrator was correct in concluding that the parties to the contract here involved implicitly incorporated into it, as separately enforceable conditions of their employment relationship, practices relative to food and security at lunch times which had prevailed for a time in the past, when those practices are neither repudiated in the agreement nor inconsistent with its terms, but when the contract includes a broad clause to the effect that the agreement as written is the complete agreement between the parties.[15] Although the non-inclusion of the practices in the bargaining agreement does not necessarily compel the conclusion that past practices are not impliedly so incorporated,[16] the existence in a contract of a broad integration clause, if it means anything, does clearly negate the

Mittenthal, *Past Practice and the Administration of Collective Bargaining Agreements,* 59 Mich.L.Rev. 1017, 1033–34 (1961).

15. The clause is contained in Article XXIV of the agreement and is as follows:

> "Article XXIV
>
> "1. The parties mutually agree that the terms and conditions expressly set forth in this Agreement represent the full and complete agreement and commitment between the parties thereto."

Paragraph 2 of Article XXIV provides as follows:

> "2. All items proposed by the Union, whether agreed to or rejected, will not be subject to renegotiation until negotiations for a new contract commence * * * and items included within the scope of the bargaining which were or are not proposed by the Union shall likewise not be subject to negotiation until the period specified above. * * *"

16. Wallen, *The Silent Contract v. Express Provisions: The Arbitration of Local Working Conditions,* Proceedings of the Fifth Annual Meeting of the National Academy of Arbitrators 117 (1962).

As Mittenthal pointed out in his authoritative paper, *supra* n. 11, at 47

> "Most agreements * * * say nothing about management having to maintain existing conditions. They ordinarily do not even mention the subject of past practice. The question then is whether, apart from any basis in the agreement, an established practice can nevertheless be considered a binding condition of employment. The answer, I think, depends upon one's conception of the collective bargaining agreement. * * * '[I]s the agreement an exclusive statement of rights and privileges or does it subsume continuation of existing conditions.'" (Footnote omitted.)

See also, Gilman, *Past Practice in the Administration of Collective Bargaining Agreements in Arbitration,* 4 Suffolk U.L.Rev. 689 (1970). Note *Labor Law—Arbitration and Award—Judicial Review of Labor Arbitration Awards Which Rely on the Practices of the Parties,* 65 Mich. L.Rev. 1647 (1967). See in general Griffin, *Judicial Review of Labor Arbitration Awards,* 4 Suffolk U.L.Rev. 39 (1969); Markham, *Judicial Review of an Arbitrator's Award Under Section 301(a) of the Labor Management Relations Act,* 39 Tenn. L.Rev. 613 (1972).

notion that the parties meant to include any terms or conditions, including those based *only* on past practices, not specifically incorporated in the written contract or reasonably inferable from its provisions. We think that this provision is dispositive of this case.[17] At least one arbitrator has expressly so held, *Lone Star Brewing Co.,* 53 LA 1317 (1969) (LeRoy Autrey), and we know of no decision to the contrary. See also Cox & Dunlop, *The Duty to Bargain Collectively During the Term of an Existing Agreement,* 63 Harv.L.Rev. 1097, 1116–17 (1950).

In deciding as we do, we hold only that where a collective bargaining agreement not only makes no mention whatever of past practices but does include a broad integration clause, an award which incorporates into the agreement, as separately enforceable conditions of the employment relationship, past practices which antedate the effective date of that agreement cannot be said to "draw its essence from the collective bargaining" agreement.[18] *United Steelworkers v. Enterprise Wheel and Car Corp.,* 363 U.S. 593, 596 (1960). We hasten to add that courts are not to become super-arbitrators and are bound to defer to the arbitrators' findings relative to the intent of the parties as the arbitrators perform their task of interpreting labor contracts negotiated under PERA. See *Community College of Beaver County v. Community College of Beaver County, Society of the Faculty,* 473 Pa. 576, 375 A.2d 1267 (1977). The able arbitrator in this case, however, was not so much interpreting the contract before him as he was declaring, no doubt out of his conviction of what was fair and reasonable, that the employer should be bound by a non-existent provision which the arbitrator then incorporates into the contract by implication. But there is here nothing to support the implication. Conceding that the past attitude of the management of the County's prison may have been petty, it is nevertheless a function of future bargaining to remedy the situation. For the arbitrator to seek to supply the remedy is on these facts not in accord with the approach of *Enterprise, supra,* which we have adopted as the proper one for applying the Arbitration Act in public employment contracts. The award must, therefore, be set aside.

What we have said, of course, is not to suggest that in another case the evidence may not justify a contrary conclusion. Nor do we intend to say that an arbitrator's reliance on past practices to clarify ambigu-

17. The arbitrator made note of the existence of Article XXIV, only to conclude, without explanation, that its "zipper provisions" were inapplicable. Record at 13a. It does not advance a reasoned solution of the problem presented by this case to dismiss this provision as "boilerplate," the characterization used in both dissenting opinions, *infra.* We are obliged to take the agreement as the parties wrote it. The significance of the integration clause is given emphasis by the broad language of the management rights clause (Article XII) quoted at n. 8, *supra.*

18. Mittenthal, *supra* note 11, at 48–49, articulates the theory on which many arbitrators rely in concluding that a past practice not specifically repudiated during negotiations for a contract are impliedly incorporated in the agreement which is finally reached. He then observes (p. 49, n. 39):

> "This implication, of course, would not be possible if it conflicted with the express language of the contract. For example, if a contract said the written provisions constitute the entire agreement of the parties, it would be difficult to imply that the parties meant to make practices a part of their contract."

ous language in the collective bargaining agreement, to implement general contract language or to show that a specific provision in the contract has been waived by the parties, would be improper although the agreement in question included an integration clause.

The order of the Commonwealth Court is affirmed.

ROBERTS, JUSTICE, dissenting. * * *

The majority's holding deprives the arbitrator of two of his most valuable tools in settling labor disputes whenever the collective bargaining agreement contains a boilerplate integration clause. These tools are the arbitrator's knowledge of the particular conditions in which labor and management operate and his knowledge of the rules—the "law of the shop"—which labor and management have developed to respond to these conditions. I cannot agree that the presence of an integration clause so completely alters the basic rules of the arbitration process. I therefore dissent.

The majority holds that the arbitrator failed to give proper weight to the "integration clause" in the collective bargaining agreement. In so doing, however, the majority misapplies the "essence test," the standard by which courts of this Commonwealth are to review arbitration awards. * * * This "essence test" reflects a judgment that arbitrators, and not courts, are best equipped to deal with the multitude of potential disputes which the parties agree to submit to them. This deferential standard also serves to solidify the integrity of the arbitration process by giving the parties the assurance that the decision of the arbitrator will, in the vast majority of cases, be final.

The majority's decision is contrary to these policies. The majority, by requiring the arbitrator to conform to the strict rules of contract law applied by the courts in non-labor contract cases deprives him of the opportunity to employ his knowledge of the customs and practices of the industry and the shop involved. As the Supreme Court of the United States stated in *United Steelworkers v. Warrior & Gulf Navigation Co.*, 363 U.S. 574, 579–80, 582–83 (1960):

> " 'the institutional characteristics and the governmental nature of the collective-bargaining process demand a common law of the shop which implements and furnishes the context of the agreement. We must assume that intelligent negotiators acknowledged so plain a need unless they stated a contrary rule in plain words.'
>
> . . .
>
> "The labor arbitrator's source of law is not confined to the express provisions of the contract, as the industrial common law,—the practices of the industry and the shop—is equally a part of the collective bargaining agreement although not expressed in it. The labor arbitrator is usually chosen because of the parties' confidence in his knowledge of the common law of the shop and their trust in his personal judgment to bring to bear considerations which are not expressed in the contract as criteria for judgment."

In view of the fact that the guards are required to eat their meals on the premises, the award here which covers the meals for guards and the security available to the guards while eating involves important working conditions. By allowing a boilerplate integration clause to divest the arbitrator of the ability to make an award concerning these important conditions, the majority defeats the policy which encourages arbitrators to draw upon their knowledge of the particular job setting so that a "fair solution of the problem" can be reached. The majority forces the arbitrator to treat the integration clause with more deference than the parties to the collective bargaining agreement may have intended, given their particular work situation. In so holding, the majority discourages the arbitrator from performing fully the services expected from him.

Moreover today's decision destroys the stability of the arbitration process. "[T]he arbitrators are the final judges of both law and fact and their award will not be disturbed for a mistake of either." *Ludwig–Honold Mfg. Co. v. Fletcher,* 405 F.2d 1123, 1128 (3d Cir.1969). Accord, *Sudders v. United National Insurance Co.,* 217 Pa.Super. 196, 269 A.2d 370 (1970), *aff'd,* 445 Pa. 599, 284 A.2d 500 (1971). If an award of an arbitrator is upheld by the courts so long as it is rationally based, then parties can respect the decision of the arbitrator as a final resolution of the dispute between them. If, instead, the award of the arbitrator is open to unnecessary judicial modification, the arbitrator becomes only a small step in the process of resolving labor disputes; the judgment of the arbitrator which the parties bargained for is thereby replaced with the judgment of the courts. * * *

. . .

MANDERINO, JUSTICE, dissenting: I agree with the majority that we should uphold the arbitrator's decision that this grievance filed by the Union was arbitrable. I cannot agree, however, that because this particular collective bargaining agreement contains an integration clause, the arbitrator was in error in determining that a past practice, though not specifically mentioned in the collective bargaining agreement, was implicitly incorporated in that agreement.

A collective bargaining agreement cannot possibly cover every single term and condition of employment. The existence of an integration clause does not alter this fact. Integration clauses such as the one which existed here are boilerplate, and parties to a collective bargaining agreement do not, because an integration clause is present, go to any greater lengths to insure that every term or condition of employment, from the choice of meals to the furnishing of restroom necessities, is contained within the agreement. Under the majority's reasoning, if the employer has been furnishing toilets and toilet paper but the agreement is silent about such matters, the employer can ignore the past practice and cease furnishing the restroom necessities.

Here, the arbitrator concluded that the parties *agreed* on certain conditions concerning guards' lunches, conditions which were present prior to the effective date of agreement and which the parties felt no need to spell out in the collective bargaining agreement. That conclusion should be upheld in spite of the existence of a "broad" integration clause, otherwise, collective bargaining agreements will have to be written as rolls of paper stretching endlessly....

Notes

1. Under the majority's view, would the arbitrator's award be set aside if there had been evidence from negotiating history that the "integration clause" was not intended to preclude reliance on past practice? Under Justice Manderino's view, would the award be set aside if the arbitrator found that the clause *did* preclude reliance on past practice? Under Justice Roberts' view, would there be any circumstances in which an arbitrator's award interpreting an "integration clause" would be set aside? Would the absence of an "integration clause" warrant a different result? See *Ringgold Area School District v. Ringgold Education Association,* 489 Pa. 380, 414 A.2d 118 (1980).

2. The Pennsylvania courts are not alone in expressing concern over arbitral reliance upon past practice. See Grodin & Najita, *Judicial Response to Public-Sector Arbitration,* Aaron, Najita, and Stern, Public Sector Bargaining, BNA Books, 2d Ed. 1988, pp. 243–44. Is there a principled basis for a less deferential attitude on the part of counts toward such reliance in the public sector?

3. Most state courts have accepted the *Enterprise* "essence" test, or something close to it, as the standard for judicial review; but, as in cases involving arbitrability, it is the application of the standard that counts. Courts appear reluctant to affirm awards which rely upon past practice to add to or vary the terms of an agreement, e.g., *Civil Service Employees v. City of Steuben,* 50 A.D.2d 421, 377 N.Y.S.2d 849 (1976) (overturning an award which held that a county was precluded by longstanding past practice from attempting to enforce a contract clause which required that social workers obtain written approval in advance in order to secure travel reimbursement from their homes to the homes of clients).

INTERNATIONAL BROTHERHOOD OF FIREMEN AND OILERS, LOCAL 1201, AFL–CIO v. THE BOARD OF EDUCATION OF THE SCHOOL DISTRICT OF PHILADELPHIA

Supreme Court of Pennsylvania, 1983.
500 Pa. 474, 457 A.2d 1269.

ZAPPALA, JUSTICE.

* * * Pursuant to the *Public Employee Relations Act,* Act of July 23, 1970, P.L. 563, No. 195, 43 P.S. § 1101.101 et seq. (hereafter "Act 195"), the Union called a three-day strike against the District in

February, 1981. The strike ended with the signing of a collective bargaining agreement covering the period from September 1, 1980 to August 31, 1982. The agreement provided that there would be no salary increase for the first year. There would be a four (4%) percent lump sum bonus for the period of January 1 to August 31, 1981, payable on September 1, 1981. The bonus would be incorporated into the salary schedule, and an additional ten (10%) percent increase would be given for the second year of the agreement. The District would make increased payments for health, welfare and pre-paid legal services during the second year.

In March, 1981, after approving the collective bargaining agreement, the District prepared a proposed budget for the 1981–82 school year. The budget reflected $750,207,000.00 in revenues and $902,700,000.00 in net obligations. There was a fund deficit of $71,073,000.00 in addition to the excess of net obligations over revenues reflected in the proposed budget.[1] In May, 1981, the District adopted a revised budget reflecting $761,024,148.00 in revenues; $701,005,148.00 in net obligations; and a $60,019,000.00 fund deficit. The District cut its budget by, inter alia, refusing to pay the salary and benefit increases it agreed to for the second year of the collective bargaining agreement with the Union.

Pursuant to the agreement, the Union filed a grievance over the refusal to pay the salary and benefit increases. The grievance was heard by an arbitrator. The District argued that it was excused from paying the increases on the basis of impossibility of performance in that it did not have and could not obtain sufficient funds and that the availability of funds was a condition precedent to performance. The arbitrator determined that the District had not established impossibility of performance and ordered it to pay the increases. The District filed a Petition for Review in the Court of Common Pleas of Philadelphia. The court dismissed the Petition and confirmed the arbitration award. The Commonwealth Court reversed, holding that the availability of sufficient funds was a condition precedent to the agreement and that the burden was on the Union to establish the occurrence of such condition. It ordered the case remanded to give the Union an opportunity to establish the occurrence of the condition precedent. We granted the Union's Petition for Allowance of Appeal. The issues on appeal are whether there is impossibility of performance, whether there is a condition precedent and, if so, whether the Union has the burden to establish it, whether the arbitration award must be upheld as being rationally derivable from the collective bargaining agreement, and whether the award is consistent with law and public policy.

We will first consider the claim of impossibility of performance. The District bases the claim on an inability to obtain sufficient funds. The District operates under a home-rule charter adopted under the *First Class City Public Education Home Rule Act,* Act of August 9,

1. The fund deficit reflected a shortage of funds for the previous year.

1963, P.L. 643, 53 P.S. § 13201 et seq. The charter requires a balanced budget, § 12–303(a). It also provides that school board members are appointed by the mayor, § 12–1201. Under Article 3, § 31 of the Constitution of the Commonwealth, "the General Assembly shall not delegate to any special commission * * * any power * * * to levy taxes * * *" This provision prevents an appointed body such as the Philadelphia School Board from being empowered to levy taxes. *Danson v. Casey,* 484 Pa. 415, 399 A.2d 360 (1979). The District is therefore dependent on funds appropriated by the Philadelphia City Council.[2] It contends that its dependence on funds so appropriated and its inability to incur a deficit renders performance of the contract impossible. The arbitrator rejected the claim on the basis that the refusal to honor the contract was based on the District's unilateral decision as to how to balance its budget without a showing that it had tried to honor the contract by all possible means.

We accept the arbitrator's finding that impossibility of performance was not established. In *Moore v. Whitty,* 299 Pa. 58, 149 A. 83 (1930), this Court held that a strike or the threat thereof did not excuse a building contractor from performing on a contract. It was found that mere inconvenience, although it works a hardship, does not excuse performance and that a party who wishes to be excused from performance on the basis of a subsequently occurring condition has a duty so to provide in the contract and will not be excused otherwise if performance is lawful and possible in itself. *Luria Engineering Co. v. Aetna Casualty & Surety Co.,* 206 Pa.Super. 333, 213 A.2d 151 (1965), was another case where a labor dispute was found not to excuse performance of a contract. The court held that an act of a third party that makes performance of a contract impossible will not excuse performance if it is foreseeable and not provided for in the contract. In the instant case, we find that the District was required to establish impossibility of performance and failed to do so in the absence of a showing that it attempted performance by all possible means. Furthermore, there is nothing in the agreement stating that a balanced budget or any particular level of funding is a condition precedent to the payment of the agreed on salary and benefit increases. We find that the District had a duty to make such provision in the agreement if it wished to be excused. In *Danson v. Casey,* supra, we took note of the fact that the Philadelphia School District has had a history of funding difficulties. We find that the District's financial condition was foreseeable and did not excuse performance on the basis of action of a third party, i.e.

2. The Court of Common Pleas noted that the Mayor and other officials of the city administration participated in the contract negotiations in an advisory capacity. They discussed, inter alia, funding possibilities. The court further noted that the District requested a higher appropriation and concomitant tax levies for the year in question, but the city council refused the request. We find that the City Council knew or should have known of the contractually mandated salary and benefit increases, as they were agreed to during the previous year and city officials participated in the negotiations.

failure of the city council to appropriate sufficient funds or any other basis.

Our finding that the District's financial condition does not excuse performance is further supported by cases dealing specifically with labor relations. The award of an arbitrator in a labor dispute is not improper on the basis of its fiscal impact when the legislative body charged with appropriating the necessary funds has not rejected the award, *Board of Education of the School District of Philadelphia v. American Federation of State, County & Municipal Employees, Local 1660, District Council 33, AFL–CIO,* 66 Pa.Cmwlth. 346, 444 A.2d 813 (1982). Here the City Council appropriated funds for the District to allocate as it saw fit and did not reject the arbitration award.

In the instant case, the matters in question are proper terms and conditions of employment. Wages are specifically made subject to collective bargaining by Act 195, § 701, 43 P.S. § 1101.701. Fringe benefits are also a proper subject of collective bargaining, *Costigan v. Philadelphia Finance Department Employees, Local 696, American Federation of State, County, and Municipal Employees, AFL–CIO,* 462 Pa. 425, 341 A.2d 456 (1975). The parties have not cited and we have not found any applicable statutory or home rule charter provision that prohibits the salary and benefit increases provided for in the collective bargaining agreement and enforced by the arbitration award. The finding of impossibility of performance would, under the circumstances here announced, be improper without a showing of the capabilities or lack of the same to implement the award. While the Court is cognizant of the potential difficulties that may occur when one body negotiates a contract and another is required to act to guarantee its implementation, the solution lies in bargaining or with legislative enactment and not with decision-making.

Our acceptance of the arbitration award is required, given the applicable standard of review. An arbitration award based on an interpretation of a collective bargaining agreement must be accepted by the courts if the interpretation can in any rational way be derived from the agreement, viewed in light of its language and context and any other indicia of the parties' intent, *Ringgold Area School District v. Ringgold Education Association, PSEA/NEA,* 489 Pa. 380, 414 A.2d 118 (1980). In light of our discussion supra, we find that the arbitrator's interpretation that the district agreed to pay the disputed salary and benefit increases without any condition precedent based on its financial condition was rationally derivable from the agreement and must be accepted.

Finally, we find that the arbitration is proper under the law and public policy. As we have noted, the matters in dispute are proper subject of collective bargaining. The provisions of the agreement enforced by the arbitrator do not violate any applicable law. Act 195, § 101, 43 P.S. § 1101.101 declares that it is the public policy of the Commonwealth to "promote orderly and constructive relationships between all public employers and their employes * * * by (1) granting to public employes the right to organize and choose freely their representatives; (2) requiring public employers to negotiate and bargain with employe organizations representing public employes and to enter into written agreements evidencing the result of such bargaining; and (3) establishing procedures to provide for the protection of the rights of the public employe, the public employer and the public at large." Our decisions requiring public employers to do all in their power to implement a lawful award or contract and establishing a narrow scope of review for arbitration awards reflect a public policy. This policy favors the resolution of disputes by bargaining and arbitration where appropriate, as here, and the acceptance by the courts of the results thereof. Our upholding of the arbitration award in the instant case is in accord with public policy.

The Order of the Commonwealth Court is reversed and the Order of the Court of Common Pleas is reinstated.

D. JUDICIAL REVIEW AND PUBLIC NORMS

While arbitration has traditionally been viewed as a means of giving effect to the parties' agreement, arbitrators are increasingly being asked to take laws into account, either for the purpose of interpreting the agreement, or because the parties have agreed that disputes over the application of laws to the workplace will be resolved through arbitration. And, laws (or "public policies") external to the agreement may be relied upon by a party seeking to overturn an arbitration award.

The movement toward consideration of public norms is common to both private and public sector arbitration, but in the public sector it is more advanced, simply because in that sector public norms have always played a greater role. The cases which follow illustrate the interplay between arbitration and public norms in a variety of contexts.

CITY OF MADISON v. POLICE OFFICERS ASSOC.

Supreme Court of Wisconsin, 1988.
144 Wis.2d 576, 425 N.W.2d 8.

HEFFERNAN, CHIEF JUSTICE.

This case comes to us on a petition by the Madison Professional Police Officers Association (MPPOA) to review a decision of the court of appeals. In that decision, the court of appeals reversed the order of the circuit court for Dane county, Susan Steingass, circuit judge. The circuit court held for MPPOA and resolved the dispute over the applicability of the City of Madison's residency requirement to the members of the MPPOA, by finding that under MPPOA's "me too" clause,[2] because the city had moderated the residency requirement for

2. A "me too" clause is one which gains for the employees in whose contract it appears concessions which another second group of employees have won under the

another group of city employees, the MPPOA members must also be allowed to live outside the city. The court of appeals reversed, finding that the City of Madison's residency ordinance controlled over the "me too" clause of the MPPOA contract, and that therefore MPPOA members had to abide by the residency requirements. * * *

* * * The ordinance in question, Madison General Ordinance (MGO) sec. 3.27, reads in relevant part:

> "No person shall be eligible for * * * employment * * * unless he shall reside in the City of Madison unless permission to reside outside of the City of Madison shall be expressly granted by the Mayor. In the event that any such City * * * employee * * * shall cease to reside in the City of Madison, his * * * employment shall be automatically forthwith vacated. * * *"

This ordinance has been unchanged since 1956.

The underlying problem in this case began in 1970, when the City of Madison accepted federal funds for its bus system. This aid was provided under the Urban Mass Transit Act (UMTA), 49 U.S.C.App. sec. 1601 *et seq.* Section 13(c) of the UMTA provided that, as a condition of receiving federal funds, the city had to make "equitable arrangements" to protect the employees "affected by such assistance." Among other things, the city had to preserve all rights under existing collective bargaining arrangements.

The bus employees were employed by the private Madison Service Corporation, and represented in collective bargaining by the Teamsters Union. Although it was assumed that bus employees were not city employees, from 1970 to 1983, that union and the city executed 23 different "13(c)" agreements, designed to maintain the employees' "arrangements" as mandated under the UMTA sec. 13(c). Each of these agreements contained a clause which allowed the bus system employees to live anywhere.

In 1983, the city and the Teamsters Union, as a result of discussions between them, and also of an NLRB ruling, agreed that the bus system employees were city employees. As a result, the 24th 13(c) agreement, ratified in November of 1983, provided that the employees were now to be subject to the city residency ordinance. However, the new agreement also contained a clause stating:

> "The City and the Union agree that all employees employed on or before the 31st day of October, 1983, shall not be subject to any Ordinance requiring residency in the City of Madison as a condition of employment."

This agreement eventually triggered many problems, including the one at the root of the instant case, because other contracts which the city had with the unions representing its employees contained so-called "me too" clauses.

second group's contract. For two examples, see *infra,* notes 3 and 5.

In *City of Madison v. Local 311, International Association of Firefighters,* 133 Wis.2d 186, 394 N.W.2d 766 (Ct.App.1986), a case which is the predecessor of the case at bar, the Madison Firefighters' "me too" clause was at issue.[3] In that case, the Firefighters filed a grievance, claiming that the city, by making an exemption for the bus system employees who had been employed before October 31, 1983, had waived the residency requirement for another group.

The matter went to arbitration, where the Firefighters argued that it, too, should not be held to the residency requirement. The city countered with an argument that the exemption to the bus system employees had been mandatory under UMTA because, under UMTA, the city was required by federal law to maintain preexisting agreements, and sec. 13(c) of UMTA preempted local ordinances.

The arbitrator held for the Firefighters, on the grounds that UMTA was not meant to preempt local law and that, therefore, the city had in fact waived the requirement for the bus system employees. The city appealed the arbitrator's award to the circuit court. That court overturned the award; but on further appeal to the court of appeals, the arbitrator's award was reinstated. The court of appeals reasoned that, because its only function in reviewing an arbitrator's award was to determine whether the arbitrator made a decision so wrong as to amount to "manifest disregard" of the law, and because the arbitrator's award did not fit that category, the award must be upheld. *Local 311 Firefighters,* 133 Wis.2d 191–92, 394 N.W.2d 766. The net result of the case was to allow the firefighters to live anywhere they desired, regardless of the Madison residency ordinance.

The case at bar resembles *Local 311 Firefighters.* * * *

Specifically, the arbitrator here reasoned that, when the city by ordinance adopted the Teamsters Union contract, which allowed the bus system employees hired before October 31, 1983, to live wherever they wanted to, the city had moderated the residency requirement found in MGO sec. 3.27. Therefore, because the residency ordinance was moderated with respect to one group of employees, the MPPOA "me too" clause operated to waive the residency requirement for the police. Arbitration Award, WERC A/P M–84–228 (1985) at 10.

In addition, the arbitrator determined that, because the firefighters were allowed to live anywhere, this too triggered the MPPOA "me too" clause.[6]

3. That clause read:

"All members of the Fire Department shall be required to live within the City limits as a condition of employment. However, in the event that the City waives the City residency requirement for any group of employees, the requirement for members of the Fire Department shall be deemed to be waived."

6. Actually, because the Firefighters award was in the process of being appealed, the arbitrator recognized that it did not operate to trigger the MPPOA clause during the pendency of the appeal. However, the arbitrator held that, if the Firefighters award was upheld, then it would operate to trigger the MPPOA clause. Arbitrator's Award at 13.

The circuit court in this case upheld the arbitrator's award in its entirety, noting that the arbitrator's award was due great deference. The court of appeals, however, overturned the arbitrator's award on the ground that the arbitrator, while due great deference, had nonetheless exceeded his authority, because he had held that the terms of the MPPOA contract superseded the language in an ordinance. The court of appeals found this result erroneous, because this court, in *WERC v. Teamsters Local No. 563,* 75 Wis.2d 602, 250 N.W.2d 696 (1977), had held that an ordinance overcomes the terms of a contract. Hence, the court of appeals found that the arbitrator had made an error of law of such magnitude that, despite the deference due his decision, the decision must be overturned.

Our decision to reverse the court of appeals in this case and uphold the arbitrator's award rests on two grounds. First, we hold that the arbitrator did not exceed his authority and, hence, because of the deference due his decision, it must be reinstated. Second, we hold that, to the extent *Teamsters Local No. 563* conflicts with this holding, that case is overruled.

Turning first to the arbitrator's award: The rule concerning the deference due arbitrators' awards is settled law in this state. In the 1962 case of *Dehnart v. Waukesha Brewing Co.,* 17 Wis.2d 44, 51, 115 N.W.2d 490 (1962), this court stated that, in reviewing an arbitrator's award, this court would not substitute its judgment for that of the arbitrator because "[t]he parties contracted for the arbitrator's settlement of the grievance. * * * "

Hence, the role of a reviewing court in the arbitration context is essentially supervisory, with the goal of assuring that the parties are getting the arbitration that they contracted for. [citation omitted] Because arbitration is what the parties have contracted for, the parties get the arbitrator's award, whether that award is correct or incorrect as a matter of fact or of law. [citation omitted]

Further, the court will not overturn the arbitrator's decision for mere errors of law or fact, but only when "perverse misconstruction or positive misconduct [is] plainly established, or if there is a manifest disregard of the law, or if the award itself is illegal or violates strong public policy." [citation omitted] These narrow grounds for overturning an arbitrator's award are echoed in the controlling statute on arbitration, sec. 788.10, Stats., and especially in sec. 788.10(1)(d).[7]

Because the Firefighters award was upheld by the appeals court, the arbitrator's holding concerning the effect of that award went from being conditional to being a completed holding.

7. Section 788.10, Stats., reads in relevant part: 788.10 Vacation of award, rehearing by arbitrators. (1) In either of the following cases the court in and for the county wherein the award was made must make an order vacating the award upon the application of any party to the arbitration:

(a) Where the award was procured by corruption, fraud or undue means;

(b) Where there was evident partiality or corruption on the part of the arbitrators, or either of them;

(c) Where the arbitrators were guilty of misconduct in refusing to postpone the hearing, upon sufficient cause shown, or

Finally, it must be remembered that there is a "strong policy favoring arbitration as a method for settling disputes under collective bargaining agreements." Consistent with that policy, this court has adopted a "hands off" approach to arbitration awards.

With these principles in mind, we address the arbitrator's award in this case. Here, the arbitrator held that the Teamsters Union contract, which allowed a group of bus system employees to live anywhere, was a "moderation" of the city residency ordinance. He held that this was especially so in light of the fact that the Teamsters' contract was itself adopted as an ordinance. Hence, his reasoning was that the second ordinance "moderated" the first one.

We cannot say, given the great deference due to an arbitrator's award, that this holding is wrong. It certainly does not rise to the requisite level of a "perverse misconstruction" or "manifest disregard" of the law. There is authority in this state that a later passed ordinance modifies an earlier one. Thus, because there is authority to support the arbitrator's ruling that a later ordinance moderates an earlier one, it must be upheld. *See Local 311 Firefighters,* 131 Wis.2d at 191, 394 N.W.2d 766 ("An arbitrator cannot be said to have manifestly disregarded the law if substantial authority sustains the arbitrator[ ]. * * * ").

Also in respect to the arbitrator's alleged errors of law, the city argues in its brief that the arbitrator in this case made an error which rises to the requisite level for reversal by this court when he "manifestly disregarded" the effect of UMTA on the original Teamsters' contract. As discussed above, this amounts to an argument that UMTA preempts the Madison residency ordinance, and that, because the city had no choice but to waive residency for the bus system employees under UMTA, it is an error of law to consider this compelled waiver a "moderation" of the residency requirement.

This argument is the identical one which the city raised in *Local 311 Firefighters* and which the court of appeals disposed of there. The court wrote:

> "Respectable authority exists for the proposition that sec. 13(c) of UMTA does not preempt state law. [citation omitted]

Having referred to these same authorities, we agree with this statement of the court of appeals and adopt it as our own.

Further, even if this authority did not exist, we would still reject the city's argument that the arbitrator "manifestly disregarded" the law when he held that the Teamsters' contract waiver of residency cannot trigger the "me too" clause in the MPPOA contract because of

in refusing to hear evidence pertinent and material to the controversy; or of any other misbehavior by which the rights of any party have been prejudiced;

(d) Where the arbitrators exceeded their powers, or so imperfectly executed them that a mutual, final and definite award upon the subject matter submitted was not made.

* * *

the "mandatory" nature of UMTA sec. 13(c). This is because the city's argument rests on the assumption that it was a passive actor in the face of the UMTA provisions. However, the city was always free to reject those funds in the first place. Therefore, even were the city's position correct, and UMTA somehow operated to preempt the residency requirement, the city, in accepting the funds, would have made a choice to accept the waiver of residency that accompanied the funds.

Thus, because the arbitrator's award is due great deference, and because the arbitrator did not base his award on a perverse misconstruction of, or a manifest disregard for, the law, the award must be upheld. Indeed, given the foregoing, it is apparent that the arbitrator not only made an unobjectionable decision, but made a correct one.

The court of appeals, however, found that the arbitrator had exceeded his authority as a matter of law because in *WERC v. Teamsters Local No. 563,* 75 Wis.2d 602, 250 N.W.2d 696 (1977), this court held that an arbitrator had exceeded his authority in arbitrating whether a nonresident city employee had been dismissed on "just cause," as required by the employee's contract, when the dismissal had been done under authority of a city ordinance requiring residency. This court said that, because the contract must be considered to have been made with reference to existing law, and because the existing law required residency, the "just cause" provision could not be construed to be a waiver of the residency requirement. *Id.* at 612, 250 N.W.2d 696. The court went on to suggest that, even had the parties intended the terms of the contract to control, such an agreement would have been void, because the parties could not contract to violate a law.

In analyzing *Local 563,* we note, first, that the situation presented differed substantially from that presented here. In that case, the nonresident employee was fired for failing to comply with the residency requirement, and the arbitration was on the issue of whether failing to comply with that requirement constituted "just cause," as required by his contract, for his dismissal. Thus, the conflict between the contract provision ("just cause") and the residency requirement was an oblique one, because it was not clear from the face of the contract whether the "just cause" provision was intended to have any effect on the residency requirement.

By contrast, in this case, the conflict between the residency requirement and the contract is a direct one. The issue which both parties submitted for arbitration was the issue of whether the "me too" clause on the subject of residency controlled over the city ordinance on that same subject. In this sense these cases are very different. Hence, the principles behind *Local 563* can be said to have application only in resolving such implied, or oblique, conflicts and, therefore, is not directly relevant to resolving such direct conflict situations as the one before us here.

However, to the extent that *Local 563* can be understood to be laying down a broad rule [8] that, when a contract clause which purports to control residency conflicts with an ordinance which purports to control residency, the ordinance must prevail, that case must be overruled on the grounds of case law which is more on point than *Local 563* and, hence, more persuasive; on the grounds of public policy and logic; and on the grounds of waiver.

Turning first to case law: In *Cayo v. Milwaukee,* 41 Wis.2d 643, 165 N.W.2d 198 (1969), this court undertook to resolve a dispute over an ordinance which afforded a different treatment to city employee reservists who were veterans as opposed to those who were non-veterans. The court held that there was a rational basis to offer different reserve-period pay scales to the two different groups, but went on to note that if,

> "'* * * as a result of negotiations between representatives of city employees and the city a certain accord is reached which covers wages, hours, and other conditions of employment, then that contract supersedes any ordinance in conflict with it.'" *Cayo,* 41 Wis.2d at 651, 165 N.W.2d 198.

Thus, the court held that, if the contract negotiated had provided that both veteran and non-veteran reservists had the same pay scales for their reserve duty period, this contract would have controlled over an ordinance which purported to control the same matter.

This seems to us a correct statement of the law in a case where the ordinance being challenged is specific to certain parties, and is the subject of a contract negotiation between those same parties. While it is true, as *Local 563* states, that parties cannot contract to violate a law or ordinance, that rationale is a general statement which has no bearing where, as here, the ordinance is a specific one and is targeted at the exact audience with whom the contract negotiations are undertaken. Instead, that restriction must be limited to situations where the law or ordinance which arguably controls is one which targets a general group, so that it would be against public policy to allow one sub-group, and one sub-group only, to escape operation of the law by means of a contract.[9]

8. Under the circumstances presented here, it is apparent that the case must be at least susceptible of such an application, for it is the application which the court of appeals made. That court wrote:

> "While the facts are sufficiently different that the court's statements in *Local 563* might be considered *dicta,* such a conclusion is unwarranted. * * * We see no grounds for distinguishing *Local 563.* * * *" *Madison v. Madison Professional Police Officer Association,* 138 Wis.2d at 364–65, 405 N.W.2d 774.

9. This rationale is similar to that which underlies an equal protection analysis. We are cognizant that an argument could be constructed that allowing one group of city employees to avoid the reach of the residency requirement by action of their contract might work an inequity on other groups of city employees who are still bound by the requirement. However, this would not be a denial of equal protection between groups of city employees, because all groups of employees are free to contract, as MPPOA (and the Firefighters) have done, for a "me too" clause in their contracts as well. Further, as the city

This principle, as expounded in *Cayo,* may be illustrated using the facts of this case also. The Madison residency ordinance is directed solely at city employees. It requires these employees to live within the city limits at the risk of losing their jobs. However, the city agreed to inclusion of a "me too" clause on the specific subject of residency in the MPPOA contract. This meant the city agreed that, under certain circumstances, the requirements could be waived for the MPPOA members. The ordinance itself contemplated circumstances which would alter or vitiate the ordinance. Thus, the residency ordinance was directed at city employees and the contract terms were also directed at city employees. Under these circumstances, the contract must prevail. Were the situation otherwise, the city could make one representation at the contract table, and another through the common council. No city contract directed at a specific group would long have effect if a city ordinance directed at the same group could overcome it.

We stress, however, that this situation arises only where the groups targeted by the ordinance and the contract are identical.[10] To the extent that *Local 563* holds otherwise, it is overruled, but today's holding is not to be understood as a broad exception to the general rule that a law must take precedence over a contract, and that parties cannot avoid the action of a general law or ordinance by contract.

There is another ground also on which we hold that the contract terms here must control over the ordinance. In arbitration, as elsewhere, waiver and estoppel are established doctrines. [citation omitted] Here, as stated above, the city agreed to inclusion in the MPPOA contract of a "me too" clause on the specific topic of residency. Because this clause had the effect of agreeing that if the requirement should be waived for one group, this requirement should be waived for the police officers as well, the city was agreeing that the possibility existed that the MPPOA members might have their residency requirement waived. Now the situation has occurred where the city has waived the requirement of residency for others (*e.g.,* for the Teamsters Union under the 24th 13(c) agreement as described above), and the city cannot be heard to complain that the ordinance should take precedence over a clause which the city itself agreed to allow as a waiver or moderation in the MPPOA contract. By agreeing to the "me too" clause, the city has effectively waived its right to rely on the ordinance to the exclusion of the contract.

attorney stated in oral argument, the City of Madison deals with 13 city employee unions on a regular basis, so that the possibility of such denial, even if it existed, could be hypothetical at best.

In addition, as is further developed *infra,* there is no denial of equal protection between other groups as a result of this holding, because this holding cannot, by its terms, apply where the ordinance targets more than the same narrow group as a contract does (or could) target.

Thus, in the narrow circumstances presented by this case, we explicitly reject the suggestion made in *Local 563* that a holding allowing a contract to control over an ordinance could result in a denial of constitutional equal protection. *Id.* 75 Wis.2d 602 at 612, 250 N.W.2d 696.

10. It is because this holding is so narrow that no equal protection problem is presented. *See supra,* n. 9.

* * *

Notes and Questions

1. What is the difference between saying the arbitrator is "not wrong" and saying he is "correct"?

2. Suppose an agreement between a school district and a teachers' union incorporates by reference the provisions of a state statute governing job security, certification, and other matters affecting working conditions. Should a court defer to the arbitrator's interpretation of the statute in the same manner as it would defer to the arbitrator's interpretation of contract language independent of the statute?

3. Compare *Allegheny Valley School District v. Allegheny Education Association,* 25 Pa.Cmwlth. 559, 360 A.2d 762 (1976) (refusing to enforce arbitral award directing payment of full pay to teachers during sabbatical leave, contrary to a statute construed by the court to limit sabbatical pay to one-half) with *Fire Fighters Local 1219 v. Connecticut Labor Relations Board,* 171 Conn. 342, 370 A.2d 952 (1976) (refusing to enforce award in conflict with statutory provisions for parity pay). Note that, as discussed in Chapter 5, some states have statutes which expressly permit collective bargaining agreements to override conflicting statutory provisions.

4. Sometimes the *remedy* the arbitrator awards is challenged as conflicting with some other statute. Consider, for example, the situation of an arbitrator in a state which does not allow arbitration over the *merits* of a decision denying teacher tenure, but permits arbitration over the *procedure* used. If an arbitrator decides that school authorities did not follow the proper procedure in denying tenure to a teacher, may the arbitrator award tenure as a remedy?

5. A professor of psychology who teaches a class in "Altered States of Consciousness" at a community college is dismissed after it was discovered that he conducted a "special" meeting of the class in his apartment and provided marijuana which he and the students smoked. A nurse is dismissed after it was discovered that she failed to administer a patient's medication in a timely manner. In both cases the arbitrator concludes that the offense was not so grave as to constitute "just cause" for dismissal, and orders reinstatement. In both cases the employer moves to set aside the award on the ground that it is contrary to public policy. How should the court rule? Compare *Lansing Community College v. Lansing Community College Chapter,* 161 Mich.App. 321, 409 N.W.2d 823 (1987) with *Russell Memorial Hospital Association v. United Steelworkers of America,* 720 F.Supp. 583 (E.D.Mich.1989). The *Lansing* opinion was subsequently vacated by the Michigan Supreme Court [418 N.W.2d 95] and remanded for reconsideration in light of *United Paperworkers v. Misco,* 484 U.S. 29, 108 S.Ct. 364, 98 L.Ed.2d 286 (1987).

6. Consider the following problem: A statute provides that teachers on sabbatical leave will receive their "regular pay", notwithstanding any contrary provision of a collective agreement. The collective agreement in one school district contains a provision calling for arbitration of "any dispute concerning the interpretation or application of this agreement". A

dispute arises as to whether "regular pay" includes overtime pay. Upon what factors should the result depend in each of the following scenarios:

(a) A teacher, with union backing, seeks arbitration of her claim that she is entitled to overtime pay as part of "regular pay" on sabbatical. The district refuses to arbitrate, on the ground that the issue is statutory, and the union sues to compel arbitration. Does it matter what the agreement says about the scope of the arbitrator's authority to decide legal issues?

(b) The teacher, instead of seeking arbitration, brings suit directly on the statute, and the school district seeks dismissal of the suit on the ground that the issue belongs in arbitration.

(c) The teacher seeks arbitration, the district agrees to arbitrate, and the arbitrator decides in favor of the teacher. The district now seeks to overturn the award on the ground that the arbitrator has misinterpreted the statute.

(d) Same scenario as in (c), but the arbitrator decides in favor of the district and the *teacher* brings suit in court, claiming rights under the statute.

7. Does it make any difference to the analysis if a constitutional provision rather than a statute is involved? Consider the next section.

E. ARBITRATION AND CONSTITUTIONAL ISSUES

With some exceptions for state constitutions, constitutional claims typically depend upon a showing of governmental action, and for that reason are far more common in the public sector than in the private. Consider the following "kvetch" by Judge Kaufman of the Second Circuit Court of Appeals in a case brought by school teachers against their school board:

> "This case presents the all-too-familiar situation in which a dispute, commonplace in the private sector, becomes constitutional litigation by virtue of the fact that public employers ... are involved, rather than private entities, and the plaintiffs are, therefore, able to turn a problem of labor relations into a constitutional issue. Mindful of the undesirability of becoming entangled in the operation of local school systems, we nevertheless must address this case in a constitutional, rather than a private-law framework". *Fuentes v. Roher,* 519 F.2d 379 (2d Cir.1975).

But what if the arbitration provision of the collective bargaining agreement is broad enough to encompass the claim? In *McGrath v. State of Minnesota,* 312 N.W.2d 438 (Minn.1981) security guards at a state prison who called in sick to protest discipline imposed upon one of their colleagues after an escape were themselves disciplined for abuse of sick-leave privileges, and their union filed a grievance on their behalf. In addition the guards commenced litigation in state court alleging that their constitutional rights had been violated by the discipline and by the manner in which the investigation had been conducted. Various causes of action invoked the due process, equal protection, and free speech provisions of the federal Constitution. The court dismissed these causes of action on the ground that plaintiffs had failed to exhaust remedies under the collective bargaining agreement. The matter went to arbitration, and the arbitrator upheld the disciplinary action. On review of the trial court's order of dismissal, plaintiffs argued that because their complaint alleged constitutional issues arbitration should have been stayed. The Minnesota Supreme Court, finding the constitutional arguments to be without merit, affirmed the denial of the stay, but observed in dicta: "The fact that we decline to interfere with the arbitration process does not confer upon the arbitrator the right to decide constitutional issues. We have already indicated that arbitrators are without such authority in Minnesota * * * We now expressly hold this to be the rule in Minnesota irrespective of the language of the arbitration agreement. In the normal case, where the constitutional violations alleged are of a general nature, the arbitrator is to proceed. The alleged constitutional violations may be raised at the time of judicial review of the arbitration determination."

Justice Scott, concurring: "I concur in the result reached by the majority; however, I do not agree that an arbitrator may never have the authority to decide constitutional issues. An arbitrator's authority to decide any type of grievance should depend on the scope of the arbitration agreement. If the parties indicate a clear intent to arbitrate disputes of a constitutional dimension, such matters should be determined by an arbitrator * * * When the state is a party to a labor contract, grievances are often raised as constitutional issues. To hold that arbitrators may never consider such issues would circumvent the public policy which favors arbitration and the speedy resolution of disputes without initial resort to litigation."

1. Is there a reason to distinguish between the arbitration of constitutional and statutory claims? In deciding whether the claim is arbitrable? In reviewing the award?

2. Can a constitutional right be waived through a collective bargaining agreement? Consider the following case.

STORRS v. MUNICIPALITY OF ANCHORAGE

Supreme Court of Alaska, 1986.
721 P.2d 1146.

OPINION

MOORE, JUSTICE.

This appeal raises the question whether a collective bargaining agreement can alter the constitutional rights of covered employees to provide for post-termination review, rather than pretermination review, of a discharge and, if so, whether a discharged employee is entitled to back pay between his dismissal and eventual post-termination review. The superior court found the officer received all process due and the officer appealed. We affirm.

I. Factual and Procedural Background

John W. Storrs was a career police officer with the Municipality of Anchorage Police Department (Municipality). The Municipality claims that, while on duty, Storrs engaged in sexual activity with a woman he was driving home. Storrs denied the allegation. Following an exhaustive internal investigation, Police Chief Brian Porter fired Storrs.

Storrs is a member of a collective bargaining unit represented by the Anchorage Police Department Employees Association (APDEA). Under the collective bargaining agreement, a police officer may only be dismissed for just cause. Officers are entitled to two weeks notice or two weeks pay prior to discharge. The contract provides for arbitration of grievances only upon demand of APDEA. APDEA declined to arbitrate Storrs' dismissal.

Storrs filed suit in superior court against the Municipality for reinstatement and back pay, arguing he was deprived of due process because he did not receive a pretermination hearing. Judge Karl S. John entered a summary judgment for the Municipality, concluding that Storrs was not entitled to a pretermination hearing but that he had the right to a trial on his claim that he was terminated without just cause. Storrs appealed.

II. Federal Due Process Rights

A. Pretermination Hearing

Storrs argues that he was deprived of his constitutionally protected interest in his continued employment without due process of law because he did not receive a pretermination hearing. The Municipality contends that Storrs was not deprived of due process.

Public employees, other than those serving "at will," have a sufficient property interest in continued employment to warrant due process protection prior to termination. *Cleveland Board of Education v. Loudermill,* 470 U.S. 532, 105 S.Ct. 1487, 1491, 84 L.Ed.2d 494, 501 (1985). The collective bargaining agreement provides that Anchorage police officers may be dismissed only for just cause. Therefore, Storrs has a property interest in his continued employment; he may not be deprived of his job without due process of law. The question remains what process is due?

1. Although a trial was scheduled for January 1985, Storrs declined the opportunity to present his case in superior court.

The root of due process is the right to a hearing *before* a deprivation of property. *Loudermill,* 470 U.S. at ___, 105 S.Ct. at 1493, 84 L.Ed.2d at 503. The nature of the employee's pretermination rights varies, depending in part on the nature of subsequent proceedings available. *Loudermill,* 470 U.S. at ___, 105 S.Ct. at 1495, 84 L.Ed.2d at 506. The procedure should provide an initial check against a mistaken decision by the employer, ensuring that there are reasonable grounds to believe the allegations against the employee are true. *Id.* At a minimum, the employee must receive oral or written notice of the proposed discharge, an explanation of the employer's evidence and an opportunity to present his position. *Id.* Storrs argues that he was deprived of due process because the Municipality did not explain its evidence nor provide a meaningful opportunity to respond.

We conclude that the pretermination procedure followed by the Municipality comported with minimum federal due process requirements. The Municipality undertook an investigation on November 17 after receiving the complaint against Storrs. The investigation officers took a statement from the woman and examined the scene of the reported incident, taking photographs and casts of tire tracks. They measured the time and distance of various routes from Storrs' point of origin to the woman's residence. The woman submitted to a polygraph examination. Other officers with knowledge of the events in question were interviewed.

On November 24, the investigating lieutenant interviewed Storrs about the incident. Also present were Storrs' shop steward and a police captain. The lieutenant informed Storrs he was conducting a criminal investigation and advised Storrs of his constitutional rights. Storrs agreed to a recorded interview and gave his version of the evening's events. Storrs indicated that he did not know exactly where the woman's house was and that, although she made sexual advances toward him, no sexual contact occurred.

On November 26, Storrs voluntarily submitted to a polygraph examination. Storrs again gave his version of the facts. The state trooper who administered the test told Storrs that he appeared to be lying about certain material facts and urged Storrs to explain what really happened. The trooper informed Storrs about the contents of the woman's statements and that her allegations were supported by mileage and time measurements, the police department radio log, and tire tracks and footprints found at the scene. Storrs was also informed that the statement of another police officer indicated Storrs knew the location of a certain street and therefore Storrs' statement that he got lost on the way was less likely to be true. The trooper again urged Storrs to tell the truth. Storrs maintained that his original version was correct.

On December 6 Police Chief Porter, Storrs and Storrs' shop steward met. Porter again gave Storrs the opportunity to explain any of the evidence gathered, but Storrs merely repeated his blanket denial and did not offer any further information. At the conclusion of the interview, Porter fired Storrs.

We conclude that Storrs received notice, an explanation of the evidence against him and a sufficient opportunity to respond during the course of the investigation. The pretermination requirements of federal due process were therefore satisfied in this case.

B. Post-termination Hearing

When minimal pretermination procedures are followed, federal law entitles a public employee to a formal evidentiary post-termination hearing within a reasonable time. *Kelly v. Smith,* 764 F.2d 1412, 1415 (11th Cir.1985); *Brasslett v. Cota,* 761 F.2d 827, 836 (1st Cir.1985); *DeSarno v. Department of Commerce,* 761 F.2d 657, 660 (D.C.Cir.1985). The collective bargaining agreement provides for prompt review of grievances and binding arbitration of unresolved disputes. However, in the instant case APDEA refused to press Storrs' claim, hence no post-termination hearing occurred. In Alaska, Storrs' remedy lies in the courts; he may sue the Municipality for breach of contract. *Casey v. City of Fairbanks,* 670 P.2d 1133, 1138 (Alaska 1983).

Storrs was dismissed in December 1982. Trial was scheduled for January 1985. The question is whether, under the circumstances presented here, this delay is so unreasonable as to violate Storrs' due process rights.

Storrs did not file a complaint until June 1983, six months after the dismissal. The complaint did not request an immediate judicial hearing. In November 1983, the Municipality moved for partial summary judgment, claiming that Storrs' remedy was a judicial determination of the merits of the termination decision. Instead of joining in this suggestion and demanding an immediate trial, Storrs opposed it. Judge Johnstone granted partial summary judgment and set trial for January 1985. Storrs at no time requested an earlier trial date; instead he requested the court to enter final judgment against him so that he could appeal.

Under these specific circumstances, we cannot conclude that Storrs' federal due process rights were violated by the delay. The fact is that Storrs never requested a prompt post-termination hearing. When a post-termination hearing was offered, he refused it.

III. State Due Process Rights

A. Pretermination Hearing

Like the federal constitution, the Alaska constitution affords pre-termination due process protection to public employees who may only be terminated for just cause. *McMillan v. Anchorage Community Hospital,* 646 P.2d 857, 864 (Alaska 1982). Again we must consider the extent of the process due.

In *Nichols v. Eckert,* 504 P.2d 1359, 1365 (Alaska 1973), the court ruled that a post-termination hearing was constitutionally deficient because the discharged employee was not permitted to call witnesses on her behalf. Although a full judicial hearing is not required, the employee must be allowed to present a defense by testimonial and other evidence. *Id.* Three justices concurred in an opinion concluding that, absent extraordinary circumstances, the hearing should occur *prior* to termination. *Id.* at 1366. We therefore conclude that a public employee ordinarily has the right to an adversarial hearing before he may be effectively dismissed.

In limited circumstances, however, a collective bargaining agreement may alter the pretermination rights of covered employees. We hold that a post-termination adversarial hearing may satisfy the requirements of Alaska's Due Process Clause when a collective bargaining agreement waives the constitutionally mandated pretermination adversarial hearing. Such a substitution of a post-termination hearing for a pretermination hearing is permissible "so long as the negotiated agreement provides fair, reasonable, and efficacious procedures by which employer-employee disputes may be resolved," *Gorham v. City of Kansas City,* 590 P.2d 1051, 1058 (Kan.1979). *Accord, Antinore v. State of New York,* 49 A.D.2d 6, 371 N.Y.S.2d 213 (1975), aff'd 40 N.Y.2d 921, 389 N.Y.S.2d 576, 358 N.E.2d 268 (1976). Where, as here, a discharged employee can seek post-termination judicial review of his grievance, due process has not been offended.

B. Post–termination Hearing

The post-termination proceeding contemplated by the collective bargaining agreement did not take place in this case because the union declined to pursue the termination grievance. At that point Storrs had the right to a prompt and full post-termination hearing in the superior court. *Casey v. City of Fairbanks,* 670 P.2d 1133 (Alaska 1983). However, as we have previously explained, Storrs did not request a post-termination hearing and in fact refused one when it was offered. We therefore conclude that Storrs waived his right to a post-termination hearing by not requesting one. *See Graham v. State,* 633 P.2d 211, 216 (Alaska 1981).

Affirmed.

Notes and Questions

1. What reasons does the court give for saying that a union may waive an employee's due process right to a pretermination hearing? Do you agree with the conclusion? For critique of the *Antinore* case, upon which the Alaska Supreme Court relies, see Wallace (Comment), *Union Waiver of Public Employees' Due Process Rights,* 8 Ind.Rel.L.J. 582 (1986).

2. If the due process right to a pretermination hearing can be waived, what other constitutional rights can be waived through collective bargaining? The right not to be subject to unjustified drug testing? The right to object to a residency requirement on constitutional grounds? See *International Association of Fire Fighters, AFL–CIO, Local 55 v. City of San Leandro,* 181 Cal.App.3d 179, 226 Cal.Rptr. 238 (1986) (holding that employees were free to assert a constitutional challenge to an order of the city fire department requiring firefighters to reside within 40 road miles of the fire station, notwithstanding incorporation of that requirement in an applicable

collective bargaining agreement: "[U]nconstitutional provisions of a collective bargaining agreement are void and unenforceable").

3. In the private sector, an employee has no guaranteed right of access to the arbitration procedure provided under the collective bargaining agreement. If his union refuses to take his case to arbitration, he is out of luck unless he can persuade a court (or the NLRB) that the union violated its duty of fair representation by its refusal—and that requires a showing of hostile motive, or at least arbitrariness, on the part of union officials. In *Casey v. City of Fairbanks,* cited in the principal case, the Alaska Supreme Court rejected the federal rule, and held that if a union refuses to take a public employee's grievance to arbitration, he may sue in court on the underlying contractual commitment without any need to show the union violated its duty.

> "We are unable to adopt the federal rule in this state because it is inconsistent with our conclusion that persons who are employed other than 'at will' [citation] have a sufficient property interest in continuing their employment, absent just cause for their removal, to require that they be given notice and an opportunity to be heard under the due process clause of the Alaska Constitution (art. I, sec. 7) before their employment is terminated. [citations].
>
> "[The plaintiff in this case] was not an at-will employee, but could be terminated only for cause. Casey alleges that he was terminated because he refused to comply with illegal instructions. The Union refused to process his grievance and, under the Working Agreement, there is no other means by which Casey's claim can proceed to arbitration. If the Vaca rule were applied, Casey would be deprived of any review of the decision to terminate him unless he were able to prove that the Union acted wrongfully in refusing to process his grievance; i.e., its decision was 'arbitrary, discriminatory, or in bad faith'. [citation]. Although the evidence suggests the contrary, it is possible that the Union's decision was erroneous without being arbitrary, discriminatory or in bad faith. To deny Casey a hearing on his termination except upon proof that the Union's conduct was wrongful places too great a burden upon Casey's right to due process.
>
> "Because the Working Agreement does not permit Casey to unilaterally initiate arbitration proceedings, Casey's due process rights can be satisfied only by permitting Casey to maintain an independent action against the City of Fairbanks for breach of contract * * *
>
> "We recognize that there are legitimate reasons why an employer may prefer that employees grievances be resolved by arbitration, rather than by judicial review. * * * We note that the City of Fairbanks has recently amended its personnel ordinance to specifically permit non-union employees to process their own grievances through arbitration * * * The City is free to negotiate an amendment to its Working Agreement to similarly permit union employees to process their grievances through arbitration when their Union refuses to do so. * * *".

Do you agree with this analysis?

4. What happens when the grievant asserts constitutional rights in the arbitration proceeding? A law enforcement officer, dismissed on charges of criminal forgery, sought to exclude from his arbitration hearing evidence obtained in a search of his home. He contended that the warrant for the search was not supported by a showing of probable cause, and that the search therefore violated his rights under the Fourth Amendment. The arbitrator disagreed, and let the evidence in. Should the court defer to the arbitrator's decision on that issue? See *Minnesota State Patrol Troopers Association v. State of Minnesota Department of Public Safety,* 437 N.W.2d 670 (Minn.App.1989).

Chapter 7

STRIKES

A. INTRODUCTION

The right to strike lies at the center of federal labor policy operative in the private sector. Without the right to strike, it is hard to see how national policy (which focuses on collective bargaining) would produce a meaningful system of bilateral decision-making. As the late George Taylor once put it, the strike provides the motive power for agreement. A credible strike threat forces both sides to weigh alternatives carefully; both presumably would be hurt economically by a work stoppage; the question each must consider is whether strike costs are greater or lesser than the costs of reaching some kind of compromise.

Of course, there are exceptions. Strikes are not very effective in highly automated industries such as the generation and distribution of electrical energy or telephonic communications. Nevertheless, the right to strike remains at the core of national labor policy in the private sector. It remains an essential if collective bargaining is to be an effective instrument for fixing the terms and conditions of employment.

Most jurisdictions have made a different choice in the public sector for reasons which are detailed later in these materials. Only 13 states recognize that public employees have a right to strike. The states that permit strikes conditionally are Alaska, California (by court decision), Hawaii, Idaho, Illinois, Louisiana (by court decision), Minnesota, Montana, Ohio, Oregon, Pennsylvania, Vermont and Wisconsin. Even in those states the right is limited and dependent upon the existence of certain specified conditions. Elsewhere, strikes are prohibited or severely constrained either by statutory or decisional law.

Some statutes specifically forbid government employees to strike (District of Columbia, Florida, New Hampshire, Ohio, Tennessee [teachers], Vermont [state employees], and Wisconsin [state employees]), New York (everyone). Some states which have no law either permitting or regulating collective bargaining by public employees, for example Georgia and Texas, have particularly harsh punitive statutes applicable to strikers. Unions that participate in illegal strikes may be punished by fines as in Nevada, by withdrawal of recognition or certification as in Minnesota, or by revocation of the union's right to have dues withheld by the employer from the wages of its employees and remitted to the union, as in New York.[1]

In those states that permit public employees to strike, there are limitations. Professor Aaron has summarized these as follows:

> Typically, the state statute divides government employees into categories on the basis of whether the services they provide are "essential." Government employees who provide essential services are rarely, if ever, permitted to strike. Statutes differ as to which government employees may strike. Teachers may not strike in Alaska, but they may do so in Hawaii, Minnesota, and Vermont. Firefighters have a limited right to strike in Idaho; Pennsylvania forbids employees necessary to the functioning of the courts to strike [But strikes by other non-uniformed personnel are permitted if they do not endanger public health, safety, or welfare.], and Minnesota specifically denies the right to strike to professional engineers.
>
> * * *
>
> Many states require that [strikes are lawful only if the employees are] organized into a collective bargaining unit with an exclusive representative. Often, they must exhaust fact-finding and mediation procedures and give notice before they may strike. Many statutes provide that a government employer may petition the court for an injunction against the strike that endangers public welfare.[2]

Assumptions which are not rooted in fact frequently underlie policies which are operative in public sector collective bargaining. For example, it is assumed that the interruption of so-called "essential" services by a strike will necessarily pose an imminent threat to public health or safety. But this may not be true.

For instance, some years ago the nonprofessional hospital employees in New York City struck the state mental hospitals located there. The strike was attacked editorially by the *New York Post* as "threatening thousands of mental patients and cruelly punishing the defenseless." [Nov. 20, 1968, p. 32] However, three days into the strike, a supervising psychiatrist who was still on the job made the following statement: "We took it for granted that patients had to be helped in eating, in personal cleanliness, in making up their beds, etc. With the chips down, those who needed help, or who we thought needed help, all of a sudden were able to function. * * * I don't remember when the

1. Aaron, *The Future of Collective Bargaining in the Public Sector*, Public Sector Bargaining, 2d Ed.BNA 1988, pp. 314, 316. See comments on 1992 Alaska statute at page 285.

2. Ibid., supra, at p. 317.

building was so smoothly running, so quiet, as now." "I would never have guessed that this is what would have happened," the doctor said, referring to the increased alertness, independence and initiative which he said the patients at the hospital demonstrated. *New York Post,* November 21, 1968 at p. 6.

Public employee strikes are often ineffective. A notable example of this is a strike by public school teachers servicing a K–12 school system. Usually little economic harm is inflicted on the school district by a teachers' strike because of the money saved in unpaid salaries while the strike is going on. Although state aid may be reduced, it can usually be maintained, at least partially, by hiring enough strike replacements on a per diem basis to maintain order and keep schools open.

Thus, for example, the teachers' strike in the fall of 1989 in the City of Sacramento, California, cost teachers $1.37 million in lost wages, while the Sacramento City Unified School District's ledger sheet showed only $56,331.00 in red ink—$11,266.00 for each of the five school days the teachers missed. District expenses for the strike totalled $1.43 million, but its savings of $1.37 million in teachers' salaries helped it recoup most of the loss. The District did lose $213,295 in state revenue because thousands of students refused to cross picket lines (state revenue is based on classroom attendance). *The Sacramento Bee,* December 3, 1989, p. B3.

However, as Craig Olson has pointed out, the striking teachers may escape with minimal economic injury. School days missed are often rescheduled so that students receive the prescribed number of instructional days and teachers are paid for working the rescheduled days. Olson reports that in approximately two-thirds of the 305 teacher strikes during the decade of the 1970s, students received the mandated 180 days of instruction even though the mean strike duration was almost thirteen days.[3]

These facts underscore the proposition that public employee strikes, unlike strikes in the private sector, are not primarily economic weapons, but are, if they work at all, weapons of political embarrassment. Their success or failure depends on their ability to generate political pressure on public officials that will cause them to make concessions to end the strike.

Olson reports that the nine day strike of 2,000 nurses against state operated hospitals in Pennsylvania in 1986 for a restructured wage scale was unsuccessful. The strike's failure was due, in part, to management's ability to provide limited services using both supervisory personnel and the 25–40% of bargaining unit employees who chose not to strike. Moreover, the hospitals restricted the demand for health care services through a variety of measures, including limiting new

3. Olson, *Dispute Resolution in the Public Sector,* Public Sector Bargaining, 2d Ed. BNA 1988, p. 161.

admissions, eliminating elective surgery, and transferring patients to other facilities. Olson points out that, ironically, Pennsylvania's continuing tolerance of the right to strike is predicated in part on the fact that such strikes are often ineffective.[4]

On the other hand, there are public sector strikes which inflict serious harm and entail high risks. For example, the sixteen-day prison guard strike in New York state in the spring of 1979 cost each of the approximately 6,000 strikers thirty-two days' pay under the two-for-one penalties imposed by the Taylor Act. The state had to pick up a gross $50 million tab (estimate) for securing the perimeter of the prisons by calling out the National Guard. (This cost was offset by the fact that in New York, the struck public employer is not only responsible for collecting the monetary two-for-one penalty but it also gets to keep the money.)[5] The memory of the Attica prison riot continued to scare the public, but, in fact, the only violence was on the picket lines. The objectives sought by the striking union were not attained.

The toughest state statute in terms of prohibiting public employee strikes is the Taylor Law in New York. All concerted refusals to work are proscribed, regardless of the level of government or the type of service involved. Injunctions are virtually automatic; they are enforceable with fines and jail sentences. The striker suffers the loss of two days' pay for each day on strike. And the union stands to lose its check-off privileges by order of New York's Public Employment Relations Board.

Blanket bans on public employee strikes have uniformly been upheld against attack on constitutional grounds. See, for example, the following decision of the New York Court of Appeals in sustaining the Taylor law's blanket prohibition of public employee strikes.

B. JUDICIAL ANALYSIS

CITY OF NEW YORK v. DE LURY

Court of Appeals of New York, 1968.
23 N.Y.2d 175, 295 N.Y.S.2d 901, 243 N.E.2d 128.

[The Supreme Court of New York County granted the City's motion for an injunction against a strike and judged the defendants guilty of criminal contempt. The Appellate Division affirmed, and the defendants appealed. The question certified was: "Were the orders of the Supreme Court * * * properly made?"]

FULD, CHIEF JUDGE.

We recently decided, in Rankin v. Shanker, 23 N.Y.2d 111, 295 N.Y.S.2d 625, 242 N.E.2d 802, that public employees and labor organiza-

4. Olson, *Dispute Resolution in the Public Sector,* Public Sector Bargaining, BNA 2d Ed. 1988, pp. 160–162.

5. Olson, *Dispute Resolution in the Public Sector,* Public Sector Bargaining, BNA 2d Ed. 1988, p. 162.

tions representing them were not entitled to a trial by jury in a criminal contempt proceeding for the violation of section 210 (subd. 1) of the Taylor Law.[1] In so holding, we concluded that a legislative classification "which differentiates between strikes by public employees and employees in private industry" is reasonable and does not offend against the constitutional guarantee of equal protection of the laws (23 N.Y.2d at p. 118, 295 N.Y.S.2d at p. 631, 242 N.E.2d at p. 806). The case now before us calls upon the court to determine, primarily, whether the Taylor Law's mandate that public employees shall not strike and that labor organizations representing them shall not cause or encourage a strike violates due process requirements of the State or Federal Constitution.

At about seven o'clock in the morning of February 2, 1968, virtually all of the sanitation men in the City of New York—employees of the Department of Sanitation—failed, without excuse, to report for work.[2] Later in the day, at a demonstration in front of City Hall, members of the Uniformed Sanitationmen's Association (referred to herein as the "Union") were addressed by their president, the defendant De Lury, in these words:

> "Your sentiments before was go-go-go. I'd accept a motion for go-go-go (cheers). All in favor signify by saying yes (cheers). All opposed (boos). I didn't come here to bargain, I took a firm position with the City, I gave the members a final offer of this union. Now I want to show discipline here this morning—or this afternoon—I don't want to show where there is confusion in the members—You got a job at the locations to see that this is effective 100% (cheers)."

A nine-day strike, ending on the night of February 10, resulted. During that period, few, if any, of the sanitation men reported for work, in consequence of which garbage and refuse accumulated on the city streets at the rate of 10,000 tons a day. This constituted a serious health and fire threat; indeed, the Commissioner of Health character-

1. The Taylor Law was enacted in 1967 (L.1967, ch. 392; Civil Service Law, Consol.Laws, c. 7, art. 14, §§ 200–212) to supersede the Condon–Wadlin Act (L.1947, ch. 391, adding Civil Service Law, former § 22–a, renum. by L.1958, ch. 790, as Civil Service Law, former § 108). Like its predecessor, the Taylor Law prohibits strikes by public employees (§ 210, subd. 1) but, unlike Condon–Wadlin, it does not mandate termination of employment for its violation. The Taylor Law grants to all public employees (which, broadly speaking, includes all employees in the service of the State or any subdivision thereof) rights which in the main they did not formerly possess, namely, the right to be represented by employee organizations of their own choosing and the right to negotiate collectively with public employers and, in addition, the right to require public employers to negotiate and to enter into collective agreements with them. It sets up a Public Employment Relations Board—known as PERB—to "resolve * * * disputes concerning the representation status of employee organizations" and to assist in the "voluntary resolution" of disputes between public employers and employee organizations. * * *

2. The City and the Uniformed Sanitationmen's Association had labored long in an attempt to arrive at a new collective agreement to replace one which expired on June 30, 1967. Bargaining between the parties, which commenced in December of 1966, had dragged along for the entire year of 1967 and through January, 1968. On January 31, 1968, a mutually agreed upon mediation panel formulated a settlement agreement which, though accepted by the City, was rejected by the Union stewards.

ized the "garbage situation" as "a serious one to the health of the city" and the Fire Commissioner declared that the Fire Department "experienced a marked increase in the number of outside rubbish fires." [3]

On February 2, the very day the work stoppage began, the City instituted the present action to enjoin the defendants from "striking" and moved for a preliminary injunction. A temporary restraining order was granted which enjoined the carrying on of the strike and required the leaders of the Union to instruct the members to return to work. Three days later, on February 5, the court at Special Term granted a preliminary injunction which again contained a directive to De Lury that he shall "forthwith instruct all members [of the Union] not to engage or participate in any strike, concerted stoppage of work or concerted slowdown against the plaintiff." Although, because of the health and fire hazards involved, immediate compliance with the orders was vital, the members of the Union, as previously noted, remained away from their jobs until February 10.

An application, brought on by order to show cause, to punish the Union and De Lury for criminal contempt for willfully disobeying the restraining order, came on for hearing before the court; the testimony adduced concerning the strike and its effects, as well as the conduct of De Lury, was substantially as outlined above. When the City, through its Corporation Counsel, stated that it was prepared to call witnesses to establish that the sanitation men "had [not] received instructions from Mr. De Lury to report back to work", defense counsel conceded that, if witnesses were called to the stand—as the Corporation Counsel proposed—"they would testify that they did not receive any instructions from Mr. De Lury to go back, because Mr. De Lury did not send them out, and Mr. De Lury did nothing to bring them back. These are the facts which are known to everybody." [4]

At the conclusion of the hearings, the court, dismissing charges which had also been asserted against other officers, found De Lury and the Union guilty of criminal contempt for willfully disobeying its lawful mandate. It sentenced De Lury to 15 days in jail and fined him $250 and it fined the Union $80,000; in addition, the court ordered that the Union's right to dues check-off be forfeited for a period of 18 months.[5] The Appellate Division affirmed Special Term's orders and granted the defendants leave to appeal to our court on a certified question.

We consider, first, the defendants' contention that the Taylor Law is unconstitutional on the ground that, in prohibiting strikes by public

3. On the sixth day of the strike, a volunteer group of some 500 men collected hospital refuse, the accumulation of which created an especially dangerous threat of disease.

4. The City was ready to call 10 witnesses, having planned to issue 100 subpoenas addressed to that number of employees.

5. The fines imposed, as well as the period for which the Union's dues check-off rights were forfeited, were the maximum authorized by the applicable statute (Judiciary Law, Consol.Laws, c. 30, § 751, subds. 1, 2, par. [a]).

employees, it deprives them of due process of law. Manifestly, neither the Fourteenth Amendment to the Federal Constitution nor the Bill of Rights of the State Constitution (art. I) grants to any individual an absolute right to strike. On the contrary, that right is subject to the qualification that, if a strike is for an illegal objective, it is enjoinable at the instance of an aggrieved party. To cull from the opinion of the Supreme Court in International Union, United Auto Workers, A.F. of L., Local 232 v. Wisconsin Employment Relations Bd. (336 U.S. 245, 259–260, 69 S.Ct. 516, 524, 93 L.Ed. 651), " 'the exercise of the unquestioned right to [strike]' * * * did not operate to legalize the sit-down strike, which state law made illegal and state authorities punished. [Case cited.] Nor, for example, did it make legal a strike that ran afoul of federal law [case cited]; nor one in violation of a contract made pursuant thereto [case cited]; nor one creating a national emergency [case cited]."

Although acknowledging that the right to strike is not absolute, the defendants would have us read the opinion in the *Auto Workers* case to mean that a prohibition against strikes will be upheld only where workers strike in violation of a no-strike clause or where there is a secondary boycott, violence or a trespass such as a sitdown. There is no basis for so narrowly viewing that decision. The Supreme Court did not limit the doctrine there applied to instances of illegal strikes mentioned by it. Rather, it laid down a general rule, applicable in all cases involving illegal strikes, namely, that the State, in governing its internal affairs, had the power to prohibit *any* strike if the prohibition was reasonably calculated to achieve a valid State policy in an area which was open to State regulation. (Cf. International Brotherhood of Teamsters Local 695 v. Vogt, Inc., 354 U.S. 284, 294–295, 77 S.Ct. 1166, 1 L.Ed.2d 1347.)

Our query must, therefore, be whether the condemnation of strikes by public employees, as provided in the Taylor Law, does effectuate a valid policy of our State.

For many years, strikes against the Government have been outlawed by special legislation and by common law. Today, no less than 20 States have statutes condemning strikes by some or all of its public employees and at least seven States have achieved the same result by the application of common-law principles. (See Rubin, A Summary of State Collective Bargaining Law in Public Employment, published by Cornell University in 1968.) In addition, a Federal statute specifically provides that strikes by Federal employees are illegal (U.S.Code, tit. 5, § 7311). Substantial reasons are at hand for this almost universal condemnation of strikes by public employees. As Professor George W. Taylor, an outstanding authority in the field of labor relations and one of the architects of the Taylor Law, put it (Public Employment: Strikes or Procedures?, 20 Industrial and Labor Relations Rev. 617, 619),

> "One of the vital interests of the public which should be considered in the government-employee relationship is the ability

> of representative government to perform the functions of levying taxes and, through the budgeting of governmental resources, of establishing priorities among the government services desired by the body politic."

Quite obviously, the ability of the Legislature to establish priorities among government services would be destroyed if public employees could, with impunity, engage in strikes which deprive the public of essential services. The striking employees, by paralyzing a city through the exercise of naked power, could obtain gains wholly disproportionate to the services rendered by them and at the expense of the public and other public employees. The consequence would be the destruction of democratic legislative processes because budgeting and the establishment of priorities would no longer result from the free choice of the electorate's representatives but from the coercive effect of paralyzing strikes of public employees. (See Final Report [March 31, 1966] of the Governor's Commission on Public Employment Relations [hereafter referred to as the Taylor Report], pp. 15–16).

It was undoubtedly because of such considerations that Governor Thomas E. Dewey, in his Memorandum approving the Condon–Wadlin Act (L.1947, ch. 391)—the predecessor of the Taylor Law—declared (N.Y.Legis.Ann., 1947, pp. 36–37):

> "The duty of public employees is to the whole of society. A strike of firemen could overnight permit the destruction of a whole city. A strike of police could endanger the safety of millions of people and all their possessions. A strike of sanitation workers could almost overnight produce an epidemic threatening the lives of other millions of people".

And President Franklin D. Roosevelt expressed himself in similar fashion in 1937, some 10 years earlier (Public Papers and Addresses for Year 1937 [1941] Letter of Aug. 16, 1937, p. 325):

> "Upon employees in the Federal service rests the obligation to serve the whole people, whose interests and welfare require orderliness and continuity in the conduct of Government activities. This obligation is paramount. Since their own services have to do with the functioning of the Government, a strike of public employees manifests nothing less than an intent on their part to prevent or obstruct the operations of Government until their demands are satisfied. Such action, looking toward the paralysis of Government by those who have sworn to support it, is unthinkable and intolerable."

The courts which have dealt with the constitutional question under discussion have concluded that no provision of either the Federal or State Constitution prevents the State from outlawing strikes by public employees. * * *

* * *

In the case before us, the Legislature, after declaring (Civil Service Law § 200) that "it is the public policy of the state * * * to promote harmonious and cooperative relationships between government and its employees and to protect the public by assuring, at all times, the orderly and uninterrupted operations and functions of government", recited that such policy is best effectuated by "continuing the prohibition against strikes by public employees and providing remedies for violations of such prohibition." Furthermore, the Taylor Report, which preceded the enactment of the Taylor Law, found, after an exhaustive study of the matter, that the right of public employees to strike "is not compatible with the orderly functioning of our democratic form of representative government" (p. 19).

In view of the strong policy considerations which led to the enactment of the Taylor Law, it is our conclusion that the statutory prohibition against strikes by public employees is reasonably designed to effectuate a valid State policy in an area where it has authority to act and that the provisions of subdivision 1 of section 210 do not offend any due process rights of the defendants.

In view of our recent decision in the *Shanker* case (23 N.Y.2d 111, 295 N.Y.S.2d 625, 242 N.E.2d 802, supra), no extended discussion is required in addressing ourselves to the defendants' point that the prohibition against strikes by public employees (or their representative organizations) violates the equal protection clause of either the United States or the New York State Constitution. * * * As we had occasion to observe in *Shanker* (23 N.Y.2d, at p. 116, 295 N.Y.S.2d 629, 242 N.E.2d 805),

> "Ever since the enactment of the Norris–LaGuardia Act and our State's Little Norris–LaGuardia Act, the view has been uniformly and consistently held that a legitimate distinction between public and private employment is constitutionally permissible. This has been recognized * * * with regard not only to the prohibition against strikes but also to the issue, now confronting us, affecting jury trials."

There are a number of factual differences between employment in the public and private sectors which furnish reasonable justification for disparate treatment vis-a-vis the right to strike. Thus, for instance, the necessity for preventing goods or services being priced out of the market may have a deterrent effect upon collective bargaining negotiations in the private sector, whereas, in the public sector, the market place has no such restraining effect upon the negotiations and the sole constraint in terms of the negotiations is to be found in the budget allocation made by responsible legislators. Again, the orderly functioning of our democratic form of representative government and the preservation of the right of our representatives to make budgetary allocations—free from the compulsions of crippling strikes—require the regulation of strikes by public employees whereas there is no similar countervailing reason for a prohibition of strikes in the private sector.

(See Taylor Report, pp. 15–16.) Nor does the fact that many employees in private industry also perform essential services render the distinction unreasonable. As to this, it is sufficient to note that, although the Legislature is not barred from enacting laws regulating the relationship between the State or its subdivisions and public employees, it cannot regulate labor relations in the private sector with respect to most industries (e.g., privately owned railroads, airlines, etc.) where a strike could paralyze a city without, as we observed in the *Rankin* case, running into conflict with Federal legislation, such as the National Labor Relations Act and the Railway Labor Act, and thereby violating "the exclusive primary jurisdiction of Federal administrative agencies vested with the authority to deal with such matters" (23 N.Y.2d, at p. 118, n. 3, 295 N.Y.S.2d 631, 242 N.E.2d 806).

In view of the basic differences between public and private employment, it may not be said that a classification which prohibits strikes by public employees while failing to legislate against strikes by employees in the private sector is unreasonable, especially when it is considered that strikes by public employees, unlike private employees, have always been subject to injunctions by the courts. Consequently, we conclude here, just as we did in Rankin (p. 119, 295 N.Y.S.2d 632, 242 N.E.2d p. 629) that, "as of the present [time], legislative differentiation between public and private employees, insofar as restrictions on their right to strike and to jury trials are concerned, is reasonable."

The defendants' argument—that they are entitled to a trial by jury despite their failure to request one—may be disposed of summarily. In our decision in Rankin v. Shanker (23 N.Y.2d 119, 295 N.Y.S.2d 632, 242 N.E.2d 807, supra), as the lines already quoted from the opinion in that case establish, we expressly held that a jury trial in a criminal contempt proceeding such as this (under Judiciary Law § 753–a and Labor Law § 808) is not available to public employees, or to officers of labor organizations representing them, charged with violation of the Taylor Law (Civil Service Law § 200 et seq.). This, of course, applies equally to the present defendants.

Nor is there any substance to the further contention that the city failed to prove there is evidence that De Lury disobeyed any mandate of the court. The strike was open and notorious. Its devastating impact on the City of New York and its inhabitants, including the danger of fire and the hazard to health, was known to the defendant, as it was to all New Yorkers. The court's order that the strike be terminated and that De Lury, as president of the Union, instruct his men "not to engage or participate in" the strike was clear beyond cavil. The defendant not only failed to obey that injunction but, going to the other extreme, actually urged the men to make the strike "effective 100%". What the proof convincingly demonstrated, the concession of the defendant's counsel rendered indisputable. We cannot accept the highly technical or hair-splitting arguments urged upon us in an attempt to evade compliance with the court's lawful mandates. Indeed, when confronted with a somewhat similar situation in United States v. Mine

Workers (330 U.S. 258, 307, concurring opn., 67 S.Ct. 677, 91 L.Ed. 884)—a case in which an adjudication of criminal contempt was based on disobedience of an order enjoining a strike—Mr. Justice Frankfurter, after observing that we are " 'a government of laws and not of men' " (p. 307, 67 S.Ct. 677, p. 703), went on to say in language most appropriate here (p. 312, 67 S.Ct. 677, p. 705):

> "In our country, law is not a body of technicalities in the keeping of specialists or in the service of any special interest. There can be no free society without law administered through an independent judiciary. If one man can be allowed to determine for himself what is law, every man can. That means first chaos, then tyranny. Legal process is an essential part of the democratic process. For legal process is subject to democratic control by defined, orderly ways which themselves are part of law. In a democracy, power implies responsibility. The greater the power that defies law the less tolerant can this Court be of defiance. As the Nation's ultimate judicial tribunal, this Court, beyond any other organ of society, is the trustee of law and charged with the duty of securing obedience to it."

We have considered each of the other arguments advanced by the defendants and find them so tenuous as to require no comment.

In conclusion, then—subdivision 1 of section 210 of the Civil Service Law, designed to prevent the paralysis of Government, offends against no constitutional guarantee or requirement. Self-interest of individual or organization may not be permitted to endanger the safety, health or public welfare of the State or any of its subdivisions. There was here indisputable proof not only of deliberate disobedience of the explicit provisions of the Taylor Law but willful defiance of the court's lawful mandates as well. Such defiance, the more egregious when committed by employees in the public sector, is not to be tolerated.

The order appealed from should be affirmed, with costs, and the question certified answered in the affirmative.

All concur.

BURKE, BERGAN and KEATING, JJ., on constraint of this court's decision in Rankin v. Shanker (23 N.Y.2d 111, 295 N.Y.S.2d 625, 242 N.E.2d 802) insofar as the right to a jury trial is concerned.

Order affirmed, etc.

Notes

1. The federal courts have taken a similar view. In *United Federation of Postal Clerks v. Blount,* 325 F.Supp. 879 (D.D.C.1971), *aff'd without opinion* 404 U.S. 802, 92 S.Ct. 80, 30 L.Ed.2d 38 (1971), the court had before it the constitutionality of 5 U.S.C.A. § 7311(3) which prohibits an individual from accepting or holding a position in the federal government or in the District of Columbia if he participates in a strike against the Government of the United States or the government of the District of Columbia. The

court held that in the absence of a statute, public employees do not have the right to strike. Therefore, it is permissible for the government to prohibit strikes by those in public employment whether because of the prerogatives of the sovereign or some sense of higher obligation in order to secure the continuing function of the government without interruption and to protect public health and safety. Accordingly, the constitutionality of the statute was upheld. Judge Wright concurred but expressed reservations about the proposition that the right to strike does not exist unless it is statutorily guaranteed.

2. Title 18 U.S.C.A. § 1918 provides that an employee of the government of the United States who participates in a strike, or asserts the right to strike, against the government is guilty of a felony and, upon conviction, shall be fined not more than $1,000 or imprisoned not more than one year and a day, or both.

3. Section 7116(b)(7) of the Federal Civil Service Reform Law prohibits a labor organization from calling, or participating in, a strike, work stoppage, or slow down, or picketing an agency in a labor-management dispute if such picketing interferes with an agency's operations.

4. The proposition that strikes by public employees are unlawful at common law and in the absence of a statutory grant appears to have been accepted by all the courts which have considered the question.

However, the California Supreme Court found that the statutory right of public employees to strike has been established inferentially, not expressly. Consider the following case.

COUNTY SANITATION DIST. v. SEIU LOCAL 660

Supreme Court of California, 1985.
38 Cal.3d 564, 214 Cal.Rptr. 424, 699 P.2d 835.

Full Text of Opinion

Broussard, Justice:—Defendants appeal from a judgment awarding plaintiff sanitation district damages and prejudgment interest in connection with defendant union's involvement in a labor strike against plaintiff. The case squarely presents issues of great import to public sector labor-management relations, namely whether all strikes by public employees are illegal and, if so, whether the striking union is liable in tort for compensatory damages. After careful review of a long line of case law and policy arguments, we conclude that the common law prohibition against all public employee strikes is no longer supportable. Therefore, the judgment for the plaintiff finding the strike to be unlawful and awarding damages, interest and costs must be reversed.

I. Statement of the Case.

Defendants union (Local 660 or the union) is a labor organization affiliated with the Service Employees International Union, AFL–CIO, and has been the certified bargaining representative of the blue collar employees of the Los Angeles Sanitation District since 1973. Plaintiff is one of 27 sanitation districts within Los Angeles County [1] and is charged with providing, operating and maintaining sewage transport and treatment facilities and landfill disposal sites throughout the county.[2] The District employs some 500 workers who are directly or indirectly responsible for the operation and maintenance of its facilities and who are members of, or represented by, Local 660. Since 1973, the District and Local 660 have bargained concerning wages, hours and working conditions pursuant to the Meyers–Milias–Brown Act (MMBA). (Gov.Code, §§ 3500–3511.) Each year these negotiations have resulted in a binding labor contract or memorandum of understanding (MOU). (See Glendale City Employees' Assn. v. City of Glendale (1975) 15 Cal.3d 328, 90 LRRM 2603.)

On July 5, 1976, approximately 75 percent of the District's employees went out on strike after negotiations between the District and the union for a new wage and benefit agreement reached an impasse and failed to produce a new MOU. The District promptly filed a complaint for injunctive relief and damages and was granted a temporary restraining order. The strike continued for approximately 11 days, during which time the District was able to maintain its facilities and operations through the efforts of management personnel and certain union members who chose not to strike.[3] On July 16, the employees voted to accept a tentative agreement on a new MOU, the terms of which were identical to the District's offer prior to the strike.

The District then proceeded with the instant action for tort damages. The trial court found the strike to be unlawful and in violation of the public policy of the State of California and thus awarded the District $246,904 in compensatory damages,[4] prejudgment interest in the amount of $87,615.22 and costs of $874.65.

II. The Traditional Prohibition Against Public Employee Strikes.

Common law decisions in other jurisdictions at one time held that no employee, whether public or private, had a right to strike in concert

1. Each such district is a separate and autonomous political subdivision of the State of California authorized by Health and Safety Code section 4700 et seq. County Sanitation District No. 2 of Los Angeles County is authorized by a joint powers agreement to act on behalf of itself and the 26 other districts in numerous matters, including personnel and labor relations. (These 27 sanitation districts are hereinafter jointly referred to as the District.)

2. In 1976, the facilities operated by the District included 6 sanitary landfills which together received about 15,000 tons of solid waste each day, 11 treatment plants processing 450 million gallons of raw sewage per day, 4 maintenance yards, and 46 pumping stations. In maintaining these operations, the District served approximately 4 million residents of the county.

3. The union maintains that the strike settled on July 12, while the trial court's findings agreed with the District's contention that the strike settled on July 16. In addition, the District maintained that the strike was not entirely peaceful and had alleged various acts of vandalism were committed by the strikers. The union denied these charges in full.

4. This figure represents the following strike-related damages: Wages and FICA payments: $304,227; earned compensatory time off valued at $16,040; miscellaneous security, equipment and meal expenses; $55,080; health care benefits paid to striking employees: $6,000; less a $134,443 set off in wages, FICA and retirement benefits that the District did not have to pay out on behalf of striking workers.

with fellow workers. In fact, such collective action was generally viewed as a conspiracy and held subject to both civil and criminal sanctions.[5] Over the course of the 20th century, however, courts and legislatures gradually acted to change these laws as they applied to private sector employees; today, the right to strike is generally accepted as indispensable to the system of collective bargaining and negotiation, which characterizes labor-management relations in the private sector.[6]

By contrast, American law continues to regard public sector strikes in a substantially different manner. A strike by employees of the United States government may still be treated as a crime,[7] and strikes by state and local employees have been explicitly allowed by courts or statute in only ten states.

Contrary to the assertions of the plaintiff as well as various holdings of the Court of Appeal,[9] this court has repeatedly stated that the legality of strikes by public employees in California has remained an open question. In Los Angeles Met. Transit Authority v. Brotherhood of Railroad Trainmen (1960) 54 Cal.2d 684, 687–688, 46 LRRM 3065, this court stated in dictum that "[i]n the absence of legislative authorization public employees in general do not have the right to strike * * *" but proceeded to hold that a statute affording public transit workers the right "to engage in other concerted activities for the purpose of collectively bargaining or other mutual aid or protection"

5. See Commonwealth v. Pullis (Mayor's Ct.Phil. 91806) reported in 3 Commons, Documentary History of American Industrial Society (1910) p. 59; Walker v. Cronin (1871) 107 Mass. 555; Vegelahn v. Guntner (1896) 67 Mass. 92 [44 N.E. 1077]; Loewe v. Lawlor (1908) 208 U.S. 274.

6. Congress gradually, through a series of legislative enactments, not only granted private sector employees a right to strike and to engage in other concerted activities, but also deprived employers of their traditional remedies of injunction and damage suits. (See 38 Stat. 730 (1914) [Clayton Antitrust Act], codified as amended at 15 U.S.C. §§ 15, 17, 26 (1970), 29 U.S.C. § 52 (1970); 47 Stat. 70 (1930) [Norris–La Guardia Act], codified at 29 U.S.C. §§ 101–115 (1970); 47 Stat. pt. II 577 (1926) [Railway Labor Act], codified as amended at 45 U.S.C. §§ 151–88 (1970); 49 Stat. 449 (1935) [Wagner Act], codified as amended at 29 U.S.C. §§ 141–197 (1970)).

7. Employees of the federal government are statutorily prohibited from striking under 5 United States Code section 7311 (1976), which prohibits an individual from holding a federal position if he "participates in a strike, or asserts the right to strike against the Government of the United States. * * *" In United Federation of Postal Clerks v. Blount (D.D.C.1971) 325 F.Supp. 879, 76 LRRM 2932, affd., 404 U.S. 802, 78 LRRM 2463 (1971), the court upheld the constitutionality of the strike prohibitions, yet declared unconstitutional the "wording insofar as it inhibits the *assertion* of the right to strike. * * *" (Id. at p. 831 [emphasis in original].) In 1947, Congress originally denied federal employees the right to strike in section 305 of the Labor Management Relations Act (Taft–Hartley Act), chapter 120, 61 Statutes at Large 136 (1947). This act was repealed and ultimately replaced by section 7311.

9. See, e.g., Stationary Engineers v. San Juan Water District (1979) 90 Cal.App.3d 796, 801, 103 LRRM 2098; Pasadena, Unified School District v. Pasadena Federation of Teachers (1977) 72 Cal.App.3d 100, 96 LRRM 2363; Service Employees' International Union, Local No. 22 v. Roseville Community Hospital (1972) 24 Cal.App.2d 400, 408, 80 LRRM 2098; Trustees of California State Colleges v. Local 1352, S.F. State etc. Teachers (1970) 13 Cal.App.3d 863, 867, 76 LRRM 2265; City of San Diego v. American Federation of State etc. Employees (1970) 8 Cal.App.3d 308, 310, 74 LRRM 2407. Almond v. County of Sacramento (1969) 276 Cal.App.2d 32, 35, 72 LRRM 2182.

granted these employees a right to strike. However, in our very next opinion on the issue, In re Berry (1968) 68 Cal.2d 137, 67 LRRM 2657, we invalidated an injunction against striking public employees as unconstitutionally overbroad, and *expressly* reserved opinion on "the question whether strikes by public employees can be lawfully enjoined." (Id., p. 151.) * * *

Before commencing our discussion, however, we must note that the Legislature has also chosen to reserve judgment on the general legality of strikes in the public sector. As Justice Grodin observed in his concurring opinion in El Rancho Unified School District v. National Education Assn., supra, 33 Cal.3d 946, 964, 115 LRRM 2235 "the Legislature itself has steadfastly refrained from providing clearcut guidance." With the exception of firefighters (Labor Code, § 1962), no statutory prohibition against strikes by public employees in this state exists.[12]

The MMBA, the statute under which the present controversy arose, does not directly address the question of strikes.

The MMBA sets forth the rights of municipal and county employees in California.[13] (Gov.Code, §§ 3500–3511.) The MMBA protects the right of such employees "to form, join, and participate in the activities of employee organizations * * * for the purpose of representation on all matters of employer-employee relations." It also requires public employers to "meet and confer" in good faith with employee representatives on all issues within the scope of representation. As explained in

12. For just one example, the Winton Act (former Ed.Code, § 13080 et seq.), which governed the relationship between local school boards and teachers' unions, neither affirmed nor rejected the teachers' right to strike. In 1975 the Legislature repealed the Winton Act and added new provisions to the Government Code to establish an Education Employment Relations Board (see Gov.Code, § 3540 et seq.); the new enactment also does not prohibit strikes by teachers. It also bears mention that the California Assembly Advisory Council on Public Employee Relations in its final report of March 13, 1973, concluded that, "[s]ubject only to [certain specified] restrictions and limitations ... public employees should have the right to strike" (p. 24) and proposed a statute to carry out these goals (Appen. A). However, this proposed statute was never enacted into law, perhaps further reflecting a legislative decision to leave the ultimate determination of this thorny issue to the judiciary.

13. The MMBA revised its predecessor, the Brown Act, in 1988. The MMBA amendments, however, apply only to local government employees because the MMBA deleted reference to the "State of California" and explicitly defined "public employee" as one employed by any political subdivision of the state. (See Gov.Code, § 3501.) Presently, state employees are governed by the State Employer–Employee Relations Act (Gov.Code, §§ 3512–3524).

Additional groups of employees were excepted from coverage under the Brown Act by previous legislation. These employees are consequently not covered by the MMBA. (See Pub.Util.Code, §§ 25051–25052, added by Stats.1955, ch. 1036, § 2 at pp. 1960–1961 [governing bargaining between employees of the Alameda–Contra Costa Transit District and their employers]; Pub.Util.Code, Appen. 1, § 3.6(b)–(g) [governing bargaining in the Los Angeles Metropolitan Transit Authority]; Ed.Code, §§ 13080–13089 [governing education employees].)

For a detailed discussion of the scope and purposes of the MMBA, see Grodin, *Public Employees Bargaining in California: The Meyers–Milias–Brown Act in the Courts* (1972) 23 Hastings L.J. 719; Note, Collective Bargaining Under the Meyers–Milias–Brown Act—Should Local Employees Have the Right to Strike (1984) 35 Hastings L.J. 523.

its preamble, one of the MMBA's main purposes is to improve communications between public employees and their employers by providing a reasonable method for resolving disputes. A further stated purpose is to promote improved personnel relations by "providing a uniform basis for recognizing the right of public employees to join organizations of their own choice." [14]

On its face, the MMBA neither denies nor grants local employees the right to strike. This omission is noteworthy since the Legislature has not hesitated to expressly prohibit strikes for certain classes of public employees. For example, the * * * prohibition against strikes by firefighters was enacted nine years before the passage of the MMBA and remains in effect today. Moreover, the MMBA includes firefighters within its provisions. Thus, the absence of any such limitation on other public employees covered by the MMBA at the very least implies a lack of legislative intent to use the MMBA to enact a general strike prohibition.[15]

Plaintiffs have suggested that section 3509 of the MMBA must be construed as a general prohibition on the right to strike because it specifically precludes the application of Labor Code section 923 [16] to public employees. Labor Code section 923 has been construed by this court to protect the right of private sector employees to strike (see Petri Cleaners v. Automotive Employees, Local 88 (1960) 53 Cal.2d 455, 45 LRRM 2664); yet, an examination of other California statutes governing public employees makes it perfectly clear that section 3509 was *not* included in the MMBA as a means for prohibiting strikes.

14. However, the MMBA contains no clear mechanism for resolving disputes. It merely provides that if the parties fail to reach an agreement, they *may* agree to appoint a mediator or use other impasse resolution procedures agreed upon by the parties. Additionally, the MMBA does not authorize the establishment of an administrative agency to resolve controversies arising under its provisions. In contrast, statutes governing other public employees in California authorize the Public Employee Relations Board (PERB) to resolve disputes and enforce the provisions of the legislation. (See Gov.Code § 3541.3 (setting the powers and duties of the PERB under the Educational Employment Relations Act (EERA)); and Gov.Code, § 3513, subd. (g) [making the powers and duties of the PERB under the EERA applicable to the State Employees Relations Act].)

15. Apparently this decision was the result of political compromise and/or a desire that the courts would take the difficult first step of unambiguously indicating whether public employees generally have the right to strike. As one noted commentator explains, "The entire subject of strikes and impasse resolution procedures is avoided, except for the declaration that the parties may elect to engage a mediator. What emerges is a rather general legislative blessing for collective bargaining at the local governmental level without clear delineation of policy or means for its implementation. The courts have, on the whole, done an admirable job of exegesis, but their decisions cannot help but reflect the underlying weakness of the text." (Grodin, op. cit. supra, 23 Hastings L.J. at p. 761.)

16. Section 923 provides in pertinent part: "* * * the individual workman [shall] have full freedom of association, self-organization, and designation of representatives of his own choosing, to negotiate the terms and conditions of his employment, and that he shall be free from the interference * * * of employers * * * in the designation of such representatives or in self-organization or in other concerted activities for the purpose of collective bargaining or other mutual aid or protection."

A provision identical to section 3509 is contained in the statutes governing educational employees and firefighters. However, an explicit strike prohibition is included in the firefighters statute *in addition* to this provision. The fact that the Legislature felt it necessary to include this express strike prohibition clearly indicates that it neither intended nor expected its preclusion of section 923 to serve as a blanket prohibition against strikes. Furthermore, in San Diego Teachers Assn. v. Superior Court, supra, 24 Cal.3d at page 13, this court interpreted section 3549 of the EERA, a provision *identical to* section 3509 of the MMBA, as specifically *not* prohibiting strikes. Therefore, plaintiff's assertion that section 3509 must be read as a legislative prohibition of public employee strikes cannot be sustained.[17]

In sum, the MMBA establishes a system of rights and protections for public employees which closely mirrors those enjoyed by workers in the private sector. The Legislature, however, intentionally avoided the inclusion of any provision which could be construed as either a blanket grant or prohibition of a right to strike, thus leaving the issue shrouded in ambiguity. In the absence of clear legislative directive on this crucial matter, it becomes the task of the judiciary to determine whether, under the law, strikes by public employees should be viewed as a prohibited tort.

III. THE COMMON LAW PROHIBITION AGAINST PUBLIC EMPLOYEE STRIKES.

As noted above, the Court of Appeal and various lower courts in this and other jurisdictions have repeatedly stated that, absent a specific statutory grant, all strikes by public employees are per se illegal. A variety of policy rationales and legal justifications have traditionally been advanced in support of this common law "rule," and numerous articles and scholarly treatises have been devoted to debating their respective merits. The various justifications for the common law prohibition can be summarized into four basic arguments. First—the traditional justification—that a strike by public employees is tantamount to a denial of governmental authority/sovereignty. Second, the terms of public employment are not subject to bilateral collective bargaining, as in the private sector, because they are set by the legislative body through unilateral lawmaking. Third, since legislative bodies are responsible for public employment decision making, granting public employees the right to strike would afford them excessive bargaining leverage, resulting in a distortion of the political process and an improper delegation of legislative authority. Finally, public employees provide essential public services which, if interrupted by strikes, would threaten the public welfare.

Our determination of the legality of strikes by public employees necessarily involves an analysis of the reasoning and current viability of each of these arguments. The first of these justifications, the

17. Since the present case involves employees subject to the MMBA, we do not consider whether provisions of statutes governing other employees could be interpreted to limit the right of such employees to strike.

sovereignty argument, asserts that government is the embodiment of the people, and hence those entrusted to carry out its function may not impede it.[19] This argument was particularly popular in the first half of the 20th century, when it received support from several American Presidents.[20]

The sovereignty concept, however, has often been criticized in recent years as a vague and outdated theory based on the assumption that "the King can do no wrong." As Judge Harry T. Edwards has cogently observed, "the application of the strict sovereignty notion—that governmental power can never be opposed by employee organizations—is clearly a vestige from another era, an era of unexpanded government * * *. With the rapid growth of the government, both in sheer size as well as in terms of assuming services not traditionally associated with the 'sovereign,' government employees understandably no longer feel constrained by a notion that 'The King can do no wrong.' The distraught cries by public unions of disparate treatment merely reflect the fact that, for all intents and purposes, public employees occupy essentially the same position vis-a-vis the employer as their private counterparts." (Edwards, *The Developing Labor Relations Law in the Public Sector* (1972) 10 Duq.L.Rev. 357, 359–60.[21]

In recent years, courts have rejected the very same concept of sovereignty as a justification for governmental immunity from tort liability. In California, the death knell came in Muskopf v. Corning

19. For example, in City of Cleveland v. Division 268 of Amalgamated Assn. (1949) 41 Ohio Op. 236, 239 [90 N.E.2d 711, 715, 25 LRRM 2225], the court stated that "[i]t is clear that in our system of government, the government is a servant of all of the people. And a strike against the public, a strike of public employees, has been denominated * * * as a rebellion against government. The right to strike, if accorded to public employees * * * is one means of destroying government. And if they destroy government, we have anarchy, we have chaos." A California case which relied on this sovereignty argument is Nutter v. City of Santa Monica (1946) 74 Cal. App.2d 292, 18 LRRM 2156.

20. Commenting on the Boston police strike, Calvin Coolidge asserted that "[t]here is no right to strike against public safety by anybody, anywhere, at any time" (quoted in Norwalk Teachers Ass'n v. Board of Educ. (1951) 138 Conn. 269, 273 [83 A.2d 482, 484, 28 LRRM 2408]). Woodrow Wilson, commenting on the same strike, stated that the strike is "an intolerable crime against civilization" (quoted in id., at p. 273 [83 A.2d at p. 484]).

In another famous pronouncement of the sovereignty argument, President Franklin Roosevelt stated: "[M]ilitant tactics have no place in the functions of any organization of Government employees. * * * [A] strike of public employees manifests nothing less than an intent on their part to prevent or obstruct the operations of government until their demands are satisfied. Such action, looking toward the paralysis of Government by those who have sworn to support it, is unthinkable and intolerable." (Id. at pp. 273–274 [83 A.2d at p. 484] [quoting a letter from President Roosevelt to the president of the National Federation of Federal Employees (Aug. 16, 1937)].)

21. See also Anderson Federation of Teachers v. School City of Anderson (Ind. 1989) 251 N.E.2d 15, 20, 72 LRRM 2466 (dis.opn. of DeBruler, C.J.). ("[Sovereign immunity] is not a rationale argument at all but a technique for avoiding dealing with the merits of the issue [of whether public employees may strike]. * * * The conflict of real social forces cannot be solved by the invocation of magical phrases like 'sovereignty.' ")

Chief Justice DeBruler also notes that where the government has discretion over the terms and conditions of employment, "any decision within this discretionary area is authorized by government, and therefore, obviously does not deny the authority of government." (Id., at p. 20.)

Hospital Dist. (1961) 55 Cal.2d 211, where this court stated that, "[t]he rule of governmental immunity for tort is an anachronism, without rational basis, and has existed only by the force of inertia." (55 Cal.2d at p. 216.) As noted by this court in Muskopf, perpetuation of the doctrine of sovereign immunity in tort law led to many inequities, and its application effected many incongruous results. Similarly, the use of this archaic concept to justify a per se prohibition against public employee strikes is inconsistent with modern social reality and should be hereafter laid to rest.

The second basic argument underlying the common law prohibition of public employee strikes holds that since the terms of public employment are fixed by the Legislature, public employers are virtually powerless to respond to strike pressure, or alternatively that allowing such strikes would result in "government by contract" instead of "government by law." (See City of Los Angeles v. Los Angeles etc. Council (1949) 94 Cal.App.2d 36, 46, 21 LRRM 2600. This justification may have had some merit before the California Legislature gave extensive bargaining rights to public employees. However, at present, most terms and conditions of public employment are arrived at through collective bargaining under such statutes as the MMBA.

* * * The overall framework of the MMBA represents a nearly exact parallel to the private sector system of collective bargaining—a system which sets forth the guidelines for labor-management relations in the private sphere and which protects the right of private employees to strike. By enacting these significant and parallel protections for public employees through the MMBA, the Legislature effectively removed many of the underpinnings of the common law per se ban against public employee strikes. While the MMBA does not directly address the issue of such strikes, its implications regarding the traditional common law prohibition are significant.

This argument was eloquently explained by Justice Grodin in his concurring opinion in El Rancho Unified Sch. Dist. v. National Education Assn., supra, 33 Cal.3d at page 963, where he pointed out that "[t]he premise underlying the court's opinion in City of L.A. [94 Cal. App.2d 36—that it is necessarily contrary to public policy to establish terms and conditions of employment for public employees through the bilateral process of collective bargaining rather than through unilateral lawmaking—has since been rejected by the Legislature. The heart of the statute under consideration in this case [the Educational Employment Relations Act] for example, contemplates that matters relating to wages, hours and certain other terms and conditions of employment for teachers will be the subject of negotiation and agreement between a public school employer and organizations representing its employees. (Gov.Code, §§ 3543.2, 3545.3, 3543.7.) Thus, the original policy foundation for the 'rule' that public employee strikes are illegal in this state has been substantially undermined, if not obliterated."

The remaining two arguments have not served in this state as grounds for asserting a ban on public employee strikes but have been advanced by commentators and by courts of other states. With the traditional reasons for prohibiting such strikes debunked, these additional reasons do not convince us of the necessity of a judicial ukase prohibiting all such strikes.

The first of these arguments draws upon the different roles of market forces in the private and public spheres. This rationale suggests that because government services are essential and demand is generally inelastic, public employees would wield excessive bargaining power if allowed to strike. Proponents of this argument assume that economic constraints are not present to any meaningful degree in the public sector. Consequently, in the absence of such constraints, public employers will be forced to make abnormally large concessions to workers, which in turn will distort our political process by forcing either higher taxes or a redistribution of resources between government services.[22]

There are, however, several fundamental problems with this "distortion of the political process" argument. For one, as will be discussed more fully below, a key assumption underlying the argument—that all government services are essential—is factually unsupportable. Modern governments engage in an enormous number and variety of functions, which clearly vary as to their degree of essentiality. As such, the absence of an unavoidable nexus between most public services and essentiality necessarily undercuts the notion that public officials will be forced to settle strikes quickly and at any cost. The recent case of the air-traffic controllers' strike [23] is yet another example that governments have the ability to hold firm against a strike for a considerable period, even in the face of substantial inconvenience. As this court concluded in Los Angeles Met. Transit Authority v. Brotherhood of Railroad Trainmen, supra, "Permitting employees to strike does *not* delegate to them authority to fix their own wages to the exclusion of the employer's discretion. In collective bargaining negotiations, whether or not

22. See, e.g., United Federation of Postal Clerks v. Blount, supra, 325 F.Supp. 879, 884, 76 LRRM 2932. ("In the private sphere, the strike is used to equalize bargaining power, but this has universally been held not to be appropriate when its object and purpose can only be to influence the essentially political decisions of Government in the allocation of its resources.")

For an even more extensive elaboration of this "distortion of the political process" argument, *see* Wellington & Winter, *The Limits of Collective Bargaining in Public Employment, supra,* 78 Yale L.J. 1107.

23. In August 1981, the Professional Air Traffic Controllers Organization (PATCO) launched a nationwide strike against the federal government. President Ronald Reagan ordered the discharge of 11,000 striking controllers who had not returned to work within a two-day grace period. Up to the time of this writing, the Administration has rejected all suggestions for a general amnesty, its position being that the strikers, by violating the federal government's prohibition on strikes and their own "no-strike" oath, have forfeited their jobs with the Federal Aviation Administration forever. Federal courts upheld the government's position in PATCO v. Federal Labor Relations Auth. (D.C.Cir.1982) 685 F.2d 547, 110 LRRM 2676. For a more detailed analysis of the strike, see Meltzer & Sunstein, *Public Employee Strikes, Executive Discretion, and the Air Traffic Controllers* (1983) 50 U.Chi.L.Rev. 731.

the employees strike, the employer is free to reject demands if he determines that they are unacceptable." (54 Cal.2d at p. 693, italics added.)

Other factors also serve to temper the potential bargaining power of striking public employees and thus enable public officials to resist excessive demands: First, wages lost due to strikes are as important to public employees as they are to private employees. Second, the public's concern over increasing tax rates will serve to prevent the decision-making process from being dominated by political instead of economic considerations. A third and related economic constraint arises in such areas as water, sewage and, in some instances, sanitation services, where explicit prices are charged. Even if representatives of groups other than employees and the employer do not formally enter the bargaining process, both union and local government representatives are aware of the economic implications of bargaining which leads to higher prices which are clearly visible to the public. A fourth economic constraint on public employees exists in those services where subcontracting to the private sector is a realistic alternative. For example, Warren, Michigan resolved a bargaining impasse with an American Federation of State, County and Municipal Employees (AFSCME) local by subcontracting its entire sanitation service; Santa Monica, California, ended a strike of city employees by threatening to subcontract its sanitation operations; in fact, San Francisco has chosen to subcontract its entire sanitation system to *private* firms. If this subcontract option is preserved, wages in the public sector clearly need not exceed the rate at which subcontracting becomes a realistic alternative.[24]

The proponents of a flat ban on public employee strikes not only ignore such factors as the availability of subcontracting, but also fail to adequately consider public sentiment towards most strikes and assume that the public will push blindly for an early resolution at any cost. In fact, public sentiment toward a strike often limits the pressure felt by political leaders, thereby reducing the strike's effectiveness. * * *

In sum, there is little, if any empirical evidence which demonstrates that governments generally capitulate to unreasonable demands by public employees in order to resolve strikes. The result of the strike in the instant case clearly suggests the opposite. During the 11–day strike, negotiations resumed, and the parties subsequently reached an agreement on a new MOU, the terms of which were *precisely the same* as the District's last offer prior to the commencement of the strike. Such results certainly do not illustrate a situation where public employees wielded excessive bargaining power and thereby caused a distortion of our political process.

The fourth and final justification for the common law prohibition is that interruption of government services is unacceptable because they are essential. As noted above, in our contemporary industrial society

24. See further discussion in Burton & Krider, *The Role and Consequences of Strikes by Public Employees,* supra, 79 Yale L.J. 418, 425–427.

the presumption of essentially of most government services is questionable at best. In addition, we tolerate strikes by private employees in many of the same areas in which government is engaged, such as transportation, health, education, and utilities; in many employment fields, public and private activity largely overlap.

In a dissenting opinion in Anderson Federation of Teachers, Local 519 v. School City of Anderson, supra, Chief Justice DeBruler of Indiana observed that the source and management of most service enterprises is irrelevant to the relative essentiality of the services: "There is no difference in impact on the community between a strike by employees of a public utility and employees of a private utility; nor between employees of a municipal bus company and a privately owned bus company; nor between public school teachers and parochial school teachers. The form of ownership and management of the enterprise does not determine the amount of destruction caused by a strike of the employees of that enterprise. In addition, the form of ownership that is actually employed is often a political and historical accident, subject to future change by political forces. Services that were once rendered by public enterprise may be contracted out to private enterprise, and then by another administration returned to the public sector." (251 N.E.2d at p. 21.)

* * *

We of course recognize that there are certain "essential" public services, the disruption of which would seriously threaten the public health or safety. In fact, defendant union itself concedes that the law should still act to render illegal any strikes in truly essential services which would constitute a genuine threat to the public welfare. Therefore, to the extent that the "excessive bargaining power" and "interruption of essential services" arguments still have merit, specific health and safety limitations on the right to strike should suffice to answer the concerns underlying those arguments.

In addition to the various legal arguments advanced to persuade the courts to impose a judicial ban on public employee strikes—arguments which, as we have seen, are decidedly unpersuasive in the context of modern jurisprudence and experience—there is the broader concern that permitting public employees to strike may be, on balance, harmful to labor-management relations in the public sector. This is essentially a political argument, best addressed to the Legislature. We review the matter only to point out that the issue is not so clear cut as to justify judicial intervention, since the Legislature could reasonably conclude that recognizing public employees' right to strike may actually enhance labor-management relations.

At least ten states have granted most of their public employees a right to strike; and the policy rationale behind this statutory recognition further undercuts several of the basic premises relied upon by strike-ban advocates. As the aforementioned Pennsylvania Governor's Commission Report concluded: "The collective bargaining process will be strengthened if this qualified right to strike is recognized. It will be some curb on the possible intransigence of an employer; and the limitations on the right to strike will serve notice on the employee that there are limits to the hardships that he can impose." (251 Govt.Empl. Rel.Rep., supra, at p. E–3)

It is unrealistic to assume that disputes among public employees and their employers will not occur; in fact, strikes by public employees are relatively frequent events in California. For example, 46 strikes occurred during 1981–1983, which actually marks a significant decline when compared to the number during the five previous years.[27] Although the circumstances behind each individual strike may vary somewhat, commentators repeatedly note that much of the reason for their occurrence lies in the fact that without the right to strike, or at least a credible strike threat, public employees have little negotiating strength. This, in turn, produces frustrations which exacerbate labor-management conflicts and often provoke "illegal" strikes.

* * *

It is universally recognized that in the private sector, the bilateral determination of wages and working conditions through a collective bargaining process, in which both sides possess relatively equal strength, facilitates understanding and more harmonious relations between employers and their employees. In the absence of some means of equalizing the parties' respective bargaining positions, such as a credible strike threat, both sides are less likely to bargain in good faith; this in turn leads to unsatisfactory and acrimonious labor relations and ironically to more and longer strikes. Equally as important, the possibility of a strike often provides the best impetus for parties to reach an agreement at the bargaining table, because both parties lose if a strike actually comes to pass. Thus by providing a clear incentive for resolving disputes, a credible strike threat may serve to avert, rather than to encourage, work stoppages.

* * *

A final policy consideration in our analysis addresses a more philosophical issue—the perception that the right to strike, in the public sector as well as in the private sector, represents a basic civil liberty.[31] The widespread acceptance of that perception leads logically

27. Public employee strikes in California, 1970–1983: *

1970	1971	1972	1973	1974	1975	1976
20	14	18	15	45	44	23

1977	1978	1979	1980	1981	1982	1983
59	29	87	55	20	6	20

* Source: *An Analysis of 1981–1983 Strikes in California's Public Sector* (1884) (Mar. 1984 Inst. of Ind.Rel., U.C. Berkeley) 60 Cal.Pub.Empl.Rel. 7, 9. Public employees include all workers in public agencies in California, excluding federal service and public utilities.

31. Another interesting and related policy argument in support of granting a right to strike to public employees rests on a recognition of the changing shape and values of the American economic system itself. In essence, it focuses on the fact that

to the conclusion that the right to strike, as an important symbol of a free society, should not be denied unless such a strike would substantially injure paramount interests of the larger community.

Plaintiff's argument that only the Legislature can reject the common law doctrine prohibiting public employee strikes flies squarely in the face of both logic and past precedent. Legislative silence is not the equivalent of positive legislation and does not preclude judicial reevaluation of common law doctrine. If the courts have created a bad rule or an outmoded one, the courts can change it.

* * *

For the reasons stated above, we conclude that the common law prohibition against public sector strikes should not be recognized in this state. Consequently, strikes by public sector employees in this state as such are neither illegal nor tortious under California common law. We must immediately caution, however, that the right of public employees to strike is by no means unlimited. Prudence and concern for the general public welfare require certain restrictions.

The Legislature has already prohibited strikes by firefighters under any circumstances. It may conclude that other categories of public employees perform such essential services that a strike would invariably result in imminent danger to public health and safety, and must therefore be prohibited.

While the Legislature may enact such specific restrictions, the courts must proceed on a case-by-case basis. Certain existing statutory standards may properly guide them in this task. As noted above, a number of states have granted public employees a limited right to strike, and such legislation typically prohibits strikes by a limited number of employees involved in clearly essential services. In addition, several statutes provide for injunctive relief against other types of striking public employees when the state clearly demonstrates that the continuation of such strikes will constitute an imminent threat or

our market economy has evolved from its classical model into an increasingly mixed and pluralistic form. In this process of increased government intervention, the line between public and private enterprise has become increasingly blurred. At the same time, a concomitant blurring has occurred between traditional political and economic activity, and it is this latter overlap which renders a flat ban on all public sector strikes so difficult to defend.

The argument then analogizes the deviation of the American system from classical economic models and the corresponding reevaluation of public strike prohibitions to the Solidarity-inspired developments in Poland prior to the latest military crackdown. Ironically, the traditional common law argument that public sector bargaining and striking is antidemocratic and inimical to our political process, closely mirrors the Polish government's view that unions and strikes are antisocial—indeed revisionist and reactionary—conduct in a system operated purportedly for the benefit of all. Deviations from classical models and beliefs thus confront both ideological viewpoints. The argument for a right to strike for public employees in a capitalist system clearly gains strength as society evolves away from the classical ideal of a pure market economy where the public and private sectors are clearly separated. Similarly, the case for a right to strike in a socialist system grows stronger as that society deviates from the classical ideals of the socialist model. For a more detailed analysis of this theory, see Hanslowe & Acierno, supra, 67 Cornell L.Rev. at pp. 1072–1073.

"clear and present danger" to public health and safety. Such an approach guarantees that essential public services will not be disrupted so as to genuinely threaten public health and safety, while also preserving the basic rights of public employees.

After consideration of the various alternatives before us, we believe the following standard may properly guide courts in the resolution of future disputes in this area; strikes by public employees are not unlawful at common law unless or until it is clearly demonstrated that such a strike creates a substantial and imminent threat to the health and safety of the public. This standard allows exceptions in certain essential areas of public employment (e.g., the prohibition against firefighters and law enforcement personnel) and also requires the courts to determine on a case-by-case basis whether the public interest overrides the basic right to strike.

Although we recognize that this balancing process may impose an additional burden on the judiciary, it is neither a novel nor unmanageable task.[34] Indeed, an examination of the strike in the instant case affords a good example of how this new standard should be applied. The 11–day strike did not involve public employees, such as firefighters or law enforcement personnel, whose absence from their duties would clearly endanger the public health and safety. Moreover, there was no showing by the District that the health and safety of the public was at any time imminently threatened. That is not to say that had the strike continued indefinitely, or had the availability of replacement personnel been insufficient to maintain a reasonable sanitation system, there could not have been at some point a clear showing of a substantial threat to the public health and welfare.[35] However, such was not the

34. Legislation in several states already requires the courts to make this precise determination. (See e.g., the relevant statutory provisions in Alaska, Ore., Pa. and Wis.) For just one example, under the Pennsylvania Public Employee Relations Act, public employees are not prohibited from striking after they have submitted to mediation and fact finding, unless or until such a strike creates a clear and present danger or threat to the health, safety and welfare of the public. (Pa.Stat.Ann., tit. 43, § 1101.1003.) In such cases, the employer may petition for equitable relief, including injunctions, and is entitled to relief if the court finds that the strike creates the danger or threat. (Id.) The Pennsylvania courts have applied this standard to several classes of public employees. (See, e.g., Bethel Park School Dist. v. Bethel Park Federation of Teachers, Local 1607, Am. Fed'n of Teachers (1980) 54 Pa.Commw. 49, 52 [420 A.2d 18] (teacher's strike constituted a clear and present danger to the public's health, safety and welfare and school district entitled to back-to-work order in view of potential losses of state subsidies, instructional days vocational job, higher education opportunities, counseling, social and health services, extracurricular enrichment programs and employees' work opportunities and wages); Bristol Township Education Ass'n v. School District (1974) 14 Pa.Commw. 463, 468–470 [322 A.2d 767, 87 LRRM 2018] (school district entitled to injunction against teacher's strike under similar circumstances); Highland Sewer and Water Auth. v. Local Union 459, I.E.B.W. (1973) 67 Pa.D. & C.2d 564, 565–567 (sewer and water authority not entitled to injunction forcing striking employees back to work since there was no clear and present danger in view of the fact that the services provided by the authority could still be performed during the strike, apparently by supervisors, with relatively little inconvenience).

35. Had such a showing been made, the trial court would then have had the authority to issue an injunction and declare the strike illegal. In cases involving sanitation strikes, it is often the *length* of the

case here, and the legality of the strike would have been upheld under our newly adopted standard.[36]

Defendant union has also urged this court to find that a per se prohibition of all public employee strikes violates the California Constitution's guarantees of freedom of association, free speech and equal protection. They do not contend that such a constitutional infringement is present when a court exercises its equitable authority to enjoin a strike based on a showing that the strike represents a substantial and imminent danger to the public health or safety. Instead, the union argues that in the absence of such a showing, per se prohibition is constitutionally unsupportable.

The right to form and be represented by unions is a fundamental right of American workers that has been extended to public employees through constitutional adjudication as well as by statute; in this case, it is specifically mandated by the provisions of the MMBA itself. In addition, " '[i]t is now settled law that workmen may lawfully combine to exert various forms of economic pressure upon an employer, provided the object sought to be accomplished thereby has a reasonable relation to the betterment of labor conditions, and they act peaceably and honestly. [Citations.] This right is guaranteed by the federal Constitution as an incident of freedom of speech, press and assemblage, [citations] and it is not dependent upon the existence of a labor controversy between the employer and his employee.' " (In re Blaney (1947) 30 Cal.2d 643, 648, 20 LRRM 2645, quoting Steiner v. Long Beach Local No. 128 (1942) 19 Cal.2d 676, 682, 10 LRRM 393.)

As the union contends, however, the right to unionize means little unless it is accorded some degree of protection regarding its principal aim—effective collective bargaining. For such bargaining to be meaningful, employee groups must maintain the ability to apply pressure or at least threaten its application. A creditable [sic] right to strike is one means of doing so. As yet, however, the right to strike has not been accorded full constitutional protection, the prevailing view being that "[t]he right to strike, because of its more serious impact upon the public interest, is more vulnerable to regulation than the right to organized and select representatives for lawful purposes of collective bargaining

strike which will ultimately require issuance of an injunction. (See, e.g., Highland Sewer and Water Auth. v. Local Union 459, I.B.E.W. (1973) 67 Pa.D. & C.2d 564, 565–567.) In addition, if particular jobs performed by striking sanitation or other public employees require unique skills and training, it is conceivable that a public agency might be unable to find adequate replacements. In the instant matter, however, replacement personnel adequately maintained needed sanitation services without any significant threat of harm to the public. Further, the District's allegations of vandalism by the strikers (see fn. 4, ante), while perhaps citing individual illegal acts, were by no means enough to render the entire strike illegal or even a substantial public threat.

36. The trial court in this matter had no reason to make a finding regarding the threat to public health and safety posed by the strike. The court merely relied on prior Court of Appeal opinions, which had held that public employee strikes were per se illegal in the absence of a specific statutory grant. In the future, trial courts will clearly be required to make such a finding. In these cases, the scope of appellate review will ordinarily be limited to determining whether reasonable grounds existed for the trial court's decision.

which this Court has characterized as a 'fundamental right * * *.' " (International Union, UAW, Local 232 v. Wisconsin Employment Relations Board (1949) 336 U.S. 245, 259, 23 LRRM 2361.)

Further, the federal ban on public employee strikes has been specifically upheld as constitutionally permissible. (See United Federation of Postal Clerks v. Blount, supra, 325 F.Supp. 879, 884, 76 LRRM 2932; affd. (1971) 404 U.S. 802, 78 LRRM 2463.) In the absence of any explicit constitutional protection of the right to strike, the Blount court reasoned that the law prohibiting only public employees from striking need only have a rational basis to avoid offending constitutional guarantees. The court then easily found that the common law policy justifications (discussed in detail above) did indeed provide a rational basis for the per se prohibition. (See, United Federation of Postal Clerks v. Blount, supra, at p. 883.)

Thoughtful judges and commentators, however, have questioned the wisdom of upholding a per se prohibition of public employee strikes. They have persuasively argued that because the right to strike is so inextricably intertwined with the recognized fundamental right to organize and collectively bargain, some degree of constitutional protection should be extended to the act of striking in both the public and private sectors.

* * *

We are not persuaded that personal freedoms guaranteed by the United States and California Constitutions confer an *absolute right* to strike,[38] but the arguments above may merit consideration at some future date. If the right to strike is afforded some constitutional protection as derivative of the fundamental right of freedom of association, then this right cannot be abridged absent a substantial or compelling justification.

As this court stated in Vogel v. County of Los Angeles (1967) 68 Cal.2d 18, 22, which invalidated a loyalty oath requirement for public employees in this state, "even where a compelling state purpose is present, restrictions on the cherished freedom of association protected by the First Amendment and made applicable to the states by the Fourteenth Amendment must be drawn with narrow specificity. First Amendment freedoms are delicate and vulnerable and must be protected wherever possible. When government seeks to limit those freedoms on the basis of legitimate and substantial governmental purpose * * * those purposes cannot be pursued by means that broadly stifle fundamental personal liberties when the end can be more narrowly achieved. Precision of regulation is required so that the exercise of our most precious freedoms will not be unduly curtailed except to the extent

38. As stated in the United States Supreme Court in Dorchy v. Kansas: "Neither the common law nor the Fourteenth Amendment confers the absolute right to strike." (Dorchy v. Kansas (1926) 272 U.S. 306, 311.) Similarly, we do not find that the comparable personal freedoms guaranteed by the California Constitution confer an absolute right to strike. (See, e.g., In re Porterfield (1946) 28 Cal.2d 91, 114, 19 LRRM 2585.)

necessitated by the legitimate governmental objective. (Keyishian v. Board of Regents, supra, 385 U.S. 589, 602–603; Elfbrandt v. Russell, 384 U.S. 11, 15, et seq.; N.A.A.C.P. v. Button, 371 U.S. 415, 432–433; Shelton v. Tucker, 364 U.S. 479, 488; Bagley v. Washington Township Hospital Dist., supra, 65 Cal.2d 499, 506–509; Fort v. Civil Service Com., supra, 61 Cal.2d 331, 337–338.)"

As discussed at length above, the traditional justifications espoused in favor of a per se prohibition cannot withstand a significant degree of judicial scrutiny. Indeed, since not all public employee services are essential and many private employees perform services more vital to the public health and safety than do their counterparts in the public sector, the simplistic public/private dichotomy does not constitute a "compelling" justification for a per se prohibition of public employee strikes. Thus the constitutional arguments of defendant union and several amici cannot easily be dismissed, particularly since we will retain the limitation that public strikes may be prohibited when they threaten the public health or safety.[39]

Since we have already concluded that the traditional per se prohibition against public employee strikes can no longer be upheld on common grounds, we do not find it necessary to reach the issue in constitutional terms. Although we are not inclined to hold that the right to strikes rises to the magnitude of a fundamental right, it does appear that associational rights are implicated to a substantial degree. As such, the close connection between striking and other constitutionally protected activity adds further weight to our rejection of the traditional common law rationales underlying the per se prohibition. (Cf. Environmental Planning and Information Council v. Superior Court (1984) 36 Cal.3d 188, 195.)

We conclude that it is not unlawful for public employees to engage in a concerted work stoppage for the purpose of improving their wages or conditions of employment, unless it has been determined that the work stoppage poses an imminent threat to public health or safety. Since the trial court's judgment for damage in this case was predicated

39. Contrary to the characterization of our dissenting colleague, we neither applaud nor disapprove of strikes by public employees as a matter of social policy, for in the present state of the law that is not our function. The old rule in this state, to the effect that strikes by public employees are unlawful, rested expressly upon the premise that wages and conditions of employment for public employees may only be set by unilateral action of the public employer, and that collective bargaining for such employees in itself was contrary to public policy. *It is the Legislature which has removed the underpinnings from the old rule, by sanctioning a system of collective bargaining for local government employees.* At the same time, the Legislature has maintained a stony silence regarding the status of public employee strikes under the new statutory scheme. To the extent that we examine alternative justifications which have been asserted in support of a ban on such strikes, we do so only to determine whether there are any such justifications which are so compelling as to require acceptance by the courts even in the absence of legislative action. We find an affirmative answer only as regards those strikes which imperil public health or safety. As to other strikes, we conclude that the policy questions involved are highly debatable, and best left to the legislative branch in the first instance.

upon an erroneous determination that defendant's strike was unlawful, the judgment for damages cannot be sustained.

The judgment is reversed.

MOSK and GRODIN, JUSTICES, concur.

* * *

DISSENTING OPINION

LUCAS, JUSTICE, dissenting:—I respectfully dissent. In my view, public employees in this state neither have the right to strike, nor should they have that right. In any event, in light of the difficulty in fashioning proper exceptions to the basic "no strike" rule, and the dangers to public health and safety arising from even a *temporary* cessation of governmental services, the courts should defer to the Legislature, a body far better equipped to create such exceptions.

The majority paints a glowing picture of the public strike weapon as a means of "enhanc[ing] labor-management relations" (ante, p. ___ [maj. opn. at p. 28]), "equalizing the parties' respective bargaining positions," (p. ___ [32]), assuring "good faith" collective bargaining (p. ___ [32]), and "providing a clear incentive for resolving disputes" (p. ___ [32]). Indeed, so enamored is the majority with the concept of the public strike that it elevates this heretofore *illegal* device to a "basic civil liberty." (P. ___ [33].) Though wholly unnecessary to its opinion, the majority in dictum even suggests that public employees may have a *constitutional* right to strike which cannot be legislatively abridged absent some "substantial or compelling justification." (P. ___ [46].)

Thus, in the face of an unbroken string of Court of Appeal cases commencing nearly 35 years ago which hold that public strikes are illegal, we suddenly announce our finding that public strikes are not only lawful in most cases, but indeed they may constitute a panacea for many of the social and economic ills which have long beset the public sector. One may wonder, as I do, why we kept that revelation a secret for all these years. (See El Rancho Unified School District v. National Education Assn. (1983) 33 Cal.3d 946, 962 [conc. opn. by Richardson, J.].)

Despite the majority's encomiums, the fact remains that public strikes may devastate a city within a matter of days, or even hours, depending on the circumstances. For this reason, among many others, the courts of this state (and the vast majority of courts in other states and the federal government) have declared *all* public strikes illegal. * * *

* * *

The decision to allow public employee strikes requires a delicate and complex balancing process best undertaken by the Legislature, which may formulate a comprehensive regulatory scheme designed to avoid the disruption and chaos which invariably follow a cessation or interruption of governmental services. The majority's own proposal, to withhold the strike weapon only where "truly essential" services are involved (p. ___ [27]) and a "substantial and imminent threat" is posed (p. ___ [38]), will afford little guidance to our trial courts who must, on a "case-by-case" basis (p. ___ [38]), decide such issues. Nor will representatives of labor or management be able to predict with any confidence or certainty whether a particular strike is a lawful one or, being lawful at its inception, will become unlawful by reason of its adverse effects upon the public health and safety. In short, the majority's broad holding will prove as unworkable as it is unwise.

Of the few states that permit strikes by public employees, virtually all do so by comprehensive statutory provisions. Some of the statutory schemes begin by creating classifications of employees, distinguishing, for example, workers whose services are deemed essential (e.g., police, firefighters), those who services may be interrupted for short periods of time (e.g., teachers), and those whose services may be omitted for an extended time (e.g., municipal golf course attendants). These schemes typically define various prerequisites to the exercise of the right to strike for those categories of workers permitted that option. The prerequisites include a period of mandatory mediation as well as advance notice to the employer. In addition, some statutory schemes lay out the ground rules for binding arbitration.

In contrast, the majority's new California rule is hopelessly undefined and unstructured. In addition to the breadth of the majority's "truly essential" standard, the statutes presently provide no systematic classification of employees according to the nature of their work and the degree to which the public can tolerate work stoppages. Only firefighters are expressly prohibited from striking and giving recognition to picket lines. (Lab.Code, § 1962.) Moreover, the four principal statutory schemes regulating other public employees establish widely differing approaches to labor relations for different types and levels of employees. (Compare Gov.Code, §§ 3500–3510 [Meyers–Millias–Brown Act, covering local government employees]; 3512–3524 [State Employer–Employee Relations Act, covering state employees]; 3540–3549.3 [Ed.Employment Relations Act, covering public school employees]; 3560–3599 [governing employment in higher education].) Thus, these statutes produce inconsistent results when, as here, the right to strike is given recognition almost across the board.

The Meyers–Milias–Brown Act, for example, provides "no clear mechanism for resolving disputes" between local governments and their workers. (Ante, p. ___ [10], fn. 14.) In the absence of an administrative agency to settle charges of unfair labor practices and compel such remedies as mediation, presumably all strike-related issues will go to the courts in the first instance, but the courts are poor forums for the resolution of such issues. On the other hand, issues arising out of work stoppages by public school employees are to be resolved by the Public Employee Relations Board (PERB) on the basis of PERB's own set of remedies. Of course, this anomalous situation is in large part the product of this court's tolerance of strikes by teachers (El Rancho

Unified Sch. Dist. v. National Ed. Assn., supra, 33 Cal.3d 946; San Diego Teachers Assn. v. Superior Court (1979) 24 Cal.3d 1, 101 LRRM 2461) and PERB's correlative expansion of its authority so that it may compel mediation or adopt other remedies in labor disputes in public education (see Cal.Admin.Code, tit. 8, § 3600 et seq.).

Finally, nothing in PERB's explicit statutory powers (Gov.Code, § 3541.3) extends to mandatory arbitration, for example, so it remains to be established whether state employees, also under PERB's jurisdiction (id., § 3513, subd. (g)), will be governed by the same ground rules as educational employees, or whether some of them, perhaps deemed "truly essential," will be subject to binding arbitration under rules that do not now exist.

I would affirm the judgment.

Justice Kaus wrote an opinion concurring in the judgment (joined by Justice Reynoso) insofar as it held that a common law tort action for damages does not lie against a public sector union for a peaceful strike. The two justices reserved judgment on the question of whether such a strike is legal or illegal in an abstract sense or whether and under what circumstances an injunction might issue.

Justice Grodin wrote a separate concurrence agreeing with Justices Broussard and Mosk that the Meyer–Milias–Brown Act had removed the underpinning for the doctrine that public employee strikes are tortious and expressing his view that a blanket prohibition of all public employee strikes would raise substantial constitutional questions.

Chief Justice Bird concurred on the ground that the right to withhold personal services in concert is protected by the First, Thirteenth, and Fourteenth amendments.

Some jurisdictions have followed California's lead. In *Davis v. Henry,* 555 So.2d 457 (La.1990), the Supreme Court of Louisiana held that all public employees have the right to strike, with the exception of strikes which clearly endanger the public health and safety. To the argument that strikes by public employees are illegal under the common law, the Louisiana Court said that this argument was inoperative since Louisiana is not a common law jurisdiction.

C. DISSONANT TREATMENT OF STRIKES: MORE ABOUT CALIFORNIA

1. In *County of San Francisco v. United Assn. of Journeymen,* 42 Cal.3d 810, 230 Cal.Rptr. 856, 726 P.2d 538 (1986), the California Supreme Court reiterated the view, per Justice Broussard, that public employee strikes are illegal only if they endanger the public health or safety.

2. In *City of Santa Ana v. Santa Ana Police Benevolent Assn.*, 207 Cal.App.3d 1568, 255 Cal.Rptr. 688 (1989), the Court held that police work stoppages remain *per se* illegal irrespective of whether the stoppage (in this case "blue flu") endangered public health or safety. At issue was the following concerted action: On July 9, 1987, 16 of 18 police officers on the graveyard shift called in sick. As a result, 24 evening shift officers had to stay on duty and work overtime for several hours. Later the same day, 41 evening shift officers called in sick. On the following morning, 83 day shift officers claimed to be ill, and the entire graveyard shift remained on duty so that normal police operations could continue.

Both the City and the Association stipulated that all police functions were adequately staffed during both July 9 and 10 by working officers overtime on extra shifts. The Association argued that a concerted sick-out is not enjoinable when it is organized in a manner calculated to avoid an imminent threat to public health or safety—the requirement of *Sanitation Workers.* The court disagreed.

3. California's Public Employment Relations Board has distinguished *L.A. County Sanitation District* and elected not to follow it. PERB has found a teacher strike to be unlawful and enjoinable where it disrupts the educational process and causes a "total breakdown in education." *Compton Unified School District v. Compton Education Assn., CTA/NEA,* Case No. LA–CO–396, 11 PERC 18067 (1987).

The distinction between *L.A. County Sanitation District* and *Compton* drawn by PERB is that the former involved a statute which is judicially enforced, calls for a kind of collective bargaining, and is silent on the subject of strikes. The latter involved a statute which is administratively enforced and which contains provisions establishing unfair labor practices which PERB interpreted to mean that intermittent strikes (as in *Compton*) are unlawful and enjoinable.

4. California's PERB has distinguished between strikes that occur prior to the exhaustion of statutory impasse machinery (mediation and fact-finding) and those that occur thereafter.

If a strike occurs prior to the exhaustion of impasse procedures, there is a rebuttable presumption that the striking union is either refusing to negotiate in good faith or refusing to participate in impasse procedures. A leading case is *Modesto City Schools v. Modesto Teachers Association,* 7 PERC 14090 (March 8, 1983).

In the *Modesto* case, the school district took unilateral action and instituted its final offer before the parties got to a bargaining impasse. This was found to rebut the presumption. PERB found that the strike had been provoked by the employer's improper unilateral action. Accordingly, it was not unlawful.

In the case of *Sacramento City Unified School District v. Sacramento City Teachers Association,* 11 PERC 18053 (February 17, 1987), the unfair practice which the Association contended justified the strike was the District's conditioning of settlement on the Union's withdrawal of pending unfair practices and grievances. PERB ruled that even in the presence of an employer's unfair labor practice, the employee organization must show a causal connection between the employer's conduct and the strike. The District's conditioning settlement of the contract on the Association's withdrawal of pending unfair practices was not a sufficient provocation for a work stoppage. Therefore, the District was entitled to seek an injunction to halt the strike.

PERB's position with respect to strikes that occur after statutory impasse machinery has been exhausted is not clear. In *Fremont Unified School District v. Fremont Unified District Teachers Association,* 14 PERC 21107 (1990), the Union (post-exhaustion of statutory impasse machinery) engaged in intermittent strikes of fixed duration without notice to the employer. PERB found that post-impasse intermittent strikes were unprotected (strikes were subject to discipline) and unlawful (possibly subject to restraint) on the ground that they support an inference that the union had not been bargaining in good faith. However, the Board rejected the District's request for injunctive relief on the ground that to seek it would not be just and proper.

PERB also held that partial strikes and slow downs are unprotected, but it is not clear whether they are also unlawful when they occur after the parties have exhausted impasse machinery.

D. STATUTORY APPROACHES: LEGALIZING STRIKES

Most state statutes explicitly forbid strikes by public employees. However, some states permit strikes in the public sector, although on a limited basis:

The Hawaii statute provides that employees may strike after they have exhausted statutory procedures, including a cooling-off period. It also provides, however, that if the strike endangers the public health or safety, the public employer involved may petition the Hawaii public employment relations board, which is charged with the responsibility for enforcing the statute, to make an investigation. If the board finds that there is imminent or present danger to public health or safety, "the board shall set requirements that must be complied with to avoid or remove any such imminent or present danger." [1]

Pennsylvania prohibits strikes by guards at prisons or mental hospitals or by employees directly involved with and necessary to the functioning of the courts, by police and firemen, and by municipal transit employees.[2] However, Pennsylvania permits, subject to exhaustion of statutory procedures, other employees to strike unless or until such a strike creates a clear and present danger or threat to the health,

1. Hawaii Rev.Stat. §§ 89–11, 89–12.

2. Pa.C.S.A. tit. 43 § 1101.1001.

safety, or welfare of the public. In that event, the courts may be petitioned for relief.[3] In 1992, the Pennsylvania legislature enacted a new statute (SB 727) which bans selective strikes where teacher union members stage walkouts on a day-to-day or building-to-building basis. Teachers are now required to give school districts 48 hours notice of a strike and are not allowed to strike more than twice in a school year. (GERR, July 20, 1992).

Vermont denies the right to strike to state employees.[4] However, municipal employees in Vermont are permitted to strike if public health, safety, or welfare is not endangered.[5] Furthermore, strikes by teachers in Vermont are nonenjoinable in the absence of a finding by a court after a hearing that the commencement or continuance of a strike "poses a clear and present danger to a sound program of school education which in the light of all relevant circumstances it is in the best public interest to prevent." [6]

The Alaska statute is a variation of the Hawaii, Pennsylvania, and Vermont models. It divides public employees, for strike purposes, into three categories:

(1) Those employees whose services may not be given up for even the shortest period of time (police and fire protection employees, jail, prison, and other correctional institutional employees, and hospital employees). Employees in this category are forbidden to strike under any circumstances.

(2) Employees whose services may be interrupted for a limited, but not for an indefinite, period of time (public utility, snow removal, sanitation, and public school and other education institution employees). Employees in this category are permitted after mediation to strike for a limited time, the limit being determined by the interests of the health, safety, or welfare of the public, as decided by a superior court upon a showing that the strike has begun to threaten these interests.

(3) Employees who perform work of such a nature that stoppages may be sustained for extended periods without serious effects on the public (all other public employees). Employees in this category may engage in a strike if a majority in the bargaining unit vote by secret ballot to do so.[7] While AS 23.40.200 permits public school and other educational institutional employees to engage in limited strikes, AS 23.40.250 explicitly excepts teachers from the definition of public employee. Therefore, in Alaska, public school teachers are not allowed to strike. See *Anchorage Educ. Assn. v. School Dist.*, 648 P.2d 993 (Alaska 1982). However, in 1992, the Alaska legislature included public school employees as class a(3) employees entitled to strike after advisory arbitration Gerr, vol. 30, p. 454 (March 30, 1992) BNA, 1992. See AS § 23.40.200(c), (d) and § 23.40.215(c)(6)(7) (1992).

Under the Oregon statute policemen, firemen, and guards at correctional institutions or mental hospitals are prohibited from striking

3. Pa.C.S.A. tit. 43 §§ 1101.1002, 1101.-1003, 1101.1004.

4. Vt.Stat.Ann. tit. 3, Sec. 903(b).

5. Vt.Stat.Ann. tit. 21 § 1730.

6. Vt.Stat. tit. 16, Sec. 2010 (Supp.1972).

7. Alaska Stat. § 23.40.200 (1972).

or recognizing a picket line of a labor organization while in the performance of official duties.[8] Other employees are permitted to strike subject to the following conditions: (1) the strikers must be part of an appropriate unit in respect of which collective bargaining has been established; (2) the unit cannot be one in which the parties have agreed to submit disputes to final and binding arbitration; (3) the organization must have exhausted the mediation and fact-finding procedures of the statute and, where appropriate, procedures for preventing unfair labor practices; (4) 30 days must have elapsed since the fact-finding board made its recommendations; (5) the organization must have given 10 days notice of its intention to strike; (6) the strike must not create a clear and present danger or threat to the health, safety or welfare of the public, as determined by a trial court.[9]

In Minnesota, strikes are generally prohibited but it is a defense to the prohibition in the case of non-essential employees that the employer has refused to submit to arbitration or has failed to comply with a valid arbitration award.[10] See *General Drivers v. City of St. Paul,* 270 N.W.2d 877 (Minn.1978).

Montana permits strikes by employees of public or private health care facilities, provided there exists another such facility within a 150-mile radius, and provided the union gives 30 days notice of the service.[11]

Illinois prohibits strikes by peace officers, fire fighters, and paramedics employed by fire departments and fire protection districts. Other public employees are permitted to strike only after the exclusive bargaining representative has requested a mediator and at least 5 days has elapsed after notice of intent to strike has been given to the public employer.[12]

Ohio denies the right to strike to public employees who are members of a police or fire department, members of the state highway patrol, deputy sheriffs, dispatchers employed by a public employer to dispatch police, fire, sheriff's department, or emergency medical or rescue personnel and units, an exclusive nurse's unit, employees of any public employee retirement system, corrections officers, guards at penal or mental institutions, special police officers, psychiatric attendants employed at mental health forensic facilities and youth leaders employed at correctional facilities. Should the aforementioned public employees engage in a strike, the public employer may seek an injunction against such strike. An unfair labor practice by a public employer is not a defense to the injunction.

Other Ohio public employees have the right to strike provided that the employee organization representing the employees have given a

8. Oregon Rev.Stat. § 143.736.

9. Oregon Rev.Stat. § 243.726. If the court finds that the strike creates a clear and present danger or threat to the health, safety, or welfare of the public, it shall grant appropriate relief, including an order that the dispute be submitted to final and binding arbitration within 10 days after entry of the order.

10. M.S.A. § 179A18.

11. MCA § 39-32-110.

12. Ill.—S.H.A. ch. 48, ¶ 1617.

ten-day written notice of an intent to strike to the public employer and to the state employment relations board.[13]

Idaho prohibits strikes by firefighters.[14] However, in *Local 1494 of the Int'l Ass'n of Firefighters v. City of Coeur d'Alene,* 99 Idaho 630, 586 P.2d 1346 (1978), the Idaho Supreme Court held that in the period of time after an old contract expires and before a new one is consummated, strikes are not prohibited. In *School Dist. No. 351 v. Oneida Education Ass'n,* 98 Idaho 486, 567 P.2d 830 (1977), the Idaho Supreme Court held that the common law is in effect in Idaho unless expressly abrogated by statute. Therefore, school teachers, as public employees, did not have a right to strike even though there was no express statutory prohibition.

Wisconsin permits strikes by all municipal employees (except firefighters and police) if *both* parties withdraw final offers and there is no judicial finding that the strike "poses an imminent threat to the public health or safety." Wisconsin has also deemed it an unfair labor practice for state employees to engage in strikes. Should state employees engage in a strike, the employer may either seek an injunction or file an unfair labor practice charge with the state employment relations commission, or both.[15]

Do any of these approaches appeal to you as a sensible way to deal with public employee strikes?

E. WHAT IS A STRIKE?

1. HEALTH AND SAFETY

Following destruction by fire of the building in which they normally worked, employees of the New York State Unemployment Insurance Department refused to work in a temporary location (for which no Certificate of Occupancy had been issued) on the ground that working conditions were hazardous and uncomfortable. The building was unheated because the boiler was not operating. The wires from the space heaters lying along the floor made walking hazardous, the electricity was deficient, the exits were limited, and one toilet was clogged.

The Taylor law's blanket prohibition against strikes reads as follows: "No public employee or employee organization shall engage in a strike, and no public employee or employee organization shall cause, instigate, encourage or condone a strike." A strike is defined as "any strike or other concerted stoppage of work or slowdown by public employees." Was the concerted action described above a violation of the Taylor law? See, *Acosta v. Wollett,* 55 N.Y.2d 761, 447 N.Y.S. 241,

13. Ohio R.C. tit. 41, §§ 4117.14, 4117.-15.

14. I.C. § 44-1811.

15. Wis.Stat.Ann. §§ 111.70, 111.80-111.94. Section 111.77 refers only to police and firefighters impasse procedures and includes a strike prohibition.

431 N.E.2d 966 (1981). See also, *Local 252, Transport Workers Union of America v. New York State Public Employment Relations Board,* 58 N.Y.2d 354, 461 N.Y.S.2d 262, 448 N.E.2d 116 (1983) where bus drivers in concert refused to operate buses which violated the requirements of the Vehicle and Traffic Law.

2. WORK-TO-RULE

While negotiations over a new agreement were in progress, the Union urged its members to refrain from (1) completing student progress reports and grades, (2) attending after-school meetings and activities, (3) supervising students except in the classroom, (4) completing attendance registers, (5) administering standardized tests, (6) providing coverage for other employees, and (7) submitting any records to school officials. Is this conduct a strike? Or do you need additional facts in order to answer the question?

See *Los Angeles Unified School District v. United Teachers of Los Angeles,* 14 PERC 21082 (1990). The Board distinguished between work which is mandatory (required by the contract of employment), discretionary (the decision to perform or not to perform is left to the professional judgment of the teacher), and work that is voluntary. Are these categories useful in determining whether the conduct is a strike? How would you categorize the following activities: Participating in teacher evaluations; submitting lesson plans to the building principal; attending weekly faculty meetings; selling tickets at sporting events; chaperoning dances and assemblies; advising student clubs?

3. SANCTIONS

A sanction is a formal expression by a teacher organization, such as NEA or the American Association of University Professors, of disapprobation or condemnation of a school system or other educational institution for specified reasons such as failing to maintain adequate standards of academic freedom. The term used by the AAUP is "censure."

In 1968, the New Jersey Education Association sanctioned the school district in Union Beach, New Jersey. The "Notice of Professional Sanctions" quoted an NEA resolution advising teachers that accepting employment in Union Beach while sanctions were in effect would be regarded as a violation of the NEA Code of Ethics and that NEA and its affiliates would develop procedures for disciplining members who violated the sanctions. The Notice was distributed to 60,000 members of the New Jersey Education Association, as well as to the Presidents and Placement Directors of all teacher colleges in New Jersey, and to like officials and others connected with state preparatory colleges in Pennsylvania, New York, West Virginia, Connecticut, Delaware, and Maryland, and to all State Education Association Executive Secretaries.

NJEA also sent a letter to teachers considering employment in Union Beach warning them that if a contract was signed while a sanction was in effect, the teacher would be in violation of the NEA Code of Ethics. Finally, the New Jersey Association proclaimed publicly (per a press release) that it would be a violation of the Code of Ethics for any teacher to accept employment in Union Beach or for any administrator who was a member of NJEA to offer employment in Union Beach as long as the sanctions remained in effect.

The New Jersey Supreme Court upheld a lower court injunction (a) restraining the NJEA from issuing any press releases, notices, or statements that a sanction had been or was being applied to the school system, and from threatening any action against persons who accepted teaching jobs in that system, and (b) directing NJEA to advise each person or agency to whom it sent the "Notice of Professional Sanctions" that the Notice was illegal.

The New Jersey Court equated sanctions and strikes, interdicting both with the following language: "Unlike the private employer, a public agency may not retire. The public demand for services which makes illegal a strike against government inveighs against any other concerted action designed to deny government the necessary manpower, whether by terminating existing employments in any mode or by obstructing access to the labor market. Government may not be brought to a halt." *Board of Education, Borough of Union Beach v. New Jersey Education Association,* 53 N.J. 29, 247 A.2d 867, 872 (1968).

Can this decision be reconciled with the free speech protections of the First and Fourteenth amendments?

Would your opinion be influenced by the fact that the invoking of sanctions by the New Jersey Education Association was preceded by mass resignations by the local teachers? Although these were genuine abandonments of employment, and were accepted by the school board, the New Jersey Court viewed the "scheme of sanctions" as a "backup" to the resignations, the two being inextricably entwined in a concerted effort to deny necessary manpower to the Union Beach school system. This decision is analyzed and discussed in greater detail in Wollett and Chanin, *Resolving Impasses in Negotiations,* in the "Law and Practice of Teacher Negotiations," 2d Ed. 1974 at pp. 6:101–6:110.

4. LOCKOUTS

Striking teachers applied for unemployment compensation. They had gone on strike when their employer, the Philadelphia School Board, insisted on renegotiating the collective bargaining agreement which it had agreed to eight months earlier because the City Council had refused its budget requests. The proposed budget would have created a deficit of about $102 million during the upcoming school year if the terms of the collective bargaining agreement were honored. Since the union refused renegotiation, the School Board unilaterally made several changes in the labor agreement, including the elimination of a wage increase. The teachers went on strike. The Pennsylvania Supreme Court found that the work stoppage was a lockout, not a strike, because the School Board was the first party to violate the agreement by altering the *status quo* on working conditions. See, *Odgers v. Unemployment Compensation Board of Review,* 514 Pa. 378, 525 A.2d 359 (1987).

5. RESIGNATIONS

If an employee, dissatisfied with working conditions, chooses to resign his job he is not "striking," is he? What if a number of employees tender their resignations at the same time; is that a "strike"? What if the resignations are executed collectively by the signing of petitions, are delivered to and held by the union for submission to the employer only if a satisfactory contract is not reached, and are set in a context of plans for picketing and other activities commonly associated with strikes? See *Board of Education v. Shanker,* 54 Misc.2d 641, 283 N.Y.S.2d 432 (1967), *aff'd without opinion* 29 A.D.2d 634, 286 N.Y.S.2d 453 (1967). On the other hand, if the mass resignations are bona fide and do not therefore constitute a strike or a threat to strike, may they nevertheless constitute unlawful "collective action"? See *Board of Education v. New Jersey Education Association,* 53 N.J. 29, 247 A.2d 867 (1968). If such action is unlawful, what remedy is available, considering the Thirteenth Amendment prohibition of involuntary servitude? See Wollett & Chanin, *The Law and Practice of Teacher Negotiations* (2d ed. 1974), pp. 6:105–6:108.

What do you think of the following reasoning, contained in an opinion of the California Court of Appeals (*In re Webb,* 91 LRRM 2018 (1975))? The case involved court clerks and a court reporter adjudged guilty of contempt for violating a court order which required them to return to work:

> "When petitioners undertook to withdraw their labor by engaging in a strike they effectively terminated their employment. Since a public employee doesn't have the right to strike his cessation or withdrawal of his labor by way of a strike is tantamount to a termination of the employment relationship. * * *
>
> "When petitioners terminated their employment by virtue of their strike against their public employer the employer was at liberty to employ and engage other persons to perform work previously performed by petitioners.[5]

5. [Footnotes numbered as in original.—Ed.] We do not deem the nature of petitioners' work to be such as to render it indispensable to the function of the superior court. We apprehend that other persons would be available to serve in the place and stead of petitioners from other sources. Court clerks would be available from the civil service lists and the private sector, and court reporters could be obtained through the services of private reporting agencies. It should be noted here that the record does not disclose that the work of the court was impeded or frustrat-

"However, since petitioners had quit their employment they were no longer under the control or direction of their employer. Hence, they could not be ordered to perform the duties incident to their former employment because, having elected to exercise their constitutional right to withhold their services, they were no longer employees of the County of Santa Clara. Accordingly, since the employment relationship no longer existed they could not be found in contempt for refusing to perform duties which they were not obliged to perform. Code of Civil Procedure section 1209 contemplates that the person wilfully neglecting or refusing to perform the duty enjoined upon him must be an officer or employee of the court."

6. INDUCEMENTS TO STRIKE

a) A state court in California issued an injunction forbidding a social workers' union, its officers and directors, and 750 unidentified "Does" and "Doe" associations, and "all persons in active concert or participation with them or in concert among themselves" from "directly or indirectly by any means, method or device whatsoever" engaging in the following conduct: (1) ordering, asking, requesting "or otherwise inducing or attempting to induce" any employee of the County to stop working for the County; (2) intimidating, threatening, molesting or coercing" the County or its representatives, employees, suppliers, or invitees; (3) striking or engaging in a work stoppage or other similar "concerted activity" against the County, or "inducing" such strike, stoppage, or similar concerted activity; and (4) picketing or causing picketing, or "causing, participating in or inducing others to participate in any demonstration or demonstrations" on any grounds or street or sidewalk adjoining grounds owned or possessed by the County on which structures are located which are occupied by county employees or in which such employees "are assigned to work."

The California Supreme Court held that the order was "unconstitutionally overbroad in that it improperly restricts the exercise of First Amendment freedoms, and further that it is too vague and uncertain to satisfy the requirements of notice and fair trial which are inherent in the due process clause of the Fourteenth amendment." Can you draft an order which would satisfy these objections? See *In re Berry,* 68 Cal.2d 137, 65 Cal.Rptr. 273, 436 P.2d 273 (1968).

b) In the context of a strike by city workers in San Francisco, a state court issued a preliminary injunction enjoining union leaders, and others, from the following conduct:

"1. Striking, or calling or inducing or giving notice of a strike, against the plaintiff, City and County of San Francisco.

ed because these petitioners quit their employment. The court clerks and court reporters who remained in employment continued to perform their duties during the strike. Notwithstanding the inconvenience caused the court by petitioners' having terminated their employment, the court continued to function.

"2. Picketing said plaintiff's facilities, buildings, and properties in support, promotion or advocacy of a strike against said plaintiff;

"3. Hindering, delaying or interfering with work at the facilities, buildings and properties of said plaintiff, in support, promotion, or advocacy of a strike against said plaintiff."

Certain union leaders were adjudged in contempt of the injunction by authorizing the publication of a newspaper advertisement which called upon the board of supervisors to negotiate in good faith, and stated, "The only way to end its impasse is through hard, determined, around-the-clock good faith negotiations." The advertisement gave the address of strike headquarters, and stated that the strike was endorsed by the local labor council and various other councils and unions. The state court of appeals upheld the contempt convictions, but a federal district judge held the convictions impermissible on constitutional grounds. Declining to determine the facial validity of the injunction, the court focused on the constitutionality of its application in the particular case:

"The only remaining question then, and the one dispositive of these petitions, is whether the injunction could be constitutionally applied to the publication of the advertisement, the language of which the state court found to constitute a 'hortatory declamation' which compelled the 'inference' that the petitioners were 'abetting and advising the striking unions and others to ignore the court orders and escalate their efforts.' (Memorandum Opinion at 10–11.)

* * *

"The Supreme Court has articulated the standards for regulating speech. For the injunction here to apply to the advertisement, and thus to justify a finding of contempt, the court was required to find that the speech involved was 'directed to inciting or producing imminent lawless action and * * * likely to incite or produce such action'. *Brandenburg v. Ohio,* 395 U.S. 444, 447 (1969). * * *

* * *

"The advertisement here in question simply urged the Board of Supervisors to negotiate by engaging in collective bargaining. The finding that it was a 'hortatory declamation * * * abetting and advising' disregard for court orders and escalation of strike effects is questionable at best. However, assuming the finding is supported by the evidence, petitioners' publication may reasonably be seen as mere advocacy of lawlessness. At most, it can be viewed as directed toward producing imminent lawless action. In either case, the *Brandenberg* standard is not met as the finding makes no mention of the likelihood that the publication would effect the result supposedly intended, nor does the record indicate such likelihood.

"Thus, this Court is constrained to find that regardless of its facial validity *vel non*, the injunction could not constitutionally be applied to the publication in question. The contempt judgment based on petitioners' supposed violation of the injunction must, therefore, be held impermissible."

Glen v. Hongisto, 438 F.Supp. 10, 17, 18 (N.D.Cal.1977), *aff'd per curiam* Ct. of App., 9th Cir. (Unreported).

F. REMEDIES FOR ILLEGAL STRIKES

1. INJUNCTIONS

SAN DIEGO TEACHERS ASSN. v. SUPERIOR COURT

Supreme Court of California, 1979.
24 Cal.3d 1, 154 Cal.Rptr. 893, 593 P.2d 838.

[In this case, the California Supreme Court held that the Public Employment Relations Board, not the employer, has the exclusive authority to seek a court injunction against a strike by school teachers under EERA which arguably involves conduct prohibited or protected by that statute. In the course of its opinion, the Court made a number of comments about the role of injunctive process in labor disputes.]

NEWMAN, JUSTICE.

It is contended, however, that even if PERB could have applied for judicial relief against the strike the grounds on which this might have been done would not necessarily encompass all grounds on which a judicial order could be granted. It is argued that PERB's determination to seek an injunction, as well as its application to the court, would reflect only a narrow concern for the negotiating process mandated by the EERA and would ignore strike-caused harm to the public and particularly the infringement on children's rights to an education. An analogy is drawn to the rule that NLRB jurisdiction to remedy unfair practices does not preempt state suits that present different issues. (See, e.g., *Sears, Roebuck & Co. v. Carpenters* (1978) 436 U.S. 180 [56 L.Ed.2d 209, 98 S.Ct. 1745] (antipicketing injunction based on location, rather than on means or objective of pickets); *Farmer v. Carpenters* (1977) 430 U.S. 290 (damages action for union's intentional infliction of mental distress); *Youngdahl v. Rainfair, Inc.* (1957) 355 U.S. 131 (injunction against pickets' violence).)

That argument erroneously presupposes a disparity between public and PERB interests. The public interest is to minimize interruptions of educational services. Yet did not an identical concern underlay enactment of the EERA? The Legislature was aware of the increase in public employee work stoppage despite the availability and use of injunctions and other sanctions to prevent or punish them. (See Cal.Assem.Advisory Council, Final Rep. (Mar. 15, 1973) pp. 197–98; Cebulski, *An Analysis of 22 Illegal Strikes and California Law* (1973) 18

Cal.Pub.Employment Rel. 2; Comment, *Public Employee Legislation: An Emerging Paradox, Impact, and Opportunity, supra,* 13 San Diego L.Rev. 931, 935). It does not follow from the disruption attendant on a teachers' strike that immediate injunctive relief and subsequent punishment for contempt are typically the most effective means of minimizing the number of teaching days lost from work stoppages. As observed in *City and County of San Francisco v. Cooper, supra,* 13 Cal.3d 898, 917, the question of appropriate sanctions for illegal strike activity is complex. Harsh, automatic sanctions often do not prevent strikes and are counterproductive. PERB's responsibility for administering the EERA requires that it use its power to seek judicial relief in ways that will further the public interest in maintaining conflicts between California agencies and courts. (*United Farm Workers v. Superior Court* (1977) 72 Cal.App.3d 268, 273 [140 Cal.Rptr. 87] (declaratory relief unavailable when issue could be raised in ALRB proceeding); cf. *Morton v. Superior Court* (1970) 9 Cal.App.3d 977 [88 Cal.Rptr. 533] (police officers' suit over terms of employment precluded by failure to resort to grievance procedure).)

There are marked similarities between EERA and NLRA (29 U.S.C. § 151 *et seq.*). Both are administered by fulltime boards (§ 3541, subds. (a), (c); 29 U.S.C. §§ 153(a), 154(a)). Both boards employ a general counsel (§ 3541, subd. (e); 29 U.S.C. § 153(d)), have rulemaking power (§ 3541.3, subd. (g); 29 U.S.C. § 156) as well as authority over questions of representation (§§ 3541.3, subds. (a), (c), 3544.5, subd. (d), 3544.7, 3545; 29 U.S.C. §§ 153(b), 159) and can investigate, adjudicate, and issue orders against unfair practices (§§ 3541.3, subds. (i), (j), 3541.5; 29 U.S.C. §§ 160, 161). Courts that review or enforce those orders must treat board findings as conclusive if supported by substantial evidence. (§ 3542; 29 U.S.C. §§ 160(e), 160(f).)

Further, as if exclusive initial jurisdiction were not amply implied by the comprehensiveness of the EERA scheme, section 3541.5 declares: "The initial determination as to whether the charges of unfair practices are justified, and, if so, what remedy is necessary to effectuate the purposes of this chapter, shall be a matter within the exclusive jurisdiction of the board." In his amicus brief PERB member Gonzales contends that a comparison of that provision with section 3541.3, subdivision (i), giving PERB power to deal with "unfair practice charges or alleged violations of this chapter," demonstrates that there is no exclusive initial jurisdiction over EERA violations other than unfair practices. He argues that a strike violates section 3549 and, therefore, is outside the exclusive initial jurisdiction. As pointed out above, however, section 3549 does not prohibit strikes but simply excludes the applicability of Labor Code section 923's protection of concerted activities. Moreover, EERA specifies no "unfair practices" but only acts that are "unlawful" (§§ 3543.5, 3543.6) and thus does not segregate unfair practices from other violations.

It is contended that to require the district to apply to PERB before suing for injunctive relief would be to require an idle act because, if

PERB had then refused to apply to the court for relief, the district would have been entitled to do so—on the theory that exhaustion of remedies is not required if completion of the administrative proceeding would result in irreparable injury. (See *Abelleira v. District Court of Appeal* (1941) 17 Cal.2d 280, 296 [109 P.2d 942, 132 A.L.R. 715]; *Greenblatt v. Munro* (1958) 161 Cal.App.2d 596, 605–606 [326 P.2d 929].) But the EERA gives PERB discretion to withhold as well as pursue, the various remedies at its disposal.[5] Its mission to foster constructive employment relations (§ 3540) surely includes the longrange minimization of work stoppages. PERB may conclude in a particular case that a restraining order or injunction would not hasten the end of a strike (as perhaps neither did here) and, on the contrary, would impair the success of the statutorily mandated negotiations between union and employer. A court enjoining a strike on the basis of (1) a rule that public employee strikes are illegal, and (2) harm resulting from the withholding of teachers' services cannot with expertise tailor its remedy to implement the broader objectives entrusted to PERB.

If PERB had declined not only to seek injunctive relief but also to issue an unfair practice complaint, would the district have been without a remedy because a decision of nonissuance is not judicially reviewable? (See § 3542, subd. (b). Since no declination was made here we need not decide what effect it might have had on the district's right to proceed in court. (Cf. *San Diego Unions v. Garmon,* 359 U.S. 236, 245–46 [NLRB refusal to exercise jurisdiction does not necessarily empower state court to act].)

The contempt orders are annulled on the ground that PERB had exclusive initial jurisdiction to determine whether the strike was an unfair practice and what, if any, remedies PERB should pursue. Our holding is limited to injunctions against strikes by public school employee organizations recognized or certified as exclusive representatives (§ 3540.1, subd. (e)).

TOBRINER, ACTING C.J., MOSK, J., and KAUS, J., concurred.

RICHARDSON, J.: I respectfully dissent * * *.

CLARK and MANUEL concurred in the dissent.

Notes and Questions

The California Supreme Court's decision in *San Diego Teachers* gives PERB vast discretion in deciding whether or not to seek preliminary injunctive relief; and, if it does so decide, to seek a form of relief which facilitates rather than impairs the success of the statutorily mandated

5. Compare *Motor Coach Employees v. Lockridge,* 403 U.S. 274, 288: "The rationale for preemption, then, rests in large measure upon our determination that when it set down a federal labor policy Congress plainly meant to do more than simply to alter the then-prevailing substantive law. It sought as well to restructure fundamentally the processes for effectuating that policy, deliberately placing the responsibility for applying and developing this comprehensive legal system in the hands of an expert administrative body rather than the federalized judicial system."

negotiations between the parties. This means that PERB's General Counsel must make some sensitive judgment calls. The first inquiry might be the traditional one in equity proceedings: Does the alleged misconduct (the strike) threaten irreparable harm for which there is no adequate remedy? The following questions would also be relevant: Who is being hurt? In what way? The cessation of what service is inflicting this harm? Can the injury be remedied in some way other than by injunction? How much activity should the injunction cover?

For example, the evidence in a teachers strike case might show that only four weeks were left in the school year, that study for college entrance examinations by senior high school students had been interrupted, and that failure to pass those examinations would prejudice the students' ability to gain admission to a college or a university. These proofs might be sufficient to support an order limited to requiring a resumption of work by the responsible teachers.

On the other hand, interruption of teaching services which the evidence showed was inconvenient or annoying but where the harm could be remedied by holding makeup classes after the strike's termination might not be the subject of restraint.

Finally, what kind of injunctive relief would have the most salutary impact on the bargaining process? For example, should requiring the complainant to bargain in good faith as a condition of obtaining injunctive relief be part of the court order?

Consider the following hypothetical:

The teachers went on strike prior to the exhaustion of statutory impasse machinery. The union filed a charge alleging that the School Board took unilateral action inconsistent with its last and best offer and failed to provide pertinent financial information, thereby provoking and prolonging the strike.

Suppose the union claims that the misconduct by the School Board is so egregious that it makes a finding as to the union's good faith both in the impasse procedures and at the bargaining table impossible to make. Should a court get into these questions? Would it be permissible for a court, in the exercise of its equitable discretion, to enjoin the union from continuing to strike and to require the School Board to rescind its unilateral acts, remanding both parties to the bargaining table, with the court reserving jurisdiction to deal with questions of good faith if they should arise? Or should the court simply ignore these considerations and deal with the question of the enjoinability or non-enjoinability of the strike? See *Modesto City Schools v. Modesto Teachers Association, CTA/NEA* (March 12, 1980) PERB Order No. IR–12, 4 PERC 11034. See also, *Public Employment Relations Board v. Modesto City Schools,* 136 Cal.App.3d 881, 186 Cal.Rptr. 634 (1982).

Excerpts from the following decision manifest the Supreme Court of Idaho's disagreement with the proposition that illegality of the act at issue necessarily requires the issuance of an injunction.

ONEIDA COUNTY v. ONEIDA EDUCATION ASSN.

Supreme Court of Idaho, 1977.
98 Idaho 486, 567 P.2d 830.

The trial court ruled as a *matter of law* that the injunction should issue and we must assume, in the absence of any evidentiary record, that he concluded that a strike by teachers is illegal in Idaho. Assuming without deciding that he was correct in this conclusion, nevertheless, mere illegality of an act does not require the automatic issuance of an injunction. *Anderson v. Trimble,* 519 P.2d 1352 (Okl.1974), cert. denied, 419 U.S. 995, 95 S.Ct. 308, 42 L.Ed.2d 269; *Nathan H. Schur, Inc. v. City of Santa Monica,* 47 Cal.2d 11, 300 P.2d 831 (1956); *State v. Davis,* 65 N.M. 128, 333 P.2d 613 (1958); *Eckdahl v. Hurwitz,* 103 P.2d 161 (Wyo.1940). Contra, *Kleinjans v. Lombardi,* 478 P.2d 320 (Hawaii 1970). See, *Carroll v. President & Commissioners of Princess Anne,* 393 U.S. 175, 89 S.Ct. 347, 21 L.Ed.2d 325 (1968).

That logic has been expressly applied to situations involving teacher strikes and the automatic issuance of an injunction has been refused and condemned. *School Dist. for City of Holland v. Holland Educ. Assoc.,* 380 Mich. 314, 157 N.W.2d 206 (1968); *School Com. v. Westerly Teachers Assoc., supra; Timberlane School Dist. v. Timberlane Educ. Assoc.,* 114 N.H. 245, 317 A.2d 555 (1974).

In the private sector the right to strike is viewed as an integral and necessary part of the collective bargaining process. However, in the public sector the denial of the right to strike has the effect of weighing the scales heavily in favor of the government during the collective bargaining process. In Idaho our legislature has made the policy judgment as to the merits of *not* providing public employees with the right to strike. Rather, it has developed statutory alternative processes to resolve labor disputes between teachers and school boards. It would not be an appropriate judicial function to fault the legislature in those determinations.

We cannot ignore an *alleged* refusal to abide by and engage in those legislatively authorized procedures for resolution of impasse situations. While neither we nor the trial court should condone or approve the calling of an illegal strike by appellants (although the record does not appear to demonstrate actual engagement in strike and picketing procedures), neither should we or a trial court condone or approve the failure to abide by and utilize the statutorily prescribed procedures for possible resolution of the problem. It has long been a basic maxim of equity that one who seeks equitable relief must enter the court with clean hands.

We hold that the trial court erred in issuing the orders complained of here in what was effectively an ex parte proceeding. If testimony had been permitted and required and the trial court had accepted as correct the allegations of the appellant regarding the bad faith of the school board he might have issued the injunction, but also as a corollary thereof required the school board to engage in the statutorily mandated impasse procedure. Such order did issue but not for some months following the issuance of the preliminary injunction.

Since the dispute between the parties and the threatened strike which resulted from non-resolution of that dispute has ended we see no necessity for a remand for further proceedings. We reverse the orders of the trial court, remand the cause and order that the temporary and permanent injunctions be dissolved. No costs allowed.

McFadden, C.J., and Donaldson, J., concur.

Bistline, Justice, concurring.

I concur in the majority's conclusion that before an injunction may issue, the district court must hold a hearing at which both the teacher's union and the school board may present their cases.

The majority addresses the question of whether public employees such as teachers have a constitutionally protected right to strike which may never be abridged under any circumstances. I concur in the majority's conclusion that *that* question must be answered in the negative—though not for the reasons cited by the majority. If, as a matter of law, the teachers had an absolute right to strike, then an injunction could never issue and the hearing procedures mandated by today's opinion would never come into play.

The question actually raised by the teachers on this appeal, however, is whether such public employees, under any conceivable circumstances, ever have a right to strike. A negative answer to this question of law, as Judge Rasmussen clearly perceived below, would likewise render unnecessary the hearing procedures mandated by today's opinion. Such a *per se* rule would also be an unwise policy for this Court to adopt in the absence of an express statutory requirement that we do so:

> "I think it is a very unwise policy to allow a trial court to enjoin a peaceful strike, in the absence of any way to insure that the underlying dispute will be discussed and settled amicably. To prohibit a strike in a context where this amounts to ending any pressure on the employer to bargain in good faith with representatives of the employees is to invite arbitrary action by the employer, illegal strikes, violence, and bitter feelings which may do longlasting damage to the community." *Anderson Federation of Teachers v. Anderson,* 252 Ind. 558, 251 N.E.2d 15, 22 (1969), (Chief Justice DeBruler, dissenting).

It seems clear, therefore, that the question is not to be answered in the negative. The authorities relied upon by the majority make it clear that the equitable remedy of an injunction should issue only after all parties have been heard and the district court has considered whether recognized methods of settlement have failed, whether negotiations were conducted in good faith, and whether the public health, safety and welfare would be substantially harmed if the strike were allowed to continue. An injunction will then issue if the district court determines that the disruption of a strike would, under the circumstances, be so great as to warrant overriding the legitimate interest of the striking public employees in having an effective means to insure good-faith bargaining by their employer. See also *School Dist. v. Holland Education Asso.*, 380 Mich. 314, 157 N.W.2d 206 (1968); *Timberlane Regional School Dist. v. Timberlane Regional Education Asso.*, 114 N.H. 245, 317 A.2d 555 (1974); *Armstrong Education Asso. v. Armstrong School Dist.*, 5 Pa.Cmwlth. 378, 291 A.2d 120 (1972). It is upon this understanding of today's opinion that I base my concurrence.

BAKES, J., concurring in the judgment and dissenting in part:

I concur in the judgment in Part IV of the majority opinion which holds that the trial court committed reversible error by entering the injunctions under the circumstances of this case. However, I disagree with the reasoning and the law expressed in Part II of the majority opinion.

Regarding Part II and the legality of teachers' strikes, it seems to me that the majority is saying that teachers' strikes are prohibited, i.e., that they are illegal, although that point is not entirely clear. But there is no Idaho statute which prohibits a strike by public school teachers. Although I.C. § 33–1271 provides for labor negotiations by public school teachers, that statute says nothing about strikes. In contrast, the statute which provides for labor negotiations by firefighters expressly prohibits strikes by firefighters. I.C. § 44–1811. In the absence of a direct statutory prohibition, what basis is there for saying that teachers' strikes are illegal?

The majority, pursuant to I.C. § 73–116, looks to the common law for the applicable rule, concluding that at common law public employees had no right to strike and that therefore the public school teachers today in this state have no right to strike. Although the majority opinion cites no authority for that common law rule, some courts have indicated that at common law no employees—public or private—had a right to strike in concert with fellow workers and that such collective action was often held to be an illegal conspiracy. However, with the passage of Section 7 of the National Labor Relations Act, 49 Stat. 449, 452, 29 U.S.C. § 157 (1935), the conspiracy element was removed and the private employee's right to strike became fully protected. *International Union, U.A.W.A., A.F. of L. Local 232 v. Wisconsin Employment Relations Board,* 336 U.S. 245, 69 S.Ct. 516, 93 L.Ed. 651 (1949). Nevertheless, some courts have continued to hold that the common law rule was not abrogated with respect to public employees. *School Committee v. Westerly Teachers Assn.*, 111 R.I. 96, 299 A.2d 441 (1973); *United Federation of Postal Clerks v. Blount,* D.C., 325 F.Supp. 879 (1971).

Even assuming that at common law public employees did not have the right to strike, that rule does not, by virtue of I.C. § 73–116, become *ipso facto* the controlling rule of law in this state. Long ago this Court stated with reference to the precursor of I.C. § 73–116:

> "By the adoption of that section this state did not adopt the common law of England when such common law was inapplicable to the conditions of the state. The territory and state of Idaho, following the lead of other states having similar statutory provisions, only adopted such provisions of the common law as were applicable to the conditions of the state." *Northern Pacific Ry. Co. v. Hirzel,* 29 Idaho 438, 161 P. 854 (1916).

Moreover, the common law was not composed of unalterable or immutable rules which survived the reasons or conditions on which they were founded. Common law rules were flexible and evolving rules which adapted to changing social conditions and practical realities of the times. That was the genius of the common law. R. Pound, The Spirit of the Common Law, ch. VIII (1921). In *Good v. Good,* 79 Idaho 119, 311 P.2d 756 (1957), this Court stated:

> "[I]t does not follow that the rule of the common law must forever remain fixed and unyielding in all cases and under all circumstances. The contention ignores or denies one of the basic virtues of the common law system. The common law is not immutable. It is a flexible legal system capable of expansion and change necessary to meet new and changed problems and conditions, or to meet a new or altered public policy evolving from such changed conditions in an expanding and developing social order." 79 Idaho at 123–124, 311 P.2d at 759.

See also Funk v. United States, 290 U.S. 371, 54 S.Ct. 212 (1933).

The changing rights of women is a good example of this common law flexibility. The common law rule regarding the legal rights of married women was, in essence that the husband and the wife were one in the law—that one being the husband. The legal existence of the woman was suspended during marriage. Blackstone, Commentaries, 189 (B. Cavit ed. 1941). The changes which have evolved in the common law rights of women are apparent—and most recently dramatic. *Reed v. Reed,* 404 U.S. 71, 92 S.Ct. 251, 30 L.Ed. 225 (1971); *Turner v. Dept. of Employment Sec., Etc.,* 423 U.S. 44, 96 S.Ct. 249 (1975); *Planned Parenthood of Central Missouri v. Danforth,* 428 U.S. 52, 96 S.Ct. 2831, 49 L.Ed.2d 788 (1976); *Harrigfeld v. District Court of Seventh Jud. Dist.,* 95 Idaho 540, 511 P.2d 822 (1973). *Cf. Williams v. Paxton,* 98 Idaho 155, 559 P.2d 1123 (1977). If we were today confronted with a gap in our statute regarding the rights of married women this Court would certainly not feel bound through I.C. § 73–116 to impose the old common law rule on women in our present society. Why then has the majority reached back into antiquity to resurrect the common law anti-strike conspiracy rule which is equally as outmoded?

The relationship between employers and workers is very different today from that in which the common law rule against strikes by workers developed. Today, collective bargaining between employers and employees in the private sector is protected—even mandated under most circumstances—by federal law. Similarly, our legislature has expressly provided for labor negotiations between public school teachers and the school districts. I.C. §§ 33–1271 *et seq.* It is also a practical and historical fact of life thoroughly recognized by judicial decisions, that the strike, or at least a threat to strike, is what brings the employees' interests to bear upon the employer. *American Steel Foundries v. Tri–City Council,* 257 U.S. 184, 209, 42 S.Ct. 72, 78, 66 L.Ed. 189 (1921). *N.L.R.B. v. Erie Resistor Corp.,* 373 U.S. 221, 233–234, 83 S.Ct. 1139, 1148, 10 L.Ed.2d 308 (1963). A labor organization that can make no credible threat to strike is simply impotent in labor negotiations.

After concluding that strikes by school teachers are prohibited and illegal the majority equivocates, it seems to me, suggesting that the trial court did not have to grant an injunction for the "illegal strike" of the school teachers if it found that the school board was acting in bad faith, citing the "basic maxim of equity that one who seeks equitable relief must enter the court with clean hands." *Ante* at 835. There is some authority for the proposition that school boards must negotiate in good faith in order to obtain an injunction to prohibit a strike as shown by the following quote from *Timberlane Regular School Dist. v. Timberlane Regular Education Assn.,* 114 N.H. 245, 317 A.2d 555 (1974):

> "Accordingly, it is our view that in deciding to withhold an injunction the trial court may properly consider among other factors whether recognized methods of settlement have failed, whether negotiations have been conducted in good faith, and whether the public health, safety and welfare will be substantially harmed if the strike is allowed to continue." 317 A.2d at 559.

It seems to me that the problem is compounded by this line of reasoning. Thus, now by mandate of this Court, not only can teachers not strike, but by judicial *fiat,* school boards must now negotiate in good faith or lose the availability of a court injunction.[1] This effectively means that the final arbiters in wage negotiations between teachers and school districts are going to be the courts who must decide whether the parties are negotiating in good faith, imposing or withholding the court's injunctive powers based upon the outcome of that finding. I doubt the wisdom of placing the courts in such a position. It is not every social ill which can be resolved by the courts. It is my considered view that, in the absence of legislation holding otherwise, our society

1. The Professional Negotiations Act provides that "the board of trustees of each school district * * * shall * * * enter into a negotiation agreement with professional employees and negotiate with such employees in good faith on those matters specified in any such negotiation agreement * * *." I.C. § 33–1271. *See also* I.C. § 33–1272(3). However, that act does not require the school district to negotiate in good faith with respect to the negotiation agreement which specifies the matters subject to negotiation. Consequently, the act does not prohibit an arbitrary or bad faith refusal by the school district to include important matters in the negotiation agreement. By exercising this unqualified power to limit the subject matter of the negotiations the school district can avoid the statutory obligation to negotiate in good faith or negotiate at all with respect to the excluded matters.

would be better served in most instances by a rule which permitted teachers to strike and school boards to negotiate within the statutory framework, whether in good or bad faith, letting economic and other social factors finally forge the conclusion of that conflict, rather than interjecting the courts into the fray where the threat of an injunction dangles over the head of teachers, but only if, in the opinion of the court, the school board has negotiated in good faith.

Our legislature, when it enacted the Professional Negotiations Act, I.C. § 33–1271 *et seq.*, which provided for negotiations between teachers' organizations and their employers, the school districts, was presumably well aware of the present state of labor relations in this country, which generally favors an economic, rather than judicial determination of wage disputes. In adopting that act the legislature might have prohibited strikes by teachers as it did in the legislation providing for labor negotiations by firefighters. I.C. § 44–1811. Having made no provision prohibiting strikes by teachers in their negotiations with school boards, it seems to me that the legislature has itself opted for an economic rather than a judicial determination of wage disputes between teachers and school boards. Therefore I cannot concur with the majority of this Court when they state, albeit by dictum, that teachers' strikes are prohibited and illegal and that courts should employ their injunctive powers to prohibit strikes by school teachers. In concluding otherwise it is not necessary to assert that the right of teachers to strike is a constitutionally protected right. It is merely enough to observe that the legislature has not prohibited strikes by teachers, and the common law strike/conspiracy rule is totally inappropriate to present day circumstances, *Good v. Good, supra.* Therefore, the right of teachers to strike is neither prohibited nor illegal.

For this reason, as well as the procedural reason expressed in Part IV of the majority opinion, I would join in the decision of the majority reversing the orders of the trial court which granted the injunctions. In light of the foregoing, it is not necessary to reach the constitutional issue in Part I, or the anti-injunction statute issue addressed in Part III of the Court's opinion.

Notes

1. The *Holland, Westerly Teachers Association,* and *Timberlane Regional School District* line of cases upon which the Idaho Court relies express a minority view. The majority position is illustrated by *Anchorage Education Association v. Anchorage School District,* 648 P.2d 993 (Alaska 1982), which holds that the illegality of a strike is itself sufficient harm to justify injunctive relief. Implicit in these cases is the recognition that by making a public sector strike illegal, the legislature has decided that it causes irreparable harm.

2. The Supreme Court of Pennsylvania held in *Gulnac v. South Butler County School District,* 526 Pa. 483, 587 A.2d 699 (1991), that parents and students who are disadvantaged by a teachers strike of nearly two months'

duration lack standing to seek injunctive relief against the striking teachers.

3. Despite the common availability of injunctive relief, some public employers have displayed reluctance to seek injunctions, or to enforce them after they have been obtained. One investigator reports that, in the case of 22 strikes or other forms of presumably unlawful concerted action which occurred in the San Francisco Bay–Sacramento areas between January 1969 and mid-July 1972, legal sanctions were sought in 18. Of these 18, the employer sought a general temporary restraining order in 14 cases, and in 13 cases a temporary restraining order issued. But in these 13 cases there were only three in which the public employer attempted to enforce the order by anything more coercive than merely serving it on pickets organization leaders, and only one individual in one strike (out of a large number cited in that strike) was eventually found to be guilty of violating the court's order. All other attempts at enforcement were dismissed or dropped as amnesty for strikers as part of the settlement or because of proof problems in court proceedings. In only two of the strikes did the order clearly result in cessation of the strike. Cebulski, *An Analysis of 22 Illegal Strikes and California Law,* 18 Cal.Pub.Employee Rel. 2 (1973). If you were counsel to a public employer confronted with an illegal strike, would you advise seeking an injunction? The same investigator reports that strikes with legal sanctions lasted twice as long (23½ days) as those without (11½). Might that be a factor in your decision? Some statutes require the public employer to seek an injunction. Is that a wise policy?

4. In some states, violation of an injunction has led to substantial contempt penalties. See, e.g., *County of Orange v. Civil Service Employees Ass'n,* 54 A.D.2d 921, 388 N.Y.S.2d 120 (1976) (fine of $200,000 reduced to $100,000). Some statutes prescribe penalties for violation of injunction. In Wisconsin, for example, a union which violates a no-strike injunction is subject to penalty of $2 per member per day, not to exceed $10,000 per day; and individuals who strike after an injunction issues are subject to fine in the amount of $10 per day. Wis.Stat.Ann. § 111.70(7m)(c)1.b.

5. See also Geiger, *A Right to Strike and the Rodda Act: A Shift in Bargaining Power,* 10 Pac.L.J. 971 (1979).

2. STATUTORY PENALTIES

Some statutes provide for express sanctions against striking unions and employees. Again, the New York Taylor Act is among the most elaborate. A union which violates the strike ban is subject to forfeiture of the right to dues check-off and to agency shop fees for a period to be determined by the state PERB, and to possible decertification as bargaining representative. N.Y.–McKinney's Civ.Serv.Law § 210(3)(f). An employee who violates the strike ban, in addition to being subject to removal or other disciplinary action provided by law for misconduct, is subject to mandatory monetary penalty in an amount equal to twice his daily rate of pay for each day in which he participated in prohibited conduct. § 210(2).

The severity of a statutory sanction which suspends a union's check-off privileges may not be readily apparent. But consider the following case.

UNITED FEDERATION OF TEACHERS, LOCAL 2, NYSUT, AFT, AFL–CIO

New York PERB, 1982.
15 N.Y.PERB 3091.

Upon the Charge of Violation of Section 210.1 of the Civil Service Law.

Before HAROLD R. NEWMAN, CHAIRMAN; DAVID C. RANDLES:

BOARD DECISION ON MOTION

This matter now comes to us on a motion made by the United Federation of Teachers, Local 2, NYSUT, AFT, AFL–CIO (Federation) on July 8, 1982. It moves this Board for an order reducing the duration of the dues deduction forfeiture penalty imposed upon it on October 8, 1976 (9 PERB ¶ 3071). The motion was supplemented on August 4 and 9, 1982 by an affirmation that it "does not assert the right to strike against any government, nor to assist or participate in any such strike, nor to impose an obligation to conduct, assist or participate in any strike" and that it does not adhere to a "no contract, no work" policy.

The dues deduction forfeiture was imposed as a penalty because the Federation engaged in an illegal five-day strike between September 9 and 16, 1975. The 1976 order of the Board provided that the dues deduction privileges of the Federation would be forfeited for an indefinite period of time, but that the Federation was authorized to apply for its reinstatement at any time after the passage of two years from the effective date of the forfeiture upon an affirmation that it no longer asserted the right to strike against any government and an indication that it no longer adhered to a "no contract, no work" policy. Moreover, the Federation was authorized to apply, after the expiration of only 14 months, for a suspension of the balance of the forfeiture upon the same conditions that it would apply 10 months later for the full restoration of its dues deduction privileges. By reason of court litigation in which the 1976 order of this Board was challenged, the forfeiture ordered by this Board was not effectuated until May 1, 1982.

The basis of the motion is that the loss of dues deduction privileges has impaired the Federation's ability to provide representational services to the employees in the negotiating units that it represents. In support of this proposition the Federation has submitted evidence that it has made substantial efforts to collect the dues by several, reasonably available alternatives.[1] Notwithstanding these efforts, and for only the

1. These include direct membership payment of a year's dues with a 10% discount; automatic checking account deduction authorization cards; and Teachers' Retirement System loans with a 10% discount. The cost of developing these proce-

months of May and June, the Federation has suffered a loss of income from dues and agency shop fee payments in the amount of $870,355, or approximately 30% of its normal income from these sources.[2] This loss has forced it to curtail services that it normally renders to unit employees. Most particularly, it refers to the temporary closing of its borough offices [3] through which it provides such services as representation in unsatisfactory rating hearings, pension advice, workshops on contract rights, and consultation in connection with grievance and arbitration hearings. The Federation indicates that these offices, the focal point for rendering assistance may have to be closed permanently if its financial problems are not relieved. It also indicates that it has had to lay off employees and since March 1, 1982 left vacancies unfilled; thus further interfering with its ability to service the employees in the negotiating units it represents.

. . .

We find the evidence submitted by the Federation to be persuasive. Although that evidence concerns only two months, a third has now passed. As the two-month loss of income is more than $870,000, the Federation has already lost more than $1.3 million in income when the third month is considered. It is more difficult to project the Federation's expenses in trying to collect its dues through reasonably alternative means, because the evidence regarding those costs does not indicate which are one-time only, start-up costs as opposed to recurrent operational costs. It is reasonable, however, to conclude that as of this date the expenses of the Federation and its loss of income aggregate about $2,000,000.

As the Corporation Counsel states, the Taylor Law, and our Order of 1976, both contemplate that the Federation would suffer some significant impact on its daily operations by reason of its strike. But neither realized the magnitude of the dues checkoff forfeiture so far suffered and as would be projected for another 11 months. * * *

Basically, the Taylor Law is designed to punish employee organizations that strike by putting them to the task of collecting their dues without the assistance of dues checkoff privileges. It does not impose a forfeiture of that dues income. This is readily apparent in the concern expressed in the Law that the financial resources of the employee organization be a factor in determining the extent of the penalty. It is also apparent in the Legislature's rejection of the recommendation of the Taylor Committee that a striking employee organization be denied

dures and applying them through June, 1982 has exceeded $500,000.

2. Our order of October 8, 1976 did not refer to agency shop fee payments. The reason for this is that the Taylor Law did not authorize agency shop fee payments until September 2, 1977. In 1977, the Legislature authorized negotiation of agency shop fee deduction privileges on behalf of employee organizations that had not forfeited dues deduction privileges. [Civil Service Law, § 208.3(b)]. The Federation has negotiated for an agency shop fee and receives approximately $77,000 a month from this source.

3. These offices usually close for the summer recess, however this shut down period has been extended.

its right to represent the negotiating unit by withdrawing its certification. The employee organization's continuing status as the certified (or recognized) negotiating representative clearly contemplates a continuing income to enable it to act in that capacity. Indeed, the last factor was emphasized by the Corporation Counsel when it previously wrote:

> It is important, as I see it, that there be in existence a viable union to carry out the complex labor relations that will exist on an ongoing basis between the Board of Education and the Teacher's Union and the teachers.[5]

The difficult and most delicate role of this Board is to balance the statutory dictate of punishment for engaging in a strike and the need to preserve the solvency of the negotiating agent so that it may fulfill its statutory purpose of representing all unit employees in the negotiation and administration of collective bargaining agreements.

This is not the first time that the Federation has sought relief from our order of dues forfeiture.[6] Previously its assertion that the dues forfeiture would threaten its solvency was denied as being "based upon conjecture." Now, however, its financial straits are real. The Federation has demonstrated that, despite substantial vigorous and costly efforts, it has been unable to collect necessary income; it has shown that representational services have already been impaired and that the continuation of the penalty will lead to the elimination or diminution of other necessary and material services to the public employees. This justifies reconsideration and modification of the forfeiture.[7]

Now, therefore, we modify our order to the extent that the forfeiture of the Federation's dues deduction privilege is suspended; that such suspension is subject to revocation in the event of a strike or strike threat. The Federation may apply to this Board, on notice to the Corporation Counsel, in April 1984 for full restoration of its dues deduction privileges.

3. DAMAGES

CITY AND COUNTY OF SAN FRANCISCO v. UNITED ASSOCIATION OF JOURNEYMEN AND APPRENTICES OF THE PLUMBING AND PIPEFITTING INDUSTRY OF THE UNITED STATES AND CANADA, LOCAL 38

Supreme Court of California, 1986.
42 Cal.3d 810, 230 Cal.Rptr. 856, 726 P.2d 538.

BROUSSARD, JUSTICE.

In *County Sanitation Dist. No. 2 v. Los Angeles County Employees Assn.* (1985) 38 Cal.3d 564, 214 Cal.Rptr. 424, 699 P.2d 835, cert. denied,

5. 9 PERB ¶¶ 3071, 3127 (1976).

6. 14 PERB ¶ 3073 (1981).

7. We are not persuaded by the Corporation Counsel's argument that we lack authority to modify our own order.

___ U.S. ___, 106 S.Ct. 408, 88 L.Ed.2d 359 (hereafter *County Sanitation*), we held that a public employees' strike is illegal only if it poses an imminent threat to public health or safety. (P. 592, 214 Cal.Rptr. 424, 699 P.2d 835.) Our opinion specifically reserved the question whether an employer could recover damages in tort for an illegal strike. (*Id.* at p. 592, fn. 40, 214 Cal.Rptr. 424, 699 P.2d 835.)[1] We address that question today, and conclude that, until the Legislature provides otherwise, the maintenance of an illegal strike is not a tort for which damages may be recovered. We disapprove *Pasadena Unified School Dist. v. Pasadena Federation of Teachers* (1977) 72 Cal.App.3d 100, 140 Cal.Rptr. 41 (hereafter *Pasadena*), the only decision in the country to uphold a damage award in such a setting, and the decision on which the trial court relied in awarding $4,080,000 in damages to the City of San Francisco in the present case.

On March 11, 1976, defendant, Local 38 of the United Association of Journeymen and Apprentices of the Plumbing and Pipefitting Industry of the United States and Canada, and every other San Francisco building trades union went on strike against plaintiff city. About two weeks after the strike began, the city successfully moved for a preliminary injunction against the striking unions and their leaders. The unions appealed from this order. Before the appeal was decided, the strike settled. The Court of Appeal nevertheless retained the case as one presenting recurrent issues of public importance. (*City and County of San Francisco v. Evankovich* (1977) 69 Cal.App.3d 41, 45, fn. 2, 137 Cal.Rptr. 883 (hereafter *Evankovich*).)

The principal issue argued in the *Evankovich* appeal was whether the injunction was affected by the enactment of Code of Civil Procedure section 527.3. The Court of Appeal held that this section, which limits the right of a court to enjoin a strike, was inapplicable to strikes by public employees. (*Evankovich,* pp. 50–53, 137 Cal.Rptr. 883.) Before reaching that issue, however, the Court of Appeal rejected the union's argument that its strike was conduct protected under the First Amendment, stating that "in the absence of an authorizing statute, public employees do not have a right to strike." (Pp. 47–48, 137 Cal.Rptr. 883.) The unions sought to distinguish prior cases on the ground that there was no showing that the strike was violently conducted or induced violence, but the court rejected that distinction, describing the enjoined conduct, picketing and advocacy of a strike against the city, as conduct seeking an unlawful object. (P. 49, 137 Cal.Rptr. 883.) Thus the *Evankovich* court, by clear implication, held the San Francisco strike illegal.

Shortly before the Court of Appeal decision came down, the city filed the present action for tort damages allegedly suffered as a result of the strike. All of the unions except defendant signed consent

1. Justice Kaus, joined by Justice Reynoso, expressed the view that the courts should not "embrace the 'solution'" of damage suits as a remedy for public employee strikes. (38 Cal.3d 564, 592, 214 Cal.Rptr. 424, 699 P.2d 835 (conc. opn.).)

decrees, agreeing to refrain from engaging in a strike for five years in return for dismissal from the city's tort action.

The case went to trial against defendant. The court instructed the jurors that the strike was illegal, and directed them to find defendant liable if they found that either Local 38 conspired with other labor unions to engage in a public employee strike, or was a concurrent tortfeasor with other labor unions engaged in a public employee strike. Rejecting the union's claim that wages and salaries saved should be set off against damages incurred, the court instructed that damages should be awarded for lost revenues, increased operating expenses, and employee overtime, but that "salaries of striking workers, paid or unpaid, have no bearing on * * * the subject of damages." The jury then returned a verdict for the city of $4,080,000 in compensatory damages. No punitive damages were sought.

Defendant appealed. Before the appeal was decided, we held in *County Sanitation* that public employee strikes were illegal only if they endangered the public health or safety. The Court of Appeal, however, found the union collaterally estopped by the *Evankovich* decision from challenging the finding that the San Francisco strike was illegal. The court then relied on *Pasadena* to uphold the damage award, rejecting the claimed deduction for wages and salaries saved as "inequitable." [2]

The petition for review presented three issues: (1) whether the union is collaterally estopped to deny the asserted illegality of the strike, (2) the availability of damages as a remedy for an illegal strike, and (3) the measure of damages. Our conclusion as to the second issue—that an illegal strike is not, in itself, a sufficient basis for the award of tort damages—is conclusive of the case. We therefore do not decide the issues of collateral estoppel or the measure of damages.

Although many states prohibit public employee strikes generally, and virtually all states prohibit such strikes under certain circumstances (see *County Sanitation,* 38 Cal.3d 564, 569, 214 Cal.Rptr. 424, 699 P.2d 835), very few decisions discuss whether such a strike gives rise to a cause of action for damages. *Pasadena* appears to be the only reported appellate decision in the country upholding a damage award to a public employer in the absence of specific legislation authorizing such an award.[3] We therefore begin our discussion with an analysis of that opinion.

The Pasadena Unified School District sought damages against a local teachers' union for loss occasioned by a one-day work stoppage. The trial court upheld the union's demurrer, and the school district appealed. Reversing the judgment, the Court of Appeal first said, in accord with then-current Court of Appeal authority, that public employee strikes were unlawful. It then held that damages could be recovered

2. The Court of Appeal also decided questions of setoff and jury misconduct which were not raised by the petition for review.

3. Eight states authorize damage suits by statute. (See Note, *Damage Liability of Public Employee Unions for Illegal Strikes* (1982) 23 B.C.L.Rev. 1087, 1090, fn. 24.)

on either of two theories: (1) "tortious inducement of breach of contract," and (2) "direct liability for harms resulting from unlawful acts." (72 Cal.App.3d 100, 111, 140 Cal.Rptr. 41.)

With regard to the first theory, the Court of Appeal noted that all of the teachers were certificated employees working under contract. Although the contracts contained no explicit prohibition against strikes, the court reasoned that because (in its view) all such strikes would be illegal, the obligation not to strike was an implicit term of the contract. Consequently, it concluded, the allegation that the union induced the teachers to breach this term of their contracts stated a cause of action for damages.

Pasadena's second theory was based upon the principle that "[t]he law of this state imposes upon everyone the duty 'to abstain from injuring the person or property of another, or infringing upon any of his rights.' (Civ.Code, § 1708.) There is a breach of such legal duty when one who performs an act not authorized by law * * * causes a substantial material loss to another. That breach constitutes the commission of a tort * * * for which an action in damages will lie." (*Pasadena,* p. 112, 140 Cal.Rptr. 41, quoting *Garmon v. San Diego Bldg. Trades Council* (1958) 49 Cal.2d 595, 606, 320 P.2d 473.)[4] Since the union aided and abetted an unlawful act causing material injury to the district, the court concluded it was liable in tort.

In the present case, the city does not allege a contractual relationship with the striking workers, or assert a cause of action for tortious interference with contract. The case went to the jury solely on the theory that an illegal strike was tortious per se, and that a union which conspired to strike or aided a strike was a joint tortfeasor liable for damage caused by the strike.

This theory (which cases refer to as a theory of prima facie tort), has been rejected by other jurisdictions. In *Lamphere Sch. v. Lamphere Fed. of Teachers* (1977) 400 Mich. 104, 252 N.W.2d 818, the Michigan Supreme Court considered a suit by a school district seeking damages from striking teachers and their union. A Michigan statute prohibited public employee strikes, but provided only for injunctive relief, plus discipline or discharge of strikers. The court declined to provide a common law remedy, stating that in "states which have statutes

4. The quoted *Garmon* decision involved a suit by a nonunion employer seeking injunctive relief and damages against organizational picketing. Our decision held that injunctive relief was preempted by the National Labor Relations Act, but that the employer retained a state right to sue for damages. The United States Supreme Court reversed, holding that state court jurisdiction in cases falling within the NLRB's statutory jurisdiction was limited to strikes and picketing involving violence or threatened violence. (*San Diego Bldg. Trades Council v. Garmon* (1959) 359 U.S. 236, 79 S.Ct. 773, 3 L.Ed.2d 775.)

Subsequently in *Petri Cleaners, Inc. v. Automotive Employees, etc., Local No. 88* (1960) 53 Cal.2d 455, 2 Cal.Rptr. 470, 349 P.2d 76, this court considered whether an employer retained a state cause of action in cases not within the preemptive reach of federal law. Our decision held that organizational picketing did not violate California law, and expressly overruled *Garmon.* (53 Cal.2d at p. 475, 2 Cal.Rptr. 470, 349 P.2d 76.)

prohibiting public employee strikes, the principle permitting a cause of action in tort for damages has not been *judicially* adopted." (252 N.W.2d p. 828; *emphasis added.*) In *City of Fairmont v. Retail, Wholesale, etc.* (W.Va.1980) 283 S.E.2d 589, the West Virginia Supreme Court of Appeals reviewed a suit by the city against striking hospital workers. Finding no cause of action, the court rejected the prima facie tort theory of *Pasadena,* and distinguished *Pasadena* 's cause of action for interference with contract on the ground that the hospital workers had no written employment contracts.

* * *

Our principal objection to *Pasadena* 's prima facie tort theory, however, relates not to the lack of precedential support, but to the relative roles of the courts and the Legislature in establishing rules to govern labor-management relations. The history of the courts in applying common law doctrines to issues of labor law has been an unhappy one. Drawing back from the prosecutions for criminal conspiracy and the sweeping injunctions of early days, the judiciary has been steadily withdrawing from this field. The first Restatement of Torts, for example, discussed at length the tortious character of illegal strikes (4 Rest.Torts (1939) pp. 91–181; the Restatement Second dismissed the subject with a brief statement that "the law of labor disputes * * * has ceased to be regarded as a part of Tort Law and has become an integral part of the general subject of Labor Law, with all of its statutory and administrative regulations" (4 Rest.2d Torts (1979) p. 2).

Parallel to this withdrawal of judicial remedies has been a steady growth of statutory and administrative regulation. California teachers are now governed by the Education Employment Relations Act (Gov. Code, § 3540 et seq.); we recently held that the authority of the Public Employment Relations Board under this act to adjudicate unfair labor practices preempts superior court jurisdiction to award damages for an unlawful strike. (*El Rancho Unified School Dist. v. National Education Assn.* (1983) 33 Cal.3d 946, 192 Cal.Rptr. 123, 663 P.2d 893.) State employees are governed by the similar State Employer–Employee Relations Act (Gov.Code, § 3512 et seq.), which also vests authority to adjudicate unfair labor practice claims in the Public Employment Relations Board. Most local employees fall within the scope of the Meyers–Milias–Brown Act (Gov.Code, § 3500 et seq.), which contains various provisions for the resolution of labor disputes.[5] Other local employees are covered by local charters, ordinances and regulations which provide methods of resolving controversies. There remain today relatively few cases in which the imposition of a judicial remedy of tort damages would not impinge directly upon an established administrative mechanism for resolving disputes between a public employer and its

5. San Francisco city employees are subject to the Meyers–Milias–Brown Act, but only to the extent that its provisions are not inconsistent with the city charter. (See *Building Material & Construction Teamsters' Union, Local 216 v. Farrell* (1986) 41 Cal.3d 651, 224 Cal.Rptr. 688, 715 P.2d 648.)

employees. The possible scope of a damage remedy has been so greatly narrowed that one senses that it would be fundamentally unfair to hold a few public employee unions liable for damage awards when teachers' unions, state employee unions, and many local employee unions would not be liable for the same conduct.

In *City and County of San Francisco v. Cooper* (1975) 13 Cal.3d 898, 120 Cal.Rptr. 707, 534 P.2d 403, we observed that "[t]he question as to what sanctions should appropriately be imposed on public employees who engage in illegal strike activity is a complex one which, in itself, raises significant issues of public policy. In the past, several states have attempted to deter public employee strikes by imposing mandatory, draconian statutory sanctions on striking employees; experience has all too frequently demonstrated, however, that such harsh, automatic sanctions do not prevent strikes but instead are counterproductive, exacerbating employer-employee friction and prolonging work stoppages." (P. 917, 120 Cal.Rptr. 707, 534 P.2d 403, fns. omitted.)

Our opinion in *County Sanitation* sounded the same theme of judicial restraint, observing that the policy questions involved in public employee strikes "are highly debatable, and best left to the legislative branch in the first instance." (38 Cal.3d at p. 591, fn. 39, 214 Cal.Rptr. 424, 699 P.2d 835.) Justice Kaus, concurring, applied this theme to the question of damages, concluding that "[i]n the absence of a determination by the Legislature that a tort action, resulting in a money damage award determined by a jury many years after the strike, is the appropriate method for dealing with public employee strikes, I do not believe the judiciary should, on its own, embrace this 'solution' to the problem." (P. 592, 214 Cal.Rptr. 424, 699 P.2d 835.)

The courts of other states agree. The Michigan Supreme Court, in rejecting a damage suit against a teachers' union, said that "the ultimate legislative goal is to achieve a prompt, fair resolution of disputes while avoiding the disruption of the educational process. To recognize alternative tort remedies would result in a substantial negative impact upon such purposes. It would encourage future school board inaction. Eventual settlements could be prolonged pending the resolution of multiple tort claims and counterclaims. The inevitable result would be to create labor law logjams in our courts and, at the same time, to exacerbate labor-management disputes." (*Lamphere Sch. v. Lamphere Fed. of Teachers, supra,* 252 N.W.2d 818, 830.)

The West Virginia Supreme Court of Appeals noted that "in most other states the legislature has made an effort to make some statutory accommodations to the labor relation problems that exist in the public sector. Indeed, it was the initial inability of the courts to judicially resolve the competing interests of private employees and private employers that led to federal legislation in the labor law field. Most if not all commentators in the labor law area agree that the complex issues in this field are ill suited to any comprehensive judicial solution." (*City of Fairmont v. Retail, Wholesale,* etc., *supra,* 263 S.E.2d 589, 595.)

And the Washington Supreme Court observed that "[i]nherent in the doctrine of judicial restraint is a recognition that the delicate balance of labor relations is now primarily the province of the legislature." (*Burke & Thomas, Inc. v. International Organization of Masters, supra,* 600 P.2d 1282, 1288.) It concluded that "all factors considered * * * in view of the delicate balance to be sought in public employee labor relations, and of the legislature's active role in regulating this process, that in the absence of a legislatively created cause of action for damages sustained by third parties, a rule of judicial restraint regarding recognition of a new cause of action for damages in favor of third parties is the appropriate rule to be followed at this time." (P. 1290.) As that court recognized (see p. 1289), the same reasoning would bar a damage action by the employer.

Those who argue in favor of a tort remedy assert that it will deter illegal strikes. (*State v. Kansas City Firefighters Local No. 42, supra,* 672 S.W.2d 99, 110; Note, *op. cit. supra,* 23 B.C.L.Rev. 1087.) The deterrent effect, however, varies inversely with the strength of the union, and the threat of damages may prolong any strike which does occur. The striking union, in negotiating a settlement, will have to consider that the employer can bring a suit for enormous damages—often far more than the union treasury—at any time before the tort statute of limitations runs. The only sensible course of action for the union is to insist, as a term of any settlement, that the employer waive its right to tort damages, and to prolong any strike until the employer agrees. Thus only the weakest unions, whose strikes may fail utterly, will be deterred by the threat of a destructive damage award; the stronger unions will face little risk. The cause of action thus may have a destabilizing effect, prolonging public employee strikes and exacerbating inequalities in bargaining power. " '[T]o allow damage suits by the employer against the union * * *, far from promoting a balance of bargaining between the parties, would probably only aggravate any existing imbalance. In situations in which the union possesses the preponderance of power, the employer would be unlikely to invoke the damage remedy for fear of exacerbating relations; and when the employer holds the power, the availability of such a further remedy would merely increase his advantage.' " (*Lamphere Sch. v. Lamphere Fed. of Teachers, supra,* 252 N.W.2d 818, 831, quoting Comment, *Collective Bargaining for Public Employees and the Prevention of Strikes in the Public Sector* (1969) 68 Mich.L.Rev. 260, 293.)

In sum, *Pasadena* 's prima facie tort theory was unsupported by prior precedent from any jurisdiction, and has been rejected by all subsequent decisions. It stands alone in opposition to the steadily growing recognition that judicial intervention to weight the bargaining balance in favor of public employers, by threatening to impose ruinous judgments on unions, is not a desirable or workable method of dealing with public employee strikes.

We therefore disapprove the *Pasadena* court's holding that an illegal strike is prima facie grounds for recovery in tort. The selection of remedies for an illegal strike is, we believe, a matter for the Legislature, and in the absence of legislative authorization courts should not draw upon commonlaw precedent to create a right to sue for damages.

We do not preclude all damage actions by employers. An employer will retain the right to sue for breach of an explicit no-strike clause.[6] (See Labor Management Relations Act, § 301, 29 U.S.C. § 185(a); *A.I. Gage Plumbing Supply Co. v. Local 300 of Internat. Hod Carriers* (1962) 202 Cal.App.2d 197, 20 Cal.Rptr. 860.) It may also sue for tortious acts occurring during the conduct of a strike. (See *United Construction Workers v. Laburnum Construction Corp.* (1954) 347 U.S. 656, 74 S.Ct. 833, 98 L.Ed. 1025; *Fibreboard Paper Products Corp. v. East Bay Union of Machinists* (1964) 227 Cal.App.2d 675, 39 Cal.Rptr. 64.) We hold only that, until the Legislature enacts to the contrary, the illegality of a strike without more is not grounds for a damage suit by the employer.

The judgment of the Court of Appeal is reversed.

BIRD, C.J., and MOSK, REYNOSO, PANELLI, and SIDNEY FEINBERG*, JJ., concur.

LUCAS, JUSTICE, dissenting.

I respectfully dissent. In *County Sanitation Dist. No. 2 v. Los Angeles County Employees Assn.* (1985) 38 Cal.3d 564, 214 Cal.Rptr. 424, 699 P.2d 835, my colleagues held that, except in limited cases presenting an "imminent threat" to public health or safety, public employees now have a right to strike in this state. I dissented, observing that this holding was contrary to the federal rule and to the vast majority of cases in other states; indeed, until *County Sanitation,* it was well established in California that *all* public strikes were illegal. (*Id.* at p. 610, 214 Cal.Rptr. 424, 699 P.2d 835 [dis. opn.].) The fact that at least *nine* California appellate decisions (cited in my dissent) had so ruled, and that no statutes were enacted to change that rule, indicated to me a legislative acquiescence therein. The majority held otherwise.

Now the majority holds that even if a strike was unlawful (posing the requisite "imminent threat" to public health or safety), affected public agencies are limited to their injunctive or administrative remedies and may not sue to recover the financial losses proximately caused by the strikers' unlawful conduct. This decision is again contrary to accepted California law. (See *Pasadena Unified School Dist. v. Pasadena Federation of Teachers* (1977) 72 Cal.App.3d 100, 111–114, 140

6. We reject, however, the reasoning of *Pasadena* that a clause prohibiting illegal strikes is implicit in every public employee contract. The conduct of the parties to this action demonstrates the contrary. After *Evankovich* held the city employee strike illegal, and before *County Sanitation* cast doubt upon that holding, the city nevertheless agreed to dismiss its lawsuit against unions which would agree to an explicit five-year no-strike provision.

* Retired Associate Justice, Court of Appeal, First Appellate District, assigned by the Chairperson of the Judicial Council.

Cal.Rptr. 41 [hg. den.].) As the Court of Appeal observed in the present case, "It is established in California that public employee unions which engage in strikes are liable for the damages which are thereby proximately caused to a municipal employer." Not anymore.

Pasadena's principal theory for sustaining damage awards for unlawful public strikes was quite elementary, and quite irrefutable: An unlawful strike is no different than any other *tort* which proximately causes injury. In *upholding* a damage award against a striking union, we stated nearly 30 years ago that, "The law of this state imposes upon everyone the duty 'to abstain from injuring the person or property of another, or infringing upon any of his rights.' (Civ.Code, § 1708.) There is a breach of such legal duty when one who performs an act not authorized by law infringes upon a right another is entitled to enjoy, or causes a substantial material loss to another. That breach constitutes the commission of a tort, under the laws of this state, for which an action in damages will lie. * * * It is further established in this state that by an unlawful and unauthorized labor practice an employer who is damaged thereby may recover damages in a tort action." (*Garmon v. San Diego Bldg. Trades Council* (1958) 49 Cal.2d 595, 606, 320 P.2d 473.)

The majority disapproves *Pasadena, supra,* 72 Cal.App.3d 160. Do my colleagues also disapprove the general tort principles noted in *Garmon, supra,* 49 Cal.2d 595, 320 P.2d 473, and abrogate section 1708 of the Civil Code? Ironically, the majority claims that its "principal objection" to *Pasadena* relates to "the relative roles of the courts and the Legislature in establishing rules to govern labor-management relations." (*Ante,* p. 859 of 230 Cal.Rptr., at p. 541 of 726 P.2d.) The majority explains that it is quite reluctant to tamper or interfere with legislative treatment of public strike issues. But the majority's reliance upon principles of "judicial restraint" rings particularly hollow in light of its abrogation of the long-standing California rule, which had been acquiesced in by the Legislature, forbidding *all* public strikes. Where was the majority's "restraint" in 1985, when it decided *County Sanitation?*

The fact remains that unlawful public strikes (which, by the majority's own definition, pose "imminent threats" to public health or safety) can result in devastating financial injury to the affected municipality. To deprive public agencies of their right to recompense for such unlawful conduct, a right enjoyed by all other persons in the absence of *statutory* limitation, is not only unsound and short-sighted, but also constitutes unprecedented discrimination against California municipalities.

I would affirm the judgment of the Court of Appeal.

WHITE v. INTERNATIONAL ASSOCIATION OF FIREFIGHTERS, LOCAL

Missouri Court of Appeals, Western District, 1987.
738 S.W.2d 933.

BERREY, JUDGE.

Plaintiffs, Loretta White and Charles A. White, brought suit against the International Association of Firefighters, AFL–CIO, Local 42 of the International Association of Firefighters, eight (8) named individuals who were union officers or representatives of Local 42 and "John Doe 1–8–70," for property damage sustained during a fire fighters' strike or work stoppage against Kansas City, Missouri. The trial court granted the defendants' motion to dismiss for failure to state a claim on which relief could be granted. Plaintiffs' contend the trial court erred in granting defendants' dismissal because a private citizen may maintain a cause of action under a theory of intentional tort against the fire fighters' union for damages occurring during an illegal strike by public employees. The judgment of the trial court is affirmed.

Plaintiffs' petition, framed in two counts, alleges in Count I that on March 17, 1980, the defendants began a strike and refused to respond to fire alarms or calls; established picket lines to hinder the City's normal operations; engaged in acts of sabotage against the City's fire fighting equipment and facilities; and that these actions were in violation of § 105.530 RSMo 1978, the prohibition against public employee strikes. It was further alleged that on March 20, 1980, a fire was discovered on plaintiffs' property located at 4003 Prospect and with the inexperienced personnel and inadequate equipment available, the fire was not brought under control and totally destroyed their real and personal property. Plaintiffs contend that had defendants "been performing the duties for which they were employed, the fire could have been brought under control with inconsequential damages to the premises and its contents." Count II of plaintiffs' petition incorporates the allegations of Count I and asserts defendants' actions established the tort of outrage.

In determining whether the trial court erred in dismissing plaintiffs' petition, this court must decide if plaintiffs' allegations invoke principles of substantive law which may entitle them to relief. *Enyeart v. Shelter Mutual Insurance Co.,* 693 S.W.2d 120, 124 (Mo.App.1985). Plaintiffs draw upon the principles set forth in this court's decision in *State v. Kansas City Firefighters Local 42,* 672 S.W.2d 99 (Mo.App.1984), in support of their assertion that a private citizen has a cause of action for damages intentionally inflicted by the firefighters who failed to perform their duty in providing firefighting services.

This court's decision in *Kansas City Firefighters, supra,* a lodestone for legal commentary, *see* Note, Illegal Public Employee Strikes: Allowing a Civil Suit for Damages, 33 UMKC L.Rev. 299 (1985), and *Note,*

Prima Facie Tort—a Judicial Reaction to Public Employee Strikes in Missouri, 50 Mo.L.Rev. 687 (1985), held that a public employer could maintain a cause of action, implied by the state statute prohibiting public employees strikes, under the theory of intentional tort for damages it incurred during an illegal public employee firefighters strike. *Id.* at 116. There, on October 3, 1975, after long unsuccessful negotiations with the City on the issue of remuneration, the firefighters' union struck the City and union members failed to report for firefighter duty. With the City in a critical situation, the Governor of the State, ordered the state militia into emergency duty. The strike ended on October 7, 1975, after the state had incurred $128,782.72 in expenses for the militia's services during this period. The State, in its amended petition,[1] pled for recovery in tort for reimbursement of those expenses. *Id.* at 104.

The *Kansas City Firefighters* court relying on the doctrine of implied rights as set forth in Restatement (Second) § 874(A), found the policy behind the Public Sector Law precluding public employee strikes § 105.530, that is, to "ensure the uninterrupted delivery of services vital to the public welfare," would be furthered by allowing a civil remedy for damages sustained during an illegal strike. *Id.* at 109–110. The court found the function of the firefighters was indispensible to public safety but confined the scope of liability to extend to only these public employees on the basis it refused to exercise its judicial power in this "delicate area of public employment." The court's decision was further restricted to those cases where it is pleaded and proven that the action intended to produce the resulting harm, or that the result was a natural and probable consequence of the intended act—requirements for the claim of an intentional tort.

The court, in its analysis of the implied cause of action, acknowledged another limitation: "the suitor must be a member of the class for whose especial benefit the statute was enacted." *Id.* at 110. The Kansas City Firefighters' court stated that the Public Sector Law was enacted for the benefit of the public body or the public employer and found the State—who provided the essential services—succeeded to the rights and remedies of the City and was the public employer, or intended beneficiary, for the purposes of the action. In this regard, the court did not further describe other potential beneficiaries but specifically stated, ["w]e need not, and do not, decide whether the policy of the Public Sector Labor Law benefits a third party other than the public employer." *Id.* at 110.

Whether a cause of action inures (beyond the public employer) to third party has been examined in only a few jurisdictions, *Boyle v. Anderson Fire Fighters Association,* 497 N.E.2d 1073 (Ind.App. 2 Dist. 1986); *Burke & Thomas, Inc. v. International Organization of Masters,*

1. An earlier action was brought by the State on a quasi-contractual theory. This court in *State ex rel. Danforth v. Kansas City Firefighters Local 42,* 585 S.W.2d 94 (Mo.App.1979), found the union was not liable under contractual theory but remanded the cause for further proceedings based on its allegations of tortious conduct.

92 Wash.2d 762, 600 P.2d 1282 (banc 1979); *Jamur Productions Corp. v. Quill,* 51 Misc.2d 501, 273 N.Y.S.2d 348 (N.Y.Sup.Ct.1966); *Caso v. District Council 37,* 43 A.D.2d 159, 350 N.Y.S.2d 173 (N.Y.Sup.Ct.1973); *Burns Jackson Miller, ETC v. Linder,* 59 N.Y.2d 314, 464 N.Y.S.2d 712, 451 N.E.2d 459 (N.Y.Ct.App.1983); *Fulenwider v. Firefighters Association Local Union 1784,* 649 S.W.2d 268 (Tenn.1982). Two of the decisions have allowed private citizens to maintain damage actions, one under a nuisance theory; *Caso v. District Council 37, supra,* 350 N.Y.S.2d at 178; and the other under an intentional tort theory, *Boyle v. Anderson Fire Fighters Association Local 1262, supra,* 497 N.E.2d at 1079–83. While these two cases rest upon different theories of recovery, both decisions tend to focus upon the same policy consideration: the public's need to have uninterrupted essential governmental services which, if suspended, would have the potential of endangering the health and welfare of the people. In *Caso v. District Council 37, supra,* the court found New York's Taylor Law involving public employee relations was to be liberally construed to effectuate its purpose and that remedies, beyond those set forth in the statute, were not precluded. Thus, the Caso court found a common law nuisance action against striking sewage plant employees could be maintained. *Caso v. District Council 37, supra,* 350 N.Y.S.2d at 178. In *Boyle v. Anderson Fire Fighters Association Local 1262, supra,* 497 N.E.2d at 1081, the court, relying heavily on the decision in *Caso* and this court's decision in *Kansas City Fire Fighters, supra,* found the Anderson City's Fire Department acknowledged in its rules and regulations that it had a duty to protect the lives and property of its citizenry and that the labor agreement with the union expressly recognized this duty. Thus, the *Boyle* court concluded the fire fighters had an affirmative ministerial duty to property owners to fight the fire and that the firefighters wilfully and wantonly failed to do so in reckless disregard of the consequences. *Id.*

The cases refusing to allow private causes of action present equally diverse analysis in reaching their conclusions. In *Jamur v. Quill, supra,* 273 N.Y.S.2d at 352–353, the New York Supreme Court held it would not imply an action because the legislature failed to expressly or implicitly provide for a cause of action and thus, refused to allow a damage suit against New York public transit workers who illegally struck. The *Jamur* court, citing to *Schmidt v. Merchants Despatch Transportation Co.,* 270 N.Y. 287, 305, 200 N.E. 824, 829, 104 A.L.R. 450 (1936), stated that "[w]hen the statute merely defines, in the interest of the general public, the degree of care which shall be exercised under specified circumstances, it does not 'create' a new liability." The Supreme Court of Washington in *Burke & Thomas, Inc. v. International Organization of Masters, supra,* 600 P.2d at 1289, similarly refused to allow a private damage action against public ferry workers who illegally struck the city under a theory of tortious inference of business relationships. The court found that the careful balancing of public employment would be disturbed and the function of the State Public

Employment Relations Commission, which is to resolve labor disputes, would be effectively usurped. *Id.* In *Burns Jackson Miller, etc. v. Lindner, supra,* 451 N.E.2d at 466, the New York Court of Appeals found the Taylor Law, previously dealt with in *Caso v. District Council 37, ASCME, supra,* 350 N.Y.S.2d at 179, did not give rise to an *implied private cause of action* because such implication is inconsistent with one of the primary purposes of the legislation: the elimination of tensions in public employer-employee relations and the maintenance of labor peace. The court noted that the Taylor Law, undergoing many amendments, including creating a Public Employment Relations Board, from the time *Caso, supra,* was decided, revealed an intent to protect the labor union's demise. *Id.* 451 N.E.2d at 466. And finally, the Supreme Court in Tennessee in *Fulenwider v. Firefighters Association Local Union 1784, supra,* 649 S.W.2d at 272, found a private action for damages against a fire fighters union and its members could not be maintained where there was no allegation of wilful or even negligent destruction of property by direct action. The court stated the claim was based only upon " 'secondary' or incidental harm as a by-product of the work stoppage." *Id.*

These cases disclose that regardless of the theories upon which the action is brought, that is, common law tort, breach of contract or statutory implied rights doctrine, the courts weigh competing policy considerations that exist between the public's need for vital governmental services and the need for harmony in public employment relations. As noted in *Kansas City Firefighters,* one of the requirements of the doctrine of implied rights is that the purpose of the Public Sector Law be furthered by the allowance of a civil cause of action. *State v. Kansas City Firefighters Local 42, supra,* 672 S.W.2d at 109. The *Kansas City Firefighters* court determined a damage suit by a public employer would further one of the primary policies of the Public Sector Law, the uninterruption of essential governmental services, a policy consideration relied on in other jurisdictions to justify other theories of recovery against Unions who participate in illegal work stoppages. The *Kansas City Firefighters* court, however, recognized (although in a footnote) "the other cognate, primary policy of the statute is to vouch-safe to public employees a means to acquit the right conferred by the United States and Missouri Constitutions of peaceable assembly and to petition for redress of grievances." *Id.*

One cannot doubt that the potential for numerous private civil actions would be an influencing factor in the firefighters' decision to strike and may effectively curtail further walkouts. As one commentator noted, however, "[a]ctions by third parties for wrongful death or destruction of valuable property * * * are more likely to threaten the existence of a union than suits for compensation for replacement labor such as *K.C. Firefighters.* This is due to the potentially greater number and virtually unlimited monetary risk involved in the former type of suit." Blackwood, *Illegal Public Employee Strikes: Allowing Civil Suit for Damages,* 53 UMKC L.Rev. 299, 309 (1985). The possibility of financial collapse of the union by large damage verdicts may also be antagonistic toward the City providing continued firefighting services. First, individual firefighters could be subject to unlimited liability under the doctrine of virtual representation, *Helton v. Hake,* 564 S.W.2d 313, 322 (Mo.App.1978), and although firefighters who do not assent to strike will not be held responsible, *State v. Kansas City Firefighters Local 42, supra,* 672 S.W.2d at 125, this potential for liability may prevent competent persons from pursuing careers as firefighters. Secondly, the bargaining process between the City and the Union could be stymied:

> It need hardly be said that indemnification for tort liability would or could quickly become a subject for bargaining which every public employee union would or could insist upon as clause in its contract thus creating costly burdens to one or another of the parties thereby complicating further the bargaining process.

Burke v. Thomas, Inc. v. International Organization of Masters, supra, 600 P.2d at 1290; *see also Lamphere Schools v. Lamphere Federation of Teachers,* 400 Mich. 104, 131, 252 N.W.2d 818, 830, 84 A.L.R.3d 314 (1977); and *City and County of San Francisco v. Local 38,* 42 Cal.3d 810, 230 Cal.Rptr. 856, 726 P.2d 538 (1986).[2] It is not hard to imagine a scenario whereby a strike is prolonged, with the possibility of liability incurring, because of the union's insistence upon indemnifications from tort actions like the one sub judice.

The decision to foreclose plaintiffs' right to sue is further buttressed by the Kansas City Firefighters court's analysis of the implied rights doctrine in which there is a limitation that "the suitor must be a member of the class for whose especial benefit the statute was enacted." *Id.* at 110. The court stated that the Public Sector law was enacted for the benefit of the *public body* or public employer, and found that the State, who provided the replacement labor, succeeded to the rights and

2. This recent decision by the California Supreme Court which held an illegal public employee strike was not a tort for which damages could be recovered, the court reversed the decision of *Pasadena Unified School District v. Pasadena Federation of Teachers,* 72 Cal.App.3d 100, 140 Cal.Rptr. 41 (1977), discussed in *Kansas City Firefighters,* and stated:

> Those who argue in favor of a tort remedy assert that it will deter illegal strikes. The deterrent effect, however, varies inversely with the strength of the union, and the threat of damages may prolong any strike which does occur. The striking union, in negotiating a settlement, will have to consider that the employer can bring a suit for enormous damages—often far more than the union treasury—at any time before the tort statute of limitations runs. The only sensible course of action for the union is to insist, as a term of any settlement, that the employer waive its right to tort damages, and to prolong any strike until the employer agrees. Thus only the weakest unions, whose strikes may fail utterly, will be deterred by the threat of a destructive damage award; the stronger unions will face little risk. The cause of action thus may have a destablizing effect, prolonging public employee strikes and exacerbating inequalities in bargaining power.

City and County of San Francisco v. Local 38, supra, 230 Cal.Rptr. at 861, 726 P.2d 538. The *City and County of San Francisco* court also discussed the holding in *Kansas City Firefighters.* It *incorrectly* stated that this court found liability to the public employer based upon quasi-contractual recovery. *See State ex rel. Danforth v. Kansas City Firefighters Local 42, supra,* note 1.

remedies of the City, and was the public employer, the intended beneficiary, for the purposes of the action. We note that in *Burke and Thomas, Inc. v. International Organization of Masters, supra,* 600 P.2d at 1286, the court stated "the primary function of [a] strike * * * is usually as a tool to gain bargaining leverage during contract negotiations with the employer. The object of the work stoppage is typically not to injure any third party, but rather to apply pressure to the employer. * * *" Under § 105.500 RSMo 1986, "public body" is defined as "the state of Missouri, or any officer, agency, department, bureau, division, board or commission of the state, or any other political subdivision of or within the state." These entities listed are those likely to engage in the bargaining process with public employees and be the direct recipients of the leverage mechanism, the strike. Thus, the intended beneficiaries of the Public Sector Law are not, individuals like the plaintiffs, but governmental instrumentalities.

In this same vein, we note that public officers are not liable to individuals for injuries or damages for the failure to carry out those duties which are owed to the general public. *Lawhon v. City of Smithville,* 715 S.W.2d 300, 302 (Mo.App.1986); *Berger v. City of University City,* 676 S.W.2d 39, 41 (Mo.App.1984). In *Lawhon v. City of Smithville, supra,* 715 S.W.2d at 302, this court acknowledged that a municipal fire department is fashioned for the benefit of the entire community and that no cause of action accrues to an individual based on a breach of duty for failure to perform services due to the public at large. It should be noted that plaintiffs' petition did not allege that the union (or its members) started the fire at plaintiffs' home or did any specific acts which prevented the personnel who responded to the call from combating the fire. Such acts go beyond the protection of the public duty doctrine. *See Berger v. City of University City, supra,* 676 S.W.2d at 42.

For the foregoing reasons, this court affirms the trial court's order dismissing plaintiffs' petition.

All concur.

Chapter 8

RESOLUTION OF BARGAINING IMPASSES

A. INTRODUCTION

One of the growth industries in this country is third party intervention in interest disputes in public sector bargaining—boards, panels, commissions, full-time neutrals, retired judges, clergymen and academics serving as mediators, fact-finders, and arbitrators. Interests disputes do not involve arguments over the interpretation and application of agreed-upon language. They are controversies over what the terms and provisions of the collective bargaining agreement should be. It is this type of dispute which, if unresolved, most frequently results in concerted job action of one kind or another.

Intervention in interests disputes is a function of the widespread intolerance of strikes in the public sector and the continuing search for substitutes. Public aversion to the proposition that employees in the public sector should have the right to engage in concerted work stoppages poses a dilemma. If the ability to strike or to make a credible strike threat is the motive power which causes the bargaining parties to make a maximum effort to reach agreement, how is the system to work if the rules, prescribed by decisional or statutory law, eliminate the strike or the threat of a strike from the process?

During the past 25 years, state legislatures have devised a multiplicity and diversity of procedural arrangements designed to make the bargaining process work without resort to strike action. These range from mediation, which is the least invasive form of intervention, to arbitration, which is the most invasive. In between are fact-finders who make recommendations and advisory arbitrators whose awards are not binding.

Where binding arbitration is the form of intervention, there are variations. Conventional arbitration involves a hearing at which testimonial and documentary evidence is received, findings of fact are made and applied to specified criteria, and a binding award is issued. In this kind of arbitration, the arbitrator frequently concludes that compromises between the final offers of the two parties are appropriate.

There are two other types of binding arbitration which foreclose the arbitrator from compromise. Both of these are called final-offer arbitration because the arbitrator must choose between the final proposals of the parties. He/she can select nothing in between.

The first type of final-offer arbitration involves a comparison by the arbitrator of each party's position on each matter at issue and an award, issue by issue. The other type is package arbitration which compels the arbitrator to make a choice between the bundle of proposals made by one party as compared to the bundle of proposals made by the other party.

Finally, there is a combination intervention called "med-arb" (for mediation-arbitration). In this procedure, the designated neutral starts slowly, with minimally intrusive activities, in an effort to persuade the parties to reach their own agreement; failing that, he/she imposes a binding settlement.

B. MEDIATION AND FACT-FINDING

AARON (CHRMN.), FINAL REPORT OF THE ASSEMBLY ADVISORY COUNCIL ON PUBLIC EMPLOYEE RELATIONS

March 15, 1973, pp. 207–8.

* * *

(1) Mediation. There is widespread agreement that mediation is the most desirable technique of third-party intervention. * * * The broad support for mediation probably stems from the fact that it involves minimal interference with the bargaining process.

The function of a mediator is to help the parties reach their own agreement. It is not his job to make an agreement for them. The theory is that an experienced, impartial outsider who brings a fresh, clinical perspective to a dispute can be an effective catalyst in moving the parties toward agreement by helping them to surmount problems of communication, to overcome hostility and suspicions, and to re-evaluate proposals and re-assess positions more realistically.

Mediation has a long and respectable history of success in the private sector; it has been provided primarily by the Federal Mediation and Conciliation Service (FMCS) and by similar state agencies. * * *

A former Director of the FMCS has described the mediation process in the following terms:

> "At one end, the spectrum begins by a decision not to intervene at all—to provide no third party assistance. At the other end of the band, the mediator can issue public recommendations: A major principle is to maximize bargaining and minimize the role of the

mediator—to exercise enough patience to let bargaining work. But the mediator must also be able and willing to "grasp the nettle"—to recognize when patience is not a virtue and to act accordingly. Most mediation decisions are decisions as to strategy and timing—not decisions on the specified issues.

"In the hands of a skilled mediator, facts are potent tools. It is seldom that publication of facts is either necessary or desirable. But they can be most useful in hard-hitting deflation of extreme positions. This is accomplished in separate head-to-head conferences or meetings, absent the embarrassment of the other side's presence and certainly not in the press. Public reference to the facts, if required at all, comes after a settlement to help save face." [110]

Mediation is employed more than any other method in public-sector interests disputes. * * *

* * *

Note

In most states mediation can be requested by either party. However, under statutes in at least six states, both parties must request this service. In some states, such as Kansas and New York, the Public Employment Relations Board will intervene either by request or on its own initiative.

The concept of "required" mediation or mediation when *both* parties have not invited it, is an inconsistency in terms because this type of intervention depends for its success on the acceptability by the parties of the process as well as its results. Nevertheless, some states have mandated mediation.

KOLB, THE MEDIATORS *

1983.
Pp. 157–159; 162–163.

DISCREPANCIES AND INDIVIDUAL ADAPTATION IN STATE PRACTICE

The state context is different. The institutional framework that developed in the private sector has, with certain modifications, been imposed on the public sector, with the exception that in time it will mature like its counterpart. The problem is that the ideology of free collective bargaining as exists in the private sector is anomalous in certain respects when translated to the public sector. First, management is not capital but government officials elected to represent the majority public interest. The framework is, therefore, multilateral, not

110. W.E. Simkin, "Fact–Finding: Its Values and Limitations," a speech to the National Academy of Arbitrators, Montreal, 1970. Published in D.H. Wollett & D.W. Sears, *Collective Bargaining in Public Employment* (Wash., D.C., 1971) pp. 201–202.

* The MIT Press—Cambridge, Massachusetts; London, England.

[Footnotes are omitted from text.]

bilateral * * *. Second, unions have options in addition to the negotiating table for voicing their stands on compensation and working conditions—electoral politics, lobbying activities, and civil-service protection.

These differences between the role of government in relation to management and labor as they exist in private- and public-sector institutions seem to underlie the images invoked by the state mediators when they describe the discrepancies in public-sector practice. Their accounts are not couched in terms of these broader institutional issues, however, but rather in terms of the immediate behavioral problems they encounter on a case. Thus the mediators emphasize the absence of decisionmaking authority on a management committee, for example, and not the underlying political structure that makes such behavior almost inevitable. The state mediators' definition that the problems in the public sector are behavioral and not structural allows them to mediate in a way that they believe compensates for the critical dynamics missing in public-sector collective bargaining and mediation. Another interpretation of the dealmaker's role may be, therefore, that it is an effort on the part of the mediators to create the dramatic impression that the ideology of free collective bargaining applies in the public sector and that the problems they face are ones primarily of development and maturity. This may explain why the state mediators frequently allude to the teaching function they perform.

The specific actions the state mediators take are consistent with this interpretation that dealmaking creates the impression that bargaining is bilateral and that the parties at the table possess the resources to reach their own accommodation. The mediators frequently try to deny or to minimize the influence of other governmental bodies. In the Reed School Committee case, for example, mediator Richards articulated this view when the school committee tried to argue that they were constrained by the town budget:

> Town Negotiator: The money in the budget is finite.
>
> Mediator: I know school committees can do whatever they want. You can make an agreement here and go back to your town meeting and get it.

In the Sheridan and Ulster School Committee cases, the mediators refused to bring the entire school committees to the session until the negotiating committees made concessions on their own. And in the Tulane Firefighters case, the mediator tried to convince the attorney to override the mayor's position on EMT. In each of these examples, the state mediators pressed the bargaining committees to act as if they had authority to settle, ignoring the multilateral context in which the parties operated.

The mediators also use their own behavior to compensate for the dynamics they believe are missing in the public sector—the pressure from a strike. This occurs in several ways. On occasion, they will actually encourage the parties to strike. In the Regis School Committee case, for example, mediator Richards made this suggestion and provided the union with numerous examples from his case experience where the union had done so to its advantage. More commonly, the mediators see themselves in a way as a substitute for a strike. As I noted in the Reed School Committee and Tulane Firefighters cases, they openly adopt an advocacy role to compensate for whatever power imbalance they perceive and do so to preserve the semblance that bargaining is bilateral between parties of equal strength. They also adopt a frenetic, high-pressured building strategy that they seem to believe compels the parties to make concessions akin to their images of the way the strike works. Mediator Richards's use of time to pressure the school committees in the Rutgers School Committee case provides an example of this. The management attorney wanted the mediator to adjourn the session so that his committee would have time to prepare its final offer. Richards responded, "You know I have to keep the pressure on. Tell them this is it. If they don't move, I'm going to certify an impasse and they'll have to go to factfinding."

The common thread in each of these examples is the way the various state mediators tried to preserve the semblance of bilateral bargaining under pluralistic assumptions consistent with their image of its application in the private sector. The outcomes of their efforts, however, suggest a different pattern—the parties did not strike, did not make concessions until the full school committee attended, and did not usurp authority from town executives. The divergence between their images and their experience seems to place the mediators in a role that is problematic for them. As they try to manage these impressions, they tend to minimize the political realities of the situation, and so risk damaging their own credibility and their relationships with the parties that they often undercut the agenda they set for themselves * * *.

* * *

Implications: The Mobilization of Bias

Collective bargaining and the institutions that support it are intended to control the ever present conflict in the system of industrial relations (Slichter, 1949). Mediation is but one of these institutions. As Simkin (1971) notes, "The primary purpose prompting the establishment and operation of every governmental (mediation) agency is the public desire 1) to prevent strikes and 2) to terminate those that get started" (p. 34).

Does mediation achieve this goal? Practicing mediators overwhelmingly believe that without mediation the number of industrial strikes would increase considerably (Indik et al., 1966, p. 33). Evidence is scarce to judge whether these practitioners are correct. Strike activity has remained relatively constant over the last quarter-century, with variations attributed primarily to changes in the business cycle and the level of real wages (Kauffman, 1978). In the public sector, resort to other impasse procedures (factfinding and arbitration) are interpreted as an indicator of the degree to which mediation fulfills its mandate. Empirical research in this sector suggests that although certain mediator strategies are more likely to lead to mediated settlements, overall the ultimate outcomes are determined by political and economic forces over which the mediator has minimal control. These findings echo Kerr's assertion that mediation may avert strikes only when they are caused by misunderstandings and faulty communications. The mediator can correct these problems. But, Kerr suggests, strikes arise from these sources when the parties are inexperienced, a transient situation. For the vast majority, he concluded, "mediation is part of the game, but not an essential one".

My observations of mediators at work support this view. * * * The state mediators, with fewer pros on their cases, attempt a more substantive contribution in the form of a deal. Yet in this sector the evidence is quite clear that the success of mediation rests more on the external forces in the dispute than on the strategic efforts of the individual mediator. This is not to suggest that the mediators' contributions are unimportant, but rather that it may be wrong to assess a particular mediation approach primarily in terms of whether the institution serves its stated goals. For there are indications in the data that suggest that mediation may be important, not for the outcomes it achieves, but for the way the process serves to preserve and reinforce the institution of collective bargaining.

* * *

AARON (CHRMN.), FINAL REPORT OF THE ASSEMBLY ADVISORY COUNCIL ON PUBLIC EMPLOYEE RELATIONS

March 15, 1973, pp. 209–12.

* * *

(2) Fact-finding. Unlike the private sector, where fact-finding is limited primarily to emergency labor disputes under the Railway Labor Act, legislation and practice in the public sector rely heavily on this technique in attempting to resolve impasses in interests disputes. * * *

The term is misleading because it implies that the sole function of a fact-finder or a panel of fact-finders is to hear and weigh evidence and make findings of fact. The truth is that, with few exceptions, fact-finders, after reaching their findings, make recommendations to the parties reflecting their judgment as to what would be a fair settlement of the dispute. Although there is some disagreement, there is an overwhelming consensus that fact-finding without recommendations is in most instances a sterile and meaningless process. * * *

The theory underlying the fact-finding process has been explained as follows:

"Fact-finding requires the parties to gather objective information and to present arguments with reference to these data. An unsubstantiated or extreme demand from either party tends to lose its force and status in this forum. The fact-finding report and recommendations provide a basis to inform and to crystallize thoughtful public opinion and news media comment. Such reports and recommendations have a special relevance when the public's business is involved. The public has a special right to be informed when the issues, contentions and merits of disputes involve public employees." [113]

This theory does not appear to be supported by experience. There seems to be surprisingly little public interest in the make-up of the fact-finding panels, the procedures they follow, the evidence they elicit, and the recommendations they make. * * *

If these conclusions are correct, the argument that the recommendations ensuing from fact-finding will, if they are made public, attract a substantial body of supportive community opinion which will generate compelling pressure upon the parties to accept them as the basis for settlement is not persuasive.

Notes

It does not follow, however, that fact finding is not useful.

1. Fact finding has demonstrated its usefulness in situations in which the union has some bargaining power serving to counter-balance the power of the employer (perhaps by reason of the union's ability and willingness to strike) and where fact finding is really an extension of mediation.

The findings of Yaffe and Goldblatt, while they are more than 20 years old, have been confirmed by subsequent studies:

> "The parties must be persuaded that the fact finding recommendations accurately reflect the terms of employment both parties would probably have agreed to if fact finding were not available as a strike substitute. If the fact finder is successful in persuading the parties that his recommendations accurately reflect the agreement that would have been reached based upon the power relationship between the parties, the recommendations will probably satisfy the 'acceptability' criterion." [1]

A study by Professor Thomas Kochan, *Dynamics of Dispute Resolution of the Public Sector,* in Public Sector Bargaining, 1978, IRRA Series, (1979), 150–190 confirms these findings:

> "The fact finding process involves more than the searching-out of the factual basis of the parties' positions; it also involves an effort to identify an acceptable compromise settlement. Most studies have found that fact finders tend to give the greatest weight to some variant of comparability. The criteria of ability to pay, cost of living, interest and welfare of the public, and 'good' labor relations practice tend to follow in mixed order as secondary factors. Underlying the application

113. Final Report, N.Y. Taylor Committee (1966), pp. 50–51.

1. Yaffe and Goldblatt, Fact Finding in Public Employment Disputes in New York State: *More Promise than Illusion,* ILR Paperback No. 10 (Cornell University, New York State School of Industrial Relations, June, 1971).

of these criteria, however, is a search for an acceptable compromise. Thus, the effort to frame a recommendation that the parties will accept or use as the basis for negotiating an agreement captures the heart of the fact finding process in the public sector. In a sense, when applied in this fashion, fact finding is little more than mediation with written recommendations." [2]

Professor John Dunlop put the point differently in his recommendations as a fact finder which ended a teachers strike in Newark, New Jersey:

> [My] recommendations * * * are designed to achieve the point toward which the negotiations of the parties were tending to converge before the strike." [3]

In other words, Professor Dunlop's judgment was based upon his prediction as to where the parties would have finally settled if they had been involved in free collective bargaining where both parties are motivated to work toward agreement by their distaste for the consequences of failure, e.g., a work stoppage.

This mediative view of the function of fact finding is particularly appropriate where, while no strike has occurred or been threatened, the history of labor relations between the parties suggests that job action is a credible, if not imminent, possibility. Both parties have bargained on the assumption that each has bargaining power. Both have been motivated to avoid circumstances in which one or the other would feel constrained to assert that power; indeed, both are committed to a system of agreed-upon settlements without overt power assertions. Accordingly, the fact finders should seek out the ground of mutual acceptability, as distinguished from each party's expressions of its "druthers," no matter how eloquently they have been stated.

The search should be guided by two other considerations.

First, in the world of collective bargaining stability and continuity are values of primary importance. The status quo is not realistically subject to major alteration or modification unless (a) there is demonstrable evidence that the status quo has proved to be unworkable or mischievous, or (b) external evidence establishes "changed circumstances" which impel modification, or (c) there is a perceptible trade-off in which the party seeking change has "bought" agreement.

Second, as far as "add-ons" are concerned, that is, proposals which break new ground, the judgment as to where the parties might have ended up if they had been involved in free collective bargaining is no more than a projection based upon an evaluation of the evidence, including the past and present negotiating environment. Fact-finders can only hope that those judgments have sufficient mutual appeal to form the basis for settlement. The same thing is true, of course, where changes from the past are indicated, of recommendations with respect to the degree of those changes.

The mediative approach to fact-finding probably works best with a tripartite panel with equal representation from each party. This is so

2. Kochan, Pages 182–183.

3. Authors' files.

because, if the objective is to arrange peace, the 'just' settlement is one that correctly assesses the relative bargaining power of the adversaries and what they will accept, and contains recommendations predicated upon that intelligence. If the neutral fact-finder is to look for accommodations to the relative power of the two parties (i.e., acceptability), it is helpful to have persons in the executive sessions of the panel who can give him informed judgments as to what will work.

2. The early enthusiasm for fact-finding as a substitute for strike action without impinging on the authority of elected political officials to make final decisions with respect to the terms and conditions of employment has waned. A practitioner in Michigan put the point as follows:

> The notion that when the public really appreciates the ultimate facts of a dispute it will generally respond constructively and compel a solution along the lines recommended is * * * a romantic illusion. Fact-finding reports are rarely publicized, rarely heeded by anyone other than the parties, and their intellectual quality is generally so low that neither party is persuaded, though one or the other may accept the recommendations for political or strategic reasons.[4]

3. Do the parties, in discharge of their mutual obligation to bargain with each other and follow impasse resolution procedures in good faith, have a duty to meet and confer and discuss the recommendations of the factfinder point-by-point?

California's PERB has answered the question in the negative. The Board specifically rejected the suggestion that the employer has an obligation to enter into a face-to-face and item-by-item explanation of its reasons for rejecting the factfinder's report. See *Charter Oak Educators Association, CTA/NEA v. Charter Oak Unified School District,* 15 PERC 22067 (1991). It is enough, said PERB, if the employer in good faith considers the factfinder's report and the union's offer to accept it, rejecting both; the impasse that precipitated factfinding continues and the employer may implement its last best offers—"policies reasonably comprehended within previous offers."

C. ARBITRATION AND OTHER FORMS OF IMPOSED SETTLEMENTS

Limitations inherent in nonfinal systems of dispute resolution have led to increased consideration of procedures by which settlements are imposed upon the parties. The most common procedure is arbitration, referred to in this context as "interests" arbitration to distinguish it from the arbitration of grievances under an existing agreement.

4. Letter in Authors' files.

SCHNEIDER, PUBLIC-SECTOR LABOR LEGISLATION—AN EVOLUTIONARY ANALYSIS *

Of the 38 statutes, 16 involve a variation on conventional arbitration, for example, last-best-offer by package or issue by issue, systems designed to shift responsibility for final terms to the parties and away from the arbitrator, thereby extending the bargaining process. Although more final-offer systems exist today than 10 years ago, it could not be said that there is a trend in that direction. Tanimoto's compilations for 1976 indicate that seven of 18 arbitration statutes at that time were based on final-offer, 39 percent of the total as opposed to 42 percent in 1986. Currently, the breakdown by type is 22 conventional, 8 final offer issue by issue, and 5 final-offer package; three offer a choice.

The overriding expressed consideration in the passage of these laws has been the need to develop peaceful procedures for resolving impasses. This objective appears over and over again in statutory policy statements and in the arguments of proponents of compulsory arbitration. By shifting finality to a third party, compulsory arbitration is intended to create a substitute both for the strike and for employer unilateralism. At one stroke a sort of balance is created between the parties by divesting them of their ultimate weapons, equity is achieved by settling impasses through a quasi-judicial forum, and the public interest is protected in that we have real collective bargaining, no strikes, and fair awards.

Few would argue that we have achieved this ideal. Compulsory arbitration is challenged most often on three grounds: (1) it does not deter strikes, (2) it has a chilling effect on the bargaining process, and (3) it involves an unacceptable delegation of governmental authority.

Notes

1. Some of the substitutes for strike action conceived by statutory law are imaginative, innovative, and complex. For example, the Iowa law blends fact-finding with arbitration by deeming the fact-finder's report a final offer which is included with the offers from each party, from which the arbitrator may select if a case goes to arbitration. The parties understand that selection of the fact-finder's report is the likely outcome if they take the arbitration step. Accordingly, proceeding to arbitration may appear to be futile. The arbitration usage rate in Iowa is 3.8% of reported disputes, one of the lowest in the country, if not the lowest.

A 1991 amendment to Iowa law exempts teachers from the fact-finding process (I.C.A. Section 20.21). In the absence of an impasse agreement between the parties or the failure of either party to utilize it, the Public Employment Relations Board will, at the request of either party, appoint an impartial and disinterested person to act as mediator (I.C.A. Section 20.20). If mediation fails, the parties must go to arbitration.

* Reprinted by permission from Public Sector Bargaining 2d Ed. BNA 1988, pp. 205–206.

The Connecticut statute governing the labor relations of municipal employees calls for the selection of a tripartite arbitration panel in the event that the parties are unable to agree on the report of the factfinder. The arbitration panel conducts hearings. At the end of the hearings, the panel certifies to the parties the unresolved issues, and each party is given twenty days to file a statement of its last-best offer on each issue. The panel must issue its decision on all unresolved issues, treating each "unresolved issue as a separate question." CGSA Section 7–474.

Under the teachers bargaining statute in Connecticut, if a school board and a teachers union cannot reach agreement, either party may submit the issues to the Commissioner of Education for mediation. If mediation does not produce a settlement, the parties may agree on a single arbitrator to deal with the dispute or they may each select an arbitrator and certify him/her to the Commissioner for appointment of a neutral chairman.

The parties are required to submit to the arbitrators their respective positions on "each individual issue" in the form of a "last-best offer." The decision of the arbitrators is final and binding. And it is not "subject to rejection by the legislative body or the local or regional school district or by referendum." However, it is subject to judicial review upon the filing of a motion to vacate or modify. The grounds for review are exceeding statutory or constitutional authority, proceeding unlawfully, making some other error of law, rendering a decision clearly erroneous in view of the substantial evidence on the whole record, or abuse of discretion. CGSA § 10–153.

The new law in Ohio is a blend of fact-finding, final-offer arbitration, and the possibility of a strike. It is described by Schneider as follows:

> The end of the routine negotiations process comes, at most, seven days after the fact-finder's recommendations. If both sides agree, the recommendations are accepted as is or as modified by the parties. If rejection is considered, votes must be taken. Either the employer or the union membership may reject the recommendations by three-fifths majority of the total body. (In the case of the state, a 60% vote of the members of both houses is necessary to reject the contract.) If the vote by both is at least 41% in favor, the contract is ratified. If either rejects the recommendation, an impasse exists and the findings are published. If there is still no agreement within seven days, designated safety services go to final-offer arbitration. Other employees may strike after ten days' notice (unless they have selected another procedure, e.g., arbitration) in advance.[2]

2. "Med-arb" has four essential characteristics. First, the parties have agreed to forego resorting to a work stoppage. Second, the intervention by the neutral is continuous throughout the negotiations process from the moment it enters the med-arb stage. Third, the neutral initially directs his/her energies toward achieving a mediated settlement—one to which the parties themselves agree. Finally, failing that, he/she imposes a settlement which the parties have agreed in advance to accept as binding.

2. Schneider, *Public Sector Labor Legislation*, Public Sector Bargaining, 2d Ed., BNA 1988, pp. 201–202.

In the mediation phase of med-arb, intervenor is a mediator who can alter the parties' bargaining power by controlling the alternative to a negotiated settlement. Through that modification of bargaining power, the intervenor has considerable leverage in pressing the parties to "accept" a settlement.

In the arbitration phase, the format is adversarial, that is, the evidence is developed and positions are taken "on the record" in a hearing.

3. The Public Service Staff Relations Act of 1967, covering Canada's federal employees, gives unions the option of referring a dispute to a conciliation board with the ultimate right to strike, or to binding arbitration before a permanent tribunal. The option must be exercised before bargaining commences. If a union chooses the strike route, agreement must be reached on a list of "designated employees," performing essential services, who will remain on the job. If a union chooses the arbitration route, it is prohibited from striking.

Early experience reflected a high degree of utilization of the arbitration option and a high degree of settlement before arbitration. Arthurs, *Collective Bargaining by Public Employees in Canada: Five Models* in Comparative Studies in Public Employment Labor Relations, Institute of Labor and Industrial Relations, University of Michigan (1971). In recent years, however, a significant number of bargaining units have switched their original option. "By 1986, . . . 64 bargaining units, representing 190,064 employees in the Central Administration, had specified the conciliation-board route; 12, representing 17,816 employees had specified the arbitration route. Thirty-six of the 39 bargaining units in the Central Administration for which PSAC is the bargaining agent and 22 of the 26 units represented by PIPSC are among those now on the conciliation-board/strike option." Goldenberg, *Public Sector Labor Relations in Canada,* Public Sector Bargaining, 2d Ed. BNA 1988, pp. 266, 305.

4. The *Triborough* doctrine that the status quo must be maintained until a new agreement is reached, even after the parties have bargained to impasse, creates difficulties where there are mandated procedures for the resolution of interest disputes. In New York State, for example, even though nonmandatory subjects must be continued in effect, disputes over their modification or elimination are not subject to the impasse procedures imposed by law, unless there is a waiver.

These problems are discussed by Professor Mary Helen Moses.

> "The practical result of the interpretation of various PERB decisions concerning the Triborough law and impasse resolution is that once a nonmandatory subject gets into a collective bargaining agreement, it remains there unless both parties agree to delete it. This effect seems to go far beyond the Triborough Doctrine's earlier concept of a legally imposed 'balance' of power (status quo in return for strike prohibition) that merely modified the private sector rule because of the public employees' inability to strike. By removing the distinction between mandatory and nonmandatory subjects for contract continuation purposes, but continuing it for negotiation and impasse resolution purposes, the artificial balance undermines the collective bargaining process and creates a material disincentive for the employer to include nonmandatory terms in collective bargaining agreements because of the practical and legal inability to treat them as nonmandatory once

the contract expires. Assume that a public employer wishes to delete a nonmandatory clause in an expired agreement from a successor contract. It attempts to open negotiations by proposing that the clause be removed or altered in some way. If the union refuses to negotiate about that issue, it has not violated the Taylor Law, because it is not required to bargain about a nonmandatory topic. If the employer continues to insist on the removal or alteration of the nonmandatory term to impasse, it is violating the Taylor Law. Similarly, the employer is prohibited from submitting the issue to factfinding, interest arbitration, or legislative determination unless the union consents." "Scope of Bargaining Under the Taylor Law: New York's Unique Situation," 56 Albany Law Review 53 (1992).

5. A fundamental question pertaining to interests arbitration is whether it is compatible with democratic values. An interests arbitrator may be called upon to decide issues with wide-ranging public significance, monetary and otherwise. Is it appropriate for such issues to be determined by a person not accountable to the political process in the normal ways in which public officials are accountable? George Taylor pointed out many years ago that binding interests arbitration cuts against our political grain: "[A] strike of government employees interferes with the orderly performance of the functions of the representative government. Compulsory arbitration is a greater threat—it entails a delegation to 'outsiders' of the authority assigned by the electorate to elected officials, who are subject to the checks and balances of our governmental institutions." Taylor, *Public Employment: Strikes or Procedures?,* 20 Industrial Labor Relations Review 617, 632 (1967).

The threat to which Professor Taylor alluded is accentuated when, as is usual, the interests arbitration is *ad hoc,* thus permitting the arbitrator to exercise his power without significant judicial or political control. Furthermore, many issues arise, such as what the manning scale for firefighters should be, whether police should patrol a route alone or in pairs, and the length of school days, which may seem inappropriate for disposition by the apolitical process of arbitration. Such questions are dealt with in the following case.

FIRE FIGHTERS, LOCAL 412 v. CITY OF DEARBORN

Supreme Court of Michigan, 1975.
394 Mich. 229, 231 N.W.2d 226.

[A Michigan statute provides for arbitration of police and fire department labor disputes by a tripartite panel consisting of one delegate selected by each party and an arbitrator/chairman selected by the two delegates. In the event the two partisan delegates are unable to agree upon a third member, the arbitrator/chairman is appointed by the chairman of the Michigan Employment Relations Commission.

In 1970 negotiations between the City of Dearborn and unions representing its police and fire personnel reached impasse, and both unions initiated arbitration proceedings. The city declined to name its delegate to either panel. As a result, the MERC chairman appointed the neutral and each panel proceeded to conduct hearings and render an award on an *ex parte* basis. The city refused to comply with the awards, and the unions brought action for enforcement.

The city challenged the constitutionality of the arbitration statute on a variety of grounds, the principal ground being that it represented an unconstitutional delegation of legislative power. The Michigan appellate court upheld the statute against these attacks. On appeal, the four participating justices of the Michigan Supreme Court divided evenly as to the constitutional validity of the delegation, thus affirming the lower court's ruling that the delegation was valid. Justice Levin, with whom Chief Justice Kavanagh concurred, was of the opinion that the delegation was unconstitutional on the ground that *ad hoc* arbitrators lack adequate political accountability. Justice Coleman regarded the statute as constitutional without qualification. Justice Williams, who in a sense provided the swing vote, was prepared to hold the statute constitutional as applied in the particular case, on the limited ground that the arbitrator was appointed by the MERC chairman rather than selected by the parties. Following are excerpts from the lengthy opinions of Justices Levin and Williams]:

LEVIN, JUSTICE: * * *

The constitutional principle restricting the delegation of legislative power is invoked against this delegation of the power to resolve a labor dispute to persons other than governmental officials or tribunals.

Also implicit in the legislative power to enact laws providing for the "resolution of disputes concerning public employees" is the power to delegate the resolving authority; clearly it was not intended that the Legislature itself decide each and every dispute.

The nondelegation doctrine, Professor Davis has written, is "almost a complete failure." In his treatise, State Administrative Law, Professor Cooper demonstrated that it is not possible to devise a "true test" for determining whether a particular delegation will be sustained, one articulating and enumerating all the factors that motivate the judicial response. In the final analysis, courts, "weighing the advantage of [the] delegation against the hazards involved," make a pragmatic analysis of whether the consequences of the delegation are so undesirable as to require judicial intervention.

Another writer pertinently notes that while "the old delegation doctrine" has been rightly repudiated as an "absolutist legal theory," the "doctrine has an underlying core of validity in that it requires that those who have been selected by a given process and from a given constituency retain the power to make ultimate policy decisions and override decisions made by others." * * *

* * *

A number of states have enacted legislation similar to Michigan's providing for binding arbitration as the terminal step in the bargaining process between municipalities and policemen, firemen and some other public employees. The highest courts of several states have upheld the constitutionality of compulsory arbitration.

Despite the uniformity of the judicial response in upholding compulsory arbitration provisions, the analysis is neither consistent nor persuasive.

The Supreme Court of Wyoming avoided the real issue by refusing to characterize as a delegation of legislative power the arbitrator's power to decide "wages, hours of service, and working conditions." [22]

The Rhode Island Supreme Court acknowledged that the arbitrator's "power to fix the salaries of public employees [is] clearly a legislative function," but analyzed a challenge to the constitutionality of the delegation in a manner which has been correctly criticized as "wholly tautological." [23]

In Rhode Island, as in Michigan, the arbitration panel consists of three members.[24] Each party selects an "arbitrator" and the arbitrators "agree upon and select and name a third arbitrator" to serve as chairman of the panel. If the parties could not agree, the third arbitrator was selected by the Chief Justice of the Rhode Island Supreme Court.

The Rhode Island Supreme Court said that the determinative question was whether decisional authority had been delegated to public officials or improperly to private persons. It reasoned that since the panel enjoys the legislative "power to fix the salaries of public employees, * * * without control or supervision from any superior" and its term of service and duties are specified by statute, each member of the panel (including the union arbitrator and the public-employer arbitrator) is a "public officer and that collectively the three constitute a public board or agency." Such nominalistic reasoning both begs the question and reduces the analysis of the issue to a reason-free debate over labels. Such reasoning could countenance the syllogism that all enactments of the Legislature are constitutional because the Legislature cannot pass an unconstitutional law.

In *Harney v. Russo,* 435 Pa. 183, 255 A.2d 560 (1969), the Pennsylvania Supreme Court upheld the constitutionality of a compulsory arbitration statute against a challenge based on the absence of statutory guidelines or standards. The Court's decision rested heavily on the

22. [Footnotes numbered as in original—Ed.] The reasoning of the Wyoming Court has been described as "superficial at best." Smyser, *Public Employees and Public Employees Unions: Their Rights and Limitations in South Dakota,* 17 S.D.L.Rev. 65, 72 (1972).

23. Comment, *Collective Bargaining for Public Employees and the Prevention of Strikes in the Public Sector,* 68 Mich.L.Rev. 260, 284 (1969). *See, also,* McAvoy, *Binding Arbitration of Contract Terms: A New Approach to the Resolution of Disputes in the Public Sector,* 72 Colum.L.Rev. 1192, 1206 (1972).

24. R.I.Gen.Laws Anno., § 28–9, 1–8.

passage, subsequent to a judicial decision striking down a compulsory arbitration statute, of a constitutional amendment authorizing the legislature to enact laws making the findings of panels or commissions in policemen and firemen disputes binding on public employers. Because of the unique constitutional history of the Pennsylvania statute, obviating analysis of the question before us, its opinion is of little assistance.

In *Pleasant Ridge v. Governor,* 382 Mich. 225, 169 N.W.2d 625 (1969), this Court sustained the constitutionality of a statute providing for compulsory arbitration to select a highway route. The principal challenges concerned the adequacy of the standards prescribed to guide the administrative commission/arbitration board in the exercise of the delegated power and the failure to provide for judicial review of the decision. This Court did not consider whether there was an unlawful delegation of legislative power to an independent and politically unaccountable person.

In *Pleasant Ridge,* in contrast to the broad-ranging power of a police or fire department arbitration panel, the power delegated—to choose between alternative highway routes—was limited. After the Legislature had itself made the decision to proceed with construction of the highway and to expend the necessary public funds and, after the location of the alternative routes was outlined, the Legislature delegated a narrow responsibility to the panel.

* * *

VI

Section 1 of article 1 of the Constitution states a fundamental principle:

> "All political power is inherent in the people. Government is instituted for their equal benefit, security and protection."

We generally classify the powers of government as legislative, executive and judicial. Of the three kinds of public officers, only judges are independent in the sense that they are not supposed to be accountable for their decisions through the political process. Persons who exercise legislative and executive power are, in contrast, expected to be politically accountable for their decisions.

When a judge considers a case, we expect independence and impartiality. We often speak of an independent judiciary, independent decision-makers in the adjudicatory function. When an arbitrator is called upon to resolve a *grievance* arising in the administration of a negotiated labor agreement, we also expect independence and impartiality.

Under the act, the arbitrator/chairman exercises delegated legislative power, political power, the kind of power the Legislature and the Governor possess. But, in contrast with the Legislature, the Governor, established agencies of government and other appointees who exercise a continuing responsibility for the administration of delegated legislative power, the arbitrator/chairman is not accountable through normal political processes for the critical decisions affecting the distribution and level of public services and the allocation of public revenues which he independently makes.

* * *

Some commentators consider the arbitrator/chairman's political unaccountability a virtue in that delegation to an outside person relieves both the union leaders and the public employer of the need to make an unpopular decision. "Rather than accepting criticism for making critical concessions, the public employer and union leaders can explain to the public and union members respectively that the blame must be shouldered by the arbitrator. It was he, and not the parties, who formulated the final award." [33]

Others have recognized this aspect of the resolution of impasses by independent and politically unaccountable outsiders:

> "By relying upon arbitration, a governmental official can avoid an unpleasant decision for which he would otherwise be politically accountable." [34]
>
> "[T]he arbitration route is becoming more interesting to some public officials who see it cynically as a way out. The arbitration board can be blamed for the tax hike which follows the pay increase." [35]
>
> "Public officials may prefer to use the arbitrator as a scapegoat rather than attempt to justify an agreement to a legislative body or the electorate.[36]

Robert G. Howlett, chairman of the MERC, the public official who, if the parties cannot agree, picks the arbitrator/chairman of the panel under the challenged act, has similarly observed:

> "One advantage of legislated arbitration, as in grievance arbitration, is the post-award expendability of the arbitrator. An award, in an emotionally charged situation, may prevent criticism from constituents or remove the threat to the re-election of a mayor or union president." [37]

Defenders of tripartite compulsory arbitration frequently cite the decision of the Rhode Island Supreme Court which concluded that the members of the panel are "public officers," a characterization at odds

33. Garber, *Compulsory Arbitration in the Public Sector: A Proposed Alternative,* 26 Arb.J. 226, 230 (1971).

34. Comment, *Collective Bargaining for Public Employees and the Prevention of Strikes in the Public Sector,* 68 Mich.L.Rev. 260, 288 (1969).

35. Gershenfeld, *Compulsory Arbitration is Ready When You Are,* 23 Labor Law J. 153, 155 (1972).

36. McAvoy, *Binding Arbitration of Contract Terms: A New Approach to the Resolution of Disputes in the Public Sector,* 72 Colum.L.Rev. 1192, 1209 (1972).

37. Howlett, *Contract Negotiation Arbitration in the Public Sector,* 42 U. of Cinc. L.Rev. 47, 71 (1973).

with the acknowledged political unaccountability of the independent arbitrator/chairman.

While delegation of authority to resolve the dispute to an independent outsider may resolve the immediate crisis and relieves the public employer and union officials of the need to justify the result, this approach to legislative decision-making, precisely because it is designed to insulate and, in fact, does insulate the decision-making process and the results from accountability within the political process, is not consonant with proper governance and is not an appropriate method for resolving legislative-political issues in a representative democracy.

VII

Generally, when legislation is challenged as an invalid delegation of legislative power, the controversy revolves around the adequacy of the standards[38] and whether there are other safeguards such as a hearing opportunity to introduce evidence, a written statement of findings and conclusions and judicial review.[39]

The challenged act provides the traditional safeguards. A hearing is required; testimony and other evidence is received; a verbatim record is made; written findings of fact and a written opinion are issued; generalized standards to guide the exercise of this delegated power are stated;[40] and the decision is subject to judicial review. All that is generally required has been done.

38. See majority and dissenting opinions, *People v. Fields* (on rehearing), 391 Mich. 206, 216 N.W.2d 51 (1974).

39. See the extensive writings of Professor Kenneth Culp Davis, e.g., Davis, Administrative Law Treatise (1970 Supp.), § 2.00, *et seq.*

40. "Where there is no agreement between the parties, or where there is an agreement but the parties have begun negotiations or discussions looking to a new agreement or amendment of the existing agreement, and wage rates or other conditions of employment under the proposed new or amended agreement are in dispute, the arbitration panel shall base its findings, opinions and order upon the following factors, as applicable:

"(a) The lawful authority of the employer.

"(b) Stipulations of the parties.

"(c) The interests and welfare of the public and the financial ability of the unit of government to meet these costs.

"(d) Comparison of the wages, hours and conditions of employment of the employees involved in the arbitration proceeding with the wages, hours and conditions of employment of other employees performing similar services and with other employees generally:

"(i) In public employment in comparable communities.

"(ii) In private employment in comparable communities.

"(e) The average consumer prices for goods and services, commonly known as the cost of living.

"(f) The overall compensation presently received by the employees, including direct wage compensation, vacations, holidays and other excused time, insurance and pensions, medical and hospitalization benefits, the continuity and stability of employment, and all other benefits received.

"(g) Changes in any of the foregoing circumstances during the pendency of the arbitration proceedings.

"(h) Such other factors, not confined to the foregoing, which are normally or traditionally taken into consideration in the determination of wages, hours and conditions of employment through voluntary collective bargaining, mediation, fact-finding, arbitration or otherwise between the parties, in the public service or in private employment. M.C.L.A. § 423.239; M.S.A. § 17.455(39).

Generally, however, discretionary power of this kind is vested in a governmental officer or agency with continuing responsibility for the day-to-day exercise of the delegated power in similar cases. The decision maker is not "expendable" but, rather, is responsible through the appointing authority to the electorate for the manner in which he exercises the delegated power.

Because decision making is concentrated in one person or agency exercising the delegated power on a continuing basis, the public can focus on the manner in which the power is exercised and can hold the appointing authority accountable.

Here decision-making power has been dispersed through so many individual, independent arbitrators that it is not possible to hold any public official or authority responsible for the manner in which the delegated power has been exercised.

A.

It is argued that while the act is susceptible of such an unconstitutional delegation, there is no unconstitutional delegation of power under the facts of this case because the arbitrator/chairman of each panel was appointed by the chairman of the MERC and if the city had named delegates to the panels, each panel would have consisted of a majority of publicly responsible arbitrators.

(On the other hand, if the city had named a delegate and the delegates named by the union and the city had, as contemplated by the act, agreed on an arbitrator/chairman for each panel, the panels would not have consisted of a majority of publicly responsible arbitrators, and this legislation as applied would then, presumably, have been unconstitutional. In this analysis, the provision of Act 312 [41] authorizing the delegates selected by the parties to select the arbitrator/chairman is unconstitutional because if the delegates do in fact select the arbitrator/chairman there could not be a majority of publicly responsible arbitrators—with the result that the act is constitutional to the extent it does not work as contemplated).

The chairman of the MERC is indeed appointed by and accountable to the Governor. The chairman of the MERC, if the parties cannot agree on the arbitrator/chairman of the panel, is, however, required to choose as arbitrator/chairman an "impartial" person.[42]

Political intervention would be regarded as an unwarranted intrusion on the independence of the "impartial" decision maker. It would be regarded as improper for the chairman of the MERC or higher governmental authority to attempt to influence the arbitrator/chairman.

41. M.C.L.A. 423.235; M.S.A. 17.455(35).

42. "[A]n impartial, competent and reputable citizen." M.C.L.A. 423.235; M.S.A. 17.455(35).

Additionally, as the present chairman of the MERC observed, the arbitrator/chairman appointed by him is "expendable." (See text accompanying fn. 37.) The arbitrator/chairman's decision relieves city and union officials from responsibility for the result and, if the other publicly responsible arbitrator dissents from the arbitrator/chairman's decision, also relieves him from responsibility for the result.

The chairman of the MERC and his superior, the Governor, properly do not regard themselves to be and are not generally regarded by the citizenry as responsible or accountable for the decisions of the *ad hoc,* outside arbitrator/chairman. The statutory duty of the chairman of the MERC is to appoint an "impartial" person as arbitrator/chairman. He is not expected to appoint an arbitrator/chairman who will render a decision which will have the support of the electorate or of their elected representatives.

After the award is made, the arbitrator/chairman goes back to his other pursuits. He does not answer to the chairman of the MERC nor does his livelihood depend on retaining the chairman's favor. The *ad hoc* relationship between the arbitrator/chairman of an arbitration panel and the chairman of the MERC is too attenuated to provide political accountability. Interdependence and continuity—not expendability—are characteristic of accountability.

B.

It has been contended that the arbitrator/chairman exercises quasi-judicial power.

One can accept the characterization that the arbitrator/chairman's decision is in the nature of an adjudication of the differences that exist between the parties without accepting the conclusion that this delegation is constitutional.

Viewed as a method of determining the wages and working conditions of particular persons employed by a particular employer, the arbitrator/chairman's decision is indeed in the nature of an adjudication. As such, the process by which the decision is reached properly includes the procedural safeguards of a hearing, fact finding and judicial review.

But his decision does more than resolve the differences between the parties. It affects the allocation of public resources, the level of public services provided the community as a whole and the cost of government. It also establishes precedents affecting the terms and conditions of public employment generally in both the directly-affected and other units of government.

The arbitrator/chairman cannot formally mandate, but his decision may necessitate, an increase in taxes. In this instance, Dearborn being a "city * * * the tax limitations of which are provided by charter or by general law," [43] there is no constitutional impediment to levy by

43. Const. 1963, art. 9, § 6.

the city of additional taxes. But other taxing units to which this method of resolving collective bargaining impasses might be extended, e.g., school districts, are subject to the 15–mill limitation and the levy of additional millage ordinarily requires a vote of the people. Cf. *Advisory Opinion re Constitutionality of 1973 PA 1 and 2,* 390 Mich. 166, 180 *et seq.,* 211 N.W.2d 28 (1973).[44]

It may not be prudent or possible to cut expenditures or reduce personnel. There is a level below which police and fire services cannot safely be reduced. Additionally if in response to a wage increase awarded by the arbitrator/chairman the city were to lay off, as an economy measure, policemen or firemen, a reduction in manpower so timed would no doubt be viewed by the unions as retaliatory, as a bad faith attempt to circumvent the arbitrator/chairman's decision, and could precipitate the strike which compulsory arbitration is said to "foreclose."

Viewed from the governmental perspective, from the perspective of the citizens/taxpayers, the decision is legislative-political.

* * *

C.

The PERA, like the NLRA, provides that it is the mutual obligation of the employer and the representative of the employees to bargain collectively regarding "wages, hours, and other terms and conditions of employment." [45]

Michigan has adopted a broad view of "conditions of employment," making most issues mandatory subjects of collective bargaining and, presumably, subject to arbitration under Act 312. See *Detroit Police Officers Association v. Detroit* [391 Mich. 44, 214 N.W.2d 803], holding that residency and the employees' retirement plan are mandatory subjects of collective bargaining.[46]

Act 312 provides a means of resolving impasses in policemen and firemen collective bargaining. Act 312 arbitration panels decide the

44. We advised the Legislature that an act providing for repayment with non-voted millage of school district notes issued to fund accumulated operating deficits does not violate the 15–mill limitation.

We also noted * * * that "[t]he Legislature may impose whatever limitations it deems necessary to prevent deficit spending and the issuance of bonds and other evidence of indebtedness."

A statute provides that school districts receiving state school aid "shall not adopt or operate under a deficit budget and a district shall not incur an operating deficit in any fund in any fiscal year. Each district shall submit its adopted budget for the current fiscal year to the department before November 1. If the department determines that the district is in violation of this section, the district shall not be allotted or paid any further sum under this act until a new budget is submitted and determined by the department to be in compliance with this section. However any district with a deficit as of June 30, 1973 that demonstrates progress in eliminating this deficit is not in violation of this section." M.C.L.A. 388.1202; M.S.A. 15.1919(602).

See, also, concurring opinion of Justice Williams at p. 185.

45. M.C.L.A. § 423.215; M.S.A. § 17.-455(15); § 8(d) of the NLRA (29 U.S.C. § 158[d]).

46. Cf. *Regents of the University of Michigan v. Employment Relations Commission,* 389 Mich. 96, 109, 204 N.W.2d 218, 82 LRRM 2909 (1973).

legislative-political questions involved in determining the wages, hours and the other terms and conditions of employment of policemen and firemen.

The only issue remaining unresolved in the pending Detroit police officers arbitration proceeding is the manifestly legislative [47]–political question whether Detroit residency should continue to be a condition of police employment. An arbitration panel recently concluded that supervisory police officers in the City of Inkster need no longer reside within the environs of that city.[48]

The Court of Appeals, relying [49] on federal cases, which have held that workloads, work rules, management-right clauses and safety are among the conditions of employment,[50] ruled that an Act 312 arbitration panel has "jurisdiction" to make a "manpower award," to decide the number of firemen to be on duty at a particular time, on the rationale that such a decision affects "the firemen's safety." [51]

A broad range of questions may affect the safety of firemen and policemen—and concomitantly the safety of the entire community—e.g., whether policemen shall patrol or ride in squad cars, alone, in pairs or in greater numbers, how many firefighters shall be assigned to each pumper and what kind of firearms and firefighting equipment shall be used. Act 312 panels have made precisely those kinds of decisions.

The arbitrator/chairman might, in making a decision regarding crew size, require an increase in the total work force and is in a position to preclude a reduction in force (assuming for the moment that

47. "[T]he question of whether or not to make residence within a city a condition of employment is one which must be largely addressed to the legislative branch of government." *Williams v. Civil Service Commission of the City of Detroit,* 383 Mich. 507, 517, 176 N.W.2d 593 (1970).

48. The "command" officers of the Inkster Police Department were in a separate bargaining unit from the patrolmen. The arbitration panel's decision concerned the command officers' contract only. *In the Matter of the Arbitration between The City of Inkster and Teamster Local # 214 Police Command Unit,* MERC Mich. PA–312—Interest Arbitration opinion of M. David Keefe, Chairman, March 4, 1975.

49. "In construing the provisions and ramifications of the PERA, this Court has frequently looked to decisions of the Federal courts which construe and apply the National Labor Relations Act." *Kaleva–Norman–Dickson School District v. Kaleva–Norman–Dickson Teachers' Association,* 393 Mich. 583, 590–91, 227 N.W.2d 500, 503 (1975).

50. See Morris, *The Developing Labor Law,* pp. 404, 405, 409, 410.

51. "The union representative testified that the number of firemen on duty affected not only the public safety, but also the firemen's safety. This position was supported by extensive testimony concerning fire fighting practices and procedures. *A safety practice is a condition of employment.* [Emphasis supplied.] *NLRB v. Gulf Power Co.,* 384 F.2d 822, 66 LRRM 2501 (CA5, 1967): *NLRB v. Miller Brewing Co.,* 408 F.2d 12, 70 LRRM 2907 (CA9, 1969); *Fibreboard Paper Products Corp. v. NLRB,* 379 U.S. 203, 57 LRRM 2609 (1964), Mr. Justice Stewart concurring; see Annotation, *Subject of Mandatory Collective Bargaining Under Federal Labor Relations Act* 12 A.L.R.2d 265. We hold, therefore, that the manpower award was within the subject matter and jurisdiction of the arbitration panel." *Alpena v. Alpena Fire Fighters Association,* AFL–CIO, 56 Mich.App. 568, 575; 224 N.W.2d 672, 88 LRRM 3304 (1974).

Similarly, see *City of Detroit, Police Department v. Detroit Police Officers Ass'n,* ___ Mich.App. ___, ___ N.W.2d ___ (1975), No. 20926, decided 5/30/75.

such a reduction would otherwise be feasible) which would alleviate to some extent the costs of any wage increase or other benefits he has ordered.

D.

There are innumerable "disputes" difficult of resolution which may become hot political issues—e.g., zoning, the location of public buildings, school hours and school programs. These can all be viewed as "disputes" or "differences" between the property owners, parents or school teachers immediately affected and the government. It would be an enormous departure from present concepts of responsible exercise of governmental power if the practice were to develop of resolving difficult political issues in an arbitrator's conference room as an alternative to facing up to vexing problems in the halls of state and local legislatures.

Reposing power to resolve political issues in a person called an arbitrator and characterizing the issue a "dispute" or "difference" and his decision an "adjudication" does not obviate the need for political accountability of the manner in which political issues are resolved.

E.

The unions rely on the provision for judicial review of the arbitrator's result.

Although there have been more than a hundred awards, many of them controversial, there is no reported opinion of the Court of Appeals and we are aware of no circuit court opinion where "court review" resulted in modification of an arbitration award because it was not supported "by competent, material and substantial evidence." [52]

Judicial review of the manner in which delegated legislative power is exercised is a safeguard against arbitrary exercise of discretionary power. Within the range of reasonableness, the choice of the Legislature or its delegate is not subject to judicial alteration.

Most disputes in public employment will present a wide range of reasonable alternatives each of which is supported by "competent, material and substantial evidence on the whole record." Providing for judicial modification of those few decisions not so supported is not a substitute for political accountability and review of the choice between reasonable alternatives. Judicial review cannot fulfill the constitutional need for review and accountability through the political process.

The Legislature's ultimate political responsibility for the establishment and success of Act 312 cannot sustain this legislation. Such "accountability" is present in every legislative enactment. Similar logic would sustain legislation delegating any or all legislative power to any group or person.

* * *

52. M.C.L.A. 423.242; M.S.A. 17, 455(42).

H.

It is the unique method of appointment, requiring independent decision makers without accountability to a governmental appointing authority and the unique dispersal of decision-making power among numerous *ad hoc* decision makers, only temporarily in office, precluding assessment of responsibility for the consequences of their decisions on the level of public services, the allocation of public resources and the cost of government, which renders invalid this particular delegation of legislative power.

* * *

To avoid possible misunderstanding, we add that our holding does not preclude the Legislature from vesting the authority to resolve disputes concerning public employees in a governmental officer or agency with continuing responsibility for the day-to-day exercise of that delegated power. Such a decision maker (arbitrator) would not be "expendable" but, rather, would be responsible through the appointing authority to the electorate for the manner in which the delegated power is exercised.

* * *

WILLIAMS, JUSTICE: * * *

Compulsory arbitration is a practical response to the impasse experienced from time to time in collective bargaining where the public welfare cannot endure the impact of a work stoppage while awaiting the resolution of problems through normal negotiations. Thus, where public employees are prohibited from striking, some states have chosen to experiment with legislated compulsory arbitration in order to develop some mechanism to settle disputes and keep labor peace in these sectors. The areas of fire and police protection are prime examples. Compulsory arbitration has won popular support because it has effectively resolved conflicts and minimized the interruption of services. It has the prestige of success.

* * *

Superficially, the Michigan and out-of-state precedents without further analysis could be said to uphold the constitutionality of our Michigan statute. The big problem is that most of the cases have not dug below the surface of the challenge of delegation to a private person, or better, to a non-publicly accountable person. Also, if we thought of using the Rhode Island method of finding the party-appointed arbitrators public officials we would be confronted by the simplistic tenure rule ascribed to the *Freedland* case. As we have seen, from the Rhode Island court's attempt to grapple with the puzzle, it may be a medieval scholastic question whether an individual is a private or public person. The private or public label the person wears is not the whole answer by any means. We must reach the underlying reality.

* * *

Professor Frank Cooper in his treatise, *State Administrative Law,* observed that courts "weighing the advantage of delegation against the hazards involved make a pragmatic judgment as to whether the constitutional protections have been observed." From the pragmatic judgments we have reviewed, *supra,* we find that, implicitly or explicitly, courts have tended to rely on certain criteria in making their determinations.

The criteria used in the balances to determine these pragmatic judgments can be clustered into four categories:

First, how close by appointment is the person or agency to the elective process and political accountability? In other words, a person appointed by the governor is going to have a high degree of responsibility and accountability because his actions will reflect directly on the chief elected official.

Second, how closely restricted is the operation of the person or agency by standards written into the law and the possibility of judicial review?

Third, how much is the person or agency held to public accountability by the length of tenure on and the public exposure of the job?

There is a fourth criterion that as far as public accountability goes may act as kind of counterweight to the other three. It is the importance and breadth of power granted. In other words, while a certain amount of public accountability in all things is required, greater accountability is probably desirable where important power and broad discretion are simultaneously granted.

Obviously from the "scale of justice" metaphor, we suggest that the balances react to the total weight of all four criteria. We also suggest that if the constitutional importance and strength of one criterion is particularly great it might make up for a degree of weakness in another. In a word no single criterion is wholly dispositive. Rather it is the total effect of all the criteria that affects the balance of judgment.

* * *

A. PROXIMITY TO ELECTIVE PROCESS

Collective bargaining in the public sector is part of the public process, and thus persons bearing the ultimate political responsibility must not isolate themselves from the process. While it is not necessary that elected officials themselves do the arbitrating, citizens should be able to identify every elected official responsible for the result of the arbitration—either because he was an arbitrator or appointed the arbitrator.

The present case presents two alternative approaches to appointment. First, the law provides that parties to the dispute may select their own arbitrators and these arbitrators may select the third. This would present a situation similar to our hypothetical of minimum accountability on this point. It would be a weak argument for constitutionality when weighed with the other criteria. Since, however, as a point of fact, the city did not select an arbitrator, making impossible the joint selection of the third, the chairman of MERC appointed the arbitrator/chairman, the second method.

The MERC chairman is an appointee of the Governor, making proximity of the appointing authority to election by the people very close. Although the appointing authority is not elected, he or she is appointed by the highest elected official in the state. Furthermore, the chairman of MERC is the Governor's primary representative in employment relations. Public responsibility therefore is of a high order.

The fact of the matter is that appointment by the chairman of MERC created considerable political accountability in this case. If the chairman of MERC had appointed as arbitrator/chairman a person who would have "given away the store," the possibility of either chairman or Governor not receiving complaints from the City of Dearborn or Dearborn citizens would be very remote indeed.

We end up with the situation then where one alternative method of appointment tends strongly to unconstitutionality but the other strongly toward constitutionality. However, in construing the constitutionality of statutes we must "seek to save what we can" of public policy expressed in the statute. *People v. Bricker,* 389 Mich. 524, 529, 208 N.W.2d 172, 174 (1973). The public policy of this state as expressed in the arbitration statute has been to proscribe strikes of public employees and to substitute instead a system of binding arbitration. The Legislature, as the representative of the people, has offered two alternative methods of constituting the panel to help realize this goal. Thus, both are part and parcel of the same statute. Both are means to the end of achieving this legislative goal. We may, if we have to, sever the unconstitutional method without sacrificing the statute.

B. Sufficiency of Standards of Delegation

Of statutes requiring arbitration upon request of one party, Michigan is one of only three states (the others are Nebraska and Wisconsin) containing criteria for guiding the arbitrators. * * * [W]e observed that the standards [see p. 287 and note 40 for these criteria] relate to providing wages, hours and other conditions of employment as good as but not out of line with persons in public and private employment in comparable communities. We noted particularly the requirement to review the financial ability of the governmental unit to meet proposed costs. Col.L.Rev. 1192, 1200, fn. 41. While the Michigan law gives arbitrators a great deal of freedom in determining which criteria are most applicable to a particular case, the consensus is that the arbitration panels are using these standards and have, in written opinions, rationalized their decisions in terms of these categories. See, e.g., Smith, Edwards, Clark, Labor Relations Law in the Public Sector, 833–58.

Further restriction on the untrammelled exercise of power is the provision for judicial review. M.C.L.A. § 423.242; M.S.A. § 17.455(42). While not as broad as the South Dakota "appeal de novo," 72 Col.L.Rev. 1192, 1204 n. 73, the Michigan statute covers all appropriate bases for reviewing from an arbitration award, without permitting the relitigation which would whittle away at the binding authority behind the arbitration concept.

Thus, it is clear, the restrictions on the authority of arbitrator are both apparent and real, and serve effectively to close the gap between the people and the arbitrators.

C. Length of Tenure and Character of Job

It is suggested that the statutory system gives rise to a kind of "hit-and-run" decision-making process which permits the city to first insulate itself from unpopular decisions by delegating from elsewhere, and then further insulating itself by leaving no one around to take the blame.

However, long tenure does not guarantee publicly conscientious and accountable public servants, nor does short service automatically equate with irresponsibility. As we have seen too many times in the past, development and perpetuation of a bureaucracy may be but another method of insulating and camouflaging the real decision-maker. The issue is that of responsibility to the people. The Legislature has resolved this in the past, and may choose to do so in the future, with both long- and short-term bodies.

We should not have overmuch concern with the temporal nature of the arbitration panels. There is much to be said for selecting an arbitrator with particular expertise concerning a specific dispute, perhaps an arbitrator with roots in the community involved. Long terms in office would conceivably, by removing the arbitrators from everyday relationship to the parties, militate against this important type of responsibility.

While all parties are working on an ad hoc short-term basis, all are engaged as well in long-term relationships in the field of arbitration with other employers and employees. The arbitrator is in a profession where his reputation for impartiality and reasonableness is important to future employment, whether by these parties or someone else. He has to maintain the short-term and long-term confidence of both sides, or else suffer an inability to perform well in this and other appointments. The public employer remains responsible for the quality of its labor negotiators, and in the event of arbitration, for the performance of its appointed representative, for the effectiveness of its presentation to the arbitration panel, for the reasonableness of its offer, and for its role in the maintenance of the type of employer-employee relations which avoid open warfare and extremism. Further, it is doubtful that the citizens of the governmental unit will long tolerate an administration which consistently proves itself unable to resolve labor problems without crisis. The union must maintain its long-term credibility, or else its demands will be met with a jaundiced eye and the union leadership itself will suffer because of a loss of confidence by its membership and the community.

The short period during which arbitrators operate is a period of high visibility, where publicity is focused on the process of bargaining. While their role in the appointment strengthens the accountability of the appointers, such public attention also serves to strengthen the accountability of appointees. They are the focal point of general interest during this intense session of activity, and attempts to do otherwise than follow the legislative mandate will be, at the very least, soundly criticized.

The tripartite arbitration setup is more properly thought of as a kind of adversary proceeding, rather than the type of labor court which results from a permanent tribunal setup. The latter was not the legislative intent in designating arbitration panels to achieve impasse resolution.

The Legislature was undoubtedly familiar with the success of compulsory arbitration by ad hoc panels specially chosen to cope with a given impending crisis. They were choosing from history rather than trying to make history.

D. Kind of Power Delegated

The Legislature made only a narrow grant of power, consisting of submission of unresolved issues on wages and working conditions to a panel and a decision by that panel made according to legislatively-mandated standards which is final and binding on both parties. It is apparent that by the time problems reach the arbitration panel, the issues already have been sharpened by the process of negotiation. The panels operate with a great deal of independence within this narrow spectrum but a well-articulated series of standards and a broad provision for judicial review serve to channel these efforts.

Individuals to whom such limited discretion is delegated require less accountability than recipients of a broad, unlimited grant of power. The greatest discretion is properly exercised only by officials elected directly by the people, where accountability is accordingly greatest. Where less-independent operation is possible, accountability must still be present, but it may be less.

The three criteria we have discussed, *supra,* operate within the framework of this fourth one, and, at the same time, all four relate with one another. Ultimately, a subjective judgment is required to determine whether all four factors balance one another in a network which constitutes a delegation with sufficient accountability.

Thus, a statute delegating a narrow grant of power need not contain as direct lines to the electorate as one where the power was far broader. Further, if the narrow power is defined by well-drawn standards and adequate provision for judicial review, other requirements, such as permanence in office, are concomitantly lessened. Such is the scheme drawn by the Michigan compulsory arbitration statute.

* * *

Summing up we believe this case presents us an important and successful social experiment carefully drafted by the Legislature in specific response to the Constitution with the hazards of delegation carefully protected against by the provision of a high degree of political and legal accountability and substantial degree of personal accountability. We therefore feel that there has been no violation of the constitutional proscription against delegation of power to a nonpublicly accountable person where the appointment to the panel of the arbitration/chairman is made by the Chairman of MERC.

* * *

Notes and Questions

1. Do you agree with Justice Williams that appointment of the neutral arbitrator by the MERC chairman assures political accountability? Do you, on the other hand, agree with Justice Levin that a standing panel of arbitrators would assure political accountability? What does political accountability mean in this context anyway? First of all, to what constituency is it expected the arbitrator will be politically accountable? To the constituency of the local community in which the dispute arises? If that's the sort of accountability we want, then why not let the dispute be decided by the officials elected by that constituency? All of the justices in the instant case appear to assume that the requirement for political accountability would be satisfied if the arbitrator were in some way accountable to state authority. But does the state have a policy as to what the police and firemen of a particular municipality ought to be paid? Or as to how their interests ought to be balanced with the interests of others in the community with respect to the various issues, both fiscal and nonfiscal, which might arise? If the state has such a policy, why doesn't it implement that policy directly, through an administrative agency governed by statutory criteria? And if the state has no such policy, on the basis of what standards will the arbitrators be held accountable? Isn't there a fundamental problem with applying constitutional notions of delegation of legislative authority to a procedure which is intended primarily as an extension of the negotiating process? See Grodin, *Political Aspects of Public Sector Interest Arbitration,* 1 Ind.Rel.L.J. 1 (1976).

2. If you were the neutral arbitrator in a tripartite interest arbitration proceeding, and you became aware that the parties, while unwilling to assume public responsibility for a particular result, would nevertheless find that result "acceptable," would you see any ethical problem in framing your award to suit their expectations? Is the situation different from the "rigged award" in a grievance arbitration situation?

3. Justice Levin is correct, is he not, in noting that the kinds of issues which a public sector interest arbitrator may be called upon to decide often entail policy considerations which reach far beyond the immediate dispute? If you were an arbitrator and had to decide whether a city could impose a

residence requirement upon its police, how would you deal with the city's argument that it believes the requirement would lessen the psychological distance which exists between police and certain segments of the community?

4. Grodin, *Judicial Response to Arbitration,* Public Sector Bargaining, 2d Ed., 1988, BNA, pp. 253–254.

> Statutes mandating interest arbitration for public employees have been challenged on a variety of state constitutional grounds, most of them involving either the relationship of state to local authority, the relationship of arbitration to the legislative process, or a combination of the two. The first category of challenge—that the statute intrudes impermissibly upon the autonomy of a "home rule" city or county—has been uniformly rejected by the courts and need not concern us here. The second category, involving the relationship of arbitration to the legislative process, may take a variety of forms: that the statute constitutes an unlawful delegation of legislative power to private parties, that the statute contains insufficient standards or safeguards to guide or check arbitral discretion, that it represents an unconstitutional delegation of the taxing power, or that the method by which arbitrators are chosen violates the "one man, one vote" principle. The third category of challenge stems from the provisions, known as "ripper clauses," found in 18 state constitutions and prohibiting the legislature from delegating to a "special or private body" any power to interfere with "municipal moneys or to perform municipal functions."
>
> Prior to 1975, Pennsylvania was the only state in which interest arbitration was held constitutionally impermissible, and that was on the basis of a ripper clause that has subsequently been amended to permit arbitration. After that amendment, the state interest-arbitration statute was sustained. The supreme court of Wyoming upheld that state's interest-arbitration statute despite a ripper clause in the state's constitution, and the courts of Rhode Island, Maine, and Nebraska (which have no ripper clauses) rejected constitutional challenges based on other grounds. The supreme court of Maine was equally divided on the question of unlawful delegation, but since the lower court had sustained the statute, the effect of the division was to affirm. Thus, by the end of 1974 the score stood 5–0 in favor of constitutionality.
>
> Since that time, interests arbitration's constitutional batting average has been rising. The highest courts in Connecticut, Maine, New Jersey, Minnesota, New York, Massachusetts, Washington, and Michigan have sustained the constitutionality of interest arbitration in those states; and courts in South Dakota, Colorado, Utah, and Maryland have reached the opposite conclusion. While each of the latter state constitutions contains ripper clauses, the decisions in Colorado and Utah went beyond those clauses to rely generally on unconstitutional delegation doctrine. In California, the supreme court in a footnote in one case rather summarily dispensed with a constitutional attack raised by an amicus curiae to the constitutionality of a city-charter provision calling for binding interest arbitration; however, the vitality

of that footnote is dampened somewhat by the reasoning of the same court in an opinion which holds that an arrangement by a general-law city for interests arbitration would constitute an impermissible delegation of wage-fixing authority under a state statute providing that "by resolution or ordinance the city council shall fix the compensation of all appointive officers."

5. There are at least two problems with binding interests arbitration which appear to be unyielding. The first is that it necessarily invades to some extent the power of democratically-elected legislative bodies to make choices with respect to how public monies are to be spent. Second, it is a conservative and unimaginative process. Consider the following.

a. Excerpts from a recent arbitration opinion (Unreported):

"The City devotes almost 40 percent of its 128–page brief to its claim of inability to pay more money than it offered in the bargaining that preceded the impasse. It asserts that 'salary increases anywhere close to what the Union is demanding is a strike issue for the City.'

"The facts do demonstrate that the City's budget is tight. Revenues were down in the last fiscal year. Federal funds and State bail-out monies are substantially less in the current year.

"But the claim of inability to pay must be placed in context. Public employers have more limited options than private employers for making concessions in collective bargaining because of competing claims on the tax dollar and the limited sources of public revenue. Generally speaking, wage increases cannot be passed on to the consumer except in the form of higher taxes. Some public services cannot be eliminated; others cannot be significantly curtailed. The political imperatives of governmental decision-makers, the demands of particular constituencies, and the necessity of providing responsible and responsive public management all combine to constrain the choices made by government at the bargaining table.

"However, the fact is that inability to pay is nothing more than an assertion that other expenditures cannot be maintained at contemplated levels, absent new taxes or other revenue sources, if the economic demands of a particular union are met. The problem, in reality, is not one of ability or inability to pay—it is a problem of priorities.

"The City recognizes this in its brief. It states that it is 'not appropriate for the * * * arbitrator * * * to engage in reordering priorities established by elected representatives of the people of the City * * * 'Grabbing money set aside for reasonable improvements elevates employees above the citizenry. * * * Absent evidence of deliberate actions taken to avoid payment of salaries, and absent excessive fund balances uncommitted to reasonable priorities, it is simply not proper to second guess on policy decisions which are made independent of the bargaining process.'

"I have two difficulties with this point of view. The first has to do with the standards which I am compelled to follow by the terms of the City Council Resolution.

"The fifth standard directs the arbitrator to take into account the 'financial condition and resources of City government,' but there is nothing to suggest that this criterion is to be given greater weight than the others. It, like the others, is a guideline, not an immutable principle.

"It is the understanding of the arbitrator that he is authorized and directed by his appointment to apply *all* the standards to the record evidence. The weight to be given to that evidence as those criteria are brought to bear on it is committed to his judgment.

"This leads to my second difficulty with the City's position. If it is indeed inappropriate for the arbitrator to make decisions which require the reordering of priorities that have been established by City management, there is little meaningful function left for him to perform. He is, as I understand the argument, to do nothing more than look at the fiscal picture. If he cannot find evidence of deliberate actions taken by the City to avoid payment of salaries or excessive fund balances unreasonably committed to other priorities, he should place his imprimatur on the City's position. Such a sterile view of the proper function of an interests arbitrator is unacceptable.

"If the statutory criteria support a finding that additional monies should be made available to the employees represented by the Union, a direction to reorder priorities is an order within the dimensions of arbitral authority."

Do you agree? Suppose the following: you are the arbitrator in a dispute involving salaries for classroom teachers. How would you deal with the school district's argument that, on a budget fixed by constitutional or statutory limitations, the only way teachers could be paid more than the district has already offered would be to cut out some program that the school board and parents considered essential?

b. Consider the following remarks offered by Arbitrator Norman Brand:

> [A]rbitration is not an innovative process. If it were, the parties would be better advised to spend their energies preparing an arbitration case than to waste them bargaining. The genius of collective bargaining is that the parties can create new grievance procedures, employee benefits, and bargaining structures—while acting to their mutual advantage. They can decide whether the risks of innovation are consistent with the benefits they hope to achieve by their new creation. They can thoroughly clarify a proposal and ask all the "what ifs," based upon their intimate knowledge of the work place culture, physical limitations, and administrative constraints. Most importantly, they can balance the risks and benefits of one proposal against those associated with another proposal, and make the compromises that are the hallmark of successful collective bargaining.
>
> A neutral arbitrator—who has only a surface knowledge of the work place culture, physical limitations and administrative constraints—is ill-equipped to understand the full implications of a totally new proposal. The arbitrator is in a poor position to evaluate risks, ask the right

questions, and have sufficient information to impose one party's "new idea" on the other side. It is my view that arbitration is not the forum for innovations by either party. If the parties want to innovate, they must negotiate.

Why is this so?

6. Final Offer Arbitration. The arbitration statute involved in the *Dearborn* case calls for conventional arbitration by a tripartite board. Final-offer arbitration raises the same constitutional questions. However, it has special difficulties of its own, particularly where the choice is made on an issue by issue basis requiring the identification of each "impasse item." Consider the following case.

WEST DES MOINES EDUCATION ASS'N v. PUBLIC EMPLOYMENT RELATIONS BOARD

Supreme Court of Iowa, 1978.
266 N.W.2d 118.

MASON, J.: The Public Employment Relations Board (PERB) appeals from the judgment of the Polk District Court reversing a declaratory ruling issued by PERB upon petition submitted to it by the West Des Moines Education Association (Association). In its ruling PERB held the phrase "impasse item" as used in Sections 20.22(3) and 20.22(11) of the Public Employment Relations Act (Act) as it existed in the Code of 1973 meant subject category and, consequently it held the parties must submit their final offers of a subject category to the arbitrator. The court in its judicial review of the PERB ruling reversed the PERB and determined the phrase "impasse item" referred to any word, clause, phrase, sentence or paragraph upon which the parties were in disagreement.

At this point it is necessary to explain certain matters about arbitration and to explain how the Public Employment Relations Act works. In its brief to this court the PERB set out explanations of both matters which are particularly succinct. It stated:

> "In labor relations law, there are two basic kinds of binding arbitration of labor disputes. Arbitration is most frequently used for the resolution of grievances. The term-of-art for this type of arbitration is 'rights' arbitration. The second principal type of arbitration is used in the resolution of a contract negotiations dispute. This type of arbitration, which is of the type at issue here, is called 'interest arbitration.'
>
> "Interest arbitration itself is of two basic types. 'Final offer' arbitration or 'conventional' arbitration. In conventional arbitration the arbitrator simply arrives at a result and makes his award either on the position advocated by one of the parties or at a point between the positions of the parties.
>
> "In 'final offer' arbitration the arbitrator must select the position of one of the parties and may *not* select a compromise position.

"It is the 'final offer' system which the Iowa legislature incorporated into our statute. Final offer arbitration must be distinguished from conventional arbitration.

"As we stated to the court below, the differences between the forms of arbitration were recently summarized as follows:

" 'In conventional arbitration, the arbitrator tailors a resolution which resolves the bargaining impasse. The arbitrator can, and many times does, fashion a remedy somewhere between the last offers of the parties.

" ' * * *

" 'However, a problem commonly perceived concerning a conventional arbitration is its "narcotic effect." This problem is believed to stem from the arbitrator's real or imagined tendency to "split the difference" between the parties' positions. Management argues that because the employee organization is primarily the demanding party in negotiations, with conventional arbitration as an end result, true collective bargaining will not occur if the employee representative feels ultimate victory lies in the hands of the arbitrator rather than at the bargaining table. In other words, the availability of conventional arbitration will have a "chilling" effect on the parties' incentives to bargain in good faith.

" 'In order to limit this chilling or narcotic effect, Legislatures have developed a form of arbitration which circumscribed the arbitrator's discretionary power—final-offer arbitration. Final-offer arbitration limits the arbitrator to choosing between the last and the best offer of one party or the other on an entire package basis or on an issue-by-issue basis based upon a rule of reasonableness generally spelled out in the enabling legislation. The virtue of this type of arbitration is that it is final and binding on the parties based upon their proposed last and best offers without granting the arbitrator an undue amount of discretion. Thus, there is an element of coercion which encourages mutual agreement because a third party will select one of the offers as binding without compromise between them. In other words, "final offer arbitration should not have a chilling effect because it will function as a 'strikelike' mechanism by posing potentially severe costs of disagreement in a manner that conventional arbitration does not." If the parties are sensitive to what will be perceived as reasonable by the arbitrator, they will tend to tailor their final offer in that manner.'

"(Rynicki and Gausden, *Current Trends in Public Sector Impasse Resolution,* State Government, Autumn 1976 at 274–76).

"We now describe the context in which collective bargaining negotiations take place when an 'impasse' exists, i.e., where the parties cannot agree on the terms of the collective bargaining agreement they may seek the assistance of a series of 'neutrals' in resolving the dispute.

"Arbitration under the Public Employment Relations Act is but the last of three steps in the statutory procedure. The first step in this process is mediation. Section 20 of the Public Employment Relations Act provides for the appointment of a mediator at the request of either party to the dispute. The mediator's function is to guide the parties toward a resolution of the dispute by persuasion, by analysis, and by seeking modifications in each side's position. Mediation is not an adjudicative or quasi-adjudicative process. The number of issues which are unresolved going into mediation is reduced substantially during this process and typically, where complete settlement is not achieved, only a handful of issues remain for the next step in the process.

"Failing a settlement of the dispute in mediation, Section 21 of the Public Employment Relations Act requires the appellant Board to appoint a *fact-finder.* The fact-finder is required to conduct a hearing, take evidence and issue written findings of fact and a recommendation for the resolution of the dispute. The fact-finder is not limited to the final offers of the parties when making his recommendation but is permitted to recommend any solution. We submit that the definition of impasse item sought by the appellee is more appropriately restricted to a proceeding in front of a fact-finder who does not function under a statutory mandate wherein he must choose one of two offers submitted to him.

"Frequently, after the fact-finding stage of the process, the parties reach agreement on some of the issues and typically the arbitrator is asked to resolve fewer issues than was the fact-finder.

"The parties are not compelled, however, to accept the fact-finder's report and either party may request, under § 22 of the Public Employment Relations Act, the appointment of a panel of three arbitrators or a single arbitrator.

"The panel or the single arbitrator conducts a hearing, takes evidence and issues an award which is final and binding on the parties.

"The Iowa 'final offer' scheme contains a wrinkle not found elsewhere and not at issue here wherein the arbitrator may choose among not only the offers of the parties, but also may choose the position taken by the fact-finder on the issue.

"Thus, in a contract negotiation, the parties would ordinarily commence with all items at issue and unresolved and would proceed through few or many negotiation sessions to seek and reach agreements on numbers of issues.

"Then if they require the help of neutral third parties, the Public Employment Relations Act provides a system which clearly contemplates a continued narrowing or reduction of the unresolved

> issues. This process continues to the last point, final offer arbitration, known also as last offer arbitration, or forced-choice arbitration, which is designed to encourage hard bargaining by the parties before they resort to arbitration. Final offer interest arbitration enables 'the parties to retain maximum participation all the way up to finalization of a decision with minimum exercise of power by a third party.' "

(Emphasis in original.)

[In a declaratory ruling, the state PERB had opined that, if the parties had reached agreement on all elements of a grievance procedure except the question whether a grievance could be filed by the association (as distinguished from an employee), that question would be an "impasse item" within the meaning of the statute. If there were disagreements over that question and a number of other questions relating to the grievance procedure as well (e.g., whether the procedure should apply to claimed violations of school board policy as well as contract violations, the time limits applicable to the filing of grievances, whether group grievances should be permitted, and whether arbitration should be binding or advisory), then all the points in dispute relating to the grievance procedure would collectively constitute an "impasse item," and the arbitrator would choose between the positions of the parties on a "package" basis. The association, contending that each point in dispute constituted a separate "impasse item," sought review of PERB's decision in court, and was successful at the trial level. Portions of the Supreme Court opinion discussing the applicable procedure and standard for review are omitted.]

III. The phrase "impasse item" is not defined in chapter 20, The Code. The parties here do not dispute the meaning given the word in the Act: " 'Impasse' means the failure of a public employer and the employee organization to reach agreement in the course of negotiations." Section 20.3(10), The Code, 1975. Their disagreement centers around the word "item." The Association contends the word refers to any word, clause, phrase, sentence or paragraph while the other parties here argue it refers to a subject category of negotiable items.

This court must determine the intent of the legislature. Our construction of this statute must be sensibly and fairly made with a view of carrying out this intent. *In re Marriage of Williams,* 199 N.W.2d 339, 344 (Iowa 1972).

Our research indicates the majority of researchers and writers on the topic of final offer arbitration agree that where subject category or package final offers, rather than issue by issue final offers, must be submitted to the arbitrators, the goals of final offer arbitration are more nearly fulfilled.

In *Final Offer Selection—Panacea or Pandora's Box?,* 19 N.Y.L.F. 567, 578–79 (No. 3, 1974), appear the following pertinent comments by Arnold M. Zack:

"The choice in final offer selection should be between total packages rather than issue by issue. Although it is true that a more equitable resolution might be achieved if the decisions were made on an issue by issue basis, and certainly the arbitrators would be more comfortable with this arrangement, it must be borne in mind that the sense of reasonableness on the part of the arbitrator and the achievement of the most equitable or desirable agreement, are not the primary purposes of final offer selection. Rather, the objective is independent settlement by the parties. The greater the risk to each party of submitting a final offer, the greater the likelihood of settlement. Each party must run the risk of its whole package being thrown out because of the unreasonableness or unacceptability of even one element therein. Only in that way can the greatest pressure be exerted on the parties for direct settlement. Indeed, to the extent that a whole package may be thrown out because of one element which is deemed objectionable by the arbitrator, * * * the prospect is improved for future voluntary settlements.

"Issue by issue arbitration encourages leaving political and low priority demands on the table, wasting the time and money of both parties and cluttering the procedure. Forcing the parties to drop such demands or place them in the final offer, is likely to dispose of most, if not all, such items. There are, of course, situations where it is not politically feasible for a party to voluntarily withdraw such items. To provide for situations where the negotiators on both sides of the bargaining table recognize the need for saving face, there should be a mechanism permitting them to 'get off the hook.' A fact-finding or an ancillary 'informed award' [occurs when the negotiators privately work out a settlement of the impasse and the arbitrator adopts the results thereof as his award] arbitration procedure would serve such end.

"It should be noted that the final offer selection procedure does not easily lend itself to issue by issue determination. Multiple proposals are too often intertwined and dependent upon one another. For example, whether certain fringe benefits should be granted, or more para-professional aides hired, depends upon the total amount of money allocated to the entire package. Twin issues such as whether or not an additional step should be added to the increment schedule, or longevity increases granted, cannot practically be separated in an issue by issue final offer selection. Such related items are best handled on the package basis."

See also *Final Offer Arbitration: The Last Word in Public Sector Labor Disputes,* 10 Colum.J.L. & Soc.Prob. 525, 550–53, 558–59, 562–63 (1974); James L. Stern, Charles M. Rehmus, J. Joseph Loewenberg, Hirschel Kaspter & Barbara D. Dennis, Final–Offer Arbitration, Ch. 7 (1975) [hereinafter cited as Stern]. Contra *Compulsory Arbitration in the Public Sector: A Proposed Alternative,* 25–26 Arb.J. 226, 231–32 (1970–71). See generally *Impasse Resolution Mechanisms and Teacher Strikes,* 7 U.Mich.J.L.Ref. 575 (No. 1 1973); *Final Offer Selection in*

National Emergency Disputes, 27 Arb.J. 85 (1972); *and Political Aspects of Public Sector Interest Arbitration,* 64 Calif.L.Rev. 678 (1976).

If the objectives of final offer arbitration are to be carried out it is plain they will best be carried out through a system whereby the parties must make final offers on subject categories.

Chapter 20 contains provisions which indicate to us the legislature intended to carry out the objectives of final offer arbitration through a system mandating subject category final offers.

Section 20.9 delineates the scope of negotiations between the parties. It provides in pertinent part as follows:

> "The public employer and the employee organization shall meet at reasonable times, including meetings reasonably in advance of the public employer's budget-making process, to negotiate in good faith with respect to '*wages, hours, vacations, insurance, holidays, leaves of absence, shift differentials, overtime compensation, supplemental pay, seniority, transfer procedures, job classifications, health and safety matters, evaluation procedures, procedure for staff reduction, in-service training* and other matters mutually agreed upon.'" (Emphasis supplied.)

As the IASB correctly points out the emphasized portion of this provision deals with subjects of negotiation, not with the individual words, phrases, clauses, sentences or paragraphs of these subjects. This provides strong evidence the legislature intended subject categories to be submitted to the arbitrator.

Sections 20.21 and 20.22(11) also provide indications the legislature intended to achieve the objectives of final offer arbitration through establishment of a system of subject category final offers. Section 20.21 provides for a fact-finder who is to make recommendations for resolution of the impasse reached between the public employer and public employee organization. Section 20.22(11) makes clear the arbitrator may choose only one of three positions, that of either party or that of the fact-finder.

In our system the fact-finder is a neutral who would be expected to recommend to the arbitrator the most reasonable offer. The arbitrator, mindful of the fact-finder's neutrality, will often be prone to choosing the fact-finder's position in making his award. This propensity will force the parties to make more reasonable offers because the party who wins over the fact-finder will enter arbitration with a powerful ally. The party which fails to have the fact-finder recommend its position will be forced to think long and hard before it continues on to arbitration.

In addition, section 20.22(4)(d) makes the "losing" party at fact-finding level even less likely to continue on to arbitration. This section requires the parties to pay the costs of arbitration. A losing party who continues on to arbitration and loses will have a difficult time explaining to its constituents why it incurred the expense of arbitration when the probability of losing was so great.

In our opinion these sections are an attempt to carry out the objectives of final offer arbitration. Together they make it imperative that the parties present reasonable offers at the fact-finding stage, which in itself promotes settlement. They encourage settlement after fact-finding and prior to arbitration.

The Association points out the example of Michigan's experience with final offer arbitration. The Michigan system clearly provides for issue-by-issue final offer arbitration. We have studied this system and find it does not seek as strongly as does our system to carry out the objectives of final offer arbitration.

In Stern, Final Offer Arbitration, at pp. 70–71, appear the following pertinent comments about the Michigan experience:

> "Settlement of negotiations by the parties themselves, with or without mediation, is still the rule rather than the exception. After five years of experience under mandated binding arbitration, in over half of the public safety negotiating relationships in Michigan no petition for arbitration has ever been filed. In over two-thirds of these relationships, no arbitration award has ever been rendered. Under these circumstances, it is clear that a rough equality of bargaining power has been created between most organized public safety officers and their employers. It is equally clear that the possibility of arbitration has not eroded significantly the ability of the large majority of these parties in most of their negotiations to settle amicably upon terms and conditions of employment.
>
> "It is equally clear, however, that the substitution of binding final-offer arbitration on each economic issue for conventional arbitration has not significantly discouraged recourse to arbitration.... On balance, it does not appear that the final-offer variant in Michigan has had any major impact on either the frequency of settlements or the likelihood of impasses requiring arbitration.
>
> "Final-offer arbitration of each economic issue does not appear to have reduced significantly the number of issues the parties take to arbitration. In half of the first 14 awards rendered under the final-offer amendment, 15 or more issues were submitted to the arbitration panel. The average number of issues per case in which awards have been rendered is 12, which figure is almost identical with the average number taken to arbitration under the Michigan conventional arbitration statute. To the extent that it was originally theorized that final-offer arbitration would at least reduce the necessity for awards except on the most intractable and toughest issues, the promise of the theory has not been borne out in practice.
>
> * * *

"Of course an arbitration statute has the ultimate purpose of providing an acceptable procedure for dispute resolution without disruption of vital services. During the 39 months of conventional arbitration in Michigan, there were no strikes by firefighters and only a few by police. All but one of these were of short duration and only one was against an arbitration award. There have been no strikes, work stoppages, or significant job actions by public safety officers since the final-offer amendment was adopted. By this test of statutory effectiveness, final-offer arbitration by economic issue has fared well—although no claim of causality is advanced."

The issue-by-issue system as used in Michigan does not carry out major objectives of final offer arbitration. It fails to reduce the number of arbitration cases or the number of issues presented to the arbitrator by the parties.

It is our view the legislature in adopting final offer arbitration between public employers and employees intended to provide for the carrying out of all the objectives of such arbitration through a system mandating subject category final offers. The Association's reliance upon the Michigan experience is misplaced.

In order to carry out this legislative intent we interpret the phrase "impasse item" means subject categories which requires the parties to submit to an arbitrator their final offer on a subject category basis. Each subject category submitted shall constitute an impasse item.

The PERB was correct in its interpretation of the phrase and in its answers to the questions presented by the Association. The trial court was incorrect in its interpretation and in its answers.

The Association in its written brief and argument asserts there is a third basic type of arbitration, namely, package final arbitration where the arbitrator takes either the final offer of the public employer on all issues in the dispute or the final offer of the employee organization on all issues in dispute. In reaching the foregoing conclusion we have not deemed it necessary to deal specially with this type of arbitration.

In reaching this conclusion we have considered every other contention urged by the Association in support of the trial court's ruling whether specifically mentioned or not and find none which persuade us to reach a different conclusion.

The case is therefore reversed.

Notes

1. Iowa's use of the factfinder's recommendation in its final offer, issue-by-issue arbitration is a unique form of final offer arbitration which has attracted much interest because parties typically settle after factfinding since experience has shown that arbitrators often favor the factfinder's recommendations.

2. As Arnold Zack (quoted with approbation by the court in the *West Des Moines* case) stated, issue-by-issue final-offer arbitration may produce decisions with which the arbitrator is comfortable, but it is not as likely as package-by-package final-offer arbitration to produce overall settlement by the parties.

Furthermore, some proposals are intertwined and dependent upon others. Realistically they cannot be separated. The reverse is also sometimes true, that is, a matter may be characterized as presenting one issue when in reality there are two issues.

Finally, although the positions of both parties may be objectionable to the arbitrator, he is required by the process to endorse one or the other.

Consider the following arbitration decision.

SAN MATEO COUNTY FIREFIGHTERS, INTERNATIONAL ASSOCIATION OF FIREFIGHTERS, AFL–CIO	OPINION AND AWARD OF BOARD OF ARBITRATION
	CSMCS Case # 88–1–525
and	
THE CITY OF REDWOOD CITY	July 1990

BEFORE A TRIPARTITE ARBITRATION BOARD

FOR THE FIREFIGHTERS: STEVE KRAUSE

FOR REDWOOD CITY CITY: JOHN LIEBERT

CHAIRMAN: PROFESSOR ERWIN ERZATZ

This three member Board of Arbitrators was constituted by the parties in August of 1989 pursuant to the provisions of Section 96 of the City's Charter dealing with "impartial and binding arbitration for fire department employee disputes." The Chairman was selected from a list submitted to the parties by the California State Mediation and Conciliation Service. Thereafter, the Board conducted 20 hearings, beginning on August 2, 1989, covering 200 hours of hearing time and dealing with 84 issues about which the parties were in dispute. During the course of those hearings, the parties generated almost 3,000 pages of transcript, 10 joint exhibits, 44 Union exhibits, and 92 City exhibits.

* * *

The format of the decision is as follows. Each issue shall be considered and decided by determining which of the final offers of each party more nearly conforms with those "factors traditionally taken into consideration in the determination of wages, hours, and other terms and conditions of public and private employment, including, but not limited to, changes in the average consumer price index for goods and services, the wages, hours, and other terms and conditions of employment of other employees performing similar services, and the financial condition of the City and its ability to meet the cost of the Award."

[Clearly the availability of the arbitration procedure as the final step in resolving the overall dispute did not induce the parties to settle, although 56 of the 84 issues were settled, sometimes through mediation by the Chairman, during the protracted hearing process. These settlement agreements were adopted and incorporated as part of the Award.

Of the 28 issues which were resolved by an Award, the following four seem particularly pertinent.]

DECISION OF THE BOARD OF ARBITRATION

Issue No. 1 (Length of Agreement)

* * *

Unanimous Opinion: The position of the Union for a Memorandum of Understanding which covers a period of three and one-quarter years is closer to the norm than the four and one-quarter year period proposed by the City. For this reason, at about the midpoint in these hearings the Chairman opined that he preferred the Union's position. However, I have changed my mind.

Stability is also an important traditional value. These proceedings have gone on for almost a year. They have been time-consuming, expensive, and sometimes aggravating—although less so as we neared the end.

After this Award has been finalized and the retroactive settlements have been put in place, the remaining period of two years hardly seems long enough. The parties, in my judgment, need more time to adjust to a substantially revised labor agreement and to improve their working relationships.

Award: The proposal of the City is adopted and incorporated in the award.

ALL CONCUR

Issue No. 4 (Salaries)

* * *

Majority Opinion: The Chairman finds that the Union's last offer more nearly conforms with those factors traditionally taken into consideration in the determination of wages, hours, and other terms and conditions of public and private employment than the City's. Tradition is the key benchmark under Section 96 of the City Charter; and traditionally, with one interruption, the comparisons utilized historically in the negotiations between these parties have been between firefighters and fire engineers or firefighters and firefighter engineers.

Captain Richard Salter's testimony on this point was instructive:

> In past negotiations we have always been compared to the Engineer's position with the exception of the 1987 negotiations. In an effort to reach an agreement during the 1987 negotiations, we agreed to take the average of the Firefighter's position and the Firefighter–Engineer's position. (TR at 372)

The salary increase negotiated in 1987—a two year agreement—was substantial, close to 24% over the two-year period. (TR at 343)

It can be argued that the City was willing to agree to such a substantial increase in order to "buy out" of the past practice of comparing firefighters to firefighter-engineers. However, there is no evidence of this. There is no explanation in the record of why the parties in 1987 departed from a comparability formula in reaching their settlement on economic issues. There is no evidentiary basis for concluding that this departure from tradition was anything more than a one-time agreement in order to reach a peaceable settlement, admittedly a generous one. Certainly there is no evidence to support an inference that the parties were abandoning tradition and agreeing that henceforth comparisons would be utilized on a different basis.

Nor is there any basis for concluding that prior to 1987 comparisons had been made between firefighters and firefighters. Captain Salter's testimony was very clear. He referred to "past negotiations," that is, negotiations prior to 1987, during which, according to his testimony, the comparability formula was firefighter to firefighter-engineer. Captain Salter's testimony on this point is unchallenged and unrebutted. Accordingly it must stand.

The tradition of comparing firefighters in Redwood City to the fire engineer position in other jurisdictions has a rational basis. Redwood City does not have a separate fire engineer classification, but firefighters must have the skills of a fire engineer or if they do not presently have them, be in the process of obtaining them. (TR at 337, 346) There are no permanent assignments to fire engineer functions; rather, these tasks are rotated among the various firefighters in the department. (TR at 348) This means that most of the Redwood City firefighters have the responsibilities of functioning as fire engineers. (TR at 348–49)

Leo Mittendorf, formerly the Union's chief negotiator, was categorical on this point. He testified that while Redwood City does not have an engineer classification, all firefighters in the City have to be engineers. (TR at 325) According to Mittendorf, the functions of a fire engineer are performed in Redwood City by all the firefighters.

> Each firefighter * * * has to have all of the skills of a firefighter and all of the skills of an engineer, just as a fire captain has to have all of the skills of a firefighter and all of the skills of a fire engineer. When you look at Redwood City, their fire captains do everything that a firefighter does in another agency, plus he does whatever an engineer does in another city that has the classification of fire engineer. (TR at 337)

* * *

If one accepts the legitimacy of comparing firefighters to engineers or to firefighter-engineers, as I do, Redwood City is consistently on the bottom of comparison cities.

The Union's comparative data show that the salaries of the fire personnel whom it represents have lagged; they show a negative differential of 13.6%. The Union's proposal is to remove 7.6% of this lag in the first year and the remainder of it in the second year, with parity being achieved during the third year. Data demonstrating the lag, comparing the top step firefighter rates in Redwood City to the average of the top step fire engineer rates, or in the absence thereof, to the average of the top step firefighter rates, are set forth in Appendix A attached to the Union's Brief.

* * *

Finally, there is the question of the financial condition of the City and its ability to meet the costs of the Union's proposal. Obviously municipal corporations, like other governmental entities, have finite resources. Only the federal government which has the capacity to print money can afford the luxury of deficit financing. Usually, however, the question of whether a city or any other governmental entity can afford to pay a given salary increase is not a question of ability to pay; it is, rather, a question of priorities. How are these limited resources to be deployed and expended? Redwood City put into the record a good deal of evidence establishing that much of its revenue is use-restricted; and that, accordingly, the funds cannot be utilized for other purposes such as firefighters' compensation. However, the Chairman is not convinced that these restrictions, insofar as they are imposed by law, leave the City so constrained in its choices that it cannot fund the Union's proposal. There are enough restrictions that are imposed, not by law but by practice and by City Council choice, so that the funds could be made available without transgressing legal limitations.

The City asserts that its salary proposal standing alone would cost an average of about $429,000 in new money for each year of the MOU. The City states further that the Union's salary proposal standing alone would cost an average of over $529,000 in new money for each year of the MOU. In sum, the City claims that the Union's proposal would cost the City $100,000 more per year than the City proposal. (City Brief at 9–10) The evidence does not support a finding that the City is unable, because of use-restraints imposed by law, to find the additional amount of money necessary in order to fund the Union's proposal, which is closer to traditional comparisons than the City's.

The City argues (at page 41 of its brief, footnote 40) that the percentage of the total package increase under the Union proposal is 35.05% over three years, an average annual increase of 11.68%, while the total package increase under the City package is 26.34% over four years, an average annual increase of 6.59%. However, the Chairman is not awarding the total package increase which the Union proposes; he is dealing only with the salary package.

The cost figures set forth in Tab 2 (cost of City proposals) and Tab 4 (cost of Union proposals) document these costs as the City sees them. But these figures do not square with those set forth in the City's brief at pages 9–10. The explanation appears to be that Tab 4 assumes that all of the other Union proposals that cost money would also be granted. The figures in Tab 4 as a measure of the costs of the *salary* proposals are therefore inaccurate.

Award: The Union's proposal is adopted and incorporated in the Award.[3]

* * *

The employer's dissenting opinion is omitted.

Issue No. 26 (Credit for Unused Sick Leave)

* * *

Majority Opinion: (A) The Union argues that retiring personnel should receive service credit for unused sick leave because of the City's agreement that this is an equitable benefit. The cost, contends the Union, is miniscule and the fact that other Redwood City employees do not receive this benefit is immaterial. The City's opposition to these proposals, according to its brief (pp. 23–25), is based largely on cost.

The Chairman prefers the City's position on this issue. The Union's proposal is not supported by comparative data.

(B) The Union supports its proposal for a payout of unused sick leave at the time of retirement or death on the basis of comparative data. It argues that of the sixteen cities represented in City Exhibit 50, twelve allow for payment of unused sick leave at the time of retirement. Furthermore, other Redwood City employees receive this benefit. This is true in Redwood City with respect to the payment of accrued sick leave benefits to dependents in the MOU of the Redwood City Police Officers Association, of the Management Employees Association, and of the Service Employees International Union.

3. The settlements that Redwood City reached with [two other Unions] were not considered by the Board of Arbitration because these settlements were not offered in evidence until the record had been closed.

The Arbitration Board's adoption of the City's proposal governing the length of the contract coupled with the determination of a Board majority accepting the Union's proposal on salaries means that the salary adjustment, if any, for the period from July 1, 1992 until June 30, 1993 will be a function of the results of the study called for by Section 7.2 of the Union's proposal. That calls for a review of the list of comparable cities and the establishment of comparability guidelines which, effective July 1, 1992 and thereafter, will be the formula for salary-setting. This proposal, in context, is the functional equivalent of a wage reopener during the final year of the agreement. Wage reopeners are, of course, not uncommon in the labor relations world. Sometimes the negotiations over a wage reopener, since in terms they are restricted to one issue, yield to settlement only with great difficulty. However, that risk is substantially reduced in this instance by the endorsement of a comparability formula as the basis for settlement.

The City's opposition is based upon the fact that fire personnel presently may "cash-out" unused sick leave credits for any calendar year at the rate of twenty-five percent of the value of those sick leave credits. The City's opposition is again grounded on cost factors. However, the Union's proposal with respect to payment of unused, accumulated sick leave with a cap of twenty-five percent is supported by the data.

It is extraordinarily difficult to make a choice here. In a memorandum dated March 2, 1990, the Chairman identified for the parties the matters remaining at issue. This list was modified by the Chairman on March 12, 1990 in response to objections made by both of them.

Issue No. 26, which is what is being considered here, was presented to the parties as one issue to which they were required to respond with last best offers. This determination went unchallenged, and the parties responded in kind.

The difficulty is that while there is a common denominator—accrued sick leave—there are really two issues. This apparent error cannot be modified at this juncture. It is too late for that. The arbitration panel must lump the two together and make a choice.

This is a tough call. The Chairman's judgment, weighing the City's proposals in total opposition to any change, against the Union proposals which were modified substantially between its initial positions and its final positions, is that the latter conform more closely to traditional factors, primarily comparative data, than the former.

In cost terms, unused sick leave payout at retirement, a change which is supported by the data, is more significant than unused sick leave crediting, which is not. Sick leave crediting is important, but comparatively speaking it is a trailer. Tab 4, attached to the City's Brief, shows a projected cost difference between the two items of over $17,000 a year ($24,544.63 for buyout as compared to $7,174.38 for crediting).

Award: The Union's proposal will be adopted as part of the Award of the Board of Arbitration.

* * *

The employer's dissenting opinion is omitted.

Issue No. 44 (Drug Testing)

* * *

Majority Opinion: The Chairman of the Board has difficulties with the proposals of both parties. The principal objection that he has to the City's proposal is that in effect it provides for random drug testing of any applicant for promotion.

The Chairman's objections to the Union's proposal are as follows: First, limiting testing to the situation where the "reasonable suspicion determination" is made by at least two supervisory employees on the basis of direct observational evidence is inordinately restrictive.

Second, the procedures spelled out under the heading "Notice of Required Testing," are unnecessarily detailed. The Chairman has no difficulty with any of the six requirements, but he is of the belief that it is adequately covered by the City's proposal that the implementation of drug testing must meet the standards of procedural due process. The Chairman is concerned by the City's phrase "as required by law," but he interprets this to mean the common law of the shop which has been developed by arbitrators in dealing with such matters.

Third, the Chairman is not persuaded that the drug test should be limited to urinalysis.

Next, the Chairman is of the view that it is unnecessary (indeed, undesirable) to spell out in precise detail the chain of possession procedures. If an employee tests positive and challenges the accuracy of the results, and the matter goes to arbitration, the arbitrator will require proofs that the integrity of such procedures has not been violated.

Similarly, the Chairman is not persuaded that a twelve month period of being "clean" after rehabilitation is always a sensible basis for wiping the slate clean, nor does he agree that all records of the events should always be removed from all files and destroyed.

Finally, it is not necessary to spell out that the issues under the drug testing program are grievable and arbitrable. If an employee refuses to take a test, the question of whether or not there was "reasonable suspicion" is one with which an arbitrator must deal in order to decide whether the refusal was permissible or was a type of insubordination. Similarly, if the results are positive, considerations of "just cause" for discipline or for refusal to follow procedures other than discipline will be considered by an arbitrator.

It is also noteworthy that the Union's proposal does not deal with drug or alcohol involvements other than demonstrated impairment affecting work performance. Impairment in my view is not the only basis for discipline. Possession while on duty should also be a disciplinary offense, as should selling or providing.

In conclusion, the Chairman finds that the City's proposal is less objectionable than the Union's.

Award: The City's proposal shall be adopted as part of the Award of the Board of Arbitration.

* * *

The Union's dissenting opinion is omitted.

D. JUDICIAL AND LEGISLATIVE REVIEW

CITY OF BUFFALO v. RINALDO

New York Court of Appeals, 1977.
41 N.Y.2d 764, 396 N.Y.S.2d 152, 364 N.E.2d 817, 95 LRRM 2776.

FUCHSBERG, JUDGE: By these proceedings, originally brought pursuant to Article 78 of the CPLR against the Buffalo Police Benevolent Association (PBA), the State Public Employment Relations Board (PERB) and the members of an *ad hoc* public arbitration panel, the City of Buffalo sought to vacate a determination by which the panel had granted a salary increase to the police bargaining unit represented by the PBA.[1] The Appellate Division vacated the award because it concluded that the City was without the means to fund the increase.

The genesis of the proceedings were collective bargaining negotiations for a new contract between the City and the PBA for the fiscal year July 1, 1975 through June 30, 1976. After all attempts, including mediation and fact-finding, to resolve an impasse in their negotiations had failed to resolve their differences, the dispute was referred for compulsory binding arbitration by a public panel in accordance with the procedures set forth in Civil Service Law Section 209, subd. 4, par. c.

After entertaining extensive proof and argument proffered by both sides, the panel awarded a five percent salary increase retroactive to July 1, 1975. In doing so, it rejected the PBA's demand for a ten percent increase and an improvement in other conditions of employment; it also thereby rejected the fact finder's earlier recommendation, unacceptable to both parties, that the police be granted a fifty dollar increase in uniform allowance and a non-recurring salary bonus in an amount equivalent to six percent of base salary.

Although the Appellate Division confined itself to a consideration of proof of the financial ability of the public employer to pay (Civil Service Law § 209, subd. 4, par. [c], cl. [v], sub. cl. [b]), considerable evidence had been presented to the panel and, earlier, presented to the fact finder, whose findings of fact and recommendations for settlement go to the panel on a variety of issues. Included in that presentation was proof on such other vital issues as the comparability of the benefits received by the employees involved in the arbitration proceeding with those of similar employees in public or private employment in comparable communities, the training hazards peculiar to police work and other such matters to which the statute also specifically directed the attention of the panel (Civil Service Law § 209, subd. 4, par. [c], cl. [v], sub. cl. [a], [c], [d]).

1. [Footnotes numbered as in original.–Ed.] Pursuant to CPLR 7804(g), Special Term transferred the proceeding to the Appellate Division which, correctly treating it as one under Article 75, properly dismissed it against PERB and the panel (See *Caso v. Coffey*, 41 N.Y.2d 153, 156, 160, 94 LRRM 2195).

Before further alluding to the considerations which may have motivated the panel, we note that the source of judicial power to review findings in compulsory interest arbitrations conducted under Section 209, subd. 4, is not to be found in the statute, which itself is completely silent on the matter, but rather in the requirements of due process, so "that the contract imposed by the arbitrator under the power conferred by statute have a basis not only in his good faith, but in law and the record * * *" (*Mount St. Mary's Hosp. v. Catherwood,* 26 N.Y.2d 493, 507, 74 LRRM 2897, 2902).

For such purposes there must be a sufficient form of review. Thus, since the statute here contained detailed standards which are to be considered, though only "so far as [the panel] deems them applicable in arriving at its determination" (Civil Service Law § 209, subd. 4, par. [c], cl. [v]), it is appropriate to review whether that requirement has been followed (*Guardian Life Insurance Co. v. Bohlinger,* 308 N.Y. 174, 183). And, since, as we only recently had occasion to make clear, "the essential function of these compulsory arbitration panels is to 'write collective bargaining agreements for the parties' (*Mount St. Mary's Hosp. v. Catherwood,* 26 N.Y.2d 493, 503, 74 LRRM 2897, *supra*), it follows that such awards, on judicial review, are to be measured according to whether they are rational or arbitrary and capricious in accordance with the principles articulated in *Mount St. Mary's Hosp. v. Catherwood (supra)* (see CPLR 7803, subd. 3, for parallel language)" (*Caso v. Coffey,* 41 N.Y.2d 153, 158), 94 LRRM 2195, 2197).

Turning now to the three-man panel's determination in this case, both the majority and minority opinion and a voluminously documented record reveal that the PBA introduced considerable evidence that, among other things, the wages, hours and working conditions of a Buffalo police officer compare unfavorably with those in contiguous or other comparable areas, that his services must be performed on a police force of diminishing size in the face of the growing hazards of an increasing crime rate and that an unusually high rise in the cost of living in the Buffalo area had substantially reduced the employees' real wages.

The City did not seriously dispute these contentions, but relied on proof of property abandonment, shrinking tax collections, fleeing population and industry, high unemployment and a declining tax rate base, all of which, it contended, combined to compound the City's financial problems. However true, this picture did not go uncontroverted. On this issue, the PBA introduced analyses and proof of its own so that the record reveals important differences between the parties on the probability and amount of a projected increase in sales tax, on the anticipated availability of Federal funds under the Public Works and Economic Development Act of 1965, on State revenue sharing, on the City's residual tax ability and on other fiscal measures available to it.

In the end, the panel came to the conclusion that "the fiscal problems of the City must be weighed against the services performed by a police officer." In making its award, it went on to state that "Buffalo police officers can surely be asked to share in this fight, but cannot be expected to bear the full burden of the City's fiscal problems."

On this record, it cannot be said that the panel's award was irrational. It was within its province, under the applicable statute, not only to judge the facts but choose the priorities to which, in its judgment, some matters were entitled to over others. It had a right to balance the ability of the City to pay against the interest of the public and the PBA members. Under Section 209, subd. 4, the panel is the one to determine what constitutes "a just and reasonable determination of the matters in dispute" (Section 209, subd. 4, par. [c], cl. [v]). It was therefore for it, and not for the courts, to decide what weight to give to each matter *vis-a-vis* the others.

It could be argued that a finding of the City's ability to pay based on expectations of increased revenue sharing, or even the availability of grants under Federal public works programs, might be so speculative as to approach irrationality. Even were that position to be accepted, there here remain other identified, nonspeculative sources of additional revenue. Beyond any such analysis, however, and most significant, it must be recognized that the statute, the wisdom of which it is for others to decide, vests broad authority in the arbitration panel to determine municipal fiscal priorities within existing revenues. Thus, even if the statute were to mandate consideration of municipal ability to pay (rather than as at present only to identify ability to pay as one of the factors to be taken into consideration "so far as it deems them applicable"), the panel would still be confronted with responsibility and vested with authority to determine priorities among all relevant factors in a balancing process. The panel might determine that a particular increase in compensation should take precedence over other calls on existing or even diminishing municipal revenues.

The reviewing court could only inquire whether there was support based on all the statutory criteria. The economic evidence was received in relation to all the "matters in dispute." It was the judgment of the majority of the panel that the evidence relating to comparability and other matters denors the City's ability to pay was such as to require increases in salary. Ability to pay was only one of the considerations to be weighed by the panel. The applicable statute, reading as it does, empowered the arbitrators to conclude that it was not dispositive. What must be assumed is that the City's ability to pay was considered: the opinion of the panel demonstrates a reasonable basis for its determination.

Conceivably, rare circumstances might arise when the cost of a particular award, when taken against particular economic conditions in a municipality and other relevant factors, would, on review, be found to be irrational. But this is not such a case. Here the Appellate Division should not have drawn its own conclusions from the weight of the evidence or substituted its judgment for that of the arbitrators.

Accordingly, the order of the Appellate Division should be reversed and the award of the arbitrators reinstated, without costs.

Order reversed, without costs, and the award of the arbitrators reinstated.

Opinion by FUGHSBERG, JUDGE, BREITEL, CHIEF JUDGE, and JASEN, GABRIELLI, JONES, WACHTLER, and COOKE, JUDGES, concur.

Notes and Questions

1. The New York court's insistence upon some judicial review, despite statutory silence on the matter, is typical. See Note, *Compulsory Arbitration: The Scope of Judicial Review,* 51 St. John's L.Rev. 604 (1977). But is the standard of review applied by the court adequate to protection of the public's interest? Can you suggest a better standard?

2. Where the arbitrator's award is deemed to conflict with some substantive constitutional or statutory provision courts have no hesitation in setting the award aside. E.g., *City of East Providence v. Firefighters Local 850,* 117 R.I. 329, 366 A.2d 1151, 94 LRRM 2571 (1976) (award imposing contractual obligation beyond the one-year limit permitted by statute); *Superintending Schools Committee v. Town of Winslow,* 363 A.2d 229, 93 LRRM 2398 (1976) (award establishing impermissible limitations upon school district's authority to terminate probationary teachers).

3. Statutory Directions to the Arbitrator Enforced by Judicial Review

The assumption has been (and is) that judicial review of interest arbitration awards is not only constitutionally required, but that it also is a mechanism for constraining arbitral excesses. However, the New York studies in the mid- and late 1970s shed substantial doubt on the latter proposition.

Thus, Professor Kochan reported in a 1976 study of police and firefighter tripartite arbitration held under a statute which includes standard criteria:

> The arbitration awards are largely negotiated and mediated * * * the awards of the arbitrators, and more importantly, the justifications or rationale accompanying these awards bear little relationship to the actual factors that shape the award. Thus, given the nature of this decision-making process and the way in which the statutory criteria are used or not used in framing the awards, it would be impossible for a court to effectively rule whether the award is arbitrary or capricious or has a reasonable basis.

In 1977, the New York statute was amended in an effort to tighten judicial review by requiring that the arbitration panel specify the basis for its findings. N.Y.—McKinney's Civ.Serv.Law § 209, subd. 4, p(c), cl. (v). The intent of this language was described by Governor Carey's supporting memorandum of June 7, 1977:

> This bill tightens the standards and procedures in the compulsory arbitration process, so that review of arbitration determinations by the courts will henceforth be meaningful. * * * This bill is intended to narrow the expansive authority accorded to arbitrators by the court of

> appeals in *City of Buffalo v. Rinaldo* and to make it clear that arbitrators must make findings with respect to each statutory criterion [including ability to pay] which the parties put in issue, that such findings must have an evidentiary basis in the record and that arbitrators must specify in their final determination what weight was given to each finding and why.

N.Y.Legis.Ann., 1977, p. 129.

A follow-up study in 1979 by a Cornell University group led them to conclude that the Governor's admonition had not been heeded. In most instances, the criteria were carefully listed somewhere toward the front of the report and studiously ignored thereafter. In only a minority of the awards was there any evidence that the arbitration panel had specified the basis for its findings. Comparability and cost of living remained the two most significant criteria. Ability to pay was only given lip service.

However, in 1980, a New York Supreme Court vacated an interest arbitration award on the ground that the arbitration panel failed to make specific findings with respect to each and every statutory criterion placed at issue by the parties, including ability to pay. *City of Buffalo v. Buffalo Police Benevolent Assn.,* 77 A.D.2d 789, 432 N.Y.S.2d 862 (1980).

In 1981, the Appellate Division sustained this determination but decided that the appropriate remedy, in lieu of vacating the arbitration award, was to remand the case to the arbitration panel so that it would have an opportunity to specify the basis for its findings as required by the statute. The court noted that the arbitration board made salary comparisons between the police in Buffalo and those in other cities, but had not taken into consideration the conditions of employment among the police forces in other jurisdictions and had made no comparison with any general public employees as required by the statute. Furthermore, while the panel had commented in passing on the city's ability to pay, it had presented no factual basis for its conclusion that the higher salaries requested by the police union would bankrupt the city while the awarded increase would not. Finally, the court noted that the panel had failed to specify the basis for its determination of about 20 other contract demands other than to state generally that all economic issues had been considered. *Buffalo Police Benevolent Assn. v. City of Buffalo,* 82 A.D.2d 635, 443 N.Y.S.2d 107 (1981).

Arvid Anderson noted:

> The awards were set aside because the arbitrators merely had written an essay stating that they had considered the statutory standards and had arrived at a particular result. Such a practice can no longer be followed successfully.

Anderson, *Interest Arbitration in New York City,* 37 The Arbitration Journal No. 4, p. 17 (December 1982).

In *City of Cohoes v. Cohoes Firefighters Local 2562,* 15 PERB ¶ 7530 (Sup.Ct.1982), the court refused to confirm or modify an ambiguous interest arbitration award; instead it remanded the case to the arbitration panel for clarification. *See also City of Yonkers v. Mutual Aid Association of Paid Fire Department Local 628,* 80 A.D.2d 597, 436 N.Y.S.2d 1009 (1981), in which an interest arbitration award that had previously been sent back to the arbitration panel with directions that it specify the basis for the award was confirmed on its second trip to the court. More recently, in *City of Batavia v. Local 896, Batavia Firefighters Association,* 19 PERB ¶ 7510 (Sup.Ct.1986), the court imposed upon the arbitration panel the obligation to explore each statutory criterion not simply as an arbiter, but also as a quasi-legislative body to the extent that, even where a statutory criterion is not put in issue, the panel should "nevertheless elicit the position of the parties and/or pertinent facts and consider the significance of such in its decision."

Thus, it seems that the judicial review is having a significant impact on interest arbitration in the State of New York. Arbitrators must make findings with respect to each statutory criterion which is in issue, including ability to pay, the findings must have an evidentiary basis in the record, and the arbitrators must specify, where the criteria point in different directions, the basis for choosing one over the other. This requires an explanation of the interplay between ability to pay, comparability of wage rates and total compensation, the cost of living and other relevant factors.

As Anderson points out, this places a special burden on the arbitrator as well as on the parties in a tripartite system to make certain that, whether the award is produced by adjudication or by the med-arb process described by Professor Kochan in his 1976 report, it is supported by the evidentiary record.

4. The Power of a Legislative Body to Refuse to Implement Awards

a. *Minnesota*

A severe and conventional restraint on arbitral authority is illustrated by *Minnesota Education Association v. State of Minnesota,* 282 N.W.2d 915 (Minn.1979), *appeal dism'd* 444 U.S. 1062, 100 S.Ct. 1001, 62 L.Ed.2d 744 (1980). The Minnesota Supreme Court reversed a lower court judgment holding that the state, as a public employer, committed an unfair labor practice when it failed to implement a final and binding arbitration award submitted to the State Legislature for review pursuant to a state statute which provided for legislative review of wage-related "agreements" entered into by a state employer (Minn.Stat.Ann. § 179.74, subd. 5). The Legislature passed a statute which lowered the salary structure in the award. The union contended that only negotiated provisions of its contract, and not the terms of an arbitration award, were subject to legislative modification. Concluding that the legislature had reserved the right to modify all contracts, the Supreme Court found that the arbitration award was incorporated into the written contract between the union and the state and it was this contract, "clearly an 'agreement' within the meaning of the statute," that was submitted to the Legislature for review. In *AFSCME Councils 6, 14, 65 and 96, AFL–CIO v. Sundquist,* 338 N.W.2d 560 (Minn. 1983), the Supreme Court extended its opinion in *Minnesota Education Association* to apply to legislative enactments which unilaterally change the terms and conditions of employment after the legislature had previously approved a collective bargaining agreement. The Supreme Court's construction of section 179.74, subdivision 5 (repealed 1984 c 462 s 28) has now been codified in Minnesota Statutes section 179A.22, subdivision 4 which provides that negotiated agreements *and arbitration awards* shall be submitted to the legislature to be accepted or rejected.

b. *New York State*

At the other end of the spectrum is New York's Taylor Law which expressly does not subject the arbitration panel's determination of matters in dispute to the approval of any local legislative body or other municipal authority. N.Y.—McKinney's Civ.Serv.Law § 209(4)(c)(vi).

c. *New York City*

Impasse panel recommendations in New York City are final and binding if not rejected or appealed by a party to a dispute within prescribed time limits. However, if implementation of any part of an impasse award requires the enactment or amendment of a law, the provision does not become binding until the appropriate legislative body enacts such a law. Thus, if there are insufficient funds in the budget to cover recommended wage increases, the award may not be implemented until the necessary appropriation is made. Anderson and Krause, *Interest Arbitration: The Alternative to the Strike,* 56 Fordham L.Rev. 153, 175 (1987); Anderson and London, *Collective Bargaining and the Fiscal Crisis in New York City: Cooperation for Survival,* 3 Fordham Urban Law Journal 373, 390 (1981–82); see New York City Administrative Code, ch. 54, §§ 1173–7.0(c)(3)(e) and (4)(3) (1975); § 12–311c(4)(e) (1986).

d. *New York Metropolitan Transit Authority*

In 1982, the New York State Legislature enacted short-term legislation authorizing New York's PERB, upon the request of either the employer or the union, to appoint an arbitration panel to resolve any impasses that might arise in the 1982 contract negotiations. In that instance, the panel was not tripartite; all three members were to be impartial. The determination of the panel was to be final and binding except that any provision thereof which required the enactment of a law for its implementation would not be binding until such law was enacted. Act of March 19, 1982, Ch. 19, § 2(a), (g), 1982 N.Y.Laws § 28–30. After expiration of that legislation and renewal thereof in 1985 (Act of March 31, 1985, Ch. 15, 1985 N.Y.Laws § 18), the New York Legislature amended the Taylor Law, which regulates labor disputes between state and local government employers and employees, to require the New York Metropolitan Transit Authority and the unions representing its employees who are subject to the Taylor Law to submit collective bargaining impasses to final and binding arbitration. Act of December 31, 1986, Ch. 929, § 33.5(a), 1986 N.Y.Laws §§ 2339, 2369–70; N.Y.—McKinney's Civ.Serv.Law § 209(5); *see* Anderson and Krause, supra, at p. 154.

e. *Pennsylvania*

A Pennsylvania statute provides that the awards in binding interest arbitration involving security personnel at prisons or mental hospitals "which would require legislative enactment to be effective shall be considered advisory only." 43 P.S. §§ 1101.101, 1101.805. [This statutory requirement is not to be confused with the statute dealing with awards for police and firefighters which, by constitutional amendment, mandates implementation of awards by local governments, including legislative bodies.]

The leading case is *Franklin County Prison Board v. Pennsylvania Labor Relations Board,* 491 Pa. 50, 417 A.2d 1138, 11 PPER 1162 (1980), holding that the awards pursuant to this statute are binding on the employer unless and until it can demonstrate that the legislative body responsible for providing funds has met, considered and rejected the award. Unless and until that happens, the award is binding.[1] See also *Commonwealth v. PLRB,* 64 Pa.Cmwlth. 84, 438 A.2d 1061, 13 PPER 13036 (1982); *County of Lawrence v. PLRB,* 79 Pa.Cmwlth. 14, 469 A.2d 1145, 13 PPER 1374 (1983); *County of Allegheny v. Allegheny Association of Professional Employees,* 67 Pa.Cmwlth. 277, 446 A.2d 1370, 13 PPER 13230 (1982); *Pennsylvania Labor Rel. Bd. v. Clarion County,* 65 Pa.Cmwlth. 158, 442 A.2d 374, 13 PPER 13076 (1982).

In *Association of Pennsylvania State College and University Faculty v. Kline,* 58 Pa.Cmwlth. 164, 427 A.2d 684, 13 PPER 13043 (1981), the Pennsylvania Commonwealth Court held that an arbitration award providing for a retroactive wage increase to university faculty members was binding, not advisory, because it had not been specifically repudiated by the General Assembly. The court stated that the employer—the executive branch—has the responsibility for setting salaries pursuant to an arbitration award unless and until it is considered and rejected by the general assembly in the exercise of its authority to enact appropriations. The employer argued that an arbitration award is not binding until it has been specifically considered by the General Assembly. The court rejected this argument, stating that it in effect would make all arbitration awards calling for salary increases automatically advisory, a conclusion which would make arbitration ineffective in resolving negotiation impasses. In other words, the award is binding until rejected; upon rejection, and only then, it becomes advisory.

In *Commonwealth of Pennsylvania v. Commonwealth of Pennsylvania, Pennsylvania Labor Relations Board,* 64 Pa.Cmwlth. 84, 438 A.2d 1061 (1982), the Commonwealth Court affirmed a decision of the Pennsylvania Labor Relations Board which found that the Commonwealth had committed certain unfair labor practices based on the Commonwealth's refusal to implement an arbitration award increasing salaries. The Board's decision included an order that the Commonwealth submit legislation implementing the salary increase to the General Assembly which was then to make an appropriate minimum legislative response. Relying on *Franklin County's*

1. The court noted:

However, the Prison Board can only implement the award to the extent permitted by Art. III, section 31 of the constitution, thus the Prison Board can only submit to the Salary Board the financial items of the arbitration award and the Salary Board must fix the salary and compensation in accordance with the award. If, at that point, legislative enactment is required—that is, if taxes must be levied or funds appropriated—then our holding herein cannot be read to override the constitutional prohibition against improper delegation of legislative powers. Where it is demonstrated by the public employer that the lawmaking body has met, considered and rejected an arbitration award concerning financial items, then Art. III, section 31 and the proviso of section 805 become operative, and the award is thereby rendered advisory only.

holding that an arbitration award is binding absent consideration and rejection of the award by the appropriate legislative body, the Commonwealth Court concluded that the Board's order did not exceed the Board's authority because the order was a reasonable exercise of the Board's remedial power to insure the enforcement of the Public Employees Relation Act.

In *County of Allegheny v. Allegheny Court Association of Professional Employees,* 517 Pa. 505, 539 A.2d 348 (1988), the Supreme Court stated that *Franklin County* had imposed upon the public employer the burden of demonstrating that an award is advisory only. To meet this burden, the public employer must establish "(1) that 'legislative enactment,' i.e., the levying of taxes or appropriation of funds, is necessary to implement the award and (2) if so, that the public employer has, in fact, met, considered and rejected the award." The Supreme Court approved the holding of the lower court that the county must administratively transfer money to implement the arbitration award because the transfer of funds from one line item of the budget to another constitutes ordinary administration and not legislative enactment and because it was not shown that money was unavailable in the general fund or from other items with surplus funds. Further, a *pro forma* resolution adopted by the Board of County Commissioners did not constitute compliance with the mandate to meet, consider and reject or accept the award because the resolutions summarily rejected the arbitration award without considering either the merits or the fiscal impact of the award.

5. Do the foregoing notes persuade you that binding interests arbitration can function to resolve public sector labor disputes without grossly invading legislative authority?

Is it fair to restrict arbitration to the uniformed services and other strategically situated public employees such as transit workers? Does the restriction operate to disadvantage other public employees who have less bargaining power? See Chapter 1.

Chapter 9

THE UNION–EMPLOYEE RELATIONSHIP

A. THE DUTY OF FAIR REPRESENTATION

BELANGER v. MATTESON

Supreme Court of Rhode Island, 1975.
115 R.I. 332, 346 A.2d 124.

[An agreement between the Warwick School Committee and the Warwick Teachers Union provided, with respect to promotions, that "candidates shall be recommended on the basis of qualifications for the position," and that "where qualifications are considered equal, seniority in the Warwick School System shall prevail." In 1972 the school committee appointed Belanger to a vacant promotional position as business department head of a high school. Matteson, who had greater seniority than Belanger, requested that the Union file a grievance on his behalf. The Union did so and, after proceeding through the grievance steps of the agreement, took the case to arbitration as the agreement provided. After a hearing in which both Belanger and Matteson testified, the arbitrators ruled that Matteson was entitled to the appointment.]

After a full year on the job, Belanger found himself deprived of his promotion and back in the classroom. He wrote to his principal and the Union and requested that a grievance be filed on his behalf as he wished to challenge this demotion.

The Union president responded that, although the Union would be happy to file a grievance for him alleging that the School Committee had not adequately represented or protected his interest in his former position as department head, it would not ask for his reinstatement in that position because: "We [the Union] cannot, at this time, however, ask for a remedy which in effect would reverse a decision which was a result of a grievance filed by the Union. This would be illogical and inconsistent with our role as bargaining agent and our obligation under the contract. We have, after all, agreed to make binding arbitration the final step in our grievance procedure."

Thereafter, Belanger instituted this litigation in the Superior Court. He named as defendants Matteson, the Union, the arbitrators, and the School Committee and asked the court to overturn the arbitrators' decision and reinstate him. His suit was based on two grounds: (1) that the arbitrators exceeded their jurisdiction, and (2) that the Union breached its duty to fairly represent his interests when it decided to pursue Matteson's grievance.

The trial justice found that there existed a duty of fair representation which the Union had breached, and that the award was in excess of the arbitrators' power and thus void. He vacated the award, and reinstated Belanger. Matteson and the Union appealed. We will first consider the duty of fair representation facet of this appeal and then go on to discuss the finding that the arbitrators had exceeded their power by usurping duties and responsibilities which the Legislature has committed to the school committees of the various municipalities and nobody else.

The question of the duty owed by a union to its members is one of first impression in this court. It has, however, been extensively litigated in other jurisdictions, most notably in the federal courts, in cases arising under the National Labor Relations Act, 29 U.S.C.A. § 151 *et seq.* (1973), the Labor Management Relations Act, 1947, 29 U.S.C.A. § 141 *et seq.* (1973), and the Railway Act. 45 U.S.C.A. § 151 *et seq.* (1972).

The first of what has become a long line of cases was *Steele v. Louisville & Nashville R.R.*, 323 U.S. 192, 15 LRRM 708 (1944). There, the Court held that the Railway Labor Act, in providing that an organization chosen by the majority of employees would be the exclusive representative of all the employees within its class, mandated a concomitant duty "to act for and not against those whom it represents," and "to exercise fairly the power conferred upon it in behalf of all those for whom it acts * * *" *Id.* at 202, 203, 15 LRRM at 712. This duty has also been found in unions governed by the NLRB. *Ford Motor Co. v. Huffman*, 345 U.S. 330, 337, 31 LRRM 2548 (1953). By taking away the right of individual employees to further their interests individually or to organize into numerous small units to deal with their employer, Congress has given a union power and control over the working lives of each of its members. A corollary of such power is the duty to act for the benefit of its members.

Our Legislature has created a structure of labor regulations which parallels in many significant respects the federal scheme. Our focus here is G.L.1956 (1968 Reenactment) § 28–9.3–1 et seq. entitled Arbitration of School Teacher Disputes. Section 28–9.3–1 declares it to be the public policy of this state to grant public school teachers the right to organize, to be represented, and to bargain on a collective basis with school committees relevant to "hours, salary, working conditions and other terms of professional employment." Section 28–9.3–3 mandates that the school committee recognize the labor organization chosen by the teachers to be their "sole and exclusive" bargaining agent. Thus, a labor organization representing teachers of this state has the same broad authority in the negotiation, administration, and enforcement of the collective bargaining agreement as does a union regulated by federal law. We find ourselves in agreement with the persuasive logic of the Steele opinion and its progeny, and, therefore hereby recognize, as implicit in our Act, a statutory duty on the part of an exclusive bargaining agent to fairly and adequately represent the interests of all of those for whom it negotiates and contracts, not only those who are members, but all those who are part of the bargaining unit.[1]

The union and its bargaining unit are necessarily composed of many individuals with diverse views and oft-times conflicting employment demands. The whole purpose behind the creation of the union is, however, to present a solid, unified front to the employer. "In unity there is strength," went the old organizing slogan, and it was the truth. In dealing with the employer, the union gains its negotiating power from the fact that it speaks with one voice for all the employees.

That we find a duty on the part of the union does not, however, solve the controversy before us. We must define the parameters of the duty, and then apply it to the facts as found by the Superior Court.

We believe at the start that we must recognize that "[a] wide range of reasonableness must be allowed a statutory bargaining representative in serving the unit it represents. * * *" *Ford Motor Co. v. Huffman, supra,* 345 U.S. at 338, 31 LRRM at 2551. Recognizing conflict[s], the Court found that the union did not breach its duty to its members by bargaining for a seniority provision in the contract which favored some employees, but caused the layoff of others because of their newly lowered position on the seniority lists.

The union must be an advocate for its membership and where its members disagree, the union should not be forced into a neutral position by a court-enforced obligation not to take a stand. In *Humphrey v. Moore,* 375 U.S. 335, 55 LRRM 2031 (1964), a multiemployer union found itself representing the employees of two trucking companies who were merging their businesses. The employees from the dissolved outfit had an interest in retaining their seniority within the absorbing company. That company's employees obviously did not favor such a happening. The contract signed by both employers and the

1. [Footnotes numbered as in original.—Ed.] General Laws 1956 (1968 Reenactment) § 28–9.3–7 provides that teachers shall be free to decline to join an organization even if it is certified as the exclusive representative of all teachers within a unit. The union, however, is still the sole representative for those who choose not to join its organization, and owes them the same duty as it does its dues-paying members. *Steele v. Louisville & Nashville R.R.* 323 U.S. 192, 15 LRRM 708 (1944). We have approved a provision in collective bargaining agreements requiring teachers who are not members of the union to pay their proportionate share of the costs of the benefits conferred upon all members of the bargaining unit. *Town of North Kingstown v. Teachers Ass'n,* 110 R.I. 698, 297 A.2d 342, 82 LRRM 2010 (1972).

union was ambiguous. The contract question was put before a joint labor-management committee. The union took the side of the absorbed employees, some of the other employees were "bumped" and they sued their union and their employer. The Court, expanding upon the *Huffman* holding, said:

> "Just as a union must be free to sift out wholly frivolous grievances which would only clog the grievance process, so it must be free to take a position on the not so frivolous disputes. Nor should it be neutralized when the issue is chiefly between two sets of employees. Conflict between employees represented by the same union is a recurring fact. To remove or gag the union in these cases would surely weaken the collective bargaining and grievance processes." *Id.* at 349–50, 55 LRRM at 2037–38.

Given these facts of life in the labor-management world, the duty of fair representation which is imposed on the union must not be such as to squelch union advocacy of position, nor must it weaken the union's ability to act when it does for all its members, even those whose interests may not be served but who are nonetheless bound by the majority vote. The entire scheme of federal and state labor regulations would be pointless if the minority in a union were not bound by the majority will. For example, what would be the efficacy of statutes requiring an employer to bargain exclusively with the duly elected union if the minority of employees who voted against ratification of a collective bargaining contract could then turn around and require the employer to contract with them individually.

Whether or not the minority should be bound by the majority in the control of the conditions of their employment is not a matter for us to decide. The Legislature has unequivocally declared that to be the policy and we cannot say otherwise. However, concurrent with the union's power to bind the minority flows the duty which we define today.

In the negotiation process, we hold that a union must make an honest effort to serve the interest of all of its members, without hostility to any, and its power must be exercised in complete good faith and with honesty of purpose. *Ford Motor Co. v. Huffman, supra.*

Where the union and the employer have provided by contract for the internal settlement of disputes by means of grievance and arbitration procedures, and where these settlement procedures can be initiated and continued solely by the union, the union is likewise subject to a duty of fair representation in its handling of employee grievances. As in contract negotiations, the union as it deals with grievances must often take a position which is detrimental to some employees as it is helpful to others. The duty upon the Union here is to " * * * in good faith and in a non-arbitrary manner, make decisions as to the merits of particular grievances." *Vaca v. Sipes,* 386 U.S. 171, 194, 64 LRRM 2369, 2378 (1967), and, if it decides to pursue a grievance, it must not do so in a perfunctory manner.

For a union to make a decision affecting its members without investigating the underlying factual situation is a clear breach of the duty of fair representation. *De Arrovo v. Sindicato De Trabajadores Packinghouse, AFL–CIO,* 425 F.2d 281, 74 LRRM 2028 (1st Cir.1970). In an examination of the union's conduct in its discharge of its duty to the members of the bargaining unit, there are three possible foci for our analysis; the union's motives, its decision-making procedures, and the reasons for its acting as it did. A court's investigation into the first two questions is proper and necessary. We will, however, be more careful in any review of the merits of the Union's decision. An inquiry into the merits would open the way for our substituting our judgment for that of the Union, and that is not our role. It will be enough protection for an employee represented by a union if we inquire into motives and ensure that the union has fairly considered both sides before taking a stand.

In examining the record presented to us, we find no evidence of bad faith by the Union. However, the Union's decision to press on with Matteson's grievance without making any effort to assess the relative qualifications of the respective candidates was patently defective. Thus, the Union breached its duty to represent fairly the interests of one of its members—Belanger.

[In the balance of its opinion, the court decided that despite the union's breach of duty the award should not be overturned. It reached this conclusion on the ground that Belanger had participated fully in the arbitration proceeding, and that the arbitrators had fully considered the respective qualifications of the two candidates. Distinguishing *Vaca,* the court observed that "the Union's breach did not foreclose a fair utilization of the contractual remedy; and the employer, who had done no wrong, should not be subjected to a relitigation of the question. * * *" The court also rejected Belanger's contention that the award should be overturned because the arbitrators exceeded their powers. One Justice, dissenting in part, was of the view that the school committee's authority to promote employees was not subject to arbitration.]

Notes

1. The principal case is typical of cases in which courts, in the absence of express statutory guidance, have followed private sector principles in developing a duty of fair representation on the part of public sector unions. See Aaron, *Procedural Due Process and the Duty of Fair Representation in Public Sector Grievance Disputes,* Part V, in *Labor Relations Law in the Public Sector,* ed. Knapp (ABA Labor Law Section 1977), p. 179.

2. Some statutes provide explicitly for some duty on the part of an exclusive bargaining representative toward employees within the bargaining unit. E.g., Hawaii Rev.Stat. § 89–8(a) ("As exclusive representative it shall have the right to act for and negotiate agreements covering all employees in the unit and shall be responsible for representing the interests of all such employees without discrimination and without regard to employee organization membership"); West's Ann.Cal.Gov't Code § 3544.9

("The employee organization recognized or certified as the exclusive representative for the purpose of meeting and negotiating shall fairly represent each and every employee in the appropriate unit").

New York's Taylor Law was amended in 1990. See N.Y.Laws 1990–91, c. 8, § 217 p. 83. The amendments establish a four-month statute of limitations for civil actions against a union on duty-of-fair-representation grounds and those against an employer where the union's DFR breach is essential if the plaintiff is to prevail. Moreover, the amendments make a violation of a union's duty of fair representation an improper practice. See Section 209–a2. An amendment to Section 209–2.3. requires that a public employer be made a party to any DFR charge where the claim arises out of the improper processing or failure to process a claim against the employer on the ground that it violated the collective bargaining agreement. Section 205.5(b) is amended to give PERB the power, when it has found a DFR breach involving the administration of the labor agreement, to direct the union and the employer to process the grievance in accordance with the grievance machinery in the contract. Finally, PERB is empowered to apportion damages between the union and the employer.

3. Public employees have certain constitutional due process rights where their expectation of entitlement in their jobs rises to the level of a "property interest." *Board of Regents v. Roth,* 408 U.S. 564, 92 S.Ct. 2701, 33 L.Ed.2d 548 (1972); *Perry v. Sindermann,* 408 U.S. 593, 92 S.Ct. 2694, 33 L.Ed.2d 570 (1972). *Cf. Arnett v. Kennedy,* 416 U.S. 134, 94 S.Ct. 1633, 40 L.Ed.2d 15 (1974). Would an employee in Belanger's position have a due process right to be notified of and to participate in the arbitration hearing? *See Sedita v. Board of Education,* 82 Misc.2d 644, 371 N.Y.S.2d 812 (1975); *Ricciotti v. Warwick School Comm.,* 319 F.Supp. 1006 (D.R.I.1970). Would due process require a higher standard of care in processing grievances than is normally applied under the duty-of-fair-representation doctrine? Consider the following:

> "* * * Policy arguments regarding the *Vaca* doctrine appear to apply roughly as well in the public sector as in the private sector. The additional element in public sector analysis, however, is the due process requirement that unless there is a strong countervailing public interest, a discharged employee should receive reasonably accurate factfinding. At minimum, the aggrieved employee ought to be entitled to expect his union to exercise due care and reasonable prudence in handling his grievance. Arguably, he receives due process only if the union's failure to pursue his grievance is based on a fair consideration of the merits of that grievance. Hence the constitutional duty of fair representation must be somewhat stronger than the *Vaca* rule; procedural negligence even in the absence of bad faith should constitute a breach." Comment, *Public Sector Grievance Procedures, Due Process, and the Duty of Fair Representation,* 89 Harv.L.Rev. 752, 785 (1976). Refer back to Chapter 6, Section E.

4. As will be explored below, some states preclude the negotiation of union security arrangements whereby payment of dues or their equivalent is made a condition of employment. Should that preclusion affect the union's duty of fair representation?

5. Do considerations of procedural due process give the aggrieved employee the right to sue on the contract if the union refuses to take his grievance to arbitration? See Chapter Six, p. 250, note 3.

B. CHECK-OFF OF MEMBERS' DUES

Dues check-off arrangements, whereby the employer deducts the amount of monthly union dues from each employee's paycheck and transmits such amount to the union, are quite common in the public sector, as in the private. Many statutes which do not recognize any other form of union security explicitly permit the check-off; and in some states check-off arrangements exist even in the absence of statutory authorization.

In the absence of statutory authorization, is there any problem, do you think, with a public employer granting check-off rights *exclusively* to the majority union while denying such rights to other unions which may have members within the same bargaining unit? In *Board of School Directors v. WERC,* 42 Wis.2d 637, 168 N.W.2d 92 (1969), the Wisconsin Supreme Court held that to be a prohibited practice on the ground that "those rights and benefits which are granted exclusively to the majority representative, and thus denied its minority organizations, must in some rational manner be related to the functions of the majority organization in its representative capacity, and must not be granted to entrench such organization as the bargaining representative." The court reasoned that the "sole and complete purpose of exclusive check-off is self-perpetuation and entrenchment. While a majority representative may negotiate for check-off, he is negotiating for all the employees, and, if check-off is granted for any, it must be granted for all."

Other state courts which have considered the question have reached an opposite result. The New York Court of Appeals, for example, found exclusive check-off to be "plainly consistent with the scheme set forth in the Taylor Act for according recognition, and a degree of union security, to bargaining agents for public employees." *Bauch v. City of New York,* 21 N.Y.2d 599, 289 N.Y.S.2d 951, 237 N.E.2d 211 (1968), *cert. denied* 393 U.S. 834, 89 S.Ct. 108, 21 L.Ed.2d 105 (1968). *Accord: Sacramento County Employees Organization v. County of Sacramento,* 28 Cal.App.3d 424, 104 Cal.Rptr. 619 (1972). Which result do you consider to be more sound in terms of public policy?

The minority unions in the *Bauch* case also argued that the exclusive dues check-off arrangement deprived them of due process and equal protection of the laws, and of their rights of freedom of association guaranteed by the First and Fourteenth Amendments. How do you think a court should deal with that issue? Consider that question in light of the following case, which dealt with the other side of the coin: may a public employer constitutionally refuse to grant check-off rights to *any* union under circumstances in which it allows deductions from paychecks for other purposes?

CITY OF CHARLOTTE v. LOCAL 660, INT'L ASS'N OF FIREFIGHTERS

Supreme Court of the United States, 1976.
426 U.S. 283, 96 S.Ct. 2036, 48 L.Ed.2d 636.

MR. JUSTICE MARSHALL delivered the opinion of the Court.

The city of Charlotte, N.C., refuses to withhold from the paychecks of its firefighters' dues owing to their union, Local 660, International Association of Firefighters. We must decide whether this refusal violates the Equal Protection Clause of the Fourteenth Amendment.

I

Local 660 represents some 351 of the 543 uniformed members of the Charlotte Fire Department. Since 1969 the union and individual members have repeatedly requested the city to withhold dues owing to the union from the paychecks of those union members who agree to a check off. The city has refused each request. After the union learned that it could obtain a private group life insurance policy for its membership only if it had a dues checkoff agreement with the city, the union and its officers filed suit in federal court alleging, *inter alia,* that the city's refusal to withhold the dues of union members violated the Equal Protection Clause of the Fourteenth Amendment. The complaint asserted that since the city withheld amounts from its employees' paychecks for payment to various other organizations, it could not arbitrarily refuse to withhold amounts for payment to the union.

On cross-motions for summary judgment, the District Court for the Western District of North Carolina ruled against the city. The Court determined that although the city had no written guidelines, its "practice has been to allow check offs from employees' pay to organizations or programs as required by law or where the check off option is available to all employees within a single employee unit such as the Fire Department." 381 F.Supp. 500, 502 (1974). The Court further found that the city has "not allowed check off options serving only single employees or programs which are not available either to all City employees or to all employees engaged in a particular section of City employment." *Ibid.* Finding, however, that withholding union dues from the paychecks of union members would be no more difficult than processing any other deduction allowed by the city, the District Court concluded that the city had not offered a rational explanation for its refusal to withhold for the union. Accordingly, the District Court held that the city's refusal to withhold moneys when requested to do so by the respondents for the benefit of Local 660 "constitutes a violation of the [respondents'] rights to equal protection of laws under the Fourteenth Amendment." *Id.,* at 502–503. The Court ordered that so long as the city continued "without clearly stated and fair standards to withhold moneys from the paychecks of City employees for other purposes," it was enjoined from refusing to withhold union dues from the paychecks of the respondents. *Id.,* at 503. The Court of Appeals for the Fourth Circuit affirmed, 518 F.2d 83 (1975), and we granted certiorari. 423 U.S. 890 (1975). We reverse.

II

Since it is not here asserted—and this Court would reject such a contention if it were made—that respondents' status as union members or their interest in obtaining a dues check off is such as to entitle them to special treatment under the Equal Protection Clause, the city's practice must meet only a relatively relaxed standard of reasonableness in order to survive constitutional scrutiny.

The city presents three justifications for its refusal to allow the dues checkoff requested by respondents. First, it argues, North Carolina law makes it illegal for the city to enter into a contract with a municipal union, N.C.Gen.Stat. 95–98, and an agreement with union members to provide a dues check off, with the union as a third-party beneficiary, would in effect be such a contract. See 40 N.C.Atty.Gen. Rep. 591 (1968–1970). Thus, compliance with the state law, and with the public policy it represents of discouraging dealing with municipal unions, is said to provide a sufficient basis for refusing respondents' request. Second, it claims, a dues check off is a proper subject of collective bargaining, which the city asserts Congress may shortly require of state and local governments. Under this theory, the desire to preserve the checkoff as a bargaining chip in any future collective-bargaining process is in itself an adequate basis for the refusal. Lastly, the city contends, allowing withholding only when it benefits all city or departmental employees is a legitimate method for avoiding the burden of withholding money for all persons or organizations that request a check off. Because we find that this explanation provides a sufficient justification for the challenged practice, we have no occasion to address the first two reasons proffered.

The city submitted affidavits to show that it would be unduly burdensome and expensive for it to withhold money for every organization or person that requested it, App. 17, 45, 55, and respondents did not contest this showing. As respondents concede, it was therefore reasonable, and permissible under the Equal Protection Clause, for the city to develop standards or restrictions to determine who would be eligible for withholding. *Mathews v. Diaz,* ___ U.S. ___, ___, slip op., at 14–15 (1976). See Brief for Respondents 9. Within the limitations of the Equal Protection Clause, of course, the choice of those standards is for the city and not for the courts. Thus, our inquiry is not whether standards might be drawn that would include the union, but whether the standards that were drawn were reasonable ones with "some basis in practical experience." *South Carolina v. Katzenbach,* 383 U.S. 301, 331 (1966). Of course, the fact that the standards were drawn and applied in practice rather than pursuant to articulated guidelines is of no import for equal protection purposes.

The city allows withholding for taxes, retirement-insurance programs, savings programs, and certain charitable organizations. These categories, the District Court found, are those in which the checkoff option can, or must, be availed of by all city employees, or those in an entire department. Although the District Court found that this classification did not present a rational basis for rejecting respondents' requests, 381 F.Supp., at 502, we disagree. The city has determined that it will provide withholding only for programs of general interest in which all city or departmental employees can, without more, participate. Employees can participate in the union check off only if they join an outside organization—the union. Thus, Local 660 does not fit the category of groups for which the city will withhold. We cannot say that denying withholding to associational or special interest groups that claim only some departmental employees as members and that employees must first join before being eligible to participate in the check off marks an arbitrary line so devoid of reason as to violate the Equal Protection Clause. Rather, this division seems a reasonable method for providing the benefit of withholding to employees in their status as employees, while limiting the number of instances of withholding and the financial and administrative burdens attendant thereon.

Given the permissibility of creating standards and the reasonableness of the standards created, the District Court's conclusion that it would be no more difficult for the city to withhold dues for the union than to process other deductions is of no import. We may accept, *arguendo,* that the difficulty involved in processing any individual deduction is neither great nor different in kind from that involved in processing any other deduction. However, the city has not drawn its lines in order to exclude individual deductions, but in order to avoid the cumulative burden of processing deductions every time a request is made; and inherent in such a line-drawing process are difficult choices and "some harsh and apparently arbitrary consequences. * * *" *Mathews v. Diaz,* ___ U.S., at ___, slip op., at 15. See *id.,* at ___, slip op., at 14–16; *Dandridge v. Williams,* 397 U.S. 471, 485 (1970). Cf. *Schilb v. Kuebel,* 404 U.S. 357, 364 (1972); *Williamson v. Lee Optical,* 348 U.S. 483, 489 (1955).

Respondents recognize the legitimacy of such a process and concede that the city "is free to develop fair and reasonable standards to meet any possible cost problem." Brief for Respondents, at 9. Respondents have wholly failed, however, to present any reasons why the present standards are not fair and reasonable—other than the fact that the standards exclude them. This fact, of course, is insufficient to transform the city policy into a constitutional violation. Since we find a reasonable basis for the challenged classification, the judgment of the Court of Appeals for the Fourth Circuit must be reversed, and the case remanded for further proceedings consistent with this opinion.

It is so ordered.

MR. JUSTICE STEWART concurs in the judgment upon the ground that the classification challenged in this case is not invidiously discriminatory and does not, therefore, violate the Equal Protection Clause of the Fourteenth Amendment.

C. THE PROBLEM OF THE FREE RIDER

STATE OF CALIFORNIA DECISION OF THE PUBLIC EMPLOYMENT RELATIONS BOARD

DON HAGOPIAN, Charging Party,	)	
v.	)	6 PERC 13159 (1982)
SAN FRANCISCO FEDERATION OF TEACHERS, LOCAL 61, CFT/AFL–CIO, Respondent.	)	

The Federation is the exclusive representative for a unit of certificated employees in the San Francisco Unified School District (District). The Charging Party is a member of this unit, but is not a member of the Federation. The collective agreement negotiated by the Federation and the District contains a provision covering involuntary transfers, provides for binding arbitration of grievances, and gives the Federation the *exclusive* right to appeal a grievance to arbitration. The agreement does *not* include an agency fee provision. The Federation filed a class action grievance challenging several involuntary transfers and represented the entire class, including the Charging Party, at the lower steps of the grievance procedure. Julie Koppich, a Federation representative, made arguments on behalf of individual members of the class and specifically on behalf of Mr. Hagopian. At the arbitration stage of the grievance procedure the Federation invoked the policy which gives rise to the instant proceeding. In accordance with that policy, the Federation agreed to represent its members in the arbitration, but refused to represent the Charging Party unless he agreed to pay his pro-rata share of arbitration costs or the equivalent of annual Federation dues, whichever was less. The Charging Party refused to comply with this policy. The basis of the Federation's refusal to represent the Charging Party is not that he is a nonmember. Rather, the Federation refused to represent Mr. Hagopian at the arbitration because he would not agree to this policy. If Charging Party had agreed to pay his pro-rata share of arbitration costs or the equivalent of annual Federation dues, whichever was less, the Federation would have represented him at the arbitration. On February 13, 1979, the Federation appealed the grievance involving the involuntary transfers to arbitration. The appeal consisted of a class of 21 teachers, including other nonmembers who complied with the Federation's policy. Mr. Hagopian was not included in the appeal and his individual grievance was not arbitrated. The record does not reflect the outcome of the arbitration for the other teachers nor what, if any, job related or monetary harm Charging Party has suffered.

Mr. James Ballard, Federation president and executive officer, testified that the Federation incurs costs in processing grievances through steps one and two of the grievance procedure, including costs stemming from staff time, preparation and paperwork. Despite these costs, the Federation represents all bargaining unit employees at the first two steps of the grievance procedure. It is only at step three, the arbitration stage, that the policy to which Charging Party objects is applied.

Mr. Ballard further testified that the high costs associated with arbitration prompted the Federation's executive board to adopt the policy. Costs cited by Mr. Ballard include staff time for preparation, attorney fees, Xeroxing fees, arbitrator fees, court reporter and transcript fees, and possibly room rental fees.

Discussion

In this case we are faced with the issue of whether an exclusive representative may charge nonmembers for representation in arbitration proceedings. The Charging Party excepts to the hearing officer's conclusion that such a charge does not violate either the duty of fair representation or discriminates against an employee for the exercise of the right to refuse to participate in the activities of an employee organization.

We conclude, for the reasons stated below, that the Federation's policy breached the duty of fair representation and the charging party's rights under section 3543 [2] in violation of the unfair practice subsection 3543.6(b). (See, *King v. Fremont Unified District Teachers Association, CTA/NEA,* (4/21/80) PERB Decision No. 125.)

2. Section 3543 states that:

Public school employees shall have the right to form, join, and participate in the activities of employee organizations of their own choosing for the purpose of representation on all matters of employer-employee relations. Public school employees shall also have the right to refuse to join or participate in the activities of employee organizations and shall have the right to represent themselves individually in their employment relations with the public school employer, except that once the employees in an appropriate unit have selected an exclusive representative and it has been recognized pursuant to Section 3544.1 or certified pursuant to Section 3544.7, no employee in that unit may meet and negotiate with the public school employer.

Any employee may at any time present grievances to his employer, and have such grievances adjusted, without the intervention of the exclusive representative, as long as the adjustment is reached prior to arbitration pursuant to Sections 3548.5, 3548.6, 3548.7, and 3548.8 and the adjustment is not inconsistent with the terms of a written agreement then in effect; provided that the public school employer shall not agree to a resolution of the grievance until the exclusive representative has received a copy of the grievance and the proposed resolution and has been given the opportunity to file a response.

By authorizing the negotiation of service fee arrangements,[3] the Legislature has recognized the financial burden of the duty of fair representation placed upon exclusive representatives. By requiring the employer's agreement to such arrangements and, under given circumstances, the approval of unit employees expressed through the authorization election, the Legislature has also indicated its refusal to impose an absolute obligation on nonmembers. By its action here, the union goes beyond the Legislature's concession to its 'free-rider' concerns.

The Federation's policy, in effect, creates a distinction between members and nonmembers which impinges on the Charging Party's right not to join or participate in the activities of the Federation. The Federation requires the charging party to first agree to pay a specified sum of money in order to take his grievance to arbitration. Members of the local are *not* required to make such a payment.

Section 3543 guarantees employees the right to refuse to join or participate in the activities of an employee organization.[4] Conditioning representation of nonmembers upon payment of costs unlawfully discriminates, interferes with, restrains and coerces such members in the exercise of rights guaranteed by section 3543. Article 18 of the agreement between the Federation and the District details the grievance procedure covering the employees in the bargaining unit and states that the union has the *exclusive* right to appeal to arbitration the decision of the superintendent or designee. Thus, under the agreement, the union is the only one to decide when to appeal to arbitration. The charging party can't appeal on his own. He is faced with either paying the fee or not being able to have his grievance processed through arbitration. The right to have a meritorious grievance processed is a fundamental right. *Machinist, Local 697,* (1976) 91 LRRM 1529, 1531. Once an agreement provides for a grievance procedure as in the instant case, it must apply equally and fully to all the employees in the unit, whether members or non-members.

The Federation's Policy Violates the Duty of Fair Representation

EERA, unlike the National Labor Relations Act (NLRA), has a statutory duty of fair representation.

Government Code section 3544.9 states:

3. Subsection 3546(a) states that:

(a) An organizational security arrangement, in order to be effective, must be agreed upon by both parties to the agreement. At the time the issue is being negotiated, the public school employer may require that the organizational security provision be severed from the remainder of the proposed agreement and cause the organizational security provision to be voted upon separately by all members in the appropriate negotiating unit, in accordance with rules and regulations promulgated by the board. Upon such a vote, the organizational security provision will become effective only if a majority of those members of the negotiating unit voting approve the agreement. Such vote shall not be deemed to either ratify or defeat the remaining provisions of the proposed agreement.

4. Of course, the right not to participate is not absolute. The service fee provision in the Act constitutes an exception to such a right.

> The employee organization recognized or certified as the exclusive representative for the purpose of meeting and negotiating shall fairly represent *each and every* employee in the appropriate unit. (Emphasis added.)

In the *Wallace Corporation v. NLRB,* 323 U.S. 248, 255–256, 65 S.Ct. 238, 241–242, 89 L.Ed. 216, 15 LRRM 697 (1944) the Supreme Court stated:

> "The duties of a bargaining agent selected under the terms of the Act extend beyond the mere representation of the interests of its own group members. By its selection as bargaining representative it has become the agent of all the employees, charged with the responsibility of representing their interests fairly and impartially."

Similarly, the National Labor Relations Board (NLRB) has long held that an exclusive bargaining agent has taken on the responsibility to act as a genuine representative of all the employees in the bargaining unit, "irrespective of union membership. * * *" *Peerless Tool and Engineering Co.,* 111 NLRB 853, 858, 35 LRRM 1598 (1955) enfd. sub nom. *NLRB v. Die and Tool Makers Lodge No. 113, International Association of Machinists, AFL,* 231 F.2d 298, 37 LRRM 2673 (7th Cir.1956), *cert. denied* 352 U.S. 833, 77 S.Ct. 50, 1 L.Ed.2d 53, 38 LRRM 2717.

In *Machinist, Local 697, supra,* the NLRB explained that what is involved is a quid pro quo—in exchange for the protection of the Act, the bargaining representative must represent all unit employees.[5]

Under EERA the duty of fair representation is breached when the exclusive representative's conduct towards a member of the bargaining unit is arbitrary, discriminatory or in bad faith. *Mt. Diablo Unified District,* (8/21/78) PERB Decision No. 68; and *Redlands Teachers Association,* (9/25/78) PERB Decision No. 72. See also *Rocklin Teachers Professional Association* (3/26/80) PERB Decision No. 124. We do find that the Federation's policy is discriminatory. Since the Federation does not condition the processing of arbitration by dues-paying members on their paying a specific fee for arbitration, the Federation has drawn a distinction between members and nonmembers, and to this extent discriminated against the Charging Party.[6]

5. Although *Machinists Local 697* expressly stated that resolution of its proceeding did not turn upon the duty of fair representation under the NLRA, but focused on whether respondent's discrimination against nonmembers is such that it restrains and coerces them in the exercise of Section 7 rights; we nonetheless find the rationale expressed in the above cases to be persuasive to support not only a finding that the Federation's policy interfered and coerced the Charging Party in his exercise of section 3543 rights, but also to support a finding that the Federation breached the duty of fair representation it owes to the Charging Party.

6. This case is distinguishable from one of the leading private sector cases *Vaca v. Sipes,* 386 U.S. 171, 87 S.Ct. 903, 17 L.Ed.2d 842, 64 LRRM 2369 (1967) because in that case the labor organization based its decision of whether or not to take the case to arbitration on its good faith assessment on the *merits* of the case given the conflicting medical opinions it had received regarding the grievant's capacity to work.

* * *

ORDER

Upon the foregoing facts, conclusions of law and the entire record in this case, it is found that the San Francisco Federation of Teachers, Local 61, CFT/AFL–CIO has violated subsection 3545.6(b) of the Educational Employment Relations Act. It is hereby ordered that the Federation and its representatives shall:

1. TAKE THE FOLLOWING AFFIRMATIVE ACTIONS DESIGNED TO EFFECTUATE THE POLICIES OF THE EERA:

(a) Within five (5) working days of service of this Decision issues, mail a copy of the enclosed Appendix to each and every Federation member in the certificated unit of the San Francisco Unified School District as well as the nonmember grievants who complied with the policy.

(b) Within five (5) working days of date of service of this Decision, post copies of the Appendix attached hereto for thirty (30) working days at its headquarters office.

(c) At the end of the posting period, notify in writing the San Francisco regional director of the Public Employment Relations Board of the actions the Federation has taken to comply with this Order.

By: ________________________ ________________________

Irene Tovar, Member Harry Gluck, Chairperson

____

John W. Jaeger, Member

Notes

1. Florida has a different view of this issue.

447.401 "All public employees shall have the right to a fair and equitable grievance procedure administered without regard to membership or nonmembership in any organization, except that certified employee organizations shall not be required to process grievances for employees who are not members of the organization. A career service employee shall have the option of utilizing the civil service appeal procedure, an unfair labor practice procedure, or a grievance procedure established under this section, but such employee is precluded from availing himself to more than one of these procedures."

The labor organization exercised its discretion based on legitimate criteria. In the instant case, the refusal to take the Charging Party's case to arbitration was based on his refusal to tender payment for the cost of arbitration. This is not a legitimate criteria because it results in a failure to fairly represent every member of that unit without regard to membership.

Our holding should not be read to imply we are intruding into the area of union discretion in the processing of employee grievances, as long as that discretion is not exercised in an arbitrary, discriminatory or bad faith manner.

2. Getman and Pogrebin, *Labor Relations: The Basic Processes, Law and Practice,* (The Foundation Press 1988), pp. 322–324.

A proviso to Section 8(a)(3) [of the NLRA] specifically legalizes:

"making any agreement with a labor organization * * * to require as a condition of employment membership therein on or after the thirtieth day following the beginning of such employment or the effective date of such agreement whichever is the latter. * * * Provided further that no employer shall justify any discrimination against an employee for non-membership in a labor organization if * * * he has reasonable grounds for believing that membership was terminated for reasons other than failure of the employee to tender the periodic dues and initiation fees uniformly required as a condition of acquiring or retaining membership."

The stated purpose of the proviso, which contravenes both the policy of section 8(a)(2) and the policy against discrimination on the basis of union activity, was to permit unions to deal with the problem of "free riding," i.e., employees who obtain the benefits of union representation without paying for it. The decision to permit such an exception was sufficiently controversial that Congress in section 14(b), included by the Taft–Hartley Amendments, permitted states to prohibit such agreements, and Congress also initially provided that such agreements had to be authorized by a majority vote of the affected employees. This latter provision was quickly dropped at the instance of employers, who were its initial supporters. It turned out that the authorization votes, which were disruptive in terms of time spent and sentiment stirred, were overwhelmingly favorable to the inclusion of such clauses. These results reflected the strength of employee sentiment in unionized enterprises concerning free riding, and they gave great impetus to the unions' claim.

Section 14(b) giving jurisdiction to the states has been far more significant and lasting. Twenty states now have laws prohibiting the type of union security arrangements permitted by the proviso. (In some of these "right to work" states the union is permitted to charge an "agency fee" whereby non-members are required to pay to cover the costs of collective bargaining.) It is not clear how important such laws have been. Early studies suggested that they have little or no impact on union membership or power, but these studies have recently been subject to sophisticated methodological criticism and the validity of their findings is subject to doubt.

CITY OF HAYWARD v. SERVICE EMPLOYEES LOCAL 390

California Courts of Appeal, 1976.
54 Cal.App.3d 761, 126 Cal.Rptr. 710.

CHRISTIAN, JUSTICE: The City of Hayward and its city manager appeal from a judgment declaring that an "agency shop" agreement between the City and respondent United Public Employees, Local 390, is lawful.

Respondent (hereinafter "the Union") is a labor organization affiliated with the Service Employees International Union, AFL–CIO; certain employees of the City are members of the Union. On July 11, 1972, the Union and the City entered into a "Memorandum of Understanding," whereby the City recognized the Union as representing a majority of the employees in the City's Maintenance and Operations Unit.

The agreement covered wages, hours, and other terms and conditions of employment, about which there is no controversy. A dispute arose, however, over the validity of section 1.02 of the agreement, which provides that, although employees are not to be required to join the Union, all employees in the Maintenance and Operations Unit, including nonmembers of the Union, "shall, as a condition of continued employment, pay to the union an amount of money equal to that paid by other employees in the appropriate unit who are members of the union, which shall be limited to an amount of money equal to the union's usual and customary initiation and monthly dues."

Except as may be authorized by statute, public employees have no right to bargain collectively with the employing agency. * * * In 1961, California became one of the first states to create a right on the part of government employees to organize and confer with management as to the terms and conditions of their employment.[1] Another enactment, the Meyers–Milias–Brown Act (Gov.Code §§ 3500–3510 [hereinafter "MMBA"]) has created certain additional rights of organization in employees of municipalities and local agencies, and authorized representatives of labor and management to enter into written agreements for presentation to the governing body. (Gov.Code, §§ 3505–3505.1)[2]

The memorandum of understanding entered into by the parties was negotiated by means of procedures which conform to the MMBA. The sole question presented is whether the MMBA permits the creation of an agency shop in an agency of local government. An agency shop agreement is to be distinguished from a union shop agreement, which conditions the continuance of an employee's job on union membership; a union shop is prohibited by statute in public employment. (§ 3502.) In an agency shop, union membership is not a condition of employment, but all employees, including those who do not choose to join the union, must pay union dues. The MMBA does not explicitly refer to agency shop agreements; no reported decision has previously addressed the issue of the legality of this type of agreement.

Section 3502 provides: "Except as otherwise provided by the Legislature, public employees shall have the right to form, join, and participate in the activities of employee organizations of their own choosing for the purpose of representation on all matters of employer-employee relations. Public employees also shall have the right to refuse to join or participate in the activities of employee organizations *and shall have*

1. [Footnotes numbered as in original.—Ed.] The George Brown Act now Government Code sections 3525–3526, still governs relations between the state and its employees.

2. Unless otherwise indicated, all statutory references hereinafter are to the Government Code.

the right to represent themselves individually in their employment relations with the public agency." (Emphasis added.)

Section 3506 prohibits both public agencies and employee organizations from interfering with, intimidating, restraining, coercing or discriminating against public employees "because of their exercise of their rights under Section 3502." The freedom of choice provisions of each of these sections must be construed as prohibiting the extraction of union dues, or their equivalent, as a condition of continued employment. Otherwise the statutory right of employees to represent themselves would be defeated.

The trial judge did not address either of these sections; instead, he found that the agency shop provision was a "reasonable rule or regulation" adopted pursuant to the authority conferred by section 3507.

Section 3507 provides:

"A public agency may adopt reasonable rules and regulations after consultation in good faith with representatives of an employee organization or organizations for the administration of employer-employee relations under this chapter (commencing with Section 3500).

"Such rules and regulations may include provisions for (a) verifying that an organization does in fact represent employees of the public agency (b) verifying the official status of employee organization officers and representatives (c) recognition of employee organizations (d) exclusive recognition of employee organizations formally recognized pursuant to a vote of the employees of the agency or an appropriate unit thereof, subject to the right of an employee to represent himself as provided in Section 3502 (e) additional procedures for the resolutions of disputes involving wages, hours and other terms and conditions of employment (f) access of employee organization officers and representatives to work locations (g) use of official bulletin boards and other means of communication by employee organizations (h) furnishing nonconfidential information pertaining to employment relations to employee organizations (i) such other matters as are necessary to carry out the purposes of this chapter.

"Exclusive recognition of employee organizations formally recognized as majority representatives pursuant to a vote of the employees may be revoked by a majority vote of the employees only after a period of not less than 12 months following the date of such recognition.

"No public agency shall unreasonably withhold recognition of employee organizations."

The trial judge reasoned that the agency shop provision could be lawfully enacted under section 3507 because "(a) it obligates the Union to represent all employees, (b) it requires nonmembers to share the cost of the benefits which such representation is intended to provide, and (c) it clearly relates to the administration of employer-employee relationships." He recognized the inconsistency of the provision with the employees' statutorily guaranteed freedom of choice, but reasoned that the right of the individual should be subordinated to a policy in furtherance of collective bargaining "as a vehicle for improving employment relationships and avoiding the harsh consequences of labor disputes involving public services."

Courts must, if possible, harmonize statutes, reconcile seeming inconsistencies and construe them to give force and effect to all provisions thereof. (*Hough v. McCarthy* (1960) 54 Cal.2d 273, 279.) A court may not add to or detract from a statute or insert or delete words to accomplish a purpose that does not appear on its face or from its legislative history. (*Estate of Simmons* (1966) 64 Cal.2d 217, 221.)

The MMBA was enacted to promote "full communication between public employers and their employees by providing a reasonable method of resolving disputes regarding wages, hours, and other terms and conditions of employment. * * *" (§ 3500.) It was not intended to supersede existing systems for the administration of employer-employee relations in the public sector, but to strengthen such systems by improving communication. (*Ibid.*)

It is argued that an agency shop agreement is a reasonable method of resolving labor disputes and that, since it is not specifically prohibited, it should be held permissible under the MMBA. But that construction would render the provisions of sections 3502 and 3506 meaningless. Section 3502 implicitly recognizes that employees may choose to join or participate in different organizations. (See, e.g., *Sacramento County Employees Organization, Local 22 etc. Union v. County of Sacramento, supra,* 28 Cal.App.3d 424, 81 LRRM 2841.) It also confers upon each employee the right not to join or participate in the activities of any employee organization. Section 3506 not only prohibits management from interfering with an employee's section 3502 rights, but also imposes the same ban on employee organizations.

Without common law collective bargaining rights, public employees enjoy only those rights specifically granted by statute. Statutes governing the labor relations of other public employee groups indicate that when the Legislature has authorized union security devices, it has done so with explicit language. * * * Although the MMBA has been amended from time to time since its enactment, the Legislature has never modified the language of sections 3502 and 3506 nor added provisions limiting or enlarging the rights created therein.

Those rights cannot reasonably be reconciled with an agency shop provision. The forced payment of dues or their equivalent is, at the very least, "participation" in an employee organization. Practically, it would have the effect of inducing union membership on the part of unwilling employees. While increased participation and membership is a legitimate goal of labor organizations, coercion toward that end is forbidden by statute. Such union security devices as the agency shop must await authorization by the Legislature.

The courts of other states having similar statutes recognizing the right of a public employee not to join or participate in an employee organization have held the agency shop to be unlawful. (See *Smigel v. Southgate Community School District* (Mich.S.Ct. 1972), 388 Mich. 531, 202 N.W.2d 305, 81 LRRM 2944; *New Jersey Turnpike Employees' Union, Local 194 v. New Jersey Turnpike Authority* (N.J.Super.Ct.App.Div. 1973), 123 N.J.Super. 461, 303 A.2d 599, 83 LRRM 2250, *aff'd* (N.J.S.Ct. 1974), 64 N.J. 579, 319 A.2d 224, 86 LRRM 2842; *Farrigan v. Helsby* (S.Ct.1971), 68 Misc.2d 952, 327 N.Y.S.2d 909, 68 LRRM 2360, *aff'd* (S.Ct.App.Div.1973), 42 A.D.2d 2653, 346 N.Y.S.2d 39, 83 LRRM 3052; *Pennsylvania Labor Relations Board v. Zelem* (1974), 329 A.2d 477, 88 LRRM 2524.) Apparently, only Rhode Island has held that there is a common law right to include an agency shop provision in a collective bargaining agreement. (*Town of N. Kingstown v. North Kingstown Teach. Assn.* (1972), 110 R.I. 698, 297 A.2d 342, 344–45, 82 LRRM 2010 [statute merely gave teachers the right "to join or to decline to join" any employee organization].)

This conclusion is further supported by a comparison with federal statutes. Recognizing that many state labor enactments have followed federal models, California courts have often looked to interpretations of federal labor legislation when construing similar state statutes. * * * The National Labor Relations Act, 29 U.S.C. § 151 *et seq.* (hereinafter "NLRA"), contains provisions similar to sections 3502 and 3506 of the MMBA with one major difference. Section 7 of the federal act provides: "Employees shall have the right to self-organization, to form, join, or assist labor organizations, to bargain collectively through representatives of their own choosing, and to engage in other concerted activities for the purpose of collective bargaining or other mutual aid or protection, and shall have the right to refrain from any or all of such activities except to the extent that such right may be affected by an agreement requiring membership in a labor organization as a condition of employment as authorized in section 158(a)(3) of this title." (29 U.S.C. § 157.) Sections 8(a)(1) and 8(a)(3) make it unfair labor practices for an employer to threaten, restrain, or coerce employees in the exercise of their section 157 rights or to encourage or discourage union activity by discrimination in employment except for union shop agreements. (*Id.*, §§ 158(a)(1), (a)(3).) The Supreme Court has held that, without the express provisos in section 7 and 8(a)(3), conditioning employment upon union membership would be an unfair labor practice. (*Retail Clerks v. Schermerhorn* (1963) 373 U.S. 746, 756, 53 LRRM 2318.) The court has further held that the agency shop is the practical equivalent of the union shop. (*Id.*, 373 U.S. at p. 751; *Labor Board v. General Motors* (1963) 373 U.S. 734, 743, 53 LRRM 2313.)

The provisos permitting union security arrangements were enacted by Congress in 1935 and 1947. Sections 3502 and 3506 of the MMBA were not enacted until 1961, and major revisions were made in 1968. It is reasonable to infer that the California Legislature was aware of the analogous provisions of the NLRA, and the construction thereof, and chose not to permit the agency shop in public employment in California. (Cf. *Fire Fighters Union v. City of Vallejo, supra,* 12 Cal.3d 608 at pp. 615–17, 87 LRRM 2453.)

The judgment is reversed with directions to enter a new judgment declaring the agency shop provisions of the agreement to be unlawful.

CALDECOTT, PRESIDING JUSTICE, and EMERSON, JUDGE, concur.

* * *

Notes and Questions

1. Some legislatures have unequivocally outlawed all forms of mandatory membership or payment. Consider, for example, Iowa's Public Employee Relations Act, Sec. 8(4): "Public employees shall have the right to * * * Refuse to join or participate in the activities of employee organizations, including the payment of any dues, fees, or assessments or service fees of any type." I.C.A. tit. V, § 20.8.

At the other extreme, consider Connecticut's policy with respect to state employees (Conn. PERA § 5–280):

> "If an exclusive representative has been designated for the employees in an appropriate collective bargaining unit, each employee in the unit who is not a member of the exclusive representative shall be required, as a condition of employment, to pay to such organization for the period that it is exclusive representative, an amount equal to the regular dues, fees, and assessments that a member is charged." Conn. Stat.Ann. § 5–280(a).

Compare Hawaii Rev.Stat. § 89–4:

> (a) Upon receiving from an exclusive representative a written statement specifying the amount of regular dues required of its members in the appropriate bargaining unit, the employer shall deduct this amount from the payroll of every member employee in the appropriate bargaining unit and remit the amount to the exclusive representative. Additionally, the employer shall deduct an amount equivalent to the regular dues from the payroll of every nonmember employee in the appropriate bargaining unit, and shall remit the amount to the exclusive representative; provided that the deduction from the payroll of every nonmember employee shall be made only for an exclusive representative which provides for a procedure for determining the amount of a refund to any employee who demands the return of any part of the deduction which represents the employees' pro rata share of expenditures made by the exclusive representative for activities of a political and ideological nature unrelated to terms and conditions of employment. * * *

2. What policy considerations underlie an approach which makes payment of a service fee mandatory by statute rather than by agreement between the public employer and the union? And what considerations support the different approaches to such a fee in the two states?

3. A number of statutes permit agreements making either membership or the payment of certain fees a condition of continued employment. Pennsylvania is unique among these states in permitting only a maintenance of membership agreement, i.e., an agreement whereby "all employees who have joined an employee organization or who may join the employee organization in the future must remain members for the duration of the collective bargaining agreement." Pa.C.S.A. tit. 43, § 1101.401.

4. Statutes permitting agreements imposing a requirement of "membership" as a condition of employment are rare in the public sector, and these vary in approach. The Vermont statute applicable to municipal employees, for example, uses language patterned after the federal union shop model, permitting membership as a condition of employment after 30 days but precluding dismissal where membership is terminated for any reason other than the failure to tender periodic dues. Vt.Stat.Ann. tit. 21, § 1726(a)(8).

The Alaska Public Employees Relations Act, on the other hand, permits a requirement of membership as a condition of employment after 30 days but does not impose a similar limitation on grounds for termination. Alaska Stat. § 23.40.110. Do you suppose this means a union can expel a member for some disciplinary offense and insist upon his removal from employment?

5. Most statutes which authorize union security arrangements in the public sector speak, as the Michigan statute, Mich.Comp.Laws Ann. § 423.-210(3), does, in terms of an "agency shop fee" or "service fee" or "fair share fee" rather than in terms of membership. Some of these make clear that the fee to be charged is equivalent to dues. E.g., R.I.Gen.Laws § 36–11–2.

Is there any difference between such an arrangement and the sort of union shop arrangement authorized in Alaska? Cf. NLRB v. General Motors Corp., 373 U.S. 734, 83 S.Ct. 1453, 10 L.Ed.2d 670 (1963).

Others suggest or require that the amount of the service fee be less than the amount of dues. The Minnesota statute, for example, provides for a fair share fee in an amount "equal to the regular membership dues of the exclusive representative, less the cost of benefits financed through the dues and available only to members of the exclusive representative, but in no event shall the fee exceed 85 percent of the regular membership dues." Minn.Stat.Ann. § 179A.08.

6. The Massachusetts Public Employment Relations Act (Mass.Gen. Laws Ann. c. 150E, § 12) provides that the service fee "shall be commensurate with the cost of collective bargaining and contract administration." The state PERB has issued the following regulations under this section (Article IX, § 3):

Section 3. Elements of a Service Fee.—

"(a) Any service fee imposed in compliance with the provisions of this Article shall be presumed valid by the Commission.

"(b) The service fee shall be proportionately commensurate with the costs of collective bargaining and contract administration.

"(c) The service fee imposed upon employees in a bargaining unit shall be uniform.

"(d) Costs not related to collective bargaining and contract administration include:

"(i) Contributions to political parties or candidates for or holders of public office;

"(ii) Contributions to charitable, religious or political organizations or causes;

"(iii) Fines, penalties or damages arising from the unlawful activities of a bargaining agent or a bargaining agent's officers or agents or members;

"(iv) Costs of social or recreational activities;

"(v) Costs of educational activities unrelated to collective bargaining and contract administration;

"(vi) Costs of medical insurance, retirement benefits or other benefit programs;

"(vii) Costs incurred by the bargaining agent to organize employees who are not included in the bargaining unit;

"(viii) Other costs unrelated to collective bargaining and contract administration."

7. Some statutes authorizing union security arrangements attach other conditions. California's Educational Employment Relations Act, for example, permits the public employer to insist that such arrangement be put to special vote among the employees in the bargaining unit, and provides that the union's authority to negotiate such an arrangement may be rescinded by vote of the employees. West's Ann.Cal.Gov't Code § 3546. Washington requires accommodation to the religious beliefs of employees by permitting payments to be made to a charity where the employee asserts a religious objection to payment to the union. West's RCWA § 41.56.122.

8. Some statutes have nothing specific to say about union security arrangements. Most, however, contain language patterned after Section 7 of the NLRA, 29 U.S.C.A. § 157, guaranteeing employees the "right to refrain" from union membership or activities. Under such a statute, would an agency shop, requiring payment of amounts equivalent to union dues, be permissible?

D. THE USE OF FUNDS OBTAINED UNDER AGENCY SHOP AGREEMENTS

JAMES P. LEHNERT, ET AL. v. FERRIS FACULTY ASSOCIATION ET AL.

Supreme Court of the United States, 1991.
___ U.S. ___, 111 S.Ct. 1950, 114 L.Ed.2d 572.

JUSTICE BLACKMUN announced the judgment of the Court.

* * *

This case presents issues concerning the constitutional limitations, if any, upon the payment, required as a condition of employment, of dues by a nonmember to a union in the public sector.

I

Michigan's Public Employment Relations Act (Act), Mich.Comp. Laws §§ 423.201 *et seq.* (1978), provides that a duly selected union shall serve as the exclusive collective-bargaining representative of public employees in a particular bargaining unit.[1] The Act, which applies to faculty members of a public educational institution in Michigan, permits a union and a government employer to enter into an "agency shop" arrangement under which employees within the bargaining unit who decline to become members of the union are compelled to pay a "service fee" to the union.[2]

Respondent Ferris Faculty Association (FFA), an affiliate of the Michigan Education Association (MEA) and the National Education Association (NEA), serves, pursuant to this provision, as the exclusive bargaining representative of the faculty of Ferris State College in Big Rapids, Mich. Ferris is a public institution established under the Michigan Constitution and is funded by the State. See Mich. Const. Art. VIII, § 4. Since 1975, the FFA and Ferris have entered into successive collective-bargaining agreements containing agency-shop provisions. Those agreements were the fruit of negotiations between the FFA and respondent Board of Control, the governing body of Ferris. See Mich.Comp.Law § 390.802 (1988).

Subsequent to this Court's decision in *Abood v. Detroit Board of Education,* 431 U.S. 209 (1977), in which the Court upheld the constitutionality of the Michigan agency-shop provision and outlined permissible uses of the compelled fee by public-employee unions, Ferris proposed, and the FFA agreed to, the agency-shop arrangement at issue here. That agreement required all employees in the bargaining unit who did not belong to the FFA to pay a service fee equivalent to the amount of dues required of a union member.[3] Of the $284.00 service

1. The statute provides:

"Representatives designated or selected for purposes of collective bargaining by the majority of the public employees in a unit appropriate for such purposes, shall be the exclusive representative of all the public employees in such unit for the purposes of collective bargaining in respect to rates of pay, wages, hours of employment or other conditions of employment, and shall be so recognized by the public employer. * * *" Mich. Comp.Laws § 423.211 (1978).

2. The statute reads:

"[N]othing in this act or any in any law of this state shall preclude a public employer from making an agreement with an exclusive bargaining representative as defined in section 11 [§ 423.211] to require as a condition of employment that all employees in the bargaining unit pay to the exclusive bargaining representative a service fee equivalent to the amount of dues uniformly required of members of the exclusive bargaining representative * * *." § 423.210.

3. The agency-shop provision of the collective-bargaining agreement for 1981–1984 provided in pertinent part:

"A. Each employee covered by the negotiated Agreement between the Board of Control of Ferris State College and the Ferris Faculty Association (Dated November 19, 1981) shall, as a condition of employment, on or before thirty-one (31) days from the date of commence-

fee for 1981–1982, the period at issue, $24.80 went to the FFA, $211.20 to the MEA, and $48.00 to the NEA.

Petitioners were members of the Ferris faculty during the period in question and objected to certain uses by the unions of their service fees. Petitioners instituted this action, pursuant to 42 U.S.C. §§ 1983, 1985, 1986, in the United States District Court for the Western District of Michigan, claiming that the use of their fees for purposes other than negotiating and administering a collective-bargaining agreement with the Board of Control violated rights secured to them by the First and Fourteenth Amendments of the United States Constitution. Petitioners also claimed that the procedures implemented by the unions to determine and collect service fees were inadequate.

After a 12–day bench trial, the District Court issued its opinion holding that certain union expenditures were chargeable to petitioners, that certain other expenditures were not chargeable as a matter of law, and that still other expenditures were not chargeable because the unions had failed to sustain their burden of proving that the expenditures were made for chargeable activities. 643 F.Supp. 1306 (1986).

Following a partial settlement, petitioners took an appeal limited to the claim that the District Court erred in holding that the costs of certain disputed union activities were constitutionally chargeable to the plaintiff faculty members. Specifically, petitioners objected to the District Court's conclusion that the union constitutionally could charge them for the costs of (1) lobbying and electoral politics; (2) bargaining, litigation, and other activities on behalf of persons not in petitioners' bargaining unit; (3) public relations efforts; (4) miscellaneous professional activities; (5) meetings and conventions of the parent unions; and (6) preparation for a strike which, had it materialized, would have violated Michigan law.

The Court of Appeals, with one judge dissenting in large part, affirmed. 881 F.2d 1388 (CA6 1989). After reviewing this Court's cases in the area, the court concluded that each of the challenged activities

ment of professional duties or July 1, 1981, whichever is later, join the Ferris Faculty Association or pay a service fee to the Association equivalent to the amount of dues uniformly required of members of the Ferris Faculty Association, less any amounts not permitted by law; provided, however, that the bargaining unit member may authorize payroll deduction for such fee. In the event that a bargaining unit member shall not pay such service fee directly to the Association or authorize payment through payroll deduction, the College shall, at the request of the Association, deduct the service fee from the bargaining unit member's salary and remit the same to the Association under the procedure provided below.

* * *

"D. Bargaining unit members paying the service fee provided for herein or whose service fees have been deducted by the College from their salaries may object to the use of their service fee for matters not permitted by law. The procedure for making such objections is that officially adopted by the Association. A copy of the Association policy will be provided by the Association upon a request of a bargaining unit member." Union defendants' Exh. I, § 2.6; see *Lehnert v. Ferris Faculty Association–MEA–NEA*, 643 F.Supp. 1306, 1308, n. 3 (WD Mich.1986).

was sufficiently related to the unions' duties as the exclusive bargaining representative of petitioners' unit to justify compelling petitioners to assist in subsidizing it. The dissenting judge concurred with respect to convention expenses but disagreed with the majority's resolution of the other items challenged. *Id.,* at 1394. Because of the importance of the issues, we granted certiorari. ___ U.S. ___ (1990).

* * *

It was not until the decision in *Abood* that this Court addressed the constitutionality of union-security provisions in the public-employment context. There, the Court upheld the same Michigan statute which is before us today against a facial First Amendment challenge. At the same time, it determined that the claim that a union has utilized an individual agency-shop agreement to force dissenting employees to subsidize ideological activities could establish, upon a proper showing, a First Amendment violation. In so doing, the Court set out several important propositions:

First, it recognized that "[t]o compel employees financially to support their collective-bargaining representative has an impact upon their First Amendment interests." 431 U.S., at 222. Unions traditionally have aligned themselves with a wide range of social, political, and ideological viewpoints, any number of which might bring vigorous disapproval from individual employees. To force employees to contribute, albeit indirectly, to the promotion of such positions implicates core First Amendment concerns. See, *e.g., Wooley v. Maynard,* 430 U.S. 705, 714 (1977) ("[T]he right of freedom of thought protected by the First Amendment against state action includes both the right to speak freely and the right to refrain from speaking at all").

Second, the Court in *Abood* determined that, as in the private sector, compulsory affiliation with, or monetary support of, a public-employment union does not, without more, violate the First Amendment rights of public employees. Similarly, an employee's free speech rights are not unconstitutionally burdened because the employee opposes positions taken by a union in its capacity as collective-bargaining representative. "[T]he judgment clearly made in *Hanson* and *Street* is that such interference as exists is constitutionally justified by the legislative assessment of the important contribution of the union shop to the system of labor relations established by Congress." 431 U.S., at 222.

In this connection, the Court indicated that the considerations that justify the union shop in the private context—the desirability of labor peace and eliminating "free riders"—are equally important in the public-sector workplace. Consequently, the use of dissenters' assessments "for the purposes of collective bargaining, contract administration, and grievance adjustment," *id.,* at 225–226, approved under the RLA, is equally permissible when authorized by a State vis-a-vis its own workers.

Third, the Court established that the constitutional principles that prevent a State from conditioning public employment upon association with a political party, see *Elrod v. Burns,* 427 U.S. 347 (1976) (plurality opinion), or upon professed religious allegiance, see *Torcaso v. Watkins,* 367 U.S. 488 (1961), similarly prohibit a public employer "from requiring [an employee] to contribute to the support of an ideological cause he may oppose as a condition of holding a job" as a public educator. 431 U.S., at 235.

The Court in *Abood* did not attempt to draw a precise line between permissible assessments for public-sector collective-bargaining activities and prohibited assessments for ideological activities. It did note, however, that, while a similar line must be drawn in the private sector under the RLA, the distinction in the public sector may be "somewhat hazier." *Id.,* at 236. This is so because the "process of establishing a written collective-bargaining agreement prescribing the terms and conditions of public employment may require not merely concord at the bargaining table, but subsequent approval by other public authorities; related budgetary and appropriations decisions might be seen as an integral part of the bargaining process." *Ibid.*

Finally, in *Ellis,* the Court considered, among other issues, a First Amendment challenge to the use of dissenters' funds for various union expenses including union conventions, publications, and social events. Recognizing that by allowing union-security arrangements at all, it has necessarily countenanced a significant burdening of First Amendment rights, it limited its inquiry to whether the expenses at issue "involve[d] *additional* interference with the First Amendment interests of objecting employees, and, if so, whether they are nonetheless adequately supported by a governmental interest." 466 U.S., at 456 (emphasis added).

Applying that standard to the challenged expenses, the Court found all three to be properly supportable through mandatory assessments. The dissenting employees in *Ellis* objected to charges relating to union social functions, not because those activities were inherently expressive or ideological in nature, but purely because they were sponsored by the union. Because employees may constitutionally be compelled to affiliate with a union, the Court found that forced contribution to union social events that were open to all imposed no additional burden on their First Amendment rights. Although the challenged expenses for union publications and conventions were clearly communicative in nature, the Court found them to entail little additional encroachment upon freedom of speech, "and none that is not justified by the governmental interests behind the union shop itself." *Ibid.* See also *Keller v. State Bar of California,* ___ U.S. ___ (1990), and *Communication Workers v. Beck,* 487 U.S. 735 (1988).

Thus, although the Court's decisions in this area prescribe a case-by-case analysis in determining which activities a union constitutionally may charge to dissenting employees, they also set forth several guidelines to be followed in making such determinations. *Hanson* and *Street* and their progeny teach that chargeable activities must (1) be "germane" to collective-bargaining activity; (2) be justified by the government's vital policy interest in labor peace and avoiding "free riders"; and (3) not significantly add to the burdening of free speech that is inherent in the allowance of an agency or union shop.

III

In arguing that these principles exclude the charges upheld by the Court of Appeals, petitioners propose two limitations on the use by public-sector unions of dissenters' contributions. First, they urge that they may not be charged over their objection for lobbying activities that do not concern legislative ratification of, or fiscal appropriations for, their collective-bargaining agreement. Second, as to nonpolitical expenses, petitioners assert that the local union may not utilize dissenters' fees for activities that, though closely related to collective bargaining generally, are not undertaken directly on behalf of the bargaining unit to which the objecting employees belong. We accept the former proposition but find the latter to be foreclosed by our prior decisions.

A

The Court of Appeals determined that unions constitutionally may subsidize lobbying and other political activities with dissenters' fees so long as those activities are " 'pertinent to the duties of the union as a bargaining representative.' " 881 F.2d, at 1392, quoting *Robinson v. New Jersey,* 741 F.2d 598, 609 (CA3 1984), cert. denied, 469 U.S. 1228 (1985). In reaching this conclusion, the court relied upon the inherently political nature of salary and other workplace decisions in public employment. "To represent their members effectively," the court concluded, "public sector unions must necessarily concern themselves not only with negotiations at the bargaining table but also with advancing their members' interests in legislative and other 'political' arenas." 881 F.2d, at 1392.

This observation is clearly correct. Public-sector unions often expend considerable resources in securing ratification of negotiated agreements by the proper state or local legislative body. See Note, Union Security in the Public Sector: Defining Political Expenditures Related to Collective Bargaining, 1980 Wis.L.Rev. 134, 150–152. Similarly, union efforts to acquire appropriations for approved collective-bargaining agreements often serve as an indispensable prerequisite to their implementation. See Developments in the Law: Public Employment, 97 Harv.L.Rev. 1611, 1732–1733 (1984). It was in reference to these characteristics of public employment that the Court in *Abood* discussed the "somewhat hazier" line between bargaining-related and purely ideological activities in the public sector. 431 U.S., at 236. The dual roles of government as employer and policymaker in such cases make the analogy between lobbying and collective bargaining in the public sector a close one.

This, however, is not such a case. Where, as here, the challenged lobbying activities relate not to the ratification or implementation of a dissenter's collective-bargaining agreement, but to financial support of the employee's profession or of public employees generally, the connection to the union's function as bargaining representative is too attenuated to justify compelled support by objecting employees.

We arrive at this result by looking to the governmental interests underlying our acceptance of union security arrangements. We have found such arrangements to be justified by the government's interest in promoting labor peace and avoiding the "free-rider" problem that would otherwise accompany union recognition. *Chicago Teachers v. Hudson,* 475 U.S. 292, 302–303 (1986); *Abood,* 431 U.S., at 224. Neither goal is served by charging objecting employees for lobbying, electoral, and other political activities that do not relate to their collective-bargaining agreement.

Labor peace is not especially served by allowing such charges because, unlike collective-bargaining negotiations between union and management, our national and state legislatures, the media, and the platform of public discourse are public fora open to all. Individual employees are free to petition their neighbors and government in opposition to the union which represents them in the workplace. Because worker and union cannot be said to speak with one voice, it would not further the cause of harmonious industrial relations to compel objecting employees to finance union political activities as well as their own.

Similarly, while we have endorsed the notion that nonunion workers ought not be allowed to benefit from the terms of employment secured by union efforts without paying for those services, the so-called "free-rider" concern is inapplicable where lobbying extends beyond the effectuation of a collective-bargaining agreement. The balancing of monetary and other policy choices performed by legislatures is not limited to the workplace but typically has ramifications that extend into diverse aspects of an employee's life.

Perhaps most important, allowing the use of dissenters' assessments for political activities outside the scope of the collective-bargaining context would present "additional interference with the First Amendment interests of objecting employees." *Ellis,* 466 U.S., at 456. There is no question as to the expressive and ideological content of these activities. Further, unlike discussion by negotiators regarding the terms and conditions of employment, lobbying and electoral speech is likely to concern topics about which individuals hold strong personal views. Although First Amendment protection is in no way limited to controversial topics or emotionally charged issues, see *Winters v. New York,* 333 U.S. 507, 510 (1948); *Buckley v. Valeo,* 424 U.S. 1, 14 (1976); *Abood,* 431 U.S., at 231, and n. 28, the extent of one's disagreement with the subject of compulsory speech is relevant to the degree of impingement upon free expression that compulsion will effect.

The burden upon freedom of expression is particularly great where, as here, the compelled speech is in a public context. By utilizing petitioners' funds for political lobbying and to garner the support of the public in its endeavors, the union would use each dissenter as "an instrument for fostering public adherence to an ideological point of view he finds unacceptable." *Maynard,* 430 U.S., at 715. The First Amendment protects the individual's right of participation in these spheres from precisely this type of invasion. Where the subject of compelled speech is the discussion of governmental affairs, which is at the core of our First Amendment freedoms, *Roth v. United States,* 354 U.S. 476, 484 (1957); *Mills v. Alabama,* 384 U.S. 214, 218 (1966); *Buckley v. Valeo,* 424 U.S., at 14, the burden upon dissenters' rights extends far beyond the acceptance of the agency shop and is constitutionally impermissible.

Accordingly, we hold that the State constitutionally may not compel its employees to subsidize legislative lobbying or other political union activities outside the limited context of contract ratification or implementation.

B

Petitioners' contention that they may be charged only for those collective-bargaining activities undertaken directly on behalf of their unit presents a closer question. While we consistently have looked to whether nonideological expenses are "germane to collective bargaining," *Hanson,* 351 U.S., at 235, we have never interpreted that test to require a direct relationship between the expense at issue and some tangible benefit to the dissenters' bargaining unit.

We think that to require so close a connection would be to ignore the unified-membership structure under which many unions, including those here, operate. Under such arrangements, membership in the local union constitutes membership in the state and national parent organizations. See 643 F.Supp., at 1308. See also *Cumero v. Public Employment Relations Board,* 49 Cal.3d 575, 603–604, 778 P.2d 174, 192 (1989) (noting the inherent "close organizational relationship").

The essence of the affiliation relationship is the notion that the parent will bring to bear its often considerable economic, political, and informational resources when the local is in need of them. Consequently, that part of a local's affiliation fee which contributes to the pool of resources potentially available to the local is assessed for the bargaining unit's protection, even if it is not actually expended on that unit in any particular membership year.

The Court recognized as much in *Ellis.* There it construed the RLA to allow the use of dissenters' funds to help defray the costs of the respondent union's national conventions. It reasoned that "if a union is to perform its statutory functions, it must maintain its corporate or associational existence, must elect officers to manage and carry on its affairs, and may consult its members about overall bargaining goals and policy." 466 U.S., at 448. We see no reason why analogous public-sector union activities should be treated differently.[4]

We therefore conclude that a local bargaining representative may charge objecting employees for their pro rata share of the costs associated with otherwise chargeable activities of its state and national affiliates, even if those activities were not performed for the direct benefit of the objecting employees' bargaining unit. This conclusion, however, does not serve to grant a local union carte blanche to expend dissenters' dollars for bargaining activities wholly unrelated to the employees in their unit. The union surely may not, for example, charge objecting employees for a direct donation or interest-free loan to an unrelated bargaining unit for the purpose of promoting employee rights or unionism generally. Further, a contribution by a local union to its parent that is not part of the local's responsibilities as an affiliate but is in the nature of a charitable donation would not be chargeable to dissenters. There must be some indication that the payment is for services that may ultimately enure to the benefit of the members of the local union by virtue of their membership in the parent organization. And, as always, the union bears the burden of proving the proportion of chargeable expenses to total expenses. *Chicago Teachers v. Hudson,* 475 U.S., at 306; *Abood,* 431 U.S., at 239–240, n. 40; *Railway Clerks v. Allen,* 373 U.S., at 122. We conclude merely that the union need not demonstrate a direct and tangible impact upon the dissenting employee's unit.

C

JUSTICE SCALIA would find "implicit in our cases since *Street,*" the rule that "to be constitutional, a charge must *at least* be incurred in performance of the union's statutory duties." *Post,* at 9. As the preceding discussion indicates, we reject this reading of our cases. This Court never has held that the First Amendment compels such a requirement and our prior decisions cannot reasonably be construed to support his stated proposition. See, *e.g., Ellis,* 466 U.S., at 456 ("Petitioners may feel that their money is not being well-spent, but that does not mean they have a First Amendment complaint"); see also *Keller, supra* (distinguishing between statutory and constitutional duties in the context of integrated state bar membership).

Even if viewed merely as a prophylactic rule for enforcing the First Amendment in the union-security context, Justice Scalia's approach

4. The Michigan Employment Relations Commission—the state agency responsible for administering the Act—has reached the same conclusion in applying the statute to local affiliates of the MEA and the NEA. In determining that the involvement of the NEA and the MEA in local contract administration and grievance adjustment was a legitimate aspect of the local's service fee, the agency explained that "to restrict chargeability to only those activities directly relating to the local bargaining unit is to totally ignore the fact of affiliation." *Bridgeport-Spaulding Community Schools,* 1986 MERC Op. 1024, 1057. See also *Garden City School District,* 1978 MERC Op. 1145, 1155–1156. While the agency's conclusions of law are without effect upon this Court, we find persuasive its factual findings regarding the structure and operation of labor organizations within its jurisdiction.

ultimately must be rejected. As the relevant provisions of the Michigan Act illustrate,[5] state labor laws are rarely precise in defining the duties of public-sector unions to their members. Indeed, it is reasonable to assume that the Michigan provisions relating to collective-bargaining duties were purposefully drafted in broad terms so as to provide unions the flexibility and discretion necessary to accommodate the needs of their constituents. Here, as in the RLA context, "[t]he furtherance of the common cause leaves some leeway for the leadership of the group." *Street,* 367 U.S., at 778 (Douglas, J., concurring), quoted in *Abood,* 431 U.S., at 222–223.

Consequently, the terms of the Act provide a poor criterion for determining which charges violate the First Amendment rights of dissenting employees. The broad language of the Act does not begin to explain which of the specific activities at issue here fall within the union's collective-bargaining function as contemplated by our cases. Far from providing a bright-line standard, Justice Scalia's "statutory duties" test fails to afford courts and litigants the guidance necessary to make these particularized distinctions.

More important, Justice Scalia's rigid approach fails to acknowledge the practicalities of the complex interrelationship between public employers, employees, unions, and the public. The role of an effective representative in this context often encompasses responsibilities that extend beyond those specifically delineated in skeletal state labor law statutes. See *Abood,* 431 U.S., at 236. That an exclusive bargaining representative has gone beyond the bare requirements of the law in representing its constituents through employee contributions does not automatically mean that the Constitution has been violated, at least where the funded activities have not *transgressed* state provisions. "The very nature of the free-rider problem and the governmental interest in overcoming it require that the union have a certain flexibility in its use of compelled funds." *Ellis,* 466 U.S., at 456.

We therefore disagree with Justice Scalia that any charge that does not relate to an activity expressly authorized by statute is *constitutionally* invalid, irrespective of its impact, or lack thereof, on free expression. In our view, his analysis turns our constitutional doctrine on its

5. As relevant here, § 11 of the Act provides:

"Representatives designated or selected for purposes of collective bargaining by the majority of the public employees in a unit appropriate for such purposes, shall be the exclusive representatives of all the public employees in such unit for the purposes of collective bargaining in respect to rates of pay, wages, hours of employment or other conditions of employment, and shall be so recognized by the public employer. * * *" Mich. Comp.Laws § 423.211 (1978).

Section 15 provides in pertinent part:

"[T]o bargain collectively is the performance of the mutual obligation of the employer and the representative of the employees to meet at reasonable times and confer in good faith with respect to wages, hours, and other terms and conditions of employment, or the negotiation of an agreement, or any question arising thereunder, and the execution of a written contract, ordinance or resolution incorporating any agreement reached if requested by either party, but such obligation does not compel either party to agree to a proposal or require the making of a concession." § 423.214.

head. Instead of interpreting statutes in light of First Amendment principles, he would interpret the First Amendment in light of state statutory law. It seems to us that this proposal bears little relation to the values that the First Amendment was designed to protect. A rule making violations of freedom of speech dependent upon the terms of state employment statutes would sacrifice sound constitutional analysis for the appearance of administrability.

We turn to the union activities at issue in this case.

IV

A

The Court of Appeals found that the union could constitutionally charge petitioners for the costs of a Preserve Public Education (PPE) program designed to secure funds for public education in Michigan, and that portion of the MEA publication, the Teacher's Voice, which reported these activities. Petitioners argue that, contrary to the findings of the courts below, the PPE program went beyond lobbying activity and sought to affect the outcome of ballot issues and "millages" or local taxes for the support of public schools. Given our conclusion as to lobbying and electoral politics generally, this factual dispute is of little consequence. None of these activities was shown to be oriented toward the ratification or implementation of petitioner's collective-bargaining agreement. We hold that none may be supported through the funds of objecting employees.

B

Petitioners next challenge the Court of Appeals' allowance of several activities that the union did not undertake directly on behalf of persons within petitioners' bargaining unit. This objection principally concerns NEA "program expenditures" destined for States other than Michigan, and the expenses of the Teacher's Voice listed as "Collective Bargaining" and "Litigation." Our conclusion that unions may bill dissenting employees for their share of general collective-bargaining costs of the state or national parent union is dispositive as to the bulk of the NEA expenditures. The District Court found these costs to be germane to collective bargaining and similar support services and we decline to disturb that finding. No greater relationship is necessary in the collective-bargaining context.

This rationale does not extend, however, to the expenses of litigation that does not concern the dissenting employees' bargaining unit or, by extension, to union literature reporting on such activities. While respondents are clearly correct that precedent established through litigation on behalf of one unit may ultimately be of some use to another unit, we find extra-unit litigation to be more akin to lobbying in both kind and effect. We long have recognized the important political and expressive nature of litigation. See, *e.g., NAACP v. Button,* 371 U.S. 415, 431 (1963) (recognizing that for certain groups, "association for litigation may be the most effective form of political association'"). Moreover, union litigation may cover a diverse range of areas from bankruptcy proceedings to employment discrimination. See *Ellis,* 466 U.S., at 453. When unrelated to an objecting employee's unit, such activities are not germane to the union's duties as exclusive bargaining representative. Just as the Court in *Ellis* determined that the RLA, as informed by the First Amendment, prohibits the use of dissenters' fees for extra-unit litigation, *ibid.,* we hold that the Amendment proscribes such assessments in the public sector.

C

The Court of Appeals determined that the union constitutionally could charge petitioners for certain public-relations expenditures. In this connection, the court said: "Public relations expenditures designed to enhance the reputation of the teaching profession * * * are, in our opinion, sufficiently related to the unions' duty to represent bargaining unit employees effectively so as to be chargeable to dissenters." 881 F.2d, at 1394. We disagree. Like the challenged lobbying conduct, the public-relations activities at issue here entailed speech of a political nature in a public forum. More important, public speech in support of the teaching profession generally is not sufficiently related to the union's collective-bargaining functions to justify compelling dissenting employees to support it. Expression of this kind extends beyond the negotiation and grievance-resolution contexts and imposes a substantially greater burden upon First Amendment rights than do the latter activities.

Nor do we accept the Court of Appeals' comparison of these public-relations expenses to the costs of union social activities held in *Ellis* to be chargeable to dissenters. In *Ellis,* the Court found the communicative content of union social activities, if any, to derive solely from the union's involvement in them. 466 U.S., at 456. "Therefore," we reasoned, "the fact that the employee is forced to contribute does not increase the infringement of his First Amendment rights already resulting from the compelled contribution to the union." *Ibid.* The same cannot be said of the public-relations charges upheld by the Court of Appeals which covered "informational picketing, media exposure, signs, posters and buttons." 643 F.Supp., at 1313.

D

The District Court and the Court of Appeals allowed charges for those portions of the Teachers' Voice that concern teaching and education generally, professional development, unemployment, job opportunities, award programs of the MEA, and other miscellaneous matters. Informational support services such as these are neither political nor public in nature. Although they do not directly concern the members of petitioners' bargaining unit, these expenditures are for the benefit of all and we discern no additional infringement of First Amendment rights that they might occasion. In short, we agree with the Court of

Appeals that these expenses are comparable to the *de minimis* social activity charges approved in *Ellis*. See 466 U.S., at 456.

E

The Court of Appeals ruled that the union could use the fees of objecting employees to send FFA delegates to the MEA and the NEA conventions and to participate in the 13E Coordinating Council, another union structure. Petitioners challenge that determination and argue that, unlike the national convention expenses found to be chargeable to dissenters in *Ellis,* the meetings at issue here were those of affiliated parent unions rather than the local, and therefore do not relate exclusively to petitioners' unit.

We need not determine whether petitioners could be commanded to support all the expenses of these conventions. The question before the Court is simply whether the unions may constitutionally require petitioners to subsidize the participation in these events of delegates from the local. We hold that they may. That the conventions were not solely devoted to the activities of the FFA does not prevent the unions from requiring petitioners' support. We conclude above that the First Amendment does not require so close a connection. Moreover, participation by members of the local in the formal activities of the parent is likely to be an important benefit of affiliation. This conclusion is supported by the District Court's description of the 13E Coordinating Council meeting as an event at which "bargaining strategies and representational policies are developed for the UniServ unit composed of the Ferris State College and Central Michigan University bargaining units." 643 F.Supp., at 1326. As was held in *Ellis,* "[c]onventions such as those at issue here are normal events * * * and seem to us to be essential to the union's discharge of its duties as bargaining agent." 466 U.S., at 448–449.

F

The chargeability of expenses incident to preparation for a strike which all concede would have been illegal under Michigan law, Mich. Comp.Laws § 423.202 (1979), is a provocative question. At the beginning of the 1981–1982 fiscal year, the FFA and Ferris were engaged in negotiating a new collective-bargaining agreement. The union perceived these efforts to be ineffective, and began to prepare a "job action" or, in more familiar terms, to go out on strike. These preparations entailed the creation by the FFA and the MEA of a "crisis center" or "strike headquarters." The District Court found that, "whatever label is attached to this facility, prior to a strike it serves as a meeting place for the local's membership, a base from which tactical activities such as informational picketing can be conducted, and serves to apply additional pressure on the employer by suggesting, whether true or not, that the local is prepared to strike if necessary." 643 F.Supp., at 1313.

Had the FFA actually engaged in an illegal strike, the union clearly could not have charged the expenses incident to that strike to petitioners. We can imagine no legitimate governmental interest that would be served by compelling objecting employees to subsidize activity that the State has chosen to disallow. See *Male v. Grand Rapids Education Association,* 98 Mich.App. 742, 295 N.W.2d 918 (1980), appeal denied, 412 Mich. 851, ___ N.W.2d ___ (1981) (holding that, under Michigan law, compulsory-service fees cannot include money allocated to the support of public-sector strikes). Similarly, one might expect the State to prohibit unions from using dissenters' funds to threaten or prepare for such conduct. The Michigan Legislature, however, has chosen not to impose such a restriction, and we do not find the First Amendment to require that limitation.

Petitioners can identify no determination by the State of Michigan that mere preparation for an illegal strike is itself illegal or against public policy, and we are aware of none. Further, we accept the rationale provided by the Court of Appeals in upholding these charges that such expenditures fall "within the range of reasonable bargaining tools available to a public sector union during contract negotiations." 881 F.2d, at 1394. The District Court expressly credited trial testimony by an MEA representative that outward preparations for a potential strike serve as an effective bargaining tool and that only one out of every seven or eight "job action investigations" actually culminates in a strike. 643 F.Supp., at 1312. The Court of Appeals properly reviewed this finding for clear error. See *Anderson v. Bessemer City,* 470 U.S. 564, 575 (1985).

In sum, these expenses are substantively indistinguishable from those appurtenant to collective-bargaining negotiations. The District Court and the Court of Appeals concluded, and we agree, that they aid in those negotiations and enure to the direct benefit of members of the dissenters' unit. Further, they impose no additional burden upon First Amendment rights.[6] The union may properly charge petitioners for those costs.

V

The judgment of the Court of Appeals is affirmed in part and reversed in part, and the case is remanded for further proceedings consistent with this opinion.

6. That Justice Scalia's "statutory duties" test is unworkable is evidenced by the fact that he apparently is unwilling to apply it fully to the charges at issue in this case. He agrees with our determination that dissenting employees may be charged for the local's contribution to the collective-bargaining activities of state and national parent associations. Yet the parent organizations are not bound by statute or by contract to provide collective-bargaining support to the local. Nor is the local statutorily required to affiliate with or contribute to its larger parent associations. The Justice concludes, as do we, that there is "no reason to insist that, in order to be chargeable, on-call services for use in the bargaining process be committed by contract rather than by practice and usage." *Post,* at 11. But this conclusion appears to be out of line with his view that dissenters may be charged only for services that the State has *required* the union to provide. Under his analysis, that the benefits of affiliation as a practical matter may *aid* the local union in performing its "statutory duties" should be irrelevant. Thus, he would prohibit charges for strike preparations despite his admission that "visible preparations for a strike [may] strengthen the union's position in negotiations." *Post,* at 12. In our view, this inconsistency highlights the unfeasibility of Justice Scalia's approach.

It is so ordered.

JUSTICE SCALIA, with whom JUSTICE O'CONNOR and JUSTICE SOUTER join, and with whom JUSTICE KENNEDY joins as to all but Part III–C, concurring in the judgment in part and dissenting in part.

While I agree with the Court's disposition of many of the challenged expenditures, I do not agree with the test it proposes. In my view today's opinion both expands and obscures the category of expenses for which a union may constitutionally compel contributions from dissenting nonmembers in an agency shop. I would hold that contributions can be compelled only for the costs of performing the union's statutory duties as exclusive bargaining agent.

I

* * *

I would hold that to be constitutional a charge must *at least* be incurred in performance of the union's statutory duties. I would make explicit what has been implicit in our cases since *Street:* a union cannot constitutionally charge nonmembers for any expenses except those incurred for the conduct of activities in which the union owes a duty of fair representation to the nonmembers being charged.

* * *

JUSTICE KENNEDY, concurring in the judgment in part and dissenting in part.

I join all except for [that part of Justice Scalia's opinion concerning strike preparation activities]. * * *, I agree with the majority that these are indistinguishable in substance from other expenses of negotiating a collective bargaining agreement. I would find, under Justice Scalia's test, that it was reasonable to incur these expenditures to perform the duties of an exclusive representative of the employees in negotiating an agreement.

The separate opinion of JUSTICE MARSHALL is omitted.

Notes

1. Procedurally a union has the obligation to provide sufficient information to potential objectors to enable them to gauge the propriety of the fee. This was the holding of *Chicago Teachers' Union, Local No. 1 v. Hudson,* 475 U.S. 292, 106 S.Ct. 1066, 89 L.Ed.2d 232 (1986). A more recent decision involving the same parties holds that a 39–page notice given by the union to the objectors setting forth its methods of cost allocation and its definition of legitimate collective bargaining expenditures is adequate to satisfy this obligation. The protecting agency fee payers must first file a claim through the internal union procedures, which include some form of impartial arbitration, before going into court to challenge the accuracy of the fee calculation. If the decision by the impartial decision-maker is adverse to the claimants, they may then seek review in federal court. But the courts will not micro-manage the calculations beforehand. *Hudson v.*

Chicago Teachers' Union, Local No. 1, 922 F.2d 1306 (7th Cir.1991), *cert. denied* ___ U.S. ___, 111 S.Ct. 2852, 115 L.Ed.2d 1020 (1991).

2. The New York Taylor Act, as amended in 1977, provides that agency shop arrangements are applicable only "in the case of an employee organization which has established and maintained a procedure providing for the refund to any employee demanding the return of any part of an agency shop fee deduction which represents the employee's pro rata share of expenditures by the organization in aid of activities or causes of a political or ideological nature only incidentally related to terms and conditions of employment." (Sec. 208(b).)

Index

†